lonely 🌍 planet

Western Europe

AF215429

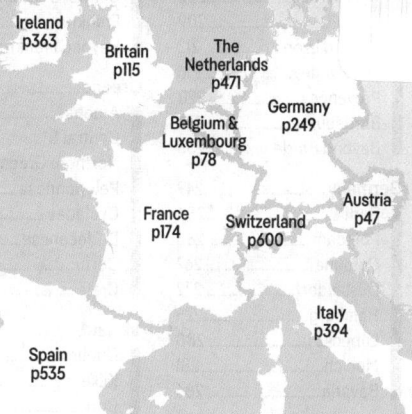

Ireland
p363

Britain
p115

The
Netherlands
p471

Germany
p249

Belgium &
Luxembourg
p78

France
p174

Switzerland
p600

Austria
p47

Italy
p394

Portugal
p498

Spain
p535

Greece
p318

**Anthony Ham, Kate Armstrong, Cristian Bonetto,
James March, Catherine Le Nevez, Isabella Noble,
Anna Richards, Helena Smith, Joana Taborda,
Kerry Walker, Nicola Williams, Barbara Woolsey**

CONTENTS

Plan Your Trip

The Guide

King's Guard, Buckingham Palace (p122), London, Britain

Park Güell (p558), Barcelona, Spain

FROM LEFT: LAURIE NOBLE/GETTY IMAGES, ALEXANDER CHAIKIN/SHUTTERSTOCK, SYLVAIN SONNET/GETTY IMAGES

Austrian National Library's State Hall, Hofburg (p52), Vienna, Austria

Toolkit

Storybook

DALU/SHUTTERSTOCK

Schloss Neuschwanstein (p288), Germany

WESTERN EUROPE

THE JOURNEY BEGINS HERE

Western Europe is a magical confluence of enlightened human culture and soaring natural beauty. Each of the countries covered in this book possesses both elements in abundance. Sometimes you'll experience this in the world-class galleries, architecture both medieval and contemporary, or in the fabulous food and drink. On other occasions, it will happen when surrounded by glorious mountain ranges, beaches or iconic rivers. There are also times when you get to enjoy the two simultaneously – at a fairy-tale castle high in the Austrian, German or Swiss Alps, for example, or as you linger over lunch in a gorgeous village alongside a dramatic stretch of coastline in Spain, Portugal or Italy. There are countless moments such as these, and all of them highlight one overriding truth: Western Europe is one beautiful region whose inhabitants really know how to live.

Anthony Ham

@AnthonyHamWrite

Anthony travels the world in search of stories. He has written two books of narrative nonfiction and he lived for 10 years in Madrid.

My favourite experience There is one Western European view that I love above all others. Some 5km northeast of **Füssen** (p288) in Bavaria, the view of baroque church, Alps and Schloss Neuschwanstein is perfection.

WHO GOES WHERE

Our writers and experts choose the places that, for them, define Western Europe.

My home, **Lyon** (p209), is wonderfully close to the Alps – a city for people who secretly hate cities. My perfect day in summer is spent hiking in the mountains (pictured); in winter I swap my hiking boots for skis. Come evening, you'll find me enjoying the city buzz in a gourmet restaurant or wine bar.

Anna Richards

@annahrichards

Anna lives in Lyon with two dogs who accompany her on adventures. She's won several awards for her work and is the author of Paddling France *for Bradt Guides. She curated the France chapter.*

I loved hopping on a train from Den Haag to **Gouda** (p484) for the traditional cheese market (pictured). It wasn't the Gouda itself that I loved but rather, an entire smorgasbord of Dutch snacks including *stroopwafel* (syrup waffles), *koekjes* (cookies), *kibbeling* (battered fish chunks) and fresh seafood.

Barbara Woolsey

@xo.babxi

Based in Germany for over a decade, Barbara has authored over 30 Lonely Planet guidebooks. When not researching, she's DJing in Berlin's nightclubs. She curated the Germany and Netherlands chapters.

My favourite experience is the **Slea Head Drive** (p381), a journey through millennia of history (beehive huts, ring forts, inscribed stones, early Christian sites) along spectacular edge-of-the-world coastline, ending in an inviting music-filled Dingle pub.

Catherine Le Nevez

lonelyplanet.com/authors/catherine-le-nevez

A Lonely Planet author since 2004, contributing to over 100 guides in two dozen countries, Catherine has a Doctorate of Creative Arts in Writing and insatiable wanderlust. She curated the Ireland chapter.

It's hard to play favourites in Italy, but my heart belongs to **Naples** (p444). Nowhere else thrills or moves me quite so deeply. It's a visceral, esoteric place – an old-world New Orleans littered with contradiction, magic and a raw energy both invigorating and fatalistic. As elegant and erudite as it is coarse and gritty, Napoli has almost 3000 years of tales to tell – in its ghostly catacombs, gilded royal palaces and beautiful hilltop vistas. Dive in.

Cristian Bonetto

@cristian_alessandro_bonetto

Born in Australia to Italian parents, Cristian has made a career from straddling two continents and cultures. He has penned over 60 Lonely Planet titles, many covering Italy. He curated the Italy chapter.

Bruges is brilliant at combining ancient and modern. I was blown away by **Museum Sint-Janshospitaal** (p96). I know the Memling paintings well, and the magnificent wooden structure of the 12th-century hospital that commissioned his work. But now, contemporary works inspired by the hospital's founding principles have been woven into the collection. They speak of compassion and care, and their dialogue with the historic collection is fascinating.

Helena Smith

@helenasmithpix

Helena loves to write about ecotravel, community and the outdoors. She curated the Belgium & Luxembourg chapter.

Few places feel as magical for me as the **Costa de la Luz** (p592) of Cádiz province in Andalucía, where I spend time every year. It's something to do with the crisp natural light beaming across wild blonde beaches, catching a glimpse of Morocco just across the Strait of Gibraltar, and wandering through the whitewashed streets of ancient, buzzing towns like Tarifa and Vejer (pictured). The food here is some of Spain's best, too.

Isabella Noble

@isabellamnoble

Andalucía-raised travel journalist, Isabella is based between Barcelona and Málaga and has written over 50 Lonely Planet guidebooks. She curated the Spain chapter.

A romantic collection of widescreen valleys, chocolate-box villages and stately homes, the **Peak District** (p142) in northern England is my favourite place to get lost for a little while. The wind-sculpted hills of the Hope Valley (pictured) are the most spectacular stretch, with some sublime hiking trails and craggy cliff faces for more audacious pursuits like rock climbing and hang-gliding. I'm just as happy in a rustic rural pub.

James March

@jmarchtravel

James is a Birmingham-based travel writer who has contributed to several Lonely Planet books. He curated the Britain chapter.

My favourite place in Portugal is **Alqueva Lake** (p527) in the Alentejo region. This is Europe's largest artificial lake. I love swimming in its warm river beaches (a pleasant alternative to the brisk Atlantic waters), walking among its surrounding villages like Monsaraz, and capturing the clear starry skies above me, preferably with a glass of Alentejo wine in hand.

Joana Taborda

@cityodes

Joana is a Portuguese travel writer with a deep passion for her country's artisanal crafts and festival traditions. She curated the Portugal chapter.

Nafplio (p336) is my Greek magnet. I love wandering through the alleyways to evoke aspects of the past. Even these days, as children play in the plazas, locals stroll the waterfront and fishmongers bellow their prices at the market, the essence of life here continues as it has for centuries. The crowds don't detract from Nafplio's soul: the Venetian houses, the maze of pedestrian lanes and the generosity of its locals.

Kate Armstrong

katearmstrongtravelwriter.com

Kate first visited Greece aeons ago and has finally put her roots down there. She writes for publications around the world, and has contributed to 65-plus Lonely Planet titles. She curated the Greece chapter.

There are higher mountains in Austria, but few are more upliftingly beautiful than the **Tennengebirge** (p61) – ragged spires of limestone that fling up above the village of Werfen and Eisriesenwelt, the world's largest accessible ice caves. Walking high on this karst plateau, you are often alone with your own thoughts, footsteps and the occasional screech of a golden eagle wheeling overhead.

VADYM LAVRA/SHUTTERSTOCK

Kerry Walker

@kerryawalker

Kerry is a lifelong fan of the Austrian Alps, an avid hiker and the author of multiple Lonely Planet guidebooks. She curated and contributed to the Austria chapter.

My favourite experience is crunching over crevasses with crampons, roped to a guide, on the mammoth **Aletsch Glacier** (p616) – it will be gone by 2100. The rumbling of water flowing deep beneath your feet is an emotive song to the glacier's immensity and fragility. Should you trip and fall, razor-sharp ice crystals can shred the skin of your hands like glass. Yet, on this monumental sea of ice on a hot day in July, 80 cu metres of ice melt every second.

JAMES O'NEIL/GETTY IMAGES

Nicola Williams

@tripalong

Nicola lives on Lake Geneva. She is a travel writer and editor, specialising in France, Italy and Switzerland for Lonely Planet, The Telegraph and others. She curated the Switzerland chapter.

V_E/SHUTTERSTOCK

Amsterdam (p476), Netherlands

9

Edinburgh
Watch sunset from an extinct volcano (p153)

Amsterdam
Savour Rembrandt and Van Gogh (p476)

Chamonix
Take France's highest cable car (p203)

Camino de Santiago
Walk Europe's most popular pilgrim path (p575)

Algarve
Surf or swim Portugal's best beaches (p516)

La Albufera
Go in search of the perfect paella (p579)

Rhine Valley
Tour vineyards, castles and wine villages (p309)

Zugspitze
Climb Germany's highest mountain (p288)

Mayrhofen
Discover a fine alpine village near Innsbruck (p70)

Zermatt
Relax in the Matterhorn's shadow (p614)

Naxos
Explore Greece's idyllic shoreline (p342)

Piedmont
Take a wine tour to find the perfect red (p415)

Rome
Admire Michelangelo's Sistine Chapel masterpiece (p400)

Crete
Hike Samaria Gorge and surrounding canyons (p352)

500 km
250 miles

NORWAY
OSLO
SWEDEN
DENMARK
COPENHAGEN
Baltic Sea
RUSSIA
MOSCOW
Lübeck
Rostock
Hamburg
Bremen
Hanover
GERMANY
BERLIN
Potsdam
WARSAW
UKRAINE
Essen
Düsseldorf
Magdeburg
POLAND
Kassel
Cologne
Leipzig
Erfurt
Dresden
Frankfurt-am-Main
Nuremberg
PRAGUE
CZECHIA
Mannheim
Stuttgart
SLOVAKIA
Strasbourg
VIENNA
Basel
Munich
Linz
BRATISLAVA
Zürich
Salzburg
AUSTRIA
BUDAPEST
ROMANIA
BERN
Innsbruck
Graz
HUNGARY
Black Sea
SWITZERLAND
SLOVENIA
Milan
Trento
Trieste
Turin
Verona
Venice
ZAGREB
Parma
Bologna
CROATIA
Genoa
Pisa
Ravenna
Ligurian Sea
Florence
Ancona
Corsica
Siena
Perugia
Adriatic Sea
ITALY
Pescara
BULGARIA
Ajaccio
ROME
Foggia
TIRANA
NORTH MACEDONIA
Serres
Komotini
Sassari
Bari
ALBANIA
Katerini
Alexandroupoli
Sardinia
Naples
Taranto
Lecce
Ioannina
Thessaloniki
Amalfi
Larissa
İzmir
Tyrrhenian Sea
Corfu
GREECE
Volos
Aegean Sea
TURKEY
Cagliari
Catanzaro
Halkida
Agrinio
Corinth
Hora (Naxos)
Palermo
Messina
Reggio di Calabria
Ionian Sea
Patras
ATHENS
Rhodes Town
Sicily
Catania
Kalamata
Tripoli
Rhodes
Syracuse
Hania
Iraklio
MALTA
Mediterranean Sea
Crete

MOUNTAIN MAJESTY

Western Europe's mountains rank among the most beautiful on earth. The Alps (Germany, Austria, Switzerland and Italy), the Dolomites (Italy), the Pyrenees (France and Spain), the Picos de Europa (Spain) and the Sierra Nevada (Spain) are both backdrop and destination in their own right. Ski in winter, hike in summer or just sit back and admire the view. Whichever you choose, building your trip around the region's summits and valleys is a wonderful way to go.

High Point

Western Europe's highest peaks are in the Alps. France's Mont Blanc (4805m; pictured) is tallest, followed by Monte Rosa (4634m) and Dom (4545m), both in Switzerland.

Hiking in Spain

Spain is a walker's wonderland, whether you're scaling peaks in the Pyrenees, the Sierra Nevada (pictured) or the Picos de Europa, or hiking between villages at lower altitudes.

Gear Up

Especially in the Alps, it's eternal winter above 3000m, even in July and August. Come prepared for snow, wind and sun glare.

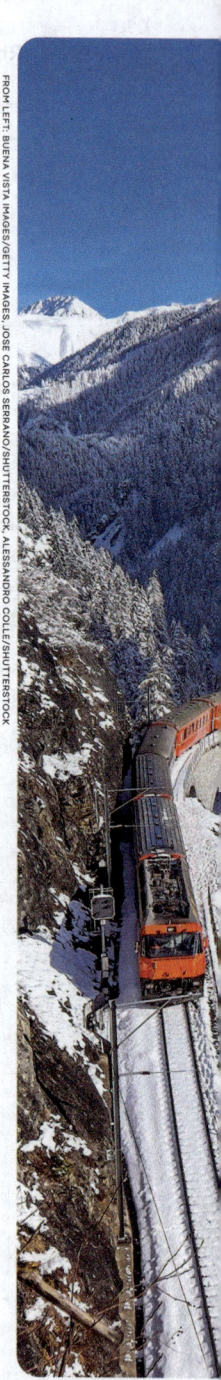

BEST MOUNTAIN EXPERIENCES

Head to Chamonix and take France's highest cable car to **❶ Aiguille du Midi** (3842m) in the Massif du Mont Blanc. (p205)

Take the cog railway up to, and the cable-car back down, from glorious **❷ Zugspitze** (2962m) on the German–Austrian border. (p288)

Soak up snow-encrusted peaks, the Aletsch Glacier and Black Forest from **❸ Jungfraujoch**, Europe's highest train station at 3454m. (p616)

Hike the high ridge lines and superb canyons of the Valle de Ordesa in Spain's Pyrenean **❹ Parque Nacional de Ordesa y Monte Perdido**. (p568)

Tackle the thrilling hiking trails in Granada's **❺ Parque Nacional Sierra Nevada**, including mainland Spain's tallest peak: Mulhacén (3479m). (p594)

BEACH LIFE

Europe's beaches are spectacular, from wild Atlantic shores to more sheltered Mediterranean coves. If you're planning on swimming, summer months are crowded but ideal weather. The rest of the year, you may have some of them all to yourself, while non-summer months can be ideal for surfing or long beach walks.

BEST BEACH EXPERIENCES

Go kitesurfing on the superb beaches of Portugal's Algarve, especially around **❶ Lagos**. (p519)

Seek out sparkling *calas* (coves) all along the Costa Brava, but especially near **❷ Cadaqués**. (p566)

Roam around the coastal paradise of **❸ Cabo de Gata**, whose gold-sand beaches are some of Andalucía's best. (p594)

Try a new beach every day on **❹ Naxos**, where one glossy strand of white sand merges right into the next. (p342)

Experience the wild beauty of Sicily's golden-sand beaches, especially around **❺ Taormina**. (p460)

Beach Seasons

Dates vary across the region, but most beaches are patrolled by lifeguards from at least June (May in some countries) to August or mid-September.

Accessible Beaches

Portugal has over 200 accessible bathing areas, with reserved parking, walkways and adapted toilets. Some spots have amphibious wheelchairs for easier water access.

Surf's Up

Northern Spain is a surfer's dream, particularly the Basque Country, Cantabria, Asturias and Galicia. Tarifa (Andalucía) is renowned for kitesurfing and windsurfing.

FROM LEFT: ANTOINEZK/SHUTTERSTOCK, ROBERT PAUL VAN BEETS/SHUTTERSTOCK

SINA ETTMER PHOTOGRAPHY/SHUTTERSTOCK

BEST ALPINE TOWN EXPERIENCES

Soak up the Swiss Alps beneath the Eiger, with geraniums cascading from the balconies of ❶ **Grindelwald**. (p616)

Rub shoulders with well-heeled celebrities and look down on postcard-perfect ❷ **Verbier** from a cable car. (p613)

Explore the gabled alpine town of ❸ **Garmisch-Partenkirchen**, close to Zugspitze and Oberammergau in Germany's south. (p288)

Immerse yourself in the world of Austrian alpine villages near Innsbruck, especially in ❹ **Mayrhofen** and further around ❹ **Zillertal**. (p70)

Linger in ❺ **Zermatt**, a postcard-perfect alpine town with gabled architecture and uninterrupted Matterhorn views. (p614)

Zermatt (p614), Switzerland

ALPINE TOWN CHARMERS

The mountain ranges of Western Europe may be spectacular natural phenomena, but they are lent scale, depth and chocolate-box beauty by the towns that nestle in the mountains' valleys or cling to hilltop perches. From the Pyrenees of the south to the Alps of central Europe, no two villages are alike – and many are utterly gorgeous.

Swiss & Sustainable

Peruse pages of beautiful Swiss villages on *swissvillages.org*. Bead your journey with those labelled 'Swisstainable' – it means they're championing a more sustainable tourism.

Spain's Prettiest

Such is the beauty of Spain's many, varied villages that there's an official list and association of them: **Los Pueblos Más Bonitos de España** (*lospueblosmas bonitosdeespana.org*).

15

GLORIOUS ART

Western Europe is perfect for those who love European art. From the Middle Ages onwards, royal patronage of the great artists of the day produced an astonishing output from master painters including Van Gogh and Rembrandt, Velázquez and Goya, Leonardo da Vinci and Michelangelo. In more recent centuries, artists like Dalí, Picasso and Toulouse-Lautrec and the artistic trends they led, from Impressionism to surrealism, have come to define much of what we know as European art.

Arty Amsterdam

Amsterdam's world-class museums draw millions of visitors each year. You can't walk a kilometre without bumping into a Van Gogh, Rembrandt or Mondrian masterpiece.

Klimt in Austria

Start your gold-kissed Klimt journey at Vienna's Schloss Belvedere and continue at the Leopold Museum, Beethoven Frieze–bedecked Secession (pictured) and Kunsthistorisches Museum.

On Picasso's Trail

Pablo Picasso was born in Málaga, but spent his life in Madrid, Barcelona and Paris. Each city has a world-class gallery devoted to the master.

BEST ART EXPERIENCES

Tour Amsterdam's fabulous museums – there's none finer than the mighty **❶ Rijksmuseum** and **Van Gogh Museum**. (p477)

Take a wonder-struck tour of European masterpieces at the **❷ Musée du Louvre**, the pick of the gallery treasure-troves that adorn Paris. (p186)

Seek out celebrated masterpieces and lesser-known jewels of Madrid's golden triangle of art, including the **❸ Museo del Prado**. (p546)

Gaze heavenwards at Michelangelo's celebrated frescoes in the **❹ Sistine Chapel**, the papal church and the grand finale in the Vatican Museums. (p408)

Go face to face with world-famous Renaissance paintings at Florence's premier art museum, **❺ Galleria degli Uffizi**. (p435)

GARY PERKIN/SHUTTERSTOCK

Camel Trail (p129), Padstow, Britain

OUTDOOR ADVENTURES

Western Europe is a fabulous place to get active. The region's bountiful natural gifts – mountain ranges, lakes and rivers, ocean shores – provide opportunities for exploring wild Europe. Whether you're hiking, skiing, kayaking, horse riding, cycling or just about anything you can do outdoors, Western Europe has something to get excited about.

Biking Britain

The UK's National Cycle Network has 8400km of traffic-free paths, alongside 12,101km on-road. Bicycle rental places are never far away.

Hiking Season

The best hiking weather at lower altitudes is spring (April to June) and early autumn (September), but higher altitudes are best in summer (July to August).

BEST OUTDOOR EXPERIENCES

Walk Spain's ❶ **Camino de Santiago** in whole or in part for Western Europe's best long-distance walk. (p575)

Hike Crete's gorges, from spectacular ❷ **Samaria Gorge** to its equally breathtaking and less crowded nearby canyons. (p355)

Walk, cycle or cruise through the romantic ❸ **Rhine Valley**, past vineyards, castles and half-timbered wine villages. (p309)

Walk with the gods on the ❹ **Sentiero degli Dei**, a thrilling coastal trail that runs along the mountains of the Amalfi Coast. (p453)

Scare yourself stupid hurtling down the world's oldest bobsleigh run near ❺ **St Moritz** in Switzerland. (p617)

FABULOUS FOOD & WINE

Ranked among the culinary giants of world cuisine, France, Greece, Spain and Italy are glorious places to make food a centrepiece of your trip. Other countries, like Belgium and Portugal, are also brilliant if you know where to look. And France, Spain and Italy make some of the best wines anywhere in the world.

Portuguese Cod

In Portugal, there are 365 ways of cooking *bacalhau*. It requires patiently soaking the salted cod for at least 24 hours and changing the water regularly.

Italian Wines

Italy's wines are classified: DOCG, DOC, IGT, *vino da tavola* (table wine). Spain and France have similar classification systems.

Seafood & Siesta

A seafront taverna lunch in summer is a Greek cultural mainstay, with its parade of dips and dishes, followed by a decadent siesta.

FROM LEFT: LINGXIAO XIE/GETTY IMAGES, ELENA KATKOVA/SHUTTERSTOCK

BEST FOOD & WINE EXPERIENCES

Combine a medieval village setting with world-class artisan cheesemaking in Switzerland's **❶ Gruyères**. (p608)

Road-trip through the **❷ Loire Valley** with its wineries and walking trails that take you to the heart of good taste, France-style. (p216)

Try the original recipe of the world-famous *pastel de nata* (custard tart), freshly baked at **❸ Pastéis de Belém** in Lisbon. (p506)

Get a taste of the Basque Country's celebrated culinary creativity on a *pintxo*-bar crawl around **❹ Donostia-San Sebastián**. (p571)

Hunt down the perfect paella in its Valencia homeland of **❺ La Albufera**, where you can dine overlooking the rice crops. (p579)

19

REGIONS & CITIES

Find the places that tick all your boxes.

Ireland

ANCIENT HISTORY, SPELLBINDING SCENERY AND SPIRITED CULTURE

If it weren't for the weather, half the world would live in Dublin. This fun-loving, yet deeply cultured city opens out onto a world of villages and small towns, wild highland landscapes and even wilder coastlines out west. Best of all are the spirited people of this small but eternally fascinating land.

Ireland
p363

France

WINE, CHEESE AND WILDLY VARIED SCENERY

Paris, fairy-tale Mont St-Michel, the Loire Valley with its châteaux and vineyards, the near-perfect world of Provence, the Mediterranean, the French Alps, the Riviera... France's attractions read like a roll-call of European charm. And you'll eat and drink like a king wherever you go.

Portugal

A LAND SHAPED BY THE ATLANTIC

Like some decadent, ageless beauty on the continent's southwestern rim, Portugal deserves as much time as you can spare. Graceful, intriguing Lisbon is a must, but the same can be said of Porto, Coimbra, the Algarve and the Alentejo. Fine foods and soulful music are at the heart of Portuguese life.

Portugal
p498

Spain
p535

Britain

AN ANCIENT AND INSPIRING ISLAND

Britain is one of the continent's cultural giants. Storied London is the gateway to many a fine adventure that could include glorious cities (Bristol, Edinburgh), quaint village life (as in the Cotswolds) and wildly beautiful landscapes, from Cornwall to the Scottish Highlands and islands.

The Netherlands

CYCLING, CANALS AND DUTCH COURAGE

Amsterdam is one of Europe's most memorable cities, a world of canals and superb museums. It sets the scene for a country where clichés appear reliably often, from cheese markets and windmills to tulips and cycling. In fact, it can all seem like one beautiful impressionist masterpiece.

Belgium & Luxembourg

GABLED BUILDINGS AND OFFBEAT CHARM

Belgium's capital, Brussels, is the political heart of Europe. It also has fabulous medieval cities like Bruges and Ghent, and everywhere you go, expect beer, chocolate and other culinary stars. Meanwhile, Luxembourg's gorge setting crowned by a castle is big on more than novelty value.

Spain

A SOULFUL, SUNNY, FIESTA-LOVING LAND

Spain is a vibrant, passionate world unto itself. Its cities (Madrid, Barcelona, Seville) are repositories of all that's great about Spanish life – the food, the flamenco, the irresistible spirit coursing through its streets. And then there's the Moorish architecture, the wild northern coast and the beautiful Balearics.

Britain
p115

The Netherlands
p471

Belgium & Luxembourg
p78

France
p174

Switzerland

ALPINE TRADITION, OUTDOOR ACTION AND URBAN FUN

It's impossible not to fall in love with Switzerland. The Alps adorn almost every corner of this splendid country, its cuckoo-clock architecture and small villages offset by soaring mountains and lakes, achingly scenic train rides, and elegant cities like Lucerne, Bern, Geneva, Zürich and Lausanne.

Germany
p249

Austria
p47

Switzerland
p600

Italy
p394

Italy

EUROPE'S CULTURAL AND CULINARY PARADISE

It's impossible to overstate Italy's appeal. Perhaps you'll find it in the artistic riches of Rome and Venice, in the rolling hills of Tuscany or the soaring Dolomites of the north. Maybe you'll fall in love with the dramatic Amalfi Coast or the gritty charm and history of Sicily. Wherever you go, it will happen.

Germany

TRANQUIL LANDSCAPES AND FESTIVE TRADITIONS

Traditions reign supreme in every aspect of German life, from the medieval core, old Weinstüben and half-timbered architecture in vibrant modern cities to the wonderfully preserved villages of the Romantic Road. Berlin, the nation's heartbeat, is one of Western Europe's coolest cities.

Austria

WHERE CULTURE HITS THE HEIGHTS

Once the centre of its very own empire, Austria has some of the loveliest cities in Western Europe. The imperial capital of Vienna, as well as Innsbruck and Mozart's Salzburg, are simply superb. At the same time, the Alps are a constant and spectacular presence in this magnificent country.

Greece

THE PLACE FOR EPIC ADVENTURES

Blessed with iconic natural beauty and overlaid with an ancient story of soaring civilisation, Greece is filled with stories to discover. Everything begins in Athens, but islands like Crete, Corfu and Rhodes mean you could easily spend weeks here and still barely scratch the surface.

Greece
p318

VUNAV/SHUTTERSTOCK

La Sagrada Família and Barcelona (p555), Spain

ITINERARIES

Iconic Cities

Allow 2 weeks **Distance** 2650km (1647 miles)

To go to the heart of Western European culture, pick five of its most celebrated cities and build an itinerary around them. With only two weeks, you'll need to fly between them. This is a whirlwind tour, and you'll long for more time in each city – but what a fabulous trip awaits.

①

DUBLIN ⏱ 2 DAYS

Dublin (p366) is a special city and a glorious place to begin any exploration of urban Western Europe. Go on a literary pub crawl, wander the lively streets, visit the fabulous portfolio of museums and graceful architectural highlights. Yet more than any of these, Dublin is an idea, a relatively small city with a big heart and always up for a good time.

②

LONDON ⏱ 3 DAYS

London (p120) is a giant in so many ways, a place where so many icons of British culture and architecture stand tall: Big Ben, Buckingham Palace, Tower of London, the British Museum, the Shard. And yet, you'll love London just as much for the chance it offers to catch a show and enjoy a meal and a pint in a historic pub.

③

PARIS ⏱ 3 DAYS

There's nowhere on Earth like **Paris** (p180). This is a timeless city of elegant boulevards and streetside cafes, of world-class art galleries like the Musée du Louvre or the Musée d'Orsay, and landmarks like the Eiffel Tower or the reborn Notre Dame. But it's more than mere architecture or the city's joie de vivre. Paris is simply magical.

Glasgow
EDINBURGH
START
GREAT BRITAIN
North Sea
DENMARK
SWEDEN
Baltic Sea
Dublin
1
Liverpool
Leeds
IRELAND
Birmingham
London
2
CARDIFF
Bristol
Bremen
Hamburg
AMSTERDAM
BERLIN
POLAND
Rotterdam
Hanover
Antwerp
Leipzig
Dresden
Düsseldorf
Cologne
BRUSSELS
Lille
GERMANY
CZECHIA
Atlantic Ocean
Rouen
Paris
3
Rennes
Strasbourg
Stuttgart
Nuremberg
VIENNA
Linz
Salzburg
Munich
Nantes
Dijon
Zürich
Innsbruck
Graz
Bay of Biscay
FRANCE
BERN
Geneva
2hr
Lyon
Milan
Venice
Turin
CROATIA
Bordeaux
Genoa
Bologna
Gijón
Bilbao
Toulouse
Montpellier
SAN MARINO
Nice
Florence
Valladolid
Marseille
Zaragoza
Rome
5
MADRID
Barcelona
4
1¾hr
ITALY
Bari
SPAIN
Mediterranean Sea
END
Naples
Valencia
Palma de Mallorca
0 500 km
0 250 miles
Cagliari

4 BARCELONA 3 DAYS

Few Western European cities pulse with life quite like **Barcelona** (p555). This beguiling Spanish-Catalan city is adorned with the miraculous architecture of Antoni Gaudí and infused with a culinary culture that ranks it among the finest places to eat anywhere in Western Europe. Three days here might just be the start of a lifelong love affair with the city.

5 ROME 3 DAYS

Italy's eternal city is steeped in history that dates back millennia and echoes at every turn in the Colosseum, temples and monuments grand and ancient. **Rome** (p400) is also a city that lives the Italian dolce vita to the fullest, in its elegant public squares, homely *trattorias* and cafes. Then there's the Vatican, incredible museums and so much more.

St Peter's Basilica (p409), Vatican City

FROM LEFT: V_E/SHUTTERSTOCK, VIACHESLAV LOPATIN/SHUTTERSTOCK, PAOLO BONA/SHUTTERSTOCK

ITINERARIES

Mountains of Western Europe

Allow 2 weeks **Distance** 935km (581 miles)

The Alps rise above the Western European heartland and it's a fairy-tale world of storybook castles, postcard-perfect mountain villages, cable cars to high summits, ski resorts and idyllic lakes. The journey covers four countries (Austria, Germany, Switzerland and France), beginning in stately Salzburg and ending in the shadow of Western Europe's highest mountain.

1 SALZBURG ⏱ 3 DAYS

Welcome to one of Western Europe's most graceful cities, known as the city of Mozart. **Salzburg's** (p57) architectural gems line up along the river with a tight huddle of medieval streets. It's a compact city, but one worth lingering over for a couple of days.

🔺 *Detour: On day three, take a day trip to the mountain-ringed, jewel-like* **Hallstätter See** *(p62) in the Salzkammergut region.*

2 GARMISCH-PARTENKIRCHEN ⏱ 1 DAY

Where the plains of southern Bavaria come up against the soaring rocky spires of the Alps, **Garmisch-Partenkirchen** (p288) is a pretty alpine village and gateway to a whole other world. An old-fashioned cog railway runs from here to the summit of Zugspitze, Germany's highest peak. Go skiing and gaze out across one of the most spectacular views anywhere in the Alps.

3 FÜSSEN ⏱ 1 DAY

Further west along the northernmost boundary of the Alps, **Füssen** (p288) is a pretty, strollable old town. For all its charms, Füssen is thoroughly overshadowed by King Ludwig II's fairy-tale castle Schloss Neuschwanstein nearby, as well as the slightly more muted Schloss Hohenschwangau and a museum dedicated to Bavaria's legendary kings. The views in these parts are simply splendid.

4 ST MORITZ ⏱ 2 DAYS

There aren't many corners of Switzerland not covered by the Alps, and it can be difficult to choose which superb alpine village to use as a base. We'll make it easy: first pick one of Switzerland's ritziest ski resorts, **St Moritz** (p617), where you can ride the *Bernina Express* mountain railway. It's the kind of place you'll never want to leave.

AARONCHENP52/SHUTTERSTOCK ©

Glacier Express (p617) to St Moritz, Switzerland

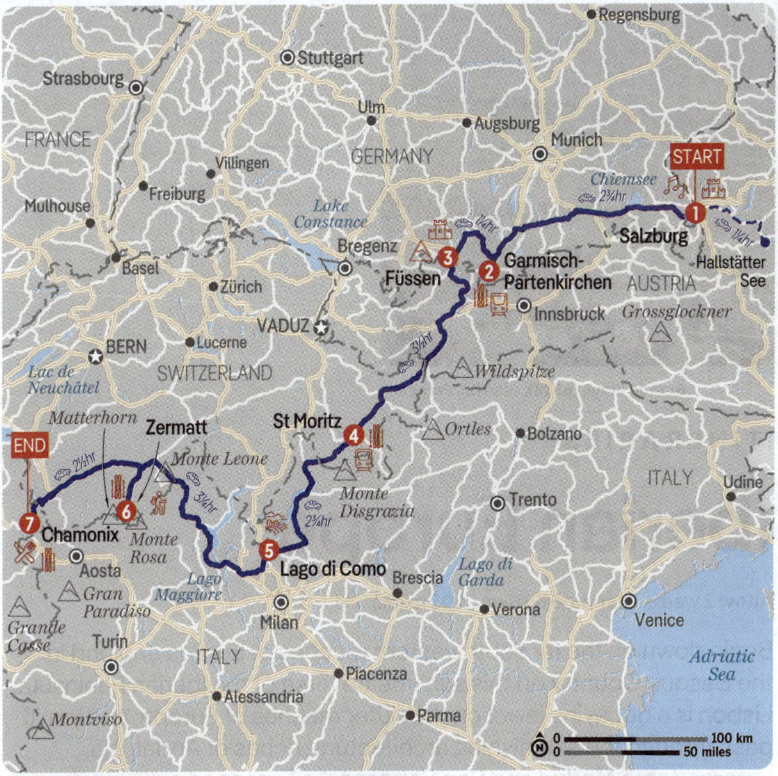
Regensburg
Stuttgart
Strasbourg
Ulm
Augsburg
Munich
START
FRANCE
Villingen
GERMANY
Chiemsee
2¾hr
Freiburg
Mulhouse
Lake Constance
1¼hr
1
Salzburg
1¼hr
Bregenz
3
2
Garmisch-Partenkirchen
Hallstätter See
Basel
Füssen
AUSTRIA
Zürich
Innsbruck
Grossglockner
VADUZ
BERN
Lucerne
3¼hr
Lac de Neuchâtel
SWITZERLAND
Wildspitze
Matterhorn
Zermatt
St Moritz
4
Ortles
Bolzano
END
2¼hr
Monte Leone
ITALY
Udine
3¼hr
6
Monte Disgrazia
Trento
2¾hr
7
Chamonix
Monte Rosa
5
Aosta
Lago di Como
Brescia
Lago di Garda
Gran Paradiso
Lago Maggiore
Milan
Verona
Venice
Grande Casse
Turin
ITALY
Adriatic Sea
Piacenza
Alessandria
Parma
Montviso
0 100 km
0 50 miles

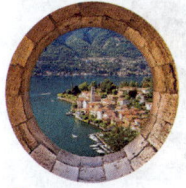

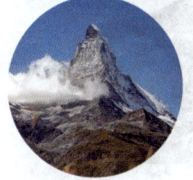

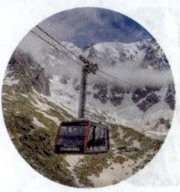

5

LAGO DI COMO ⏱ 3 DAYS

A Europe without borders is a privileged luxury for European travellers, and it's easy enough to dip down into Italy from Switzerland. Northern Italy is something of a playground for Europe's jet-set, especially the sparkling lake of **Lago di Como** (p420) beneath the towering peaks, with its exquisite Bellagio village. Three days is a minimum for exploring this most elegant of shorelines.

6

ZERMATT ⏱ 2 DAYS

Most Swiss alpine villages have chocolate-box charm in abundance, but few can match **Zermatt** (p614) when it comes to views. The Matterhorn – arguably Switzerland's most recognisable and shapeliest mountain – watches over the town, opening up all kinds of opportunities for skiing, hiking or simply staring at the view from a fireside cafe.

7

CHAMONIX ⏱ 2 DAYS

Of all the French ski towns, **Chamonix** (p203) carries the greatest cachet. Not only does it have Mont Blanc, Western Europe's highest summit, for company, it also has the continent's highest cable car, and some outrageously good skiing and hiking high on the slopes. The town itself oozes classic French elegance, with fine foods available on seemingly every street corner.

FROM LEFT: XBRCHX/SHUTTERSTOCK, L_B_PHOTOGRAPHY/SHUTTERSTOCK, JULIA MOUNTAIN PHOTO/SHUTTERSTOCK

Grande Plage (p238), Biarritz, France

ITINERARIES

Iberian Europe

Allow 2 weeks **Distance** 1938km (1205 miles)

Begin down on the far southwestern reaches of Europe and end in the Basque Country on this sublime traverse of the Iberian Peninsula. Lisbon is a decaying jewel on the outer reaches of Europe, and you'll pass through the astonishing architectural riches of Andalucía, unforgettable Madrid and San Sebastián, a European culinary giant.

① LISBON ⏱ 3 DAYS

It's difficult not to fall in love with **Lisbon** (p504), a decadent city that very much holds fast to its traditions and unique character. Wander its ancient streets, take in the views from its high lookouts, admire the soaring monuments to the days when Portugal ruled the seas, sample irresistible Portuguese cuisine and take in a fado performance.

② SEVILLE ⏱ 2 DAYS

When you think of Spain's Andalucian south, chances are you're thinking of **Seville** (p585). The grandeur of this ancient city is expressed in old-world, whitewashed neighbourhoods and intimate squares lined with some of Spain's most enjoyable tapas bars. A glorious cathedral, bejewelled architecture from the days of Al-Andalus and fabulous flamenco make for one special city.

③ CÓRDOBA ⏱ 2 DAYS

A rival to Seville when it comes Andalusian magic, **Córdoba** (p590) has a whitewashed old town, elegant courtyards and La Mezquita, one of Spain's most beautiful buildings. From its fruit-tree-filled gardens to the delicate arches of the interior, this is Al-Andalus at its finest.

🚗 *Detour: Head for **Granada** (p593) to visit La Alhambra, explore the Albaicín quarter and enjoy great food.* 🚌 *1 day*

The following map labels appear:

Atlantic Ocean

Bay of Biscay

FRANCE
• Bordeaux

• A Coruña
Santiago de Compostela
Vigo
Oviedo • Gijón
Santander
Bilbao
END
6 Donostia-San Sebastián
• Toulouse
León
Vitoria-Gasteiz
Pamplona
Perpignan
Porto
Valladolid
Burgos
Logroño
Zaragoza
PORTUGAL Salamanca
Segovia
Ávila
5 Madrid
SPAIN
Lleida
Girona
Tarragona
Barcelona
Coimbra
Cáceres
Toledo
Valencia **4**
Palma de Mallorca
START
1 Lisbon
Badajoz
Mérida
Ciudad Real
Albacete
Alicante
Faro
Huelva
Seville **2**
Córdoba **3**
Murcia
Mediterranean Sea
Cádiz
Málaga
Granada
Almería
Strait of Gibraltar

MOROCCO

ALGERIA

0   200 km
0   100 miles

4 VALENCIA ⏱ 2 DAYS

Across the high plateau and down to Spain's Mediterranean shore, **Valencia** (p576) belongs to a whole other world. The light seems brighter here along the coast, and it shines even brighter with the stellar Ciutat de les Arts i les Ciències. You can also glimpse the Holy Grail (pictured) and enjoy Spain's best paella by the beach or in La Albufera.

5 MADRID ⏱ 3 DAYS

You could spend weeks in **Madrid** (p540) and only scratch the surface, but a couple of days in the capital provides a good intro. Cycle around Retiro park, wander the renowned galleries and dive into the tapas scene and lively markets.

🚌 **Detour**: *Visit one of southern Castilla y León's historical cities, Segovia (p551) or Ávila (p551).* 🚌 *1 day*

6 DONOSTIA-SAN SEBASTIÁN ⏱ 2 DAYS

One of the world's great culinary cities, **Donostia-San Sebastián** (p571) is the perfect welcome to the north, with its cliff-edged beaches and buzzing old town. Go bar-hopping around the *pintxo* spots, try surfing, chill out on lovely Playa de la Concha and hike along the lush coastline.

🚌 **Detour**: *Catch a bus to Bilbao (p570) and dive into the Museo Guggenheim.* 🚌 *1 day*

ITINERARIES

Through the Heart of Western Europe

Allow 2 weeks **Distance** 2287km (1421 miles)

This journey traverses the Western European heartland, through countries that showcase centuries of the continent's cultural and architectural sophistication. As with all of these itineraries, you'll long for more time in each and pass by many tempting sideroads. But these fantastic cities are just the start.

❶ FLORENCE ⏱ 2 DAYS

Florence (p433) is a masterpiece cast in stone, a medieval triumph of style and sophistication that makes a strong case for being Italy's most beautiful city. The Duomo and the Galleria degli Uffizi are the crowning glory of this remarkable city, but the street life, the culinary excellence, the quiet public squares and palaces add up to something approaching urban perfection.

❷ VENICE ⏱ 2 DAYS

With its photogenic canals, stunning palazzi and slender gondolas, **Venice** (p425) gets you in the mood. If Piazza San Marco with its basilica and Palazzo Ducale are too crowded, seek out art in the Peggy Guggenheim Collection, admire Basilica di Santa Maria della Salute, scour seafood stalls at Rialto Market, bar-hop along Fondamenta dei Ormesini and snack on *cicheti* (Venetian tapas).

❸ MILAN ⏱ 2 DAYS

Stay in style in **Milan** (p417), Italy's fashion and finance capital. Marvel at the architectural excess of the Duomo and Leonardo da Vinci's *Last Supper* before browsing designer styles in the boutiques of the Quadrilatero d'Oro and catching a performance at La Scala. Dine on *risotto alla milanese* and toast the road ahead with a canal-side *aperitivo* in the Navigli area.

❹ PROVENCE ⏱ 3 DAYS

Provence (p220) is as much an idea as a place, a dreamy countryside of charming French villages, farm-to-table restaurants, medieval markets and centuries-old wineries. Base yourself (or simply begin) in Marseille, a gritty port city reborn into a cultural powerhouse of southern France, and one of the country's most rewarding culinary destinations.

PANI GARHYDEN/SHUTTERSTOCK

Vieux Port, Marseille (p226), France

5 PARIS ⏱ 2 DAYS

The bird's-eye city view from the Eiffel Tower is a breathtaking introduction to the capital that doesn't tire. Experience it at night, or gorge on the **Paris** (p180) panorama unfurling atop Arc de Triomphe instead. Don't miss a concert in the soul-soaring Sainte-Chapelle and Versailles. Factor in ample time for cafe lounging, bistro lunches and Seine-side strolls.

6 BRUGES ⏱ 1 DAY

Bruges (p94) has it all: romantic canals lined by picture-perfect houses, a towering belfry, a mysterious secret in a medieval church, an idyllic *begijnhof* (cluster of old terraced houses) and great museums. Ideally visit out of season, stay overnight, and rework your itinerary if necessary to avoid being here at weekends when visitor numbers peak.

6 AMSTERDAM ⏱ 2 DAY

Spend two days in **Amsterdam** (p476) to take in a couple of world-class museums and a canal cruise, as well as ample strolling around historic neighbourhoods. The perfect itinerary covers Jordaan, De Pijp, the Jewish Cultural Quarter and trendy Noord, with plenty of time allocated for getting lost and whiling away an hour or two watching the world pass by from a cafe.

FROM LEFT: ERIC ISSELEE/SHUTTERSTOCK, SERGII FIGURNYI/SHUTTERSTOCK, S. VINCENT/SHUTTERSTOCK

WHEN TO GO

Western Europe is magnificent all through the year, but the weather, festival calendars and visitor numbers should all play into your decision.

European summers are legendary for a reason – the weather can be glorious, everything's open and the whole world seems happy. But many places are paying for their own popularity with overtourism that causes long queues, high prices and even rumbling resentment among locals. From Barcelona to Venice, Amsterdam to the Greek islands, there may be better times to visit.

June is probably the pick of the summer months, with crowds yet to build but fine summer weather likely. The shoulder months of May and September can also be superb, with everything from fun festivals to spring wildflowers or autumn colours.

Winter can also be fabulous, with far fewer visitors, lower prices and greater hotel availability. It's also an excuse – if any were needed – to seek refuge inside cosy British and Irish pubs, visit German Christmas markets, go alpine skiing or seek out fun festivals like Carnival.

⊗ I LIVE HERE

TULIP FEVER

Jurriaan Teulings is a Dutch travel photographer living in De Pijp, Amsterdam @jurrpix

My perfect spring day is catching 'tulip fever' in less touristic East Amsterdam. Enjoy breakfast or lunch in Javastraat, stroll through blooming Flevopark, and cross the bridge over the Amsterdam-Rijnkanaal railings adorned with tulips. End up at Oranjesluizen, a pretty set of sluices you can walk across. Opposite, Schellingwoude is an incredibly picturesque Dutch village, or walk west to Noord and ferry back.

SUMMER RAIN?

The best bet for a blue-sky holiday in Germany, Netherlands and surrounding countries isn't in mid-summer but May, June and September. July and August often bring heatwaves, which can trigger sudden and intense thunderstorms, especially in the afternoons and evenings.

Tulips at the Rijksmuseum (p477), Amsterdam, the Netherlands

Weather through the Year: Paris

JANUARY	FEBRUARY	MARCH	APRIL	MAY	JUNE
Avg. daytime max: **6.9°C**	Avg. daytime max: **8.1°C**	Avg. daytime max: **11.6°C**	Avg. daytime max: **15.2°C**	Avg. daytime max: **18.6°C**	Avg. daytime max: **22.1°C**
Days of rainfall: **9**	Days of rainfall: **8**	Days of rainfall: **8**	Days of rainfall: **9**	Days of rainfall: **9**	Days of rainfall: **8**

MEDITERRANEAN WARMTH

The waters of the Mediterranean Sea are Europe's warmest, rising to around 26°C or 27°C during summer, around 16°C or 17°C in winter. Inland, cities like Spain's Seville and Córdoba can push close to 50°C in July and August.

Big-Ticket Festivals

The run-up to Lent, **Carnival** is celebrated with street partying, costumed parades, satirical shows and general revelry. The biggest parties are in Germany (Düsseldorf, Cologne and Mainz), Italy (Venice) and Spain (Sitges, Ciudad Rodrigo and the Balearics). 🌐 **February**

Sombre, compelling celebrations take over Spain during **Semana Santa** (Holy Week), which sees endlessly elaborate *pasos* (holy figures) paraded through the streets. It's especially big in Seville,

Málaga, Lorca, Cuenca, Zamora and Ávila. 🔆 **March/April**

LGBTIQ+ tourists from all over the world take part in the Saturday parade down Paseo del Prado for **Madrid Orgullo** (p547), the largest Pride festival in Europe. 🔆 **July**

Considered one of Western Europe's premier cultural festivals, **Edinburgh Fringe Festival** (p153) features live performances and all manner of events for all ages over three weeks. 🔆 **August**

Local & Quirky Festivals

Spain's's most important pilgrimage sees up to a million devotees join the **Romería del Rocío** (p589) in Andalucía's Huelva province on Pentecost (Whitsunday) weekend. 🔆 **May/June**

Belgium's 1815 **Battle of Waterloo** (p105) is re-enacted to dramatic effect with hundreds of costumed 'soldiers'. Held annually, but on an epic scale every five years (next in 2030). 🔆 **June/July**

Siena's Piazza del Campo sets the stage for **Palio** (p442), a daredevil horse race between costumed jockeys. Each rider represents one of the city's medieval *contrade* (districts). 🔆 **July/August**

Barcelona's post-summer extravaganza, **Festes de La Mercè** (p559) is riotous fun, with *castells* (human towers), *gegants* (papier-mâché giants) and *correfocs* (fire-running). 🔆 **September**

Praia da Ribeira d'Ilhas Ericeira, Portugal (p498)

SNOWFALL

Snow typically falls in the Alps, Apennines and Pyrenees from November to March. It also snows at lower altitudes, although this is increasingly unpredictable – and scant. Sicily's Mt Etna or Spain's Sierra Nevada are snowcapped most years from December to April.

JULY	AUGUST	SEPTEMBER	OCTOBER	NOVEMBER	DECEMBER
Avg. daytime max: 24.2°C	Avg. daytime max: 24°C	Avg. daytime max: 20.9°C	Avg. daytime max: 16.4°C	Avg. daytime max: 10.7°C	Avg. daytime max: 7.5°C
Days of rainfall: 8	Days of rainfall: 7	Days of rainfall: 6	Days of rainfall: 8	Days of rainfall: 9	Days of rainfall: 10

GET PREPARED FOR WESTERN EUROPE

Useful things to load in your bag, your ears and your brain.

Clothes

Smart casual Acceptable streetwear rarely dips below smart casual in most countries. Pack at least one smarter outfit for an evening out.

Comfy shoes Cobblestones and uneven pavements are everywhere, including archaeological sites. Opt for closed-toe flats with good grip (or hiking shoes).

Layers Rain is possible at any time, especially the further north you go. Pack versatile layers, a waterproof coat or rain jacket and all-weather sturdy shoes.

Summer gear All across the Mediterranean south, breezy clothes are best during the hot summers, along with hats, sunglasses, swimwear and sun cream.

Manners

Greetings Always say a greeting when entering a shop, restaurant or business in most countries.

Learn how to kiss It's two kisses on meeting casual acquaintances and friends in Spain, up to four in parts of France.

Language Always learn a few words in the local language and use them – locals will love you for trying.

Shawl or scarf These serve a double purpose – warmth on cool evenings and for entering churches in Italy, Spain and elsewhere.

📖 READ

And Their Children After Them (Nicolas Mathieu; 2018) Goncourt Prize–winning 'coming of age' novel set in post-industrial Lorraine.

The Leopard (Giuseppe Tomasi di Lampedusa; 1958) Historical novel evoking the social tremors that shook Sicily during Italian unification.

Homeland (Fernando Aramburu; 2016) Highly acclaimed novel revolving around the ETA terror campaign.

Stasiland (Anna Funder; 2003) The Stasi's vast spying apparatus from the perspectives of both victims and perpetrators.

Words

FRENCH
Bonjour 'Good morning' or 'Hello'; switch to *bonsoir* (good evening) in late afternoon
Salut More casual way of saying 'hello' or 'hi'
Comment allez-vous? How are you?
S'il vous/te plaît Please (pol/inf)
Merci Thank you
De rien You're welcome

GERMAN
Guten Morgen Good morning; *hallo* can be used any time of day
Guten Tag/Abend Good day/evening
Auf Wiedersehen Goodbye; *Tschüss* (bye) will do among friends
Sprechen Sie Englisch? Do you speak English?
Ich verstehe nicht I don't understand

ITALIAN
Ciao 'Hi' or 'bye' to friends or family
Buongiorno Good morning; *Buona sera* is 'good afternoon/evening'
Arrivederci Goodbye
Per favore Please
Grazie 'Thank you', to which the response is *Prego,* 'You're welcome'
Come stai? The informal version of 'How are you?'

SPANISH
Hola Hello
Buenos días Good morning
Buenas tardes/noches Good afternoon/night
¿Qué tal? An informal way of saying *¿Como estás?* (How are you?)
Por favor Please
(Muchas) Gracias Thank you (very much)
¿Habla/Hablas inglés? Do you speak English? (pol/inf)

▶ WATCH

The Crown (2016–23) Historic drama series about England's royal family, during the life and reign of Queen Elizabeth II.

L'Amour ouf (Gilles Lellouche; 2024) A teenage love story amid a life of crime in '80s and '90s mining communities near Dunkirk.

La dolce vita (Federico Fellini; 1960) Marcello Mastroianni and Anita Ekberg frolicking in Rome's Trevi Fountain.

Run Lola Run (Tom Tykwer; 1998) Stylish, fast-paced thriller with killer techno soundtrack capturing Berlin's late-'90s energy.

Todo sobre mi madre (Pedro Almodóvar; 1999) An early Almodóvar classic tackling complex issues, set in Barcelona.

🎧 LISTEN

DNK (Aya Nakamura; 2023) Top-selling album by the French-Malian sensation who opened the 2024 Paris Olympics.

Geschichte ist Gegenwart: The New Germany (Katja Hoyer & Oliver Moody; 2022–25) Podcast with insights into culture, society and politics.

Un briciolo di allegria (Mina & Blanco; 2023) Smash-hit duet by best-selling Italian artist of all time Mina and disruptive rapper Blanco.

El mal querer (Rosalía; 2018) Show-stealing second album by Spanish superstar Rosalía, known for her R&B-influenced flamenco tracks.

Rijksmuseum (p477), Amsterdam, the Netherlands

HOW TO...

Enjoy Western European Museums

Whether you're an experienced aficionado or a curious beginner, Western Europe will satisfy your inner art lover. World-class galleries and museums stand at the centre of cultural life here, and we strongly recommend making some of these galleries a centrepiece of your journey.

Buying Tickets

You might get away with simply turning up and buying a ticket in the depths of winter. But during the rest of the year that's a recipe for disappointment, especially in major galleries. Check the galleries' websites and buy a ticket as far in advance as you can.

Usually, you're not just choosing a date but a time slot as well. The time listed on your ticket is not a hard-and-fast rule – we've turned up before our allocated time slot and been allowed in. Don't count on it, and always turn up right on time. But if you happen to be early, don't be afraid to ask.

Beat the Crowds

The best times to visit most art museums is outside the summer months and on weekdays; locals often visit these galleries on weekends. In the peak summer season, try and organise your visit for the earliest opening hours of the day – even during the busiest times, it can be mid- or even late morning before queues really start to form or online tickets sell out.

Saving Money

London's big-hitter museums give free entry to their permanent collections. Elsewhere, museums and galleries have free- or reduced-admission days (often the first Sunday of the month); for example, as part of the Domenica al Museo initiative, many state museums in Italy are free on the first Sunday of the month from March to October. In other countries, it may be one evening during the week. In Madrid's major galleries, admission is often free for the last two hours of the day. Some cities with lots of art galleries may offer multi-museum tickets. In Madrid, for example, the Paseo del Arte ticket covers three museums and will save you 20% off the individual ticket prices.

MUST-SEE GALLERIES

France: Musée du Louvre (p186), Musée d'Orsay (p184) and Musée National Picasso-Paris (p190) (Paris)
Spain: Museo del Prado (p546), Museo Thyssen-Bornemisza (p546) and Centro de Arte Reina Sofía (p546) (Madrid); Museo Guggenheim Bilbao (p570) (Bilbao); Teatre-Museu Dalí (p567) (Figueres)
Netherlands: Rijksmuseum (p477) and Van Gogh Museum (p477) (Amsterdam)
Italy: Vatican Museums (p408) (Rome); Basilica di Santa Maria delle Grazie (p420) (Milan); Galleria degli Uffizi (p435) (Florence); Gallerie dell'Accademia (p430) (Venice)
Austria: MuseumsQuartier (p54) and Leopold Museum (p54) (Vienna)
Britain: Tate Modern (p125) (London)

IRINA MELIUKH/SHUTTERSTOCK

Moussaka

THE FOOD SCENE

Culinary traditions run deep on this continent, and every country is its own wonderful world of gastronomy.

When it comes to stellar world cuisines, the countries of Western Europe have colonised the planet. And going to the source and sampling French, Spanish, Italian and other cuisines on their home terrain is one of the greatest joys of travelling the region.

Every Western European nation has its own specialities (Irish seafood chowder, Italian pasta and pizza, Spanish tapas and paella, French crêpes and croissants, Swiss fondue, Austrian Wiener schnitzel, German bratwurst, Greek souvlaki and moussaka...) that are known well beyond its borders. But these are merely the best-known dishes to emerge from regional cuisines of astonishing richness. Within each country, especially in southern Europe, local specialities can vary from one village to the next. Plotting your path through Western Europe with this in mind will add depth and great flavour to your trip. Put another way, locals in these parts make food a centrepiece of lives lived well – why not approach your trip with the same philosophy?

Sampling the Starters

With so much to choose from, it can be daunting to find your entry point into the cuisine of any particular country. An excellent starting point is to order the starters that cover a wide range of specialities in one sitting. Spanish tapas is a case in point – they can be anything as long it's a bite-sized morsel, and most Spanish dishes make an appearance in some form as a tapa. Charcuterie boards – as a Spanish *ración*

Best Western European Dishes

GAZPACHO
Chilled Spanish garlic-and-tomato soup; *salmorejo* is a thicker version from Córdoba.

QUICHE LORRAINE
French eggs, milk or cream and bacon bits, baked in a pastry shell.

SOUPE À L'OIGNON
French onion soup traditionally served with a slide of cheesy toast on top.

MOUSSAKA
Greek dish with layers of aubergine, cheese sauce, minced meat and potato.

(with *jamón*, chorizo, *lomo, salchichón*) or Italian antipasto (with salami, prosciutto and *mortadella*) – is like a crash course in Mediterranean culinary obsessions. Cheeses can serve a similar purpose, from world-famous Spanish and French varieties (Manchego, Brie, Camembert) to Dutch Gouda and Maasdam, or Swiss Gruyère. Best of all, many of these can be purchased in supermarkets or, better still, delicatessens.

Regional Variety

France is an obvious place to begin. Go to Burgundy and Bordeaux for wine-based cooking; Normandy for cream, apples and cider; Brittany and the Atlantic Coast for seafood; Lyon for offal; Corsica for earthy dishes smacking of the herbal maquis; Languedoc-Roussillon for Catalan cuisine; and Pays Basque for a slice of Spanish spice.

There's a whole world of Spanish cuisine to experience between the seafood of Galicia, Asturias and the Basque Country and the olives, *jamón* (ham), *pescaíto frito* (fried fish) and sangría of Andalucía; or between the roasted meats and hearty stews of Madrid and the interior, and the abundant rice dishes of Catalonia, Valencia and the Balearics.

In Italy, what type of pasta, ham or cheese you'll find depends on where you are in the country. Umbrians have *strangozzi* and Puglians can't get enough of *orecchiette*. In Emilia-Romagna cooks love egg pastas like *tagliatelle* and *tortellini*. Similarly, there are endless variations of hams and cured meats, ranging from Parma's celebrated prosciutto to *mortadella* (pork cold cut) from Bologna.

Oktoberfest (p253), Munich

FOOD & DRINK FESTIVALS

Brum Brew Fest (p139; August) Spend a weekend crawling through Birmingham's best pubs.

Galway International Oyster & Seafood Festival (p383; September) Galway Bay is the source of Ireland's famous oysters, and Galway City hosts the world's oldest oyster festival.

Fête du Vin Nouveau et de la Brocante (p234; October) France's Bordeaux region hosts this two-day wine festival in Chartrons.

Oktoberfest (p253; September/October) Balance those litre-sized beers with roast chicken, pork and pretzels at Munich's late-September classic.

Chestnut Festival & Amphora Wine Day (p526; November) The Alentejo region of Portugal has roasted chestnut (Marvão) and *talha* wine (Vidigueira) tastings.

Jamón tapas

TAGLIATELLE AL RAGÙ	SPAGHETTI ALLE VONGOLE	ARROCES	TAPAS/PINTXOS	POFFERTJES
The original Italian spag bol: long pasta ribbons with meat sauce.	Much-loved Italian seafood pairing of spaghetti and clams.	There's a world of Spanish rice dishes beyond paella, including *fideuà* (with noodles).	From *jamón* (ham) to cheeses, Basque-style *pintxos* are slivers of bread with toppings.	Puffy Dutch mini-pancakes generously layered with butter and powdered sugar.

Local Specialities

Sweet Treats

Mince pie Sweet fruit pie often served at Christmas in the UK.
Apfelstrudel Flaky German pastry filled with apples and served with vanilla custard.
Cannoli Italy's biscuity pastry tubes packed with creamy ricotta.
Tiramisu Italian *trattoria* staple of coffee, chocolate, mascarpone and ladyfingers.
Churros con chocolate Spain's deep-fried doughnut strips for dipping in rich hot chocolate.

Cannoli

Street Food

Pie and mash Traditional working-class London meal.
Wurst German sausages, from bratwurst to *Currywurst*, *Bockwurst* or *Weisswurst*.
Pizza al taglio Pizza by the slice is the perfect Roman snack.
Arancini Sicilian fried-rice balls stuffed with *ragù* (meat sauce) and cheese.
Gouda Traditional cheeses at a historic Dutch market.

Cheap Eats

Pork pie Traditional English meat pie – cold pork wrapped in crimped pastry.
Croque monsieur France's toasted ham-and-cheese sandwich.

Pa amb tomàquet Catalonia's beloved bread with tomato, salt and olive oil.
Tortilla de patatas Classic Spanish potato omelette, with or without onion.
Croquetas Spain's deep-fried breaded parcels, stuffed with *jamón*, mushrooms and more.

Dare to Try

Black pudding A type of sausage made from pig's blood, originating from Britain.
Marmite British salty spread made from yeast extract.
Il quinto quarto Roman gourmands prize 'the fifth quarter' (the animal's interiors).
Percebes Goose barnacles, a claw-like Galician favourite.
Callos Tripe in a herby tomato sauce, particularly popular in Madrid.

MEALS OF A LIFETIME

Auberge Sauvage (p196) A Michelin-starred haven near Mont St-Michel, set in a 16th-century presbytery.
Casa Perbellini (p422) World-class, three-star Michelin dining in Verona (tasting menus from €220).
La Taverna di San Giuseppe (p441) This historic Siena eatery, set in a 12th-century building, offers an overload of Tuscan flavours.
Tasca Zé dos Cornos (p507) Homemade Portuguese meals are the speciality at this family-run *tasca* (tavern) in Lisbon.
Mercado de San Miguel (p541) A 19th-century Madrid market turned gastronomic hub; great for tapas.
StreetXO (p546) Vibrant younger sibling of Madrid's famous Michelin-starred restaurant, DiverXo, led by Spanish chef Dabiz Muñoz.

THE YEAR IN FOOD

SPRING

Fresh fruits and vegetables come to the fore; asparagus is a favourite in France, Germany and the Netherlands, as is everything from wild garlic and artichokes to strawberries. Easter lamb is popular throughout.

SUMMER

Markets are bursting with fresh fruits, while seafood is a recurring theme by the coast. Andalucía's cold soups gazpacho and *salmorejo* (pictured), plus Mediterranean rice dishes, are the key ingredients of a Spanish summer.

AUTUMN

Grape harvests produce plenty of local brews – cider in Britain, wine in France, Spain and Italy, and *raki* in Greece. Mushrooms (Spain), wild boar and truffles (Italy), come to the fore.

WINTER

Christmas markets in Germany and surrounding countries come with gingerbread and mulled wine. Just about everywhere, hearty winter stews and roasted meats keep everyone warm. *Turrón* (nougat) is a Spanish Christmas treat.

39

Lago di Como (p420), Italy

THE OUTDOORS

Western Europe's outdoors is ripe for exploration, from hiking through its wild mountain ranges to winter sports, kayaking, surfing monstrous Atlantic waves and more.

Western Europe is a beautiful place of rich diversity, and its landscapes are a call to adventure and immersion through outdoor activities of extraordinary variety. Hiking is possible for much of the year in the hut-dotted ridges and valleys of the Alps, Pyrenees and Dolomites. Those same mountains host skiers and snowboarders in the snow-clad Western European winter. And throughout the year, the region's lakes and rivers offer exploration opportunities of their own, from kayaking to white-water rafting.

Walking & Hiking

Bring your hiking boots: Western Europe is a world-class hiking destination. The Alps (Switzerland, Austria, Germany and Italy), rising above 4000m, the jagged Pyrenees along the France–Spain border, Spain's village-speckled Sierra Nevada, Italy's pink-tinged Dolomites – each range beckons with everything from day walks to multi-day, hut-to-hut treks.

Highlights among many include France's Tour du Mont Blanc, Spain's pilgrim-favourite Camino de Santiago, Scotland's Munro-skimming West Highland Way, Crete's gasp-inducing Samaria Gorge or the Fishermen's Trail on the Rota Vicentina in Portugal's southwest. Out in Ireland's west, Connemara has some fabulous hill walks, as does Snowdonia in Wales.

For hiking resources, **Cicerone** (*cicerone.co.uk*) gives you a head-start with well-researched walking guides. **Kompass** (*kompass.de*) produces reliable maps, and handy apps include **AllTrails** (*alltrails.com*). For self-guided and guided walking holidays in Europe, check out the likes of **Ramble Worldwide** (*rambleworldwide.co.uk*), **Headwater** (*headwater.com*) and **Macs Adventure** (*macsadventure.com*).

Adrenaline Activities

BOBSLEDDING
For a minute in the life of an Olympic bobsleigh racer, ride the **Olympia Bob** (p69) in Igls in the Alps of Tyrol.

RAFTING & CANYONING
Race through white water in Switzerland's raging rivers and gorges near **Interlaken** (p615).

PARAGLIDING
Drift above the monastery-topped rocks of **Meteora** (p333) in Greece on a tandem or motorised paragliding flight.

Skiing & Snowboarding

Europe's mountains call to skiers and snowboarders from whenever temperatures start to drop and snow begins to fall. Funiculars and cable cars climb slopes where you'll find cross-country trails, downhill slopes from beginner trails to black runs, and even summertime glacier skiing.

The season generally runs from December to Easter. Ski passes aren't cheap, but avoiding school holidays and favouring low-key villages over upscale resorts make it easier to enjoy the slopes on a budget. Bigger resorts have ski schools offering individual and group lessons. Runs are colour-coded according to difficulty: blue (easy), red (intermediate) and black (expert). Skis, snowboards, boots, poles and helmets can be rented at sport shops, including **Intersport** (*intersportrent.com*), which covers 14 countries in Europe.

The choice of resorts is endless all across the Alps and the Pyrenees. Spain's Sierra Nevada is Europe's southernmost ski destination.

Water Sports

From the foaming rivers of the Alps to deep dives in the crystal-clear Med, Europe is ideal for (mostly summer) watery adventures.

On the coast, sea kayaking raises pulses, with highs including paddling Italy's crazily pretty Cinque Terre. Summer (June to September) is best for divers plunging to reefs, wrecks and grottoes; **PADI** (*padi.com*) gives the inside scoop on sites and courses.

Winter (November to February) brings the biggest swells, with waves bashing Atlantic beaches in surf magnets like Portugal, the Canary Islands, the UK and Norway. **Surf Atlas** (*thesurfatlas.com*) has details on surf resorts, camps and schools.

Don't forget Europe's rivers, lakes and wild Atlantic coast. Highlights include stand-up paddleboarding in Austria's Wörthersee, or sea kayaking at various points along the Portuguese coast.

ACTION AREAS

See p42

Skiing in Sierra Nevada (p594), Spain

VIA FERRATA
Flirt with mountaineering around **Lake Como** (p421); these fixed climbing routes deliver thrills and knockout views.

SURFING
Surf the world-famous left-hand barrel of **Mundaka** (p572) along Spain's northern Basque coast.

BLACK RUN
Thunder down Europe's longest black run at the speed of light skiing in **Alpe d'Huez** (p208).

ZIPLINING
Zipline down through the otherworldly landscapes of a former quarry at **Blaenau Ffestiniog** (p152) in North Wales.

ACTION AREAS

Where to find Western Europe's best outdoor activities.

Surfing

1 Mundaka (p571), Spain
2 Playa de Somo (p573), Spain
3 El Palmar (p593), Spain
4 Plage de la Côte des Basques (p238), France
5 Nazaré (p510), Portugal
6 Costa Vicentina (p518), Portugal
7 Newquay (p131), Britain

Shetland Islands

Orkney Islands

SCOTLAND
Inverness
Aberdeen
Outer Hebrides
Glasgow
Dundee
EDINBURGH
North Sea
NORTHERN IRELAND
Derry
BELFAST
Newcastle-upon-Tyne
Galway
IRELAND
DUBLIN
Manchester
Liverpool
Leeds
NETHERLANDS
Limerick
Kilkenny
Sheffield
Nottingham
Rotterdam
Killarney
Irish Sea
Leicester
AMSTERDAM
Cork
Waterford
Birmingham
ENGLAND
WALES
CARDIFF
Oxford
LONDON
Den Haag
Bristol
Antwerp
St Ives
Portsmouth
Brighton
Ghent
BELGIUM
Plymouth
BRUSSELS
Lille
English Channel (La Manche)
Caen
Rouen
Reims
Nancy
Brest
PARIS
Rennes
Le Mans
Troyes
Nantes
Orléans
Dijon
Tours
Bourges
Geneva
Bay of Biscay
Poitiers
FRANCE
Lyon
La Rochelle
Clermont-Ferrand
Grenoble
A Coruña
Gijón
Donostia-San Sebastián
Bordeaux
Nîmes
Santiago de Compostela
Lugo
Bilbao
Bayonne
Toulouse
Nice
Vigo
León
Pau
Montpellier
Marseille
Burgos
Pamplona
Porto
Vila Real
Valladolid
Zaragoza
Girona
Perpignan
PORTUGAL
Salamanca
Barcelona
Coimbra
MADRID
Tarragona
Atlantic Ocean
Cáceres
Toledo
Valencia
Balearic Islands
Menorca
LISBON
Évora
Badajoz
SPAIN
Albacete
Mallorca
Seville
Córdoba
Alicante
Palma de Mallorca
Faro
Granada
Murcia
Ibiza
Cádiz
Málaga
Cartagena
Mediterranean Sea
Gibraltar (UK)
Almería

MOROCCO

Wineries

1 Rhine Valley (p311), Germany
2 Bordeaux (p232), France
3 Loire Valley (p216), France
4 La Rioja (p575), Spain
5 The Algarve (p516), Portugal
6 Nemea (p338), Greece

Beaches

1 The Algarve (p516), Portugal
2 Costa Brava (p566), Spain
3 Cabo de Gata (p594), Spain
4 Naxos (p342), Greece
5 Sicily (p455), Italy

Hiking
1. Camino de Santiago (p573), Spain
2. Tour du Mont Blanc (p203), France
3. West Highland Way (p163), Britain
4. Samaria Gorge (p355), Greece
5. Rota Vicentina (p518), Portugal
6. Connemara National Park (p385), Ireland
7. Eryri National Park (Snowdonia; p150), Britain

Skiing/Snowboarding
1. Kitzbühel (p70), Austria
2. Innsbruck (p68), Austria
3. Chamonix (p203), France
4. Les Trois Vallées (p208), France
5. Alpe d'Huez (p208), France
6. Portarró d'Espot (p568), Spain
7. Zermatt (p614), Switzerland
8. St Moritz (p617), Switzerland

THE GUIDE

Ireland
p363

Britain
p115

The
Netherlands
p471

Germany
p249

Belgium &
Luxembourg
p78

France
p174

Switzerland
p600

Austria
p47

Italy
p394

Portugal
p498

Spain
p535

Greece
p318

Chapters in this section are organised by
countries, with each country split into hubs
and their surrounding areas. Each hub includes
unique experiences, local insights, insider tips
and expert recommendations. It's also your
gateway to the surrounding area, where you'll
see what and how much you can do from there.

Douro Valley (p515), Portugal

For places to stay in Austria, see p73

LIUDMILA KIERMEIER/SHUTTERSTOCK

Above: Stift Melk (p54), Melk; Right: Skiing, Kitzbühel (p70)

Curated by
Kerry Walker

Austria

WHERE CULTURE HITS THE HEIGHTS

No country waltzes so effortlessly between urban and outdoors as Austria. One day you're cresting alpine summits, the next you're swanning around imperial Vienna.

For such a tiny country, Austria is ridiculously big on inspiration. This is the land where Mozart was born, Strauss taught the world to waltz and Julie Andrews grabbed the spotlight with her twirling entrance in *The Sound of Music*. It's where the Habsburgs ruled over their spectacular, sprawling 600-year empire.

These past glories still shine in the resplendent baroque palaces and chandelier-lit coffee houses of Vienna, Innsbruck and Salzburg. Over centuries, the Habsburgs channelled immense wealth into the fine arts and music, collecting palaces the way others do stamps. You'll feel their cultural reverberations today – be it hearing the work of classical masters echo at lavishly gilded concert halls, eye-

balling avant-garde art in born-again baroque riding stables, or catching a summer music festival against an uplifting lakeside or mountain backdrop.

Beyond its storybook cities, Austria's trump card is its astonishing natural beauty, which waltzes joyously from the romance of the vine-strewn Wachau to the crystal-clear lakes of Carinthia. Whether you're schussing down the legendary slopes of Kitzbühel, spotting an ibex in the fiery light of sunset as you crest a mountain ridge in Hohe Tauern National Park, or freewheeling along the banks of the mighty Danube, you'll find the kind of landscapes to which no well-orchestrated symphony or singing nun could ever quite do justice.

GEVISION/SHUTTERSTOCK

THE MAIN AREAS

Find Your Way

Austria's public transport network is a dream, with swift, inexpensive trains linking towns and cities, and buses filling the gaps. Car hire gives you greater freedom to explore the country's remotest corners.

CAR

Autobahn (motorways) are well maintained. You can only drive on them with a *Vignette* (motorway tax), available from border crossings and petrol stations. Be prepared for exposed, sharply twisting roads in the Alps.

TRAIN

Austria's rail network is fast, efficient, inexpensive and wide-reaching. Österreiche Bundesbahn (ÖBB; Austrian Federal Railway; oebb.at) is the main operator. The best deals are *Sparschiene*, heavily discounted tickets sold up to six months ahead.

Vienna, p50

Baroque streetscapes and imperial palaces set the stage for Vienna's artistic and musical masterpieces alongside its coffee-house culture and vibrant epicurean and design scenes.

Salzburg, p57

Legends have been made and born on these grand baroque streets, where you can explore Mozart's 'hood, climb to a medieval castle and catch one of Europe's greatest summer festivals.

Innsbruck & Tyrol, p67

Cultured Innsbruck is the springboard for mountains that make you want to yodel out loud, from summer's patchwork pastures to Christmas-card scenes in winter.

Graz & the South, p64

Castle-topped Graz beguiles with medieval looks and edgy art, while beyond rolling hills, vines, orchards and pristine mountain lakes entice.

CZECHIA

SLOVAKIA

GERMANY

SWITZERLAND

LIECHTENSTEIN

ITALY

SLOVENIA

HUNGARY

Bratislava

Neusiedl am See

Neusiedler See

VIENNA

Eisenstadt

Szombathely

Laa an der Thaya

Mistelbach

Retz

Hollabrunn

St Pölten

Tulln

Baden bei Wien

Wiener Neustadt

Neunkirchen

Oberpullendorf

Oberwart

Feldbach

Bad Radkersburg

Maribor

Klagenfurt

Völkermarkt

Wolfsberg

Feldkirchen im der Glan

St Veit an der Glan

Spittal an der Drau

Villach

Lienz

Klaach

Judenburg

Murau

Knittelfeld

Leoben

Theben

Liezen

Mürzzuschlag

Kapfenberg

Hartberg

Gleisdorf

Leibnitz

Bad Gleichenberg

Graz

Köflach

Tamsweg

Radstadt

Bischofshofen

Bad Gastein

Gmünd

Zwettl

Horn

Krems an der Donau

Melk

Amstetten

Steyr

Enns

Wels

Linz

Freistadt

České Budějovice

Lambach

Gmunden

Ebensee

Bad Ischl

Ried

Mattighofen

Braunau am Inn

Landshut

Munich

Rosenheim

Kufstein

Wörgl

Kitzbühel

Zell am See

Saalfelden

Mittersill

Jenbach

Zell am Zillter

Innsbruck

Imst

Landeck

St Anton am Arlberg

Bludenz

Feldkirch

Vaduz

Chur

St Gallen

Konstanz

Memmingen

Kempten

Sonthofen

Bregenz

Dornbirn

Salzburg

Mondsee

Bodensee

Zugspitze

Wildspitze

Piz Buin

Schesaplana

Hoher Dachstein

Grossglockner

Hohe Tauern National Park

Nationalpark Kalkalpen

Großvenediger

Ötztaler

Landeck

Merano

Bolzano

Bressanone

Danube (Donau)

Drava (Drau)

100 km

50 miles

Cycling in the Zillertal (p70)

Plan Your Time

Austria looks deceptively small on a map, but as most of it is vertical there's always a mountain pass, alpine view or hidden hamlet to discover. Avoid peak season for better deals.

Vienna to Salzburg

● Begin with palaces, parks, galleries and world-class concert halls in **Vienna** (p50). An hour west is **Wachau** (p55) on the River Danube, home to twin-spired baroque abbey **Stift Melk** (p55). Next stop is UNESCO-stamped **Hallstatt** (p62). Continue west to **Werfen** (p61) and the **Eisriesenwelt** (p61) ice caves, before rounding out with fortress-topped **Salzburg** (p57).

Into the Tyrolean Alps

● Admire soaring peaks in **Innsbruck** (p67). Roam the Altstadt's medieval lanes, before breezing up to 2334m **Hafelekarspitze** (p69). Skip east to **Swarovski Crystal Worlds** (p69) in Wattens. Detour south to the **Zillertal** (p70) for mountain biking, hiking, whitewater rafting and skiing. From here, head east to **Kitzbühel** (p70) for more action on Olympic slopes.

SEASONAL HIGHLIGHTS

SPRING
Meadows and parks bloom. Snow polishes the highest Alps, but there's cycling and hiking in valleys. Easter markets dazzle.

SUMMER
Light, warm days entice hikers. Cities host open-air festivals, including Vienna's **Donauinselfest** (p53).

AUTUMN
New wine in *Heurigen* (taverns) and highs like **Steirischer Herbst festival** (p65). Cows descend from pastures at the **Almabtrieb** (p72).

WINTER
Alpine slopes buzz, Christmas markets sparkle and Vienna waltzes into ball season. Salzburg gets orchestral at **Mozartwoche** (p59).

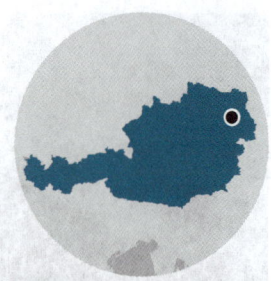

Vienna

REGAL HISTORY | HIGH CULTURE | CUTTING-EDGE ARTS

GETTING AROUND

Vienna's historic centre and inner districts are easy to explore on foot, including the Hofburg, museum complexes, modern neighbourhoods with landmarks and low-key nightlife. Schloss Schönbrunn can be easily reached by bus, tram and metro from the centre. Get information at *wienerlinien.at*.

Few cities in the world waltz so effortlessly between past and present, urban and outdoors like Vienna, a capital that has clocked up Mercer's 'most liveable city in the world' for many consecutive years. Its splendid historical face is easily recognised: grand imperial palaces and bombastic baroque interiors, revered opera houses, magnificent squares and art-vault museums curated over the 600-year reign of the Habsburgs.

But Austria's capital isn't bound by its vintage time bubble. Dig deeper, and you'll see a multifaceted Vienna on a spectrum from grandeur to gritty that bridges the classical and the contemporary. You'll need to cover some ground, though – which is easy to do via Vienna's excellent and cheap public transport system.

A stone's throw from Hofburg (the Imperial Palace), the MuseumsQuartier houses provocative and high-profile contemporary art behind a striking basalt facade. In the Innere Stadt (Inner City), up-to-the-minute design stores sidle up to old-world confectioners, and Austro-Asian fusion restaurants stand alongside traditional *Beisln* (small taverns).

Seeking Out Stephansdom

Vienna's symbolic landmark cathedral

Vienna's Gothic masterpiece **Stephansdom** (*stephanskirche. at)* soars above. A mosaic of 230,000 glazed roof tiles crests in between, stamped with the imperial double-headed eagle. It's free to venture into the vaulted, prismatic glass site. You have to pay to enter the central **nave** (*adult/child €7/3, cash only*) for a closer look at the 16th-century sandstone masterwork on the **Pilgramkanzel** (Pilgrim pulpit) and the commanding baroque black marble **High Altar** consecrating the holy space some 100 years later.

Austria's largest bell, the 21-tonne *Pummerin,* is accessible via an elevator journey to the **North Tower** (*adult/child €7/3)*

☑ **TOP TIP**

There's an easy way to know when you've left the circular centre. The grandiose architectural loop of the Ringstrasse surrounding the Innere Stadt, completed on one side of the Danube Canal, is a great orientation point. Beyond this boulevard border, you enter the fringes of the inner districts.

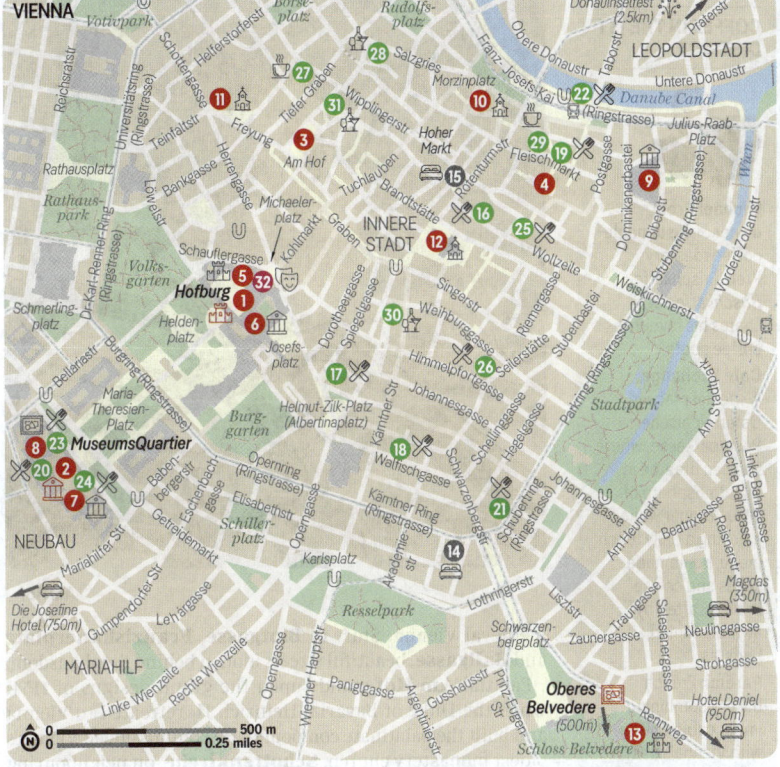

platform overlooking Stephansplatz. Sweeping city views from the **South Tower** (adult/child €6.50/2.50) require enough stamina to climb 343 precarious, winding steps to access the peering **Türmerstube** (tower room).

Step into the Middle Ages

Medieval squares and backstreets

Narrow trader alleys, age-old market squares and hidden courtyards – pockets of the Innere Stadt are a window into

COFFEE IN THE 1ST DISTRICT

Michael Prem, owner of sustainable coffee roastery Prem Frischkaffee *(frischkaffee.at)*, shares his favourite coffee spots.

Café Exchange: A special place in Österreichische Postsparkasse, where you can breathe in the atmosphere of Otto Wagner while enjoying a daily lunch menu, homemade cakes and coffee brews crafted by award-winning baristas.

Parémi: French bakery combining impeccable coffee with Vienna's best croissant.

Fenster Café: Unique hole-in-the-wall cafe near Schwedenplatz serves its own roast. This is not a space you can enter, but it is the place to get a speciality brew when passing by.

Am Hof

medieval Vienna. Start in **Blutgasse**, **Franziskanerplatz** and **Ballgasse**, beautiful streets hidden behind Stephansdom.

Palatial **Am Hof** stands upon the grand designs of 1154, when the Duke of Bavaria, Heinrich II, retreated to Vienna and built the palatinate compound. He commissioned Vienna's oldest monastery church, **Schottenkirche**, on neighbouring Freyung in 1170.

The courtyard curiosity of **Heiligenkreuzerhof** has its foundations in the 1135-founded Heiligenkreuz Abbey. A time-warp passage between Schönlaterngasse and Grashofgasse, today's courtyard was added in 1771. Neighbouring **Ruprechtskirche**, from 1200, is the oldest in Vienna, overlooking Schwedenplatz and perched on an elevated weave of cobbled alleys that chart the prettiest route down to the Danube Canal.

Habsburg Grandeur at the Hofburg

A palace to out-pomp them all

Nothing epitomises the Habsburgs' extravagant reign more than the humongous 240,000-sq-metre **Hofburg**. Home to

 EATING IN INNERE STADT: WIENER SCHNITZEL

Figlmüller: Proclaimed inventors, where the original *Wiener Schnitzel* (breadcrumbed veal cutlet) has been served since 1905. *11am-10.30pm* €€

Meissl & Schadn: Before feasting, watch the schnitzel beaten and baked through the open salon kitchen in front of the restaurant. *11.30am-11pm* €€€

Gasthaus Reinthaler: It's like time stopped still in this 1977 *Beisl*, one of the historic district's last remaining authentic taverns. *11am-11pm Mon-Fri* €€

Gasthaus zur Oper: Contemporary venue of classic culinary institution Plachutta serves perfectly prepared house recipe *Wiener Schnitzel. 11.30am-midnight* €€

the imperial family for 700 years until 1918, the palace is a tapestry of heritage across its 18 wings and 19 courtyards, showcasing a staggering collection of cultural artefacts and art masterpieces.

Roll back the times in the **Alte Burg** (Old Castle). Enter the **Sisi Museum** and **Kaiserappartements** (*Imperial Apartments; sisimuseum-hofburg.at; adult/child €20/12*) via the marbled Emperor's Staircase – as visitors seeking an audience with Emperor Franz Joseph I once did – and meander through resplendent rooms of court life accompanied by a 75-minute audio guide. Move to the bedazzling belt of living spaces, including bedrooms and bathrooms, studies and saloons, preserved with their chandeliered ceilings, decked walls, regal red silk upholstery and royal gold embellishments.

Burrowed within the wings of the **Schweizerhof** (Swiss Courtyard) are the coveted crown jewels of Austria. The **Kaiserliche Schatzkammer** (*Imperial Treasury; kaiserliche-schatzkammer.at; adult/child €18/free*). Make a beeline to the bejewelled Crown and Holy Lance of Emperor Rudolf II (Room 2), and the distinguished insignia of the Order of the Golden Fleece (Room 15).

The Hofburg residents today are world-famous white Lipizzaner stallions. Classical skills of horse-riding art and equestrianism have been practised at the UNESCO-listed **Spanische Hofreitschule** (*Spanish Riding School; srs.at; adult/child from €26/reduced*) since 1565. Horses dance gracefully in musical performances in the baroque **Winter Riding School** arena.

Baroque at the Belvedere

Find the world's most famous kiss

Prince Eugene of Savoy's 1723 baroque palace is a masterpiece; the art connoisseur filled it with his collections, which Empress Maria Theresia turned into the Imperial Picture Gallery in 1777, opening Vienna's first public museum. The dual complex is a trove of Austrian art from the Middle Ages to the present day and displays the world's largest collection of Klimt works.

Begin at the **Oberes Belvedere** (*adult/child €21/free; 9am-7pm*). Top billing goes to Gustav Klimt's most famous work, *Der Kuss* (The Kiss), which, of his 22 paintings here, never leaves the gallery. Stroll the terraced, fountain-splashed, sculpture-strewn gardens down to the **Unteres Belvedere** (*adult/child €18/free, Combi ticket adult/child from €31.50/free; 10am-6pm*) to explore Prince Eugene's illustrious world. He commissioned

BEST FREE MUSIC FESTIVALS

The city of music has events throughout the year, though summer to autumn is when festivities abound.

Film Festival Rathausplatz: Open-air music films from concert and stage greats, plus pop-up eats at the City Hall square. *Jul-Sep*

Kultursommer Wien: Music, theatre and dance performances are staged at parks, squares and gardens across the city. *Jun-Aug*

Gürtel Night Walk: Up-and-coming artists and local bands perform outside the Gürtel (belt) road of bars. *last weekend in August*

Donauinselfest: Europe's biggest free open-air music festival brings the party to the Donauinsel (Danube Island). *last weekend in June*

 EATING IN THE HISTORIC CENTRE: OUR PICKS

Motto am Fluss: Canal-anchored boat with cafe and restaurant serving contemporary Austrian cuisine. *6-11pm Mon-Sat, to 10.30pm Sun, bar to midnight* €€

Griechenbeisl: Feast on *Wiener Schnitzel* and *Kaiserschmarrn* (sweet pancake) in the city's oldest *Beisl. noon-11pm* €€

Tian: This Michelin-star gourmet vegetarian restaurant is rooted in rare ingredients and experimental cooking. Book well ahead. *6am-11pm Tue-Sat* €€€

Die Cafetière: Revived mid-century modern cafe and purveyors of the tastiest Viennese cheese-and-ham toastie. *7.20am-6pm Mon-Fri, 9am-4pm Sat* €€

ALESTA/SHUTTERSTOCK

mumok

baroque starchitect Johann Lucas von Hildebrandt to design the opulent summer residence.

A Cultural Dive into the MuseumsQuartier

Tune into Vienna's on-the-pulse arts scene

The former baroque imperial stables have been reborn as **MuseumsQuartier** *(MQ; mqw.at; courtyard open 24/7, museum entry times vary)*, one of the world's largest cultural districts with its arsenal of 11 exhibition spaces.

For modernist art in a brightly lit marble interior, hit the **Leopold Museum** *(leopoldmuseum.org)*, where star exhibits include the world's most comprehensive Egon Schiele collection and Gustav Klimt's *Death and Life* masterwork. Across the way, **mumok** *(mumok.at)* presents a galaxy of contemporary art: from expressionism to the experimental pop of the 1960s and 1970s, and the taboo and tragic in 20th-century Viennese actionism.

Save on individual entry with the MQ Fab 5 ticket *(€39)*; discounted or free entry for children across all museums.

 DRINKING IN THE HISTORIC CENTRE: BARS

Dino's Apothecary Bar: Dark wood-panelled, low-light, classic cocktail bar. Extensive experimental menu. *5pm-2am Tue-Thu, to 3am Fri & Sat*	**Loos American Bar:** Celeb magnet and cult-status bar designed by Viennese modernism architect Adolf Loos. *noon-4am*	**Lamée Rooftop Bar:** The chic and colourful rooftop bar of Hotel Topazz Lamee, with one of the best views of Stephansdom. *11am-1am Sun-Thu, to 2am Fri & Sat*	**Needle Vinyl Bar:** A trendy, retro-styled, record-spinning bar lounge, mixing music and signature cocktails. *5pm-2am*

Beyond Vienna

Waltz beyond the Austrian capital to find some of the country's greatest treasures – from grand abbeys to romantic castle ruins.

Providing popular day-trip material from Vienna, Lower Austria possesses the country's most vibrant cultural landscape: a combination of vineyards and art, monasteries and low wooded hills. Through this enchanting scene flows the mighty Danube, which forms the famous Wachau – one of Europe's most fascinating valleys, watched over by castles and medieval villages.

The stretch of Danube between Krems and Melk is arguably the loveliest along the entire length of this long, long river. Both banks are dotted with ruined castles and medieval towns, and lined with terraced vineyards. You can also indulge in some of Austria's best wines, and local and seasonal dishes at low-key but enormously welcoming *Heurigen* (wine taverns).

Places
Melk p55
Dürnstein p56

Melk

TIME FROM VIENNA: **45MIN**

Benedictine abbey: the Wachau's baroque masterpiece

Perched on a granite outcrop overlooking the Danube, **Stift Melk** *(stiftmelk.at; adult/child €16/8)* is one of Europe's finest ensembles of baroque architecture. Built on the site of a castle, which Leopold II of Babenberg gave to Benedictine monks from Lambach in Upper Austria, it's a huge and imposing place.

The abbey church shines with frescos by baroque master Johann Michael Rottmayr, and Paul Troger, a highly influential painter who ditched the characteristic dark palette of baroque painting in favour of lighter, more vibrant colours. His huge, illusionistic ceiling painting is in the abbey's **Marble Hall**. Around two dozen monks reside in the abbey and surrounding parishes. English-language guided tours of the abbey take place two or three times a day and last around 50 minutes.

The Wachau by boat

Taking a cruise along the Danube is almost part and parcel of spending time in the **Wachau Valley**. It's a nice, lazy way to spend half a day, and the views from the upper deck, enhanced and unobstructed, are very enjoyable – so order yourself a cool spritzer from the onboard bar, sit back and watch the world go by. Tables on the upper deck tend to fill up fast. You can easily combine a boat cruise with a return journey by train or bicycle; don't forget to reserve a place for your bike

GETTING AROUND

Lower Austria is the largest of the country's nine states; however, given Vienna's proximity, transport links are frequent and efficient. There are good rail connections between Vienna and Krems via St Pölten. Along with the famous **Danube Cycle Path**, many areas of Lower Austria are fantastic for cycling, and bikes can easily be rented locally. Bring walking boots, too, as trails above the river lace hills and vines.

ON YOUR BIKE

The **Danube Cycle Path** is one of Europe's greatest long-distance cycle routes – and one of its most beautiful sections is between Krems and Melk, through the UNESCO-listed Wachau Valley. The path follows both banks of the Danube, so you can cycle along one bank and return along the other. Even better, you can take your bike on a boat from Krems to Melk, visiting Dürnstein and Spitz – or on a train from Krems to Emmersdorf (the town opposite Melk), stopping at Dürnstein, Spitz and other places. This makes it nice and easy to combine a river cruise or train ride through the area's legendary vineyards, stopping to soak up some of the Wachau's celebrated cultural sites while sampling its excellent wines.

Kuenringerburg castle, Dürnstein

TRABANTOS/SHUTTERSTOCK

when you book). **DDSG Blue Danube** (*ddsg-blue-danube.at*) offers cruises on the river between Krems and Melk, calling at Dürnstein and Spitz.

Dürnstein

TIME FROM VIENNA: **1HR 10MIN**

Romantic castle ruins

The pretty little town of Dürnstein stands on an impossibly photogenic curve in the Danube, backed by low hills. Rising high above the town, **Kuenringerburg** is the castle where Richard I of England – yes, the Lionheart – was once imprisoned. He ended up here due to a dispute with Leopold V, Duke of Austria, during the Third Crusade. Leopold had Richard incarcerated on his way back from the Holy Land. Leopold was excommunicated for imprisoning a fellow Crusader, and was obliged to have Richard released (following the payment of a sizeable ransom – 35 tonnes of silver).

Only ruins of the castle remain, but they can still be visited, and the view is lovely. It takes 20 minutes to walk up from town following a clearly marked trail.

EATING & DRINKING IN THE WACHAU: OUR PICKS

Gasthof Prankl: Deservedly popular, with delicious food and local wines, in a 500-year-old former ship-owner's house in Spitz. *8am-10pm Fri-Tue €€*

Landgasthaus Essl: Refined dining on Danube's right bank between Spitz and Dürnstein. *11.30am-2.30pm & 6-11pm Wed-Fri, 11.30am-3.30pm & 6-11pm Sat, 11.30am-4pm Sun €€€*

Gasthof Goldenes Schiff: Family-run traditional restaurant and guesthouse, right in the centre of town, with a nice big terrace. *11.30am-8pm Thu-Tue €€*

Klosterhof Spitz: Set in a vineyard on the east side of Spitz, with tables in an atmospheric brick-vaulted interior. *11.30am-7pm Wed-Sun €€*

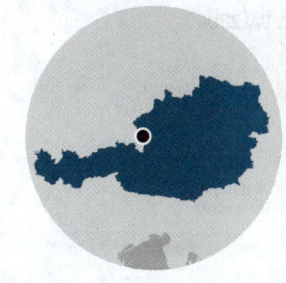

Salzburg

BAROQUE BRILLIANCE | MOZART'S BIRTHPLACE | ALPINE BACKDROP

The joke 'If it's baroque, don't fix it' could be a perfect maxim for Salzburg: the storybook Altstadt burrowed below steep hills looks much as it did when Mozart lived here 250 years ago. Beside the fast-flowing Salzach River, which divides the city in two, your lifted gaze is raised bit by bit to graceful domes and spires, the formidable clifftop fortress and the mountains beyond. It's a backdrop that did the lordly prince-archbishops and Maria proud.

Beyond Salzburg's two biggest money-spinners – Mozart and *The Sound of Music* – hides a city with a burgeoning arts scene, wonderful food, manicured parks, quiet side streets where classical music wafts from open windows, and concert halls that uphold musical tradition 365 days a year. Everywhere you go, the scenery, the skyline, the music and the history send your spirits soaring higher than Julie Andrews' octave-leaping vocals.

> ☑ **TOP TIP**
>
> During the summer holidays (July and August), Salzburg gets swamped. In December, when the city brims with Christmas markets and festival sparkle, it can get busy and expensive, too. Come in spring or autumn for cheaper flights, lower room rates and fewer crowds.

Salzburg on High

Get a ringside city view

Salzburg is at its most entrancing from above, with domes, spires and rooftops spreading out before you and the turquoise Salzach River unfurling into the mountains. One of the most memorable ways to see the city away from the masses is to get out and stride. Puff up the Nonnbergstiege to Benedictine abbey

---

 GETTING AROUND

Walking is the only way to get a true feel for Salzburg's pedestrianised backstreets. This is one of Austria's most cycle-friendly cities, with a superb network of bike paths along the river, making the transition from city to mountains seamless. Rent touring and e-bikes at **aVelo** at Staatsbrücke.

Getting around by public transport *(salzburg-verkehr.at)* is quick, easy and inexpensive. If you're planning on zipping about town, a *Tageskarte* day pass is better value than single tickets.

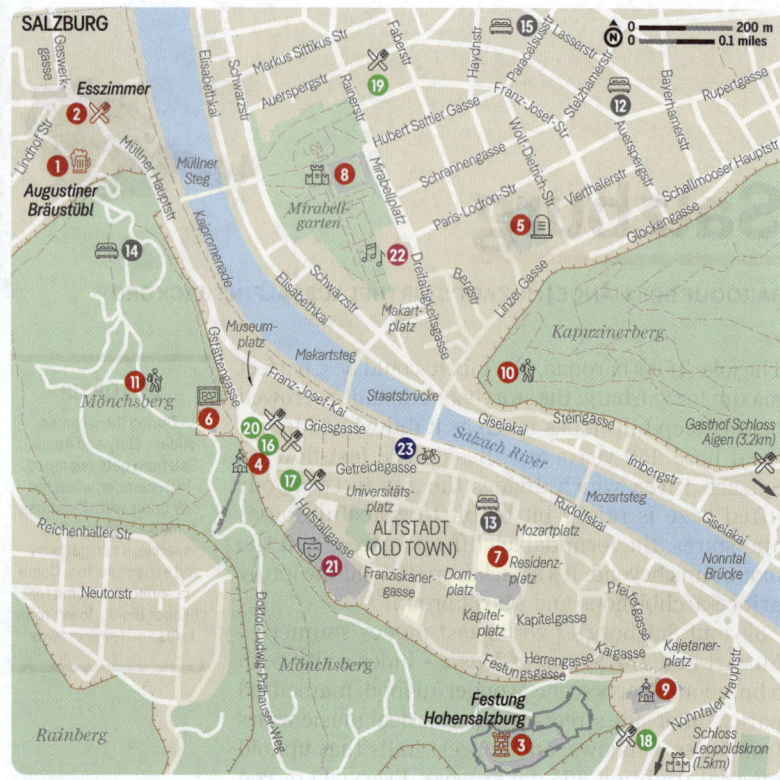

SALZBURG

Stift Nonnberg (p60), then continue your short but scenic walk along Hoher Weg and Festungsgasse to **Festung Hohensalzburg** (*festung-hohensalzburg.at; adult/child €13.60/5.20*). The city's crowning-glory fortress has dress-circle views of the baroque Altstadt. Time your walk for midday to hear bells ring out across the city.

You can easily devote an afternoon to wandering the 540m peak of **Mönchsberg**, the cliffs that give Salzburg its dramatic edge. Its sheer, wooded heights are crisscrossed by walking trails. A highly scenic hike leads 3km on from Festung Hohensalzburg, past the **Museum der Moderne** (*museumder moderne.at; adult/child €14/free*) and through woods of beech,

Capuchin abbey

MOZART MAGIC

Mozart's symphonies, sonatas and concertos live on in Salzburg. **Mozarteum:** Opened in 1880 and revered for its supreme acoustics, the Mozarteum highlights the life and works of Mozart through chamber music (October to June), concerts and opera. *mozarteum.at* **Mozart Week:** In late January, when much-lauded orchestras, conductors and soloists celebrate Mozart's birthday with an 11-day music feast. **Schlosskonzerte:** A fantasy of coloured marble, stucco and frescos, the baroque Marmorsaal (Marble Hall) at Schloss Mirabell is the exquisite setting for chamber-music concerts *(adult/child from €42/28)* where internationally renowned soloists and ensembles perform works by Mozart and other well-known composers such as Haydn and Chopin. *schlosskonzerte-salzburg.at*

sycamore, linden and oak, to the jovial monastery-founded brewery **Augustiner Bräustübl** *(augustinerbier.at)*. Here you can rest up with a cold foamy one under the chestnut trees in the beer garden.

A leap over the river to the Right Bank brings you to the forested, 640m-high hump of **Kapuzinerberg**, which frames the Altstadt like a postcard. Paths twist past Way of the Cross chapels to the Capuchin abbey at the top. Despite the glorious views, it's rarely busy – hence the reason it is still home to a colony of nimble-footed chamois, which you might spot if you're lucky (and quiet).

The Hills Are Alive
The Sound of Music trail

Ever since Hollywood box-office smash *The Sound of Music* hit big screens in 1965, Salzburg has been inseparable from the world's most famous singing nun. Channel your inner Julie Andrews by devising your own self-guided tour of the movie locations. Start at the very beginning with a cable-car ride to the summit of **Untersberg** *(untersbergbahn.at; return cable car adult/child €34/17)*, where Maria makes her twirling entrance through blooming alpine pastures and the Trapp family flee from the Nazis at the end.

 EATING IN SALZBURG: BEST ROMANTIC RESTAURANTS

| **Gasthof Schloss Aigen:** This 15th-century country manor does Austrian home cooking with panache. *5.30-10pm Thu, 11.30am-10pm Fri-Sun* €€ | **Blaue Gans Restaurant:** In 650-year-old vaults, this restaurant riffs on regional cuisine in season-spun dishes. *noon-midnight Mon-Sat* €€ | **Glass Garden:** Ingredient-driven sensations at Hotel Schloss Mönchstein's glass-domed, Michelin-starred restaurant. *noon-10pm Thu-Mon* €€€ | **Esszimmer:** Andreas Kaiblinger puts an innovative spin on market-driven French cuisine at this art-slung, Michelin-starred stunner. *noon-10pm Tue-Sat* €€€ |

ESCAPE THE CROWDS

Hildegard Strohmeyer, an official Salzburg city and hiking guide *(hildastroh. com),* divulges some peaceful spots.

Friedhof St Sebastian: Mozart's father, Leopold, and wife, Constanze, are buried in this cemetery, established in 1600 as an Italian 'campo santo'. Its centrepiece is the mausoleum of Prince-Archbishop Wolf-Dietrich of Raitenau.

Bürgerspitalskirche St Blasius: The civic hospital church near Getreidegasse has an inner courtyard with Renaissance arcades. A Gothic church with 12th-century roots, it impresses with its vault, stained-glass windows and mystical interior.

Waldbad Anif: Rent a bike to pedal south along the Salzach River to this emerald-green lake, perfect in summer.

Schloss Mirabell gardens and Festung Hohensalzburg (p58)

At the foot of Mönchsberg's cliffs, the **Felsenreitschule** is the dramatic backdrop for the **Salzburger Festspiele** (Salzburg Festival) in the movie, where the Trapp Family Singers win the audience over with 'Edelweiss' and give the Nazis the slip with 'So Long, Farewell'. Close by is **Residenzplatz**, where Maria belts out 'I Have Confidence' and playfully splashes the spouting horses of the Residenzbrunnen fountain. Hoof it uphill from here to Benedictine **Stift Nonnberg** *(nonnberg.at; free),* where the nuns waltzed on their way to mass, including the ever-problematic Maria. To see the abbey at its most atmospheric, arrive for the 6.45am Gregorian chant.

Palaces, you say? Romantically rococo **Schloss Leopoldskron** *(schloss-leopoldskron.com),* a 15-minute stroll south of the centre, is where the lake scene was filmed. Its Venetian Room was the blueprint for the Trapps' opulent ballroom, where the von Trapp kids bid their heart-melting farewells. Now you can stay the night in its elegant hotel.

Back in town, the Pegasus fountain, gnomes and steps with fortress views in the **Schloss Mirabell** *(salzburg.info; free)* gardens might inspire a rendition of 'Do-Re-Mi' – especially if there's a drop of golden sun.

 EATING IN SALZBURG: TOP LUNCH SPOTS

Afro Café: Go for fair-trade coffees, lavish brunches and creative day specials at this Afro-chic cafe. *9am-8pm Mon-Sat* €

Green Garden: Tapping into plant power, this vegan cafe rustles up tasty Buddha bowls, brunches and superfood salads. *1-9pm Wed-Fri, 10am-9pm Sat & Sun* €

Heart of Joy: Ayurveda-inspired cafe: all-vegetarian, part-vegan, mostly organic menu of bagels, salads, homemade cakes, juices, daily specials. *8am-7pm* €

Humboldt: Like a blast of nouveau alpine chic, the vibe is cool yet cosy. A good buzz and all-organic, season-driven menu. *10.30am-11pm* €€

Beyond
Salzburg

Salzburg is the curtain-raiser to Alps that will make your heart soar and cinematic backdrops that will prompt you to yodel out loud.

You don't need to venture far from Salzburg for high alpine drama. For a memorable day trip, take the quick train ride to Werfen, which thrills with a showstopping medieval castle and the world's biggest ice caves, Eisriesenwelt. Here cliff-skimming trails thread through the rugged peaks of the limestone Tennengebirge, where eagles wheel, winds blow and silence reigns.

Further east, the Salzkammergut wows with alpine and subalpine lakes, deeply carved valleys, high hills and rugged, steep mountains rising to almost 3000m. Rugged paths wind to mountain-top restaurants, caves and salt mines, where the region's 'white gold' once filled the coffers of Habsburg rulers. Swinging south, the unmissable road trip is the Grossglockner High Alpine Road, helter-skeltering below the country's highest peak, 3798m Grossglockner.

Werfen

TIME FROM SALZBURG: **40MIN** OR **1HR**

Cue the world's biggest ice caves

High above Werfen, the pointed peaks of the Tennengebirge rise like a theatre curtain of solid limestone over the river-woven Salzach Valley. Take the cable car, then hoof it up the steep, scree-strewn trail to **Eisriesenwelt** *(eisriesenwelt.at; adult/child €42/21)*, open from May to October. Stepping through the huge 20m-wide gash in the rock, feeling the frosty blast of 0°C air and seeing the ice twinkle is like pushing through the wardrobe into Narnia.

An old-fashioned carbide lamp illuminates your passage through this pitch-black, glittering underworld of frozen tunnels and passageways, where you will be blown away by the scale and beauty of the ice. But most impressive of all is the echoing, cathedral-like **Eispalast** (Ice Palace), with icicles as big as organ pipes and ice-veined walls.

Big views and birds of prey at Burg Hohenwerfen

Slung high on a wooded clifftop and cowering below the gnarly peaks of the Tennengebirge, **Burg Hohenwerfen** *(burg-hohen werfen.at; adult/child incl lift €17.90/6.10, with guided tour €20.90/7.60)* is visible from afar. For 900 years this turreted beauty of a castle has guarded the Salzach Valley. You'll be mostly captivated by the mountain views from the 16th-century belfry,

GETTING AROUND

Much of the region beyond Salzburg is accessible by public transport (bus and train), removing the need to hire a car unless you crave the independence. There are regional and S-Bahn trains from Salzburg running frequently to Hallein (15 minutes) and Werfen (40 minutes). The two-hour journey to Obertraun often involves a bus-train combo via Bad Ischl.

WATER & WHEELS ON HALLSTÄTTER SEE

Swimming:
Hallstätter See reaches about 24°C from June to August. Obertraun and Untersee (near Steeg) have free public beaches with facilities.

Cycling & kayaking:
Hire touring bikes, mountain bikes and e-bikes at Dormio Resort Obertraun. For standard city/e-bikes per hour, expect to pay €20/30. There's a charging station at the cable car valley station. Kayak hire for the first hour is €10, and €5 after that.

Lake Connections:
Hallstättersee Schifffahrt (hallstattschifffahrt. at) connects the train station on the eastern shore with the town of Hallstatt year-round, timed to trains. From May to September it does southern-end lake circuits and boat rental.

GOGENTUNC/SHUTTERSTOCK

Saltzwelten Funicular, Hallstatt

but the dingy dungeons (displaying the usual nasties, such as the iron maiden and thumbscrew) are equally worth a look.

Time your visit to catch the stunning **falconry show** *(11.15am & 3.15pm daily)* in the grounds, where falconers in medieval costume release eagles, owls, falcons and vultures to wheel in front of the ramparts. The brisk walk up from Werfen takes 20 minutes, or you can cheat by catching the lift.

Hallstatt

TIME FROM SALZBURG: **1HR 30MIN** 🚗

Descending into the salt mine

On the western shore of its exquisitely pretty lake, Hallstatt is famous for its salt mine, where mining began over 7000 years ago. Today miners still dig white gold out of the earth. After a short ferry ride across the lake from the train station, you reach a jetty that is a 15-minute walk from the **Saltzwelten Funicular** *(salzwelten.at; adult/child €24/12)*. It's a dramatic ascent into a strange alpine valley with mirrors reflecting the green landscape, a **Skywalk** with stupendous views, and an Iron Age burial ground.

From the top station, it is another 15-minute walk to the mine. After donning protective clothing, you begin the bilingual 90-minute mine tour in **Salzwelten** *(salzwelten.at/en/ hallstatt; funicular & tour adult/child €43/21)*, taking you around 2km through shafts, down miners' slides, and to an illuminated underground lake. Along the way you learn all about the formation of salt, salt mining, and conditions of the miners.

 EATING IN WERFEN: OUR PICKS

Pizzeria im Markt: Pizzas fly out of the oven perfectly thin and crisp at this cosy pick in Werfen's heart. *10am-10pm* €

Oedlhaus: At Eisriesenwelt, this 1574m woodsy hut fortifies walkers with grub like *Gröstl* (pan-fried potatoes, pork and onions) and mountain views. *8am-4pm* €€

Stiege No 1: Venison, asparagus, wild garlic – the menu sings of the seasons. In summer, sit in the lantern-lit garden. *11am-10pm Wed-Sun* €€

Obauer: Two Michelin-starred restaurant, with alpine, homegrown and locally foraged ingredients. *6-9pm Wed, noon-9pm Thu-Sun* €€€

 ## DRIVING THE GROSSGLOCKNER ROAD

Get up close and personal with the Austrian Alps on this sky-high road trip.

START	END	LENGTH
Bruck	Heiligenblut	48km; 5–6hr

Leaving **1 Bruck**, enter the mountainous Fuschertal, passing Fusch and **2 Wildpark Ferleiten**. Once through the tollgate, the road climbs steeply to **3 Hochmais** (1850m), where glaciated peaks like Grosses Wiesbachhorn (3564m) crowd the horizon. The road zigzags up to **4 Haus Alpine Naturschau** (2260m), which spotlights local flora and fauna. Further on, a 2km side road spirals up to **5 Edelweiss Spitze** (2571m), the road's highest viewpoint. Get your camera handy for **6 Fuscher Törl** (2428m), with smashing views, and gemstone-coloured lake **7 Fuscher Lacke** (2262m) nearby. Here is a small exhibition on the road's construction, built by 3000 men during the Great Depression (1930–35). The road wriggles on through high

meadows to **8 Hochtor** (2504m), the top of the pass. Next there's a steady descent to **9 Schöneck**. Branch off west onto the 9km Gletscherstrasse, passing waterfalls and Achtung Murmeltiere (Beware of Marmots) signs – you may spot one of the burrowing rodents. The Grossglockner massif slides into view on the approach to flag-dotted **10 Kaiser-Franz-Josefs-Höhe** (2369m), with memorable views of bell-shaped Grossglockner (3798m) and the rapidly retreating Pasterze Glacier. Allow time for the glacier-themed exhibition at the visitor centre and the Wilhelm-Swarovski observatory. Round out your road trip in **11 Heiligenblut**, where a 15th-century pilgrimage church lifts gazes to Grossglockner.

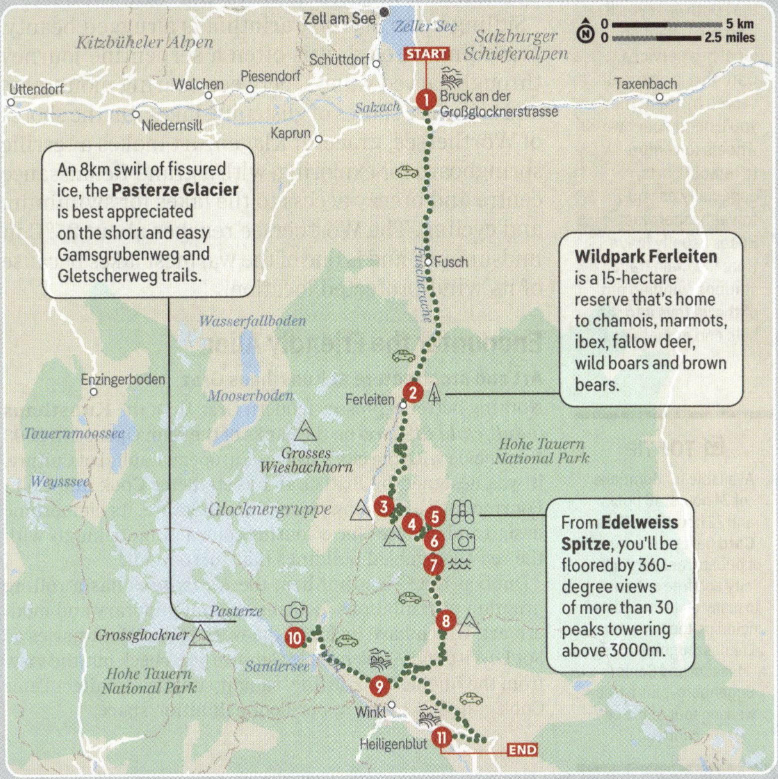

An 8km swirl of fissured ice, the **Pasterze Glacier** is best appreciated on the short and easy Gamsgrubenweg and Gletscherweg trails.

Wildpark Ferleiten is a 15-hectare reserve that's home to chamois, marmots, ibex, fallow deer, wild boars and brown bears.

From **Edelweiss Spitze**, you'll be floored by 360-degree views of more than 30 peaks towering above 3000m.

63

Graz & the South

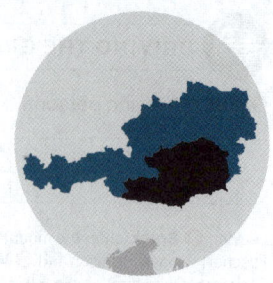

LAKES | MOUNTAINS | CULTURAL COOL

GETTING AROUND

Styria has a good rail network, with Graz being particularly easy to reach from Vienna, though for the southwest you'll be more reliant on local bus services. Carinthia is also well served by trains, but you'll need your own wheels to venture to remote parts, especially as you travel further west. Buses usually leave from the main train stations, winding out of the valleys into the hills and mountains.

☑ **TOP TIP**

Available for durations of 24 hours, 48 hours and 72 hours, the **Graz Card** gets you free use of public transport in the city and free entrance to many of its museums, including the *Kunsthaus*, Landeszeughaus, Graz Museum and Schloss Eggenberg, plus a free walking tour of the city centre.

Though Austria's south receives just a trickle of visitors compared to other regions, if you make it this far you'll be richly rewarded. Styria wings you from rolling vineyards, pumpkin fields, wildlife-rich national parks and snow-streaked limestone peaks to the beautiful sweep of the River Mur. UNESCO-listed Graz, Austria's second city, is one of its most vibrant, fizzing with avant-garde arts and a food scene buoyed by abundant farmers markets and local produce.

Sidling up to Styria, Carinthia is a rugged beauty. Travelling through it is often a serpentine journey through carved valleys, between soaring mountains and along the shores of glistening lakes. On the shores of Wörthersee, graceful Klagenfurt makes a terrific springboard for exploring, with a grand Renaissance centre and breezy access to the lakes for swimming and cycling. The Wörthersee reaches about 25°C in midsummer, and is one of the warmest lakes because of its wind-protected location.

Encounter the Friendly Alien

Art and architecture at Kunsthaus Graz

Nothing better expresses modern Graz than the **Kunsthaus** (*adult/child €12/free*) on the banks of the Mur. Opened in 2003 to coincide with the city's stint as European Capital of Culture, it was designed by British architects Peter Cook and Colin Fournier. It's a dazzling piece of architecture, its biomorphic design and intense blue colouring contrasting strikingly with the red-tiled gabled buildings that surround it.

Dubbed the Friendly Alien, the *Kunsthaus* has a rolling program of exhibitions focusing on contemporary and modern art, which have included the work of such luminaries as Sol LeWitt and Ai Weiwei. Make sure you check out the view from the furthest nozzle (the 'naughty nozzle', architect Peter Cook called it) in the upper-floor exhibition space.

GRAZ

0   200 m
0   0.1 miles

Kepler-
brücke

Schlossberg **3**

GEIDORF

Zinzendorfgasse

Sauraugasse

Paulustorgasse

Karmeliter-
platz

Stadtpark

Elisabethstr

Lendlplatz

5

6

Kaiser-Franz-Josef-Kai

Lendkai

Mur

Lendlgasse-
Josefigasse

LEND

Sackstr

Sporgasse

Freiheits-
platz

Hofgasse

Leonhardstr

Wickenburggasse

Maiffredygasse

9 ✕

Farbergasse

Dom **1**

*Kunsthaus
Graz* **2**

Mariahilferstr

Südtirolerplatz

Hauptbrücke

Hauptplatz

Belgiergasse

4

Tegetthoff-
brücke

Lendkai

Neutorgasse

Herrengasse

Schmied-
gasse

Kaiserfeldgasse

INNERE
STADT

Opernring

SANKT
LEONHARD

Glacisstr

Lessingstr

Burgring

✕ **8** Kaiser-Josef-
Platz Mandellstr

GRIES

Griesgasse

Grieskai

Marburger Kai

Griesplatz

Brückenkopf-
gasse

Radetzky-
brücke

Radetzkystr

Joanneumring

Jakomini-
platz

Reitschul-
gasse

Jakoministr

✕ **10**

Grazbachgasse

Dietrichstein-
platz

Zweiglgasse

Grazbachgasse

Wielandgasse

JAKOMINI

⭐ **HIGHLIGHTS**	⚫ **SLEEPING**	🟢 **EATING**
1 Dom	4 Das Weitzer	7 Altsteirische
2 Kunsthaus Graz	5 KAI 36	Schmankerlstube
3 Schlossberg	6 Schlossberg Hotel	8 Geniesserei am Markt
		9 Mohrenwirt
		10 Scheucher

To the Top of the Schlossberg

Graz' unassailable fortified hill

Schlossberg *(graztourismus.at),* the city's green hill, stands
at 473m high above the left bank of the Mur. The old medieval
castle underwent a makeover in the mid-16th century courtesy of Italian architect Domenico dell'Allio, who turned it
into an impregnable Renaissance fortress. The best way to
approach Schlossberg is by skipping up the zigzagging steps
from Schlossbergplatz, where it towers above you. Or take the
Schlossbergbahn *(adult/child €3.20/1.60)* funicular, which
was built in 1894 and has a gradient of 61%.

At the top, you'll find the **Bell Tower**, with its 5-tonne bell
known as Liesl, the restored casemates and the Schlossberg

BEST FESTIVALS IN GRAZ

This university
town has a flurry
of festivals, from
the International
Storytelling Festival
(May) to Assembly,
the city's Festival of
Fashion (September)
and Klangnacht, a
mesmerising light
and sound festival
(October).

Elevate: Bills itself
as a festival of 'music,
arts and political
discourse'. *Mar*

Design Month: All of
Graz' creative energy
condensed into a
one-month festival.
May

Springfestival: Live
electronic music and
art installations. *Late
May/early June*

Aufsteirern:
Traditional festival
with music, dance,
handicrafts and good
food. *Sep*

Steirischer Herbst:
Edgy, contemporary
performing-arts
festival, which has
been running for over
half a century. *Sep/
Oct*

EATING IN GRAZ: OUR PICKS

Mohrenwirt:
Traditional dishes with
a contemporary twist:
organic, seasonal local
produce. Michelin Bib
Gourmand. *11.30am-11pm
Wed-Sat* €€

Geniesserei am Markt:
Beside the Kaiser-Josef-
Platz farmers market.
Lunch or the 6pm
10-course surprise menu
(book ahead). *9am-10pm
Tue-Sat* €€€

**Altsteirische
Schmankerlstube:**
Seasonal Styrian and
classic Austrian in a
homely setting. Vaulted
ceiling and wood
panelling. *10am-11pm* €€

Scheucher: Michelin-
listed restaurant famed
for its dry-aged steaks.
*11am-2.30pm & 6am-10pm
Mon-Fri, 6am-10pm Sat*
€€€

branch of the Graz Museum. But the main thing to do up here is enjoy the view over the rooftops of Graz in the beautiful garden on the **Bürgerbastei** – a restored bastion below the clock tower.

Historic Highs in Klagenfurt
Evocative architecture and altar painting

Renaissance romance lives on in Klagenfurt's historic centre. On **Neuer Platz** square is the 16th-century **Dragon Fountain**. This blank-eyed, wriggling statue is modelled on the lindwurm (dragon) of legend, said to have resided in a swamp here long ago, devouring cattle and virgins.

Nearby is the Renaissance **Landhaus** (state parliament), where the highlight is the **Grosser Wappensaal** (Heraldic Hall; landesmuseum.ktn.gv.at; adult/child €7/free), with its magnificent trompe l'oeil gallery painted by Carinthian artist Josef Ferdinand Fromiller (1693–1760). Steps from here, on Pfarrplatz, is the **Stadthauptpfarrkirche St Egid** (kath-kirche-kaernten.at/pfarren/pfarre/C3080; free), where a climb to the 90m-high tower affords a bird's-eye view of town and the surrounding mountains.

Backtracking brings you to the **Dom** (cathedral; kath-kirche-kaernten.at/pfarren/pfarre/C3074; free), with its ornate marble pulpit, sugary pink-and-white stucco and standout altar painting in the chapel by Paul Troger dedicated to St Ignatius.

Swimming & Cycling Wörthersee
Make a splash in Carinthia's biggest lake

Framed by wooded hills and shimmering turquoise-blue, Wörthersee is an instant heart-stealer. In summer all the action is on the lake – open-water swimmers, canoeists, kayakers and stand-up paddleboarders love its placid, tepid waters.

If you prefer to pedal rather than paddle, the 40km **R4 bike route** wraps around the entire shoreline. It's an easy, well-marked ride ticking off swimming spots, beaches and viewpoints. You can hire road and e-bikes at stations in the region, including at the Klagenfurt **tourist office** on Neuer Platz. Boats departing for destinations around the Wörthersee leave from a quay just north of **Strandbad Klagenfurt** (Klagenfurt Bathing Beach). Check times at woertherseeschifffahrt.at.

PLAYING YOUR GUEST CARDS RIGHT

Play your guest cards right and you won't need to pay for travelling by regional train around Carinthia. As well as offering various discounts, the free **Wörthersee Plus Card** (woerthersee. com/card; year-round) entitles overnight visitors to free train travel throughout Carinthia, including the Sl, connecting Friesach in the north with Lienz (in Tyrol, west of Carinthia). It is valid both days of a one-night stay in a participating hotel.

The **Erlebnis Card** (visitvillach.at/de/ erlebnis-card.html), Villach's free card, also includes regional travel anywhere in Carinthia and on a few special bus services for the duration of your stay.

The **Kärnten Card** (kaerntencard.at; adult €60-89, child €31-46) provides discounts or free admission but not free transport; available in one-, two- and five-week timeframes.

EATING IN KLAGENFURT: OUR PICKS

Princs: Lively kitchen serves pizzas, plates of pasta and 'street food'. Kitchen closes at 9pm. Also with a popular bar. 10am-midnight Mon-Thu, to 2am Fri & Sat €€

Dolce Vita: Local flagship restaurant-bistretto with northern Italian cuisine and a local seasonal menu. 11.30am-3pm & 6.30-10pm Mon-Fri €€

Ricardo: Portuguese, tapas, vegetarian (and vegan) dishes, and steaks in a relaxed setting, with outdoor seating. 11.30am-2pm & 6-11.30pm Tue-Sat, 6-11.30pm Mon €€

Gasthaus im Landhaushof: Classic Austrian cuisine, with outdoor seating in the yard and a kitchen open all day. 11am-9pm Mon-Sat, to 3pm Sun €€

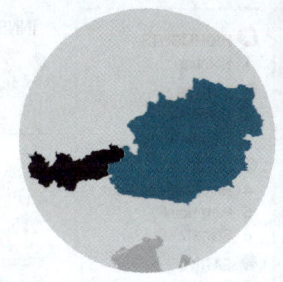

Innsbruck & Tyrol

LIVING HISTORY | HABSBURG CULTURE | HIGH ALPS

Tyrol's capital is a sight to behold. Rising like a theatre curtain above the city, the rock spires of the Nordkette range are so breathtakingly close that when you fly here, it feels as though you're going to smash right into them. It isn't just an illusion: within minutes you can whizz from the late-medieval Altstadt, presided over by a Habsburg palace, to 2000m above sea level and be up among crags where alpine choughs glide and cowbells tinkle.

Beyond Innsbruck, it's all about the outdoors, whether you're pelting down an Olympic bob run, schussing down the legendary slopes of Kitzbühel, cycling the Zillertal or hiking in the Alps with a flawlessly blue sky overhead. Welcome to a place where snowboarders brag under the low beams of a medieval tavern about awesome descents; where *Dirndls* and *Lederhosen* have street cred; and where *Volksmusik* (folk music) features on club playlists.

Palace of Dreams
MAP p68

Discover imperial Innsbruck

Grabbing attention with its pearl-white facade and cupolas, the **Hofburg** *(burghauptmannschaft.at; adult/child €9.50/ free)* imperial palace was built for Archduke Sigmund the Rich in the 15th century, expanded by Emperor Maximilian I in the 16th century and given a baroque makeover by Empress Maria Theresia in the 18th century.

Take a romp around the lavish rococo state apartments and you'll be astounded by the 31m-long **Riesensaal** (Giant's Hall), a feast of frescos, weighty chandeliers and Habsburg portraits. Right opposite is the **Hofkirche** *(tiroler-landesmu seen.at; adult/child €14/free)*, one of Europe's finest royal court churches. Top billing goes to the crazily ornate black-marble tomb of Emperor Maximilian I (1459–1519), a masterpiece of German Renaissance sculpture. The twin rows of 28 giant bronze figures guarding the sarcophagus include Dürer's legendary King Arthur. Touching the statues is now forbidden,

GETTING AROUND

Innsbruck's compact, pedestrianised, alley-woven Altstadt is a pleasure to explore on foot. Most sights are here, and ultramodern funiculars race you up into the mountains. For outlying sights, such as Bergisel and Schloss Ambras, hop on one of the **IVB** *(ivb. at)* buses; for multiple journeys, invest in a 24-hour ticket. Public transport is free with summer's Welcome Card, the guest card you receive with stays of more than two nights.

☑ **TOP TIP**

Tourist information centres on Burggraben, at the Stadtturm and the Hauptbahnhof are handy first ports of call for maps, tickets, ski passes and information.

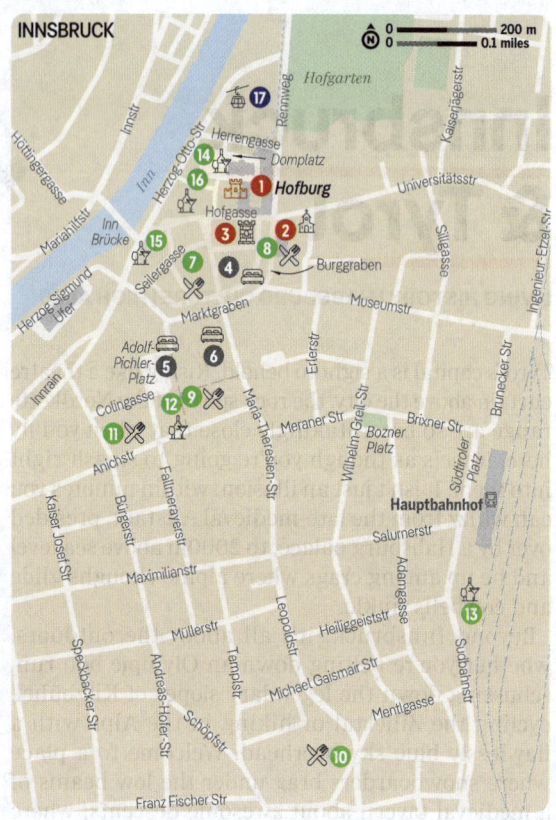

INNSBRUCK

but numerous inquisitive hands have already polished parts of the dull bronze, including Kaiser Rudolf's codpiece!

Innsbruck on High

MAP p68

From city to slopes

You'll be itching to head into the mountains on Innsbruck's doorstep. Zaha Hadid's space-age funicular **Nordketten-bahnen** *(nordkette.com; top of Innsbruck return ticket adult/child €52/31.20)* floats to the slopes in no time, stopping at Hungerburg, where you switch to a cable car to Seegrube and,

 EATING IN INNSBRUCK: OUR PICKS ──────── MAP p68

Olive: Vegetarians and vegans are in their element at this cute bistro with vintage furniture. Book – it gets busy. *5-11pm Mon-Sat* €

Die Wilderin: A modern hunter-gatherer restaurant, where season-spun menus play up farm-fresh and foraged ingredients. *5pm-midnight Tue-Sun* €€

Il Convento: Tucked into the old city walls, this Italian job has dishes like clam linguine and braised veal, and a well-stocked cellar. *11.30am-midnight Mon-Sat* €€

Oniriq: Explosive Austrian flavours are given a foraged twist in ingredient-led tasting menus at this stylishly monochrome pick. *6-11pm Wed-Sat* €€€

finally, 2256m Hafelekar. A 15-minute uphill trudge brings you to 2334m **Hafelekarspitze**, where alpine choughs ride the breeze and gnarly limestone mountains rise in great waves. The views are riveting, reaching all the way to 3798m Gross-glockner when it's clear.

Walking trails head off in all directions, including the ridge-top **Goethe Trail**, a 10km, five-hour, out-and-back stomp over meadow and mountain to the **Pfeishütte**. The steep, technically demanding **Nordkette Single Trail** draws hardcore downhill mountain bikers. In winter, the most central place to pound powder is the **Nordpark**. Fearless skiers ride the **Hafelekar Run**, one of Europe's steepest runs, with a 70% gradient.

Life in the Fast Lane

MAP p71

Pick up speed, Olympian-style

For a minute in the life of an Olympic bobsleigh racer, ride the **Olympia Bob** (*knauseder-event.at; bobsleigh ride summer/winter €55/120, skeleton €65*) at the foot of Patscherkofel mountain in **Igls**.

Zipping around 14 curves and picking up speeds of up to 120km/h, the 1.3km bob run, built for the 1976 Winter Olympics, is a single minute of pure hair-raising action. From December to March, you can either join a four-person bobsleigh or throw yourself headfirst down the run on a skeleton. Otherwise, join a pro-bobsled driver from April to October for the summer version. See the website for dates, times and bookings. To reach the bob run, take Bus J from Innsbruck Landesmuseum to Igls Olympiaexpress.

Swarovski Sparkle

MAP p71

Enter a crystal world

The dinky village of **Wattens**, a 30-minute bus ride east of Innsbruck, is the glittering heart of the Swarovski crystal empire. **Swarovski Kristallwelten** (*kristallwelten.swarovski.com; adult/child €26/8*) shines as one of Austria's most-visited attractions.

Against the backdrop of the Alps, the fantasy world begins outdoors with an ivy-swathed giant's head spouting water, a dazzling crystal cloud, bejewelled with 800,000 crystals, floating above a mirrorlike pool, and a stunning modernist, black-and-white carousel glimmering with 15 million crystals by Spanish designer Jaime Hayon. Inside, the Chambers of Wonder zoom in on Alexander McQueen's wintry *Silent Light*,

SKY-HIGH VIEWS

Stadtturm: Onion-domed medieval tower in the heart of the Altstadt. Puff up 133 steps for 360-degree views over Innsbruck's rooftops to the surrounding mountains.

360°: Knockout view of the skyline from the balcony skirting this spherical bar. Nicely chilled spot for a coffee/sundowner.

Lichtblick: Dinner at this slickly minimalist, backlit, glass-walled restaurant takes in the entire sweep of the city and its mountain backdrop.

Buzihütte: This woodsy alpine hut has a peak-gazing terrace for digging into traditional faves like *Käsespätzle* (cheese noodles).

Cloud One: On the 13th floor of Motel One, this glass-fronted bar has tremendous views. Shake your own cocktail or go for a signature pomegranate margarita.

 DRINKING IN INNSBRUCK: OUR PICKS

MAP p68

Fuchs & Hase: This vaulted bar is a mellow pick for an expertly mixed cocktail, proper coffee or glass of natural wine. *5pm-1am Tue & Wed, 3pm-1am Fri & Sat*	**Stage 12:** Backlit, gold-kissed bar with a terrace for summer imbibing, a vintage popcorn machine and talented mixologists. *noon-midnight Sun-Thu, to 1am Fri & Sat*	**Moustache:** Retro bolthole, with a terrace overlooking Domplatz. Go for cocktails, craft beers and finger food. *10am-2am Tue-Sun, 4pm-2am Mon*	**In Vinum:** Snug Altstadt wine bar: relaxed choice to sample Austria's finest wines; see website for details of the regular tastings. *11am-midnight Mon-Sat, 4-10pm Sun*

CITY TO SLOPES

The money-saving **Innsbruck Card** *(24/48/72hr €69/79/89, child half price)* gets you one visit to Innsbruck's main sights and attractions, a return cable car or funicular journey, a guided city walk and unlimited use of public transport, including the Sightseer and Kristallwelten shuttle bus.

Heading to the slopes? The surrounding region is brilliantly connected by public transport. Distances are generally short and fares inexpensive. Many connections are covered by free guest cards you receive locally, so check this before shelling out on tickets. In winter, Innsbruck's money-saving **Ski Plus City Pass** wraps up 346km of pistes in 12 ski areas around Innsbruck and the glacier-capped Stubaital, and opens the doors at 22 sights and attractions.

BIKEMP/SHUTTERSTOCK

Hikers, Kreuzjoch

South Korean artist Lee Bul's perspective-bending *Into Lattice Sun* and Mexican-Canadian artist Rafael Lozano-Hemmer's *Pulse Voronoi,* a light fantastic walk through 7000 shards of crystal inspired by a Big Bang–style blast.

Outdoor Action in the Zillertal   MAP p71

Hit the slopes

In a stupendously wild pocket of Tyrol, an hour's train ride from Innsbruck, the Zillertal is ripe for outdoor adventure. In summer, hiking trails vein the landscape. Memorable rambles in Zell am See include the 8km round hike to **Zellberg** via the wispy Talbach falls, and the tougher 14km, five-hour stomp up to the 2558m-high, cross-topped summit of **Kreuzjoch**, the highest peak in the Kitzbühel Alps. Mountain bikers are in their element on the 30km **Zillertal Radweg**. For bigger thrills, the **Aktivzentrum** *(aktivzentrum-zillertal.at)* is a one-stop shop for pulse-quickening sports, from paragliding to whitewater rafting and river bugging in raging waters.

When the snow falls, **Mayrhofen**, at the head of the valley, has the downhill edge, with 204km of well-groomed slopes, terrific off-piste and the **PenkenPark** for boarders. One ticket covers the lot: the **Zillertal Superskipass** *(zillertal.at; adult/child €79/35.50).*

Snow Legends in Kitzbühel   MAP p71

World Cup winter wonderland

Winter sparkles brightly in Kitzbühel, right up there among the world's best ski resorts. When flakes blanket the mountains,

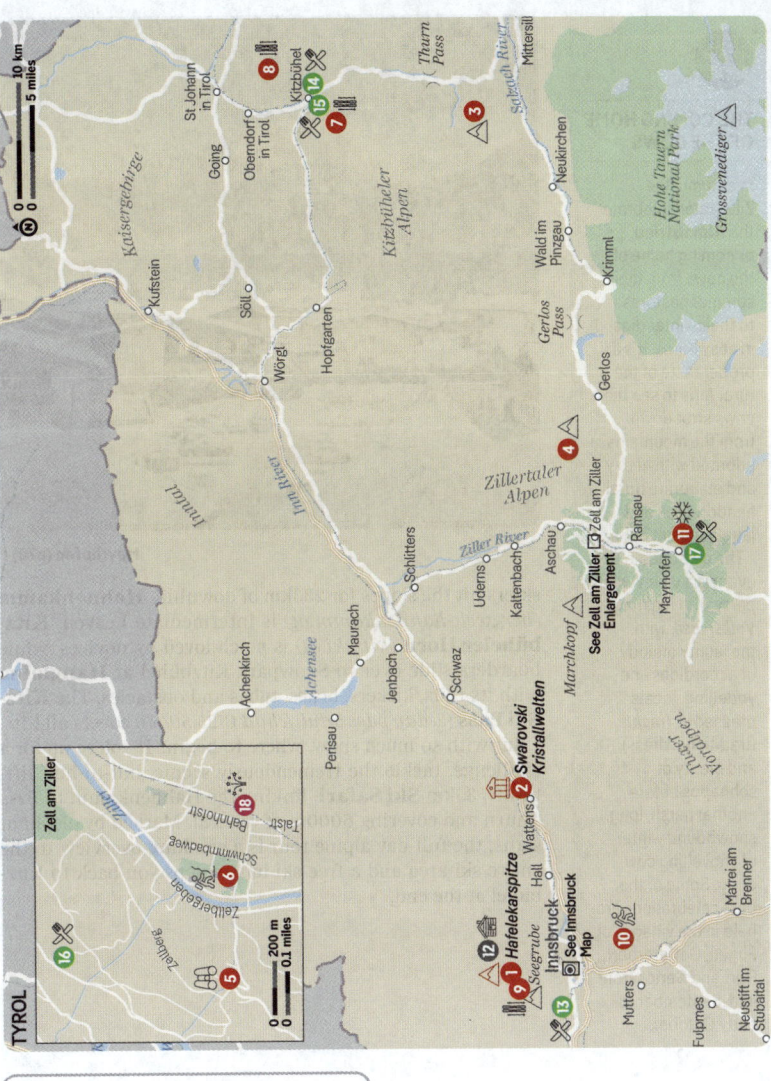

TYROL

Zell am Ziller

0   200 m
0   0.1 miles

0   10 km
0   5 miles

Hohe Tauern
National Park

Grossvenediger △

Kitzbüheler
Alpen

Thurn
Pass

Zillertaler
Alpen

Tuxer
Voralpen

★ HIGHLIGHTS
1 Hafelekarspitze
2 Swarovski
   Kristallwelten
● **SIGHTS**
3 Hanglalm
4 Kreuzjoch
5 Zellberg
● **ACTIVITIES**
6 Aktivzentrum
7 Hahnenkamm
8 Kitzbüheler
   Horn
9 Nordpark
10 Olympia Bob

11 PenkenPark
● **SLEEPING**
12 Pfeishütte
● **EATING**
13 Buzihütte
14 First Lobster
15 Huberbräu
   Stüberl
16 Schulhaus
17 Wirtshaus zum
   Griena
● **ENTERTAINMENT**
18 Almabtrieb

71

THE COMING HOME OF THE COWS

In autumn, the Zillertaler celebrate the **Almabtrieb**, or coming home of the cows from their summer pastures to their winter digs in cosy barns. It's a proper taste of the rural Alps to see the cows strut down from the mountains adorned with heavy and elaborate floral headdresses and jangling giant bells.

The centuries-old event is a valley-wide party with feasting, *Volksmusik* with the jaunty melody of accordions and yodelling, locals dressed in *Tracht* (traditional dress), and plenty of schnapps before another harsh, long, snowbound winter of shovelling cow dung. Some of the best celebrations are held in the villages of Fügen, Gattererberg, Hart and Gerlos from mid-September to early October.

ALEXANDER TOLSTYKH/SHUTTERSTOCK

Mayrhofen (p70)

skiers hit the slopes for 233km of downhill. **Hahnenkamm** (*bergwelt-hahnenkamm.at*) is intermediate heaven, **Kitzbüheler Horn** (*kitzski.at*) is much loved by novices, while boarders slide over to Snowpark Kitzbühel at **Hanglalm**, with its rails, kickers, boxes, tubes and obstacles. The **Kitz-Ski Pass** (*2-day pass adult/child €125.50/63*) covers all lifts.

But with so much snow, where to begin? If you're up for a challenge, tackle the tremendously scenic, hut-to-hut, lift-to-lift, 35km **Ski Safari**, linking the Hahnenkamm to Pass Thurn and covering 6000m of vertical. Marked by elephant signs, the full-day alpine tour is a cracking overview to the entire ski area and a free ski bus schleps you back to Kitzbühel at the end.

 ### EATING IN THE ZILLERTAL & KITZBÜHEL: OUR PICKS

Wirtshaus Zum Griena: *Schlutzkrapfen* (cheese-filled pasta) and *Specknödel* (bacon dumplings) at 400-year-old chalet in Mayrhofen. *3-11pm Mon & Thu-Sun* €€

Schulhaus: Panoramically perched above Zell am Ziller, this old schoolhouse has sublime views and a Tyrolean seasonal menu. *6-11pm Fri* €€

Huberbräu Stüberl: Old-world Kitzbühel haunt with vaults and pine benches, delivering Austrian classics like schnitzel, goulash and dumplings. *9am-11pm* €€

First Lobster: Oyster shells mounted on brick walls are a nod to the terrific fish and seafood on the menu at this slick, bistro-style restaurant. *4-11pm Mon-Sat* €€

Places We Love to Stay

€ Budget €€ Midrange €€€ Top End

Vienna
MAP p51

Hotel Lamée €€ Glamorous art deco–styled hotel near Stephansplatz, with a city-view rooftop bar.

Die Josefine Hotel €€ Boutique 49-room hotel with *Great Gatsby* vibes; home of stylish Barfly's speakeasy.

Hotel Daniel €€ Smart-luxury, minimalist-style hotel next to Belvedere, with one of the best brunches in town. Vespas and bikes for hire.

Magdas €€ Social business hotel integrating refugees. The sustainable, upcycled design supports NGOs and local artists.

Hotel Imperial €€€ Palatial hotel brimming with decadent features, from the royal staircase to rooms.

Melk & Dürnstein

Hotel Schloss Dürnstein €€€ Opulent rooms in a 17th-century castle – the height of luxury in the Wachau.

Hotel Richard Löwenherz €€€ Beautifully converted from a former medieval convent in Dürnstein, complete with serene monastery garden.

Salzburg
MAP p58

YoHo € Backpacker dream: comfy bunks, cheap beer and *The Sound of Music* screened daily.

Hotel & Villa Auersperg €€ Fuses late-19th-century flair with contemporary. Relax in the vine-swaddled garden or rooftop spa with Kapuzinerberg views.

Hotel am Dom €€ Antique meets boutique at an Altstadt hotel in an 800-year-old building.

Schloss Mönchstein €€€ On a fairy-tale perch atop Mönchsberg and set in hectares of wooded grounds, this 16th-century castle is honeymoon material.

Werfen

Weisses Rössl € Good-value *Pension* (B&B) has great views of the fortress and the Tennengebirge from its rooftop terrace.

Landgasthof Reitsamerhof €€ Rousing views of the Tennengebirge peaks at a sunny yellow, geranium-bedecked chalet just south of Werfen.

Hallstatt

Camping am See € Camping, glamping and upmarket wagons in Obertraun; lake location with beach and sauna-on-wheels.

Hallstatt Hideaway €€€ Modern, beautifully textured suites just back from the lake in Hallstatt. Sauna and private garden on the lake itself.

Graz
MAP p65

Das Weitzer €€ Excellent hotel beside the River Mur and near the Kunsthaus, with a cafe, rooftop sauna and flower-filled lobby.

Schlossberg Hotel €€ Swish art hotel in the former late-16th-century royal carpentry workshops, with an impressive art collection.

Klagenfurt & Wörthersee

Sandwirth €€ Contemporary, comfortable and central, these parquet-floored rooms and apartments are ideal for families.

Seehotel Porcia €€€ In Pörtschach, right on the Wörthersee, with a private beach and elegantly decorated rooms in antique style, some with lake views.

Innsbruck
MAP p68

Hotel Weisses Kreuz €€ This 500-year-old hotel oozes history, with creaking beams, wood-panelled parlours and a twisting staircase.

Stage 12 €€ Design-driven pick lodged in a 16th-century townhouse, with mountain-view rooms, a 6th-floor spa and an upbeat cocktail bar.

Penz Hotel €€€ Behind a sheer wall of glass, this contemporary design hotel has minimalist-chic rooms and a rooftop bar for sunset cocktails.

Zillertal

Schulhaus €€ Charismatic schoolhouse panoramically perched above Zell am Ziller. Rustic rooms, mountain views and a slow-food menu.

Alpenhotel Kramerwirt €€ Big on alpine flair, this rambling 500-year-old chalet in Mayrhofen has warm-hued rooms and a rooftop spa.

Kitzbühel

Snowbunny's Hostel € This friendly, laid-back hostel is a bunny-hop from the slopes.

Villa Licht €€ Pretty gardens, spruce modern apartments with pine trappings, balconies with mountain views – this charming Tyrolean chalet has the lot.

73

Practicalities

HEALTH

The World Health Organization (WHO) recommends all travellers should be covered for diphtheria, tetanus, measles, mumps, rubella, polio and hepatitis B. A UK Global Health Insurance Card (GHIC) or European Health Insurance Card (EHIC) from your healthcare provider covers most emergency medical care in Austria. This is no substitute for good insurance.

ANDRZEJ ROSTEK/SHUTTERSTOCK

LGBTIQ+ TRAVELLERS

Progressive and diverse, Vienna is home to the country's biggest gay community. Positive change is afoot elsewhere, too, though there is still some discrimination, especially in staunchly conservative, Catholic pockets of the country.

MOUNTAIN SAFETY

Every year people die from landslides and avalanches in the Alps. Always check weather conditions before heading out; consider hiring a guide when skiing off-piste. For challenging hikes, ensure you have the proper equipment and fitness. Inform someone at your accommodation where you're going and when you intend to return.

VISAS

Austria is part of the Schengen Agreement. Citizens of the EU, Eastern Europe, Israel, USA, Canada, Central and South America, Japan, Korea, Malaysia, Singapore, Australia and New Zealand don't need visas for stays of up to three months.

OPENING HOURS

Opening hours vary through the year and can differ between cities and small villages.

Banks 9am–3pm Monday to Friday
Cafes 8am–11pm
Post offices 8am–noon and 2–6pm Monday to Friday
Pubs & bars 5.30pm–midnight
Restaurants 11am–2.30pm & 6–11pm
Shops 9am–6.30pm Monday to Friday, to 5pm Saturday
Supermarkets 8am–8pm Monday to Friday, to 5pm Saturday

ACCESSIBLE TRAVEL

Austria scores highly with accessible travel, but a trip still requires careful planning. Ramps into buildings are common but not universal; most U-Bahn stations have wheelchair lifts, but on buses and trams you'll often be negotiating gaps and steps.

PUBLIC HOLIDAYS

New Year's Day 1 January
Epiphany 6 January
Easter Monday March/April
Labour Day 1 May
Whit Monday 6th Monday after Easter
Ascension Day 6th Thursday after Easter
Corpus Christi 2nd Thursday after Whitsunday

Assumption 15 August
National Day 26 October
All Saints' Day 1 November
Immaculate Conception 8 December
Christmas Day 25 December
St Stephen's Day 26 December

Language

The national language of Austria is German. Let's get to grips with the basics here.

Basics

Hello. Servus. *ser*-vus
Hello. Grüss Gott. grewss-got
Good morning. Moagn. *mwah*-gen
Goodbye. Auf Wiedersehen. owf *vee*-der-zay-en
Bye. Tschüss./ Tschau. chüs/chow
Yes. Ja. yah
No. Nein. nain
Please. Bitte. *bi*-te
Thank you. Danke. *dang*-ke
Excuse me. Entschuldigung. ent-*shul*-di-gung
Sorry. Entschuldigung. ent-*shul*-di-gung
What's your name?
Wie ist Ihr Name? (pol) vee ist eer *nah*-me
Wie heißt du? (inf) vee haist doo
My name is …
Mein Name ist … (pol) main *nah*-me ist …
Ich heiße … (inf) ikh *hai*-se …
Do you speak English?
Sprechen Sie Englisch? (pol) *shpre*-khen zee *eng*-lish
Sprichst du Englisch? (inf) shprikhst doo *eng*-lish
I don't understand. Ich verstehe nicht. ikh fer-*shtay*-e nikht

Directions

Where's (the station)?
Wo ist (der Bahnhof). vor ist (der *bahn*-hawf)
What's the address?
Wie ist die Adresse? vee ist dee a-*dre*-se
Could you please write it down?
Könnten Sie das bitte aufschreiben? *kern*-ten zee das *bi*-te owf-shrai-ben

Can you show me (on the map)?
Können Sie es mir (auf der Karte) zeige *ker*-nen zee es meer (owf dair *kar*-te) *tsai*-gen

Signs

Ausgang Exit
Eingang Entrance
Damen Women
Herren Men
Heiß Hot
Kalt Cold
Offen Open
Geschlossen Closed
Kein Zutritt No Entry
Rauchen Verboten No Smoking
Verboten Prohibited

Time

What time is it? Wie spät ist es? vee shpayt ist es
It's (10) o'clock. Es ist (zehn) Uhr. es ist (tsayn) oor
morning Morgen *mor*-gen
afternoon Nachmittag *nahkh*-mi-tahk
evening Abend *ah*-bent
yesterday gestern *ges*-tern
today heute *hoy*-te
tomorrow morgen *mor*-gen

Emergencies

Help! Hilfe! *hil*-fe
Go away! Gehen Sie weg! *gay*-en zee vek
I'm ill. Ich bin krank. ikh bin krangk
Call the police! Rufen Sie die Polizei! *roo*-fen zee dee po-li-*tsai*
Call a doctor! Rufen Sie einen Arzt! *roo*-fen zee *ai*-nen artst

NUMBERS	
1	eins *ains*
2	zwei *tsvai*
3	drei *drai*
4	vier *feer*
5	fünf *fünf*
6	sechs *zeks*
7	sieben *zee-ben*
8	acht *akht*
9	neun *noyn*
10	zehn *tsayn*

NATALI GLADO/SHUTTERSTOCK

Arriving

Vienna is the main transport hub for Austria, operating services worldwide. The airport is 19km southwest of the city centre. Most low-cost and European carriers operate from Terminal 1, while Terminal 3 is for long-haul flights. Salzburg, Innsbruck and Graz have small, minimal-fuss airports, operating flights to numerous destinations across Europe.

By Rail
Bordering eight countries, Austria's super-central location makes international rail travel a breeze. Vienna is an hour from Bratislava, Innsbruck is 3½ hours from Verona, Linz is four hours from Prague. You get the idea – Europe really is your oyster here.

By Car
There are numerous entry points from Germany, the Czechia, Slovakia, Hungary, Slovenia, Italy and Switzerland. Border crossing points are open 24 hours. Austria is compact – driving from Bregenz in the west to Vienna in the east takes just six hours (traffic permitting).

MONEY
Currency: Euro (€)

CREDIT CARDS
Visa and Mastercard (EuroCard) are more widely accepted than Amex and Diners Club. Upmarket shops, hotels and restaurants will accept cards. Credit cards allow you to get cash advances at ATMs and over-the-counter at most banks. Train tickets can be bought by credit card in main stations.

TAXES & REFUNDS
Mehrwertsteuer (VAT) in Austria is typically 20%. Look for the 'Global Refund Tax Free Shopping' sticker to reclaim about 13% on single purchases over €75 (by non-EU citizens/residents); see *globalrefund.com*. Refund desks are at major department stores, as well as Vienna and Salzburg airports.

TIPPING
Bars About 5% at the bar and 10% at a table.

Hotels One or two euros per suitcase for porters and valet parking in top-end hotels.

Restaurants About 10% (unless service is abominable).

Taxis About 10%.

Getting Around

Austria's public transport network is a dream, with swift, inexpensive trains linking towns and cities, and buses filling the gaps. Car hire gives you greater freedom to explore the country's remotest corners.

JULIA MOUNTAIN PHOTO/SHUTTERSTOCK

Train

Austria's rail system is excellent and inexpensive with a discount card. Österreiche Bundesbahn (*ÖBB; Austrian Federal Railway; oebb.at*) is the main operator. The best deals are *Sparschiene*, heavily discounted tickets sold online up to six months ahead.

Car

You'll find all the major car-hire companies at airports, including Sixt, Hertz and Enterprise. The minimum age for hiring small cars is 19. A valid licence is necessary. Autobahn (motorways) are well maintained. You can only drive on them with a *Vignette* (motorway tax), available from border crossings and petrol stations.

Mountain Railways

When trains stop in the Alps, the only way is up on a *Seilbahn* (funicular) or *Bergbahn* (cable car). Costs quickly mount, meaning it's often cheaper to buy a weekly pass (a ski pass in winter) or use a discount card. Some guest cards get you a free ride.

Bus

Rail routes are often complemented by Postbus (*postbus.at*) services, useful in inaccessible mountainous regions. Buses are fairly reliable, and usually depart from train stations. Aim for weekday travel; services are reduced or nonexistent on weekends.

Bike

Thousands of kilometres of well-signposted bike routes shadow rivers and lakeshores and twist up the Alps. Bike/e-bike rental is ubiquitous and many ÖBB stations rent wheels. Most regional trains transport bikes in the baggage car (you'll need a bicycle ticket). On long-distance trains, reserve online/use the ÖBB app.

DRIVING ESSENTIALS

Drive on the right.

Winter tyres are obligatory November to mid-April.

50 **100**

Speed limit is 50km/h: built-up areas, 100 km/h: open roads and 130 km/h: motorways.

Curated by
Helena Smith

Belgium &
Luxembourg

GABLED BUILDINGS AND OFFBEAT CHARM

Belgium and Luxembourg have all the showy art and architecture you could dream of, as well as little known but appealing towns, cities and verdant landscapes.

Stereotypes of comic books, chips and sublime chocolates are just the start in eccentric little Belgium, which has spent centuries producing some of Europe's finest art and architecture. Bilingual Brussels is the dynamic yet personable EU capital, also sporting what's arguably the world's most beautiful city square. Otherwise, its galleries, cafes and distinctive village-like districts are a delight to explore. Flat, Dutch-speaking Flanders has many other alluring medieval cities, all easily linked by regular train hops: Bruges is the most popular, for its art and exceptional prettiness; but Ghent also features canals, medieval art and beautiful buildings – plus an edgy student scene.

It's a region much beloved by cyclists for its flatness and for its devotion to the Tour of Flanders. Within a Frisbee throw of Bruges, coastal Ostend offers wide sandy beaches, and modern art too. The port city of Antwerp is forever associated with diamonds and the painter Rubens, but it also is known for high fashion. Much of hilly, French-speaking Wallonia is contrastingly rural – its castles and extensive cave systems easier to reach by car – though fascinating Mons is well connected by public transport. Independent Luxembourg, the EU's richest country, is compact and attractive with its own wealth of castle villages, while its capital city is famed both for banking and its fairy-tale UNESCO-listed Old Town.

PECOLD/SHUTTERSTOCK

THE MAIN AREAS

BRUSSELS
Majestic central square and characterful cafes.
p84

GHENT
Medieval magic and contemporary life.
p91

BRUGES
Postcard-perfect canal-side beauty.
p94

For places to stay in Belgium & Luxembourg, see p109

SCSTOCK/SHUTTERSTOCK

Left: *The Adoration of the Mystic Lamb* (p92), Ghent; Above: Grand Place (p84), Brussels

ANTWERP
Rubens, chocolate,
fashion and diamonds.
p100

WALLONIA
Little-visited cities,
wooded Ardennes.
p103

LUXEMBOURG CITY
Fortified bastions,
stunning gorge setting.
p106

Bruges, p94

Bruges grabs the limelight with its fairy-tale confection of pretty canals, soaring towers and step-gabled houses. If the crowds get too much, nip up a quiet side street.

Antwerp, p100

Antwerp is Belgium's second city, biggest port and fizzing hub of cultural cool, known for its glittering diamonds and the baroque canvasses of art superstar Rubens.

Ghent, p91

Ghent has quietly become the country's best-kept secret. Once a European superpower, it is now an unsung treasure with a strong artistic bent and a lively student population.

Brussels, p84

History meets bureaucracy meets bizarre in this multicultural jumble that's fabulous for art, museums, chocolate shops and unforgettable cafe-bars. Brussels' magnificent Grand Place is a global wonder.

Roosendaal

Bergen-op Zoom

Snijder-Rockoxhuis

Onze-Lieve-Vrouwekathedraal

Museum Plantin-Moretus

North Sea

Westerschelde

Knokke-Heist

Terneuzen

Zeebrugge

Blankenberge

De Haan

Ostend

Markt

Bruges

Eeklo

St- Niklaas

Antwerp

Nieuwpoort

Museum Sint-Janshospitaal

Groeninge-museum

A11

Lokeren A14

A12

Veurne

A18

The Adoration of the Mystic Lamb

Dender-monde

Willebroek

Dunkirk

Diksmuide

Torhout

A10

Gravensteen

Mechelen

Calais

Roeselare

Deinze

Belfort

Ghent

FLANDERS

A10 Aalst

Grand Place

A

Poperinge

Zonnebeke

A14

Oudenaarde

BRUSSELS

Musé Horta

Ypres A19

Kortrijk

Ronse

Ninove

Mont des Arts

Menen

Schelde

Lessines

Halle

Waterlo

Tourcoing

Mouscron

Enghien

A7

Armentières

Lille

Roubaix

Leuze

Ath

Mémorial 1815

A8

Tournai

Soignies

Nivelles

A16

La Louvière

Lens

A7

Mons

Charlero

Douai

Valenciennes

Binche

Arras

Maubeuge

Beaumont

Sambre

Couvir

Chimay

Amiens

FRANCE

Find Your Way

The train and bus services are extensive, efficient and affordable (even free in Luxembourg). Wallonia, being less populated, does not have the same coverage as Flanders and Brussels, but cities are well connected.

Reims

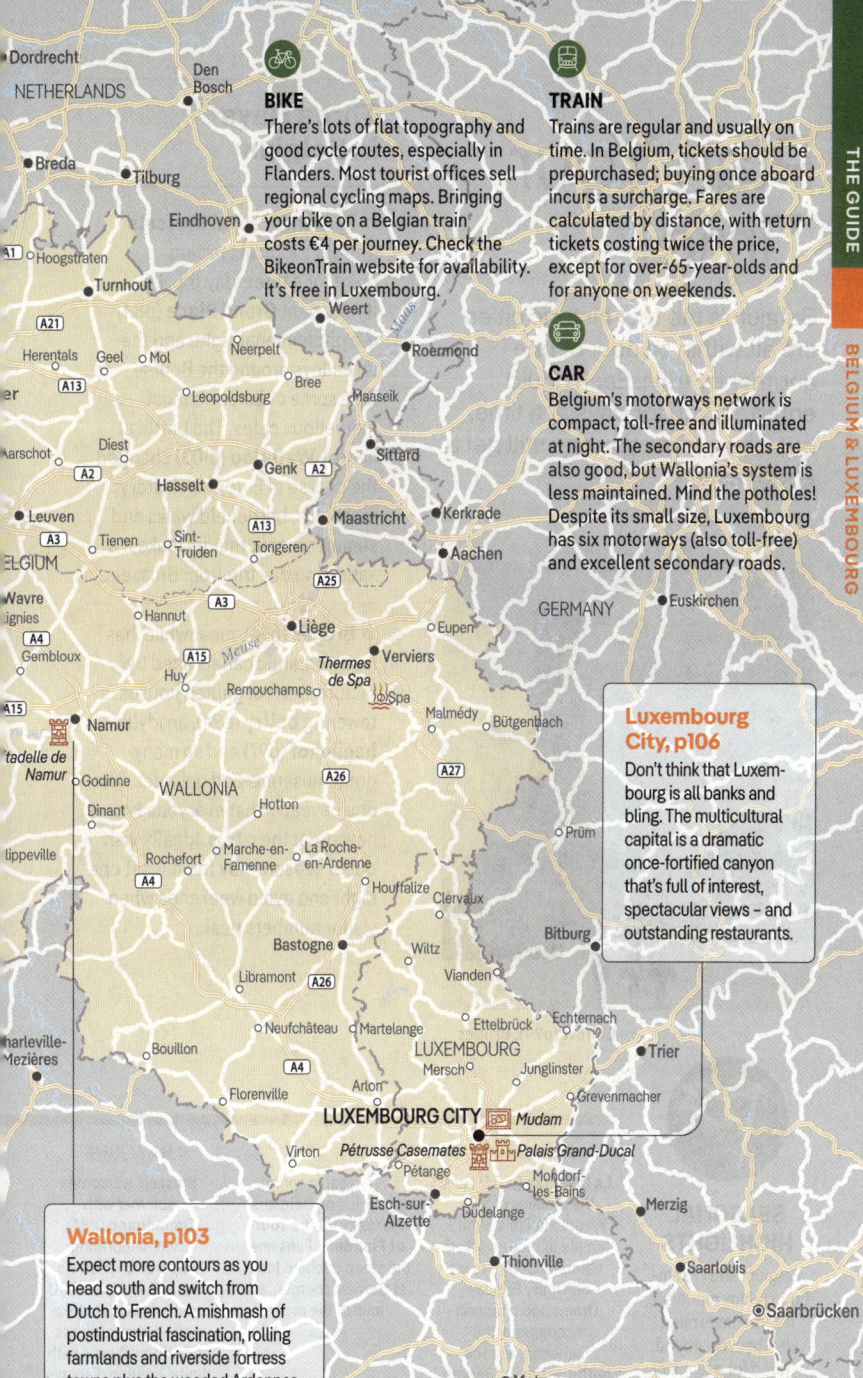

BIKE

There's lots of flat topography and good cycle routes, especially in Flanders. Most tourist offices sell regional cycling maps. Bringing your bike on a Belgian train costs €4 per journey. Check the BikeonTrain website for availability. It's free in Luxembourg.

TRAIN

Trains are regular and usually on time. In Belgium, tickets should be prepurchased; buying once aboard incurs a surcharge. Fares are calculated by distance, with return tickets costing twice the price, except for over-65-year-olds and for anyone on weekends.

CAR

Belgium's motorways network is compact, toll-free and illuminated at night. The secondary roads are also good, but Wallonia's system is less maintained. Mind the potholes! Despite its small size, Luxembourg has six motorways (also toll-free) and excellent secondary roads.

Luxembourg City, p106

Don't think that Luxembourg is all banks and bling. The multicultural capital is a dramatic once-fortified canyon that's full of interest, spectacular views – and outstanding restaurants.

Wallonia, p103

Expect more contours as you head south and switch from Dutch to French. A mishmash of postindustrial fascination, rolling farmlands and riverside fortress towns plus the wooded Ardennes.

Plan Your Time

Belgium's fab four historic cities are all within an hour of one another by train. Each could entertain you for days at a time, but with a week you can still get a good taster.

OLENA ZNAK/SHUTTERSTOCK

Belfort (p94), Bruges

Three Days in Belgium

● Belgium's capital **Brussels** (p84) is a logical starting point for a three-day trip. Its flamboyant **Grand Place** (p84) is a phenomenal sight, and the tiny alleys around the Bourse hide some of Europe's most marvellous cafes. The battle at nearby **Waterloo** (p103) changed the course of European history; museums, battlefield walks and summer reenactments make it a satisfying day trip from Brussels.

● **Bruges** (p94), meanwhile, has it all: romantic canals lined by picture-perfect gabled houses, a towering **belfry** (p94), an idyllic **begijnhof** (p97) and so many great museums and galleries. The one caveat is that everyone knows how great the city is. Ideally visit out of season, stay for at least one night and avoid weekends when visitor numbers peak.

SEASONAL HIGHLIGHTS

Belgium and Luxembourg enjoy moderate, if sometimes rainy, weather year-round – good for a range of events, festivals and gatherings.

FEBRUARY

La Ducasse (p103) sees the remains of Ste-Waudru (a 7th-century female miracle-worker) paraded around town on Trinity Sunday. Drums and chanting accompany the Lumeçon, a mock battle pitting St George against a wickerwork dragon.

APRIL

Every year in spring, cycle-loving Belgians go crazy for the **Tour of Flanders**. Fans line the steep cobbled Muur at Geraardsbergen, an icon of the race.

MAY/JUNE

Brussels welcomes summer with **Ommegang** (p84), commemorating Emperor Charles V's visit in 1549. Up to 1200 costumed locals take part – knights, giants and stilt-walkers – with digital lighting displays on the side.

A Week of Sensational Cities

● Explore Brussels and Bruges as suggested above, then head to gorgeous **Ghent** (p91) with its majestic canal views: this hip and student-filled town feels like a grittier, more lived-in version of Bruges. A day here will leave you wanting more, but it's time enough to climb the tall **belfry** (p91), take a canalboat trip, explore the city-centre medieval castle of **Gravensteen** (p91), check out a cool cafe and adore the fabled *Mystic Lamb* by Flemish Primitive artist **Jan van Eyck** (p92).

● The old core of the city of **Antwerp** (p100) has plenty more, including fabulous museums, an impossibly venerable printworks and Rubens connections at every turn. The city is also a cradle of creativity, where immersive experiences give insights into the diamond industry, chocolate making and brewing.

A Week in Wallonia & Luxembourg

● The old centre of **Namur** (p104) is a fine place to while away a day; the vast bastions of the great fortress make for great explorations and adventures. Afterwards head to **Luxembourg City** (p106) via Dinant and the Meuse Valley. This may be the capital of Europe's richest country, but while much is pricy, there are plenty of free attractions and public transport is gratis. The geography of the city is spectacular, and it is a truly multicultural place.

● The elegant original spa of **Spa** (p105) is a charmer, whether for dining well, 'taking the waters' or otherwise pampering yourself. **Liège** (p105) takes a bit of effort to love, but it's rewarding to stroll around and practise your French with the ebullient, fun-loving locals.

JUNE

Reenactments of the **Battle of Waterloo** (p105) see hundreds of costumed 'soldiers' battle it out on the very field where the conflict took place. Scale and dates vary each year (can be early July).

JULY

The fabulously raucous **Gentse Feesten** (p93) transforms the heart of Ghent into a youthful party, with free music and street theatre, dance workshops and packed streets. Be prepared to party a lot, and sleep little.

AUGUST

A week of raucous celebrations in **Outremeuse** (p105) culminates on 15 August when sermons are read in Walloon dialect, then everyone gets tipsy on *pékèt* (local gin). Expect firecrackers, puppets, dances and a procession of giants.

NOVEMBER

Late November to New Year, embrace the festive holiday spirit as lights illuminate the wonders of Luxembourg City during the winter-lights period.

Brussels

GLOBAL CITY | ARCHITECTURE | NINETEEN VILLAGES

☑ **TOP TIP**

To see a bunch of top sites, consider the **BrusselsCard** *(brusselscard.be; 24/48/ 72hr €39/51/57)*, which includes free city transport. However, avoid buying one for Mondays when much is closed, or on the first Wednesday afternoon of each month when many major museums are free.

As the capital of a trilingual country with over 180 nationalities, and as the decision-making centre for over 400 million Europeans, Brussels proudly embraces its identity as an open city.

At first glance, Brussels can seem chaotic. Years of uncoordinated urban planning, with little regard for previous heritage, have left the city scattered with mismatched architecture. Grand squares, intricate guildhalls and Gothic churches stand alongside Art Nouveau, Art Deco and sleek glass buildings. This improbable mix has become an integral part of Brussels' landscape, adding to its distinctive character.

It's a city of art, from Flemish masters in the Museum of Fine Arts to avant-garde galleries spread all around town. Comic art has deep roots here: Hergé, creator of Tintin, was born in Brussels. But most of all, the city is all about conviviality and festivities such as Ommegang. With a collection of 19 'villages' and different districts waiting to be discovered, Brussels welcomes you, just as you are.

Brussels' Crown Jewel

Admire the Grand Place

It's impossible not to gawk at the gilded guildhalls of the **Grand Place** (Grote Markt in Dutch). They are a testament to the power and resilience of the guilds and notable figures who rebuilt the Grand Place after the devastating bombing

GETTING AROUND

The heart of Brussels is compact. While the central area, known as the Pentagon, is easily covered by foot, public transport is recommended for visiting other neighbourhoods and attractions, including the distinctive Atomium. The transport network in Brussels consists of metros, trams, buses (operated by STIB/MIVB) and intra-urban trains (SNCB/NMBS). For late-night-goers, Noctis buses (on Friday and Saturday nights) and Collecto, a shared taxi service, are available.

of Brussels by the army of the King of France, Louis XIV, in 1695. The walls of the Gothic city hall remained standing as the sole testimony of the square's medieval past. Its tall and slender tower supports a golden statue of St Michel, one of Brussels' two patron saints. Since 2023, the **Hôtel de Ville** *(City Hall; bruxelles.be/hotel-de-ville; adult €15)* has been open for daily visits. Across from it, the neogothic Maison du Roi now houses the **Brussels City Museum** *(brusselscity museum.brussels; adult/under 18 €10/free)*. On the eastern side of the square, the **House of the Dukes of Brabant** is in fact several houses built under the same facade, making it

TOP EXPERIENCE

Mont des Arts & Museums

Nowhere else in Brussels will you find such a concentration of sights: the Coudenberg (Cold Hill) overlooking the lower town is home to the lovely Mont des Arts gardens and contains a plethora of museums. Here we have highlighted our favourites: you can also visit the Palais du Coudenberg archaeological site, Musée BELvue and the manuscripts and miniatures of the KBR Museum.

JOSEFKUBES/SHUTTERSTOCK

Musée des Instruments de Musique (MIM)

TOP TIPS

● The Old Masters and Magritte Museums are free on the first Wednesday of the month from 1pm, and BELVue is on the first Sunday of the month.

● Feeling peckish? **albert**, the National Library's top-floor restaurant, offers splendid views of Brussels and a lovely terrace full of greenery.

PRACTICALITIES

● mim.be, fine-arts-museum.be, coudenberg.brussels, belvue.be, kbr.be/en/museum ● Prices vary ● Museums close Mondays

Musée des Instruments de Musique (MIM)

Strap on a pair of headphones, then step onto the automated floor panels at **MIM** in front of precious instruments to hear them being played. The museum is housed in the stunning Art Nouveau Old England Building, a former department store built in 1899 by Paul Saintenoy. The rooftop cafe remains closed for renovation.

Musées Royaux des Beaux-Arts

Musées Royaux des Beaux-Arts features 15th-century Flemish Primitives, including Rogier Van der Weyden's *Pietà* with its hallucinatory sky, Hans Memling's refined portraits, and the richly textured *Madonna with Saints* by the anonymous Master of the Legend of St Lucy. Highlights continue with Bruegel the Elder *(The Fall of Icarus),* Rubens *(Four Studies of a Head)* and Van Dyck *(Portrait of an Elderly Lady).*

Musée Magritte

With new scenography, **Musée Magritte** holds the world's largest collection of the surrealist pioneer's paintings and drawings. Going from the top floor to the bottom, you can watch his style develop from colourful Braque-style cubism in 1920 through a Dalí-esque phase and a late-1940s period of Kandinsky-like brushwork to his trademark bowler hats of the 1960s.

Place du Jeu de Balle flea market

look like a palace decorated with busts of the several Dukes and Duchesses of Brabant.

A Masterful Design

Visit Horta's own house

At the turn of the 20th century, Victor Horta was already an important architect. He decided to design his own townhouse and workshop, **Musée Horta** *(hortamuseum.be; adult/student/child €14/6/3.5)* in St-Gilles, and when the two buildings were completed in 1901, it was a true work of total art. Horta meticulously created every aspect, from the letterbox to the mosaics and furniture – today the museum includes some original pieces. The living area's interior is bathed in light, thanks to the windows and a stunning glass roof, showcasing the characteristic Art Nouveau style with its emphasis on glass, metal and curves.

The Spirit of Brussels

Browse and bargain at the Marolles Flea Market

The predominantly working-class and multicultural neighbourhood of **Marolles** (Marollen in Dutch) has always had a rebellious streak and a joke on its lips. The best way to experience it is by visiting the flea market on **Place du Jeu de Balle**. Every morning, starting at 9am, vendors fill up the whole square to sell secondhand clothes, furniture, old cameras, books, paintings... Try your hand at bargaining, or simply enjoy the vibe and have a cup of coffee in one of the many cafes surrounding the square.

THE CONTINENT'S FIRST MALL

Built in 1847, the **Galeries Royales St-Hubert**, just 80m away from Grand Place, is an elegant glass-covered shopping arcade – and was the first of its kind on the continent. With a delightful array of boutiques, chocolatiers, cafes and theatres, intricate architecture and high-end shops, it exudes a timeless charm that attracts both locals and tourists. Do not miss **Tropismes**, Brussels' prettiest bookshop; and have a waffle or *speculoos* biscuit at **Maison Dandoy** or **Mokafé**. Additionally, the Galeries have residential apartments on the upper floors. Fancy living like a resident? We recommend **Hotel des Galeries** or the **Vaudeville B&B**.

EATING IN THE PENTAGON: BUDGET EATS

Mer du Nord/Noordzee: Enjoy your shrimp croquettes at this outdoor venue by a fishmonger's window. *11am-6.30pm Tue-Sun* €

Chouke: Have the best *frites* (chips/fries) in the city centre at this no-frills *fritkot*. Don't miss the homemade burgers. *noon-11pm* €

Tonton Garby: Cheese-loving brothers serve custom sandwiches worth the wait, mixing veggies, fruits and sauces. Friendly, chatty service. *11am-5pm Mon-Fri & Sat* €

Super Fourchette: Vinyl shop meets cafe–*cantine* with homemade, seasonal dishes and a chill vibe. *noon-2pm & 6.30-9.30pm Mon-Fri* €

STE-CATHERINE ON FOOT

Welcome to Ste-Catherine, one of the oldest Brussels neighbourhoods and former site of the city's inland port.

START	END	LENGTH
Place Ste-Catherine	La Bellone	1km; 45min

Start your walk at ❶ **Place Ste-Catherine**. Until 1854, the square and church area were part of Brussels' port. The city authorities closed it and filled in the basins connected to the Willebroek Canal, which leads to Antwerp. This transformation coincided with the covering of the Senne River and the construction of the Haussmann-inspired Central Boulevards. The current church, designed by Joseph Poelaert, replaced the original one – only the baroque bell tower remains. From here, head to ❷ **Vismet-Marché aux Poissons**, the public space named after the fish market established after the basins were filled in. Though dismantled in the 1950s, the surrounding streets still bear names linked to old merchandise quays. Two artificial basins and several historic fish restaurants recall the area's maritime past. At the end of the second basin, admire the ❸ **Anspach Fountain** with a bas-relief representing an allegory of the Senne River, resting in a tunnel. On the left, notice the Maison du Cheval-Marin, a former inn dating back to the 17th century. Further along, the ❹ **Pigeon Soldat Memorial** pays homage to homing pigeons and their owners during WWI. Next, head to ❺ **Rue de la Cigogne** for Brussels' prettiest street. Rue de Flandre offers an array of good restaurants and independent stores. If open, check out ❻ **La Bellone** for a beautiful surprise.

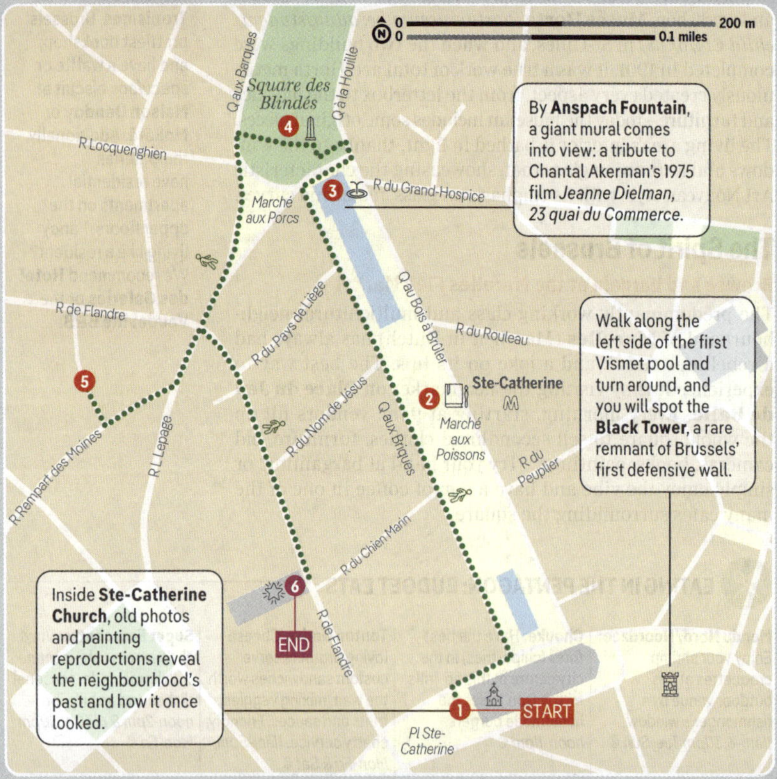

By **Anspach Fountain**, a giant mural comes into view: a tribute to Chantal Akerman's 1975 film *Jeanne Dielman, 23 quai du Commerce*.

Walk along the left side of the first Vismet pool and turn around, and you will spot the **Black Tower**, a rare remnant of Brussels' first defensive wall.

Inside **Ste-Catherine Church**, old photos and painting reproductions reveal the neighbourhood's past and how it once looked.

Q aux Barques
Square des Blindés
Q de la Houille
R Locquenghien
❹
Marché aux Porcs
❸ R du Grand-Hospice
R de Flandre
R du Pays de Liège
Q au Bois à Brûler
R du Rouleau
❺
R Rempart des Moines
R L'Epage
R du Nom de Jésus
Q aux Briques
Ste-Catherine Ⓜ
❷
Marché aux Poissons
R du Peuplier
R du Chien Marin
❻
END
R de Flandre
❶ START
Pl Ste-Catherine

0   200 m
0   0.1 miles

Beyond Brussels

Hop on a train and explore three intriguing cities, rich in history, architecture, and tasty eating and drinking options.

Places

Mechelen p89

Leuven p90

Map of the area around Brussels showing: Antwerp, Lier, Willebroek, Dendermonde, Mechelen, Aarschot, Aalst, BRUSSELS, Leuven, Anderlecht, Tienen, Halle, Waterloo, Wavre, Braine-l'Alleud, Louvain-la-Neuve, Nivelles

Mechelen (Malines in French) is an unexpected treasure of medieval architecture, with a gorgeous central square, great museums, and an astonishing selection of splendid churches as befits the seat of Belgium's Catholic primate (archbishop equivalent). If possible, time your itinerary so that you over-night here at the weekend which, in complete contrast to Bruges, is when accommodation prices typically fall. Lively Leuven (Louvain in French) elegantly combines history and fun. Today it's home to Flanders' foremost university, and with some 25,000 students in residence between mid-September and June, there's always loads going on.

Mechelen

TIME FROM BRUSSELS: **20MIN** 🚆

Mechelen's Catholic heart

Rising 97m above Mechelen's majestic Grote Markt, the 15th-century tower of **St-Romboutskathedraal** (St-Rombouts Cathedral) is a soaring landmark that you'll find variously framed down gently curved medieval streetscapes. Inside the cathedral there's a 1723 monumental pulpit and a 1630 cruci-fixion scene by Van Dyck.

Beer and history

Mechelen's landmark brewery, **Brouwerij Het Anker**, forms an incongruous addition to the little streets of the city's Grote Begijnhof. But it is heir to a beer-making tradition started here by the *begijns* themselves in 1369. Het Anker beer names are interesting for historico-cultural references relating to Mech-elen's past. There's a well-crafted blonde called Maneblusser meaning 'moon extinguisher' – that's been a self-mocking

---

GETTING AROUND

The main Mechelen train station is around a 20-minute walk south of the Grote Markt. Leuven train and bus stations are a 15-minute walk from the centre straight along Bondgenotenlaan. Dazzling Liège-Guillemins is the main long-distance, high-speed train station, with national and international connections. If you're arriving and want the historic city centre, Liège-St-Lambert station is a more convenient place to alight, though you might need to change at Guillemins.

CHANGE COMES IN WAVES

In 2025, Leuven celebrated the 600th anniversary of its university-city status by installing **Kunst en Wetenschaps-route**, a walking route linking 16 new works of outdoor contemporary art and subtitled in English 'And so, Change comes in Waves'. Many of the artworks are so subtle you need the guide pamphlet to realise that you're actually looking at them. The route starts in the attractive parkland campus around **Arenburg Castle**, where **Dwaaltuin** is the latest monumental artwork by Gijs Van Vaerenbergh. As yet, it's just a monumental steel superstructure, but over coming years the various planted creepers will grow up around the rust-coloured frameworks, creating a circular labyrinth of cascading foliage.

nickname for Mechelen townsfolk since 1687, when cloud-diffused moonlight above the cathedral tower was mistaken for a fire that they tried to put out. The Gouden Carolus range references Holy Roman Emperor 'Golden' Charles V. Ambrio is based on a recipe that was supposedly Charles' favourite ale. Hopsinjoor is a hoppy pun on Op-Sinjoorke, a folklore character.

Leuven

TIME FROM BRUSSELS: **22MIN**

A Gothic spectacular

Leuven's incredible 15th-century **Stadhuis** is an architectural wedding cake overloaded with terraced turrets, fancy stonework and colourful flags. A phenomenal 235 statues were added in the mid-19th century, each representing a prominent scholar, artist or noble from the city's history.

Flemish Last Supper

If the northwest frontage of the 1425 **St-Pieterskerk** *(free)* looks unfinished, that's because Leuven's unstable subsoil forced builders to abandon plans for a 170m-high tower. However, the interior is lavished with priceless artworks, notably *Het Laatste Avondmaal,* by Leuven-based Flemish Primitive artist Dirk Bouts, who placed Jesus' Last Supper in a typical Flemish dining hall.

Something brewing

Wander into the square called **Oude Markt** any night in the university term time (September to June) and you'll find a surging mass of happy drinkers whose chatter and whoops reverberate around the baroque gables.

Dozens of side-by-side pubs here are collectively nicknamed 'Europe's Longest Bar'. Meanwhile Leuven is home to AB InBev, the world's biggest brewing group. You'll need to pre-book to join a two-hour tour of its vast flagship **Stella Artois Brewery** *(breweryvisits.com; tour €17.50),* usually weekends only. Don't like Stella? Brewery–cafe **Domus** preempted the microbrewery trend decades ago, while **De Blauwe Kater**, open 11am to 2am, has over 100 beers and free blues or jazz gigs on term-time Monday nights.

EATING IN MECHELEN & LEUVEN: OUR PICKS

De Margriet: Courtyard of a historic Mechelen monastery with brasserie-style meals, particularly asparagus or mussels when in season. *11.30am-8.30pm Mon-Sat* €€

Graspoort: Imaginative multicourse 'New World' fusion dinners in atmospheric Mechelen alley, half engulfed by foliage. Close to the Vismarkt. *7-9pm Tue-Sat* €€€

De Werf: Eccentric Leuven student classic, with tables spilling way out into Hogeschoolplein. Popular for back-to-basics fare or just a drink. *9am-9pm Mon-Fri* €

Lukemieke: Serving vegetarian delights for over 50 years in a discreet Leuven townhouse with a rear garden. *noon-2pm & 6-8pm Mon-Fri, closed mid-Jul–mid-Aug* €€

Ghent

The seat of the Counts of Flanders, Ghent was a great cloth town that grew to become medieval Europe's largest city after Paris and Constantinople. In the early 19th century, Ghent was the first town in Flanders to harness the Industrial Revolution. Many historical buildings were converted into flax- and cotton-processing mills and the city became known as the 'Manchester of the Continent' after its industrial equivalent in England.

Despite being one of Belgium's most historic cities, Ghent remains small enough to feel cosy but big enough to be a vibrant, relevant centre for trade and culture. There's a wealth of medieval and classical architecture here, contrasted by postindustrial areas undergoing urban renewal that give the city a gritty-but-good industrial feel.

In the centre, tourists remain surprisingly thin on the ground, but Ghent's large student and youth population means there are always people about, enjoying the city's fabulous canal-side architecture, abundance of quirky bars and restaurants, and some of Belgium's best museums.

GETTING AROUND

Ghent's city centre is relatively large, but the different districts are well connected by public transport, including smoothly gliding modern trams. Download the De Lijn app *(delijn.be/en)* to find routes, buy tickets and consult up-to-date information.

Head into Ghent's Past

Medieval monuments

Ghent's UNESCO-listed 14th-century **Belfort** *(historische huizen.stad.gent/en/belfry; adult/child €11/2.20)* or belfry stands 91m high and is topped by a huge and magnificent dragon weather-vane; he's become something of a city mascot. You'll meet two previous dragon incarnations on the 350-stair climb to the top; there are elevators to help some of the way. Enter through the **Lakenhalle**, Ghent's cloth hall that was left half-built in 1445 and only completed in 1903. Hear the carillon at 11.30am Fridays and 11am on summer Sundays.

Flanders' quintessential 12th-century stone castle, the **Gravensteen** *(historischehuizen.stad.gent/en/castle-counts;*

☑ TOP TIP

CityCard Gent *(48/72hr €42/48)* gives free entrance to all of Ghent's top museums and monuments and allows unlimited travel on trams and city buses, plus a boat trip and a day's free bike hire. It's excellent value. Buy one at participating museums, major bus offices or the **tourist office**.

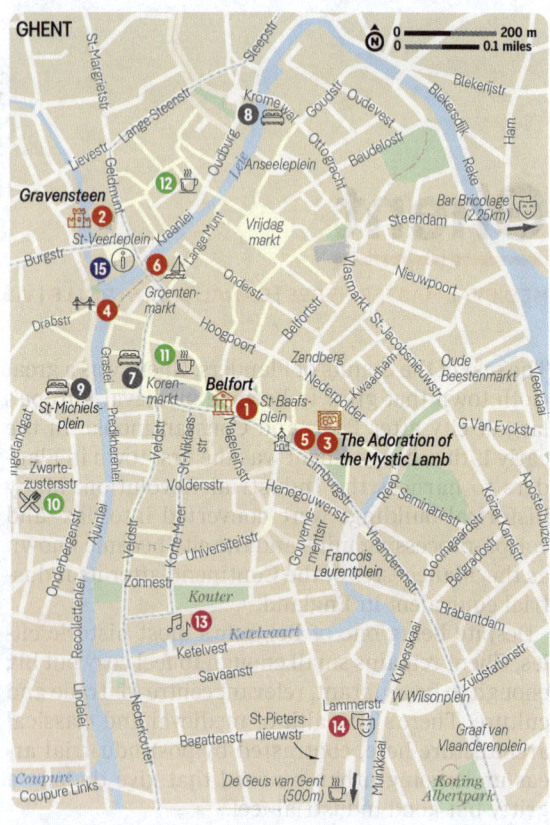

adult/child €13/2.70), comes complete with fairy-tale moat, turrets and arrow slits. It's all the more remarkable considering that during the 19th century the site was converted into a cotton mill. Meticulously restored since, the interior sports the odd suit of armour, a guillotine and torture devices. The lack of furnishings is compensated for with a handheld 45-minute movie guide, which sets a tongue-in-cheek historical costumed drama in the rooms, prison pit and battlements. There's a great castle viewpoint on St-Widostraat.

The Mystic Lamb

Flemish Primitive masterpiece

Housed in the towering interior of **Sint-Baafskathedraal** *(sintbaafskathedraal.be; adult/child €16/8)*, the Van Eyck brothers' 1432 Flemish Primitive masterpiece **The Adoration of the Mystic Lamb** is one of the earliest-known oil paintings. Completed in 1432, it has 20 luminous panels, which are in the process of a remarkable restoration.

The work represents an allegorical glorification of Christ's death: on the upper tier sits God the Father flanked by the

UHRYN LARYSA/SHUTTERSTOCK

Grasbrug bridge

Virgin and John the Baptist. On the outer panels are the nude Adam and Eve. The lower tier centres on the lamb, symbolising the sacrifice made by Christ, surrounded by religious figures and a landscape dotted with local church towers.

On the Water

Canals, bridges and boat trips

To admire Ghent's towers and gables at their most photogenic, stand just west of the little **Grasbrug** bridge over the Leie river at dusk. The appealing waterfront facades of Graslei aren't as old as they look – they were largely rebuilt to make Ghent look good for the 1913 World Fair.

Join a traditional guided **boat tour** from companies including **Rederij De Gentenaer** *(rederijdegentenaer.be; €10)*. These tours take you around the city in 45 minutes to an hour, showing all the highlights with some explanation from a local.

LIVE MUSIC IN GHENT

Liz Aku, Ghent resident, singer and music teacher, reveals her favourite live-music spots. *@lizakumusic*

Bar Bricolage: Urban oasis in Ghent's Old Docks, with sandy boardwalk paths, cultural programming, live DJs and a relaxed campfire atmosphere.

VIERNULVIER: Known for concerts and parties, particularly in the Concert Hall and the new Club Wintercircus.

Handelsbeurs Concert Hall: Beautifully restored venue: intimate setting for jazz, world, soul and acoustic performances.

Gentse Feesten: One of Europe's largest cultural festivals; 10-day celebration; free live music on every corner, from folk to punk to techno. Crowded but amazing experience for all ages.

 DRINKING IN GHENT: BEST BROWN CAFES & COFFEE SHOPS

't Oud Clooster: Atmospheric double-level cafe was once a nunnery. Well-priced meals presented with style. *11.30am–2.30pm & 6-10.15pm Mon-Sat* €€

Mokabon: Ghent's classic old-world coffee shop still serves old-school Belgian coffee with whipped cream. *9am-6pm* €

Rococo: Lit by candles, this classic late-night cafe–bar with carved wooden ceilings is ideal for cosy midnight conversations. *9pm-late Tue-Sun* €€

De Geus van Gent: Congenial cafe with eclectic decor and 20 beers from the barrel. It hosts regular jam nights and live music. *4pm-3am Mon-Fri, 7pm-3am Sat* €

Bruges

GABLED BUILDINGS | ARTISTIC TRADITIONS | TRANQUIL BACKSTREETS

GETTING AROUND

The medieval city centre is compact, and walking around it is one of the major pleasures of a visit. The relatively quiet streets also make this a great place to explore by bike. If you're coming from the station, hop on city bus 1 or 2, both of which make loops through the city centre (you can make contactless payments on board), or take a taxi to your hotel.

If you set out to design a fairy-tale medieval town, it would be hard to improve on central Bruges (Brugge in Dutch), one of Europe's best-preserved cities. Picturesque cobbled lanes and dreamy canals link photogenic market squares lined with soaring towers, historical churches and lane after lane of old whitewashed almshouses. Medieval Flemish painters were perhaps the first to use oil paint, kicking off a tradition that rivals that of Renaissance Italy. Bruges' galleries and museums are simply outstanding, with many boldly incorporating contemporary works into their historic collections.

For many, though, the Bruges secret is already out; during the busy summer months, you'll be sharing the magic with a constant stream of tourists in the medieval core. To really enjoy Bruges, stay one or two nights – day-trippers miss out on the city's stunning nocturnal floodlighting – and try to visit midweek to avoid weekend crowds.

The Historic Heart of Bruges

Marvellous Markt

The heart of ancient Bruges, **Markt**, the old market square, is lined with pavement cafes beneath step-gabled facades. The buildings aren't always quite as medieval as they look, but together they create a fabulous scene; even the neogothic former post office is architecturally magnificent. The urban panorama is dominated by the 13th-century **Belfort** *(visitbruges.be/nl/belfort; adult/child €15/13)*, towering 83m above the square like a gigantic medieval rocket. There's relatively little to see inside, but it's worth the mildly claustrophobic 366-step climb for the fine views. Look out through wide-gauge chicken wire for panoramas across the spires and red-tiled rooftops towards the wind turbines and giant cranes of Zeebrugge.

The **Historium** *(historium.be; adult/child €26/18)* occupies a neogothic building on the northern side of the Markt. The immersive one-hour audio and video tour aims to take you

☑ TOP TIP

The best times to visit are in spring, when daffodils carpet the tranquil courtyard of the historic *begijnhof* retreat, or outside of Christmas in winter, when you'll have the magnificent, if icy, town almost all to yourself.

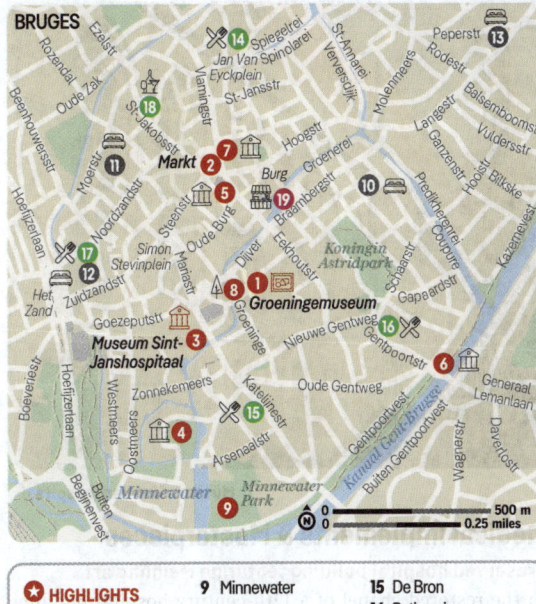

BRUGES

HIGHLIGHTS
1 Groeningemuseum
2 Markt
3 Museum Sint-Janshospitaal

SIGHTS
4 Begijnhof
5 Belfort
6 Gentpoort
7 Historium
8 Hof Arents
9 Minnewater

SLEEPING
10 B&B Amaryllis Dietiens
11 Dukes' Palace
12 Passage Bruges
13 St Christopher's Inn Hostel at The Bauhaus

EATING
14 Blackbird
15 De Bron
16 Patisserie Schaeverbeke
17 That's Toast

DRINKING & NIGHTLIFE
18 De Republiek

SHOPPING
19 Vismarkt

back to medieval Bruges; a fictional love story gives narrative structure, and you can nose around Van Eyck's studio, among other pseudo-historic experiences.

Not So Primitive Art

Artistic highlights in Bruges

The **Groeningemuseum** (*museabrugge.be/en/visit-our-museums/our-museums-and-monuments/groeningemuseum; adult/youth €15/13*) covers a huge sweep of art history, but is best known for its paintings by Flemish Primitives Jan Van Eyck, Rogier Van der Weyden, Hans Memling and Gerard David. These artists depicted the affluence and beauty of Bruges to brilliant effect. Van Eyck's portraits, like those of his counterparts, reflect the abundance of the city, while adding a further dimension of psychological depth. Memling's epic *Moreel Triptych* (1484) is one of the first large-scale group portraits ever painted.

NATALIYA NAZAROVA/SHUTTERSTOCK

Museum Sint-Janshospitaal

Medical Implements & Masterpieces

Preserved hospital building featuring Memling art

In the restored chapel of a 12th-century hospital building, the **Museum Sint-Janshospitaal** *(visitbruges.be/en/sint -janshospitaal-saint-johns-hospital; adult/child €15/7)* shows various torturous medical implements, a hospital sedan chair and a gruesome 1679 painting of an anatomy class. It also incorporates contemporary pieces such as Berlinde De Bruyckere's fallen archangel, a crumple of feathers with fragile legs emerging; and deeply moving video works muse on illness, death and mourning. But most eyes are on seven masterpieces by 15th-century artist Hans Memling, including the enchanting reliquary of St Ursula, which looks like a miniature Gothic cathedral.

 EATING IN BRUGES: VEGAN & VEGGIE-FRIENDLY

Blackbird: All-vegan cafe serving bagels, bountiful happiness bowls, pancakes, fresh juices and cakes. *9am-3pm Wed-Sat, 9.30am-1pm Sun* €

De Bron: By the time this glass-roofed restaurant's doors open, there's a queue of diners keen to get vegetarian fare from *de bron* (the source). *11.45am-2pm Mon-Fri* €

De Republiek: This is a big, buzzing modern bistro with great vegan choices on the menu. *noon-1am Wed-Sun, from 5pm Mon-Tue* €€

That's Toast: Bruges' best breakfast restaurant has gained a following for its all-day brekkies, with several vegan options. *8.30am-4pm Wed-Sun* €€

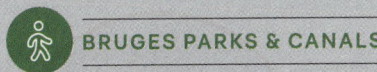

BRUGES PARKS & CANALS

This walk links some of Bruges' entrancing green spaces, by way of secluded lanes and canals.

START	END	LENGTH
Vismarkt	Vismarkt	3.4km; 2–3hr

The handsome colonnaded 1821 **①** **Vismarkt** (fish market) is still open for business most days. Check out pretty Huidenvettersplein, ringed with archetypal Bruges buildings.

Walk south along Jozef Suvéestraat for a few minutes until you reach local hangout **②** **Koningin Astridpark**, named after the Swedish wife of King Léopold of Belgium; you'll come across her bust when you reach the park. Walking through the park you'll pass a community radio station, bandstand and adventure playground. Beyond the Gothic revival Magdalen Church is scrumptious Patisserie Schaeverbeke. Continue south to **③** **Gentpoort**, one of the town's four medieval gateways. From here, a pleasant footpath leads through the greenery along the water's edge. Follow the path west until you reach **④** **Minnewater** and its eponymous park, a scenic green space with orderly flowerbeds and secluded paths.

Just north of the park, Wijngaardplein, a touristy but still irresistible square, is ringed by cafes. Over the little arched bridge from the square, the 13th-century **⑤** *begijnhof* is one of the delights of Bruges, its whitewashed buildings encircling a garden with tall trees and swathes of daffodils in spring. It's well worth visiting the church here.

One of the prettiest of this pretty city's hangout spots, **⑥** **Hof Arents** features a humpback bridge, and the clattering hooves of passing carriages that call here. From here, it's a short stroll back to Vismarkt.

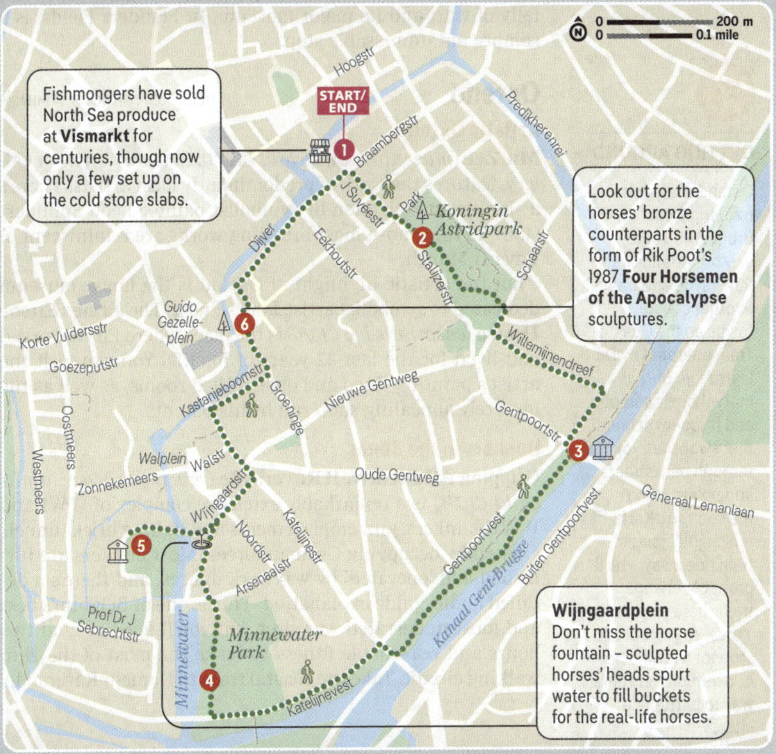

Fishmongers have sold North Sea produce at Vismarkt for centuries, though now only a few set up on the cold stone slabs.

Look out for the horses' bronze counterparts in the form of Rik Poot's 1987 Four Horsemen of the Apocalypse sculptures.

Wijngaardplein
Don't miss the horse fountain – sculpted horses' heads spurt water to fill buckets for the real-life horses.

Koningin Astridpark

Minnewater Park

0   200 m
0   0.1 mile

Beyond Bruges

Nip up to the coast at Ostend, wander the historic city of Kortrijk or explore WWI history in Ypres.

Places

Ostend p98
Kortrijk p99
Ypres p99

In a region with excellent public transport and short distances between cities and sights, Bruges makes a great jumping-off point to sample the region. Ostend is the focus of the Belgian coast, with wide sand beaches and some fantastic art attractions; take the coastal tram to fascinating Atlantikwall Raversyde to see preserved bunkers and lookouts from both wars. The city of Kortrijk isn't well known on any tourist circuit, but its beautiful historic core and standout textile museum make the place well worth a visit. Entirely rebuilt following WWI, the town of Ypres stands testament to the folly of war; and its major museum, In Flanders Fields, is a sombre but unmissable stop.

Ostend

TIME FROM BRUGES: **14MIN**

Artistic Ostend

Mu.Zee *(muzee.be; adult/child €12/3),* Ostend's foremost gallery, features the work of predominantly local artists. There's a significant collection by symbolist painter Léon Spilliaert (1881–1946), whose most brooding works are reminiscent of Edvard Munch.

But the artistic highlight of Ostend is the house museum dedicated to symbolist artist James Ensor. The **James Ensor House** *(ensorhuis.be; €13/6)* is the place where Ensor worked and lived for the last 32 years of his life. You can visit the artist's painting-lined and object-filled rooms, as well as the bizarrely appealing shop run by his parents.

Bunkers in the dunes

Gripping **Atlantikwall Raversyde** *(raversyde.be/en; adult/child €10/4)* is a remarkably extensive complex of WWI and WWII bunkers, gun emplacements and linking brick tunnels created by occupying German forces. Most bunkers are furnished and 'operated' by waxwork figures, and there's a detailed audio-guide explanation. This is one of Belgium's best and most underrated war sites, but you'll need around two hours and reasonable fitness to make the most of the 2km walking circuit. Take the coastal tram to Domein Raversijde.

GETTING AROUND

Ostend is a quick train trip from Bruges; you can explore Atlantikwall Raversyde and travel to other coastal towns on the Coastal Tram operated by De Lijn *(delijn.be/en),* a marvellously smooth and frequent service that swooshes you through backstreets and points along the seafront. Kortrijk is a slightly longer train ride away; you'll probably change trains here en route to Ypres, so you could stop for a few hours or overnight on your way to battlefield sites.

Kortrijk

TIME FROM BRUGES: 47MIN

Serene *begijnhof*

Small but utterly delightful, Kortrijk's enclosed *begijnhof* is as charming a cluster of whitewashed old terraced houses as you could hope to find. Designed for single women, the complex was founded by Johanna of Constantinople way back in 1238. The last member of the community died in 2013, and the buildings were restored and now provide affordable housing.

Get in touch with the Texture museum

It's well worth the walk to **Texture** *(texturekortrijk.be; adult/child €8/6)*, located in a 1902 flax factory. This museum focuses on the town's flax and linen industry; you'll also see a lovely collection of damasks and laces. The history of flax is told through individual accounts and is surprisingly absorbing; you can touch and smell the fabric itself. The beautifully converted building uses flax chipboard and linen drapes in homage to the museum's content.

Ypres

TIME FROM BRUGES: 1HR 45MIN

Great War experience

In Flanders Fields Museum *(inflandersfields.be; €12/6)* contains a wealth of letters, household objects, military equipment, maps, newspapers and memorabilia pertaining to WWI. But the real stars of the show are the striking video installations illustrating how families and soldiers on both sides experienced the horrors of the Great War. The audio guide *(per person €2)* includes additional, in-depth listening points. Expect to spend at least two hours here.

THE BATTLE OF THE GOLDEN SPURS

Flanders' French overlords were incensed by the Bruges Matins massacre of May 1302. Philip the Fair, the French king, promptly sent a well-equipped cavalry of aristocratic knights to seek retribution. Outside Kortrijk on 11 July this magnificent force met a ragged, lightly armed force of weavers, peasants and guild members from Bruges, Ypres, Ghent and Kortrijk. But the horseback knights failed to notice a trap: the Flemish townsfolk had disguised a boggy marsh with brushwood. Snared by the mud, the heavily armoured French were immobilised and slaughtered. The event became a symbol of Flemish resistance, and to this day 11 July is celebrated as Flanders' 'national' holiday.

Don't miss the paintings upstairs of Ostend locals.

 EATING IN OSTEND, KORTRIJK & YPRES: OUR PICKS

De Ruyffelaer: Traditional local dishes in a wood-panelled place in Ypres. Chequerboard floors, vintage decor. *11.30am-3.30pm Sun, 5.30-9.30pm Fri-Sun* €€

Frituur Franky: Lovers of the humble fry are spoiled for choice at this excellent Ostend *frituur* (chip shop). *noon-2pm & 5.30-11pm Tue-Sat, 5-10pm Sun* €

't Mouterijtje: Spacious Kortrijk brasserie with bare brickwork: good beers and signature dish *côte-à-l'os* (rib roast). *5pm-midnight Fri-Tue* €€

Bistro Beau-Site: Ostend cafe with jazz on the stereo and art books. Upstairs window seats have beach views. *11am-7pm Mon, Wed & Thu, noon-late Fri-Sun* €€

Antwerp

HIGH FASHION | **RUBENS PAINTINGS** | **LIVE MUSIC**

☑ TOP TIP

Antwerp City Pass
*(antwerpcitypass.be;
24/48/72hr €45/55/65)*
allows entry to over 20
key attractions plus free
public transport. It might
make sense if you're
visiting Chocolate Nation,
De Ruien and De Koninck
Brewery. But almost all
other Antwerp museums
are included in the all-
Belgium **MuseumPass**
*(museumpassmusees.
be; €64.95)*, which lasts a
whole year.

Belgium's second city is also its capital of cool, a fashion hub and world-leading diamond-trading hub, yet it still retains an exquisite medieval heart. By the 16th-century Antwerp had taken over from Bruges as one of Europe's main trading ports, opening the world's first specially built stock exchange. From the 1560s, iconoclasts, the Dutch Revolt and the inquisition devastated the place, exacerbated later by a blockade of Antwerp's port. Skilled workers and international trade fled north (hence Amsterdam's rise). Still, the world's first newspaper was produced here in 1606, and Rubens hung around to paint baroque masterpieces. Once the port blockade finally ended in 1863, wealth quickly returned, and by the 1920s Antwerp was important enough to host the Olympic Games and build Europe's first skyscraper. WWII destroyed much and decimated the significant Jewish population, but Antwerp rebounded, and today few cities have a more optimistic 21st-century vision.

Medieval Marvels

Antwerp's antique heart

Other than Europe's first skyscraper (the 1929 Boerentoren), central Antwerp's architecture remains relatively low-rise, such that the 16th-century belfry of **Onze-Lieve-Vrouwekathedraal** majestically dominates the cityscape. Ornately magnificent, the

🧭 GETTING AROUND

Beautiful **Antwerpen-Centraal** is the main train hub and the nearest station to the old city centre. Antwerpen-Berchem is a possible alternative for the Art Nouveau area of Zurenborg. Antwerpen-Zuid is marginally nearer Het Zuid. Antwerp has a well-developed bus and tram system, known as 'pre-metro' when tunnelling underground. The easiest way to explore the main sights is to use the Velo short-hop bicycle-hire system *(velo-antwerpen.be/en)*. Bike pickup and drop-off stands are plentiful and the system is unusually easy to use.

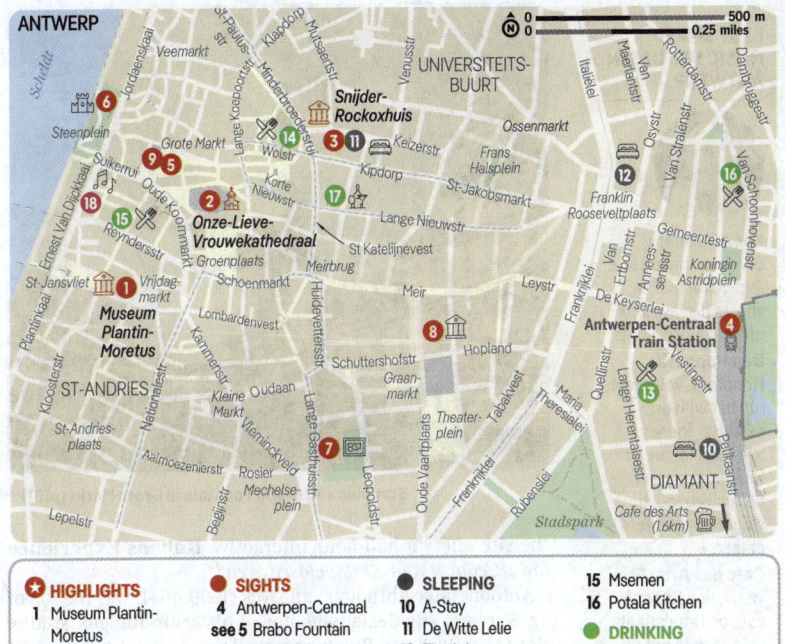

ANTWERP

UNIVERSITEITS-BUURT

Snijder-Rockoxhuis

Onze-Lieve-Vrouwekathedraal

Museum Plantin-Moretus

ST-ANDRIES

Antwerpen-Centraal Train Station

DIAMANT

Stadspark

Cafe des Arts (1.6km)

★ **HIGHLIGHTS**
1 Museum Plantin-Moretus
2 Onze-Lieve-Vrouwekathedraal
3 Snijder-Rockoxhuis

● **SIGHTS**
4 Antwerpen-Centraal
see 5 Brabo Fountain
5 Grote Markt
6 Het Steen
7 Maagdenhuis
8 Rubenshuis
9 Stadhuis

● **SLEEPING**
10 A-Stay
11 De Witte Lelie
12 The Ash

● **EATING**
13 Aahaar
14 Jam

15 Msemen
16 Potala Kitchen

● **DRINKING & NIGHTLIFE**
17 Den Beulebak

● **ENTERTAINMENT**
18 Den Hopsack

123m tower has a habit of popping into view from all kinds of intriguing angles. The cathedral itself is a Gothic masterpiece that took 169 years to finish (1352–1521).

The small streets around the cathedral are abuzz with cafe life, with bars also spilling onto the main market square, **Grote Markt** – a beautiful cobbled space that's lined on three sides by classic step-gabled medieval-style merchant houses. Behind the **Brabo Fountain** is the **Stadhuis**, Antwerp's 1565 city hall with a statue-topped palatial facade that blends Flemish and Italian styles. Inside is a fascinating, map-rich exhibition (*free*) about the city's development, setting out ambitious plans for the future.

Het Steen is Antwerp's dinky but photogenic castle dating from 1200. It contains a tourist office and free-access viewpoint.

Artistic Pedigree

Local artists: Rubens, Van Dyck and Breugel

Peter Paul Rubens (1577–1640) moved to Antwerp in 1609 after lengthy studies in Italy. The house–studio he designed is now the memorable **Rubenshuis** (*rubenshuis.be*), which is undergoing a restoration project until around 2027: meanwhile

Stadhuis and Brabo Fountain in Grote Markt (p101)

BEST SMALL MUSIC VENUES IN ANTWERP

Koen Cassiers, Berchem-based lute and guitar maker, shares his favourite offbeat music spots.

Den Hopsack: Nonprofit, volunteer-run bar with art exhibits. There's live music three or four times a week, typically acoustic singer-songwriters or jazz.

Cafe des Arts: For years, tiny Gitanes cafe on Draakplaats managed to put on little concerts which were essentially rehearsals for the bands. Now the gigs have moved to co-owned Cafe des Arts near Berchem Station, with jazz most Sundays and who knows what on Friday nights.

Den Beulebak: This cute 16th-century building, on a hidden but central courtyard square called St Nikolaasplaats, hosts occasional offbeat folk-music gigs.

the site offers a half-hour interactive **Rubens Experience** *(adult/concession €12/8; closed Wed).*

Antoon (later Anthony) Van Dyck (1599–1641) was the son of an Antwerp silk dealer who honed his art in Rubens' studio. Both Van Dyck and Rubens are well represented at the splendid 17th-century **Snijder-Rockoxhuis** *(snijdersrockoxhuis. be; adult/under-26 €10/6),* gallery–museum.

Dutch-born Pieter Breugel the Elder (c 1525–69) made his home in Antwerp from 1555, and the city still houses several of his masterpieces, notably his brilliantly grotesque 1561 *Dulle Griet* (Mad Meg). See his work at the **Maagdenhuis** *(maagdenhuis.be; adult/under-26 €10/6),* a former 16th-century orphanage/refuge.

The Print Pioneer

The world's oldest surviving presses

In a building that was a print shop from the 1550s, **Museum Plantin-Moretus** *(museumplantinmoretus.be; adult/under-26/under-18 €12/8/free),* retains half a dozen antique presses, including two that are the oldest still in existence anywhere. The medieval building is memorable in itself, with its gilt-leather 'wallpaper', 1622 courtyard garden and 1640 library, not to mention the fabulous collection of paintings.

 EATING IN ANTWERP: BUDGET EATS

Jam: Fresh, imaginative cafe (and terrace) serving flavour-packed snack-lunches inspired by world travels. *11am-6pm Thu-Mon €*

Aahaar: The €12 buffet of authentic Indian vegetarian food is a budget traveller's delight. Good mango lassis. Zero score for decor. *noon-3pm & 5.30-9.30pm €*

Msemen: Moroccan stuffed puff-pastries served with mint tea and tasty harira soup in an invitingly light, bright interior or rear garden. *11am-7.30pm Tue-Sun €*

Potala Kitchen: Simple but great-value Tibetan, Chinese and Pan-Asian meals, mostly costing under €10. On the station area's 'Chinatown' strip. *noon-10pm Thu-Mon €*

Wallonia

INTRIGUING TOWNS | SPORTY OUTDOORS | FORTRESSES

Wallonia is a place of contradictions. It is Belgium's outdoorsy rural underbelly but also the home to cities with heavy industries that brought the country wealth before decaying into an economic malaise during the 1980s. The carnivals are wild (Binche, in particular), the mindset humorous and the language a form of French that amuses visitors from France. Mons is one of Belgium's underrated cultural gems with a crazy dragon-slaying festival to boot – La Ducasse – while Wallonia's capital, Namur, has a lively cultural vibe and an urban cable car that can whisk you to the top of its signature fortress-citadel. Though scarred by 20th-century eyesores, Liège was once an independent prince bishopric and has complex historical layers that reward patient discovery. Spa is the original spa, and there are fortresses galore, from medieval castles to grand châteaux and more recent fortifications.

GETTING AROUND

Train connections are fine for Mons, Liège, Verviers, Namur and Tournai. There's a regular bus to Waterloo from Brussels and river-buses are a pleasure in Namur and Liège. In contrast to much of Flanders, having a car is a great advantage in Wallonia, where many of the attractions are rural and/or awkward to reach by public transport. Free parking is common.

Waterloo

Site of Napoleon's downfall

As you enter the main battlefield site, **Mémorial 1815** *(wat erloo1815.be; adult/under-18/under-10 €24/12/free),* you appear to be descending into the earth. Collect a lanyard to facilitate multimedia quizzes and connect to the internal wi-fi to access *visit.io* on your smartphone for written and spoken extra coverage. Suitably equipped, the museum section then explains the Battle of Waterloo's historical context, from the Enlightenment to the rise of revolutionary France. Then a parade of life-sized soldiers lead you to a 3D film – an intense experience in which you feel really in the thick of the fighting. Then there's a whole lot more about the battle and its repercussions.

Still within Mémorial 1815, continue to the contrastingly old-fashioned **Panorama de la Bataille**, a circular diorama of the battle painted in 1912. It comes complete with sound effects and foreground models of fallen troops and horses. You can

☑ TOP TIP

La Roche-en-Ardenne is the mountain-biking capital of the Benelux region. It has some good road-biking routes too, and there are plenty more in the Haute Fagnes area, with riders often basing themselves at Malmédy.

also climb the historical **Lion's Mound**, a memorial erected in the 1820s at the request of the Dutch king, whose son who had been injured while assisting Wellington in the battle here.

Mons

Up at the belfry

Mons hosts four UNESCO-listed features, including one of Europe's most memorable festivals. The medieval city developed around the hilltop site of a Roman camp.

On the highest point of the town, partly ringed by remnant fortifications, the **belfry** *(beffroi.mons.be; adult/senior/under-12 €9/6/free)* is a focal point that marks out Mons from kilometres around. There are great views without climbing it, but paying for entry gets you a lift to the 5th floor, with even finer panoramas and touchscreen view identifiers.

Namur

Bastions and tunnels

The **Citadelle de Namur** covers a whole hillside. To learn more about the city's history – and the fortress, in particular

Its speciality is pork 'berdoulle', ie smothered in thick mustard-onion-tarragon dressing.

 EATING IN WATERLOO, MONS & NAMUR: OUR PICKS

Brasserie de Waterloo: Bistro fare plus beers and spirits created on the premises in this battlefield farmstead. *11am-11pm Wed-Sat, 10.30am-7pm Sun* €€

Chez les Filles: Sweet spot between comfort food and gastronomy. Cosy shop-house on Mons' main dining street. *noon-2.30pm Wed-Sun & 6.30-10pm Wed-Sat* €€

Henri: Mons home-cooking that's been a favourite with local families since 1956. Lunch plates €8.50, cash only. *noon-2pm daily & 6.30-9pm Wed-Sat* €

Le Panorama: High in the Namur citadel, this airy pavilion does a varied menu, ranging from snacks to brasserie-style dishes. *11am-last customer* €€

– it's worth starting a visit at the **Terra Nova visitor centre** *(citadelle.namur.be; adult/student €6/5)*. Audio guides cover the key features, though if you speak French there's a lot more to learn from the swirling information boards.

With a Citadelle Pass *(adult/student €18/16)* you can also visit part of the **souterrains**, a fascinating web of dripping tunnels into which the fortress moved the majority of its key installations in more recent iterations. Guides help bring the past to life using audio-visual displays and 3-D wall projections. Temperatures hover around 13°C (55°F), so dress appropriately.

Liège

Light up the mountain

The sprawling city of Liège is like a living architectural onion, with layer upon layer of history lying beneath a craggily scarred facade; in mid-August look out for the wild **Outremeuse** festival. **Montagne de Bueren** is one of the world's most daunting public stairways, with 374 steps rising vertiginously behind Rue Hors Chateau. On the first Saturday of October, this remarkable sight is transformed into a twinkling beauty during the **Nocturne des Coteaux**, when some 20,000 candles are lit on the steps.

A severed head

In a beautifully adapted cloister-convent, the **Musée de la Vie Wallonne** *(viewallonne.be; adult/concession €7/5)* is thematically chaotic but still the best museum in Liège. In a darkened chamber is the ghoulish showstopper: an original guillotine, and the mummified head of the last man to have felt 'her kiss'.

Spa

The spa at Spa

The **Thermes de Spa** *(thermesdespa.com; 3hr €32)* is the city's contemporary spa centre, located on the hilltop directly above the town centre. It's an indulgent complex of indoor and outdoor baths, hammams and saunas. The centrepiece is a giant, light-filled pool with tall glass windows to contemplate the view. The fun way to arrive from town is by a little funicular *(return €3)* from beside the **Van Der Valk Hotel**.

WATERLOO BATTLE REENACTMENTS

In late June 2025, over 2000 men dressed up in early-19th-century military costumes and replayed scenes from the 1815 battle beside the Lion's Mound. Reenactments on this scale take place every five years, with a grandstand erected for ticketed onlookers *(€42-55)* and a running commentary. Still in character, the 'soldiers' camp overnight at La Cailliou (Napoleonic) and Hougoumont (allies), and a visit to these 'Bivouacs' (also ticketed) is nearly as interesting than the battle show.

In the four years between big reenactments, smaller ones take place, show-fighting around the gates of Hougoumont with around 200 or so participants. The exact weekend (late June/early July) depends on Belgian holidays.

 EATING & DRINKING IN LIÈGE & SPA: OUR PICKS

Amon Nanesse/Maison du Pékèt: Rambling antique Liège house with pub fare. Tasters of local gins. *bar 9am-late daily, food noon-2pm & 6-10pm Thu-Mon* €

Brasserie {c}: Medieval buildings that are tasting rooms for Liège's Curtius beer range, but also popular for Belgian food, burgers and *café liégeois*. *noon-11pm Thu-Sun* €€

Little Arthur: Cosy Spa cafe with piled cushions, William Morris wallpaper and a selection of dessert tarts and quiches. *9am-6pm Fri-Tue* €

Rest'O des Amis: Mixing Belgian brasserie and Italian culinary influences to create a locals' dining favourite in the heart of Spa. *11.30am-9pm Wed-Sun* €€

Luxembourg City

ANCIENT WALLS | TOP GALLERIES | INTERNATIONAL VIBES

 TOP TIP

Although the languages you'll most likely encounter are French and German (plus English and Portuguese in some places), Luxembourg's own Germanic language, Luxembourgish (Lëtzebuergesch) is spoken by around 430,000 people. One key word to learn is the general-purpose greeting *'Moien!'*

If you were expecting a city dominated by high-rise banks and anonymous corporate HQ buildings, Luxembourg City will prove a refreshingly charming revelation. The city's old city is in fact a UNESCO-listed layer-cake of bastion walls, footpaths and viewpoints terraced steeply down through parks and fortress remnants to the deep-cut Alzette and Pétrusse river valleys. These scenes are surveyed from many a viewpoint and panoramic walkway, most notably the Chemin de la Corniche, which has been nicknamed the 'most beautiful balcony of Europe'. The atmospheric Grund quarter lies at the riverside below, and it's only when you cross the giant red road bridge (Pont-Grande-Duchesse Charlotte) that you reach the contrastingly brash glass towers of the EU quarter on the Kirchberg Plateau. Add in summer festivals, great art, fine museums and totally free public transport – you don't even pay for the funicular – and you have a gem of a discovery.

Fit for a Grand Duke

The Grand-Ducal palace, inside and out

Luxembourg's hereditary head of state has their office in the **Palais Grand-Ducal**. Built in 1572 as the town hall, an annex was added in 1860 that today houses the Luxembourg Chamber of Deputies (ie parliament). The main building has served as

GETTING AROUND

Free transport around town includes a useful modern tram linking the main train station and airport via bus hubs and the Kirchberg EU district. Transport systems are completely integrated across the city and the whole Grand Duchy, with real-time best-choice connections given through the *mobiliteit.lu* app.

A funicular and two tall public elevators are handy for dealing with steep cliff ascents. These all run very frequently till 1am.

You do have to pay to use the Velóh *(myveloh.lu)* short-hop shared bicycle-hire scheme: €2/5 for one/three days then free for rides of up to 30 minutes.

LUXEMBOURG CITY

the royal palace since 1890. To get inside you'll need to pre-book a 75-minute **guided tour** (mid-Jul–late Aug only, adult/under-13 €18/9) online or via the **tourist office** (luxembourg-city.com/en).

Presiding over nearby **Place Guillaume II** is a bronze horseback **statue of William II**, the Grand Duke/Dutch king who in 1841 granted Luxembourg its then-liberal parliamentary constitution. Graves of the grand ducal family lie in the peaceful crypt of the **Cathédrale Notre-Dame**, guarded by bronze lions.

Formidable Fortifications
Going underground into the casemates

The defining feature of Luxembourg's extensive fortifications are **casemates**, honeycombs of military tunnels and artificial caves. Casemates have been used for cultivating mushrooms, ageing sparkling wines and, in WWII, sheltering 35,000 locals during bombardments. Today two sections are open for exploration (not feasible for those with limited mobility). At the **Pétrusse Casemates** (adult/child €18/12) you descend 242 steps and exit one-way into the valley gardens below. Visiting the **Bock Casemates** (adult/child €10/5) involves 300 steps: the real fun here comes from views out of rock-cut 'windows' overlooking the valley below.

Art & History
The greatest galleries and museums of Luxembourg City

Lëtzebuerg City Museum (citymuseum.lu; adult/senior/child €5/3/free), is an engrossing, family-friendly city history museum hosted partly in a former 'holiday home' of the Bishop of Orval. In a pretty park atop more fortifications, **Villa Vauban** (villavauban.lu/en; adult/under-26/child €5/3/free) has a rich collection of 17th- to 19th-century art with a few contemporary extras.

Nationalmusée (nationalmusee.lu/en; free), the superb national museum, covers an astounding range of genres and crosses all epochs. It's based in three 17th-century townhouses confusingly interlinked by glass skyways.

You'll find the city's most cutting-edge contemporary art at **Mudam** (mudam.com; adult/under-26/under-21 €10/7/free). While exhibitions can be fascinating, it's IM Pei's building that makes the experience here so special.

 EATING & DRINKING IN LUXEMBOURG CITY: INFORMAL SPOTS

Pizzeria Bacchus: Cheery, prompt service, decent portions and unusually good value for such a central spot. noon-9.30pm Tue-Sat €

Scott's: Casual riverside watering hole with international pub food and grills. kitchen 6-10pm Mon-Fri, noon-10pm Sat, noon-9pm Sun €€

Big Beer Company: Microbrewery with Bavarian and Luxembourgish food in the Rives de Clausen nightlife zone. 5am-late Tue-Fri, from noon Sat & Sun €€

Beim Renert: Fox-themed local cafe–bar with popular terrace and Belgo-Luxembourgish lunches. 10am-12.30am Tue-Sat, kitchen 11.30am-2.30pm €€

Places We Love to Stay

€ Budget €€ Midrange €€€ Top End

Brussels
MAP p85

Auberge de Jeunesse Jacques Brel € HI-affiliated, no-frills hostel with a great bar, lovely courtyard and free organic breakfast.

Meininger Bruxelles City Center € Set in a restored brewery by the canal, this stylish hostel has spacious rooms (dorms and private), a beautiful bar, kitchen, laundry and bike rentals.

Made in Catherine €€ With just a few rooms, this cosy stay offers a warm welcome and free drinks. Expect exposed beams, vibrant touches, comfy beds and local goodies.

Jam Hotel €€ Jam embraces raw concrete and bold colours, with industrial-chic rooms, a rooftop plunge pool, bar with cosy vibes, and standout gin and tonics.

Maison Flagey €€€ Art Nouveau flair at this characterful B&B near Flagey. Be wowed by the entrance staircase and rooms lovingly decorated with period furniture.

Mechelen

3 Paardekens € Bare-bones rooms and app-activated automated reception, but very central, with a perfect cathedral view from the breakfast terrace.

Hotel Vé €€ Artistic hotel on Mechelen's liveliest nightlife square, retaining elements of the building's former role as a fish smokery.

Leuven

Leuven City Hostel/Hotel Ladeuze € Small, low-key 'grown-ups' hostel with games lounge and quality kitchen. Budget hotel rooms too.

Fourth €€ Super-central in a photo-perfect historic building that's the fourth incarnation of a 1479 guild house.

Ghent
MAP p95

Uppelink € Within a step-gabled canal-side house, the attraction at this super-central hostel is the unbeatable view of Ghent's towers.

Simon Says €€ Get in quick to snap up one of two fashionably styled guest rooms located above its well-patronised, chilled-out coffee shop.

1898 The Post €€€ This boutique offering is housed in Ghent's twin-turreted former post office. Dark and moody in a wonderful way, with great design at every turn.

Bruges
MAP p95

St Christopher's Inn Hostel at The Bauhaus € This backpacker village incorporates a hostel, apartments, a nightclub and a chill-out room.

Passage Bruges € This small hotel has stylish, large and well-priced rooms. Located at the end of a small alleyway, they are also very quiet.

B&B Amaryllis Dieltiens €€ Old and new art fills this lovingly restored classical mansion, which remains an appealing real home run by charming musician hosts.

Dukes' Palace €€€ This large-scale five-star hotel is imposingly tall with a Disneyesque turret. It partly occupies the Prinsenhof building, Bruges' 15th-century royal palace.

Ostend

Hostel De Ploate € This HI hostel is smart, modern and minimal, with no curfew, super-helpful and friendly staff, and a great location.

Thermae Palace Hotel €€€ The beautiful, beachfront Thermae Palace is ageing gracefully and it retains appeal for folks seeking that old-school Euro-beach-resort vibe.

Kortrijk

Hotel Messeyne €€ This grand 1662 townhouse's beamed high ceilings and original fireplaces meld with stylish decor and immaculate rooms.

Center Hotel €€ Attractively modernised rooms at reasonable prices above a subtly fashionable bar with handy 24-hour reception.

Ypres

Yoaké B&B €€ Smart two-room B&B attached to a hip wellness centre. Great breakfasts and a warm welcome.

Main Street Hotel €€€ Jumbling eccentricity with historical twists and luxurious comfort, this is a one-off that oozes character.

Antwerp
MAP p101

A-Stay € The vibe of a great hostel – with common area, sociable bar–cafe, washing-machines etc – but comfortable, hi-tech rooms.

Ash € Big, functional hostel with good kitchen, bar and a handy location for the station. Can overheat in summer.

De Witte Lelie €€€ Behind a 16th-century facade, this highly distinctive design hotel has a courtyard garden.

Waterloo

Le 1815 €€ Compact rooms above the Maximus restaurant facing the battlefield, around 300m from the Lion's Mound.

Gîte Ferme d'Hougoumont €€€ Unique rental apartment above the south gateway of the historic Hougoumont farm-museum. Sleeps up to five.

Mons

Mons Dragon House € Guesthouse with stylish decor, very handy location, friendly hosts and communal sitting room/kitchen.

La Maison de la Duchesse de la Vallière €€ Genteel mansion B&B 600m south of the Grand Place set back behind wrought-iron gates. Free private parking.

Namur

Auberge de Jeunesse € It's hard to imagine a better HI hostel, set facing the river with terrace, games room and generous breakfast.

Hôtel Les Tanneurs €€ Contemporary hotel in central Namur, artfully incorporating a series of 17th-century buildings.

Liège

YUST Liège € Hostel accommodation taken to a swanky new level. The rooftop bar surveys Guillemins station. Free coffee in a comfy lounge area.

N° 5 Bed & Breakfast €€ Elegant B&B with sauna, entered through an 18th-century home in the city's most charming historic quarter.

Spa

Manoir de Lébioles €€€ Luxurious 1905 château-style mansion–hotel complex with spa and swimming pools, a 10-minute drive above Spa.

Les Bains de Spa €€€ Choose a 'heritage' room to sleep in the palatial UNESCO-listed 19th-century baths–building, revamped as a five-star hotel in 2025.

Luxembourg City   p107

Youth Hostel, Luxembourg City € State-of-the-art HI hostel. Its terrace has great views up towards the Old Town. Bring padlock for lockers.

Hôtel Français €€ Unpretentious but fair-value rooms above a classic brasserie in the city's cafe-life epicentre.

Hôtel Parc Beaux Arts €€€ Exclusive old-town property with original artworks and a 'secret' lounge in the eves.

La Pipistrelle €€€ Four gorgeous B&B suites in an 18th-century property that's carved into the cliff between Grund and the old city.

Hotel Les Jardins d'Anaïs €€€ Oasis of cultured calm with a retro twist, sitting in gardens on a bend of the river, just beyond Claussen.

VIDEO MEDIA STUDIO EUROPE/SHUTTERSTOCK

Manoir de Lébioles, Spa (p105)

Practicalities

ACCESSIBLE TRAVEL

Brussels metro stations have Braille signs and tactile tiles leading up to the platforms. Luxembourg City offers accessible public transport with low-floor buses, trams and an easy-to-use funicular. Cobblestone streets in both countries can be challenging for wheelchairs and those with vision impairments, due to uneven surfaces.

IZII8/SHUTTERSTOCK

LGBTIQ+ TRAVELLERS

Belgium and Luxembourg are among the most welcoming destinations for LGBTIQ+ travellers. Belgium was the second country, after the Netherlands, to legalise same-sex marriage. Both countries offer an inclusive atmosphere; larger cities have thriving queer communities.

ELECTRICITY

The electricity supply is 230V/50Hz. Plugs are type E (Belgium) and type F (Luxembourg).

WEIGHTS & MEASURES

Both countries use the metric system. Also note that the decimal place is indicated by a comma and the thousand by a dot.

LANGUAGES

Belgium is split into Dutch-speaking Flanders (Vlaanderen in Dutch) and French-speaking Wallonia (la Wallonie in French), as well as a small German-speaking region. French, German and Lëtzebuergesch are spoken in Luxembourg. For Dutch see p495, for French see p245 and for German see p315.

CANNABIS POLICY

Contrary to the general perception, possession of cannabis is still illegal in Belgium; it's merely decriminalised. However, carrying a small amount for personal use (3g) is tolerated if you're over 18 years. Luxembourg has passed a similar law. Smoking cannabis in public, even if some people indulge, is still prohibited.

OPENING HOURS

Banks 9am-4pm or 5pm
Bars 6pm-midnight or 1am
Cafes 8am to 8pm
Clubs 10pm-3am (L) or 6am (B)
Restaurants noon-2pm & 6-10pm
Shopping malls 9am or 10am-7pm
Shops 10am-6pm (with a possible midday break)
Supermarkets 8am-8pm

PUBLIC HOLIDAYS

New Year's Day 1 January
Easter Monday March/April
Labour Day 1 May
Europe Day (Luxembourg) 9 May
Ascension Day May
Whit Monday May/June
Luxembourg National Day 23 June

Belgian National Day 21 July
Assumption Day 15 August
All Saints' Day 1 November
Armistice Day (Belgium) 11 November
Christmas Day 25 December
Second Day of Christmas (Luxembourg) 26 December

BJÖRN BEHEYDT/SHUTTERSTOCK

Eurostar, Brussels

Arriving

Swift Eurostar trains from London arrive at Brussels Midi station. The major airports are Brussels and Luxembourg; both are about 20 minutes away from their city centres, by train or bus. Low-cost airlines mainly land at Brussels South Charleroi Airport, 45 minutes away from Brussels by shuttle.

By Train
High-speed trains have fast, easy connections between Brussels and London, and between Belgium and the broader French, Dutch and German networks, but such trains require seat reservations and can prove expensive if demand is high.

By Air
Brussels is the country's most globally connected airport and the hub for Belgium's biggest carrier Brussels Airlines *(brusselsairlines. com)*. Charleroi airport, misleadingly described as Brussels-South, attracts budget airlines. Luxembourg Airport is the country's only international airport.

MONEY
Currency: Euro (€)

DIGITAL PAYMENTS
Paying with your phone, smartwatch or contactless bank card has become commonplace since the COVID-19 pandemic. For larger purchases, you will still be asked to enter your PIN. Use contactless payment in Brussels (STIB/MIVB) and Flanders (De Lijn) public transport.

TAXES & REFUNDS
VAT is always included in both countries. Non-EU residents having bought goods with a minimum invoice of €125.01 (in Belgium) or €74 (in Luxembourg) are entitled to a VAT refund. Request your Tax Free Form, then have it stamped by customs and file it at the airport.

DISCOUNTS
Museums and sights typically offer small discounts to seniors and bigger discounts to those under 26. Accompanied children generally pay even less/go free. Students with an ISIC (International Student Identity Card) might qualify for concession rates.

Getting Around

You can easily move around by public transport in both Belgium and Luxembourg – trains are efficient and services regular. Buses serve areas that the trains don't reach. The scattered towns and villages of Wallonia and Luxembourg are more easily explored by car.

OLRAT/SHUTTERSTOCK

Public Transport
The train and bus services are extensive and affordable (free in Luxembourg), although rush hours often see trains getting delayed. Wallonia, being less populated, does not have the same coverage as Flanders and Brussels, but cities are well connected.

Trains & Trams
A good network of trains makes public transport the best way to visit northern Belgium's cities. The Belgian coast is served by a remarkable tram that runs efficiently back and forth for 70km. Luxembourg's joint railway–bus network is coordinated by CFL (*cfl.lu*).

Car
In the rustic, less populous south of Belgium, rail-lines are sparse, buses rare and, away from the traffic-jammed motorways, having your own wheels is the easiest way to get around.

Bus
Buses tend to be used in conjunction with train services rather than in competition. Reaching much of rural Wallonia especially, you're likely to need a train–bus combination. Bus frequency is highest on schooldays. Fewer operate on Saturday, while Sunday services can be scant or nonexistent.

Bike
City bikes and electric bikes can easily be hired in many cities in this bicycle-mad region: Flanders is a particularly bike-friendly region. Throughout Belgium you can take your bike on the train for a small fee.

DRIVING ESSENTIALS

Drive on the right.

Seatbelts must be worn by all occupants.

0.5MG

Blood alcohol limit is 0.5mg in Belgium, 0.25mg in Luxembourg.

For places to stay in Britain, see p169

CHRISTIAN MUELLER/SHUTTERSTOCK

Above: London Eye views (p125); Right: Urquhart Castle and Loch Ness (p162)

THE MAIN AREAS

LONDON
Traditional yet boundary-pushing; forever evolving. **p120**

DEVON & CORNWALL
Coast, cliffs and countryside. **p129**

BRISTOL, BATH & THE COTSWOLDS
Innovation, history and English charm. **p133**

THE MIDLANDS
Valleys, villages and soaring hills. **p138**

LIVERPOOL & THE PEAK DISTRICT
Cultural highs and sweeping landscapes. **p142**

Researched by
James March

Britain

AN ANCIENT AND INSPIRING ISLAND

Welcome to Britain, a small island in the North Atlantic with a huge personality. There's much to discover, so dive right in.

From the world-class museums, endless art galleries, renowned attractions, sweeping parks and riverside panoramas of London to the Cotswolds' picturesque villages of golden buildings, thatched roofs and cottage gardens, Britain is immediately enchanting. The remote southwest is a ragged, wind-blasted landscape that's equally dotted with charming coastal villages as with imposing rocks and cliffs. The Midlands is Britain's heartland, where a howling industrial past has given way to dynamic cities, but also where centuries of heritage have been preserved in the quiet, undulating countryside.

Venture out to Britain's western flank and you'll find thunderous rivers, glacial mountain ranges, wave-whipped beaches and ancient forests in Wales, alongside a deep cultural and national pride. The same can be said about Scotland, but its two biggest cities are very different from each other – Edinburgh is ethereal and alluring, while Glasgow is a gregarious delight. Scotland's Highlands bring jagged mountain peaks, brooding castle ruins and stunning drives, before its islands offer Neolithic mystery and wild scenery.

Britain is unlike anywhere else on Earth. Nowhere bombards you with such history, royal heritage, art, culture, food, natural beauty, humour and eccentricity in quite the same way. The country is but a tiny speck on the world map, but it's all right here in Britain. And it's great.

SERGII FIGURNYI/SHUTTERSTOCK

Find Your Way

Transport in Britain can be expensive compared to continental Europe. Bus and rail services are sparse in more remote parts of the country, but between them serve most destinations (expect a more sporadic service at weekends).

TRAIN

The fastest way to reach Britain's main hubs is by train. The ease of travelling between regional towns depends on the train line; if the journey involves several changes, there may be a more direct route by bus.

BUS

For short journeys and for trips outside Britain's main towns, buses are usually the best option if you don't have a car. Buses are often cheaper than trains. Most bus companies accept contactless payment by card.

CAR

Having your own wheels is helpful in most areas because of the flexibility it offers. In others, it's essential, especially in the countryside where public transport can be irregular or nonexistent. Fair warning: parking can be a nightmare in popular spots, particularly during peak seasons.

The Scottish Islands, p165

Wind-blasted shores, ancient monoliths and smoky single malts make Scotland's islands a journey into Britain's wild northern frontier.

Edinburgh, p153

With its mix of meandering medieval alleyways, stately neoclassical terraces and cutting-edge arts festivals, Edinburgh is a cultural capital for the ages.

The Scottish Highlands, p161

Jagged mountain peaks, dune-fringed beaches and brooding castle ruins reveal an untamed side to Scotland.

---

0   100 miles
0   200 km

Yell
Unst
Fetlar
Shetland
Mainland
Isle of Noss
Shetland Islands
Foula   Lerwick
Fair Isle

North Sea

Westray
Rousay   Sanday
Orkney   Brae
Islands   Skara   Kirkwall
Stromness   Mainland
Hoy   John O'Groats
Wick
Thurso   Helmsdale
Durness   Lairg   Tain   Nairn   Elgin   Banff   Fraserburgh
Lochinver   Dingwall   Inverness   Aviemore   Peterhead
Ullapool   Inverness   Castle   Huntly   Aberdeen
Gairloch   Fort   Augustus   SCOTLAND   Stonehaven
The Minch   Kyle of   Lochalsh   Ben   Montrose
Stornoway   Jacobite   Nevis   Pitlochry   Dundee
Lewis   Portree   Steam Train   St Andrews
Tarbert   Skye   Mallaig   Fort William   Perth   EDINBURGH
Harris   Rum   Tobermory   Loch Lomond &   Stirling   Edinburgh   Arthur's Seat   Dunbar
Lochmaddy   Coll   Mull   the Trossachs   Castle   Berwick-upon-Tweed
North Uist   Barra   Oban   National Park   Glasgow   M8   Galashiels
Balivanich   Castlebay   Sea of the   Greenock   M74   Johnnie   Walker
Benbecula   Hebrides   Bute   Ardrossan
South Uist   Tiree   Colonsay   Jura   Brodick
Outer Hebrides   Jura   Islay   Port Ellen
Lochboisdale   Atlantic   Arran
St Kilda   Ocean   Tarbert

Atlantic Ocean

Sea of the Hebrides

Liverpool & the Peak District, p142

Stroll Liverpool's famous waterfront before heading inland to a great widescreen playground, combined with fascinating history.

The Midlands, p138

The rolling hills and gentle farmlands of the Midlands are pockmarked by lively cities and the ruins of a pioneering past. Welcome to the heart of England.

London, p120

London's story started nearly 2000 years ago, and it's displayed through instantly recognisable landmarks from the Tower of London and Big Ben to the Shard.

North Wales, p150

Eryri is Britain's most prominent peak, but that's just the start of an adventure through old industry, sublime scenery and villages packed with character.

Cardiff & South Wales, p146

Start in a capital fizzing with creative energy before journeying to a wild coast packed with starry night skies and dense woodlands.

Bristol, Bath & the Cotswolds, p133

Bristol and Bath are a beguiling tandem, while the Cotswolds' dreamy chocolate-box charm is England at its most seductive.

Devon & Cornwall, p129

Welcome to England's wild west, where gorse-clad cliffs, booming surf, white sand and wild coastlines rub shoulders with welcoming towns.

Derry
Stranraer
Stewart
NORTHERN IRELAND
BELFAST
Isle of Man
Douglas
DUBLIN
IRELAND

Newcastle-upon-Tyne
Durham
Middlesbrough
Thirsk
Scarborough
Carlisle
Penrith
Windermere
Lancaster
Skipton
York
Leeds
Doncaster
Grimsby
Hull
Keswick
Lake District
Barrow-in-Furness
Blackpool
Preston
Blackburn
Manchester
Sheffield
Lincoln
Skegness
Liverpool
Chester
ENGLAND
Stoke-on-Trent
Derby
Nottingham
Grantham
Boston
King's Lynn
Sheringham
Great Yarmouth
Norwich
The Beatles Story
Llandudno
Bangor
Holyhead
Mt Snowdon
Ffestiniog Railway
Eryri National Park (Snowdonia)
Newtown
Shrewsbury
Birmingham
Coventry
Leicester
Peterborough
Ely
Cambridge
Ipswich
Colchester
Chelmsford
Southend-on-Sea
Shakespeare's Birthplace
Stratford-upon-Avon
Warwick Castle
Coventry Cathedral
Northampton
Luton
M1
M11
LONDON
British Museum
Tower of London
Buckingham Palace
Windsor
M4
M3
M20
Canterbury
Dover
Hastings
Brighton
Eastbourne
Portsmouth
Isle of Wight
Cowes
Southampton
Winchester
Salisbury
Stonehenge
Bath
Roman Baths
Bristol
Brunel's SS Great Britain
CARDIFF
Cardiff Castle
National Museum Cardiff
WALES
Swansea
Carmarthen
Pembroke
Fishguard
New Quay
Aberystwyth
Cardigan Bay
Hereford
Worcester
Gloucester
Oxford
Swindon
M5
Wells
Dorchester
Bournemouth
Barnstaple
Taunton
Exeter
Bude
Dartmoor National Park
Torquay
Plymouth
Truro
Newquay
St Ives School of Painting
Land's End
Penzance
Isles of Scilly
CHANNEL ISLANDS (UK)
Guernsey

Irish Sea

FRANCE
Dieppe
Rouen
Le Havre
Cherbourg
Calais
Strait of Dover
English Channel (La Manche)

117

Plan Your Time

Britain is wildly diverse, so planning ahead is key to deciding if you want city strolls, coastal drives, mountain hikes or museum mornings. Then simply choose how long to spend on them.

CRISTIAN M BALATE/SHUTTERSTOCK

Royal Pavilion (p127), Brighton

A Whirlwind Week

● You could spend a month in **London** (p120) and still not feel as though you'd seen enough. It's stuffed to the rafters with museums, bursting at the belt with restaurants to rave about, and with enough nocturnal naughtiness to keep half the world partying – you certainly won't be bored. For starters, visit the **Tower of London** (p123) and **St Paul's Cathedral** (p123).

● If you have the time, take the one-hour train down to **Brighton** (p127), the seaside party city that's England's unofficial LGBTIQ+ capital. From fish and chips along the pier to an astonishing Indian-style pleasure palace, there's nowhere quite like it.

● And for more iconic English sights, the **White Cliffs** (p128) of Dover and **Canterbury Cathedral** (p126) are also just a direct train ride away.

SEASONAL HIGHLIGHTS

Fewer crowds and good weather make the shoulder seasons (March to May, plus September and October) the best time to go.

JANUARY
At a latitude of 60° north, the Scottish island of Shetland is the best place in Britain to catch the colourful **northern lights** (p168) in winter.

MAY
Britain's premier literary festival comes to the borderlands of Hay-on-Wye in May. Catch brilliantly bookish conversations at the **Hay Festival** (p149).

JUNE
Witness the unique sight of the sun rising in line with the Stonehenge's famous stones at its **summer solstice** (p137).

Ten Days to Travel Around

● Start in **Bristol** (p133), the cool capital of the West Country before moving on to nearby **Bath** (p134), home to impeccably preserved Roman baths and remarkable Regency-era architecture.

● This tandem is flanked to the south by **Devon and Cornwall's** (p129) sandy beaches, fishing villages, rolling countryside and stark moorland, while to the north are the chocolate-box villages of the **Cotswolds** (p135).

● In the Midlands, vibrant **Birmingham** (p138) has world-class shopping, Michelin-star restaurants and intriguing industrial history. Just beyond is Shakespeare's hometown of **Stratford-upon-Avon** (p140), where you can see the Bard's birthplace, school and final resting place. Veer north to the wind-whipped scenery and stately homes of the **Peak District** (p142) before finishing in **Liverpool** (p142), home of the Beatles and Liverpool FC.

With More Time

● Kick off a Celtic odyssey exploring Welsh capital **Cardiff** (p146) with its castle, parks and museums, before hitting the remote moors and brooding mountains of **Brecon Beacons National Park** (p149). In North Wales, **Eryri's** (p150) jagged summit is Wales at its most spectacular and **Portmeirion** (p152) its most quirky.

● A Scottish adventure should start in its vibrant capital **Edinburgh** (p153), where highlights include the Royal Mile and medieval Old Town. Then head further north to explore the **Highlands** (p161), from sprawling lochs to mountain trails, lush glens and precious woodland. Don't miss the stunning islands, either. **Skye** (p165) is a misty world of jagged mountain peaks, rich river valleys and plunging cliffs, while **Orkney** (p167) and **Shetland** (p168) are ancient wonderlands illuminated by the northern lights.

AUGUST

The **Edinburgh Festival Fringe** (p153) has an event for anything you care to name – books, art, theatre, music, comedy, marching bands.

OCTOBER

Halloween is an old Celtic festival, so dress up in your spookiest costume, or at least drink in pubs festooned with bats and pumpkins.

NOVEMBER

Guy Fawkes Night (5 November) means the skies across Britain fill with fireworks honouring a failed attempt to blow up parliament back in 1605.

DECEMBER

Colourful **Christmas markets** appear around Britain in December, so get your fix of warming mulled wine amid brightly lit wooden chalets.

London

ICONIC SIGHTS | GLOBAL CUISINE | DENSE HISTORY

☑ TOP TIP

When roaming around the West End, give yourself the freedom to explore. Instead of looking at a map or your phone – simply get lost. Let your intrigue guide you through the little lanes and passages and you may discover a new secret spot. Don't forget to look up: historic details are everywhere.

London's architecture tells a unique and beguiling biography; tireless innovation is built into the city's fabric. The capital's deep-rooted past is accented by modern structures – the Shard, the Gherkin and Tate Modern – that never drown out London's centuries-old narrative. Major projects continue to move London forward, such as the 2022 opening of the Elizabeth line, the 73-mile east–west railway extending across the capital and into neighbouring counties. The regenerated Battersea Power Station, a 1940s power plant turned shopping centre, became accessible to the public for the first time in 2022 with many of its industrial features preserved.

London is a city of concrete plans but also of ideas and imagination – whether it's theatrical innovation, contemporary art, pioneering music, cutting-edge design or global cuisine. It's a place where wide-open vistas and sight-packed streets exist in unison. Add in historic neighbourhoods, leafy suburbs, charming parks and tranquil riverbanks and you have one of the world's great metropolises.

House of Important Pieces
View the world's oldest artefacts
The **British Museum** *(britishmuseum.org; free)* is the country's most popular museum (around 5.8 million visitors

---

🧭 GETTING AROUND

London is huge, but the public transport network is generally a well-oiled machine that runs reliably. The Tube, or London Underground – which includes the London Overground, Docklands Light Railway (DLR) and the Elizabeth line – is the fastest and most efficient way of getting around. Some stations are much closer together in reality than they appear on the map. The main sights are clustered around the West End, South Bank and the City of London, and if you plan well, you'll mostly walk.

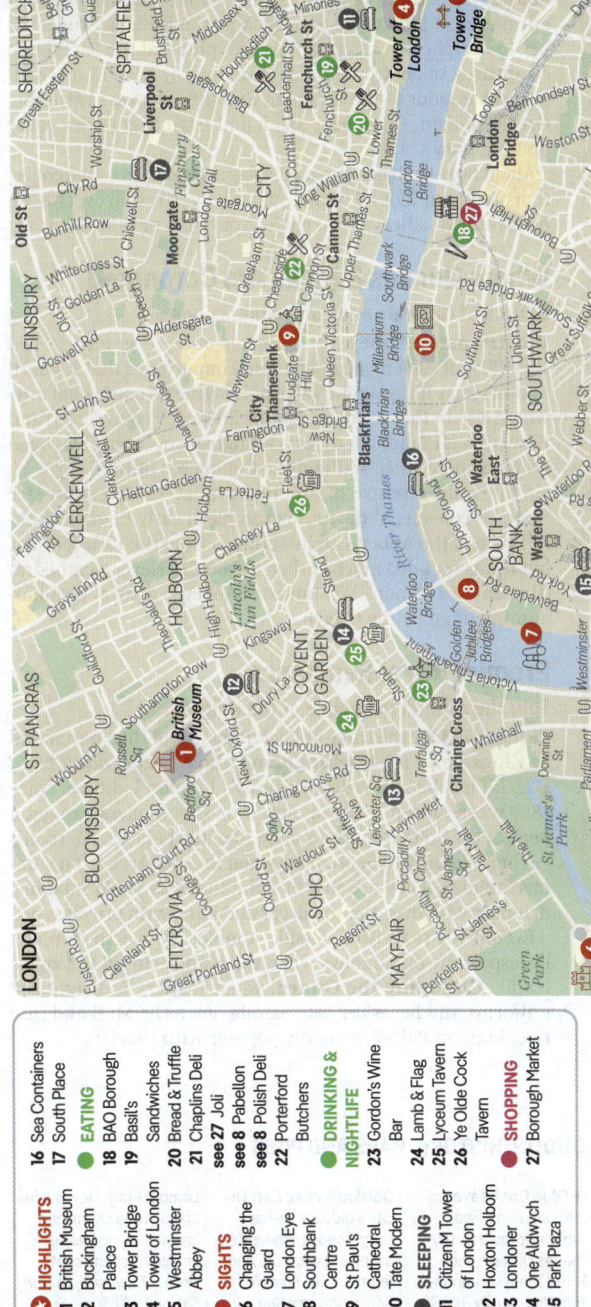

★ **HIGHLIGHTS**
1 British Museum
2 Buckingham Palace
3 Tower Bridge
4 Tower of London
5 Westminster Abbey

● **SIGHTS**
6 Changing the Guard
7 London Eye
8 Southbank Centre
9 St Paul's Cathedral
10 Tate Modern

● **SLEEPING**
11 CitizenM Tower of London
12 Hoxton Holborn
13 Londoner
14 One Aldwych
15 Park Plaza

16 Sea Containers
17 South Place

● **EATING**
18 BAO Borough
19 Basil's Sandwiches
20 Bread & Truffle
21 Chaplins Deli
see 27 Joli
see 8 Pabellon
see 8 Polish Deli
22 Porterford Butchers

● **DRINKING & NIGHTLIFE**
23 Gordon's Wine Bar
24 Lamb & Flag
25 Lyceum Tavern
26 Ye Olde Cock Tavern

● **SHOPPING**
27 Borough Market

annually) and one of the world's oldest (opened in 1759). It houses – sometimes controversially – some of the most important pieces of human history, such as the Rosetta Stone, the key to deciphering Egyptian hieroglyphs; and the Parthenon sculptures, taken from Athens' Acropolis by Lord Elgin (British ambassador to the Ottoman Empire). The vast Etruscan, Greek, Roman, European, Asian and Islamic galleries carry on humanity's story.

About 80,000 objects are on display at a time (from the collection of eight million). The museum is huge, so avoid overwhelm by picking a gallery or theme for your visit or taking a tour.

Where Queens & Kings Are Coronated
Church of funerals and commemorations

Westminster Abbey *(westminster-abbey.org; adult/child £30/13)* is of such royal and national importance that it's hard to overstress its symbolic value or imagine its equivalent anywhere else in the world. Except for Edward V (murdered) and Edward VIII (abdicated), every English sovereign has been crowned here since William the Conqueror in 1066.

A splendid mixture of architectural styles, Westminster Abbey is considered the finest example of early English Gothic. Much of the Abbey's architecture is from the 13th century, but it was founded much earlier, in 960 CE. Never a cathedral (the seat of a bishop), Westminster Abbey is a 'royal peculiar' administered by the Crown.

Premier Royal Residence
Tour the official residence of the King

Built in 1703 for the Duke of Buckingham and then purchased by King George III, **Buckingham Palace** *(rct.uk; adult/child £32/16)* has been the Royal Family's London lodgings since 1837 when Queen Victoria moved in. Commoners can get a peek at the State Rooms – a mere 19 of the palace's 775 rooms – from mid-July to September when the monarch is on summer holiday. They are just as sumptuous as you'd imagine, dripping with over-the-top decor and hung with priceless art.

Even if you're visiting outside summer, it's worth stopping by, especially on Sundays when the Mall is closed to vehicle traffic. **Changing the Guard**, when soldiers in bright-red uniforms and bearskin hats parade down the Mall and into Buckingham Palace, is madly popular with tourists.

PERFECT BIG BEN SNAPS

Millions of visitors get off the Tube at Westminster. As home to Big Ben, Westminster Bridge crossing the River Thames and the neo-Gothic Palace of Westminster, it's the perfect spot for an 'I'm in London' selfie. For the best photos, come early in the morning (ideally dusk for the perfect lighting) to avoid the crowds. And try these iconic frames:

● Beneath Westminster Bridge passageway, next to St Thomas' Hospital, for views framed by the archway.

● On the Queen's Walk in front of the Sea Life Centre – best when the clock is illuminated after sunset.

● The red phone box on the edge of Parliament Sq; come off-peak to avoid lines for this social-media-famous picture.

DRINKING IN LONDON: HISTORIC BARS AND PUBS

Lyceum Tavern: On the site of the original Lyceum Theatre; today it's a traditional oak-panelled pub. *noon-11pm Mon-Thu, to midnight Fri & Sat, to 11.30pm Sun*

Ye Olde Cock Tavern: London's narrowest pub was frequented by Charles Dickens and Alfred Tennyson. *noon-11pm Mon-Sat, to 7pm Sun*

Gordon's Wine Bar: The city's oldest wine bar is a gorgeous candlelit basement and a buzzing terrace. *11am-11pm Mon-Sat, noon-10pm Sun*

Lamb & Flag: Tiny and full of old-world charm and history – a pub has been on this West End spot since 1772. *11am-11pm Mon-Sat, noon-10.30pm Sun*

ALEXANDER CHAIKIN/SHUTTERSTOCK

Changing the Guard

A Saintly Symbol of Resilience

Step inside London's mightiest cathedral

A place of Christian worship for more than 1400 years (and pagan before that), **St Paul's Cathedral** *(stpauls.co.uk; adult/child £26/10)* is one of London's most magnificent buildings. For Londoners, the vast dome is a symbol of pride, standing tall since 1710 and surviving an onslaught of Luftwaffe incendiary bombs during the Blitz. The dome, inspired by St Peter's Basilica in the Vatican, rises more than 85m above the floor, supported by eight huge columns.

A Window of Bloody History

London's macabre 1000-year-old royal jail

The unmissable **Tower of London** *(hrp.org.uk/tower-of-london; adult/child £34.80/17.40)* offers a window into 1000 years of gruesome and compelling history. A former royal residence, treasury, mint, armoury and zoo, it's perhaps most remembered as the prison where a king, three queens and many nobles – including Anne Boleyn and Catherine Howard, Henry VIII's second and fifth wives – met their deaths. The immaculately dressed Yeomen Warders (better known as the Beefeaters) live on-site, protecting the spectacular Crown Jewels.

Walk the Thames' Icon

Cross the famous Tower Bridge

With its neo-Gothic towers and sky-blue suspension struts, **Tower Bridge** *(towerbridge.org.uk; adult/child £16/£8)* is one

THE GREAT REBUILD OF LONDON

The Great Fire of London is the reason almost none of medieval London remains and so much of it dates from the late 17th century, yet there's little popular lamentation of this 'wiping out' of the 'old London'. This is because, though London at the time was the third-largest city in the Western world, it wasn't famous for its beauty, architecture or urban design. Writer John Evelyn felt it paled in comparison to the baroque magnificence of Paris and described London as an unplanned, wooden mess. The latter was the main reason the fire spread so quickly and devastatingly, with most properties made of timber and covered in thatched roofing. What was built in their place is the magnificence we still see.

 EATING IN LONDON: BEST STREET FOOD IN THE SOUTH BANK

Pabellon: Indulge in black beans, plantains and Venezuelan arepas at South Bank Food Market. Vegan-friendly. *noon-8pm Fri, noon-11am Sat, noon-6pm Sun* ££

Joli: Singaporean and Malaysian dishes, like tender beef rendang, cooked in a traditional clay pot in Borough Market. *10am-5pm Tue-Fri, 9am-5pm Sat, 10am-4pm Sun* ££

Polish Deli: Barbequed Polish sausages are served with pickles and beer in the South Bank Food Market. *11am-8pm Fri, 10am-6pm Sat, noon-6pm Sun* ££

BAO Borough: Taiwanese joint serving beef short-rib bao buns; wash it down with a fermented pineapple soda. *noon-10pm Mon-Thu, to 10.30pm Fri & Sat, to 9pm Sun* £

A WALK AROUND HAMPSTEAD HEATH

Hampstead Heath's rolling woodlands and wild meadows feel miles away from central London, but you see the city from its hilltops.

START	END	LENGTH
Hampstead Heath station	Holly Bush pub	4 miles; 3–4 hours

Take the London Overground to Hampstead Heath station. Follow the Parliament Hill street into the park to start your climb up to the **1 Parliament Hill Viewpoint** for a panoramic scene of the city.

A web of trails to the north leads to bathing ponds (**2 mixed pond** to the west, **3 men's** and **4 women's** to the east). The men's and women's ponds are open year-round for cold-water swimming and supervised by lifeguards.

Traverse the heath to its northern edge and find the 18th-century **5 Kenwood House**. The free-to-visit gallery has a magnificent collection of art, including paintings by Rembrandt, Constable, Turner, Gainsborough and Vermeer.

Next, head to one of the wonderful pubs nearby for a restorative pint. Exit the heath via the Kenwood House car park and walk southwest along Hampstead Ln. At the heath's edge is the 1585 **6 Spaniards Inn**, where Romantic poets Keats and Byron and artist Sir Joshua Reynolds all paused for a drink.

Stroll to the Jack Straw's Castle bus stop and explore the historic neighbourhood of Hampstead. Loved by artists in the interwar years, it has retained a bohemian feel, with leafy streets, cafes and boutiques. Finish with a gastro-pub dinner at **7 Holly Bush**, a secluded pub with a splendid antique interior.

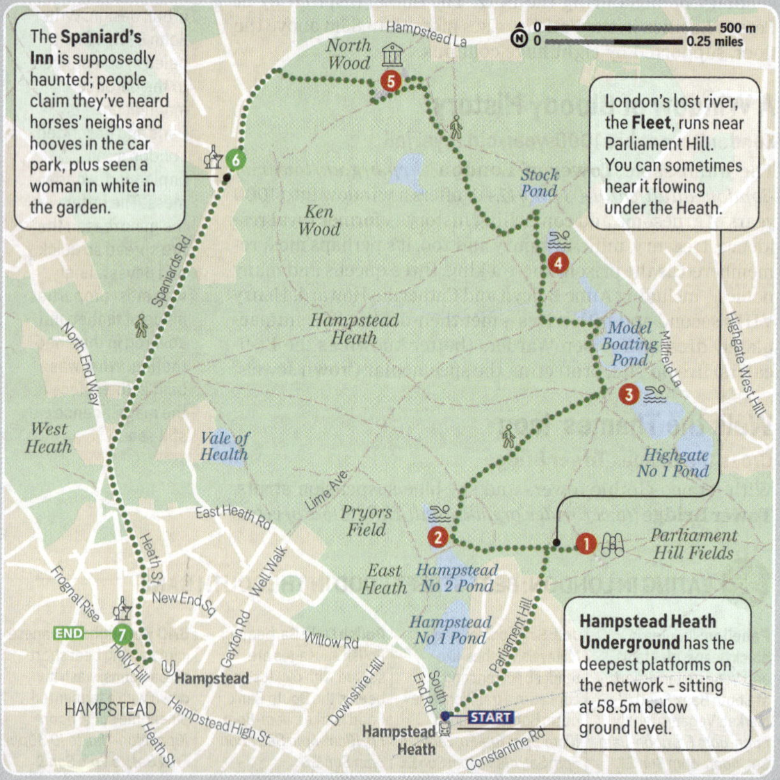

The **Spaniard's Inn** is supposedly haunted; people claim they've heard horses' neighs and hooves in the car park, plus seen a woman in white in the garden.

London's lost river, the **Fleet**, runs near Parliament Hill. You can sometimes hear it flowing under the Heath.

Hampstead Heath Underground has the deepest platforms on the network – sitting at 58.5m below ground level.

North Wood
Hampstead La
Stock Pond
Ken Wood
Hampstead Heath
Model Boating Pond
Millfield La
Highgate West Hill
West Heath
Vale of Health
Highgate No 1 Pond
North End Way
Spaniards Rd
Lime Ave
East Heath Rd
Pryors Field
Parliament Hill Fields
East Heath
Hampstead No 2 Pond
Heath St
New End Sq
Caxton Rd
West Walk
Willow Rd
Hampstead No 1 Pond
Parliament Hill
Frognal Rise
Holly Hill
END 7
Hampstead
HAMPSTEAD
Hampstead High St
Heath St
Downshire Hill
South End Rd
START
Hampstead Heath
Constantine Rd

0 — 500 m
0 — 0.25 miles

of London's most recognisable sights. The city was a thriving port in 1894 when the bridge was built as a much-needed crossing point in the east, equipped with a revolutionary steam-driven bascule (counterbalance) mechanism that could raise the roadway to make way for oncoming ships in just three minutes. The story of building the structure is recounted in the Tower Bridge Exhibition.

Sample Global Flavours
Feast your way through a historic food court

Borough Market (*boroughmarket.org.uk; free*) was initially a wholesale market for greengrocers a millennium ago, but has since transformed into the most renowned food market in London. Today, its hundred-plus high-quality food and drink vendors pull in massive crowds. There are two main areas: Three Crown Square for larger merchants and Green Market for smaller ones. In the third area, Borough Market Kitchen, you'll find street-food traders serving anything from Asian baos to Spanish paella.

Art in a Former Power Station
Dive into Tate Modern's wildest works

The outstanding **Tate Modern** (*tate.org.uk; free*) is a spellbinding synthesis of modern art and industrial brick design. This contemporary-art gallery, housed in the creatively revamped Bankside Power Station, has been extraordinarily successful in bringing challenging work to the masses, both through its free permanent collection and fee-charged temporary exhibitions. The curators have at their disposal more than 60,000 works by Henri Matisse, Andy Warhol, Mark Rothko, Jackson Pollock, Barbara Hepworth, Damien Hirst, Rebecca Horn and more.

Bird's-Eye Views
Take in panoramic scenes from a London landmark

Standing 135m high in a fairly flat city, the **London Eye** (*londoneye.com; adult/child from £29/£26*) is the world's largest cantilevered observation wheel and affords views 25 miles in every direction (as far as Windsor Castle), weather permitting. A ride in one of the 32 glass-enclosed eye-shaped pods takes a gracefully slow 30 minutes.

THE FESTIVAL THAT SHAPED THE SOUTH BANK

The genesis of Europe's largest cultural and artistic hub traces back to the Festival of Britain held between May and September 1951 at a cost of £12 million to showcase great feats in architecture, the arts, science, technology and industrial design. Dubbed a 'tonic for the nation', it was the brainchild of Labour cabinet minister Herbert Morrison to raise spirits and celebrate recovery from WWII, despite austerity, by shining a spotlight on Britain's achievements to millions of visitors. Amid nationwide festivities, South Bank emerged as a thriving focal point, amplifying the festival's resonance. Today, the site of the festival houses the iconic **Southbank Centre**.

 EATING IN LONDON: BEST SANDWICHES IN THE CITY

Porterford Butchers: There are always lunchtime queues out the door for the meat-heavy baguettes at this family-owned shop. *6am-6pm Mon-Fri* £

Basil's Sandwiches: Doorstep-sized club sarnies made with focaccia. The Italian cheese and salami fillings are legendary. *5am-5pm Mon-Fri* £

Chaplins Deli: One for spice o' files, choose from the heaped fillings at the counter of this vintage express joint. *6am-4pm Mon-Fri* £

Bread & Truffle: Freshly baked, gourmet focaccia sandwiches with pesto, mozzarella and basil. *9.30am-5pm Mon-Thu, to 9pm Fri, 10.30am-9pm Sat & Sun* £

Beyond London

South of the capital, where deep and spectacular history meets fun and flair, life is never dull.

Places

Canterbury p126
Brighton p127
Dover p128
Winchester p128

GETTING AROUND

It's easy to reach the southeast's main hubs by train from London. The ease of travelling between towns depends on the train line; if the journey involves several changes, there may be a more direct route by bus. Car is generally the easiest way to get around, particularly in rural areas, and driving affords more freedom to explore. However, parking can be expensive in urban centres and traffic can be heavy on the coast.

England's sunny southeast is where the coastline comes closest to the Continent. Historically, the region has been the frontline of defence against invasion, a past that has left reminders in the form of Norman castles and naval shipyards. This strategic position is brought into focus at Dover Castle and the shore's famous White Cliffs where, from Roman times to the Cold War, the occupiers have prepared for an attack. It's also been the seat of religious life in Britain, with Canterbury Cathedral a beacon of the country's Christianity.

Things are very different a little further west. Ever since the 19th century, when Prince George hosted all-night parties at his opulent Royal Pavilion pleasure palace, Brighton has embraced hedonism. And as home to England's biggest gay scene, it also a place that invites people to be themselves.

Canterbury

TIME FROM LONDON: 1HR 🚆

The mother church

Rich in historical significance, UNESCO-listed **Canterbury Cathedral** (*canterbury-cathedral.org; adult/child £18/free*) is the spiritual head of the Anglican church and is among Europe's finest cathedrals. Exploring its precincts offers the chance to experience moments of peace and connect with its spirituality, and guided tours illuminate the many treasures and architectural details that tell the story of the cathedral's 1400-year history.

Next to the early Tudor-era Christ Church Gate, head to the visitor centre's upstairs gallery for a superb view of the mostly Gothic cathedral exterior. Before entering the cathedral at the southwest porch, walk further around to its western-most side to see statues of historical figures including Queen Elizabeth II and Prince Philip in the exterior niches.

Inside, the signposted visitor route spotlights the cathedral's most important details. Don't miss the Martyrdom, the spot where Archbishop Thomas Becket was murdered in 1170 by two of Henry II's knights; today it's marked by a flickering candle and modern altar.

AGSAZ/SHUTTERSTOCK

Tomb of Edward, the Black Prince, Canterbury Cathedral

Brighton

TIME FROM LONDON: **1HR** 🚆

A life of hedonistic excess

Walking down from the train station, the first glimpse of the astonishing 19th-century, Indian-inspired architecture to come is the magnificent **Brighton Dome** *(brightondome. org),* now a concert hall and theatre.

Beyond the dome lies the ostentatious former party palace of King George IV, the **Royal Pavilion** *(brightonmuseums. org.uk; adult/child £19.50/£11.75)* itself. Meticulously planned to wow visitors at every turn, the pavilion's interior is an outlandish fantasy decorated with hand-painted Chinese wallpaper and mirrors to trick the eye.

Retail therapy in the Lanes

The tightly packed **Lanes** form Brighton's popular shopping district. Every twist and turn is packed with jewellers, gift shops, cafes and boutiques, selling everything from upcycled furniture to vegan shoes. Just south of the Brighton train station, the **North Laine** area has a number of partially pedestrianised streets with colourful murals and a more bohemian vibe.

The flea market **Snoopers Paradise** *(snoopersparadise. co.uk)* and nearby **North Laine Bazaar** *(northlainebazaar. com)* are fun places to search for retro collectibles and vintage clothes, records and books, while music lovers could spend hours browsing the vinyl at **Resident Music** *(resident-music.com).*

BEST TOURS IN BRIGHTON

Brighton Regency Routemaster: Afternoon-tea or gin-and-prosecco Regency architecture tours on a converted Routemaster RML 233 double-decker vintage bus.

Piers & Queers: Entertaining 90-minute LGBTIQ+ history tours Friday and Saturday, April to October, visiting famous sights and hidden bars.

Street Art Tour: Two-hour walking tour led by graffiti expert REQ, with insider info on the latest additions to Brighton's street art.

Ghost Walk of the Lanes: Actor and storyteller Rob Marks leads 80-minute Wednesday to Saturday night walks around macabre sights in the Lanes.

Brighton Diver Windfarm Tours: Board a 12m catamaran for a two-hour tour of the offshore New Rampion Windfarm.

🍺 **DRINKING IN BRIGHTON: OUR PICKS**

Lion & Lobster: Maze of nooks and crannies with three bars, two hidden gardens, a sun-drenched roof terrace and live-music stage. *noon-midnight*

Plotting Parlour: Kemptown speakeasy with ceiling murals and cocktails including seasonal infusions. *4-11pm Sun-Thu, 3pm-midnight Fri & Sat*

Cricketers: Brighton's oldest pub, with flamboyant Victorian interiors. Live music Tuesdays and Fridays. *noon-11pm Sun-Thu, to 2am Fri & Sat*

Joker: Red-brick pub with pressed-tin ceilings and a roof terrace; the cocktail bar has monthly changing cocktails. *4-11pm Mon & Tue, noon-1am Wed-Sun*

STARLING MURMURATIONS ON THE SUSSEX COAST

The sight of thousands of starlings swooping and rising as one is among nature's most mesmerising spectacles. Starling murmurations – in which the glossy black birds react in less than 100 milliseconds to adapt to their neighbours' movements and make near-instant flight-path adjustments – are believed to be a tactic to deter predators and protect the flocks within one confusing, swirling mass.

The best time to see murmurations is during autumn and winter as the late-afternoon light begins to fade. Particularly dramatic displays are often seen near the piers in Eastbourne, Hastings and Brighton, where some 40,000 starlings gather near dusk at the remains of the derelict West Pier.

Join the party at Brighton's seafront

The seafront at Brighton and Hove is an active place, with joggers and dog-walkers zipping along the promenade, past buzzing bars, beachside volleyball games and tarot-card readers. At **Brighton Palace Pier** *(brightonpier.co.uk)*, the screams of thrill-seekers compete with the crashing of waves; take a stroll past doughnut stands and arcade games to the pier-end viewing platform.

For vertical views, hop in the viewing pod to shimmy up the world's tallest moving observation tower, the **i360** *(brighton i360.co.uk; adult/child £17.95/£8.95)*, which tops out at 162m.

Dover
TIME FROM LONDON: 1HR

Visit the famous White Cliffs

Spending a day in Dover offers an introduction to 2000 years of English history and a chance to connect to the emblematic significance and natural beauty of Dover's distinctive cliffs.

Visiting Dover's **castle** *(english-heritage.org.uk; adult/child from £25.90/16.30)* gives a sense of the town's historical role at the frontline of England's defence. From the castle, head 1 mile east to the National Trust–managed **White Cliffs** *(nationaltrust.org.uk)*, standing 106m high and stretching for 8 miles on both sides of Dover; there's parking at the visitor centre on the northern side. Follow the path along the clifftops for a bracing 2-mile walk to the **South Foreland Lighthouse**, where you can eat at the cafe's picnic tables looking out towards France.

Winchester
TIME FROM LONDON: 1HR 10MIN

An awe-inspiring Gothic cathedral

With one of Europe's longest medieval naves, **Winchester Cathedral** *(winchester-cathedral.org.uk; adult/child £13.50/ free)* is an imposing Gothic landmark that can be seen from the surrounding hills. Inside, it's a beguiling jumble of architectural styles, with a Norman crypt and ornate Renaissance chantry chapels.

Near the entrance is the **grave of Jane Austen**, marked by a plaque. One of the cathedral's most striking features is the abstract patchwork of the West Window: after the original stained-glass window was destroyed by Parliamentary troops during the English Civil War, the current window was created in 1660 using fragments of shattered glass.

 EATING IN CANTERBURY AND WINCHESTER: OUR PICKS

Goods Shed: Canterbury indoor farmers market, food hall and mezzanine restaurant rolled into one. *noon-3pm Sun & Tue, noon-3pm & 5.30-9pm Wed-Sat* ££

Parrot: Dating back to 1370, this snug half-timbered Canterbury pub serves local real ales; has upstairs dining room and a leafy beer garden. *noon-9.30pm* ££

Cart & Horses: Classic pub fare and top Sunday roast are served at this country pub on Winchester's outskirts. *10am-11pm* ££

Wellhouse: All dishes served in this rustic Winchester building are cooked over an open wood-fire. *6.30-9.30pm Mon-Sat, noon-2.30pm & 6.30-9.30pm Sun* ££

Devon & Cornwall

WILD COAST | FRESH SEAFOOD | SPECTACULAR STROLLS

Flung out on Britain's far edge, the southwest is celebrated for its natural charms: craggy cliffs cloaked in gorse, rocky tors on wild moors, golden beaches washed by surf. Every year, millions of visitors flock here to feel the sand between their toes, and with miles of coastline, countryside and clifftops to explore, it's really no wonder.

If you want to experience the region's landscapes at their best, ditch the car and get active. Hiking trails and cycling paths crisscross the countryside, and the South West Coast Path winds around a stunning coastal kaleidoscope. Kayak the rivers, hike the moors, bike the back lanes, surf the waves or coasteer on the cliffs – the adventures never seem to end.

And while the southwest's popularity inevitably means crowds, with the help of a decent map and an adventurous spirit, you'll nearly always be able to find a patch of sand to call your own.

☑ TOP TIP

The southwest is packed in July and August: it's much more pleasant to visit in spring or autumn, when the big crowds have left and you can appreciate the scenery in (relative) peace and quiet. Book well ahead, too.

Padstow

Cornwall's best-known bike route

Originally a railway line, the **Camel Trail** *(cornwall.gov.uk/cameltrail)* is now Cornwall's most popular bike ride. The trail starts in Padstow and runs east through Wadebridge along the

---

 GETTING AROUND

England's southwestern peninsula is widespread and remote, with just three cities and a handful of major towns. A car brings maximum freedom, but parking can be tricky (and pricey) in popular places, and summer traffic can be a serious headache. The A30 and A38 are the main road routes into the region.

Travelling by bus in the southwest is cheap and usually reliable, but slow. Rural services

are less frequent, and in the case of some remote villages, non-existent. Seasonal, hop-on/hop-off buses often run between major attractions in popular areas.

The mainline train between London and Penzance stops at major towns and cities and includes an overnight service six days a week.

DEVON & CORNWALL

Camel Estuary before continuing through Bodmin (10.8 miles) to Poley's Bridge (18.3 miles) on Bodmin Moor. The Padstow–Wadebridge section makes a lovely half-day excursion, and the scenery is marvellous, but it does get busy in summer.

Bikes can be hired from both ends: in Padstow, try **Padstow Cycle Hire** (*padstowcyclehire.com; adult/child from £17/6*) or **Trail Bike Hire** (*trailbikehire.co.uk; adult/child from £16/8*). In Wadebridge, try **Bridge Bike Hire** (*bridgebikehire.co.uk; adult/child from £19/10*).

Fruit of the (Cornish) vines

The sheltered valleys around Padstow are home to several renowned vineyards. **Camel Valley Vineyard** (*camelvalley.com; tours adult £18*) has been producing award-winning still and sparkling English wines since 1989. Visit for one of the guided tours, run at 10.30am Monday to Friday (reduced during harvest and winter), or book a table to sip wines by the glass in the tasting room or on the sun terrace.

Closer to Padstow is **Trevibban Mill** (*trevibbanmill.com; tours £17.50*). Tours are run seasonally three times a week, or you can book a table for a wine or cider tasting. Alternatively,

 EATING IN PADSTOW: SEAFOOD SPECIALITIES

Seafood Restaurant: The restaurant that started the Stein saga: an elegant, light-filled dining room on the riverside. *noon-9pm* £££

Paul Ainsworth at No 6: TV chef Ainsworth's Michelin-starred food deserves all the plaudits; it's booked up months in advance. *noon-10pm Tue-Sat* £££

Prawn on the Lawn: Tiny, ultra-cool seafood bar where the menu changes daily depending on what its fishers have caught. *noon-10pm Tue-Sat* ££

Stein's Fish & Chips: Lines are long and prices above average, but the fresh, battered fish is undeniably good! *noon-8pm* ££

relax on the viewing balcony (open Tuesday to Saturday) with a sharing platter and a glass of still or sparkling wine or cider.

Newquay
Surf's up
Newquay is Cornwall's surf central. The north coast swells are the most consistent in the UK, and every year they attract thousands of budding boarders looking to catch their first wave or hone their skills. There are scores of schools to choose from; **Escape Surf School** (*escapesurfschool.co.uk; from £30*) and **Fistral Beach Surf School** (*fistralbeachsurfschool.co.uk; £45*) both have good reputations.

Fistral Beach is legendary for its waves, which can reach over 30ft on the infamous Cribbar Reef. Other options within easy reach of Newquay include **Crantock**, **Holywell Bay** and **Watergate Bay**, where another of the area's best surf schools is based: **Wavehunters** (*wavehunters.co.uk; £45*).

St Ives
Pick up a brush in Cornwall's art capital
With its fishers' cottages and church towers spread around a brilliant turquoise bay, St Ives is a dazzling sight. If it has inspired you to pick up a brush, book a course at the **St Ives School of Painting** (*schoolofpainting.co.uk; from £12*), which has been tutoring budding artists since it opened in 1938. Today, the school runs a range of classes and multiday courses focusing on painting in a range of mediums, covering everything from landscapes to life drawing.

Land's End
Take a photo with the Land's End sign
The clue's in the name. The rugged headland of **Land's End** (*landsend-landmark.co.uk; free*) is where Cornwall (and mainland Britain) comes to a screeching halt, and the black granite cliffs fall away into a maelstrom of white surf.

Famous as the last port of call for walkers on the 874-mile slog from John O'Groats in Scotland, the views are epic: the restless Atlantic seems to wrap itself around the horizon, shimmering in the late-afternoon light, and on a clear evening, the sunsets are out of this world. Look out for the **Longships Lighthouse**, 1.25 miles offshore, and the faint outlines of the Isles of Scilly 28 miles out to sea. The photo-op beside

RICK STEIN & PADSTOW

Celebrity chef Rick Stein opened the **Seafood Restaurant** (*rickstein.com*) on the quay in Padstow in 1975 – before he'd even learnt to cook! As his reputation grew, Stein made several TV appearances, rising to fame after his first show, *Taste of the Sea*, in 1995.

The presence of a celebrity chef's flagship restaurant helped boost Padstow's popularity as a holiday destination, turning the town into an upscale foodie hub. Stein now owns four restaurants in Padstow, plus a fishmonger, coffee shop, deli, gift shop and a cookery school – earning the town the nickname 'Padstein'. It's not always affectionately meant: while tourism massively supports the economy, many locals feel Padstow has lost its identity.

EATING IN ST IVES: OUR PICKS

Porthminster Beach Cafe: Less a beach cafe, more a bistro with a sun-trap terrace and a superb Med-inspired menu. *noon-9pm* ££

Porthminster Kitchen: The beach cafe's in-town sister restaurant, specialising in seafood. *12:30-3pm & 5:30-9pm Mon-Sat, noon-3pm Sun* ££

One Fish Street: The daily seafood-themed tasting menus depend on what's been landed that morning on the quay. *noon-3pm & 7pm-late Mon-Sat* £££

Blas Burgerworks: St Ives' burger joint has choices for carnivores, vegetarians and vegans; also serves breakfasts. *hours vary, closed Mon & Tue* ££

GREAT DARTMOOR WALKS

Lydford Gorge: The southwest's deepest gorge, home to a 30m waterfall and the magical 'Devil's Cauldron' whirlpool.

Wistman's Wood: An easy stroll from the Two Bridges pub to a mossy oak woodland straight from a fairy tale.

Bellever Forest: Several waymarked trails in a dense pine forest: climb Bellever Tor and explore Kraps Ring Bronze Age village.

Princetown Railway Track: Follow the old railway to King's Tor, passing two abandoned quarries, Swell Tor and Foggintor.

Yes Tor & High Willhays: The two highest points on Dartmoor (619m and 621m respectively) afford spectacular views of the moors.

HELEN HOTSON/SHUTTERSTOCK

Combestone Tor, Dartmoor National Park

the famous signpost (New York 3147; John O' Groats 874) is a cliché, but essential nonetheless.

Dartmoor National Park

Hike across Dartmoor's famous tors

Dartmoor's 160 tors are legendary. Though they look like they were dropped upon the landscape by a giant hand, these hilltop outcrops of granite were formed from molten rock some 280 million years ago and left exposed by millennia of erosion. The bizarre shapes of these stacks and monoliths have inspired mankind for centuries. Some were used as places of worship by Dartmoor's ancient inhabitants, others gave rise to folklore and legends that persist to this day.

Some, like the face-shaped **Combestone Tor**, can be seen from the road, while others require a walk. **Haytor** is one of the most popular and easiest to visit: a short walk uphill from the large car park nearby. The moorland trail from here to **Hound Tor** is an ideal introduction to Dartmoor, taking in disused quarries, a clapper bridge and a medieval settlement.

EATING & DRINKING IN DARTMOOR: CLASSIC COUNTRY PUBS

Warren House Inn: Legendary pub halfway along the B3212, near Postbridge, where the fire has remained lit since 1845. *hours vary* ££

Three Crowns: Chagford's lovely, part-thatched inn mixes 13th-century features and a modern atrium dining room. *10am-10pm* ££

Rugglestone Inn: Log fires and home-cooked food in a wisteria-clad stone property in charming Widecombe-in-the-Moor. *hours vary* ££

Dartmoor Inn: Organic open-fire grill cooking and some of the best views of Dartmoor, near Merrivale. *10am-10pm* ££

Bristol, Bath & the Cotswolds

ARCHITECTURE | ANCIENT HISTORY | VILLAGES

Contemporary cities rub shoulders with the ancient past in this region of pastoral landscapes, country pubs and chocolate-box villages.

Bristol is a city that's well and truly on the rise. Disused warehouses have been reimagined as art galleries and museums, old cargo containers now host restaurants serving Modern British dishes with a West Country lilt, and a world-class street-art scene adds colour.

Over in beautiful Bath, its rows of harmonious townhouses and famous crescents still exude the elegance that helped make this the most fashionable city in Georgian Britain. More than 5000 of the city's buildings are now listed by Historic England – part of the reason why Bath is the only city in Britain that's a UNESCO World Heritage site in its entirety.

Just to the north, the Cotswolds burst with charming villages of golden buildings, thatched roofs and picturesque cottage gardens.

☑ TOP TIP

Bristol Temple Meads train station is beautiful but just on the outskirts of the city centre, so if you have lots of luggage, prepare to order a taxi as the central hotels aren't really walkable.

Bristol

The world's first great ocean liner

Moored in the dockyard in which it was built, **SS Great Britain** (*ssgreatbritain.org; adult/child £19.80/£13.05*) still looks

---

⊘ GETTING AROUND

Bristol is well connected to the rest of the UK by rail and bus. Bristol Airport, 8 miles from the city centre, provides links with UK and European cities. With the possible exception of hilly Clifton, it's easy to get around on foot and by bike – Bristol is the UK's first Cycling City, and there's a good network of cycling lanes and routes, plus several bike-rental companies in the city centre. Ferries provide a fun and often quicker way of moving around the harbour.

Bath is a compact and very walkable city, with most of its sights lying in the centre or just to the north, although it's a bit of an uphill climb to reach the Circus and the Royal Crescent.

For the greatest flexibility, and the potential to get off the beaten track in the Cotswolds, having your own car is unbeatable (you just need to find a spot to park).

JANE AUSTEN

Beloved English novelist Jane Austen (1775–1817) topped a 2022 poll as the greatest British author of all time (beating Shakespeare and *Harry Potter's* JK Rowling) but didn't experience fame. Austen published her first novel, *Sense and Sensibility* (1811), anonymously as 'By a Lady', and subsequently *Pride and Prejudice* (1813), *Mansfield Park* (1814) and *Emma* (1816) only as 'By the Author of' her previous works. Austen's other completed novels, *Northanger Abbey* and *Persuasion* (1817), were published posthumously. Social commentary on upper-class, late-18th-century society, especially women's dependence on marriage for status and financial security, were pivotal in her writing, though she wasn't wealthy and didn't marry before her death aged 41.

every bit the groundbreaking steamship it once was. Designed in 1843 by Isambard Kingdom Brunel, this was one of the largest ships ever built, measuring 98m from stern to tip. Brunel used wrought iron instead of wood, allowing for a far bigger hull, and to forego conventional paddle wheels in favour of a propeller. You can see them in the **Dry Dock**, enclosed by the 'glass sea' in which the ship rests. In the **Dockyard Museum**, exhibits chart the ship's chequered history, from a passenger liner to a quarantine ship and coal hulk.

See a grand bridge

Spanning the river below the well-heeled suburb of Clifton is Isambard Kingdom Brunel's awe-inspiring **Clifton Suspension Bridge** *(cliftonbridge.org.uk)*, which took 33 years to build and wasn't finished until 1864, several years after Brunel's death. Cross the bridge to the **Visitor Centre** to discover the story behind this feat of engineering; the free **Weekend Bridge Tours** (year-round) are excellent.

Bath

The world's most famous Roman spa

For over 2000 years, visitors have been drawn to the **Roman Baths** *(romanbaths.co.uk; adult/child £28/£21)* that give the city its name. The Romans established the town of Aquae Sulis around the sight of a sacred spring here in 44 CE and within 100 years had built this ostentatious complex of baths and adjoining temple to the goddess Sulis Minerva. The baths now form one of Europe's best-preserved ancient Roman sites.

The heart of the complex is the atmospheric **Great Bath**, a lead-lined pool filled with steaming jade-coloured water. Though now open-air, the bath was originally covered by a 20m-high barrel-vaulted roof. The Great Bath was fed with water from the **Sacred Spring**, which you can see bubbling away next door.

Taking the waters

While you can't swim at the Roman Baths, you can put the healing powers of thermal waters to the test in Bath.

The cutting-edge **Thermae Bath Spa** *(thermaebathspa.com; from £42.50)* complex is split into the **New Royal Bath** (no children under 16) and, in a separate building across from the aptly named Hot Bath St, the more intimate **Cross Bath** (no kids under 12). The highlight is the open-air rooftop pool in the main building, with superb views over the cityscape (especially at dusk).

EATING IN BRISTOL: OUR PICKS

Pasta Ripiena: Stellar stuffed pasta: handmade, wrapped in front of you, deeply flavoured and delicious. *5.30–11pm Tue, noon–4pm & 5.30–11pm Wed–Sat* ££

Riverstation: Light-filled waterfront restaurant and bar serving modern European cuisine. *11am–9pm Mon–Fri, 10am–9.30pm Sat, 10am–5.30pm Sun* ££

BOX-E: Beautifully cooked seasonal British dishes served in a pair of old shipping containers on Wapping Wharf. *5.30–9.30pm Wed, noon–9.30pm Thu–Sat* ££

Bulrush: Michelin-starred restaurant with British-, French- and Scandinavian-influenced set menus. *6–9.30pm Tue–Thu, noon–1.30pm & 6–9.30pm Fri & Sat* £££

Roman Baths, Bath

The Cotswolds

Get that quintessential England shot

Many of the places for snapping that classic Cotswolds photo have fallen victim to overtourism. Go early in the morning or late in the day to avoid the crowds – it's often when you'll get the best lighting, too.

Starting in **Burford**, Sheep St has vine-covered stone houses set back from the road. In **Bibury**, looking very much like it did when it was built in the 14th century, the cottages of **Arlington Row** are the subject of the occasional visitor controversy; No 9 is available to rent through the National Trust website. While in summer it's hard to get a shot of the bridges over the River Windrush in **Bourton-on-the-Water** without dozens of people, in winter you may snap that elusive snow shot.

Other notable places to visit include the cobblestone **Chipping Steps** in Tetbury; the **Old Mill** at Lower Slaughter; Grade I–heritage listed **Grevel's House** in Chipping Norton; the unfinished, Gothic-revival **Woodchester Mansion**, near Stroud; and the ruins of **Minster Lovell Hall** on the River Windrush near Witney, or **Hailes Abbey** at Winchcombe, both managed by English Heritage.

It goes without saying, respect residents' privacy, and drive on if a coach-load of visitors arrived just before you.

BEST COTSWOLDS OUTDOOR ACTIVITIES OPERATORS

Cotswold Cycles: Rents out all kinds of bikes and has maps and route suggestions from its Moreton-in-Marsh base.

Wild Pig: Hot-air balloon trips over the Cotswolds landscapes from April to October, toasting with bubbles (or tea/coffee).

Cotswold Canoe Hire: Kayaks, open canoes and SUPs for hourly or multiday hire from Lechlade-on-Thames.

Cotswold Mountain Biking: Half- and full-day tours, from flat towpath rides to steep descents and challenging climbs, on electric and traditional mountain bikes.

Cotswold Gliding Club: Sightseeing flights with views of the villages, rivers and rolling hills, plus gliding lessons.

 ## EATING IN THE COTSWOLDS: BEST COUNTRY DINING

Woolpack Inn: Three-century-old pub near Stroud with dishes like crispy pig's cheek with dandelion. *noon-3pm Mon, noon-3pm & 6-9pm Tue-Sun* ££

Wheatsheaf Inn: Seasonal British cuisine served in an elegant dining room and garden in Northleach. *8am-10am & noon-9pm Mon-Sat, noon-8pm Sun* ££

Bull: Locally sourced ingredients cooked over a charcoal grill; near Chipping Norton. *5-10pm Mon, noon-3pm & 5-10.30pm Tue-Sat, noon-5pm Sun* ££

Quince & Clover: Lovely daytime cafe for dishes like black-pudding sausage rolls in a thatched building near Chipping Norton. *8.30am-4pm Wed-Mon* £

JOAOCCD/SHUTTERSTOCK

TOP EXPERIENCE

Stonehenge

This mystical ring of monolithic stones is the most famous prehistoric monument in Europe and one of England's most emblematic sights, attracting pilgrims, tourists and New Age travellers for over 5000 years. Despite countless theories about the site's purpose, from a sacrificial centre to an astronomical clock, no one knows exactly why Ancient Britons expended so much time and effort on its construction.

DON'T MISS

Great Trilithon

Heel Stone

Slaughter Stone

Archaeological exhibits

360-degree projection

Neolithic houses

Cursus Barrows

Stone Circle

Walking the visitor path around the circle gets you as close as 5m to the stones to ponder their mysterious origins. Building Stonehenge was a process that lasted over 1000 years. The first phase started around 3000 BCE, when the outer circular bank and ditch were created. Within this were 56 pits – known as Aubrey Holes after John Aubrey, the antiquarian who discovered them in the 1600s – in which cremated remains were buried. These are now marked by concrete plaques.

About 500 years later, Stonehenge's main sarsen stones were hewn from the Marlborough Downs, 20 miles away, and

PRACTICALITIES

● english-heritage.org.uk ● adult/child from £27.20/16.30 ● 9.30am-7pm Jun-Aug, to 5pm Oct-May

dragged to the site. The largest were erected in a horseshoe and crowned by massive lintels to make the trilithons (two vertical stones topped by a horizontal one). The huge slabs of the Great Trilithon were worked to ensure its uprights perfectly framed the setting sun on a midwinter's day.

Surrounding this horseshoe was a ring of 30 sarsens (17 of which are still standing), each one linked to the next by a similar lintel. Four Station Stones were arranged around the edge of the enclosure in a layout that, again, was governed by the movement of the sun. Two additional curving rows of smaller bluestones were hauled here from the Preseli Mountains in South Wales, an incredible 250 miles away, while in 2024 scientists discovered the Altar Stone came from northeast Scotland.

The entrance to the circle is marked by the Heel Stone and, slightly further in, the Slaughter Stone. These stones were aligned to coincide with sunrise at the midsummer solstice.

Crowds flock for **solstice and equinox celebrations**, when free managed access is allowed inside the stone circle.

Stonehenge Landscape

Stonehenge actually forms part of a huge complex of ancient monuments that you can wander around.

North of the circle lie the Cursus Barrows, a humped cemetery of Bronze Age burial mounds. From these, you can make out the ridge of the nearby Cursus itself, an elongated embanked oval built around 1000 years before Stonehenge was raised. More burial mounds, the Old and New King Barrows, sit beside the Avenue, a ceremonial pathway that linked Stonehenge with the River Avon, 1.5 miles away.

The only visible remains of the Neolithic settlement at Durrington Walls, further up the Avon and connected to the river by its own smaller avenue, is the massive henge that was built around it. It's believed Durrington housed the builders of Stonehenge, who also erected nearby Woodhenge.

The National Trust has downloadable walking trails in the Stonehenge Landscape.

Visitor Centre Exhibitions

Engaging displays at the visitor centre, which plot the site's development and show how Stonehenge fits within the landscape and the movement of the sun, give you a good sense of what you're about to see at the stone circle and surrounding landscape. The highlight is a 360-degree projection of Stonehenge, letting you experience the changing seasons (including the midsummer sunrise) from 'inside' the circle. Exhibits include finds unearthed at the site, such as axes, arrowheads and antler picks, and the strikingly lifelike model of the face of a Neolithic man who was buried in a long barrow nearby. Outside, thatch-roofed, white-chalk-walled Neolithic houses replicating those used by Stonehenge's builders were constructed using local materials and ancient methods.

VISITING STONEHENGE

From the visitor centre, frequent shuttle buses make the 1.5-mile trip to the stones. Walking is more atmospheric; ask the driver to drop you at Fargo Woods then follow the trail, past the Cursus and Cursus Barrows. Wear sturdy shoes and bring waterproofs (there's no shelter at the stones). To go inside the circle, book a hosted, out-of-hours **Stone Circle Experience** (maximum 30 people), several months ahead.

TOP TIPS

● The best times to visit are weekdays, before 11am or after 2pm.

● Tickets are by timeslot entry; you can then stay until closing.

● Download English Heritage's free audio tour (bring headphones) for comprehensive guides to the exhibitions, stone circle and surrounding landscape.

● Parking is free if you've prebooked Stonehenge tickets.

● From Salisbury, hop-on/hop-off Stonehenge Tour buses have transport only, or transport and ticket options to Stonehenge and Old Sarum, with combination tickets also available for Salisbury Cathedral. See *thestonehengetour.info*.

The Midlands

CUISINE | INDUSTRIAL HERITAGE | LITERARY LORE

☑ **TOP TIP**

Stirchley is Birmingham's neighbourhood *du jour*, particularly if you're a craft-beer fan. But its name doesn't appear on any train map. To visit, take the Cross City Line to Bourneville and exit at Mary Vale Rd.

Though it's comfortably the Midlands' largest metropolis, a combination of Luftwaffe air raids and questionable town planning gave Birmingham a somewhat dismal image during the late 20th century, but fresh new architecture, gleaming trams and the arrival of some fabulous restaurants have helped make it the Midlands' renaissance city. World-class shopping and unique museums bring the smart centre plenty of buzz, but make time for neighbourhoods like Harborne and Moseley, where creative locals put their hearts into some fine artisan shops, bars and cafes.

The leafy countryside outside the Second City reveals some serious history, from imposing castles to the home of a certain 16th-century playwright. There are also grand adventures found in Shropshire, while over in Nottingham, there's far more to the city than its famous tights-wearing outlaw, Robin Hood. These days, the crowds come to Nottingham for its bumping music scene, creative restaurants and an infectious youthful dynamism.

Birmingham

Stroll Birmingham's historic waterways

'More canals than Venice' is the tongue-in-cheek phrase often used by locals when discussing Birmingham's famous

GETTING AROUND

The Midlands is a large landlocked region in the centre of England. It features hubs of various sizes, though Birmingham is the best place to start, as it offers public transport links in every direction. Hubs can be reached quickly and easily by train, with regular departures from Birmingham New Street

station. Different train companies running various routes may feel confusing at first, but the countryside rides are smooth and relaxing.

Driving is the most practical way of exploring rural areas like Shropshire. Having your own wheels is especially handy for accessing viewing points, country houses and villages.

BIRMINGHAM

See Enlargement

New St · Moor St · DIGBETH · St Paul's Sq

EGBASTON

MOSELEY

0 — 500 m
0 — 0.25 miles

0 — 1 km
0 — 0.5 miles

🔴 **SIGHTS**
1 Barber Institute of Fine Arts
2 Birmingham Back to Backs
3 Coffin Works
4 Gas Street Basin
5 Sarehole Mill

6 Worcester & Birmingham Canal

⚫ **SLEEPING**
7 Bloc
8 Grand Hotel Birmingham

🟢 **EATING**
9 Adam's

10 Albatross Death Cult
11 Opheem
12 Shababs
13 Wilderness

🔴 **ENTERTAINMENT**
14 Moseley Folk & Arts Festival

BIRMINGHAM'S BEST FESTIVALS

Moseley Folk & Arts Festival: Laid-back three-day music festival in Moseley Park at the end of August. Bring a blanket and a fold-up chair.

Brum Brew Fest: Weekend beer trail by the Brum Beer Babs group. Visit the city's best pubs, tick them off and receive a unique badge.

Birmingham Pride: One of the UK's biggest queer celebrations. Join the colourful street party on Hurst St and watch shows in Smithfield Sq.

Birmingham Cocktail Weekend: A weekend-long showcase of Birmingham's finest mixologists at different locations, with wallet-friendly prices.

Birmingham Mela: The UK's biggest South Asian music festival in Smethwick's sprawling Victoria Park. Very family-friendly, too.

---

waterways. Once used as fume-ridden trade routes in the 18th and 19th centuries, the city's canals are clean, pleasant and pass by some of Birmingham's prettiest scenery.

With its jaunty waterside pubs, bars and bistros, **Gas Street Basin** is the lively epicentre of Birmingham's canals. Enjoy the atmosphere here before walking the 45-minute stretch of the **Worcester and Birmingham Canal** south to the Birmingham University grounds. This tranquil trail finishes amid some fine Edwardian architecture and it's just a short walk to the **Barber Institute of Fine Arts** (*barber.org.uk*;

Opheem's sensational Aloo Tuk is Birmingham's best dish.

🍴 EATING IN BIRMINGHAM: BEST FINE DINING

Albatross Death Cult: Sublime seafood-heavy 12-course tasting, with unbeatable sake pairings. *7-10pm Wed-Sat, 1.30-3.30pm Fri & Sat £££*

Adam's: Superb seven-course tour de force of creative modern British cuisine from chef Adam Stokes. *noon-5pm & 6.30pm-midnight Wed-Sat £££*

Wilderness: Ten-course tasting experience amid charcoal-black interior and pounding rock soundtrack. *6-9pm Wed-Sat, 12.30-2pm Fri & Sat £££*

Opheem: Aktar Islam's seasonal 10-course Indian fine dining is a revelation; two Michelin stars *5.30-9.30pm Wed-Sat, noon-1pm Fri & Sat £££*

SHAKESPEARE & STRATFORD

While most of William Shakespeare's greatest works were written in London, he was born in Stratford and spent his formative years here, as well as his final years.

Born on 23 April 1564, he was the third of eight children and the eldest surviving son of John Shakespeare and Mary Arden. He was likely educated at Kings New School which, amazingly, still exists. At 18, he married 26-year-old Anne Hathaway with whom he had three children.

At some point in the mid-1580s, he left for London where he became the playwright we know today. At the age of 49, he retired home to Stratford where he died three years later, in 1616.

free), a splendid collection of lesser-heralded works by European masters.

Taste the city's favourite dish

No British city after London has more Michelin-starred restaurants than Birmingham, though for a window into the city's gastronomic heritage you'll need to jump in a taxi to the **Balti Triangle** neighbourhood.

Developed by Birmingham's fledgling Pakistani community in the early 1970s, the balti is a fiery one-pot curry that's still popular today and is a symbol of the city's diversity. The Balti Triangle is the dish's spiritual home, with **Shababs** (*shababsindian.co.uk*) offering the most authentic experience.

Industrial relics

Birmingham's sleek new tramlines and gleaming glass skyscrapers mask a city built on belching black chimneys and howling factories. Relics of that industrial past can be found dotted across town.

For a window into Birmingham's pre-industrial past, head out to Hall Green's **Sarehole Mill** (*birminghammuseums. org.uk; adult/child £8.80/5.50*). Dating back to 1771, the old watermill next to the River Cole was originally used to grind wheat but years later fascinated a young JRR Tolkien, who used the bucolic surroundings in his writings.

Back in the city centre, the **Birmingham Back to Backs** (*nationaltrust.org.uk; adult/child £11/5.50*) are the last surviving 19th-century back-to-back houses, and show how working people lived as the industrial age took over British society. On a more macabre note, the quirky **Coffin Works** (*coffinworks. org; guided tour £10*) is a beautifully preserved factory where accoutrements to coffins were once made – funerals were big business in Victorian Birmingham.

Stratford-upon-Avon

Stroll through Shakespeare's hometown

While a walk through Stratford-upon-Avon starts and ends with major Shakespeare sites, the town is also a fascinating journey through medieval, Elizabethan, Georgian and Victorian architecture.

Start at **Shakespeare's Birthplace** (*shakespeare.org.uk; adult/child £25/12.50*), where the world's most famous playwright was born. Further in town lies the black-and-white timber frame of **Harvard House**, dating back to 1596 and built

DRINKING IN STRATFORD: BEST PUBS

Ya Bard: Friendly and compact five-tap craft-beer bar that feels like you're in someone's living room. *3-8pm Tue-Thu, noon-8pm Fri & Sat, noon-4pm Sun*

Dirty Duck: Classic actors' post-show haunt opposite the Royal Shakespeare Company. *noon-11.30pm Mon-Thu, to midnight Fri & Sat, to 10pm Sun*

Stratford Alehouse: The finest spot for real ale and cider, with walls covered in colourful beer mats. *3-10pm Mon-Thu, 1-10pm Fri & Sat, 1-7pm Sun*

Garrick Inn: Timber-framed and supposedly haunted, this 15th-century pub is the town's oldest. *9am-11.30pm Mon-Thu, to midnight Fri & Sat, to 11pm Sun*

by Thomas Rogers, grandfather to the benefactor of Harvard University, John Harvard. Next door is the similar-looking **Garrick Inn**, Stratford's oldest public house named after the influential 18th-century actor David Garrick. Make sure to drop by **Holy Trinity Church** *(stratford-upon-avon.org; free)*, the scene of the Bard's baptism, marriage and burial.

Warwick
A mighty fortress

With its rising turrets, formidable walls and regular reenactment events, **Warwick Castle** *(warwick-castle.com; adult/child £26/21)* resembles the sort of monolithic fortress typically seen in movies or adventure books. Its oldest parts date back to the 11th century and the entire structure is still in remarkably good condition.

Coventry
Marvel at two very different cathedrals

The fragmented walls and soaring spire of **Coventry Cathedral** *(coventrycathedral.org.uk; free)* are what provokes a reaction more than anywhere else here. Devastated by a ferocious German bombing blitz during WWII, its nave suffered a direct hit and was left a smoking ruined shell. But its survival was inspiring, and the stained-glass windows in the modernist **New Cathedral** next door reflect a gaudy kaleidoscope of colours.

Nottingham
Taste history in Nottingham inns

Residing beneath the cliff of Nottingham Castle's lofty hilltop site, **Ye Olde Trip to Jerusalem** *(greeneking.co.uk/pubs)* claims to be the oldest of Nottingham's historic watering holes. Dating back to (allegedly) 1189, its low-sloping sandstone ceilings, silver suit of armour and spectacular Rock Lounge are an alluring combination. **Ye Olde Salutation Inn** *(salutation-inn.com)* has parts dating back to 1240, yet has somehow found a new life as a lively rock-and-metal pub, whereas the **Bell Inn** *(greeneking.co.uk/pubs)* has been looking onto Old Market Sq for almost 600 years.

THE WORLD'S OLDEST FOOTBALL CLUB

Notts County aren't the most popular team in Nottingham (that distinction goes to local rivals Nottingham Forest), but one thing that can never be taken away is their status as the oldest professional football club in the world. Formed in November 1862 as Nottingham Football Club, the team predates the Football Association itself, which wouldn't be founded until 1863. But despite their pioneering history, County haven't been particularly successful on the pitch, with an FA Cup their only top-flight honour (and that was way back in 1894). Football (soccer) is the world's most popular team sport, but the basis for every club began here in Nottingham.

 EATING IN NOTTINGHAM: OUR PICKS

Bar Iberico: Spanish tapas in the heart of Hockley, with cosmopolitan outdoor seating underneath red awnings. *11.30am-10pm Mon-Sat* **££**

Restaurant Sat Bains: Two-Michelin-star restaurant on the edge of town with a sublime 10-course tasting menu. *5-7.30pm Wed-Fri, 1-7.45pm Sat* **£££**

Annie's Burger Shack: Retro American diner serving thick burgers and craft beers. *1-9pm Mon-Thu, 10am-10pm Fri & Sat, 10am-9pm Sun* **££**

Cod's Scallops: A new standard for fish and chips, especially alongside oysters, cockles and whelks. *11.30am-9pm Mon-Thu, to 9.30pm Fri & Sat* **££**

Liverpool & the Peak District

BEATLES LORE | HUGE HILLS | OPULENT HOMES

> ☑ **TOP TIP**
>
> The Peak District is lovely all year round, but autumn is arguably the finest time to visit. Its quaint villages and countryside are a beautiful canvas of red, orange and gold, while its walking trails are a little quieter after the summer's rush of visitors.

A romantic collection of yawning valleys, stone villages, soaring hills and historic homes, the Peak District is is a widescreen outdoor playground where the Midlands meets the north. From the wind-sculpted hills of the Hope Valley to charming chocolate-box towns such as Eyam and Buxton, this is England at its most alluring. At its heart is Bakewell, a small town best known for its sweet indulgent puddings but also considered a gateway into the Peak District. From here, you can wander pretty riversides or hop on a bike into rolling hills and valleys.

Once you've had enough of the elements, the lively cities of the north await and few are more captivating than Liverpool. Arguably northern England's most distinct city, with its rejuvenated waterfront and a soundtrack provided by the greatest band of all time, Liverpool has a friendly character that adds warmth to its wealth of unique attractions.

Liverpool

Liverpool from above

A trio of iconic Edwardian buildings known together as the Three Graces – the **Cunard Building**, the **Port of Liverpool Building** and the **Royal Liver Building** – make up the recognisable skyline of Liverpool's Pier Head waterfront.

 GETTING AROUND

Small-town Bakewell is comfortably walkable, but bear in mind there's no train station. Hiring a car is a good idea if you're planning to stay a few days in Bakewell, as some villages and heritage sites can be time-consuming to reach by bus and expensive by taxi. The hiking area around Edale is well served by the Hope Valley Line trains running between Sheffield and Manchester.

Liverpool is a very walkable city, albeit slightly hilly in parts. Buses or taxis are best for heading out to the football stadiums or Beatles hot spots like Penny Lane, while the train is best for Crosby Beach and heading in from Liverpool John Lennon Airport.

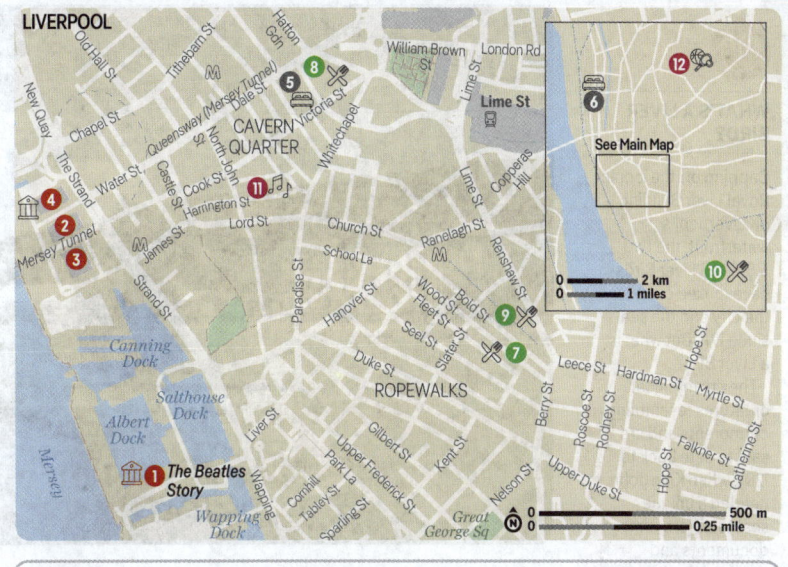

LIVERPOOL

HIGHLIGHTS
1 The Beatles Story

SIGHTS
2 Cunard Building
3 Port of Liverpool Building

4 Royal Liver Building

ACTIVITIES
see 12 Anfield Stadium Tour

SLEEPING
5 Municipal Hotel & Spa
6 Titanic Liverpool

EATING
7 Bamboo
8 Dale Street Kitchen
9 LEAF
10 Pippins Corner

ENTERTAINMENT
11 Cavern Club
12 Liverpool Football Club

Topped by the mythical Liver Birds, the Royal Liver Building (pronounced 'lie-ver') soars to a height of 98m; it's now possible to enjoy beautiful panoramic views of the city from its wind-whipped summit by taking the **Royal Liver Building 360 Tour** (*liverbuildingtour.com; adult/child £17.50/12.50*).

The Fab Four

Learn about Liverpool's most famous export at **The Beatles Story** (*beatlesstory.com; adult/child £20/11*) at the Albert Dock. Stroll north along Pier Head and grab a selfie with the excellent **statue of the band** in front of the Cunard Building. And of course, a night singing and dancing at the legendary **Cavern Club** (*cavernclub.com*) is a rite of passage (though not the original club, its atmosphere is cracking).

Make it a party with their Bottomless Brunch.

 EATING IN LIVERPOOL: BEST BRUNCH SPOTS

LEAF: Chic spot with high ceilings and a vast brunch menu, including shakshuka, and steak and eggs. *9am-10pm* ££

Dale Street Kitchen: Elegant corner spot serving award-winning breakfasts, including pancakes and a full English. *8am-5pm* ££

Bam Boo: Stylish Bold St brunch joint with floral decor and a strong French-toast game. *9am-5pm Sun-Fri, to 6pm Sat* ££

Pippins Corner: Hearty brunches with plenty of veggie options, too. Check the specials board. *9am-6pm* ££

WHAT'S A LIVER BIRD?

Capping off the iconic Royal Liver Building on Liverpool's waterfront, the two 5.5m-tall Liver Birds have looked out over the city and the sea since 1911. But what is a Liver Bird?

They're mythical creatures resembling cormorants and are said to date back to 1207, when King John needed a unique seal to differentiate documents and sterling from his territory when registering Liverpool as a borough. Centuries later, in 1797, they also appeared on the city's coat of arms.

Their cultural identity with Liverpool waned afterward, but their appearance at the summit of the city's lavish new skyscraper in 1911 shot the bird back into public consciousness – which is where it's stayed ever since.

Meet the Reds

A 15-minute bus ride from the city centre, the iconic **Anfield** stadium is the flag-waving, scarf-raising church where **Liverpool Football Club** plays, and attending a game – while not easy to get a ticket – should be a bucket-list item for any football fan. Failing that, the **stadium tour** (*bookings.liverpoolfc.com/stadiumtours; adult/child £25/16*) will get you up close to the famous Kop End and into the team dressing rooms.

Bakewell

Enter a grandiose world

The handsome landscape surrounding Bakewell is the backdrop for some of England's most opulent historic estates. **Chatsworth House** (*chatsworth.org; adult/child £35/10*) is a lavish 16th-century mansion recognisible for its appearances in various adaptations of Jane Austen's *Pride & Prejudice*. The grand estate contains the famous Devonshire art collection and a majestic 105-acre garden. Nearby **Haddon Hall** (*haddonhall.co.uk; adult/child £28/free*) has a medieval chapel on-site and a marvellous 16th-century Long Gallery, while **Hardwick Hall** (*nationaltrust.org.uk; adult/child £21/10.50*)

 EATING & DRINKING IN BAKEWELL: BEST PUBS

Red Lion: This 17th-century coaching inn with oak beams and stained-glass windows has excellent Sunday roasts. *noon-10pm £*

Manners: Slightly away from Bakewell's busy centre, with quality cask ale and pub classics. *noon-11pm Mon-Sat, to 10pm Sun £*

Rutland Arms: At this Georgian landmark hotel there's a fine front terrace to watch the world go by. *11am-11pm*

Joiners Arms: Specialist micropub with a revolving selection of cask and keg beer on tap. *noon-11pm Sun-Thu, to midnight Fri & Sat*

Chatsworth House, Bakewell

is an Elizabethan architectural masterpiece, decked out with magnificent tapestries and oil paintings.

Taking back a trail

The trend for repurposing Britain's discontinued train lines has been a wonderful boon for those who love the outdoors. Free for walking, cycling and jogging, the **Monsal Trail** is a meandering 8-mile delight on the old Manchester, Buxton, Matlock and Midland Junction Railway, which was built by the Midland Railway in 1863 to link Manchester with London and closed in 1968. Opened in 1981, the trail takes in dense forest, historic lime kilns and cinematic Victorian viaducts between Bakewell and the Topley Pike junction. Start in Bakewell and soak in the views from the spectacular **Headstone Viaduct** near Monsal Head.

Hope Valley

Adventures on the biggest scale

With its snaking mountain trails, ragged limestone edges and tranquil lakes, the Hope Valley provides a glorious windswept canvas for enjoying the great outdoors. The Peak District's hiking epicentre is the village of **Edale**, where several great walks begin. The panoramic views from the summit of **Mam Tor** are remarkable, and the 4.3-mile hike is moderately challenging, while the difficult **Kinder Scout Loop** climbs the Peak District's highest point. An evocative cycling trail flanks the edges of **Ladybower Reservoir** and **Derwent Reservoir** – the site where the Dambusters practised their famous Operation Chastise (a legendary WWII attack on German dams using 'bouncing bombs').

THE BEST VIEWPOINTS IN THE PEAK DISTRICT

Mam Tor: Gorgeous 360-panorama of the Hope Valley and Derbyshire from its 517m summit. It can get very blustery.

Monsal Head: A sigh-drawing English landscape – rolling hills, broccoli-like oak forests and a tall arching railway viaduct complete the scene.

The Roaches: Gritstone edges and craggy rocks looking over a sprawling pastoral scene. Including them makes for great photographs.

Bamford Edge: Rocky overhang that's a nerve-shredder to stand on. One of the Peak District's finest sunset spots.

Winnats Pass: Limestone gorge just south of Mam Tor. Rising ridges on either side are the region's most stunning drive.

Cardiff & South Wales

GRAND CASTLES | MISTY MOORS | GOLDEN COAST

Bannau Brycheiniog (Brecon Beacons) National Park

Llandrindod Wells • Hay-on-Wye • Brecon • Hereford • Abergavenny • Carmarthen • Llanelli • Swansea • Merthyr Tydfil • Bridgend • Newport • **CARDIFF** • Porthcawl • Barry

GETTING AROUND

South Wales takes up around a quarter of the country. While it looks small on a map, it's a journey of around 140 miles (three hours) from Chepstow in the east to St Davids in the west. The best way to explore is by car, especially in the remotest reaches of the mountains and coast. The region's main transport hubs (Cardiff, Swansea, Abergavenny, Haverfordwest) have decent train connections, but the smaller lines are slow (if scenic).

☑ TOP TIP

Wales attracts rain like moths to a flame, so always prepare for wet weather. Always pack a waterproof coat and shoes, especially if you're out in the sticks.

South Wales wings you from a capital fizzing with creative energy to mountains of myth and a wild coast of cliffs, coves and islands.

Buzzing with urban renewal, capital city Cardiff mixes a lively gastronomy scene with sweeping green spaces and grand historic sites. On the English border, the river-woven Wye Valley is a beer and literary haven. To the west, the Brecon Beacons hoist great sails above chequered fields, heather-misted moors and sheep-bobbled valleys, with single-track lanes forcing you to curse and reverse, trails cresting glacier-scoured summits, and country pubs filled with low beams, real ales and singsong voices.

And the coast just keeps getting better the further west you go. From the sweeping golden sands of Gower and Carmarthenshire to the cliff-flanked coves, coast path and puffin islands of Pembrokeshire, the call of the sea here is irresistible.

Cardiff

A headfirst plunge into history

Defiant and hulking, **Cardiff Castle** (*cardiffcastle.com; adult/child £16/10.50*) has presided over the capital for two millennia. These walls have seen it all: Romans (who built the first fort), Normans (the mighty motte-and-bailey keep), medieval lords (the Black Tower) and the Bute family (from 1766 to 1947), who gave it a mock-Gothic makeover in Victorian times.

Download the free Cardiff Castle app to access a self-guided audio walking tour. The keep is one of the best places to get your bearings. Climb 50 stone steps up the side of the motte, then continue to the viewing platform for panoramic views over the castle grounds and the city centre.

An engrossing romp through time

Cardiff's largest museum is the all-encompassing **National Museum Cardiff** (*museum.wales; free*). The building oozes classical style, with hefty granite steps leading to bronze front

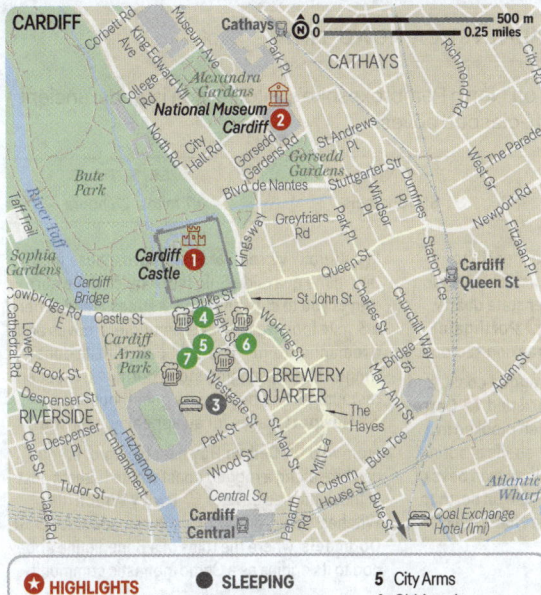

CARDIFF

CATHAYS

500 m
0.25 miles

Alexandra Gardens

National Museum Cardiff **2**

Bute Park

Sophia Gardens

Cardiff Castle **1**

Cardiff Queen St

OLD BREWERY QUARTER **4** **5** **6** **7** **3**

RIVERSIDE

The Hayes

Cardiff Central

Coal Exchange Hotel (1mi)

○ **HIGHLIGHTS**
1 Cardiff Castle
2 National Museum Cardiff

● **SLEEPING**
3 Parkgate Hotel

● **DRINKING & NIGHTLIFE**
4 Blue Bell

5 City Arms
6 Old Arcade
7 Tiny Rebel

---

doors, opening to the polished marble entrance hall capped with a 30m-high dome.

Most of the ground floor is dedicated to the **Evolution of Wales** exhibition. This fascinating walk through 4600 million years has interactive displays, space specimens, artefacts and images to illustrate how Wales came to be. The **natural history** exhibit is a snapshot of Wales' flora and fauna, from butterflies and seascapes to a 7.5m basking shark. Upstairs is all about art. The **permanent galleries** showcase over 500 years of paintings, illustrations, sculptures, ceramics and more from Wales and the world.

Hay-on-Wye

Wales' literary wonderland

Hidden in the Welsh hills, the Georgian market town of Hay-on-Wye has extraordinary cultural cachet as the host of Britain's

---

BEST ART IN THE NATIONAL MUSEUM

San Giorgio Maggiore at Dusk: This technicolour sunset, painted by Monet, is from a series of studies of an island in Venice.

Landscape at Auvers in the Rain: Finished three days before his suicide, this moving Van Gogh oil painting shows slashes of rain distorting a colourful landscape.

La Parisienne: Referred to as 'The Blue Lady', this striking Renoir oil painting is one of the museum's centrepieces.

Dorelia McNeill in a Feathered Hat: Welsh artist Augustus John painted Dorelia, his common-law wife, repeatedly for over 60 years.

The Empty Mask: A Magritte painting embodying the surrealist fascination with the subconscious.

The house bitter is worth trying.

 DRINKING IN CARDIFF: OUR PICKS

Old Arcade: Ever-popular pub with an outdoor area. Hearty food and plenty of choice on the bar. *11am-11pm Sun & Mon, to midnight Fri & Sat*

Tiny Rebel: Pub/bar from local brewery Tiny Rebel, with a great range of drinks and occasional live music. *noon-1am Sun-Wed, to 2am Thu-Sat*

Blue Bell: One of Cardiff's oldest pubs has a traditional, cosy atmosphere with locally sourced Welsh food. *11am-midnight*

City Arms: Traditional pub opposite the Principality Stadium, with a vast array of Welsh and British beers. *noon-11pm Sun-Thu, to midnight Fri & Sat*

THE GUIDE

BRITAIN CARDIFF & SOUTH WALES

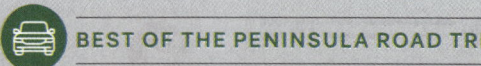

BEST OF THE PENINSULA ROAD TRIP

This 38-mile drive shows off North Pembrokeshire's wildlife-rich islands, ancient hillforts and gorgeous cliff-clasped coves.

START	END	LENGTH
St Davids	St Dogmaels	47 miles; 2½ hours

Starting in ❶ **St Davids**, meander north to ❷ **Abereiddi**, where the turquoise Blue Lagoon glimmers in a sheer-sided former slate quarry. In the hook-shaped harbour of ❸ **Porthgain** nearby, the Shed entices with cracking seafood.

Breeze 4 miles north along the ragged coast, and just past the village of Trefin you'll find ❹ **Carreg Samson**, a 5000-year-old dolmen plonked in a farmer's field. Carpeted with bluebells in spring, a wooded valley dips to the sublime twin bays of ❺ **Abermawr and Aberbach**. Push on north to lighthouse-topped ❻ **Strumble Head**, which bears the brunt of the Irish Sea.

In culturally vibrant ❼ **Fishguard**, pause for a pint in the quayside Ship Inn. A quick drive north brings you to cliff-rimmed ❽ **Dinas Head**, where a 3-mile loop walk reveals smugglers' coves and a romantic storm-ruined chapel. With its dune-fringed beach, sagging stone cottages, excellent restaurants and boutique-y guesthouses, ❾ **Newport** makes for an appealing rest stop.

From wild ❿ **Ceibwr Bay** near Moylgrove, you can hike along a ragged coast where fulmars nest in the collapsed cave of ⓫ **Pwll y Wrach** (the Witches' Cauldron). Wind up in estuary-side ⓬ **St Dogmaels**, where the ruins of a Benedictine abbey nod to its origins as a Celtic monastic community.

Carreg Samson takes its name from the local legend that 6th-century bishop and missionary St Samson of Dol lifted the 12-ton capstone into place with just his little finger.

Gorse-clad **Strumble Head** has an edge-of-the-world quality on bleak, windy days. Grab binoculars to spot Arctic skuas, storm petrels, seals and porpoises.

At **Abermawr and Aberbach**, the stumps of a drowned, 8000-year-old forest emerge at very low tide.

Irish Sea

10 km
5 miles

Cemaes Head

Cardigan

Strumble Head

Garn Fawr

Goodwick

Nevern

Mynydd CarnIngli

Fishguard

Pembrokeshire Coast National Park

Cwmcerwyn

A487

A40

PEMBROKESHIRE

St Davids Head

A487

Pembrokeshire Coast National Park

St Davids

Solva

Newgale

B4330

Ramsey Island

START

St Brides Bay

A487

Haverfordwest

A40

Addyman Books, Hay-on-Wye

THE LADY OF THE LAKE

The glacial lake of **Llyn-y-Fan Fach** appears in Welsh epic *The Mabinogion*. Legend tells that a young farmer peered into the lake and saw a beautiful maiden. He coaxed her ashore and begged for her hand in marriage. They lived happily and raised three sons, but when the farmer struck his wife three times, she returned to the fairy world forever.

Here myth merges with fact, as the sons were the first in a long line of royal healers. The village of Myddfai was a medieval centre for herbalist activity. Today, Pant-y-Meddygon (Physicians' Valley) on Mynydd Myddfai is still rich in the plants used to make the remedies described in the late-14th-century *Red Book of Hergest*.

most feted literature and arts festival. Held over 11 days from late May, **Hay Festival** *(hayfestival.com)* attracts both major and emerging talent. Politics, poetry workshops, book signings, concerts, comedy performances and kids' activities aim to generate ideas and ponder life's biggest questions.

If you can't snag festival tickets, come for a romp around the town's 20-plus independent bookshops, from the vast, immaculately catalogued shelves of **Richard Booth's Bookshop** *(boothbooks.co.uk)* to rare, out-of-print tomes at **Addyman Books** *(hay-on-wyebooks.com)*.

Bannau Brycheiniog (Brecon Beacons) National Park

Climb South Wales' highest mountain

Rain, bog and fog be damned: puffing up to the highest peak in the Brecon Beacons, **Pen-y-Fan** (886m), is irresistible. On cloud-free days, views stretch all the way over bald, glacier-scoured peaks and deep valleys to the Black Mountains, Bristol Channel and Eryri (Snowdonia) beyond.

The quickest stomp to the top begins at **Pont ar Daf** car park on the A470, 10 miles southwest of Brecon. It's a steep but straightforward ascent (4.5 miles return; allow three hours). Dodge the biggest crowds by choosing one of the longer routes on the north side of the mountain, starting at **Cwm Gwdi** car park, for instance (a 7-mile, four-hour round trip).

EATING AROUND THE BRECON BEACONS: MEALS TO REMEMBER

Felin Fach Griffin: Beamed, fire-warmed bar and stunning menus raiding the kitchen garden for ingredients. *noon-2.30pm & 6-9pm* ££

Newbridge on Usk: Exquisite regional food beside a stone bridge on the River Usk. *6-9pm Mon & Tue, noon-3.30pm & 6-9pm Wed-Sat, noon-8.30pm Sun* ££

1861: Fresh farmed and foraged produce shines in the tasting menus at this Cross Ash restaurant. *noon-3pm & 6.30-11pm Wed-Sat, noon-3pm Sun* £££

Bell at Skenfrith: Dreamy pub on the River Monnow's banks, with garden-grown produce on the creative menu. *noon-2.30pm & 6.30-8.30pm Wed-Sat* £££

North Wales

SCENERY | HERITAGE TRAINS | SEASIDE TOWNS

Llandudno
Bangor • Conwy
Caernarfon • ○ Betws-y-Coed
Yr Wyddfa (Snowdon) Blaenau
Porthmadog • Ffestiniog
Pwllheli • Portmeirion
Eryri National Park (Snowdonia) • Dolgellau
Tywyn ○ Machynlleth
Aberystwyth

☑ **TOP TIP**

One of the most photographed trees in Wales, the 'lone tree' in Llyn Padarn is a photographer's dream. If you're shooting at dawn or dusk, arrive early to secure a prime spot, and use a wide-angle lens to include Pen-y-Pass in the backdrop.

Imagine thunderous rivers, glacial mountain ranges, dune-fringed, wave-whipped beaches and ancient forests folded into 823 glorious sq miles of national park. This is Eryri (Snowdonia), the country's mountainous, Welsh-speaking, richly cultured heart. Welcome to Wales at its wildest: chockablock with trails, swim spots and scrambles over rocky terrain.

Sharp peaks pierce the heavens, with Yr Wyddfa (Snowdon) – Wales' highest mountain (1085m) – dominating the skyline. Seven trails lead to the top of Cymru's cap, with snaking queues in peak season. Beyond, adventure mounts at former quarries and historic slate mines reimagined into thrilling zipwire zones, underground trampolines, and accessible cycling routes.

Further south, rolling hills tumble into Victorian resort towns, sandy beaches and one bizarre Italianate village, while heritage rail lines showcase one of the most unique ways to see one of Britain's most cinematic landscapes.

Eryri National Park (Snowdonia)

Hike to the summit of Yr Wyddfa (Mt Snowdon)

Thousands of pro hikers and outdoor newbies flock to **Yr Wyddfa** (Mt Snowdon), Eryri's most popular and incredibly

GETTING AROUND

Covering some 5175 sq miles, this region may seem small, but the roads wrap around several mountain ranges, meander through a national park and wiggle along the coast. Take your time to enjoy it fully.

A car is helpful in most areas and essential in the countryside, where public transport can be irregular or nonexistent, though parking can

be a nightmare in popular spots, particularly during peak seasons.

Trains link many major destinations, particularly along the north and west coast (as far south as Aberystwyth). However, services are slow, and same-day travel is expensive. To get between North and Mid-Wales, you'll need to change in Shrewsbury, England.

GYVAFOTO/SHUTTERSTOCK

Llanberis Path, Eryri National Park (Snowdonia)

photogenic peak, year-round. In peak summer season, you'll see snaking queues of selfie-seekers leading to the 1085m summit.

The **Llanberis Path** is the go-to summit route for most hikers. Starting from Llanberis village, it's a more gradual ascent that follows the **Snowdon Mountain Railway** *(snowdonrailway.co.uk; prices vary),* making it a top choice for first-timers and less confident walkers. It's a steady climb, usually taking three to four hours. On a clear day, the astonishing views from the summit stretch as far as Ireland and the Isle of Man.

Blaenau Ffestiniog

Jump on a winding heritage train

Chugging away since 1832, the **Ffestiniog Railway** *(fest rail.co.uk; prices vary)* is the world's oldest narrow-gauge railway. **Mountain Spirit** is the flagship Ffestiniog Railway experience, with carriages typically pulled by 150-year-old Double Fairlie locomotives. Your epic 13.5-mile journey starts in Porthmadog and crosses the Cob Estuary, climbing steadily through lush fields, dense forests and lakes towards

STARGAZING SPOTS IN ERYRI

Eryri is designated an International Dark Sky Reserve. Here are some of the best places for stargazing.

Bwlch y Groes: As one of the highest-tarmacked passes in Wales, this site has expansive views of the Dyfi Valley, Cader Idris and the Berwyn Mountains, and unparalleled stargazing.

Llyn y Dywarchen: Situated above Drws-y-Coed in Dyffryn Nantlle, this fishing lake is a scenic dark location for stargazing, free from urban light pollution.

Llyn Geirionydd: Located in Gwydir Forest near Betws-y-Coed, this accessible star-spotting site has parking and toilets.

Llynnau Cregennen: At the foothills of Cader Idris, these twin lakes provide an atmospheric setting for stargazing and astrophotography.

 EATING & DRINKING IN BLAENAU FFESTINIOG: OUR PICKS

De Niro: Family-friendly cafe known for hearty soups, proper good toasties and veggie offerings. *10am-3pm Mon-Sat* £

Trish & Chips: Classic fish and chips; it also serves pies, sausages and scampi. *4-8pm* £

Y Manod: Classic, community-led boozer with local ales, live music and lively quiz nights. *hours vary* £

Y Pengwern: Community-owned pub in Llan Ffestiniog, with lovely wood-burning fire and classic pub grub. *hours vary* ££

Aberystwyth's **Royal Pier** *(royalpier.co.uk)* holds the accolade of being the oldest pier in Wales. This retro, Grade II-listed structure opened in 1865. It was Eugenius Birch's brainchild and initially extended 244m into the sea. Sadly, a fierce storm in 1866 took out a 30m section, but it was soon extended and refurbished, adding a tearoom and bandstand. In 1896, the Prince of Wales inaugurated a grand iron-and-glass pavilion holding 3000 people. Miraculously, the weathered pier has survived despite numerous challenges, including the Great Storm of 1938 and going into administration in 2016. Today, there's ongoing debate and plans on how best to regenerate the Victorian-era pier and restore it to its former glory.

Blaenau. Upgrade to gold service and book 'Observation Bay' seats for the best view.

Zipline over a former quarry

Situated among the former slate mines of Blaenau Ffestiniog, **Zip World Llechwedd** *(zipworld.co.uk; from £10)* is a high-adrenaline historical adventure. Strapped in on a four-person parallel zip line, you'll soar high above slate mountains dotted with patches of green and glittering lakes at speeds of over 50mph. Below you, the old slate quarry is a reminder of the area's industrious past. But it's not just about the zip-line thrills. As part of the **Titan 2** experience, a former army truck will take you to a height of 430m overlooking the human-made mountains while a guide explains the history of the mining community.

Portmeirion

A most unusual Welsh village

Resembling a technicolour fever dream, pastel-coloured **Portmeirion** *(portmeirion.wales; adult/child £20/13)* is no ordinary Welsh village. Designed by visionary architect Clough Williams-Ellis between 1925 and 1973, the Italian Riviera–style buildings hugging the Dwyryd Estuary are set amid lush woodlands and groomed gardens. Alongside its colourful architecture, the ticketed site features two historic hotels, a spa, self-catering cottages, gift shops, a swanky restaurant and an Italian-style *gelateria*.

Aberystwyth

Find beaches for all occasions

If you were to play British Seaside Holiday Bingo, Aberystwyth's three beaches would be a full house. Backed by a faded Victorian promenade, the sweeping stones of Blue Flag **North Beach** have everything you'd need for a nostalgic dip: donkey rides, chilly waters, penny arcades and a pier. On the other side of the castle is **Aberystwyth South Beach**, a quiet curl of slate-grey sand and shingle, and beyond the harbour wall is pebbly **Tanybwlch Beach**. This is where you'll find the locals.

EATING IN ABERYSTWYTH: OUR PICKS

Medina: Indie Middle Eastern cafe and food shop; come here for Neapolitan-style pizzas. *9.30am-8.30pm Mon-Fri, to 9.30pm Sat* ££

Ultracomida: Trendy Spanish deli and tapas bar. Excellent selection of continental wines, cheeses and Iberian ham. *10am-4pm Mon-Sat* ££

Mama Fay's: Caribbean-inspired dishes including spicy jerk chicken, curried goat or Jamaican potato curry. *5-10pm Tue-Sat* ££

Dragonfly Bistro: Great for vegan and vegetarian eaters; expect creative dishes that are both fresh and colourful. *hours vary* ££

Edinburgh

MAJESTIC ARCHITECTURE | TWISTING STREETS | COSY CAFES

It all began with fire and rock. The rugged landscape of modern-day Edinburgh was formed by three volcanoes, which rose 350 million years ago. The first of these (Castle Rock) is the most recognisable, with its long-extinct volcanic plug now home to moody Edinburgh Castle. The second (Calton Hill) sits to the east of the New Town, topped with mighty monuments and panorama-loving picnickers. And the third (Arthur's Seat) has become the go-to place for hikers, bikers, dog-walkers and kite-fliers, who ascend its crag-fringed slopes for views across Holyrood Park.

Most visitors to Edinburgh stick around the city's ancient, volcanic heart, with its mishmash of narrow streets, winding alleys and underground vaults. But hike up any of Edinburgh's extinct volcanoes and it becomes clear just how much lies beyond. The New Town's leafy squares, the West End's splendid architecture, Leith's fancy restaurants and Holyrood's hipster bars – varied and vibrant, Edinburgh begs to be explored.

Festival City
Edinburgh's crazy August days

August is festival season in Edinburgh, and it's the greatest show on Earth. The main attraction, of course, is the **Edinburgh Festival Fringe** *(edfringe.com)*. Over the course of three weeks, tens of thousands of performances of comedy, theatre, dance, circus, cabaret and kids' shows fill venues throughout the Old Town and beyond.

Yet the Fringe is just one of several major festivals taking place here in August. There's the **Edinburgh International Festival** *(eif.co.uk)*, with its packed program of classical music, theatre and opera. The **Edinburgh International Book Festival** *(edbookfest.co.uk)* stages talks from big-name authors from around the world. And don't miss the **Edinburgh Art Festival** *(edinburghartfestival.com)*, which sees specially commissioned artworks scattered around the city.

GETTING AROUND

With the narrow medieval alleyways of the Old Town, the grandly proportioned streets of the New Town and the well-marked footpaths snaking up Arthur's Seat, Edinburgh is a very walkable city. The tram provides hassle-free access from the airport to the city centre (a 30-minute journey), and continues to Newhaven, making it a great way to hop between the West End, New Town and Leith. Services run daily from around 4.30am to midnight.

☑ TOP TIP

For a taste of the cramped conditions of years gone by, dive off from the Royal Mile into the narrow closes on either side. Just a short walk down an alley will reveal a whole other world of quaint little courtyards, pretty whitewashed houses and surprising city views.

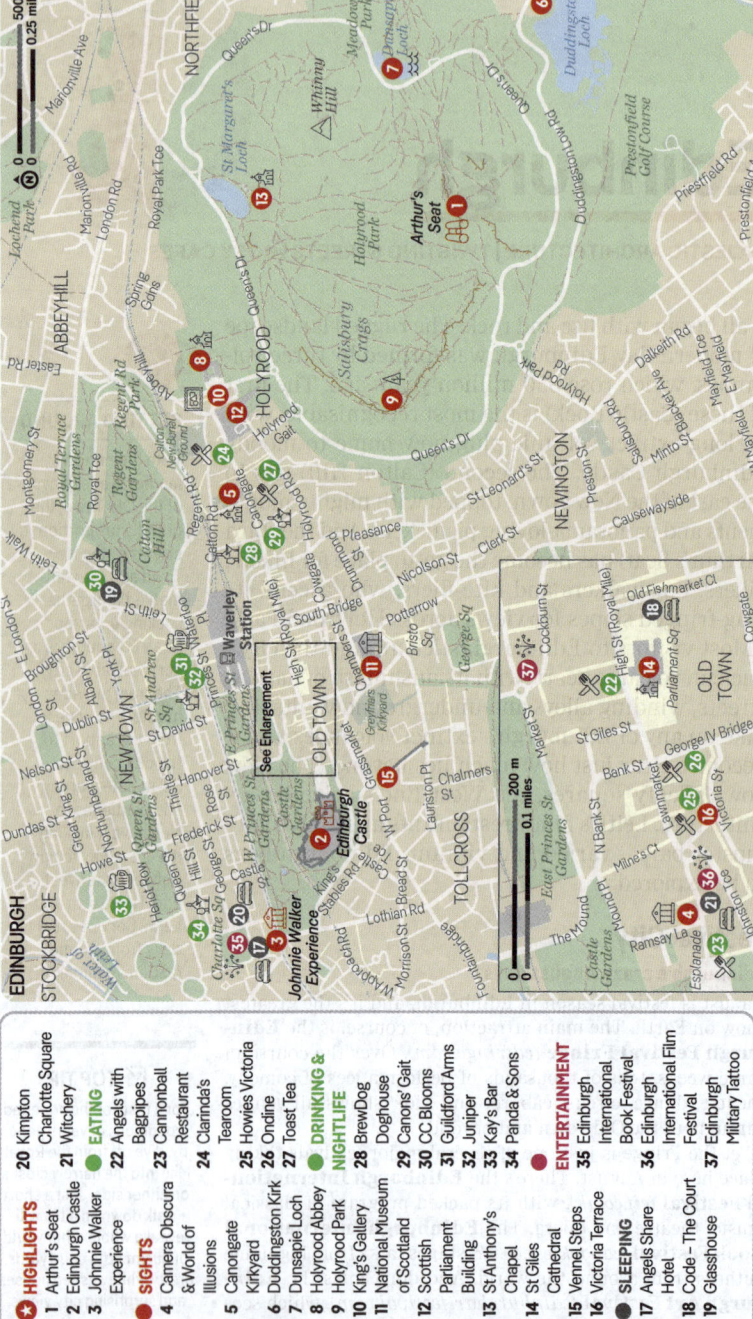

EDINBURGH

STOCKBRIDGE

NEW TOWN

OLD TOWN

See Enlargement

OLD TOWN

500 m
0.25 miles

200 m
0.1 miles

EDINBURGHCITYMOM/SHUTTERSTOCK

Edinburgh Castle from Princes St Gardens

There's also the **Edinburgh International Film Festival** *(edfilmfest.org)*, the world's oldest film festival with regular premieres and red-carpet stars. And the **Royal Edinburgh Military Tattoo** *(edintattoo.co.uk)* brings eye-popping displays of military marching bands.

Scotland's Chief Royal Castle

Visit the fortress on the hill

The most potent symbol of the Scottish capital, **Edinburgh Castle** *(edinburghcastle.scot; adult/child £21.50/13)* has stood on the brooding crags high above the city for the best part of a millennium. As well as being one of the city's most visible and recognisable sights, it's also one of its most interesting, with attractions ranging from ancient stone chapels to sparkling crown jewels.

Between April and September each year, knowledgeable guides offer 30-minute tours from just inside the Main Gate – a perfect introduction to the castle before you go and explore it for yourself.

Identity Meets Politics

Where unique architecture houses Scotland's decision-makers

The **Scottish Parliament Building** *(parliament.scot; tours free)*, conceived by Catalan architect Enric Miralles and

BEST VIEWS IN THE OLD TOWN

National Museum of Scotland: The rooftop terrace here offers far-reaching vistas of Edinburgh Castle and the city below.

Castle Esplanade: On a clear day, you can see out to Leith and beyond from this viewpoint beside the castle.

St Giles Cathedral: Accessible by guided tour, the church's roof offers great views along the Royal Mile.

Vennel Steps: Climb halfway up this staircase from Grassmarket for a remarkable view of Edinburgh Castle.

Victoria Terrace: Head down tiny Fisher's Close to emerge on this terrace with views of colourful Victoria St.

✂ EATING IN THE OLD TOWN: BEST RESTAURANTS

Angels with Bagpipes: Popular Royal Mile restaurant, named for the statue in St Giles Cathedral, serving Scottish cuisine with inventive twists. *noon-9pm* **££**

Howies Victoria: Opt for the bargain lunch menu of seasonal Scottish fare, from salmon to venison, or treat yourself to a seafood dinner. *noon-10.30pm* **££**

Cannonball Restaurant: Italian-influenced Scottish cuisine served in a chic but informal restaurant by the castle. *noon-10pm Mon-Thu, to 10.30pm Fri & Sat* **£££**

Ondine: Sample the best oysters in Edinburgh, along with other seafood specialities and seared steaks, at this fine-dining restaurant. *noon-10pm Tue-Sat* **£££**

BEST CHURCHES IN HOLYROOD & ARTHUR'S SEAT

Holyrood Abbey:
In the Palace of Holyroodhouse grounds, these ruins were once one of Europe's grandest abbeys.

Canongate Kirkyard:
This unusual-looking church (and cemetery full of famous locals) was a favourite of the late Queen Elizabeth II.

St Anthony's Chapel:
A popular stop on the way up Arthur's Seat, this ruined chapel provides great views across the city to Leith.

Duddingston Kirk:
This eye-catching Anglo-Saxon church is one of Edinburgh's oldest, built around 1124 and expanded in the 1630s.

King's Gallery:
Formerly the Queen's Gallery, this art collection is housed in the shell of the 19th-century Holyrood Free Church.

Arthur's Seat

completed by his widow, Benedetta Tagliabue, is a brazenly modern construction of polished concrete, granite and steel, without a neo-Gothic clock tower in sight. Few passers-by are immediately convinced by its starkly out-of-place exterior, but venture inside and you may just change your mind. The lobby is a playful space of concrete pillars, oak panels, glass walls and eye-catching works of art. Join a guided tour to walk the sloping corridors, see the debating chamber and learn more about the architect's intentions of creating a building to represent a national identity.

The Roof of the City

Hike to Edinburgh's highest point

An unmistakable feature of the Edinburgh skyline, the craggy, gorse-covered **Arthur's Seat** rises up behind the towers of the Palace of Holyroodhouse. Earn your porridge with a 45-minute climb to its 251m summit.

The trail starts across from the car park on Queen's Dr, and gently climbs up and away from the road. Take a short diversion to see the medieval ruins of **St Anthony's Chapel**, including fine views towards North Edinburgh, before doubling back and continuing your way into the heart of **Holyrood Park**. Divert left off the main trail onto a narrower path,

 EATING & DRINKING IN HOLYROOD & ARTHUR'S SEAT: BEST CAFES & PUBS

Clarinda's Tearoom: A Canongate institution, this quaint tearoom has been serving homemade scones for half a century. *9.30am-4.30pm Tue-Sun* £

Toast Tea: As the name suggests, this Asian cafe serves breakfast toasts alongside good coffee, tea and homemade soft drinks. *10am-6pm Mon-Sat* £

Canons' Gait: This ever-popular Royal Mile pub has a good selection of ales and unfalteringly friendly service. *noon-11pm Sun-Wed, to midnight Thu-Sat*

BrewDog Doghouse: There's craft beer galore coming out of the 30 taps here. If you find you've overindulged, simply check into the on-site hotel. *7am-1am*

which becomes increasingly steep and rocky as it approaches a plateau – a chance to catch your breath while looking over pretty **Dunsapie Loch**. From here, a final 10-minute push along the mountain ridge brings you to the top of the hill. Drink in the marvellous city panorama before heading back the way you came.

Family Fun with Victorian Roots

Escape into a world of optical illusions

It may be 170 years old, but Edinburgh's bewitching **Camera Obscura** (*camera-obscura.co.uk; adult/child £24.95/17.95*) continues to baffle and delight visitors to this day. Enter from Castlehill, near the top of the Royal Mile, and climb up to the Outlook Tower for a taste of true Victorian ingenuity. Here, live images from the streets below are projected onto a canvas table. Think CCTV, 19th-century style. The rest of the building is given over to the **World of Illusions**, a collection of hands-on exhibits showcasing a variety of optical illusions, light puzzles, mirror mazes, 3D holograms and vortex tunnels; enough to keep the kids entertained for an hour or two, but not quite matching the magic of the camera obscura above.

Bringing Whisky to Life

A spiritual experience like no other

Part animated history lesson, part interactive theatre show, part theme-park extravaganza, the no-holds-barred £150 million **Johnnie Walker Experience** (*johnniewalker.com; tours & tastings from £30*) is an all-singing, all-dancing introduction to the life and times of Mr Johnnie Walker. It starts slowly with a questionnaire (designed to work out your flavour preferences) but then the real fun begins, with the immersive, full-sensory Journey of Flavour tour. The highlight is a storytelling segment in which actors recount the brand's long journey from a humble grocer's shop to the world's best-selling Scotch, but the entire thing is an all-consuming experience of energetic live performances, top-drawer visual effects and eardrum-splitting soundscapes. After an hour or so, you emerge blinking into a tasting room, where a choice of whiskies and cocktails awaits.

LGBTIQ+ EDINBURGH

Edinburgh has a small but long-established LGBTIQ+ scene. Most of the city's gay-friendly bars and clubs are centred around the New Town's Broughton St and top of Leith Walk (also known as 'the Pink Triangle'). For two of the most popular, head to Greenside Place. Here, you'll find **CC Blooms** (*ccblooms. co.uk*), a mainstay of Edinburgh's gay scene since the early 1990s, with its two floors playing a mix of dance and disco music – as well as hosting the odd cabaret night. Just a few doors down from here is **Planet Bar & Kitchen**, a lively gay bar known for its nightly entertainment, ranging from karaoke and bingo to Showtime Fridays drag queen shows.

DRINKING IN THE NEW TOWN: BEST PUBS & BARS

Guildford Arms: Pretty pub, all wood panels and elegant plasterwork, with good beer and whisky. *11am-11pm Sun-Thu, to midnight Fri & Sat*	**Juniper:** Sip imaginative cocktails (like peaty whisky with peach iced tea) in a colourful, plant-filled interior. The steaks are tasty, too. *noon-11pm*	**Panda & Sons:** Easily missed, Prohibition-style speakeasy tucked away behind a fake barbershop exterior and down a staircase. *hours vary Tue-Sun*	**Kay's Bar:** Tiny, cosy and friendly, this coach house turned local pub has an extensive whisky selection. *11am-11pm Sun-Thu, to midnight Fri & Sat*

Beyond
Edinburgh

Where Scotland's biggest and most
gregarious city sidles up alongside a
majestic national park.

Places

Glasgow p158

**Loch Lomond & the
Trossachs National Park**
p160

Stepping out of Central Station reveals the flutter and swirl
of a metropolis. Crowds throng the sidewalks, queuing buses
and honking taxis fill the streets, and an eclectic mix of modern and Victorian architecture looms overhead. Welcome to
the heart of Scotland's biggest city.

Yet Glasgow's lively city centre is just the start of the story.
Explore the East End for the city's oldest surviving buildings,
Merchant City for some of the best restaurants, shopping and
nightlife, and the West End for bohemian bars and cafes.

Just to the north of Glasgow, the stunning Loch Lomond
and the Trossachs National Park are a majestic escape. Here
you'll find an all-you-can-explore banquet of sprawling lochs,
mountain trails, lush glens and precious woodland.

Glasgow

TIME FROM EDINBURGH: **1HR**

Classical architecture meets provocative art

Glasgow's **Gallery of Modern Art** (*glasgowlife.org.uk; free*)
features works from local and international artists, housed
in a neoclassical building on elegant Royal Exchange Sq. The
original interior is an ornate contrast to the inventive art on
display; all exhibitions are temporary and free to visit. There
are also valiant efforts made to keep the kids entertained,
from museum trails to art clubs.

Outside the museum stands the horseback **statue of the Duke
of Wellington**, which is invariably crowned with a traffic cone
– an iconic symbol of Glaswegian humour and defiance. Street
artist Banksy claims it's his favourite work of art in the UK.

 GETTING AROUND

Glasgow's grid layout makes walking easy,
albeit with steep hills. The Subway has
15 stops and travels in a loop – the most
convenient way of getting between the centre
and the West End. City bus services, mostly
run by First Glasgow, are also frequent; buy
tickets when boarding.

Loch Lomond and the Trossachs National Park
is a road-trip dream come true, with incredible
drives and 'Scenic Route Viewpoints' along
the way. Loch Lomond is easily accessed from
the Central Belt on public transport. ScotRail
services run from Glasgow to Balloch, Arrochar,
Tarbet and Ardlui.

Barrowland Ballroom, Glasgow

Marvel at medieval majesty

Glasgow Cathedral *(glasgowcathedral.org; free)* has a rare timelessness. It's a shining example of Gothic architecture and, unlike nearly all of Scotland's cathedrals, it survived the Reformation mobs almost intact.

The wooden roof has been restored many times since its original construction, but some of the timber dates from the 14th century. Many of the cathedral's stunning stained-glass windows are modern – Francis Spear's 1958 work *The Creation* fills the west window. The cathedral is divided by a 15th-century pulpitum (choir screen), decorated with carved figures that may represent Jesus' disciples. Beyond this, note the impressive shields on the roof, which create a path leading to the four stained-glass panels of the east window, also by Francis Spear and depicting the Apostles. At the northeastern corner is the entrance to the 15th-century upper chapter house, now used as a sacristy.

Take a trip to the Barras

Visiting the **Barras Market** is an essential Glasgow weekend experience. The Barras preserves a democratic old-time feel with its no-nonsense stalls, traditional cafes and the sense that some of the wares might have fallen off the back of a truck. Check out the down-at-heel secondhand market under the **Barrowland Ballroom** *(barrowland.co.uk),* a brilliant old dancehall and music venue.

GLASGOW SCHOOL OF ART

In 1896, aged 27, Charles Rennie Mackintosh won a competition to design a new building to house the Glasgow School of Art, where he had studied. Completed in phases between 1896 and 1909, the British art nouveau–style 'Mackintosh Building' (as it came to be known) was arguably his supreme architectural achievement – and became an instant city landmark. Tragically, just as it was close to reopening after a devastating 2014 fire, another (even larger) blaze in 2018 destroyed the painstakingly reconstructed interiors and severely damaged the building. The city has committed to reconstructing it in Mackintosh's distinctive style; it is scheduled to reopen in 2030.

 EATING IN GLASGOW: OUR PICKS

Finnieston: Gastropub with a below-decks atmosphere and a menu focusing on Scottish seafood. *noon-midnight Sun-Thu, to 1am Fri & Sat* ££

Mother India: A stalwart among Glasgow curry houses – the quality and innovation at this Indian restaurant are second to none. *hours vary* ££

Stravaigin: Constantly pushing the boundaries of originality without breaking the bank, this is a popular choice for a Sunday roast. *noon-midnight* ££

Hanoi Bike Shop: This upbeat Ruthven La spot has creative takes on Vietnamese food, using fresh ingredients and homemade tofu. *noon-9pm* ££

ROB ROY

The wilds of the Trossachs and the historic network of cattle-droving roads were once stomping ground for Clan MacGregor – most famously, the notorious outlaw and folk hero Rob Roy MacGregor. Born in the village of Glengyle in 1671, Rob Roy was a skilled cattle thief and an exceptional swordsman. He was an illustrious character, described as Scotland's answer to Robin Hood; his exploits are romanticised in the writings of Sir Walter Scott and played out on the big screen in the 1995 film *Rob Roy* starring Liam Neeson. Follow in his footsteps with a drink at the **Drover's Inn** (*thedroversinn. co.uk*), a reputedly haunted 300-year-old pub, and visit his **final resting place** in the graveyard at Balquhidder Old Kirk.

Disguised by an unremarkable facade, **Randall's Antique & Vintage Centre** has some two-dozen vendors peddling an excellent range of vintage objects. And look out for **Barras Art & Design** (*baadglasgow.com*), with its pop-up stalls, regular weekend events, busy courtyard bar and menu of fusion food. It's quite a contrast to the rest of the market but it works well.

Loch Lomond & the Trossachs National Park

TIME FROM EDINBURGH: **2HR**

Forests, gardens and glens

The **Great Trossachs Forest National Nature Reserve** (*lochlomond-trossachs.org*) is undergoing a major regeneration project, with two million trees already planted as part of a 200-year plan. Experience this precious medley of scenery on the 30-mile **Great Trossachs Path** from Callander to Inversnaid or choose from one of nine waymarked walking trails in Glen Finglas.

Take a leisurely, low-level walk through the woods at **Loch Ard** near Aberfoyle. Six miles away, following part of the iconic Duke's Pass, is the **Three Lochs Forest Drive**. This 7-mile driving route takes in Lochan Reòidhte, Loch Drunkie and Loch Achray.

The national park extends across to the remote Cowal Peninsula and the ever-enchanting Puck's Glen. Nearby, **Benmore Botanic Garden** (*rbge.org.uk; adult/child £9/7.80*) has 49 hectares of rare plants, vibrant rhododendrons and giant trees.

Lochs, islands and boat trips

Swarms of visitors gravitate towards Loch Lomond and its bonnie banks, especially when the sun makes an appearance. A range of water-sports activities are available with **Loch Lomond Leisure** (*lochlomond-scotland.com; rental £20-25*) at Luss and Rowardennan.

Cruise the loch for a closer look at its islands and islets: **Sweeney's Cruises** (*sweeneyscruiseco.com; adult/child from £16/10.50*) departs from Balloch, while **Cruise Loch Lomond** (*cruiselochlomond.co.uk; from £16*) offers trips and water-bus services from various locations. From Luss, take the water bus to **Inchcailloch**, a national nature reserve. Ascend the short summit path for incredible views, visit the ancient burial ground and picnic on the golden-sand beach.

EATING IN LOCH LOMOND & THE TROSSACHS NATIONAL PARK: OUR PICKS

Broch: Family-run establishment in Strathyre offering homemade soda bread, Italian coffee and full Scottish breakfasts. *10am-4pm Thu-Tue* £

Boatshed: A picture-perfect cafe with outdoor decking overlooking Loch Goil: soup, toasties, coffee and cake with a view. *10am-4pm* ££

Oak Tree Inn: Post-hike pub classics, burgers and pizzas in Balmaha; tables outside plus adjoining ice-cream parlour and coffee shop. *8am-11pm* ££

Clachan Inn: Hearty meals in Scotland's oldest licensed pub; try the haggis bonbons. Located in Drymen. *11am-11pm Mon-Thu, 12.30-11pm Sun* ££

The Scottish Highlands

EPIC DRIVES | VIEWS | DRAMATIC HISTORY

The Highland landscapes may seem timeless, but they haven't always been this empty. In the blink of an eye, following the Clearances of the late 18th century, the Highlands became some of Europe's least populated places. Centres such as Inverness, Fort William and Aviemore have bounced back, but there remain many wild and empty spaces just waiting to be explored. All you need to do is decide where to go first.

The smart city of Inverness, with its hilltop castle, is a fine starting point before escaping into the rugged hills, rock and heather of Cairngorms National Park or searching for monsters on shimmering Loch Ness. You can ascend the snow-hazed summits of the Nevis Range, or join scarf-wearing *Harry Potter* fans on the steam train to Glenfinnan.

Wherever your journey takes you, you can end each day with a warming whisky in front of a crackling pub fire.

Inverness

Discover the transformed Inverness Castle

Inverness city centre is dominated by the baronial turrets of hilltop **Inverness Castle** (*invernesscastle.scot; adult/child £20/14*). Dating from the 1840s, it replaced a medieval castle blown up by the Jacobites in 1746. The castle served as courthouse and prison until 2020, and reopened in 2025 after a regeneration project.

Gorgeous gardens and terraces surround the castle, with panoramic views south towards the Great Glen and north to the looming Ben Wyvis. Look out for the statue depicting Flora MacDonald with her collie dog, Flossie, gazing west towards Skye where she helped Bonnie Prince Charlie escape to France in the aftermath of the Battle of Culloden.

Inside the castle, colourful installations and interactive displays regale you with stories of Highland history and Gaelic culture, guided by the spirit of a *seanchaidh* (Gaelic for a traditional storyteller) and culminating in an immersive fly-through of Highland landscapes.

GETTING AROUND

The Highlands cover a huge swathe of northern Scotland, from the Cairngorms to John O'Groats. By far the best way to explore the region, having your own wheels allows you to stop whenever you like to soak up the scenery. Buses (mainly run by Scottish Citylink) and trains (run by ScotRail) connect the region's bigger towns, such as Inverness, Fort William, Aviemore, Ullapool and Wick.

☑ **TOP TIP**

Be careful when driving in this part of Scotland. Some roads can get very narrow, not to mention how remote they are, too. Prepare for all kinds of weather and watch out for sheep and deer on the roads.

THE JACOBITE REBELLIONS

The Jacobite rebellions of the 18th century were not about Scotland vs England. This was a civil war between the armed forces of the Hanoverian monarchy that had ruled Britain since 1688, and supporters of the exiled King James (hence the name 'Jacobites' – from Jacob, Latin for James) who wanted to restore a Catholic Stuart king to the British throne. From the Battle of Killiecrankie in 1689 to the final showdown at Culloden in 1746, there was no simple divide – Scots, English and Irish, Catholics and Protestants, Highlanders and Lowlanders, fought on both sides of the conflict.

QUINNY74/SHUTTERSTOCK

Culloden Visitor Centre

Comprehending Culloden

The last pitched battle ever fought on British soil took place on the eastern edge of Inverness in 1746. The Battle of Culloden saw the crushing of Bonnie Prince Charlie's dream of a restored Stuart monarchy. The Jacobite defeat sounded the death knell for the traditional Highland way of life; the horrors of the Clearances, when thousands were forcibly evicted from their homes, soon followed.

The sombre moor where the conflict took place has scarcely changed in almost three centuries. The National Trust for Scotland's **Culloden Visitor Centre** *(nts.org.uk; adult/child £16.50/12)* explains the battle, including the lead-up and the aftermath, with perspectives from both sides. An innovative 360-degree movie puts you in the middle of the mayhem. After a look around the museum, join a 45-minute guided tour of the battlefield where 1500 Jacobites were slaughtered by government forces in less than an hour.

The Nessie phenomenon

The ideal way to fathom the mystery of the Loch Ness Monster takes half a day and comes in two parts, both beginning at **Drumnadrochit** – a village seized by monster madness, its

EATING IN INVERNESS: OUR PICKS

MacGregor's: Gastropub serving Scottish food and beer by day, and traditional Scottish music by night. *11am-midnight Mon-Sat, from noon Sun* ££

Bad Girl Bakery & Cafe: Breakfast and lunch spot in the Victorian Market, with fresh pastries and top-notch coffee. *9am-6pm Mon-Sat, 10am-5pm Sun* £

Mustard Seed: Bustling riverside restaurant with a Mediterranean vibe serving seafood, steak and vegetarian dishes. *noon-2.30pm & 5-9.15pm* ££

Rocpool: Stylish bistro with a Med-influenced menu focusing on quality Scottish produce, especially seafood. *noon-2pm & 5.30-9pm Tue-Sat* £££

WEST HIGHLAND WAY IN A DAY

If you don't have time to hike the whole trail, you can walk (or mountain bike) this scenic stretch in a day.

START	END	LENGTH
Bridge of Orchy	Glencoe Mountain Resort	12 miles; 6 hours

From the train station, cross the main road to the ❶ **Bridge of Orchy** that gives the village its name, built in 1752 by General Caulfield as part of a military road-building project to pacify the Highlands.

Cross the bridge and take the footpath on the left. The trail climbs steeply over a ridge, following the route of Caulfield's road; pause at ❷ **Mam Carraigh** viewpoint for a grand panorama over Loch Tulla before descending to the Inveroran Hotel.

Continue on the tarmac to its end at ❸ **Forest Lodge**, where a gate marks the continuation of the trail along the route of the old road built by

Thomas Telford in 1811 (the main road to Glen Coe until the 1930s).

The stony trail crosses wild moorland with the hills of the Black Mount to your left, crossing Telford's ❹ **Ba Bridge** at the halfway point and passing the gloriously isolated ruin of ❺ **Ba Cottage**, a 19th-century shepherd's house.

As you round the shoulder of the hill, you'll get a ❻ **view of Buachaille Etive Mor** guarding the entrance to Glen Coe before the trail descends to ❼ **Glencoe Mountain Resort**. An hourly Citylink bus service stops at the junction with the main road and will take you back to your starting point or on to Fort William.

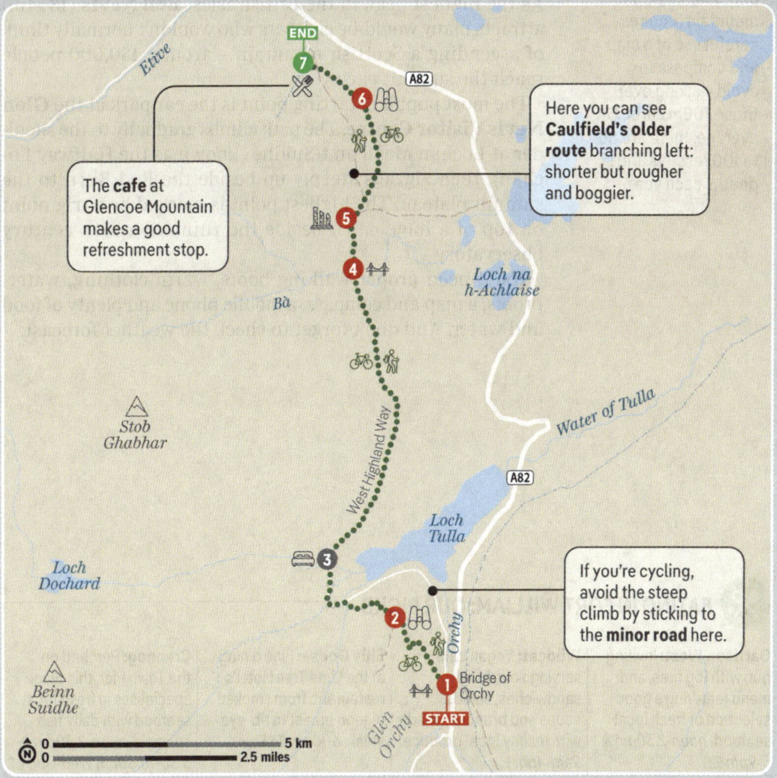

END ❼

Etive

A82

❻

Here you can see **Caulfield's older route** branching left: shorter but rougher and boggier.

The **cafe** at Glencoe Mountain makes a good refreshment stop.

❺

❹

Loch na h-Achlaise

Bà

West Highland Way

△ *Stob Ghabhar*

Water of Tulla

A82

Loch Tulla

Loch Dochard

❸

If you're cycling, avoid the steep climb by sticking to the **minor road** here.

❷

Orchy

Bridge of Orchy

△ *Beinn Suidhe*

❶ Bridge of Orchy

START

Glen Orchy

N
0 ———————— 5 km
0 ———————— 2.5 miles

BEN NEVIS FACTS

Here are a few hard facts to mull over before you try racing up the tourist track to the top of Ben Nevis.

The summit plateau is bound by 700m-high cliffs and has a sub-Arctic climate. At the summit, it can snow on any day of the year. The summit is wrapped in cloud nine days out of 10. In thick clouds, visibility at the summit can be 10m or less, and in such conditions, the only safe way off the mountain requires careful use of a map and compass to avoid walking over those 700m cliffs. On average, there are 80 to 100 rescues and six deaths each year.

gift shops bulging with Nessie cuddly toys. Take a one-hour **Deepscan Cruise** (*lochness.com/cruises; adult/child £21/18*), and get a feel for the huge size and depth of the loch while keeping a close eye on the boat's echo sounder. Then join a guided tour of the **Loch Ness Centre** (*lochness.com; adult/child £13.95/12.55*), an entertaining introduction to the history of the monster and a clear-sighted look at the evidence for and against its existence.

Fort William

All aboard the Harry Potter Express

The **Jacobite Steam Train** (*westcoastrailways.co.uk; adult/child £65/36*) travels the scenic two-hour run between Fort William and Mallaig. One of the great railway journeys of the world, the route crosses the historic Glenfinnan Viaduct, made famous in the *Harry Potter* films.

Trains depart from Fort William train station at 10.15am and (in peak season only) 2.40pm, and return from Mallaig at 2.10pm and 6.40pm. There's a brief stop at Glenfinnan station, and you get 1½ hours in Mallaig (two hours on the afternoon service).

Climbing Ben Nevis

As the highest peak in the British Isles, **Ben Nevis** (1344m) attracts many would-be climbers who wouldn't normally think of ascending a Scottish mountain – around 130,000 people reach the summit each year.

The most popular starting point is the car park at the **Glen Nevis Visitor Centre**. The path climbs gradually to the shoulder at Lochan Meall an t-Suidhe (known as the Halfway Lochan), then zigzags steeply up beside the Red Burn to the summit plateau. The highest point is marked by a trig point on top of a huge cairn beside the ruins of a 19th-century observatory.

You'll need proper walking boots, warm clothing, waterproofs, a map and compass, a mobile phone and plenty of food and water. And don't forget to check the weather forecast.

 EATING IN FORT WILLIAM: OUR PICKS

Garrison West: Inviting pub with log fires, and menu featuring a good selection of fresh local seafood. *noon-2.30pm & 5-9pm* ££

Wildcat: Vegan cafe serving sourdough sandwiches, salads, soups and brunches made with mainly local produce. *9am-4pm* £

Silly Goose: Fine dining at the Lime Tree Hotel's restaurant, from smoked pigeon breast to rib-eye steak. *6-10pm* £££

Crannog: Perched on the Town Pier, this place specialises in fresh local seafood with daily fish specials. *noon-2.30pm & 5.30-10.30pm Wed-Sun* ££

The Scottish Islands

MOUNTAINS | NEOLITHIC SITES | ISLANDS

Scotland's islands are wild, windswept and epic. These untamed corners of Britain aren't easy to travel, but the reward is some of the country's most remarkable scenery.

The main draw is Skye, an island of big landscapes: sharp-toothed mountain peaks, emerald-green river valleys and crashing cliff-edge waterfalls. Visitors flock here in their thousands to see the jagged peaks of the Quiraing or to skirt along the ridge of the Black Cuillin mountains. But there's Portree, too, a pretty harbourside settlement with colourful houses overlooking a sheltered bay, as well as top-notch whisky distilleries.

Or you can venture further afield to Scotland's far-flung northern islands like Orkney and Shetland. These starkly beautiful islands, their coastlines chiselled by North Sea storms and Atlantic gales, are a haven for wildlife and a hotbed of history. Prehistoric stone circles, Caribbean-like beaches, seabird-studded cliffs and Viking-inspired festivals await.

GETTING AROUND

Getting to the islands is easiest by ferry, either as a foot passenger or with your car. The main operators are CalMac and Orkney Ferries. Loganair flights are available between many of the islands. Once on the islands, travelling by car is by far the most efficient way of getting around.

Skye

Take to the water

The staggering landscapes of Skye can make it tempting to stay on terra firma, but those who head out to sea get to experience the island from a whole new perspective. Sign up for Rona boat trips from Portree with **Seaflower Skye** *(seaflowerskye.com; incl lunch £145)*, or get closer to the water (and the wildlife) on a sea kayak with **Sea to Skye Xperience** *(seatoskyexperience.co.uk; half-/full day £45/95)*, departing from Broadford. Prefer to be in the water rather than on it? Join a multiday diving expedition with **Dive & Sea the Hebrides** *(dive-and-sea-the-hebrides.co.uk; 3 days from £355)* to explore some of the incredible marine life, reefs and wrecks around the island. However you choose to take to the water, remember to look back at the Skye shoreline for stunning views of the Old Man of Storr and the Cuillin Hills.

☑ **TOP TIP**

These sparsely populated islands have limited accommodation, so it's important to book well in advance to secure a hotel or B&B for your time here. Also, not everything (restaurants, museums, etc) is open year-round, so plan ahead.

THE SCOTTISH ISLANDS

The drive of your life

Turning out of **Broadford** (30 minutes' drive south of Portree) and onto the B8083, it doesn't feel like you're about to embark on one of Scotland's most dazzling drives. But as the road narrows to a single-track lane, you'll notice the round-topped Beinn na Caillich mountain and know your adventure has begun.

The next 30 minutes of driving is a blur of unbelievable vistas: the picturesque valley of Strath Suardal, the roofless ruin of a church overlooking Loch Cill Chriosd, and the views of the solemn Bla Bheinn mountain across Loch Slapin. As you approach **Elgol**, traditional crofts lead the way down to the town's pier, which has perhaps the best vista of all: the Cuillin Hills jutting skywards across the water.

A duo of drams

Founded in 1830, Talisker was Skye's only legal whisky distillery for the better part of two centuries and a globally popular single malt. But today, following the 2021 release of the first whiskies by new local producers, whisky lovers can visit multiple distilleries on a day tour.

Start where it all began at **Talisker Distillery** (*malts.com; tours from £15*), around 30 minutes' drive southwest of Portree. The distillery tour and tasting allow you to sample a mix of smoky, salty classic whiskies and rare, sweet expressions matured in sherry and port casks. After a brief walk along the sands of Talisker Bay (for some sobering sea air), travel south to the Sleat peninsula to visit **Torabhaig Distillery** (*torabhaig.com; tours from £15*). Sit in the courtyard, flanked by old stone farmhouses, to savour its lightly peated, vanilla-sweetened single malt.

JUSTIN FOULKES/LONELY PLANET

Ring of Brodgar, Orkney

Orkney

A wild Neolithic heart

At the centre of Orkney, and spanning much of the West Mainland, lies the **Heart of Neolithic Orkney** *(historicenviron ment.scot)*, a UNESCO World Heritage site. This is a good starting point for the islands' wider archaeological heritage. Made up of **Skara Brae** *(adult/child £10/6)*, the **Ring of Brodgar** *(free)*, the **Standing Stones of Stenness** *(free)* and **Maeshowe** *(adult/child £10/6)*, these fascinating sites are all within a stone's throw from one another. They have forced archaeologists to rethink settlement patterns throughout Neolithic Britain and offer a tantalising glimpse into life 5000 years ago.

Entry to Skara Brae and Maeshowe should be booked online as far in advance as possible. The best plan for visiting the sites in summer is to book Skara Brae for 4pm and Maeshowe for 7pm.

BEST SIGHTS ON SKYE'S TROTTERNISH PENINSULA

Lealt Falls: Gaze upon the 90m cascade and look out for ruins of the old diatomine factory and salmon smokehouses below.

Old Man of Storr: This eye-catching, 50m-high shard of rock is a 45-minute hike from the main road car park.

Kilt Rock: Admire this high cliff face of vertical basalt columns (which look like pleats on a kilt).

Skye Museum of Island Life: Learn about traditional island crofting life at this preserved village of thatched cottages.

Fairy Glen: Explore a Hobbiton-esque landscape of impossibly green hillocks, placid pools and castle-like rock formations.

An Corran Beach: Go in search of 165-million-year-old dinosaur footprints at low tide.

 EATING IN PORTREE (SKYE): OUR PICKS

Café Arriba: Climb the steep stairs to this laid-back cafe for a hearty Scottish breakfast or seafood-filled lunch. *8am-4pm Thu-Tue £*

Pizza in the Skye: Street-food truck serving thin-crust wood-fired pizza and garlic bread. Order online in advance. *noon-8pm Tue-Sat £*

Sea Breezes: This place is all about seafood: opt for the platter with salmon, mussels and langoustines. *noon-2pm & 5.30-9pm Tue-Sat ££*

Dulse & Brose: Try modern Scottish cuisine with an Asian twist, featuring fresh Skye seafood, venison and cheese. *5-10pm £££*

THE NORTHERN LIGHTS

Shetland lies 60 degrees north of the equator, putting it at a similar latitude to Anchorage, Alaska and the southern tip of Greenland. This makes it the best place in Britain to see the northern lights (aurora borealis), known in the local dialect as the 'mirrie dancers'. Midwinter is the best time for viewing; **AuroraWatchUK** (aurorawatch.lancs.ac.uk) predicts when the aurora is likely to be visible.

Shetland's high latitude also results in the phenomenon known locally as the 'simmer dim'. A few weeks on either side of midsummer (21 June), the sun doesn't set until 10.30pm and rises again five hours later. Between sunset and sunrise there is no proper darkness, just a modest twilight. Not quite the midnight sun, but close.

THE TRIGGERHAPPYDOG/SHUTTERSTOCK

Puffins, Isle of Noss, Shetland

Shetland

Seabirds and seals

The little **Isle of Noss** (nature.scot) lies just 3 miles east of Lerwick, on the far side of Bressay. Awe-inspiring sea cliffs on its east coast rise to 180m, providing nesting sites for more than 100,000 pairs of breeding seabirds, including gannets, guillemots, kittiwakes, shags and puffins – one of the great seabird spectaculars of Shetland.

Book a two-hour boat tour with **Seabirds & Seals** (seabirds-and-seals.com; adult/child £60/30) to get up close and personal with the birds; trips depart from **Victoria Pier** in Lerwick up to six times daily.

EATING IN LERWICK (SHETLAND): OUR PICKS

Peerie Shop Cafe: An absolute gem of a place, serving the best coffee, soups, scones and sandwiches in town. 8am-4pm Tue-Sat £

Fjarå: Scandi-style cafe-bar with superb sea views and great breakfast, lunch and dinner menus. 8am-10pm Tue-Sat, 9am-5pm Sun ££

No 88 Kitchen & Bar: Hip and relaxed, with seasonal dishes championing Shetland seafood and lamb. 10am-10pm Wed-Sat, noon-4pm Sun ££

Mareel Cafe: Waterside arts-centre cafe serving locally made sandwiches, soups, wraps and salads. 10am-9pm Tue-Thu & Sun, to midnight Fri & Sat £

Places We Love to Stay

£ Budget ££ Midrange £££ Top end

London

MAP p121

Hoxton Holborn ££ Ultra-chic yet affordable, with hip rooms full of design details and leather, velvets and mid-century furniture. Its social spaces are always happening.

CitizenM Tower of London ££ If you don't get the room with windows framing Tower Bridge, there's always the roof terrace.

Londoner £££ The sexy Leicester Sq newcomer has multiple trendy eateries and a wellness retreat with a big pool.

One Aldwych £££ An independent hotel in a historic building, One has been renovated with relaxing plush, neutral decor, and has fabulous theatre views.

South Place £££ A hip, design-led five-star hotel with all the trimmings of luxury, including a Michelin-starred seafood restaurant.

Sea Containers £££ Luxury hotel with the best views of the skyline as well as a spa, a cinema and an award-winning cocktail bar.

Park Plaza £££ Four-star hotel in a central location with views to die for. You can see the London Eye right from your window.

Padstow

Trewornan Manor £££ Posh B&B in a 17th-century, Grade II–listed manor house surrounded by 25 glorious acres.

Harbour Hotel Padstow £££ Formerly the Metropole, this period beauty commands a panoramic view over the estuary.

Land's End

Old Success Inn ££ Sennen Cove's beloved seaside pub has plush, colourful rooms and glorious coastal views.

Land's End Hotel £££ Perched on the very edge of Britain, this hotel has luxurious rooms and hard-to-beat sea views.

Bristol

Artists Residence ££ Georgian townhouse with a range of industrial-chic rooms, a cafe, kitchen and lounge bar.

Number 38 £££ Upmarket B&B with sweeping city views from contemporary rooms on the edge of the Downs.

Bath

Brooks ££ A scattering of antiques meet plush modern furnishings at this comfy, fairly central bolthole with an honesty bar.

Queensberry £££ Stylish Queensberry is Bath's luxury choice. Heritage roots meet snazzy furnishings in these Georgian townhouses.

Birmingham

MAP p139

Bloc £ Smart Japanese pod-style rooms alongside golden design touches nodding to the historic Jewellery Quarter's past.

Grand Hotel Birmingham £££ Plush art deco hotel where Winston Churchill once stayed. Don't miss the indulgent afternoon tea at Parisian-style cocktail bar Madeleine.

Stratford-upon-Avon

Arden Hotel ££ Rustic rooms and a magnificent brasserie, perfectly located across the street for attending performances by the Royal Shakespeare Company.

Hotel du Vin ££ Smart Georgian boutique hotel with a French bistro, a wine cellar and 46 cosy rooms. Short walk to the train station.

Nottingham

St James Hotel ££ Stylish hotel with contemporary rooms, an art gallery and a fine location near Nottingham Castle.

Lace Market Hotel ££ Georgian townhouse in Lace Market area with 51 individual bedrooms, suites and feature rooms.

Liverpool

MAP p143

Titanic Liverpool ££ Former dockside warehouse packed with character and huge amounts of space. Don't miss the Rum bar pouring sweet spirits from Guyana, Barbados and Cuba.

Municipal Hotel & Spa £££ Lavish Victorian building topped by a soaring clock tower. Hosts a glittering palm court alongside a spa and fitness centre.

Bakewell

Rutland Arms Hotel ££ Nineteenth-century coaching inn offering 32 refurbished bedrooms, an excellent restaurant and an extensive wine menu.

H Boutique Hotel ££ Luxury boutique hotel with 10 stylish suites, each telling a local story beginning with 'H'.

Cardiff

MAP p147

Coal Exchange Hotel ££ Former hub of global coal trading transformed into a

55-room hotel with restaurant. Historic features, Jacuzzi baths and great location.

Parkgate Hotel £££ Luxury city-centre hotel next to Principality Stadium. Lovely on-site spa, bar and restaurant. Rooms are spacious and comfortable.

Bannau Brycheiniog (Brecon Beacons) National Park

Lodge ££ Blissfully poised on Llanfrynach's fringes, this B&B has country flair and lovingly tended gardens overlooking the hills.

Peterstone Court £££ On the banks of the Usk, this Georgian manor brims with period charm and Beacons views. The spa and heated outdoor pool are huge draws.

Portmeirion & Blaenau Ffestiniog

Treks Bunkhouse £ This family-run bunkhouse high in the Moelwyn mountains makes a terrific base for cycling, hiking and canoeing. There's a barbecue area with mountain views.

Hotel Portmeirion £££ Historic hotel in Portmeirion, with Dwyryd Estuary views. Gourmet dining, a heated outdoor pool and substantial breakfasts.

Edinburgh   MAP p154

Code – The Court £ Colourful, charming and cheap, this old courthouse prison turned luxury hostel has extremely comfy pod beds and tasty waffle-heavy breakfasts.

Angels Share Hotel ££ Connected to the longstanding bar of the same name, this hotel offers compact, individually designed rooms adorned with tartan and portraits of famous Scots.

Witchery £££ One of Edinburgh's most uniquely decadent stays, this historic hotel is all about plush antique furniture, indulgent themed suites and candlelit fine dining.

Kimpton Charlotte Square £££ Seven Georgian townhouses were combined to make this charming hotel, with elegant rooms and suites, a small spa and two exceptional restaurants.

Glasshouse £££ Chic, modern and luxurious, this magnificent stone- and glass-fronted hotel at the top of Leith Walk is renowned for its elegant rooftop garden.

Glasgow

Citizen M ££ Modern, business-focused hotel offering minimalist rooms with king-sized beds, decent showers and an app controlling the lighting, thermostat, blinds and more.

Glasgow Grosvenor Hotel ££ Historic hotel opposite the Botanic Gardens offering classically stylish rooms, plus a fine restaurant and gin bar.

Alamo Guest House £££ Antique furnishings and modern comforts combine in this elegant, family-run guesthouse,

located on the edge of Kelvingrove Park.

Inverness

Rocpool Reserve £££ The swishest place in town is a Georgian manor with River Ness panoramas, sunken baths, hot tubs and private balconies.

Culloden House Hotel £££ A converted mid-18th-century Palladian manor house where Bonnie Prince Charlie once stayed.

Skye

Carters Rest ££ This Neist Point–adjacent B&B has large bedrooms, great food and wonderful coastal views.

Skeabost House Hotel £££ Once a hunting lodge, this luxury lochside hotel has one of Skye's best restaurants.

Shetland

Rockvilla Guest House ££ A relaxing, welcoming retreat in a stone-built villa with a pretty garden in central Lerwick.

Belmont House £££ This 18th-century Georgian country house close to the Unst ferry pier provides luxurious B&B accommodation.

EDWARD HAYLAN/SHUTTERSTOCK

Hotel Portmeirion

Practicalities

HEALTHCARE
When Britain left the EU, it lost the reciprocal healthcare agreement provided by the European Health Insurance Card. Travellers from the EU and other nations must now have private travel insurance to cover any medical care. Choose your policy carefully and make sure you get one that includes emergency flights home.

DAVE SMITH 1965/SHUTTERSTOCK

VISAS
Citizens of Australia, Canada, EEA (European Economic Area) nations, Israel, Japan, New Zealand, Switzerland and the USA can visit Britain without a visa. Check the latest visa rules before you travel (*gov.uk/check-uk-visa*).

LGBTIQ+ TRAVELLERS
Britain is regarded as one of the most LGBTIQ+-friendly travel destinations in the world. London, Brighton, Manchester, Birmingham, Bristol, Edinburgh and Cardiff all have flourishing gay scenes, while other cities and small towns have active communities, too. However, LGBTIQ+ hate crime, particularly transphobia, is on the rise. Some areas still harbour pockets of homophobic hostility as well.

ELECTRICITY
Unlike most of the world, Britain uses the plug type G, which is the plug with three rectangular pins in a triangular pattern (on a 230V supply voltage and 50Hz) – so it's wise to bring an adaptor.

OPENING HOURS
Banks 9.30am–4pm or 5pm Monday to Friday (some to 1pm Saturday)
Pubs and bars Noon–11pm Monday to Thursday, to midnight or 1am Friday and Saturday, 12.30pm–11pm Sunday
Restaurants Lunch noon–3pm, dinner 6–9pm or 10pm (later in cities)
Shops 9am–5.30pm (6pm in cities) Monday to Saturday, 11am–5pm Sunday

LANGUAGES
The number of Welsh, Scots, Scottish Gaelic and Cornish speakers in Britain is on the rise. Meanwhile, both Polish and Romanian are spoken by over 500,000 people in the UK, with Punjabi and Urdu not far behind.

PUBLIC HOLIDAYS
New Year's Day 1 January (plus 2 January in Scotland)
Easter March/April (Good Friday to Easter Monday inclusive)
May Day First Monday in May

Spring Bank Holiday Last Monday in May
Summer Bank Holiday Last Monday in August
Christmas Day 25 December
Boxing Day 26 December

WORLDOFDOMINIC/SHUTTERSTOCK

Liverpool Street tube station

Arriving

Most visitors reach Britain by air and generally arrive at one of London's two largest airports: Heathrow (often chaotic and crowded; 15 miles west of central London) and Gatwick (busy; 30 miles south of central London). The capital has three other airports: Stansted, Luton and London City. Other options for arriving in Britain are by boat and by train.

By Air
European travellers can, for the most part, fly to all corners of Britain. Long-haul travellers will almost always fly into Heathrow. London's new Elizabeth Line is the most cost-efficient way to head into the capital once through immigration and baggage.

By Boat & Train
Britain has several passenger ports, with the most significant being Southampton, Dover and Liverpool, which handle a mix of ferries and cruise ships. Eurostar trains from Paris, Amsterdam and Brussels arrive at London St Pancras station.

MONEY

Currency: Pound sterling (£)

WAYS TO PAY
An increasing number of shops, bars and restaurants only accept card payments. While contactless is king, keep some change handy for local markets, toilets and seasonal car parking (especially on the coast).

TIPPING
Not obligatory, but tipping around 10% in restaurants and cafes is the norm. Tips may be added to your bill as a 'service charge' (12.5% in London). Unless you're eating and receiving table service, there's no need to tip bar staff.

HOW TO SAVE MONEY
Between Edinburgh's £7.50 pints and £163.40 train tickets for London to Manchester, Britain can make your credit card cry. Booking ahead saves money. Reserve B&Bs and private rooms in hostels at least two months in advance (book direct for the best deals). Swap trains for coaches (or book off-peak train travel 12 weeks in advance). Build itineraries around free museums such as the Scottish National Gallery and the British Museum.

Getting Around

Transport in Britain can be expensive compared to continental Europe. Bus and rail services are sparse in more remote parts of the country, but between them serve most destinations (expect a more sporadic service at weekends). In coastal regions, some bus services only run during the summer season.

Best Ways to Get Around
A car is useful for visiting remote regions in the countryside, mountains and on the coast. You're unlikely to need one in major cities. Trains are a good alternative, with frequent and extensive countrywide coverage. Coaches offer cheap city-to-city travel.

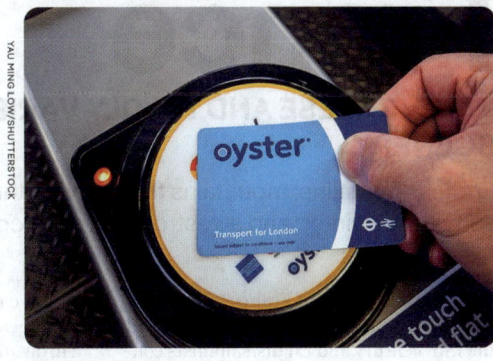

YAU MING LOW/SHUTTERSTOCK

Local Networks
Traveline *(traveline.info)* covers bus, coach, train and taxi services nationwide. It offers online timetables, a journey planner and limited fare information. **National Rail Enquiries** *(nationalrail.co.uk)* has downloadable maps of the rail network. **National Express** *(nationalexpress.com)* has interactive route maps for its coaches.

Coaches
Long-distance buses (called coaches in Britain) are nearly always the cheapest way to get around. **National Express** *(nationalexpress.com),* **Scottish Citylink** *(citylink.co.uk)* and **Megabus** *(uk.megabus.com)* are the major operators. Book early or off-peak for the cheapest fares.

Tickets & PlusBus
Ticketing in Britain is interconnected. If the train doesn't get you all the way to your destination, add a **PlusBus** *(plusbus.info)* supplement when reserving to validate your train ticket for onward travel by bus.

Driving
Having a car or motorbike means you can be independent and reach remote places. Most roads are in good or very good condition, but downsides include traffic jams, the high cost of fuel, pricey city parking and, in London, the Congestion Charge.

DRIVING ESSENTIALS

Drive on the left side

17

Driving age is 17

Speed limit is 70mph on motorways, 60mph on single-carriageway roads and generally 30mph in urban areas

Curated by
Anna Richards

France

WINE, CHEESE AND WILDLY VARIED SCENERY

Endless coastline; mountains that provide thrills, be it summer or winter; and a gastronomy so good it invented Michelin stars.

Who doesn't dream of France? Ever since rich Europeans flocked to the Riviera in the 18th century and English alpinists conquered mountain peaks to unveil tourism in the Alps, it has been a highly desirable place to go.

A little bit of everything got sprinkled into the mix in France. Beaches along the Côte d'Azur that range from sugar-soft spun gold to rocky limestone inlets, mountain giants (including the highest peak in the Alps, Mont Blanc) that soften to hills peppered with lavender fields and olive groves in Provence, châteaux that span rivers and pierce the sky with a hundred turrets. Wherever you are in the country, you're never far from a wine region, and you can bet there'll be plenty of local, AOP cheeses too.

Throw in some of the most instantly recognisable monuments in the world – the Eiffel Tower, Notre-Dame and the Louvre to name a few – and it's no surprise that France consistently hits the headlines as 'the world's top tourist destination', notching up 100 million annual visitors in 2024. Making it even easier to get around responsibly, greening public transport and encouraging longer sojourns are top priorities for a country whose new 'dream big, live slow' road map has one overriding goal: becoming the global benchmark for sustainable tourism by 2030. Travel slowly, and if you can, avoid July and August.

THE MAIN AREAS

For places to stay in France, see p242

MISTERVLAD/SHUTTERSTOCK

Left: Plateau de Valensole (p229), Gorges du Verdon; Above: Notre Dame (p185), Paris

LOIRE VALLEY
Châteaux, vineyards and cyclepaths.
p216

PROVENCE
Sun, sea and rosé
p220

BORDEAUX
Historic, wine-infused port city.
p232

Mont St-Michel, p195

When the tide rises, this monastery is completely cut off from the mainland, guarded by bobbing seals and wheeling seabirds.

Loire Valley, p216

Hundreds of châteaux framed by vineyards and waterways characterise this postcard-perfect region, which was once home to the French royal family.

Bordeaux, p232

Synonymous with wine, Bordeaux is well watered by its viticultural neighbours. Not all its history is edifying, though, and much of Bordeaux's wealth was ill-obtained.

CAR

Driving is the best way to see much of the French countryside, but it can be expensive, and *péages* (tolls) on highways quickly cost as much as, or more than, fuel. Cut costs by using a ridesharing platform like BlaBlaCar (blablacar.fr).

TRAIN

One of the best ways to get around. High-speed TGV train services link many of France's major cities, including Paris–Lyon (two hours), Paris–Bordeaux (two hours) and Paris–Marseille (3½ hours). Slower, TER services also run between cities, as well as to more rural areas.

BUS

Long-distance buses, including BlaBlaCar Bus and FlixBus, are often the cheapest way of travelling long distances (particularly into neighbouring countries like Spain, Switzerland and Italy), although they tend to take longer than the train.

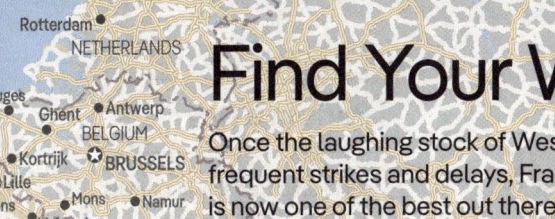

Find Your Way

Once the laughing stock of Western Europe for frequent strikes and delays, France's public transport is now one of the best out there. The strikes still happen, but they're generally scheduled in advance – check *cestlagreve.fr* for information.

Paris, p180

City of light and love, the place that inspired everyone from Hemingway to Fitzgerald, Paris' reputation precedes it.

French Alps, p202

Legendary for skiing, but increasingly a summer destination, as locals and tourists escape ever-common heatwaves to hike and mountain-bike through Europe's most dramatic scenery.

Lyon, p209

Hungry travellers arrive here guided by their stomachs, and find a city that's older than Paris, with architecture spanning Roman to Renaissance to avant-garde.

Provence, p220

A region that veers from wildly enthralling city life to tranquil village idyll – complete with fine wine, lavender fields and coastal castaway coves.

Plan Your Time

You could spend years in France and not see it all. If pushed for time, pick a region or two to savour.

ANDRE QUINOU/SHUTTERSTOCK

Château de Chenonceau (p218), Chenonceaux

Paris in a Day

● Montmartre's slinking streets and steep staircases are enchanting, especially in the early morning when tourists are few. Head to the hilltop **Sacré-Cœur** (p189) basilica to soak up views over Paris. Wander down to Pigalle for lunch, to rub shoulders with fellow diners at the long tables at **Bouillon Pigalle** (p188).

● In the afternoon, potter through the Île de la Cité, site of **Notre Dame** (p185), painstakingly restored after the 2019 fire, and climb the 422 steps up the South Tower. Then put your feet up with a good book at **Shakespeare and Company** (p189).

● In the evening, ascend the **Eiffel Tower** (p180) to experience glittering *la ville lumière* (City of Light) by night, before changing perspective over dinner and drinks at floating restaurant **Francette** (p181), looking up at the tower.

SEASONAL HIGHLIGHTS

France is strictly seasonal. Visit the Alps in May, for example, and you'll find very little open. Shoulder season often has the best of both worlds.

FEBRUARY

It's the height of **ski season** in the Alps, but the school holidays mean sky-high prices and packed pistes in ski resorts. In Provence, Nice celebrates an epic **carnival** (p224) for a fortnight in late February and early March.

APRIL

The arrival of spring means **Lyon's rivers** come to life, with *péniche* (narrowboat) beer gardens spilling onto the banks. Water levels are high for **kayaking** the Ardèche River, although it's chilly for swimming.

MAY

In a month splattered with public holidays, many choose to *faire le pont* and take long weekends. **Cannes Film Festival** (p224) turns the city into a celebrity-spotting frenzy.

A Few Days Château-Hopping in the Loire

● Start at the **Château Royal de Blois** (p217), a compelling introduction to château architecture and the bloody history of the Loire, then stroll along the riverfront and up to Blois' medieval quarter. At dinner, sample a local dry white wine.

● Spend the next day exploring **Château de Chambord** (p217), its dazzling rooftop and the formal French gardens, and take a picnic lunch. Rent a bike/boat to enjoy in the sprawling grounds in the afternoon.

● On day three, explore the yew-tree maze and architecture at castle-turned-bridge, **Château de Chenonceau** (p218), much of which was designed by women. In the afternoon, drive to **Château de Villandry** (p219), famed for its unparalleled Renaissance gardens.

A Week in Provence

● Begin in **Marseille** (p226), France's second city. Marseille develops in dog years; however often you visit, there's always new hip restaurants and bars to discover, with grab-and-go street food on every corner. Take a day to escape the city to the **Îles du Frioul** (p226), only 20 minutes away.

● Once you've had your fill of edgy bars and street art, head to the splendid coastal **Calanques** (p227) on a build-your-own adventure: kayaking, hiking or even climbing. Next, head inland for an adventure fix at the **Gorges du Verdon** (p229), France's answer to the Grand Canyon. If you're touring in June or July, tack on a detour to the purple-hued **Plateau de Valensole's lavender fields** (p229). Finish up in Avignon to visit the **Palais des Papes** (p231).

JUNE
Lavender is everywhere in Provence; for a dreamy photoshoot, visit the **Plateau de Valensole** (p229) – responsibly. **Nuits de Fourvière** (p210) brings Lyon's Roman amphitheatre back to life with almost two months of concerts.

JULY
Thousands take to the streets to embrace the wild parties and living lesson in Basque culture during Bayonne's exuberant **Fêtes de Bayonne** (p237). The French summer holidays start in early July: expect crowds in the south.

SEPTEMBER
The vendange, or **grape harvest**, begins in wine regions around the country. On the **Journées du Patrimoine** (usually the third weekend in September), many monuments usually closed to the public open their doors.

DECEMBER
Strasbourg's **Christmas markets** light up the city. Expect fairy-light-covered craft stalls, mulled wine and treats. In the Loire, Christmas spirit takes hold at châteaux, including Azay-le-Rideau, Chenonceau and Villandry.

Paris

HERCULEAN CULTURE | HISTORY | JOIE DE VIVRE

GETTING AROUND

Most international airlines fly to Aéroport de Charles de Gaulle (28km northeast) or Aéroport d'Orly (19km south). Paris also has five major train stations with international service, and trains are the easiest public transport into the city. The metro is the fastest way to get around, and RER express trains save time crossing the city and serve the suburbs and airports. With no stairs, buses are good for parents with prams/strollers and people with limited mobility.

☑ **TOP TIP**

Craving green spaces? Join joggers, families and art lovers in the former royal hunting grounds, the **Bois de Boulogne** in western Paris, or **Bois de Vincennes** in the east.

A visit to the seductive French capital is a timeless experience. Be it sipping Champagne atop the Eiffel Tower, lunching cheek by jowl in a neighbourhood bistro, or people-watching on a buzzing cafe pavement terrace, the *art de vivre* (art of living) in the City of Light is utterly contagious.

Paris' cityscapes are instantly recognisable – Notre Dame cathedral, the iron Eiffel Tower, the Arc de Triomphe guarding the glamorous Champs-Élysées, lamplit bridges spanning the Seine, cafes spilling onto wicker-chair-lined streets. A short stay or first-time visit can entice you to linger in the historic centre – the Louvre, the islands, St-Germain and the Latin Quarter – with its myriad monuments and 'must-sees'.

Dining is a quintessential part of any Parisian experience, whether at intimate restaurants, Michelin-starred temples of gastronomy, *boulangeries* (bakeries) or lively street markets.

One of the world's great art repositories, Paris' priceless treasures are showcased in palatial museums, contemporary galleries and innovative multimedia spaces.

Exploring an Icon

Metal asparagus or iron lady?

Named after its designer, Gustave Eiffel, the **Eiffel Tower** *(toureiffel.paris, 2nd floor access using the stairs adult/youth/child from €14.50/7.30/3.70)* was built for the 1889 Exposition Universelle (World's Fair). It took 300 workers, 2.5 million rivets and two years of nonstop labour to assemble. Upon completion, the tower became the tallest human-made structure in the world (324m) – a record held until the 1930 completion of New York's Chrysler Building. A symbol of the modern age, it faced opposition from Paris' artistic and literary elite, and the 'metal asparagus', as some snidely called it, was originally

The Eiffel Tower and the Seine

SPARKLES & A PAINT JOB

Every hour on the hour, the entire tower sparkles for five minutes with 20,000 6-watt lights. They were first installed for Paris' millennium celebration in 2000 – it took 25 mountain climbers five months to install the current bulbs and 40km of electrical cords. For the best view of the light show, head across the Seine to the Jardins du Trocadéro. By day, admire the paintwork. Every seven years, a 50-person crew works at night to strip the old paint and then repaint the entire structure. The tower has sported six different colours throughout its lifetime. The most recent golden hue, unveiled for the 2024 Olympics, was the yellow-brown shade originally conceived by Gustave Eiffel.

slated to be torn down in 1909. It was spared only because it proved an ideal platform for the transmitting antennas needed for the newfangled science of radiotelegraphy. Now a local nickname for the tower is *La dame de fer* (Iron Lady). Of the tower's three floors, the 1st (57m) has the most space, with a broad wooden deck for lounging, but the least impressive views. The glass-enclosed Pavillon Ferrié houses an immersion film along with a small cafe, pizza bar and souvenir shop. This level also hosts the restaurant **Madame Brasserie**. Views from the 2nd floor (115m) are grand – impressively high but still close enough to see the details of the city below. Also up here are toilets, souvenir shops, a macaron bar and Michelin-starred restaurant **Le Jules Verne** (accessible by a dedicated lift in the south pillar). Views from the wind-buffeted top floor (276m) stretch up to 60km on a clear day. At this height the sweeping panoramas are more thrilling than detailed. You'll exit the lift onto a glass-enclosed level with directional panels orienting many of the world's cities. Then take one of the two small sets of metal stairs to the highest tier, which is open-air. Celebrate your ascent with a glass of bubbly from the Champagne bar at this topmost level – or

---

 EATING NEAR THE EIFFEL TOWER: OUR PICKS

Les Deux Abeilles: Homemade delights await at this old-fashioned tearoom that's adored by regulars. *9am-7pm Tue-Sat* €

Bistrot des Fables: A zinc bar contributes to the old-world charm, along with traditional classics like herring potato salad, devilled eggs and beef stew. *hours vary* €€

Francette: Toast the tower from the deck of this floating restaurant moored right on the quay. For the best views, reserve an outside table. *noon-1am* €€

Arnaud Nicolas: The charcuterie maestro stocks a boutique and runs this restaurant with a lunch menu changing every two weeks. *noon-2.30pm & 7-10pm Tue-Sat* €€

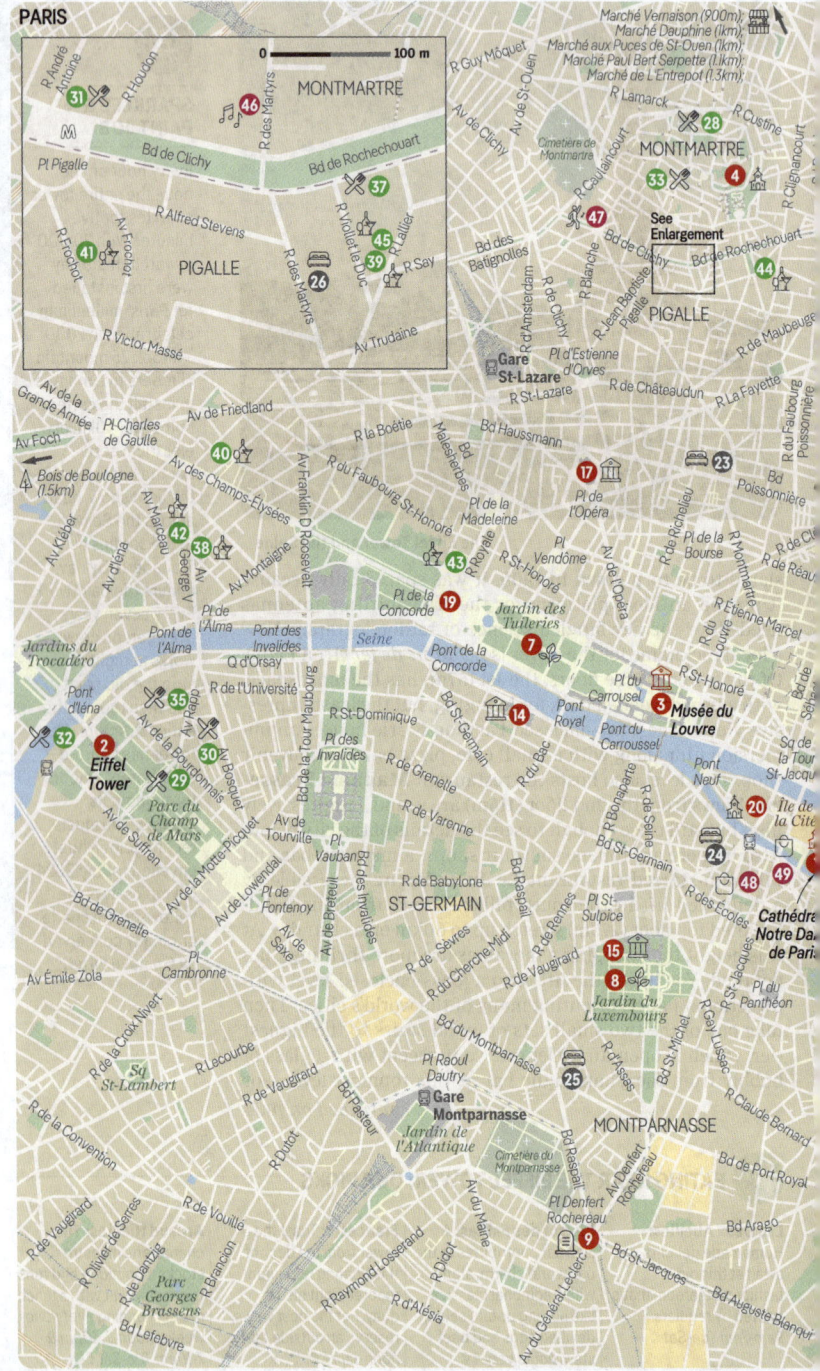

PARIS

Marché Vernaison (900m);
Marché Dauphine (1km);
Marché aux Puces de St-Ouen (1km);
Marché Paul Bert Serpette (1.1km);
Marché de L'Entrepôt (1.3km);

R Guy Môquet

MONTMARTRE

31

46

M

Pl Pigalle   Bd de Clichy   Bd de Rochechouart

R André Antoine
R Houdon
R des Martyrs

R Alfred Stevens

37

R Frochot   45   R Say

PIGALLE   41   39

26

R Victor Massé   Av Trudaine

R Lamarck   R Custine

Cimetière de Montmartre   MONTMARTRE   28

33   4

See Enlargement

47   Bd de Rochechouart

PIGALLE   44

Gare St-Lazare   Pl d'Estienne d'Orves   R de Châteaudun   R La Fayette

R St-Lazare   Bd Haussmann   23

Pl de l'Opéra   17

R la Boétie

Pl de la Madeleine   40

Av des Champs-Élysées   Pl Vendôme   43

Bois de Boulogne (1.5km)   42   38   Pl de la Concorde   19   7   Jardin des Tuileries

Jardins du Trocadéro   Pont de l'Alma   Pont de la Concorde   14

Pont d'Iéna   32   35   Pl du Carrousel   3   Musée du Louvre

2   Eiffel Tower   30   29   R St-Dominique   Pont Royal   Pont du Carrousel

Parc du Champ de Mars   Pl des Invalides   Pont Neuf   20   Île de la Cité

24   48   49

ST-GERMAIN   Pl St-Sulpice   Cathédrale Notre Dame de Paris

15   8   Jardin du Luxembourg

Gare Montparnasse   25   MONTPARNASSE

Jardin de l'Atlantique   Cimetière du Montparnasse

Parc Georges Brassens   Pl Denfert Rochereau   9   Bd St-Jacques

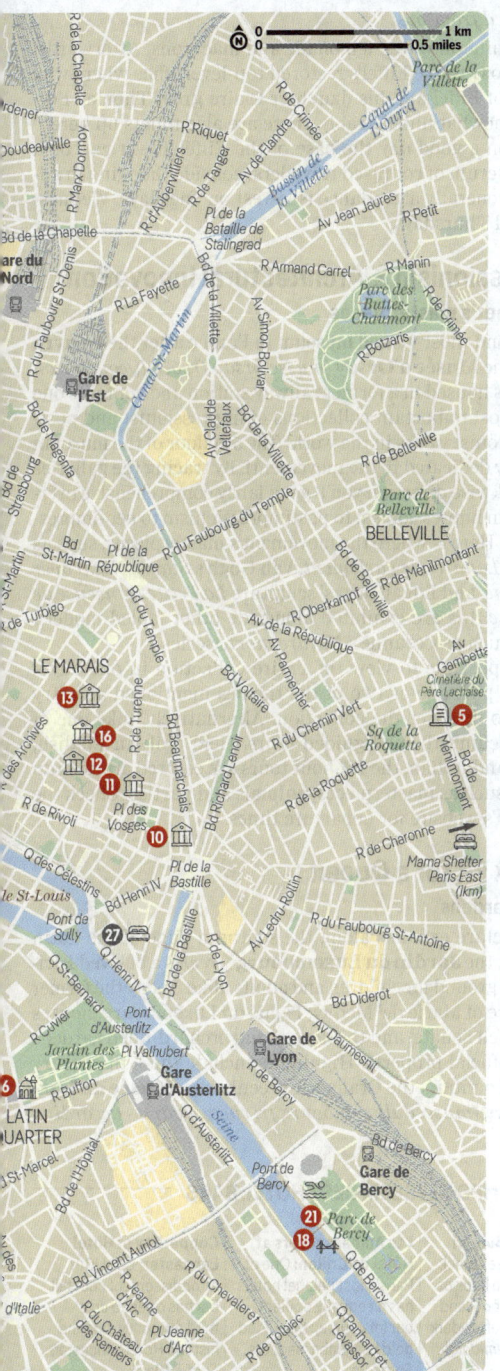

continued from p181

OFF WITH THEIR HEADS!

Created in 1772, **place de la Concorde** sits on what was once a dry moat and fields surrounding the **Jardin des Tuileries** and the former royal palace. It's famously where Louis XVI and Marie-Antoinette were guillotined in 1793 during the French Revolution, along with many others, gaining the square the name place de la Révolution. Renamed place de la Concorde in 1795, it was redesigned between 1836 and 1846 to add the two fountains, Fontaine des Mers and Fontaine des Fleuves, and the statues representing various French cities that sit around the edge of the square. But its most famous monument is the 3300-year-old Egyptian Luxor Obelisk, erected in 1836 after France received it as a gift from Egypt's ruler.

opt for mineral water, lemonade and macarons. Afterwards, peep into Gustave Eiffel's restored top-level office where wax models of Eiffel and his daughter Claire greet Thomas Edison. Somewhat unbelievably, there are also toilets up here.

Even on a good day the base of the Eiffel Tower can be a chaotic scrum of confused travellers; consider booking in advance. Generally attendance is lowest on Tuesdays, Wednesdays and Thursdays.

Impressionism & Architectural Innovation
See Monet's masterpieces

The second-most-visited museum in France after the **Louvre** (p186), the **Musée d'Orsay** *(musee-orsay.fr; adult/concession €16/13)* is housed in a former railway station and contains one of the most important collections of impressionist and post-impressionist works in the world (the 5th floor of the museum is largely dedicated to the movement). By tracing the galleries in a clockwise direction you'll get a fairly comprehensive overview from impressionism to postimpressionism to neo-impressionism. Here is where the movement's masterpieces, such as Monet's *Londres, le Parlement,* Van Gogh's *Starry Night over the Rhône,* and Edgar Degas' sculpture *La Petite Danseuse de Quatorze Ans* are exhibited alongside other fabled modern works, such as Cézanne's *Nature morte* series.

It's impossible to view the entire collection in one day – instead, pick one or two of the themes mentioned as entry points to discover the collection. Alternatively, take one of the museum's themed guided tours. Held daily in English, French and Italian, the 1½-hour tours are centred around fun themes such as masterpieces, animals and parties. Check the museum's website for departure times.

A Park Fit for a Queen
Royal gardens

A 22-hectare expanse along the southern edge of the Latin Quarter, the **Jardin du Luxembourg** *(free)* is a beloved Parisian playground for children and adults alike. Today the former residence of Marie de' Medici, Palais du Luxembourg, houses the French Senate, and the flower- and orchard-filled gardens are its official property. Highlights include the 17th-century Medici Fountain, the Orangerie greenhouse, **Musée du Luxembourg** *(museeduluxembourg.fr; charge varies according*

DRINKING NEAR THE CHAMPS-ÉLYSÉES: BEST HOTEL BARS

| **Le Bar at Four Seasons Hotel George V:** Cocktails crafted with the latest techniques at elegant and cosy gentlemen's-club-style bar. *5pm-1am* | **Bulgari Bar at Bulgari Hotel Paris:** Sleek black bar hidden at the back of Bulgari Hotel: a cool and sexy setting for after-dark cocktails. *10am-midnight* | **Les Ambassadeurs at Hôtel de Crillon:** One of Paris' most palatial hotels has an equally opulent bar (of course): the gilded gold Les Ambassadeurs. *5pm-1am* | **CopperBay at Hotel Lancaster:** Cool 10th arrondissement cocktail bar has opened up a third outpost inside the historic Hotel Lancaster. *5pm-1.30am* |

NEIRFY/SHUTTERSTOCK

Palais du Luxembourg and Jardin du Luxembourg

to exhibition) and lovely statues scattered among treelined paths. In the spring and summer months, the pond springs to life, as toy sailing boats (available to rent) race across its waters. Tennis and pétanque courts, chess tables...there's a bevy of recreational activities, not to mention the delights for young children, including a playground and Paris' oldest merry-go-round, designed by Charles Garnier (the architect of the **Palais Garnier**), and topped with an ancient ring-tilting game that's a rite of passage for Parisian kids.

Gargantuan Gargoyles
The most famous cathedral in the world

Majestic and monumental, Paris' iconic French Gothic cathedral **Notre Dame** *(notredamedeparis.fr; treasury adult/child €12/6)* reopened in December 2024 after the 2019 fire. Long considered the city's geographic and spiritual heart, it went through a massive restoration and, amazingly, because everything – including undamaged elements – was cleaned, the cathedral looks brand-new.

This is an actively working church, and also the capital's most visited free sight – more than 29,000 people come daily. The masterpiece we see today was begun in 1163 and largely completed by the early 14th century. It was badly damaged during the Revolution, prompting architect Eugène-Emmanuel Viollet-le-Duc to oversee extensive renovations between 1845 and 1864. That's when many of the magnificent forest of ornate flying buttresses that encircle the cathedral chancel and support its walls and roof were added. A constant queue marks the entrance to the Tours de Notre Dame *(tours-notre-dame-de-paris.fr)*, the cathedral's bell towers. Climb the 422 spiralling steps to the 69m top of the South Tower (the one on the right as you face the church). On your way up, you'll pass through a *continued on p188*

REBUILDING NOTRE DAME

On the evening of 15 April 2019, a blaze broke out under the roof of Cathédrale Notre Dame de Paris. Firefighters were able to control the fire and ultimately save the church, but the damage was catastrophic. The restoration involved over 1000 artists and not only repaired fire-damaged elements, but cleaned and restored everything to the untarnished condition of the era of Viollet-le-Duc. It cost about €900 million (via donations).

continued on p188

SAKO3P/SHUTTERSTOCK

TOP EXPERIENCE

Musée du Louvre

The Louvre is undeniably Paris' pièce de résistance, with 35,000 works of art on display, including iconic masterpieces, spread across four floors. Glancing at each piece for one minute would take 24 days without sleeping, not to mention the time needed to appreciate the museum's grand surroundings. Therefore, careful planning is essential to fully experience the world's largest art museum.

DON'T MISS

Mona Lisa

Winged Victory of Samothrace

Venus de Milo

The Sphinx's Crypt

Le Salon Carré

Cour Marly and Cour Puget

First Time at the Louvre?

Entering the museum for the first time can be intimidating. The key to approaching the vast collections of the Louvre is to consider them from two significant perspectives: Western Art spanning from the Middle Ages to the mid-19th century, and the art and crafts of five ancient civilisations that preceded and influenced it. Simultaneously, immerse yourself in the museum's captivating architecture shaped by multiple sovereigns. To navigate the museum, just remember that it is made of three wings: the parallel Richelieu (North), Denon (South) and Sully (East).

PRACTICALITIES
● louvre.fr/en ● adult/child €22/free ● 9am-6pm Thu & Sat-Mon, to 9pm Wed & Fri

The Louvre can be both awe-inspiring and overwhelming. Possibly the best way to visit it is to allow yourself to choose, explore and be pleasantly surprised. Don't worry about seeing every masterpiece – enjoy the journey itself!

Guided by Ancient Civilisations

The antiquities department showcases pieces dating from the Neolithic period to the decline of the Roman Empire. Exploring chronologically, the treasures of ancient civilisations will primarily lead you through the ground floor, with an additional area dedicated to Egyptian antiquities on level 1. Begin your journey in the Richelieu wing, exploring the Mesopotamian art (considered the earliest human civilisation). Continue to the Sully wing to descend into the Sphinx's Crypt and uncover Egyptian art. Proceed to the Denon wing to see Greek, Etruscan and Roman art.

Gardens of Sculptures

Sculpture enthusiasts should not miss the atmospheric Cour Marly and Cour Puget, on level 1 of the Richelieu wing. These indoor courtyards bathed in natural light house French masterpieces created under Louis XIV. The Cour Marly provides an atmospheric setting reminiscent of its original location in one of the king's residences. Interestingly, in an arrangement that may seem counterintuitive, ascending to the upper level will transport you back in time to medieval French sculpture. Moving through the Richelieu wing on the ground floor, you'll then encounter more sculptures from the 17th to 19th centuries.

A European Tour of Masterpieces

The top floors showcase European paintings and decorative arts from the Middle Ages to the mid-19th century. Many visitors explore these floors towards the end of their visit, following the sequential order of the rooms. If you're a painting enthusiast, you should prioritise these floors during your visit. They are must-visit areas for iconic artworks like the *Mona Lisa*, as well as monumental paintings such as the *Wedding at Cana* and the *Raft of the Medusa*. In addition, don't miss the impressive Great Gallery, the historic Salon Carré (the precursor to exhibition salons), and the opulent Galerie d'Apollon adorned with stunning murals and golden embellishments.

Around the Louvre, Around the World

As no ordinary museum, the Louvre takes you on a journey to different eras and continents. Don't miss the apartments of Napoléon III, almost untouched for nearly 150 years, at the end of the Richelieu wing on the first level. For a broader cultural experience, explore the small section dedicated to American, African, Asian and Oceanic arts, situated in a remote part of the Denon wing (access through level 1).

ANTIQUE MYSTERY

The oldest displayed piece is the statue of Aïn Ghazal (Room 303, Sully Wing), unearthed in the 1980s in Jordan. Its subject is still a mystery: was it a man, a child, a god? In comparison, the *Winged Victory of Samothrace* and the *Venus de Milo*, both date back to the 3rd and 1st century BCE, which means more than 8000 years separates them from the enigmatic statue!

TOP TIPS

● Make sure to book your ticket online in advance, as you won't need to line up at the museum desk and there may be special offers available.

● The website is a valuable resource for finding inspiration and planning your visit, with thematic itinerary ideas.

● Arriving early will give you the opportunity to explore the galleries with fewer crowds.

● Wear comfortable shoes – you'll be walking through 403 halls and nearly 15km of corridors!

● If you're visiting with children, take a break at the Studio (Richelieu wing, level 1), which provides creative materials for them to enjoy.

FÊTE DE LA MUSIQUE

If you are in Paris on 21 June, the longest day of the year, get ready for the Fête de la Musique (Festival of Music). During this jovial annual celebration, which was launched in 1982 by the French government to encourage and support amateur music, the city's streets are filled all day and night with every kind of music genre imaginable. Concerts include big-hitter names, and are even held in unique venues, including the Louvre, but one of the best ways to experience the festival is to just stroll around by foot in neighbourhoods like Bastille, encountering concerts by chance. Check the full schedule at *fetede lamusique-paris.fr*, concerts generally run from 6pm to midnight.

PATRICK KERWIN/SHUTTERSTOCK

Sainte-Chapelle

continued from p185

room with displays on the cathedral's history before you reach the Galerie des Chimères (Gargoyles Gallery). These grotesque statues divert rainwater from the roof to prevent masonry damage, with the water exiting through their elongated, open mouths. Although they appear medieval, they were installed by Viollet-le-Duc in the 19th century. There's a 1000-visitor maximum per day, so book your timed-entry ticket in advance.

It is absolutely worth the fee to enter the *trésor* (treasury), which houses Notre Dame's dazzling sacred jewels and relics in the cathedral's southeastern transept. Check out the wonderful Les Camées des Papes (Papal cameos), sculpted with incredible finesse in shell and framed in silver. The 268 pieces depict every pope in miniature, from St Pierre to Benoît XVI.

Shimmering Stained Glass of Sainte-Chapelle

Glorious Gothic chapel bedazzlement

No sight in Paris is as dazzling as the radiant Holy Chapel called **Sainte-Chapelle** *(sainte-chapelle.fr; adult Jun-Sep €18, Oct-May €13, incl Conciergerie Jun-Sep/Oct-May €25/20, child free)*, hidden away like a precious gem within the city's

EATING IN MONTMARTRE & PIGALLE: OUR PICKS

Aléa: Simple market-led cuisine. Local favourite. *noon-1.30pm & 7.30-9.30pm Wed & Thu, noon-1.30pm & 7.30-10pm Fri, noon-2pm & 7.30-10pm Sat, 12.30-2pm Sun €€*

La Part des Anges: Laid-back local spot with great traditional food like *magret de canard. 7pm-10.30pm Tue-Thu, 7pm-10.45pm Fri, noon-2.30pm & 7-11pm Sat €€*

Bouillon Pigalle: Terrific value, this *bouillon* is one of several not to miss for escargot and steak-frites. *noon-midnight Sun-Thu, from 11.30am Fri & Sat €*

Maggie: Vintage-style dining space (with vestiges of its days as a 1920s dancing hall) serves traditional French food. Rooftop bar with city views. *7-10pm Tue-Sat €€*

original, 13th-century Palais de Justice (Law Courts) and Palais de la Cité, the former royal residence. Paris' oldest, finest stained glass laces its sublime Gothic interior – best viewed on sunny days when light floods in, creating an entrancing rainbow of bold colours. Built in just six years and consecrated in 1248, it was conceived by French king Louis IX to house his collection of holy relics, including the famous Ste-Couronne (Holy Crown, Jesus' wreath of thorns), which he acquired in 1239 from the Emperor of Constantinople for a sum easily exceeding the amount it cost to build the chapel. There are discounts on entry on Wednesdays from April to September.

Beautiful Bookshops
English-language spots with Parisian soul

French literary giants and expatriate authors found creative refuge in both the city's cafes and bookshops, like the whimsical **Shakespeare and Company** (shakespeareandcompany.com), a hub for expats since 1919. There's also the cosy, Canadian-run **Abbey Bookshop** (abbeybookshop.org), where towering stacks of books and regular readings invite lingering. Along the Seine, the bouquinistes continue to sell vintage books, posters and magazines from green wooden stalls.

Where Cabaret Meets Cocktails
Glamour and after-dark revelry

Since the Belle Époque, Pigalle has been Paris' playground of after-dark pleasures. Its reputation truly took shape after WWII, when it became a hub for neon-lit sex shops, cabarets and smoky bars. While many of its infamous establishments are fading, Pigalle's spirit endures in legendary venues like the **Moulin Rouge** (moulinrouge.fr; adult €103), where since 1889, high-kicking dancers and extravagant sets bring the cancan to life in nightly shows at 9pm and 11pm. Cabaret **Madame Arthur** (madamearthur.fr) is a fun evening out of live music and gender-bending performances, keeping Pigalle's legacy of spectacle and seduction alive. Beyond the show lights, Pigalle's warren of small spaces has always been central to its illicit charm, once home to shadowy dens, opium-fuelled escapades and whispered rendezvous. Today, these tight quarters have found a new life as cocktail bars, where locals and visitors mingle over expertly crafted drinks. Spots like **Sister Midnight**, **Dirty Dick**, **Minore** and **Classique** shake up inventive cocktails, blending Pigalle's hedonistic past with a squeakier-clean present.

A Basilica With a View
Paris' sacred heart

Rising above Montmartre (the hill of martyrs), the **Basilique du Sacré-Cœur** (sacre-coeur-montmartre.com; adult/child/groups €8/5/6, tickets available on-site only, email for guided visits), dedicated to the Sacred Heart of Jesus, is a vantage point, a sanctuary, a Parisian rite of passage, and one of the

GHOSTS OF ARTISTS PAST

Pigalle has long been a stage for Paris' most electrifying performers and artists. In the late 19th century, Toulouse-Lautrec immortalised its cabarets, painting La Goulue and Jane Avril, the high-kicking stars of the Moulin Rouge. The district pulsed with bohemian energy, drawing poets and painters. By the 1920s, Josephine Baker mesmerised crowds at the Folies Bergère, while Édith Piaf sang in Pigalle's streets before becoming the soul of French chanson. Jazz musician and writer Boris Vian added his avant-garde flair to the area's clubs. After WWII, Pigalle's neon glow lit up a world of jazz, burlesque and underground culture. Today, its music halls, cabarets and cocktail bars keep the spirit of its legendary artists alive.

city's most visited landmarks. From its gleaming domes to one of the world's largest mosaics, its grandeur stuns. Designed in a striking Roman-Byzantine style, the basilica took five architects over four decades to complete (1875–1919). Visitors can climb the 300 steps to the dome for breathtaking panoramic views of Paris, while inside, chapels, stained-glass windows, and a crypt bathed in natural light create a contemplative atmosphere. The basilica's perpetual adoration prayer cycle, which began in 1885, continues uninterrupted, and on Sundays, the grand organ resonates through the sacred space during Mass and vespers. You can spend the night at the Basilica from 11pm to 7am if you pray for at least an hour, as part of the continuous prayer cycle, unbroken since 1885 (sign up on the Basilica website, dorms from €15).

Grab a Bargain
France's most famous flea market

Founded in 1885, the **Marché aux Puces de St-Ouen** (*puces deparissaintouen.com*) is the world's largest antiques market, located just beyond Paris' northern edge. It spans 12 distinct markets spread across 7 hectares, with antiques, vintage furniture, rare collectibles, fashion and curiosities. For serious collectors or intrigued wanderers, the mazelike alleys have endless inspiration and irresistible old-world charm.

The allure of Les Puces lies in the diversity and distinct rhythm and charm of each market. **Marché Vernaison**, the oldest, is a warren of open-air lanes lined with vintage postcards, embroidered linens and costume jewellery. **Marché Paul Bert Serpette**, the crown jewel, draws a discerning crowd of interior designers and collectors who come for 20th-century design icons, museum-worthy antiques and impeccably curated vignettes. Inside the vaulted glass pavilion of **Marché Dauphine**, the atmosphere is more freewheeling: vinyl records, retro cameras, tribal artefacts and the occasional taxidermied bird. **L'Entrepot** is one of the smallest markets but it's mighty and has a bunch of old zinc-top brasserie bars and spiral staircases from houses all over the country.

Haggling is part of the charm at Les Puces. Approach vendors with a smile, and you might knock 10% to 20% off the price. While some accept cards, cash is often preferred for smaller items or better deals.

Urban Swimming
Go for a dip in the Seine

In 1900, during the first edition of the Olympic Games in Paris, swimming races took place in the River Seine. Decades of industrialisation polluted the waters until a nadir was reached in the 1970s. After a mass clean-up operation, including the construction of water-treatment plants and rainwater-storage basins, swimming was possible once again for the 2024 Games. Since the summer of 2025, the public has also been able to bathe in the famous river,

MORE CITY DIPS
Urban 'wild' swimming is on the rise, and there are plenty of other European cities where you can take a plunge, including Barcelona, Amsterdam and **Berlin** (p652).

PETR KOVALENKOV/SHUTTERSTOCK

Grande Mosquée de Paris

including at the **Bercy swimming area** by the **Simone de Beauvoir footbridge**. The area is supervised, marked with buoys and equipped with showers and lockers.

Calm at the Paris Mosque

A North African oasis for food and relaxation

One of the biggest mosques in France, and Paris' central mosque, the **Grande Mosquée de Paris** *(grandemosqueede paris.fr)* has a striking Moorish-style minaret, which peeks out from behind smooth white walls as you approach along the street. Visit the interior to see the intricate tile work and calligraphy. There is also a North African hammam (steam bathhouse) with timings for women and men, a pretty courtyard **restaurant** *(la-mosquee.com)* that serves delicious couscous, tagines and meat skewers, as well as a tearoom with sweet, fragrant mint tea and traditional cakes. There is also the possibility of smoking shisha in the front garden.

Pay Respects to Wilde & Morrison

The resting place of artists

When commissioned to design the new Parisian cemetery, **Père Lachaise**, in the early 19th century, architect Alexandre-Théodore Brongniart envisioned a space that would embody nobility without grandiosity, and simplicity without neglect, and invoke religious sentiments without fear. Inspired by English gardens, the cemetery was meticulously planned, with winding paths and a significant portion dedicated to nature. Today, as you enter, the cacophony of the city fades away and the graves seamlessly blend into the undulating landscape, creating a feeling of beautiful strangeness, as if you were suspended between two worlds.

continued on p194

MARCHE DES FIERTÉS

Running in Paris since 1981, the **Marche des Fiertés** *(marchedes fiertes.org)* has its origins in the Gay Pride marches that began in New York. In Paris the annual parade is attended by over 500,000 people and includes support from more than 200 volunteers. Organisation of the event is led by the group Inter-LGBT, who brings together around 90 organisations. Their shared mission is to 'combat discrimination based on sexual orientation or gender identity, as part of the promotion of human rights and fundamental freedoms'. Open to all, whether you identify as an ally or part of the community, the event is a celebratory and political day filled with music, costumes, placards, floats, a final concert and dance-filled afterparties.

TAKASHI IMAGES/SHUTTERSTOCK

Hall of Mirrors

Versailles

Sprawling over 900 hectares, the monumental, 400-year-old Château de Versailles is France's most famous and grand palace. It's situated in the leafy, bourgeois suburb of Versailles, 22km southwest of central Paris. The estate is divided into three main sections: the 580m-long palace; the gardens, canals and pools to the west of the palace; and the Trianon Estate to the northwest.

DON'T MISS

The Palace

Hall of Mirrors

King's and Queen's State Apartments

Formal gardens and fountains

Lunch near the Grand Canal

History

The estate began in 1623 as a hunting lodge for Louis XIII. Subsequently, Louis XIV transformed it into a vast, baroque château. Some 30,000 workers and soldiers toiled on the property, the bills for which all but emptied the kingdom's coffers.

The Château de Versailles was the kingdom's political capital and the seat of the royal court from 1682 up until the fateful events of 1789 when revolutionaries massacred the palace guard. Louis XVI and Marie Antoinette were ultimately dragged back to Paris, where they were ingloriously

PRACTICALITIES

● en.chateauversailles.fr ● adult/child from €21/ free ● 9am-5.30pm Tue-Sun

guillotined. In the 19th century, Napoléon and Josephine lived on the estate, as did Charles de Gaulle in the 1940s.

The Palace

Work on the palace began in 1661 under the guidance of architect Louis Le Vau (Jules Hardouin-Mansart took over from Le Vau in the mid-1670s); painter and interior designer Charles Le Brun; and landscape artist André Le Nôtre, whose workers flattened hills, drained marshes and relocated forests as they laid out the seemingly endless gardens, ponds and fountains.

Le Brun and his hundreds of artisans decorated every moulding, cornice, ceiling and door of the interior with the most luxurious and ostentatious of appointments: frescoes, marble, gilt and woodcarvings, many with themes and symbols drawn from Greek and Roman mythology.

Few alterations have been made to the château since its construction, apart from most of the interior furnishings disappearing during the Revolution and many of the rooms being redecorated by Louis-Philippe (r 1830–48), who opened part of the château to the public in 1837. The château is in the final stages of a lavish €400 million restoration.

Hall of Mirrors

The palace's opulence peaks in its shimmering Galerie des Glaces (Hall of Mirrors). This 75m-long ballroom shines with 17 sparkling mirrored features comprising 357 individual mirrors on one side and an equal number of windows overlooking the gardens and the setting sun on the other.

King's & Queen's State Apartments

Luxurious, ostentatious appointments adorn every feature of the palace's Grands Appartements du Roi et de la Reine (the King's and Queen's State Apartments). Rooms are dedicated to Hercules, Venus, Diana, Mars and Mercury.

Other Notable Rooms

The **Galerie des Batailles** (Battle Gallery) is longer than the Hall of Mirrors and features 33 huge paintings that recall mostly forgotten French military victories. Savour the thematic decor in the **Salon de la Guerre** (War Room) and the **Salon de la Paix** (Peace Room), which bookend the Hall of Mirrors.

Gardens, Estate & Equestrian Academy

A walk through the sprawling and artful formal gardens, natural areas, huge Grand Canal and the Trianon palaces is a highlight. Or take in a horse show at the **National Equestrian Academy of Versailles**.

HISTORIC VERSAILLES

Don't miss the historic centre of Versailles town. Build a superb picnic at the market stalls of **Les Halles de Versailles** on the **place du Marché**. In the old St-Louis quarter, next to the **Cathédrale St-Louis**, the **Potager du Roi** (King's Kitchen Garden) dates from the time of gourmand Louis XIV.

TOP TIPS

● Prepurchase tickets on the château's website for a dedicated time slot.

● Consider getting tickets for a concert in the Royal Chapel or Royal Opera for a unique palace experience.

● Download the official Château de Versailles app – loaded with audio tours and info for the entire estate.

● The four-person rental electric carts are limited to a set route covering a fraction of the estate. Rental bikes and e-bikes allow the most freedom. Explore the Grand Canal with a rowboat. The shuttle train is very slow.

● Versailles is best reached by the RER C line, which ends at Versailles Château Rive Gauche (some trains continue elsewhere). Other stations with Versailles in their names are a much longer walk from the château and town centre.

BASTILLE'S ANCIENT FORTRESS

Nothing remains of Bastille's fortress, originally constructed in the 14th century to defend the eastern flank of Paris against the English during the Hundred Years' War. By 1417 the royal castle took on an unusual new aspect: it formally became a state prison, housing inmates for centuries until it was destroyed during the 1789 revolution. On 14 July 1789, the inhabitants of the Faubourg St-Antoine, sick of prolonged food shortages due to an ongoing siege of Paris, stormed Bastille prison. When the guards refused to surrender, rebels seized 250 barrels of gunpowder, freed prisoners and put the military governor's head on a pike. This was the first episode of the French Revolution.

Les Catacombes

continued from p191

Overlooked at the time of its inauguration, the cemetery faced challenges in gaining popularity due to its location far from the city. However, to enhance its appeal, the city of Paris relocated the graves of famous figures like Molière and La Fontaine. Over time, politicians, scientists, artists and writers followed, solidifying Père Lachaise's reputation as the eternal resting place of the renowned. Oscar Wilde's tomb has long been the object of passionate kisses believed to bring luck in love, and the ritual offerings left on Jim Morrison's grave perpetuate a cult (mainly based on alcohol). Download the cemetery map from a QR code at the entrance; this will help you locate specific graves and landmarks, and choose the right entrance. There are five different ones, but only three of them are near metro stations.

An Underground Ossuary

The ghosts of Paris past

In 1785, subterranean tunnels of an abandoned quarry were upcycled as storage rooms for the exhumed bones of corpses that could no longer fit in the city's overcrowded cemeteries. By 1810 the skull- and bone-lined catacombs – resting place of millions of anonymous Parisians – had been officially born.

The route through **Les Catacombes** (*catacombes.paris.fr; adult/child €31/12*) begins at its spacious entrance on av du Colonel Henri Rol-Tanguy. Walk down 131 spiral steps to reach the ossuary itself, with a mind-boggling number of bones and skulls of millions of Parisians neatly packed along the walls. Visits cover about 1.5km of tunnels in all, at a cool 14°C. People with claustrophobia may experience some anxiety in the confined environment. It's closed Mondays.

Mont St-Michel

BIODIVERSE BAY | TIDE-WALKING | WONDROUS ABBEY

For a millennium, Mont St-Michel has entranced visitors with majestic views that metamorphose with the tides. When the seas rise, a 1000-year-old Gothic abbey crowns the top of an island of craggy rock. Conceptualised from a dream in which an archangel bids a bishop to build a place of devotion in an impossible place, Mont St-Michel captures the imagination of anyone who crosses its sandy paths. The sometimes-island itself changes as quickly as the sea; only a handful of inhabitants live there in comparison to the millions of annual tourists who crowd the winding streets that ascend to the pointed top.

Once you've snapped your photo of the extraordinary sight and have heard the bells ring in the abbey, the next best step is to immerse yourself in the incredible biodiversity of the bay. With slow and careful observation and turning off the tourist paths, you can find yourself in a vivid, waking dream full of flora, fauna and culinary delights.

Nocturnal Visits & High Tide

A night visit to the bay

The traditional approach to the **Abbaye du Mont St-Michel** (*abbaye-mont-saint-michel.fr; adult/child €16/free*) is an established, elevated wood-plank path with guardrails, next to the road where shuttles ferry visitors back and forth all day. But in the spirit of Robert Frost: the road less travelled makes all the difference. If you're pressed for time, try to go as early as possible to avoid the crowds, and plan on eating and sleeping off the almost-island to avoid handing over a lot of cash for mediocre tourist traps.

Take the unconventional route and sink your toes in the sometimes-moving quicksand with local guide **Romain Pilon** (*labaiecderomain.fr; tours per person from €15*), native of the bay and a guide for over two decades. Fishing enthusiasts can go shrimping with Romain during select windows throughout the year, usually mid-September through October and a short

GETTING AROUND

The nearest train stop is Pontorson (just short of five hours from Paris), where buses will take you 350m from the entrance of Mont St-Michel. But a car is your best bet to get around the bay and surrounding villages, though parking near Mont-St-Michel is pricey. Getting to the island of Mont St-Michel itself is fairly straightforward: walk or queue up for an all-day shuttle bus (free). To walk across the bay, it's best to hire a guide and check tide changes: *ot-montsaintmichel .com/marees*.

☑ **TOP TIP**

Avoid the summer months (July and August) for the best views and fewer crowds. If you find yourself here during high season, try to go at dusk or dawn to beat the rush.

195

BEST ANNUAL FÊTES/FESTIVALS IN NORMANDY

Dîner sur la Digue: Join thousands of guests at this dinner party alongside the boardwalk in Cabourg. Reserve, pack your picnic or grab a meal from vendors.

Cabourg Mon Amour Festival: Annual three-day, open-air music festival, with styles from electro to rap. *cabourgmon amour.fr*

Fête des Marins: Every Pentecost weekend (the seventh Sunday after Easter), get suited in sailor stripes in Honfleur for parades, concerts, photos and more.

Offcourts Festival: September festival celebrating French and Québécois short films. Free screenings, concerts and festivities.

American Film Festival: Each September, stars gather in Deauville to celebrate American cinema. *festival-deau ville.com*

MONT ST-MICHEL

Baie du Mont St-Michel

1 Abbaye du Mont St-Michel

La Caserne

Courtils Ceaux 4 Pontaubault

3

Précey 5

Beauvoir 2 Servon

Moidrey

6

Pontorson

⊕ HIGHLIGHTS
1 Abbaye du Mont St-Michel

● SLEEPING
2 Auberge Sauvage

3 Camping La Baie du Mont St-Michel
4 Chambres d'Hôte Les Bruyères du Mont

● EATING
see 2 Auberge Sauvage
5 La Brocante
6 Le Grillon
see 1 Le Logis Sainte Catherine

window in April. But year-round, the best way to see Mont St-Michel is with his 'Sortie Nocturnes'.

Night owls will meet at 7.30pm and then skulk around the bay as evening falls. Enter a hidden world over the next few hours, bathed in the light of the spectacular sunset and surrounded by the cries of geese and migratory birds – identified by your guide – and the moving waters and sound of the shifting shores. The visit ends at 11.30pm, cloaked in the mystical magic of night, where you'll emerge with uncovered secrets and views of the bay.

 EATING NEAR MONT-ST-MICHEL: OUR PICKS

Auberge Sauvage: Michelin-starred haven set in a 16th-century presbytery. Local produce and foraged delicacies dominate. *7.30pm-midnight Thu-Mon* €€€

La Brocante: Enjoy simple snacks, sandwiches, crêpes, coffees and wines in this retrofitted old auto shop. *10am-6pm Mon, Thu & Fri, 11am-6pm Sat & Sun* €

Le Grillon: Unpretentious and unfussy spot to taste lamb chops made from the sheep that graze the salty fields. *12.30-1.30pm Sat-Wed, 7-8.30pm Fri-Tue* €€

Le Logis Sainte Catherine: Rotating menu with innovative plates like *moussette* rillettes. Dazzling terrace, elegant decor. Book online. *hours vary* €€€

Abbaye du Mont St-Michel (p195)

Go Birding or Become a Bird

Bird-watching and paragliding

If you're travelling with a group, flock together and book the **Birding Bus** (*birding-msm.com; from €10*), run by ornithologist and biologist-by-training Sébastian Provost, who showcases bird-watching as a fascinating artform that brings to life hidden worlds. At various points along the bay, you'll encounter birds, seals and even dolphins.

For those who like to fly solo, jump for a bird's-eye view of Mont St-Michel and its surroundings – literally. With experienced and competition-winning paraglider **Léo Hamard** (*parapenteenbaie.fr; flights from €80*), you can float above the abbey and the bay like a bird. Watch your feet dangle and be dazzled by the singular feeling of lightness and freedom flying on the winds. Adrenaline junkies and first-timers alike can spring for the 'acrobatic' flight option (weather contingent) for a truly head-spinning flight. Reserve a date in advance online, but the jumping-off point is dictated by the winds.

MAD FOR MOUSSETTES IN MAY

Crab lovers, take note of *moussettes*, the nickname of a variety of young spider crab (under two years old) found all over fish markets in La Manche from April to June, and especially bountiful during the month of May. They're known for their sweet, subtle and abundant flesh; enjoy them without any condiments needed, although if you're partial to one, homemade mayonnaise is the most traditional (our advice: wear a bib and gloves to avoid the mess). You can buy them cooked or boil in water for 20 minutes. As a bonus, eating *moussettes* also helps out the local ecosystem, since the spider crabs have infiltrated the Normandy region and pose a threat to mussel producers.

Beyond Mont St-Michel

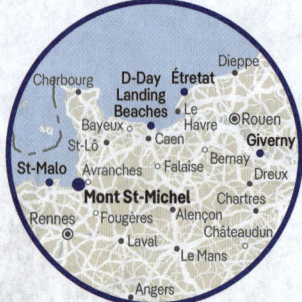

Explore the bucolic Norman countryside and wild Breton coast, toasting your adventures with crisp apple cider.

Places

Giverny p198

Étretat p199

D-Day Landing Beaches p200

St-Malo p201

GETTING AROUND

Various towns and cities like Le Havre, Étretat and St-Malo are easily accessible by direct trains from Paris. More isolated areas, including the D-Day beaches, require more planning, with sparse bus services. A car is most convenient to explore the less touristy areas (Breton highways are toll-free, Norman highways are not!). In both Normandy and Brittany, hiking and cycling are some of the best ways to take in coastal scenery.

To the east of Mont St-Michel, Normandy's breathtaking landscapes singlehandedly inspired the impressionist art movement; painter Claude Monet obsessively painted sunrise at Le Havre and his backyard water lilies in Giverny. From the world-famous and epically surreal Mont St-Michel abbey, all the way to the cliffs of Étretat, the Normandy coast is replete with famed destinations. History buffs can immerse themselves in D-Day reenactments, and even breakfast on tables made from reassembled German planes. Westwards, Brittany has some of nature's most wonderful sights with unspoiled rawness. Over 2000km of coastline, the ocean's mystical draw and mesmerising landscapes never fail to enchant visitors. That's got to be worth braving the rain.

Giverny

TIME FROM MONT ST-MICHEL: **3HR** 🚗

Skip the crowds at Monet's secret island

Monet's residence of over four decades, **Maison et Jardins de Claude Monet** (*claudemonetgiverny.fr; adult/child/under 7yr €12/6.50/free*) is a powerful testament to the lasting legacy of a visionary artist: his world-famous water lilies and his eccentric, brightly coloured home dotted with his collection of Japanese block prints are flocked to by thousands of tourists each year. The queue for the water lilies, which tears through the house at a frenetic pace, can be intimidating – but if you pause and gaze out of the window and focus on a flower, you'll surely be left with an impression of the painter's life. Reservations are strongly recommended (weekdays are slightly less crowded than the weekend) and beware of big holiday weekend crowds.

To contemplate his life with more breathing room, walk up to his humble grave and contrast it with the greatness of his legacy. Better yet, picnic at the lesser-known **Île aux Orties**, a patch of land Monet owned at the confluence of where the Epte River meets the Seine, that once turned into an island during heavy rain periods. To get there, walk past the windmill near the car parks the along the small rue des Batards

Maison et Jardins de Claude Monet, Giverny

until you reach the river for a more isolated experience of one of his rarer, inspired landscapes.

Étretat

TIME FROM MONT ST-MICHEL: 2½HR

Coast along the renowned alabaster cliffs

France's famous and trafficked cliffs, Étretat's staggering arches have been sculpted over millennia by winds and the whims of the sea, and immortalised by Monet over 80 times. More recently, the cliffs have also unfortunately been the cause of deaths due to reckless photos – skip the selfies at the top and don't stray off established paths.

Falaise d'Aval and the adjacent Aiguille are the most iconic, featuring a needle shooting from the water alongside an arch; and the **Falaise d'Amont** has a bird's-eye view of Étretat. Hikes here are choose-your-own-adventure: opt for the steep steps to the neo-Gothic stone church, **Chapelle Notre-Dame-de-la-Garde**, for a peaceful (yet windy) picnic – the view from the church is better than a visit inside. Hardcore hikers, head to the intensive and rewarding five-hour Roc Vaudieu Loop. If you're short on time, take the Porte d'Amont Loop that starts at Chemin de Criquetot. To wade deeper into the waters, head to **Voiles et Galets** (*voilesetgalets.com; rentals from €15*) in Étretat for an unforgettable kayak or paddleboard ride

IN THE PATH OF RUSSIAN PAINTERS

Stretching just 1.1km, France's shortest river runs through **Veules-les-Roses**, a tiny village of idyllic windmills and thatched-roof cottages where Russian impressionist painters found endless inspiration during the 1850s. Along the river you can see the mill and watering hole, and beachside you can see the same sea as immortalised by painters Alexei Petrovitch Bogolyubov and Vassily Dmitrievich Polenov. Near the stone bridge near the source of the river, there's a watercress mill (also painted by Polenov), and today the watercress is still enjoyed by locals with an annual festival.

 EATING IN GIVERNY: OUR PICKS

Au Coin du Pain'tre: Simple plates like quiches and baguette sandwiches. The highlight: relaxing over breakfast or lunch with a garden view. *9am-7pm €*

Cocorico: Pop-up food truck with fresh sandwiches, burgers and desserts at reasonable prices for a takeaway picnic, when the sun's out. *hours vary Apr-Oct €*

Les Nymphéas: Family-friendly garden restaurant: crêpes, fondue, raclette, burgers and salads. *9am-6pm Apr-Oct €€*

Oscar: Gourmet bistro in a stylish setting with refined plates by acclaimed chef David Gallienne. *10am-6pm Mon-Thu, to 9pm Fri & Sat €€€*

BEST WWII MUSEUMS/ MEMORIALS

Memorial Museum of Omaha Beach: Memorial of steel shooting out of the sand stops the breath, while well-curated museum pays tribute to fallen soldiers.

Utah Beach Landing Museum: Westernmost beach hosts one of biggest museums built on German fortifications. Glimpse an original B-26 bomber.

La Pointe du Hoc: View ravages of a battlefield and old bunkers at this powerfully sobering memorial point. Many stairs.

Overlord Museum: Collectors' paradise: restored trucks, vehicles, dioramas and veteran tributes.

Airborne Museum: Near historic church Ste-Mère-Église, this museum focuses on the airborne troops and hosts an original glider and a C-47 plane.

under some epic scenery; no reservations, as rentals depend on weather conditions. Don't miss a paddle out to the **Plage du Fourquet** to enjoy a secluded beach.

D-Day Landing Beaches

TIME FROM MONT ST-MICHEL: 1½HR

A night at a WWII museum

When US soldiers landed on Normandy's Omaha Beach on the morning of 6 June 1944, the ensuing crescendo to WWII left indelible scars on the French countryside. From west to east, the 80km stretch of sand comprises the American landing beaches of Utah and Omaha; Gold Beach, where the British landed; **Juno Beach** for the Canadians; and then another American landing destination, Sword Beach. Decades later, D-Day remains a monolithic legend that has left countless memorial and military sites, cemeteries, museums and remains of what was once the largest harbour in the world.

Bringing history to life are the wife-and-husband team behind guesthouse **D-Day Aviators Le Manoir** *(ddayavia torslemanoir.fr)*. Anne Florence and Paul Hontang are both pilots with passions. Paul is a history expert, constantly on the hunt to add to their impressive collection of war detritus: a plane cockpit adorns the living room, and guests breakfast on a table made from a German plane engine. Anne has a personal collection of over 500 dentelles, traditional lace bonnets and hats worn to signify the different life stages of a woman. Ask her for a peek in the garage next door. Situated in Arromanches-les-Bains, where the world's largest artificial harbour was assembled by the Allied Forces, the manor house is centrally placed for visiting all along the D-Day Landing Beaches and right next to the renovated **Musée du Debarquement** *(musee-arromanches.fr; adult/child €12.90/8.30)*, a stunningly detailed presentation of why and how the critical events of 6 June 1944 took place.

For a wilder ride, head to the family-friendly **La Batterie du Holdy Guesthouse** *(batterie-du-holdy.com)*, just south of Utah Beach. Be transported back to the events of 6 June 1944, with cinematic and immersive reenactments in the very buildings where WWII action took place. Booking a night here is well worth it – an impassioned Jeep tour is included without steep prices. The real goldmine is the anecdotes Jean generously shares with his guests, and the delight of breakfast served in a 1940s-era grocery store.

Go behind enemy lines

On the coast along the English Channel, known as La Manche, near Utah Beach, there are a few German artillery batteries to visit. The **Batterie de Crisbecq** *(batteriedecrisbecq. fr; adult/child €12.50/8.50)*, also known as the Battery of St Marcouf, is the largest and most spectacular. Built in 1941 by the German military engineering group Todt, the bunker today lets you walk in German soldiers' footsteps – the former trenches have been excavated and now serve as walking paths between the 22 blockhouses. View up-close battle scars, grenade traps and visible damage. The **Batterie d'Azeville** (*batterie-azeville.manche.fr; adult/child €8/4*) is smaller in scale, but stands intact today due to a one-in-a-million chance: on D-Day, an American destroyer successfully shot a shell through the opening of the blockhouses. The shell miraculously didn't explode but crossed through the blockhouse and ended up a dud behind the fields.

If you want to go underground in WWII sites, head to the under-the-radar **Radar Museum 1944** (*musee-radar.fr; adult/under 10yr €7.50/free*), a former German listening station that has preserved its original state. Run by friendly and impassioned volunteers, the guided visits at this lesser-known museum are well worth reserving in advance.

St-Malo

TIME FROM MONT ST-MICHEL: **50MIN**

Pirates and privateers

'Not French, not Breton, I am Malouin.' St-Malo's slogan sets the tone. Circled and protected by its commanding ramparts yet resolutely open to the sea, it takes great pride in its very distinctive identity. One of the most prosperous ports in France from the 15th century onwards, it became home to great seafarers such as Jacques Cartier, the first European to make his way to Canada in the 16th century. But St-Malo is most famous for the high number of privateers who enriched the city in the 17th and 18th centuries. Commissioned by the King of France to pillage enemy boats during war times, privateers owned hundreds of armed ships in the port of St-Malo towards the end of the 18th century. The city walls, which originally date back to the 12th century, were expanded and fortified to better defend these accumulated treasures, and quickly became emblematic of the city.

Standing imperiously on a rocky island facing the sea, St-Malo's **Fort National** (*fortnational.com; adult/child €5/3*) was built in 1689 and was originally intended to protect the city's port. Throughout the centuries, it has been the stage of legendary attacks and epic battles – and has also known darker days during WWII, when it was used as a prison by the Germans. The site is now open to visits every day in the summer, and during some school holidays and bank holidays. Opening hours depend on the time of the day: you'll need to wait for the tide to be low to walk across **Plage de l'Eventail** to reach the fort. You can book a 35-minute guided tour in English by email, with written translations also available in a number of other languages.

THE PRICE OF LIBERATION

The old town of St-Malo as we know it today came very close to not surviving at all. In August 1944, after four years of German occupation, St-Malo and its surroundings were relentlessly bombed by the Allies. When the city was liberated on 17 August 1944, 80% of the old town was destroyed. The ramparts, miraculously, were still standing. However, instead of razing the remains to the ground and rebuilding afresh, everything was reconstructed just as it was: a colossal, complex project that took years, including 18 months just to clear out the 500,000 cu metres of ruins. In 1972, when Cathédrale St-Vincent was inaugurated, St-Malo was officially completely restored.

 EATING IN ST-MALO: OUR PICKS

Doma: A cosy room and a short, tasty menu based on seasonal produce that is reasonably priced. *noon-1.30pm Wed-Sat, 7.30-9.30pm Tue-Sat €€*	**La Touline:** Classic crêperie with high-quality ingredients at the heart of the *intra muros. hours vary €*	**Les Flibustiers:** A warm spot with a terrace in the centre offering no-fuss *planches* (platters), salads, tartines, quiches and soups. *hours vary €*	**Bouliche:** Away from the crowds, near to Cité d'Alet, a local gem with creative plates. *noon-2pm Tue, 7-10pm Wed, noon-2pm & 7-10pm Thu-Sat €€*

French Alps

MOUNTAIN SCENERY | ADRENALINE | CHEESE

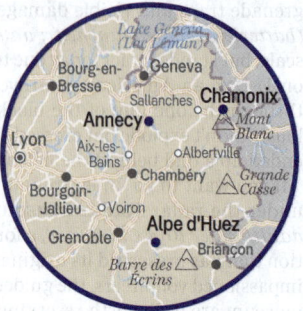

  TOP TIP

Travelling without kids? Take your skiing holiday in late January or late March: you'll miss all the school holidays (French and European) and rates are much lower. Low season in the Alps is from late April to early June and late September to late November, and many mountain towns all but shut up shop.

Heart-thumping adventure and pastoral tradition share the same starting gate in this high-octane playground, dedicated to safeguarding ancestral savoir-faire. The French Alps is where beauty of the most breathtaking nature and action collide. Glacier-carved national parks and shark-toothed mountain summits, ice-blue lakes and sky-high cols: the call of the wild is fierce in this eastern swathe of France, even more so for outdoor adventurers in town to bag the highest, longest feat – on skis, bike or simply your own two feet.

Rumbling across seven European countries, the Alps climax with western Europe's highest peak, Mont Blanc (4805m). The hypnotic snow-white crown of this storied mountain spirographs a kaleidoscope of magical shadows over the renowned ski and mountaineering town of Chamonix in Savoie (Savoy). Inhabited since prehistoric times, the French Alps have been fiercely contested since time immemorial. The desire to conquer that they arouse burns brighter

GETTING AROUND

Embracing the *départements* (departments) of Savoie, Haute-Savoie and Isère, the French Alps cover a vast area – not easy to navigate swiftly, thanks to valleys and mountains blocking direct routes. Roads to many ski stations are steep and serpentine. Snow clearing is frequent, but winter tyres or chains stowed in your trunk are obligatory from November to March. Many cols (mountain passes) are snowbound and closed in winter; in early/late summer, check road conditions before setting out. Buses link Moûtiers train station with Les Trois

Vallées and Bourg-St-Maurice station with Val d'Isère/Tignes. Modane is the rail stop for the Vanoise, linked by bus to Bonneval-sur-Arc. For Chamonix, hop on the Mont Blanc Express train at TGV station St-Gervais-Le Fayet. The long-distance GR5 or Grande Traversée des Alpes walking trail crosses the entire French Alps en route from Lake Geneva to the Med (674km). Shorter trails tackle the entire region, and are the loveliest way of slow-hopping between remote hamlets, farms and mountain *refuges* (shelters).

FRANCOIS ROUX/SHUTTERSTOCK

Mer de Glace (p204), Chamonix

than ever regardless of the season, be it the Vallée Blanche ski descent or Europe's longest black run in winter, or epic hiking trails in summer (the Tour du Mont Blanc spans three countries). Lakeside towns like Annecy offer a choice between the slow pace of life – glacial dips and languid paddleboarding in the crystalline waters of Lake Annecy – or yet more adrenaline, and it's one of the most popular spots in the country for paragliding.

All that effort tends to work up an appetite, and culinary specialities in the French Alps are of the 'roll-me-down-the-mountain' type: belt-busting troughs of fondue, gooey tartiflette and heady raclette.

Chamonix

MAP p204

Off-piste ride of a lifetime

Free-rider king of the French Alps and springboard to some of Europe's most fêted mountain adventures, Chamonix has always been one ski spin ahead of the curve. Just walking down Chamonix's pedestrian main street, loomed over by Mont Blanc's snow-white dome, it's impossible not to feel a sassy new spring in your step: the palpable buzz and anticipation of the next outdoor thrill around the corner.

Tales of skiers cruising along and suddenly disappearing from sight are rife in La Vallée Blanche annals. Then again, skiing across a snow bridge and tumbling metres like a rag doll into a dark ice-blue crevasse as the ruptured bridge collapses happens with surprising frequency.

This is just one reason why Europe's most legendary off-piste ski route – an astounding 2800m descent through a landscape of eerie, unearthly beauty – must be tackled with a certified guide. Starting at a dizzying 3842m, at the top

MOUNTAIN TOOLKIT

Lift passes: Find details of all passes at *montblancnatural resort.com*.

Mountain guides: Compagnie des Guides de Chamonix *(chamonix-guides. com),* inside the Maison de la Montagne, has guides for snowshoeing, ice-climbing, off-piste skiing, summer mountaineering, climbing and canyoning.

Trail access and conditions: The Office de Haute Montagne *(chamoniarde.com),* also in Maison de la Montagne, has information on hiking, climbing and ski-touring trails – including trail conditions.

Chamonix mobile app: Tourist office app *(en.chamonix.com):* weather forecasts, webcams, maps; purchase and top-up lift passes, too.

BEST ALTERNATIVE MOUNTAIN THRILLS IN THE FRENCH ALPS

Moon-biking: Ride snowy trails in Courchevel astride a silent, electric snow bike with front sled blade and rear caterpillar track.

Fat biking: Speed down on snow bicycles with ultra-fat tires in La Plagne.

Acro-speleology: Go with a guide to Grottes de St-Christophe caves for mixed climbing-canyoning in Massif des Chartreuse.

Electric mountain biking: Along the Via 3 Vallées, a 34km cycling itinerary links Courchevel, Méribel, Les Menuires and Val Thorens.

Mushing: Sled (up to 50km/h) with American Eskimo, Greenland or Alaskan dogs through sugar-dusted firs in several ski resorts

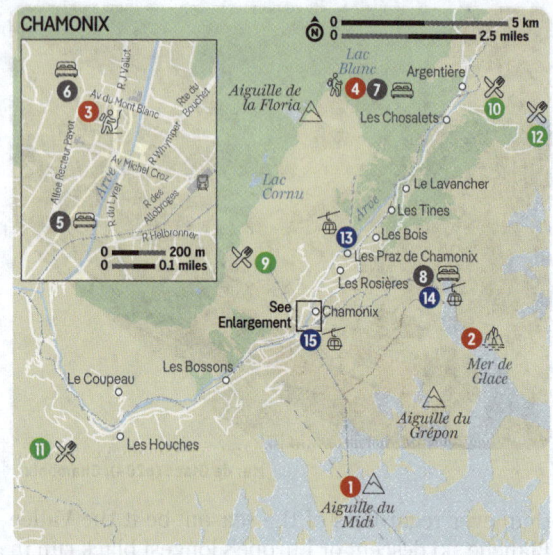

● SIGHTS	● SLEEPING	● EATING	● TRANSPORT
1 Aiguille du Midi	5 Hôtel Richemond	9 La Bergerie de Planpraz	13 Télécabine de la Flégère
2 Mer de Glace	6 La Folie Douce	10 La Crèmerie du Glacier	14 Télécabine de la Mer de Glace
● ACTIVITIES	7 Refuge du Lac Blanc	11 Les Vieilles Luges	15 Téléphérique de l'Aiguille du Midi
3 Compagnie des Guides de Chamonix	8 Refuge du Montenvers	12 Refuge de Lognan	
4 Lac Blanc			

cable-car station of the **Téléphérique de l'Aiguille du Midi** (*aiguilledumidi.montblancnaturalresort.com/en; adult/child return €78/66.30*), the challenging 20km ski route follows three serpentine glaciers down to the lower, moraine-scarred reaches of France's longest glacier, the **Mer de Glace** (Sea of Ice).

Here, at around 1700m, the glass-sided **Télécabine de la Mer de Glace** (*montenversmerdeglace.montblancnatural resort.com; adult/child return incl train, cable car & ice cave €39.50/33.60*) – a state-of-the-art cable car directly above an ice cave – whisks Vallée Blanche skiers back up to Gare du Montenvers at 1913m. From here Montenvers' cherry-red cogwheel train trundles down to Chamonix town in 20 minutes. This leg of the trip is also an exhilarating day trip for nonskiers year-round.

Late March to early April is the best time to tackle the Vallée Blanche, only suitable for confident skiers comfortable on black pistes and ungroomed terrain. Hook up with a guide from **Compagnie des Guides de Chamonix** (*chamonix-guides. com*) on a **small-group expedition** (*per person €155, plus lift passes €90*), with an overnight at 3613m at the **Refuge des Cosmiques** (*incl lift pass €425*) on the Col du Midi glacier or – most magically of all – on a **moonlight descent** (*2 people €430*).

Get up high on Chamonix's most popular hiking trail

Don trainers or sturdy walking shoes for the short but steep, rocky hike up to **Lac Blanc** (2352m). Despite horrific summertime crowds (avoid in July and August), marvelling at razor-sharp reflections of Europe's highest peak in the picture-postcard alpine lake is mind-blowing. Wild dipping in the crystalline water is prohibited.

Beat the crowds by hitting the trail at 8.30am when cable cars open; count three to four hours to cover the 8.5km return hike from the top of **Téléphérique de la Flégère** *(adult/child return €24/20.40)* at 1877m. Alternatively, overnight in Lac Blanc's lakeside mountain hut **Refuge du Lac Blanc** *(refuge-lac-blanc.fr; per person incl full board €85)* to gorge on sunrise views in splendid isolation. The WWII-era, 40-bed hut with basic cafe is open June to September.

Summiting the Aiguille du Midi

This rocky tooth of an alpine peak – **Aiguille du Midi** (3842m) in the Massif du Mont Blanc, easy to spot for miles around – ensnares France's highest cable-car station at 3777m, promising spine-tingling adventure for mountain enthusiasts and privileged access to a spectacular fairy-tale ice world for first-timers to high altitudes. Since it's weather dependent, check the website for variable hours *(aiguilledumidi.montblanc naturalresort.com; adult/child €88/68.90)*.

The giddy anticipation of new heights to be conquered is electric as you glide from Chamonix's bottom Téléphérique de l'Aiguille du Midi cable-car station to its top station at 3842m. The change of cabin at mid-station Plan d'Aiguille du Midi (2317m) is a prime opportunity to grab a coffee or *vin chaud* (warm mulled wine) at mountain hut Bar Plan d'Aiguille and acquaint yourself with the numerous aiguilles sculpting Chamonix's distinctive skyline.

At the futuristic top station, dimly lit tunnels spaghetti from the cable car, past wintertime skiers donning crampons to tackle the Vallée Blanche off-piste descent, to a succession of outdoor panoramic terraces. Information panels identify what's what in the surrounding breathtaking sea of snowy peaks.

Follow signs to Le Tube – a 34m-long metal pipe wrapped around part of the rocky spur. Take your time to traverse the cylindrical walkway, perforated with five slit windows overlooking ant-sized rock climbers in summer dangling on Pointe Rébuffat. Information boards impress with mind-blowing facts such as the 300 cu metres of concrete, 80 tons of steel and 500-plus helicopter trips it took to construct this wild, gravity-defying gallery.

CHEESY SAVOYARD SPECIALITIES

Savoyard fondue: In Savoie equal parts of grated Comté, gruyere and Beaufort cheese are melted with white wine in a garlic-smeared pot.

Tartiflette: Reblochon sliced and layered between potatoes, diced bacon, cream and nuts in this classic oven-baked dish.

Raclette: Melted raclette – occasionally smoked/peppered – is scraped from a standing grill onto boiled potatoes.

Burgdorf: Slices of Abondance cheese are oven-baked with Savioe white wine, sweet Madeira wine, nutmeg and pepper until bubbling, crisp and golden.

Crozet gratin: Savoyard 'pasta' squares are oven baked with Beaufort or Reblochon to create a gooey, crisp-crust gratin.

 EATING IN CHAMONIX: BEST MOUNTAIN LUNCHES ——————— MAP p204

Refuge de Lognan: The blueberry tart is a rite of passage at this mountain shelter on Argentière's Intégrale run. Cash only. *noon-2pm Jun-Sep & Dec-Apr €*

La Crèmerie du Glacier: A 1920s forest cabin famed for gratins, fondues and *croûtes* (wine-soaked bread, oven-baked with toppings). *11:30am-3pm €€*

Les Vieilles Luges: A roaring fire welcomes skis at the Old Sledges, an 18th-century farmhouse on the slopes in Les Houches. *12.30-3pm Tue-Sun Dec-Apr €€*

La Bergerie de Planpraz: The cozy Sheepfold gazes at Mont Blanc from its sunny terrace perched at 2000m. Order fire-grilled meat. *noon-3pm Dec-Apr €€€*

Ride the lift up to Pas dans le Vide, a glass-walled and -floored cabin overhanging a 1000m drop which, at 3830m, sits just 12m short of the summit. This is the highest point of the Aiguille du Midi tourist site, and views down are predictably exhilarating or terrifying, depending on your head for heights.

Annecy

Timeless romance in a handsome old town

Colourful facades and flower-fringed canals characterise Annecy's Vielle Ville (old town), nicknamed 'Venice of the Alps'. Commanding views across ochre rooftops and flower-festooned canals to the lake and burly Massif des Bauges beyond, **Château d'Annecy** (musees.annecy.fr; adult/under 12yr €7/free) is the crowning glory. Residence to the Counts of Geneva in the 13th and 14th centuries, it was abandoned three centuries on.

From the château, drop steeply down along stone-paved Rampe du Château to prison-turned-history museum **Palais de l'Isle** (adult/child €5/2.50). The best views of this eye-catching stone building, squatting on a triangular islet in the Canal du Thiou since 1325, are from Pont Perrière, the old town's distinctive canal bridge safeguarded by baroque **Église St-François de Salès**. The Venetian atmosphere here is undeniable.

Fly with the birds above Col de la Forclaz

It requires no skill – just guts or the dream to fly with birds – to paraglide over Lake Annecy. April to November, tandem flights take off from the **Site de Montmin** (1276m) up high near the **Col de la Forclaz** (1150m) at the lake's southern tip. They land 10 to 20 minutes later at official landing zones in Doussard (next to the D281) or in Perroix (2km south of Talloires).

Dozens of *parapente* (paragliding) schools offer tandem flights. Several operate from wooden huts at the Doussard landing field, from where minibuses shuttle clients up to the pass. In Annecy's old town, adventure-sports specialists **Takamaka** (annecy.takamaka.fr; from €95) has an office at 23 rue du Faubourg Ste-Claire where you can pick up info, check weather/flying conditions and reserve flights.

Paddling and surfing Lake Annecy

Don't let the garish rubber rings outside the *épicerie* (grocery) at the entrance to Doussard Plage on the lake's southern tip put you off. Once afloat a stand-up paddleboard (SUP), you'll find the serenity of less-tamed shores here is intoxicating.

 EATING IN ANNECY: OUR PICKS

Marché de la Vieille Ville: Open-air street market in the old town, stalls with Savoyard cheeses, charcuterie and food to go. *7am-1pm Tue, Fri & Sun* €

Les Baigneurs Café: Breakfast, brunch, specialist coffee and lunchtime tartines on a sun-soaked terrace. *8.30am-5.30pm Wed-Fri, from 9am Sat & Sun* €

Bon Pain Bon Vin: Local produce fuels this old-school buvette with 1960s interior, traditional cuisine and specials chalked on the board. *10am-1am* €€

Saba: Feast on creative French-Japanese fusion with local foodies at this sassy old-town bistro. *noon-1.30pm & 7-9pm Mon, Tue, Thu & Fri, 7-9pm Wed* €€€

CYCLING LAKE ANNECY

Lap up big mountain views and bijou villages on this 42km lake-loop ride.

START	END	LENGTH
Annecy Town	Annecy Town	42km; 3–4 hours

Hire a bicycle/e-bike from **①** **Cyclable** (annecy-bonlieu.cyclable.com) and set off clockwise (300m elevation). Pick up the two-way cycling path in front of Veyrier-du-Lac, and cruise 6km alongside the D909, past Mont Veyrier (1291m) on your left. Climb up to place de l'Église in Menthon-St-Bernard, 3km south; its fairy-tale **②** **Château de Menthon-St-Bernard** is a 2km detour uphill. At **③** **Café de la Place**, refuel on coffee and a *tarte écureuil* (caramelised walnut tart) from the bakery.

Stay alert on the steep downhill swoop to Talloires. It was in this pretty lakefront village

cradling 17th-century **④** **Abbaye de Talloires** that Cézanne painted in 1896. This is the lake's narrowest point where the built-up 'grand lac' (north) spills into the wilder 'petit lac' (south). Thirty minutes (8.7km) on a dedicated cycling path takes you to the lake's southern tip. Doussard is the springboard for walks in the **⑤** **Réserve Naturelle du Bout du Lac d'Annecy**. A greenway now takes you to Duingt: pedalling through a defunct railway tunnel heralds your arrival. Park and follow the footpath 10 minutes to hillside **⑥** **Grotte de Notre Dame du Lac** for breathtaking lake views. It's 13km back to Annecy.

Lakeside **Château de Duingt** hosts seasonal exhibitions.

Along the reserve's circular boardwalk, keep your eyes peeled for beavers.

Climb the **Tour de Brauvivier** to watch paragliders dropping over rocky Dents de Lanfon (1824m) and Lanfonnet (1793m).

SKIING LES TROIS VALLÉES

The world's largest ski area connects three valleys with 600km of pistes and 200 lifts. Key resorts:

Méribel (1450m): Best for intermediate skiers: 150km of blue and red runs, two snow parks and a wild après-ski scene. Linked by gondola to budget Brides-les-Bains (600m). *(meribel.net)*

Courchevel (1850m): Tree-fringed playground for the super-rich; La Tania (1400m) lower down is less flash. *(courchevel.com)*

Val Thorens (2300m): Europe's highest ski resort, meaning the longest snow-sure season (usually late November to mid-May. *(valthorens.com)*

St-Martin de Belleville (1450m): Traditional village option: chic accommodation and dining ranging from gourmet mountain hut to Michelin-starred. *(st-martin-belleville.com)*

Paragliding over Lake Annecy (p206), Annecy

Help yourself to an inflatable board, paddle and life vest – via the Equip Sport app – from the ingenious SUP vending machine on the lawn section of Doussard Beach. April to October, head to beach cafe **Le Cadre** *(lecadre74.com)*, at the beach's opposite end by the pleasure port, where water-sports school **SkiWake74** *(skiwake74.com; rental per hr €17)* rents kayaks and SUPs. You can also water-ski, wakeboard or surf the waves of the latest speedboat here.

Alpe d'Huez

Fly down Europe's longest black run

Winter or summer, in the ski town of Alpe d'Huez, riding the two legs of the **Télépherique du Pic Blanc** *(skipass. alpedhuez.com)* up to Lac Blanc (2700m) and beyond to Pic Blanc (3330m) is dizzying. Prepare for bitter cold on the wind-whipped glacier – frequently -20°C in winter and -10°C on a sun-scorched spring day. A spectacular ski-swoosh down to Alpe d'Huez beckons – on Europe's longest black run, 16km-long **La Sarenne** with a 2km vertical drop. Except for a handful of steep, ungroomed segments polka-dotted with moguls, the snowy descent is more like a wide, roller-coaster red with a maddeningly long green at the end. Skip the final 'flat' by cutting off at Pont du Gua to take the Chalvet chairlift up, then ski the red Campanules down. To admire Pic Blanc and its glacier in an alternative, magical light, ski La Sarenne at sunrise with a *pisteur* (ski patroller) or after sunset by head-torch with a guide; book at the tourist office *(alpedhuez.com)* on place Joseph Paganon.

Nonskiers zoom down Europe's longest black run on two wheels during April's Sarenne Snowbike *(skipass.alpedhuez .com/hiver/sarenne-snowbike)* and in July when thousands of intrepid bikers rip down ice, slush and rocks at speeds of up to 100km/h during Megavalanche, the world's longest downhill mountain-bike event.

Lyon

FINE WINE | UNPARALLELED DINING | VARIED HISTORY

First the Roman capital of the Gauls in the 1st century BCE, then European capital of the silk trade in the 16th century, Lyon's past has been multifaceted. As it industrialised and motorists began to pass through, it rose to prominence in the Michelin road guide, leading to the discovery of the city's unusual cuisine and *bouchon* restaurants.

Lyon today is wonderfully liveable, and still deservedly wears the crown as France's gastronomic capital. It has a sprinkling of everything: great food and wine, proximity to the mountains, immense parks, a buzzing nightlife (watered by fine wines from Beaujolais to the north and the Rhône Valley to the south), and architecture that yo-yos between Roman, Renaissance, Baroque and art deco. In recent years, the city council has invested in all things green, meaning that bike paths are often as wide as car lanes, and footpaths and parks run along much of the riverbanks.

> ☑ **TOP TIP**
> Some of the best art installations are under your feet. Incognito street artist Ememem is Lyon's answer to Banksy, only they're solving the city's pothole problem by filling them in with mosaics.

Before Lyon Came Lugdunum

Think about the Roman Empire

Until 43 BCE, Lyon was little more than a Gaulish village. Lucius Munatius Plancus, governor of Gaul, was sent to found a Roman colony by the Senate, and Lugdunum was born. Under Emperor Augustus (27 BCE to 14 CE) the city mushroomed, and many vestiges of its Roman origins are still standing today. The 1st-century-CE amphitheatre is home to summer

🧭 GETTING AROUND

Lyon's metro is comprehensive and reliable *(€2.10/journey)*. A **Lyon City Card** *(24hr/48hr/72hr/96hr €32/€44/€56/€68)* from **Only Lyon Tourist Office** includes entry into multiple museums, public transport, guided visits and certain boat trips. Download the Vélo'v app (electric and regular bikes) for easy, pay-per-use rental in the city. To get to the city centre from the airport, take the **Rhône Express** *(rhoneexpress.fr; one way €15.20)*, or the C200 bus *(€2.10)* to **Vaulx-en-Velin La Soie** metro.

WHAT'S A BOUCHON?

In other parts of the country, a *bouchon* is either a wine cork or a traffic jam. In Lyon, they're meat-heavy traditional restaurants formerly run by *Mères Lyonnaises* (Lyonnaise mothers), who'd feed workers cheap, cheerful and filling plates of offal, washed down with red wine. Restaurants sticking to tradition dish up *andouillette* (sausages made from pig intestines), kidney and tripe, and many of the upmarket *bouchons* manage to make it quite palatable (though beware tourist traps in Vieux Lyon). The truly traditional even serve *mâchon*: bottomless brunch with a Lyonnais twist. Instead of eggs and avocado, the menu includes *rognons de veau* (calf kidneys) and *tête de veau* (calf's head) all washed down with large quantities of wine...at 9am.

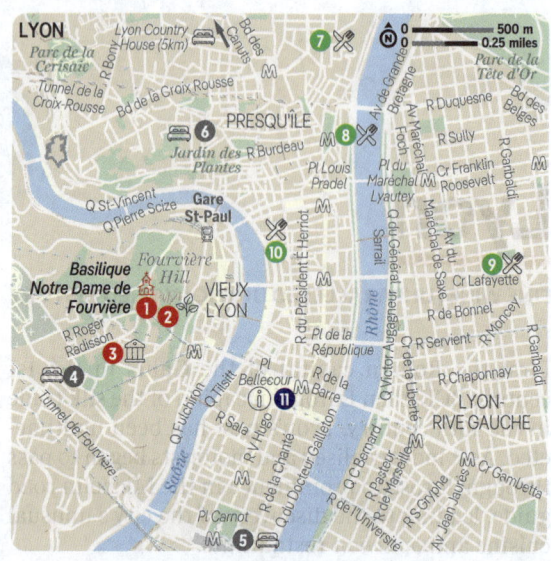

⭐ **HIGHLIGHTS**
1 Basilique Notre Dame de Fourvière

🔴 **SIGHTS**
2 Jardin du Rosaire
3 Musée Gallo-Romain de Fourvière

⚫ **SLEEPING**
4 Fourvière Hôtel
5 Hotel de Verdun 1882
6 Pilo

🟢 **EATING**
7 Alebrije
8 Astral

9 Ayla
10 Circle

🔵 **INFORMATION**
11 Only Lyon Tourist Office

concerts; **Nuits de Fourvière**, in June and July, is the largest. There's a great museum, the **Musée Gallo-Romain de Fourvière** (*lugdunum.grandlyon.com; adult/child €7/3*), that thoroughly explores Lyon's origins and has plenty of interactive displays for kids, including one section where they can dress up as gladiators.

Discover Secret Passageways
Traboules crisscross the city

Over 400 *traboules*, covered passageways originally used for transporting silk, wind their way through Lyon. Many are in private buildings, making them difficult to explore independently. Lyon's free **walking tour** (*freetourlyon.com*) – give what you like – in English and run by a Dutch expat, shows places many locals don't even know exist. Choose from a tour of Vieux Lyon (the Old Town), or Vieux Lyon and Croix-Rousse, and expect to return with a mine of fun facts. Who knew that the predecessor to computers was Lyon's silk-weaving Jacquard loom?

©GERALD VILLENA/SHUTTERSTOCK

Virgin Mary statue, Basilica Notre-Dame de Fourvière

High on the Basilica Domes

A hill with history

It's difficult to imagine Lyon without **Basilica Notre-Dame de Fourvière** *(fourviere.org; free)*, which dominates the skyline, but was only built at the end of the 19th century. The golden statue of the Virgin Mary predates the basilica: it was built by a local sculptor in 1852 and erected on the spires of the basilica to commemorate Lyon's liberation from the plague epidemic in 1643 (rumour has it that the disease never crossed the Rhône and stayed confined to the other side of Pont de la Guillotière).

Views from the top of Fourvière Hill are already impressive: they take in Lyon's twin rivers, the Saône and the Rhône, and (when you stand next to the basilica) the Alps. However, the highest point is from the basilica's domes. Inside the cathedral, stained-glass windows and ceilings adorned with golden stars and chandeliers of epic proportions create scenes straight out of a fairy tale. **Tours** *(booking.fourviere.org; adult/child €14/7)* run daily from April to September. To get here, take the funicular from Vieux Lyon, or walk up through **Jardin du Rosaire**.

 EATING IN LYON: PROPER GOOD GRUB

Circle: Six- or eight-course tasting menus where the quality of the simplest ingredients, like olive oil, shines through. *noon-1.15pm & 8-9.15pm Tue-Sat* €€€

Ayla: Franco-Lebanese sharing plates, as much of a feast for eyes as bellies. The tempura vine leaves stand out. *noon-2pm & 7.30-9.30pm Tue-Sat* €€

Astral: Classic French cuisine done well, managed by a young team. It also runs wine tastings in the cellar. *noon-2pm & 7-9.30pm Thu-Mon* €€

Alebrije: Franco-Mexican fusion from one of Lyon's top chefs, Carla Kirsch Lopez, who draws on inspiration from her two cultures. *7.30-9pm Tue-Sat* €€€

Beyond
Lyon

Towering limestone gorges, prehistoric caves and the seat of the European Parliament are easily reachable from Lyon.

Places

Strasbourg p212
Gorges de l'Ardèche p213
Gorges du Tarn p215

Limestone pillars higher than skyscrapers mask warrens of prehistoric caves, and forests teem with wildlife. The many twists and turns of the Ardèche River and Tarn River cut through their prospective limestone plateaus and snake through the middle to form the Gorges de l'Ardèche and the Gorges du Tarn. To the northeast, the impossibly photogenic city of Strasbourg is a flurry of twisting backstreets lined with crooked half-timbered houses, scenic canals, flower-filled courts and opulent shops. Inviting *winstubs* (traditional Alsatian taverns) cower beneath the soaring magnificence of the cathedral, a medieval marvel in pink sandstone. It may look like something out of a fairy tale, but Strasbourg has got its finger on the pulse, and this city is the seat of the European Parliament.

Strasbourg

TIME FROM LYON: **4HR**

Awe-inspiring architecture

Strasbourg walks a fine tightrope between France and Germany, and between a medieval past and a progressive future.

Completed in all its Gothic grandeur in 1439, **Cathédrale Notre-Dame** (*cathedrale-strasbourg.fr; astronomical clock adult/child €4/2, platform €8/5*) is the unchallenged Strasbourg icon in the heart of the city. The lace-fine facade lifts the gaze little by little to flying buttresses, leering gargoyles and a 142m spire. The interior is exquisitely lit by 12th- to 14th-century stained-glass windows. We love the quirky Gothic-meets-Renaissance astronomical clock that strikes solar noon at 12.30pm with a parade of figures portraying the lives of the Apostles. A spiral staircase twists up to the 66m-high viewing platform. To appreciate the cathedral in peace, visit in the early evening, when the crowds have thinned.

Visit the European Quarter

About 2km northeast of central Strasbourg, the European Quarter is a city within the city, with its own architecture and unique energy. Overlooking the River Ill, the oval-shaped building of the **Parlement Européen** (*europarl.europa.eu*) is striking. You can take an audioguide tour or sit in on debates ranging from lively to yawn-a-minute.

GETTING AROUND

Strasbourg is a major transport hub, and has high-speed (TGV) connections to Paris (from one hour 50 minutes). There's also an airport serving several European destinations.

Strasbourg city centre is relatively small, so easy to walk.

Both the Gorges de l'Ardèche and the Gorges du Tarn are difficult to reach using public transport: take a car to avoid wasting hours waiting for virtually nonexistent buses. The scenic roads with sweeping bends are popular with motorcyclists.

Cathédrale Notre-Dame's astronomical clock, Strasbourg

DINING AT A WINSTUB

For a memorable culinary experience in Strasbourg, dine at a *winstub*: a traditional Alsatian restaurant renowned for its warm, homely atmosphere. Most dishes are based on pork and veal; specialities include *baeckeoffe* (meat stew), *wädele* or *jambonneau braisé* (braised pork knuckles), *fleischschnäcke* (minced meat rolls) and *choucroute garnie* (sauerkraut garnished with meat or fish). Vegetarians can usually order *bibelaskäs* (soft white cheese mixed with fresh cream) and *pommes sautées* (sautéed potatoes). Also look for restaurants serving *tarte flambée* (a thin-crust pizza dough topped with crème fraiche, onions and lardons). Alsatian specialities are best accompanied with Alsatian white wines.

A futuristic glass crescent, the Council of Europe's **Palais de l'Europe** *(coe.int)* across the River Ill can be visited on free one-hour weekday tours (ask to join a group); see the website for reservations. You can also take a virtual tour at *70.coe.int/virtual-tour-en.html*.

It's just a hop across the Canal de la Marne to the swirly silver **Palais des Droits de l'Homme** *(European Court of Human Rights; echr.coe.int)*, the most eye-catching of all the EU institutions. It ensures that 46 European states abide by the European Convention on Human Rights.

Gorges de l'Ardèche

TIME FROM LYON: 3HR 🚗

Prehistoric cave paintings

Grotte Chauvet 2 *(grottechauvet2ardeche.com; adult/child 10-17/under 10yr €18/9/free)* may be a replica of the original cave, which is closed to the public to avoid damaging the cave paintings, but it's a good one. The original, discovered in 1994, is a UNESCO World Heritage Site, and features cave paintings thought to be over 30,000 years old, composed of handprints and sketches of cave bears, cave lions and mammoths. From the paintings it's possible to deduce incredible amounts of information, including the rough age and the gender of the artists. The replica includes exceptionally informative guided

EATING IN STRASBOURG: OUR WINSTUB PICKS

Chez Yvonne: Near the cathedral, Chez Yvonne is an institution. Traditional decor and excellent Alsatian dishes. *11.45am-2pm & 6.30-10pm Tue-Sat* €

Le Tire-Bouchon: Arguably the best *choucroute* of Strasbourg is served at this snug, amiable *winstub*. *11.30am-9.30pm* €

Au Pont Corbeau: The essence of Alsace quaintness: dark timber, checked tablecloths and hearty grub. *noon-2pm & 7-9.30pm Mon-Fri, noon-2pm Sun* €

Le Clou: The menu is packed with classics – *wädele, bibelaskäs* – all of which marry nicely with a glass of local pinot noir. *11.45am-2.30pm & 6-10pm* €

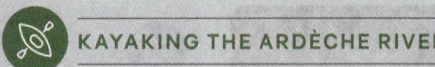

KAYAKING THE ARDÈCHE RIVER

A roller-coaster adventure by water through France's prehistoric playground. Shorter 7km and 13km routes are also possible.

START	END	LENGTH
Vallon Pont d'Arc	Sauze	32km; 7 hours/2 days

Kayaking the Ardèche River reaches motorway levels of busy in high season; a website is in place to predict how busy the river will be. Canoë Malin can be consulted via the tourist office website (*gorges-ardeche-pontdarc.fr*).

Start at ❶ **Vallon Pont d'Arc**: it's a sprawling mass of rental shops without a clearly defined centre. There's plenty of choice and, so long as your kayak is seaworthy, rentals are much of a muchness, supplying laminated maps and a watertight tub for your belongings, and organising your return transfer at the end of whichever distance you choose to tackle. Aigue Vive (*aigue-vive.com*) is helpful and efficient.

It doesn't take long to reach the showstopper, the ❷ **Pont d'Arc** (4km), but what those who've taken the land route don't see are the caves inside the rock arch itself. By kayak, you can dip in and out of the caves and crane your neck to take in the 54m-high rock arch from the water.

Keep moving with the current, over rapids (Grade II/Grade III) and between limestone cliffs, to reach two wild campsites: ❸ **Bivouac de Gaud** and ❹ **Bivouac de Gournier**. If splitting the trip over two days, you'll need to camp at one of these. For the final few kilometres to ❺ **Sauze**, the limestone cliffs shrink, and you can often see vultures wheeling overhead.

Pont d'Arc is a 60m rock arch created by thousands of years of water erosion.

Les Mazes

START

Vallon-Pont-dArc

ARDÈCHE

D4   St-Rémèze

D290

Gorges de l'Ardèche

D579

Ardèche

❸

❹

Gorge de l'Ardèche Réserve Naturelle

Sauze is the end of the (watery) road, with several riverside restaurants and bars.

Bivouacs Gaud and Gournier are open April to September. Obtain a camping permit (*€16.50*) from the tourist office in Vallon Pont d'Arc.

N   0 _____ 5 km
     0 _____ 2.5 miles

Ardèche

END   ❺   Sauze

Aiguèze   St-Martin d'Ardèche

D901   St-Julien de Peyrolas

GARD

Gorges du Tarn

BEST LONG-DISTANCE HIKES NEAR THE GORGES DU TARN

For more information, see gr-infos.com.

GR67: Considered the ultimate guide to the Cévennes on foot, the 130km GR67 is a loop hike that begins and ends in Anduze, summiting Mt Aigoual.

GR68: The GR68, aka the Mont Lozère loop, never actually climbs the mountain, rather using it as the axle around which the 115km hike revolves.

GR736: From Albi to Villefort, this 317km route encompasses the entire Causses et Cévennes.

GR4: Passes through the Causses et Cévennes on its way from the Atlantic to the Mediterranean.

GR70: The Stevenson Trail, famously trekked by Robert Louis Stevenson and his donkey Modestine, running from Le Puy-en-Velay to Alès.

visits and immersive sound-and-light shows. The visit lasts approximately one hour; factor in extra time for the sound-and-light show. Audioguides in English available.

Gorges du Tarn

TIME FROM LYON: 3½HR

Road trips and watery adventures

One of France's most spectacular natural wonders, the Gorges du Tarn, is found in the zone where the Cévennes becomes the Causses: a biodiverse region of shifting mountain-scapes. If you have a car, prepare for one of the country's truly spectacular, and slightly unnerving, drives. The gorge runs for around 50km, but a good entry point is the pretty village of Ste-Énimie. From here, the D907 balcony road scrapes its way past vertiginous cliffs, which occasionally hang right over the road.

Midway along is the stunning La Malène village, the best point to go boating. **Les Bateliers des Gorges du Tarn** (gorgesdutarn.com; €26), the revered local boaters, steer you down the river in a green wooden boat. Kayaking and canoeing are popular alternatives, and the river is safer for beginners here than Ste-Énimie. **Canoë 2000** (canoe-kayak-gorgesdu tarn.com) and **Canoe au Moulin de la Malène** (canoeblanc. com) rent all the necessary equipment and drive you back to the village at the end. In **Ste-Énimie**, try **Canoë Méjean** (canoe-mejean.com). Back on the road, at **Le Rozier** you can turn east into **Gorges de la Jonte**, which has another stunning gorge drive on wider, less crowded roads.

 EATING IN GORGES DU TARN: BEST RESTAURANTS

L'Alicanta: Seasonal ingredients (often linked to beef, pork or lamb) with good-value set menus in Le Rozier. *7-8.30pm* €€

Le Petit Paris: Try regional dishes, such as *aligot* (cheesy mashed potato served with sausage) in Ste-Énimie. *hours vary Fri-Tue* €€

Capluc Kfé: Charcuterie and cheeseboards, river trout and *aligot* with pork sausages in onion gravy are hearty at this Le Rozier favourite. *hours vary* €€

Auberge du Moulin: Terrace dining in Ste-Énimie, overlooking the gorge, with French cuisine staples such as roast leg of lamb with vegetables. *Thu-Tue Apr-Oct* €€

Loire Valley

RIVERSIDE CASTLES | VINEYARDS | SERENE CYCLING

Le Mans · St-Calais · Orléans
La Flèche · Vendôme · Beaugency
Château de Loir · **Blois** · **Chambord**
Villandry · Tours · Amboise · Romorantin-Lanthenay
Chenonceaux · Vierzon
Azay-le-Rideau · Loches
Châtellerault · Châteauroux

 TOP TIP

Thirsty? Head to one of the Loire's many *guinguettes*. A kind of pop-up riverbank restaurant with a beer-garden vibe, *guinguettes* originated in Paris during the Belle Époque. Open from spring to early autumn, they bring together wooden furniture, deckchairs, hanging fairy lights, local wine, tasty food and, often, live music.

If you're looking for French splendour, style and gastronomy, the Loire Valley will exceed your expectations, no matter how great. Poised on the crucial frontier between northern and southern France – and just a short train or *autoroute* (tolled motorway) ride from Paris – the region was once of immense strategic importance. Kings, queens, dukes and nobles came here to build feudal castles and, later on, sumptuous Renaissance pleasure palaces – that's why this fertile river valley is sprinkled with hundreds of France's most opulent aristocratic estates, many sporting crenellated towers, soaring cupolas and twinkling banquet halls.

The Loire, much of it a UNESCO World Heritage Site, is also known for its outstanding wines – reds, whites, rosés and sparkling – and vineyards stretch along both banks of the Loire from the Blésois, westward through Touraine and Anjou, to the Atlantic. A network of walking trails, bike paths and tertiary roads makes it easy to visit both glittering châteaux and vine-encircled *domaines* (wine-growing estates) in a single afternoon.

Fans of French urban life will find medium-sized cities that are renowned for their *douceur de vivre* (the gentle pleasures of life), with verve and energy added by tens of thousands of students. Tours, Angers and Nantes are graced with handsome avenues, historic

GETTING AROUND

Having your own wheels is the easiest and quickest way to visit châteaux and vineyards, but if you stay in the city centre in Tours, Angers and Nantes, a car can be a liability, as parking is in short supply and is time-limited and/or pricey. Tours-Centre, the Loire Valley's main rail hub, has direct services to over a dozen Loire destinations.

Direct TGV trains link Paris Montparnasse with St-Pierre-des-Corps (3km from Tours), Angers-St-Laud and Nantes. Zipping along backroads on a *vélo* is a fantastic way to tour the Loire.

quarters traversed by narrow medieval streets and excellent (and moderately priced) dining, as well as an abundance of lovely gardens and romantic riverside promenades.

Blois

Royal château with a bloody history

Seven French kings lived in the **Château Royal de Blois** (*chateaudeblois.fr; adult/child €14.50/7.50*). Its four grand wings were built during four distinct periods in French architecture: Gothic (13th century), Flamboyant Gothic (1498–1501), early Renaissance (1515–20) and classical (1630s). You can easily spend a half-day immersing yourself in the château's dramatic and bloody history and its extraordinary architecture. An informative audioguide costs €3; a HistoPad, offering augmented-reality views, is free at the *consigne* (checked-luggage facility). The most sumptuous part of the Gothic wing is the richly painted Estates General Room, from the 13th century. The King's Chamber was the setting for one of the bloodiest episodes in the château's history, the assassination of Duke Henri I de Guise in 1588.

Every night from early April to late September, a 45-minute **Son et Lumière** (*adult/child €12/7.50*), held in the interior courtyard, brings the château's history and architecture to life with dramatic lighting and narration.

Chambord

The Loire's most magnificent château

One of the crowning achievements of French Renaissance architecture, the **Château de Chambord** (*chambord.org; adult/child €19/free*) – with 426 rooms, 282 fireplaces and 77 staircases – is the largest, grandest and most visited château in the Loire Valley. Rising through the centre of the structure, the world-famous double-helix staircase ascends to the great lantern tower and the rooftop, where you can gaze out across the vast grounds and marvel at a mind-blowing skyline of cupolas, domes, turrets, chimneys and lightning rods. To add virtual-reality furnishings to some of the rooms, pick up – at the entrance to the château itself – a HistoPad tablet computer (*€6.50, 1½ hours*). In July and August, hour-long guided **tours** (*adult/child €7/4*) in English begin daily at 11.15am; reserve online or at the ticket counter.

WINE TOURING IN THE LOIRE

It's easy to put together a web of wonderful wine-tasting itineraries in the Loire, drawing on 350 wine cellars producing reds, rosés, whites, dessert wines and crémants (sparkling wines). A tourist office or *maison des vins* (wine visitor centre) can supply you with local options and – assuming it's reissued – *A la Découverte des Vins de Loire* (Discovering Loire Wines): a free map with an excellent, colour-coded presentation of the winegrowing areas that stretch from Blois to the Atlantic. It is produced by the region's winegrowers' association, Vins de Loire (*vinsdeloire. fr*); its website has plenty of information in English and downloadable brochures under 'Tourist circuits'.

EATING IN BLOIS: OUR FRENCH PICKS

Poivre et Sel: Traditional French cuisine served on rustic tables, with old-style wood beams overhead. *noon-1.45pm & 7-9.30pm Mon-Sat* €€

L'Arboré Sens: A city-centre brasserie with a pretty terrace, a good selection of salads, reasonable prices and, on some evenings, live music. *11am-midnight Mon-Sat* €

Côté Loire-Auberge Ligérienne: On the riverfront, French cuisine in a rustic dining room and, when it's warm, on a lovely terrace. *noon-1.30pm & 7.30-9pm Tue-Sat* €€

Au Rendez-Vous des Pêcheurs: Elegant bistro specialising in fish (salmon, cod, zander), served on gorgeous ceramic plates. *12.15-1.15pm & 7.15-8.30pm Tue-Sat* €€€

VINEYARD-HOPPING & FLOATING ABOVE THE VINEYARDS

Private companies offer well-organised minibus tours that take in various combinations of châteaux, sometimes coupled with vineyard visits, as well as specialised tours featuring cycling or wine-tasting. Tourist offices and their websites have details. Floating peacefully in a *montgolfière* (hot-air-balloon) is a gorgeously romantic way to see the Loire countryside. Operated by about a dozen companies, flights are generally possible from April to October, weather permitting, with departures early in the morning or in the evening. Tourist offices (eg Tours and Amboise) and their websites can provide contact information and help with reservations.

VICTOR TORRES/SHUTTERSTOCK

Château de Chenonceau, Chenonceau

The château is surrounded by Louis XIV-style formal gardens (château tickets required) and extensive grounds (open 24 hours). At the Embarcadère (boat dock), rent bicycles, quadricycles, electric golf carts and electric boats from early April to October. Outdoor spectacles held in the warm season include a 45-minute **equestrian show** *(adult/child €18/14.30, adult incl château €32)* in which horses and colourfully clad riders take you through five centuries of Chambord's history. Shows are held from early April to September and begin at 11.45am and/or 4pm from Tuesday to Sunday.

Chenonceaux

Elegant arches and delightful gardens

Spanning the languid Cher River atop a graceful arched bridge, the **Château de Chenonceau** *(chenonceau.com; adult/child €18/15)* is one of France's most elegant castles. It's hard not to be moved and exhilarated by the glorious setting, the formal gardens, the magic of the architecture and the château's fascinating history. Chenonceau is largely the work of several remarkable women – hence its nickname, the Château des Dames. The distinctive arches and the eastern formal garden were added by Diane de Poitiers, mistress of Henri II. Catherine de Médici completed the château's construction and added the yew-tree maze and the western rose garden. The most singular contribution of Louise of Lorraine's was her black-walled mourning room on the top floor, to which she retreated when her husband, Henri III, was assassinated in 1589.

The château's pièce de résistance is the 60m-long, checkerboard-floored Grande Galerie over the Cher River, scene of many an elegant party hosted by Catherine de Médici and Madame Dupin. Used as a military hospital during WWI, it served from 1940 to 1942 as an escape route for *résistants*, Jews and other refugees fleeing from the German-occupied zone (north of the Cher) to the Vichy-controlled zone (south of the river). There's an excellent 1¼-hour audioguide *(€5)* in 12 languages. Chenonceau's elegant restaurant, L'Orangerie, serves brunch-style French meals from noon to 3pm and becomes a *salon de thé* (tearoom) from 3pm to 4.30pm You can taste Touraine wines in the château's historic wine cellar, the Cave des Dômes (closed November to January). Chenonceaux (the name of the village has an X at the end) is an easy train ride from Tours.

Villandry
Exquisite gardens à la Française

The gardens of the **Château de Villandry** *(chateauvillandry. com; adult/child €14/8, gardens only €8.50/5.50, winter €2)* are among France's most beautiful, with more than 6 hectares of cascading flowers, ornamental vines, manicured lime trees, razor-sharp box-hedges and tinkling fountains. Try to visit when the gardens – all of them organic – are blooming (ie between April and October). Tickets are valid all day (get your hand stamped if you leave). An audioguide costs €4. For many, the highlight is the 16th-century-style *Potager Décoratif* (Decorative Kitchen Garden), where cabbages, leeks and carrots create nine geometrical, colour-coordinated squares.

Azay-le-Rideau
Renaissance castle par excellence

Romantic, moat-ringed **Château d'Azay-le-Rideau** *(azay-le-rideau.fr; adult/child €16/free)*, built almost exactly 500 years ago on a natural island in the middle of the Indre River, is wonderfully adorned with elegant turrets, exquisitely proportioned windows, delicate stonework and steep slate roofs. The famous, Italian-style loggia staircase overlooking the central courtyard is decorated with the salamanders and ermines of François I and Queen Claude. Audioguides *(€3; 1½ hours)* are available in five languages. From mid-July to late August, you can take a *flânerie nocturne* (nighttime stroll; adult/child €8/4) around the illuminated gardens, accompanied by ancient music, from nightfall until 11.15pm.

CYCLING THE LOIRE

The Loire Valley is fabulous cycling country – pedal through villages, vineyards and forests on your way from one château to the next. **La Loire à Vélo** *(Loire by Bike; loirebybike.co.uk)* maintains 900km of signposted routes from Nevers to the Atlantic; pick up a free guide from a tourist office or access information (details on route options and bike hire) from the website. Individual *départements*, including Indre-et-Loire (Touraine), Loir-et-Cher (Blésois) and Maine-et-Loire (Anjou), have their own cycling networks and brochures. Les Châteaux à Vélo *(chateauxavelo.co.uk)* maintains over 500km of marked bike routes in the Blésois. The Geovelo smartphone app recommends routes that follow bike paths and avoid heavy traffic.

Provence

SEDUCTIVE BEACHES | LAVENDER FIELDS | COLOURFUL CITIES

 TOP TIP

Don't dismiss Provence in winter. The crowds have left and prices are much lower, but the temperature remains balmy. Some of the best parties happen in winter, including Nice's carnival, which lasts for two weeks each February.

When you find yourself awash in Provence's famous light, it becomes clear why so many artists have been magnetically drawn here for centuries, seeking to unlock something bigger than themselves. This land epitomises springtime, having inspired great post-impressionist painters Cézanne and Van Gogh to create their seminal works. As the mistral wind howls down the Rhône Valley towards the sea, slamming the wooden shutters of homes throughout the night and clearing the skies for what feels like endless sunshine, it creates a climate that is not only inviting for travellers but also ideal for farming. Sampling the fresh produce nurtured here is an essential part of the journey, especially in the busy markets and endless stretches of vineyards. For a month or two every year, from June to early July, the region glows purple as Provençal lavender comes into bloom.

The region's palpitating heart is Marseille, France's second-largest city, with its vibrant cultural energy, street art, eclectic nightlife and world-class dining scene. It's constantly evolving, and increasingly attracts partygoers looking to discover 'France's Berlin'. To the east, the Côte d'Azur, France's glittering

GETTING AROUND

Away from the coast, driving in this region can be a joy. To spontaneously stop in tiny villages or wind your way to far-flung vineyards is a luxury. Provence is one of the best cycling areas in France, thanks to its endless backroad options. In the cities, ditch the car as fast as you can. Marseille has two metro lines and an extensive bus network, while Nice is best explored by bus or tram. Both cities also have pay-per-use bike-rental schemes.

The comprehensive ZOU! bus service runs lines all around the region. Great for connecting villages and sights, but, with infrequent services, it's not so great if you want to dine at a restaurant outside of town or have booked accommodation in the countryside. However, it is a good way of avoiding extortionate parking charges and summer traffic jams along the coast.

blue coast, maintains its glorious longtime allure with its intoxicating mix of sun, sea, culture, food and wine. The sun shines down 300 days a year on Nice's Renaissance old town, movie capital Cannes and the glitzy beach clubs of St-Tropez.

Whether you're stretched out by the sea, driving quiet countryside roads or lost in nature, Provence is a sensuous Mediterranean experience waiting to be discovered.

Nice

MAP p222

Soak up the history

Nice's UNESCO heritage can be seen in around 800 buildings across the city, and their art deco detailing and Belle Époque flourishes can be admired from the street. The excellent Explore Nice Côte d'Azur app (*explorenicecotedazur.com/ en/discover-the-unesco-heritage-routes*) organises some of the most noteworthy sites into a series of self-guided neighbourhood walks, complete with a pop-up historical outline of each building listed. You can also deep dive into this protected heritage at the **Musée Massena** (*massena-nice.org; adult/child €10/free*) on the **Promenade des Anglais**. Much of the permanent collection is dedicated to the history of Nice.

Cycling the Prom

The combo of Nice's public e-bike fleet and the dedicated, flat bike lane that extends the entire 6km length of the Promenade des Anglais (and then some) is one of the city's best pairings. The Prom is scattered with bike pickup and drop-off points.

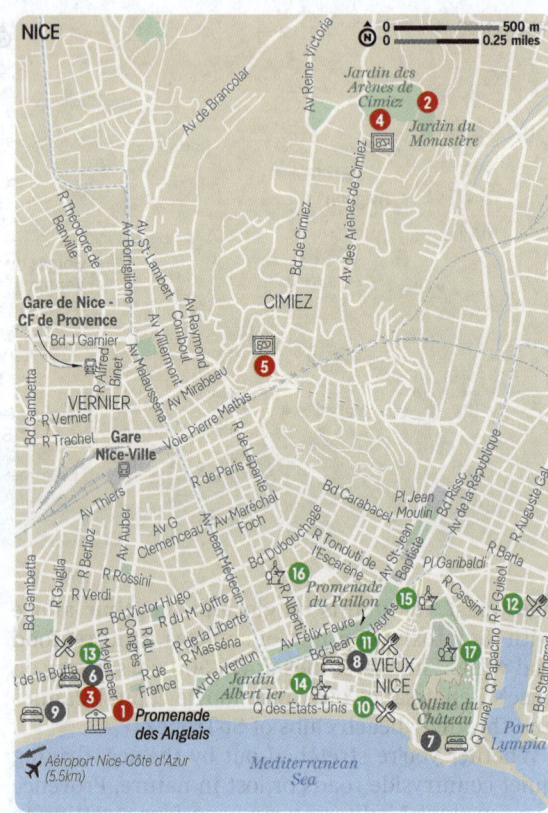

NICE

Propelled by the battery and the fresh sea air, you'll reach **Aéroport Nice-Côte d'Azur** in less than 20 minutes (if starting out at the eastern end opposite the arcades of **Vieux Nice**).

Two masters and their museums

It is a truth universally acknowledged that the light on the Côte d'Azur has an allure unlike anywhere else in the world. Countless artists have been drawn to the region in search of it: two in particular have left their mark (or, perhaps it's the other way around?): Marc Chagall and Henri Matisse. Dedicated museums to both artists occupy sprawling grounds in

 EATING IN NICE: OUR PICKS ──────── MAP p222

Lavomatique: Trendy bistro with natural wines in Vieux Nice. Shared plates cooked in an open kitchen. *noon-1.45pm & 7-10pm Tue-Fri, 7-10pm Mon* €€

Babel Babel: Med cuisine, served across from the Med. Don't miss the panisse with homemade za'atar. *10am-midnight Mon, Thu & Sun, to 2am Fri & Sat* €€

Le Bistrot de Jan: More casual sibling to the Michelin-starred Jan next door. The decor is straight from a design magazine. *noon-3pm & 7pm-12.30am Tue-Sat, 11am-3pm Sun* €€

Le Canon: Neighbourhood fave with a hyperlocal focus: each farmer is named on the menu. *noon-2pm Mon, Tue, Thu & Fri, 7.30-11.30pm Mon-Fri* €€

VV SHOTS/SHUTTERSTOCK

Musée Massena (p221), Nice

WHAT IS NIÇOISE CUISINE?

Nice's street-food culture, including chickpea-based *socca* and panisse, *pan bagnat (salade niçoise* in a bread roll) and *pissaladière* (onion-topped dough), is based on the colourful vegetables and legumes that thrive in the poor, water-deprived soils of the Mediterranean coastline. It feels closer to Italy in nature and flavour than the heavier, sauce-based cuisine of northern France. The city brims with cheap and cheerful street-food stops, as well as more classic local bistros. If you see the Cuisine Nissarde sticker displayed at a restaurant's entrance, you know their dishes respect local culinary traditions. Beyond the traditional places, a new wave of chefs is putting a fine-dining twist on local dishes, elevating them to a semi-gastronomic standing.

Cimiez, the leafy residential neighbourhood in the north of Nice, and can be visited on the same day. Start at the **Musée National Marc Chagall** *(musees-nationaux-alpesmaritimes .fr/chagall; adult/child €10/free)*, where the most extensive public collection of the Belarusian artist's work hangs. The 12 monumental canvases depicting scenes from the Old Testament are spellbinding in colour and detail, and will linger in your memory long after you've left. A further 20 minutes' walk (or Ligne d'Azur bus 5) and you'll arrive at the **Musée Matisse** *(musee-matisse-nice.org; adult/child €10/free)*. The setting, in a coral-red Genoese villa dating from the 17th century, is magic, with olive groves and ancient ruins. Matisse is buried in the **Monastère Notre Dame de Cimiez** at the eastern end of the parkland. Both museums are closed Tuesdays.

The coolest street in town

The strip and the surrounding streets of **rue Bonaparte** are Nice's hip LGBTIQ+ district, having earned the nickname le petit Marais, a nod to Paris' famous bohemian gay quarter. A part of the road is painted rainbow, à la San Francisco's Castro District, and the stretch between place Garibaldi and place du Pin is now fully pedestrianised. This is where you should head if you are looking for a guaranteed evening buzz,

DRINKING IN NICE: BEST WINE BARS

MAP p222

Rouge: Sleek spot just back from Port Lympia serving up stylish, modern tapas plates, washed down with organic wines. *noon-10.30pm*

Cave de la Tour: Enjoy 1940s jazz, an interior that has hardly changed, and Nice wine by the glass. *8am-2.30pm & 6-8.30pm Tue-Sat, 8am-12.30pm Sun*

La Part des Anges: A treasure of natural and organic wines in the city centre; voted best wine bar in France in 2020. *10am-8.30pm Mon-Sat*

Cave Bianchi: History seeps out of every nook of this atmospheric Vieux Nice wine shop and bar across from the Opera. *9.30am-7.30pm, to 10.30pm Fri & Sat*

BEST EVENTS IN NICE

Carnaval de Nice:
For two weeks in late February and early March, floats and flower battles take over the streets. One of Europe's brightest carnivals, running since the Middle Ages.

Lou Queernaval:
France's first queer carnival runs adjacent to the Carnaval de Nice; expect glitter, dazzling floats and drag queens.

Nice Jazz Festival:
Jampacked four-night calendar of performances in Jardin Albert 1er, and fringe concerts popping up all around town.

Pink Parade (Pride):
Crowds swarm Nice's main streets for July's Pink Parade (Pride); the afterparty lasts all night.

Noël à Nice: Sip bubbles with fresh oysters and ride on a giant Ferris wheel; festive Nice lights up during December.

Jardin Exotique d'Èze, Èze

as new bars or restaurants are always opening – just remember that you're still in the provinces, and even the most lively bars shutter by 1am, particularly out of season.

Èze

Exotic flowers and panoramic sea views

Although you'll increasingly need to swerve around selfie-stick-wielding visitors as you meander through it, the **Jardin Exotique d'Èze** *(jardinexotique-eze.fr; adult/child €5/free)* is still one of the region's most delightful experiences. Around the ruined 12th-century château above the terracotta rooftops of the village, a peaceful cactus garden grows: it's more than worth the entry fee for the sweeping sea views that extend beyond Cannes alone.

Cannes

Festival fever

For two weeks every May, Cannes rolls out the red carpet for a galaxy of stars during the annual **Festival de Cannes** (the Cannes Film Festival). The harbourfront **Palais des Festivals et des Congrès** is the epicentre. For the remainder of the year, the gloss barely fades. Follow the trail of over 400

 EATING & DRINKING IN CANNES: OUR PICKS

Poissonnerie Forville:
Fish counter outside Marché Forville serving fresh treats such as oysters and sea urchins (in season). *7am-2.30pm Tue-Sun €€*

Le Pompon: A menu of creative small plates that changes daily with the season. Colourful ingredients and beautiful presentation. *12.15-1.30pm & 7.15-9.30pm Tue-Sat €€*

Bar Fouquet's: Hôtel Barrière Le Majestic's bar serves artful cocktails, where homemade bitters, jellies, even edible perfumes, are standard. *10am-midnight*

Maison Grenache:
Atmospheric wine bar next to the Marché Forville with ultra-knowledgeable owners. *9am-5pm, to 10.30pm Fri & Sat*

stars who have cast their handprints in stainless steel along the **Chemin des Étoiles** (path of stars) outside the Palais. Dates for **tours** *(adult/child €6/3)* inside the Palais are only scheduled six weeks in advance by the tourist office (conveniently housed in the building), depending on the upcoming event calendar, and are only in French. When visits do run, you're given a 1½-hour behind-the-scenes insight into one of cinema's most legendary venues.

St-Tropez
Life's a beach

Sexy St-Tropez might be the most desired destination on the Côte d'Azur and a byword for lithe, tanned bodies dancing on tables at trendy beach bars along buttercream Plage de Pampelonne, but it hasn't always been the jet-set magnet it is today. The sleepy fishing village was thrust into the global spotlight in the 1950s, when a young Brigitte Bardot filmed *And God Created Woman* here. If bling isn't your thing, that doesn't mean you should bypass St-Tropez. Meander cobbled lanes in the old fishing quarter of La Ponche, watch games of pétanque beneath plane trees on place des Lices, fill your picnic basket at its produce market (don't forget a bottle of local rosé), or hike along the coast from beach to beach on the Presqu'île de Saint-Tropez peninsula. Just be aware: in summer, every inch of space is jampacked.

The seaside scene revolves around sandy clubs and restaurants, all with their own style. Most are open May to September, and advance bookings are highly recommended. Beaches also have public areas where you can lay down your towel. The 5km-long, celebrity-studded **Plage de Pampelonne** is the most famous of the beaches and has the largest selection of exclusive clubs and restaurants. It's the place to see and be seen – you'll want to reserve a lounger and lunch. Atmosphere? Indulgence, glitz and relaxation. **Le Club 55** *(leclub55.fr)* is the longest-running Pampelonne club, originally the crew canteen during *And God Created Woman* and still catering to incognito celebs. **Nikki Beach** *(nikkibeach.com/sttropez)* is favoured by dance-on-the-bar glitterati, and those who just want to be seen. For a more chill vibe, try **Le 1051** *(le1051.com)*.

Looking for a quieter beach experience without sacrificing luxury? Book ahead for **La Cabane Méditerranée** *(laca banemediterranee.com; loungers from €30)*, on the edge of **Plage d'Héraclée**. About 10km further south from St-Tropez, the beach is wilder than Pampelonne, and the club is tucked into the edge of a rock.

Hit the open seas

Get out on the water to take in the gorgeous coast. It can be as easy as taking a ride on **Les Bateaux Verts**, with boat excursions throughout the region. Or opt for a water-skimming catamaran on Golfe de St-Tropez at sunset with **Sport Decouverte** *(sport-decouverte.com; €40)*, where you can sip an *apéro* suspended in the nets of the catamaran, sandwiched between the blues of the sea and the sparkling sky.

BEST ARTS EXPERIENCES & EVENTS IN CANNES

Festival d'Art Pyrotechnique: Global competition to win best fireworks show crown. Six nights in summer.

Les Plages Électroniques: Epic three-day dance festival on the beach: eight stages and over 50,000 festivalgoers. In August.

Musée Bonnard: Neoimpressionist painter Pierre Bonnard (1867–1947) was known as the Painter of Happiness, and Le Cannet, at Cannes' northern fringes, was his happy place.

La Malmaison: Showcase of contemporary art in a historic, renovated building.

Le Suquet des Artistes: Small but avant-garde exhibition space in the former city morgue that brings local artists to the fore.

CLEANLINESS IS CLOSE TO GODLINESS

Following the cholera outbreaks of the early 1830s, which claimed thousands of lives, a plan was devised to improve public health by channelling water from the Durance River in the Alps. By 1869, Marseille's **Palais Longchamp** was opened to the public as a 'hymn to water', celebrating this remarkable engineering achievement.

Marseille's famous soap (Savon de Marseille) also played a significant role in reducing infant mortality and the spread of contagious diseases during the 19th century. Originally made with olive oil and free of colouring and perfume, it now comes in various shapes and smells. The **Savonnerie Marseillaise de la Licorne** has free daily tours of its factory.

STEFANO BOLOGNINI/SHUTTERSTOCK

Chateau d'If, Marseille

Marseille

MAP p226

Mix with the locals in lively squares

Marseille has an edge. France's second-largest city puts its arms around you as a drunken friend would – passionately and deliriously. It is a city that revels in its status as France's underdog. Sooner or later, you'll end up on the **cours Julien** (known locally as 'le cours Ju') for a drink, and for good reason. As a pedestrian area slathered with street art and bohemian yearnings, this is the home of some great bars and restaurants, which remain open day and night. Wander the narrow side streets, packed with bookshops, galleries and tattoo parlours, until you reach the noisy and elongated main square, a destination for a solid night out, and a microcosm of the city itself. You are likely to hear boomboxes blasting, guitars strumming and African drums pounding as soon as the sun comes out.

Place Jean-Jaurès, also known as La Plaine, is another vast square surrounded by bars and restaurants. For years it has been the battleground for left-wing militants and artists. Buzzing day and night in the spring and summer months, it remains a beating heart for locals escaping the tourist traps, whether in the bars or in the public seating areas beneath the trees. La Plaine is only a 10-minute walk east from cours Julien.

Escape to the Château d'If

For a quick and easy trip out to sea, hop on the Frioul-If ferry to Marseille's closest islands: the Île d'If (for historians) and the **Îles du Frioul** (for nature lovers). Commanding access to Marseille's Vieux Port, the **Chateau d'If** *(chateau-if.fr; adult/child €7/free)* was immortalised by Alexandre Dumas in his classic 1844 novel, *The Count of Monte Cristo*. At the 16th-century island prison with three towers, one giving a great view across the bay, you can wander unaccompanied or visit with an audio or guided tour; the contrast between the cells for the wealthy and the dungeon pit strikes a tone. This is the ferry's first stop; it's 20 minutes from the Vieux Port.

MARSEILLE

Mediterranean Sea

See Enlargement

Marseille

Île Ratonneau **6** **4**

Île Pomègues

9 **10**

16

La Pointe-Rouge

Parc National des Calanques

Mont Puget

1

Les Goudes

Callelongue

3 **2**

Île de Jarre

Île Calseraigne

Île de Riou

0 ———— 2 km
0 ———— 1 miles

Enlargement:

Allées Léon Gambetta

Bd de la Libération

Cours F Roosevelt

La Canebière

THIERS

11

13

Bd Garibaldi

Cours Lieutaud

R des Trois Mages

17

12

14

Pl Jean Jaurès

8

R St Saturnin

R Curiol

R Ste Pierre

5

15

0 ———— 200 m
0 ———— 0.1 miles

★ HIGHLIGHTS
1 Parc National des Calanques

● SIGHTS
2 Calanque de Morgiou
3 Calanque de Sormiou
4 Château d'If
5 Cours Julien
6 Îles du Frioul

7 Palais Longchamp
8 Place Jean-Jaurès

● SLEEPING
9 Hotel Peron
10 La Relève
11 Le Ryad

● DRINKING & NIGHTLIFE
12 Bar des Maraîchers

13 Grand Bar du Chapitre
see 10 La Relève
14 PMU le blabla

● SHOPPING
15 Bière de la Plaine
16 Cristal Limiñana
17 Savonnerie Marseillaise de la Licorne

It's another 15 minutes to the next stop, the Port du Frioul, your entry point to two of the Îles du Frioul, Pomègues and Ratonneau, which are connected by a dam. Attacking the unspoiled jagged rock of Pomègues is liberating. Following the seawall after you dock will lead to the Fort de Cavaux, leaving you lost at sea on an uninhabited island, revisiting ghosts in the bunkers of WWII. The island of Ratonneau has a few small shops and restaurants and is popular for its beaches and tiny village. There's a chapel that resembles a Greek temple and the ruins of the Hôpital Caroline, which once housed quarantined travellers, but the highlight is the St-Estève beach, where you can swim safely, protected from the wind.

The ticket pier for **lebateau ferries** (*lebateau-frioul-if.fr; 1/2 islands return €11.10/16.70*) is at the Vieux Port. When facing the port, get in line at its large booth on the left. The Château d'If is closed on Mondays.

Outdoor adventures in the Parc National des Calanques

It feels like a miracle to find a refuge like the **Parc National des Calanques** only a short distance from Marseille. In parts

---

DISCOVER THE HISTORY OF PASTIS

The apéritif pastis is easy to spot: a milky-looking concoction served in a tall glass that adorns outdoor tables across Provence. In 1932 in Marseille, Paul Ricard developed his aniseed-and-liquorice-based liqueur (*pastís* means 'mix' in Occitan) after absinthe was banned in France for fear it caused hallucinations and madness. Since then, it has become a drink that is synonymous with the city. Ricard may now be part of a multinational conglomerate based in Lille, but there are still independent producers in Marseille where you can arrange a visit, including **Cristal Limiñana** (*cristal-liminana.com*) and the independent brewery **Bière de la Plaine** (*Distillerie de la Plaine; @distillerie_de_la_plaine*).

MARAKOBS/SHUTTERSTOCK

WHAT IS A CALANQUE?

Calanques are coastal geological features typical of the Mediterranean region. These picturesque coves, formed in limestone and located between Marseille and Cassis, are characterised by steep cliffs rising above vibrant turquoise waters. When the sun shines, the small beaches within these narrow bays, comprising either pebbles or fine sand, attract crowds. Escaping to them has become a way of life for city dwellers, leading to various regulations protecting the natural sites. Access by car can be challenging, and most routes are closed between June and October as the arid conditions during this period place the parks at a high chance of wildfires. The strong mistral winds that can sweep through the area further intensify the risks.

of this diminutive 85-sq-km patch of scrubby promontories, it's easy to believe you're miles from civilisation. Then a twist in a pine-clad gully reveals the entirety of France's second metropolis spread out within apparent touching distance; the *calanques* (inlets) appear almost as its uninhabited suburbs. But with their light-shifting geometry, rich plant and animal life and idyllic hidden coves, Les Calanques are so much more than that. They are beloved of the Marseillais, who come for the sun and to hike over pine-strewn promontories, mess about in boats and generally refresh their souls.

Of the many *calanques* along the coastline, the most easily accessible are **Calanque de Sormiou** and **Calanque de Morgiou**. Remote inlets such as **Calanque d'En-Vau** and **Calanque de Port-Miou** take dedication and time to reach, either on foot or by kayak. Note that overland access is often limited from June to September, due to fire danger; always check first on the app: *calanques-parcnational.fr/fr/application-mobile-officielle-mes-calanques*. The app is also excellent for up-to-date info on the park and activities. There is also a reservation system in place for two of the most popular *calanques* in summer: **Calanque de Sugiton** and **Calanque des Pierres Tombées**. See *calanques-parcnational.fr*.

DRINKING IN MARSEILLE: BEST PASTIS BARS

MAP p226

Bar des Maraîchers: Listen to '80s radio hits with owner, Serge, who features in his own hilarious fresco of the *Last Supper. 3pm-2am*

Grand Bar du Chapitre: A young crowd in a leafy square at the top of the main thoroughfare, La Canebière. *10am-12.30am*

PMU le blabla: Super cheap and one of the best suntraps protected from the wind in the city. *6.30am-9pm*

La Relève: In the Endoume neighbourhood. Pastis can still be fancy and here it's served with great food and music. *8am-10pm Mon-Sat, 9am-5pm Sun*

Calanque d'En-Vau

There's no shortage of outdoor activities here: hiking, kayaking, stand-up paddleboarding, swimming, diving and rock climbing are all incredible. You'll find guides and gear rental in both Marseille and Cassis. From October to June, hiking trails lead through the maquis (scrub). Marseille's tourist office leads guided walks and has an excellent hiking map of the various *calanques,* as does Cassis' tourist office. For access by public transport take bus 19 from Marseille's Castellane bus station down the coast to its terminus at La Madrague, then switch to bus 20 to Callelongue. Note that the road to Callelongue is only open to cars on weekdays from mid-April to May and closed entirely from June to September.

Gorges du Verdon
Sustainable lavender visits

Dive into the new face of ecologically responsible lavender production by visiting an organic lavender farm on the **Plateau de Valensole**. To start with, look for the lavender fields that have let golden grass grow up between the rows of purple – these farms are doing their part to preserve the soil for the next generation. Many farms are open year-round to guests, but run special tours during the harvest season. And no visit would be complete without trying some lavender-based products straight from the source, such as essential oils, soaps and perfumes produced on-site using sustainable methods.

The lavender fields of Valensole are usually the highlight of a photography tour of Provence. Visit in late June or early July, but no later. During this time, the fields are alive with colour and fragrance, providing a stunning backdrop for your photos. To get the perfect shot, you'll have to get up early – sunrise has the longest 'soft-light' period, which reduces shadows and harsh glare. Don't go tramping in the fields,

LOOK UP

The Gorges du Verdon is home to one of France's most impressive bird populations, including griffon, cinereous and Egyptian vultures. These massive birds ride the thermals above the cliffs, often visible from Route des Crêtes or trail lookouts. Bring binoculars and look for their broad wingspans and slow, soaring flight – especially active on warm afternoons with rising air currents. The two-hour **Treguier Botanical Trail** (start/finish Moustiers-Ste-Marie) is a relatively easy circular walk; great for spotting birdlife. Spring is the best time for twitchers, although the wallcreeper bird tends to only make an appearance in winter.

LAVENDER FARMS ON THE PLATEAU DE VALENSOLE

La Ferme du Riou:
This organic farm runs distillery visits during the harvest season and farm visits year-round.

Lavande Bio Berenger: Organic producer with a cabin in the fields during harvest season. Otherwise, stop into the shop in Valensole.

Lavandes Angelvin:
Runs distillery visits during high season and guided visits on Tuesdays at 3pm.

Terraroma: Very photogenic lavender and almond farm, with a few sunflower fields to complete the mosaic.

Les Lavandes d'Isabelle et Sébastien:
Technically off the plateau and closer to Manosque, this little family lavender farm is less crowded and has a small boutique to find your favourite products.

Tablet in use, Palais des Papes, Avignon

but tread carefully between rows – these are precious crops for local farmers. What to wear? Consider colours that will complement the lavender fields. Soft pastels, earthy tones and neutral colours work well in this setting. Avoid wearing bright colours that may clash with the lavender or draw too much attention away from the landscape's natural beauty.

Hike the Sentier Blanc-Martel

This 16km one-way trek from **Chalet de la Maline** to **Point Sublime** is one of France's most legendary hikes. Named after the first geologists to explore the canyon, the trail hugs the cliffs and drops down to the riverbed, with ladders, tunnels and dizzying views along the way. It's demanding but not extreme – suitable for fit beginners with proper footwear. Book the Navette Blanc-Martel *(navette.parcduverdon.fr)* in advance for transport to the trailhead and pickup at the end. Hikers should carry plenty of water, snacks and a torch for the tunnel. Get an early start to avoid the heat and crowds.

Cycle the Route des Crêtes

This 24km balcony road loops out from La Palud-sur-Verdon, rising over 650m in elevation and offering heart-stopping views straight into the canyon. Originally designed for motorised day-trippers, parts of the Route des Crêtes are now restricted or closed to vehicles on select days, giving cyclists a stretch of silence and space. The ride is challenging but manageable with an e-bike – rentals are available in La Palud. Spring and autumn are the best times to ride, with cool weather and lighter traffic. Stop at *belvédères* (lookouts) along the way, where vultures and climbers share the same dizzying vertical playground. A helmet, water and good brakes are essential.

Raft the Verdon River

From April to June, when the river is flowing strong, rafting the Verdon is a wild, splashy ride through limestone corridors and rolling rapids. Most trips depart from Castellane, on the gorge's eastern end. Rapids range from easygoing to intense (Class I to IV), making this a good fit for both beginners and adrenaline junkies. Book ahead with a certified company such as **Yeti Rafting** *(verdon-rafting.net; per person from €40)* – gear and guides are included. Minimum age varies by route (usually seven to 16), and all participants must be able to swim. It's a half-day adventure that takes you deep into the canyon, with moments of calm water to catch your breath between the thrills.

Avignon

The home of seven popes

The vast rooms and shady arcades of 14th-century **Palais des Papes** *(palais-des-papes.com; adult/child €12/€6.50)* give a glimpse into medieval life, when Avignon was the centre of the Catholic world. A visit is supported by tablets (available in multiple languages) that digitally restore lost frescoes and furniture. It's a surprising example of tech that genuinely deepens the experience, bringing rooms to life with audio-visual storytelling and changing art installations. The **Great Chapel** represents the largest covered space in the palace. Construction began in 1348 but was slowed by the Black Death pandemic. In the 14th century, the windows were of stained glass with a carpeted floor and walls covered with drapery dominated by green tones.

Buy tickets online to save time at the entrance, especially during the busy summer season and July theatre festival, and don't miss the Jardins du Palais, designed in the English style and accessible from the former apartments of the Pope – his place for wandering reflection.

THE GREAT SCHISM

Avignon first gained its ramparts – and reputation for arts and culture – during the 14th century, when Pope Clement V fled political turmoil in Rome. From 1309 to 1377, seven French-born popes invested huge sums in the papal palace and offered asylum to Jews and political dissidents. Pope Gregory XI left Avignon in 1376, but his death two years later led to the Great Schism (1378-1417), during which rival popes (up to three at once) resided at Rome and Avignon, denouncing and excommunicating one another. Even after the matter was settled and an impartial pope, Martin V, established himself in Rome, Avignon remained under papal rule. Avignon and Comtat Venaissin (now the Vaucluse *département*) were ruled by papal legates until 1791.

EATING IN AVIGNON: BEST RESTAURANTS

Numéro 75: Chic restaurant in a *hôtel particulier* with a private courtyard, excellent Med menu and stellar wine list. *noon-2.30pm & 7-10pm Mon-Fri* €€€

Graines de Piment: Good-value, tasty bistro on place de la Principale that gives disadvantaged youth a chance to gain work experience. *12.15-1.30pm Mon-Fri* €

Fou de Fafa: Four-course dinners at this Avignon staple, drawing on Mediterranean and Provençal cuisines. Reserve. *7-11pm Thu-Mon* €€

L'Épicerie: Classic French bistro with rustic decor in the heart of old Avignon. Plenty of hearty meat-based dishes; vegan options too. *noon-2.15pm & 7-10pm Thu-Mon* €€

Bordeaux

WINE | GASTRONOMY | ART AND ARCHITECTURE

Bordeaux's mood board hasn't changed since French novelist Victor Hugo (1802–85) visited in 1839, waxing lyrical in letters to his wife back in Paris about the city's elegant squares and quaysides, fountains and monumental theatre that reminded him of Versailles. He wrote 'and you will love Bordeaux, even if you only drink water'.

Bordeaux's heady cocktail of old and new – not to mention its legendary wine cellars, bistros, *bars à vin* and restaurants bursting with prestigious vintages – is as intoxicating as ever. From this Gallo-Roman city's golden past as medieval wine trader and key port in Europe during the Age of Enlightenment, to famous vineyards, a spirited student population and a buoyant undercurrent of creativity, France's sixth-largest city brims with surprising and enthralling stories at every turn. Paired with an exceptional dining scene and captivating river life, there is no tastier marriage.

The Epic Story of Bordeaux Wine

Learn and taste in city museums

Bordeaux's intoxicating wine story begins in the ancient trading district of riverside Chartrons. The city's life-blood wine trade originates here. Discover the role of *négociants* (merchant traders) in the 18th and 19th centuries at the **Musée du Vin et du Négoce** *(museeduvinbordeaux.com; adult/child*

 GETTING AROUND

Tram line A is the cheapest, quickest way to get into town: 45 minutes from **Aéroport de Bordeaux** *(bordeaux.aeroport.fr)* in Merignac, 10km west. The same tickets *(single/10-ticket card €1.90/15)* are valid on Bat3 riverboats, likewise run by public-transport company

TBM *(infotbm.com)*. TBM's public bike-sharing scheme **Le Vélo** has stations with classic and electric wheels all over town. Free-floating electric scooters by **Pony** *(getapony.com)* and **Dott** *(ridedott.com)* fill the gaps.

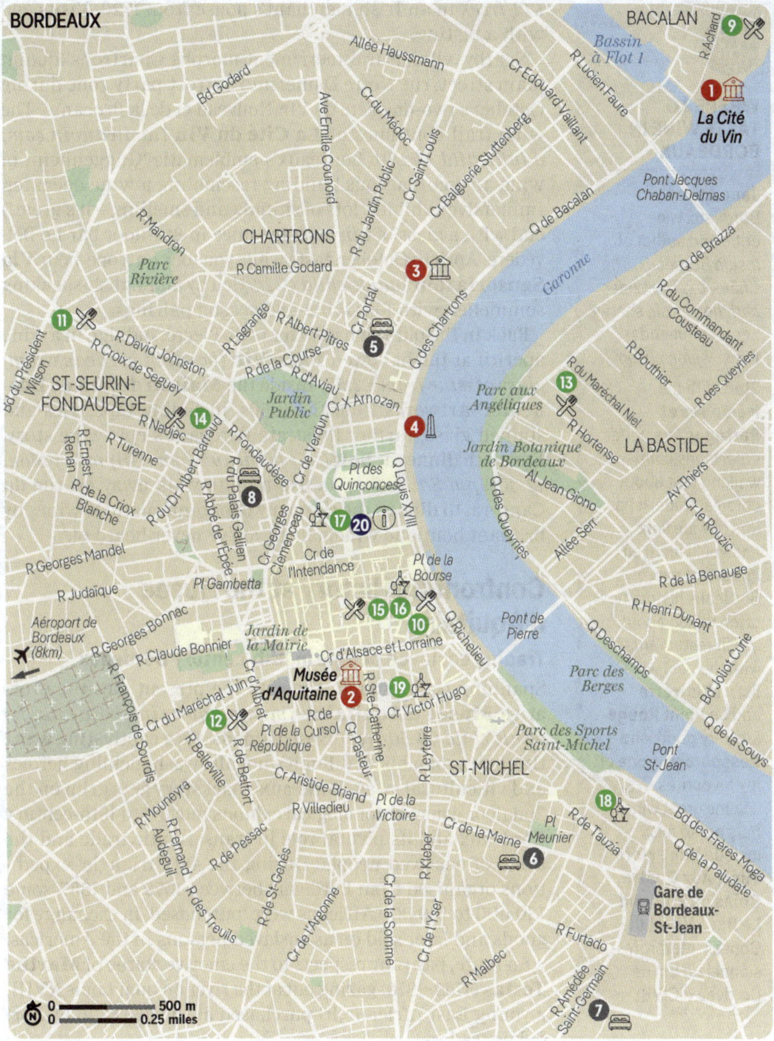
BORDEAUX
BACALAN
Bassin à Flot 1
La Cité du Vin
Allée Haussmann
Bd Godard
Cr du Médoc
Ave Emile Counord
R du Jardin Public
Cr Saint Louis
Cr Balguerie Stuttenberg
Cr Edouard Vaillant
R Lucien Faure
R Achard
Pont Jacques Chaban-Delmas
Q de Bacalan
Garonne
Q de Brazza
CHARTRONS
R Camille Godard
R Mandron
Parc Rivière
Cr Portal
R Lagrange
R Albert Pitres
R de la Course
R d'Aviau
Q des Chartrons
Cr X Arnozan
Jardin Public
Bd du Président Wilson
R David Johnston
R Croix de Seguey
ST-SEURIN-FONDAUDÈGE
R Naujac
R Turenne
R Ernest Renan
R de la Croix Blanche
R du Dr Albert Barraud
R Fondaudège
R du Palais Gallien
R Abbé de l'Epée
Cr de Verdun
Pl des Quinconces
Q Louis XVIII
Parc aux Angéliques
Jardin Botanique de Bordeaux
Al Jean Giono
Q des Queyries
R du Maréchal Niel
R Hortense
R du Commandant Cousteau
R Bouthier
R des Queyries
LA BASTIDE
Av Thiers
Cr le Rouzic
Allée Serr
R Georges Mandel
R Judaïque
Pl Gambetta
Cr Georges Clemenceau
Cr de l'Intendance
Pl de la Bourse
Aéroport de Bordeaux (8km)
R Georges Bonnac
R Claude Bonnier
Jardin de la Mairie
Cr d'Alsace et Lorraine
Q Richelieu
Pont de Pierre
R de la Benauge
R Henri Dunant
Q Deschamps
Parc des Berges
Bd Joliot Curie
R François de Sourdis
Cr du Maréchal Juin
Cr d'Albret
Musée d'Aquitaine
R Ste-Catherine
Cr Victor Hugo
R de Belfort
R Belleville
Pl de la République
R de Cursol
Cr Pasteur
R Leyteire
Parc des Sports Saint-Michel
ST-MICHEL
Pont St-Jean
Q de la Souys
Cr Aristide Briand
R Villedieu
Pl de la Victoire
Cr de la Marne
Pl Meunier
R de Tauzia
Bd des Frères Moga
Q de la Paludate
R Mouneyra
R Fernand Audeguil
R de Pessac
R des Treuils
R de St-Genès
Cr de l'Argonne
Cr de la Somme
R Kleber
Cr de l'Yser
Gare de Bordeaux-St-Jean
R Furtado
R Malbec
R Amédée Saint-Germain
500 m
0.25 miles

HIGHLIGHTS
1 La Cité du Vin
2 Musée d'Aquitaine

SIGHTS
3 Musée du Vin et du Négoce
4 Statue of Marthe Testas

SLEEPING
5 Chez Dupont
6 Hôtel La Zoologie
7 Jost
8 La Maison du Lierre

EATING
9 Bar de la Marine
10 Chiocchio
11 Le Pavilion des Boulevards
12 L'Univerre
13 Magasin Général
14 Ressources
15 Soif

DRINKING & NIGHTLIFE
16 Aux Quatre Coins du Vins
17 Bar à Vin
18 Le Point Rouge
19 Wine More Time

INFORMATION
20 Bordeaux Tourist Office

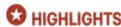

WHERE TO TASTE WINE IN BORDEAUX

Jane Anson, Bordeaux wine critic and author of *Inside Bordeaux: The Châteaux, The Wines and the Terroir,* shares her recommenda-tions. *@jane.anson*

Start with the **Mémoires et Partages** (*memoires etpartages.com*) walking tour about colonial trade. It has lots of wine links and you'll learn an important part of Bordeaux history not often talked about.

Visit restaurants with the best wine lists: **L'Univerre** and **Le Point Rouge** are very good, and **Ressources** is one of my favourites.

Some great wine bars not to miss include **Wine More Time, Aux Quatre Coins du Vins** and **Le Bar à Vin** at the Conseil Interprofes-sionnel du Vin de Bordeaux (CIVB).

€12/free), in an Irish merchant's house from 1720. Visits end with a tasting.

Nearby, viticultural merriment morphs Chartrons' quaint main street, rue Notre Dame, into a street-party zone during October's two-day Fête du Vin Nouveau et de la Brocante. The wine trail continues at **La Cité du Vin** (*laciteduvin.com; adult/child €22/9*), Bordeaux's emblematic 'Guggenheim of wine' in a curvaceous building resembling a wine decanter. Immersive exhibits (lots of sniffing and smelling – it's great!) end with a glass of *vin* or grape juice in 8th-floor bar Le Bel-védère. April to October, taste while you tour on a one-hour **Via Sensoria tour** (*adult/child €22/9*) led by an English-speaking sommelier, with four wine-and-season pairings.

Back in the old-town quarter of St-Pierre, indulge in a wine apéritif at the hallowed **Bar à Vin** (*baravin.bordeaux.com; glass of wine from €2.50*) inside the **Maison du Vin de Bordeaux**. Artworks from the 1950s, including tapestries and stained glass, further illustrate Bordeaux's epic wine story. End with dinner at **Soif** (*soif-bordeaux.com; 7-11pm Fri-Mon, 12.30-2pm Sat & Sun*), a five-minute walk away on rue du Cancera, to dine in the company of organic, natural wines by brilliant boutique winemakers you've never heard of.

Confronting History at the Musée d'Aquitaine

Trading enslaved people in 18th-century Bordeaux

Spanning Gallo-Roman times to the present day, the evoc-ative **Musée d'Aquitaine** (*musee-aquitaine-bordeaux.fr; adult/child €4.50/free*), closed Monday, is a captivating waltz through urban history. But it's not all swashbuckling heroics and viticultural swag. Bordeaux's backstory gets grim on the 2nd floor where chronological exhibits move into 18th-century Bordeaux and its pivotal role in transatlantic trade and the trade of enslaved people. During the 480 'triangle' expedi-tions organised from Bordeaux between 1672 and 1837, some 130,000 to 150,000 Africans were 'purchased' in exchange for goods and later sold on as enslaved persons in the Americas.

En route, pay your respects to the emotive statue of **Marthe Testas** (1765–1870) gazing out at the river on quai Louis XVIII, a young East African girl purchased at the age of 16 by Bor-delais traders.

 EATING IN BORDEAUX: FAVOURITE TERRACES

Magasin Général:	**Bar de la Marine:**	**Chiocchio:**	**Le Pavilion des**
France's largest organic restaurant, with vintage sofas. *8am-7.30pm Mon-Fri, from 9am Sun, to 11.30pm Fri, 9am-11.30pm Sat* €	Nothing beats the €20 three-course lunch served in a summer flower garden in Bacalan. Cool 1950s memorabilia too. *9am-5pm Mon-Fri* €	Tasty Franco-Tuscan fare on an urban terrace, foxy street art and prime people-watching on cafe-beaded place du Palais. *noon-3pm & 7-11.30pm Mon-Sat* €€	**Boulevards:** Seasonal gastronomy on terracotta-paved patio perfumed with magnolia. *noon-2pm Wed, noon-2pm & 8-10pm Tue & Thu-Sat* €€€

Beyond Bordeaux

An unmatched sensory feast, trips beyond Bordeaux deliver pink-hued cities, go-slow sea adventure and France's finest wine.

Bordeaux is a gateway to vine-ribboned countryside and Atlantic Coast sand dunes. North, where the Dordogne and Garonne Rivers meet, spills the Gironde Estuary and the prestigious vineyards of the Médoc. South of the city, the Côte d'Argent (Silver Coast) takes centre stage with endless shimmering-gold beaches backed by dark-green pine forests. Surfers catch waves and enjoy incredible sunsets in celebrity Biarritz, while Basque culture reigns supreme in Bayonne. To the southeast, the pink city of Toulouse feels lived in and laid-back, thanks to its large student population, yet still has lofty dreams of aiming for the stars: it's a hub for the manufacture of airplanes and rockets.

St-Émilion

TIME FROM BORDEAUX: 1HR 🚗

Visit an eco-winery and lunch between vines

The first vines were planted on the picturesque Troplong Mondot estate carpeting the highest point of St-Émilion in the 1700s, and by 1745 the winemaker was rich enough to have a handsome château built from the local creamy limestone on his land. Today, guided tours of **Château Troplong-Mondot** *(troplong-mondot.com; 90min guided tour with tasting €50)* walk you around one of the region's most innovative, green-thinking wineries. Vineyards are ploughed exclusively by a dozen hefty working horses; a pig and several hens recycle organic waste; and the estate's swanky barrel cellar with 12m-high cathedral ceiling is underground to avoid spoiling the centuries-old bucolic landscape.

Tours end with tastings of two vintages and there's a swish boutique where you can buy the premier *grand cru* wines. Alternatively, reserve a table at the château's Michelin-starred

---

 GETTING AROUND

A car isn't vital along the southwest coast, but needed in rural areas and those with poor public transport (northern part of the Médoc and the Basque hinterland). High-speed TGVs service Bordeaux, Biarritz and Bayonne (four hours direct from Paris Montparnasse).

Toulouse also has TGVs to Paris Montparnasse (just under five hours), and regular trains to Spain. Walking or cycling the city centre is easiest. Toulouse also has a well-served international airport.

restaurant, Les Belles Perdrix (*weekday lunch/dinner menus from €50/85*), overlooking vines, to indulge in outstanding modern French cuisine and perfect pairings. It's 20 minutes (2km) on foot from St-Émilion village to Troplong-Mondot.

LA VÉLODYSSÉE

As its evocative name suggests, **La Vélodyssée** (*cycling-lavelodyssee.com*) is a coastal odyssey by *vélo* (bike) along France's Atlantic Coast, linking Roscoff in Brittany with Hendaye on the French–Spanish border, 1270km away in Pays Basque.

The scenic Gironde stretch is 81km (four hours) from the tip of the Médoc south to Lacanau, just north of the Bassin d'Arcachon. Flat and reasonably unchallenging, the well-marked cycling itinerary kicks off with ethereal sea and Cordouan lighthouse views from Pointe de Grave (it's 108 steps up the cape's own, 28m-tall Phare de Grave lighthouse) before plunging through pine forests and past sand dunes, beaches, lake and lagoon on its route 7.5km south to Soulac-sur-Mer and beyond.

Arcachon

TIME FROM BORDEAUX: 1HR

Climb Europe's largest sand dune

Breathtakingly cold in winter and as hot as burning coals in the height of summer it might be, but barefoot is the most thrilling way to romp around the golden sands of Europe's largest dune. Local lore claims the shifting **Dune du Pilat**, 10km south from Arcachon, has swallowed trees, a road junction, even a hotel. What is certain is the spectacular panorama from the top. Looking west, see sandy shoals at the mouth of the Bassin d'Arcachon, Cap Ferret and bird-rich Banc d'Arguin. Facing east, dead black trees killed by forest fires polka-dot rich green forest.

April to November, a staircase – around 150 steps – is built on the dune's eastern slope to help tourists stagger breathlessly to the top. Otherwise, use the locals' 'secret' shortcut to arrive midway up the dune: uphill past fashionista lunch hangout **La Co(o)rniche** on av Louis Gaume, then right onto the unmarked footpath between the bike stand and No 31 on av des Dunes. To understand the fragility and diversity of Pilat's vulnerable sand scape, join a guided nature walk, sunrise or sunset hike, telescope workshop or storytelling sessions organised by the **Espace Accueil** (*ladunedupilat.com*) at the dune entrance. Snack bars and eco-boutiques here only sell local artisan fare.

Bayonne

TIME FROM BORDEAUX: 2HR

Learn about traditional Basque culture in Bayonne

Funerary rites, fishing, folklore, pastoral life and *pelota*: Petit Bayonne's riverfront **Musée Basque et de l'Histoire de Bayonne** (*musee-basque.com; adult/under 26yr €8/free; closed Mon & Thu*) has brought Basque history, culture and crafts vividly to life since 1924. Its 20 rooms fill a 17th-century warehouse, built on the wharf by a merchant to store his goods once offloaded from the ship. Get orientated with a scale model of Bayonne port in 1805, showing Grand Bayonne, which the Romans founded on a hill between the town's two rivers, and Petit Bayonne on the Nive's opposite riverbank, which flourished as a trading and shipbuilding hub from the 12th century. Spot the Gothic twin spires – one now clean-cream, the other

EATING & DRINKING IN ARCACHON: OUR PICKS

La Pâtisserie de Ma Fille: Gourmet breakfasts, brunch, crêpes and cakes on market square place des Marquises. *8am-7pm Mon-Thu, to 10pm Fri-Sun* €€

Café de la Plage – Chez Pierre: A Mira craft beer brewed next door in La Teste-de-Buch or lavish shellfish platter: this timeless seafront duo delivers. *8am-2am* €€

Coquille: All-day ceviche, burgers, bowls, salads and meat/fish mains in a cosy, sea-inspired bistro near the market. *9am-midnight Tue-Sat, to 4pm Sun* €€

Club Plage Pereire: Enjoy oysters, seafood, cocktails and a great gin made from Cognac vine blossoms at this pop-up on Plage Pereire. *10am-midnight Apr-Sep* €€

Dune du Pilat, Arcachon

FÊTES DE BAYONNE

Thousands of revellers fill Bayonne for five days during July's Fêtes de Bayonne *(fetes. bayonne.fr)*. White with a red sash and neck-scarf is the non-negotiable dress code. The street revelry starts on the last Wednesday in July or first in August with the traditional throwing of the city keys from the balcony of Bayonne's town hall. Fireworks and a *bal* (dance) follow. Brass bands, DJs and choirs perform all over town and there's folk dancing, *pelota*, omelette championships, espadrille throwing, tugs-of-war and stone lifting in *festivals de force basque* (strength competitions). Thursday's Journée des Enfants has kids' activities. Less savoury are the Basque *courses des vaches* ('running of the bulls' but with horned cows) and *corridas* (bullfights).

dirty dark-grey – of 13th-century **Cathédrale Ste-Marie** *(free)* and its peaceful cloister on place Louis Pasteur, and the 17th-century ramparts encircling the city.

Don't miss the rooms dedicated to *pelote Basque (pelota)* – the catchall name for more than a dozen traditional Basque ballgames, including *main nue* (played barehanded) and *jaï alaï* (the most high-octane variant). Art, short films and players' kit shine light on the rules, the *fronton* (*pelota* court), how to use the scoop-like basket called a *chistera*, etc. Post-museum, pass by **Trinquet St-André**, a 17th-century covered *jeu de paume* court on rue du Jeu de Paume, later adapted for *pelota*. Enjoy a drink in its bar-brasserie from 1943 and catch a game in action.

Biarritz

TIME FROM BORDEAUX: **2HR**

Lunch cheap on oysters and white wine

Fashionable surf villages and fishing ports bead the seashore south of Biarritz. Ruins of medieval ovens once used to melt whale blubber rub shoulders with trendy beach bars, bodegas and eco-boutiques. *Pintxos, poissons* and paella at Biarritz' renowned bistro-bodega **Bar Jean** *(barjean-biarritz.fr)* has been a Biarrot rite of passage since 1930. The round-the-clock festive vibe on the street terrace alone is memorable (unusually, food is served nonstop from 10.30am to 1am).

EATING IN BAYONNE: GOOD-VALUE DINING

Bistrot Pépite: Modern bistro fare: duck hearts with port, curried mussels, veggie beignets. *7.30-9.30pm Tue-Fri, noon-1.30pm & 7.30-9.30pm Sat* €

Cantine du Musée: Excellent-value bistro serves seasonal Basque fare with lashings of *'bonne humeur'*. *12.15-1.30pm Tue, 12.15-1.30pm & 7.30-9.30pm Wed-Sat* €€

Cidrerie Ttipia: A juicy *txuleta* (beef steak) for two, fries, salad and a cider is the thing at this rustic, noisy cider hall. *noon-2pm & 7-11pm Tue-Sat, noon-2pm Sun* €€

Basa: Good-value lunches in a brasserie with peaceful garden patio. Try smoked octopus with beetroot and caramelised dill. *noon-10pm Mon-Sat, to 2pm Sun* €€

237

BEST BIARROT BEACHES FOR SURFING & SUNBATHING

Grande Plage: Biarritz' main golden-sand beach, much-loved since the days of Napoléon II and Eugénie.

Plage de la Côte des Basques: Long golden sand beach with trendy bars. A surfers' and sunset lovers' favourite.

Plage d'Ilbarritz: Another strip of powder-soft sand, enlivened with the summer terrace of beach bar Blue Cargo, a dance floor after dark.

Plage de l'Océan: Fringed by protected sand dunes and a golf green, this is the wildest of Anglet's back-to-back swathe of sand beaches. Sunset drinks at beach bar Ozeanoa are a must.

Plage des Sables d'Or: Cafes, surf shops and several sandy beach-volley courts in Anglet.

ANIBAL TREJO/SHUTTERSTOCK

Capitole, Toulouse

To keep things cheap, dive into **Les Halles** *(halles-biarritz. fr; 6/12 oysters with glass of wine €8/14)* opposite. Swimming with the day's catch from 7.30am to 2pm daily, the fish hall buzzes with vendors flogging crab claws, whelks, seasonal sea urchins and an ocean of fish. Oyster farmers shuck various sized *huîtres* for seafood lovers to devour standing up or slurp around shared tables on a no-frills mezzanine upstairs.

Toulouse

TIME FROM BORDEAUX: 2½HR 🚆

It's a Capitole idea to visit Toulouse

Toulouse's city hall, the **Capitole** *(free)*, demonstrates many facets of the city's cultural character. With its rose terracotta and white brick neoclassical facade, complete with eight pink and cream marble Corinthian columns, it is one of Toulouse's signature buildings. The exterior's architectural display is balanced by the interior's impressive frescoes and paintings, which decorate the chambers and halls. Enter from the **Place du Capitole**, the city's social focal point; its perimeter arcades are packed with patrons of its Belle Époque bistros and brasseries. Inside, follow the entry signs through security. Once through, climb the elegant main staircase, overlooked by Renaissance-style murals. At the top, local artist Henri Martin's huge postimpressionist canvases fill Salle Henri-Martin, while painted scenes from Toulouse's history

 EATING IN BIARRITZ: HIP PICKS IN BIBI BEAURIVAGE

Bleach: Lunch with sassy locals over homemade food in a retro, 1950s-styled cafe in Biarritz' coolest no-tourists 'hood. *9am-3pm Mon-Fri* €

Club Sandwich: Chicken burgers, truffle clubs, falafel salad by day. Vinyl nights, DJ sets, club nights come dark. *noon-3pm & 7pm-midnight Tue-Sat, noon-3pm Sun* €

Restaurant Hernani: Spend an evening in Spanish Basque country at this lively bodega. The sangria flows. *7.30-11pm Tue-Sat* €€

Chéri Bibi: Off-grid modern neighbourhood bistro: expertly curated local produce with natural wines on a wooden people-watching deck. *7pm-midnight Thu-Sun* €€

decorate the **Salle des Illustres** (Hall of the Illustrious). The southern end of the building hosts the **Théâtre du Capitole** (*opera.toulouse.fr*), where the city's ballet and opera companies perform regularly. Try to catch one of the occasional €5 lunchtime recitals (book in advance).

Towpath adventures

The Canal de Garonne runs east from the Atlantic; the Canal du Midi runs west from the Mediterranean. They meet in Toulouse, forming one continuous, navigable coast-to-coast waterway. Exploring the towpaths, which are shaded by regimented parades of plane trees, can be as simple as a leisurely stroll or a daylong cycling trip. For the latter, rentals are available from the city's 400 bike stations using the véloToulouse (*velotoulouse.tisseo.fr*) bike-sharing app.

A more substantial waterway, the Garonne River cleaves its way through the heart of the city. Get onto the water with **Les Bateaux Toulousains** (*bateaux-toulousains.com; from €8*), with 30-minute cruises from July to October. The same boats are used for canal cruises from March to June.

Conquering the skies

Toulouse has long been seen as the world capital of aeronautics. And aviation, space and technology enthusiasts have not one, but four major landmarks in store. Of them, the most impressive is **Aeroscopia** (*aeroscopia.fr; adult/child €15/12*), which brings together scores of planes, among them some of the world's largest. You can walk through a Concorde (its 1970s style seats and complex control panels preserved in place behind perspex) and an Airbus A380 on the tarmac outside, where parts of the fuselage and flooring are stripped back to expose the complicated wiring. Nearby, **Ailes Anciennes Toulouse** (*Old Wings Toulouse; aatlse.org; €7*), open only a few days a week, holds a fine collection of 47 heritage planes, including a French Dassault Mirage, British De Havilland Vampire T11, and a US Lockheed T-33 Shooting Star. **Let's Visit Airbus** (*manatour.fr; adult/child €16/13*) runs tours of the Airbus Factory.

Nothing martials humanity's scientific advances like the exploration of space. Toulouse's contribution to our airborne feats beyond the stratosphere are celebrated at the vast **Cité de l'Espace** (*cite-espace.com; adult/child €29/22.50*) space museum. Highlights include boarding a Mir space station, riding the Apollo mission simulator and seeing real pieces of moonrock.

CITY OF VIOLETS

It is dubbed the Rose City but Toulouse is also a city of violets. Specifically, the flowers that are cultivated locally in winter and used to make *liqueur de violette* (a popular ace up the sleeve with local mixologists); *violettes de Toulouse* candies; and Paris-Toulouse pastries, consisting of hazelnut praline and violet-infused Chantilly cream. If used well, violet flowers create a subtle fragrant note, rather than the soapy flavour you might expect. To buy violet products, check out **La Maison de la Violette**, a shop in a canal barge. In a nod to this violet heritage, the local football team, Ligue 1's Toulouse FC, play in purple and even released a third kit in the 2024–25 season emblazoned with violet flowers.

EATING IN TOULOUSE: OUR PICKS

Chez Tran: Playful neon lighting and paper lanterns. Try its signature bo buns. On rue Pargaminières, known as the 'street-food half-mile'. *hours vary* €

Au Bon Graillou: Try the excellent-value seasonal three-course menu for lunch, using ingredients from Marché Victor Hugo downstairs. *noon-3pm Tue-Sun* €€

L'Oncle Pom: Sagely takes a potato-forward approach: first, select your preparation (gratin, French fries etc) before choosing a meat or fish to accompany. *hours vary* €€

Restaurant Emile: Michelin Guide–level *cassoulet* served in clay bowls. Book ahead for terrace seating. *noon-1.30pm & 7.30-9.30pm* €€€

HELP ME PICK:

Where to Taste Wine

The French thirst for wine dates to Roman times when oenophiles identified fertile pockets of Gaul to plant *vignobles* (vineyards) to spawn France's most celebrated wine regions: Burgundy, Bordeaux, Champagne, Alsace, the Loire and Rhône valleys, Provence and Languedoc. Quality wines in France are Appellation d'Origine Contrôlée (AOC) or Appellation d'Origine Protégée (AOP): the wine has met stringent regulations governing where, how and under what conditions it was grown and bottled. Some regions have a single AOC (like Alsace); others dozens. Bordeaux has 65!

Where to go if you love...

Full-Bodied Reds

Monks in Burgundy began making wine in the 8th century, believing divine spirits in the soil spoke to them through wine. Burgundy vineyards remain small and are divided into *climats* – a viticultural patrimony UNESCO-listed since 2015. Winegrowers in **Côte d'Or**, **Chablis**, **Châtillon** and **Mâcon** produce small quantities of excellent reds from pinot noir grapes. The best Bourgogne vintages demand 10 to 20 years to age. Despite Burgundy's global fame (and the sky-high prices its wines now fetch), many winemakers remain modest – owner-operators who prune their own vines and consider themselves caretakers rather than creators.

Bubbles

Champagne's beloved bubbles were once thought to be a fault in the region's still wine. It wasn't until Dom Pierre Pérignon, a Benedictine monk at Hautvillers Abbey, started to master the art of winemaking that the sparkling wine began to be appreciated. 'Come quickly, I am tasting the stars!' is what he reportedly exclaimed upon tasting Champagne in 1693. For centuries, Champagne was the celebratory drink for French coronations, giving it the reputation as 'the wine of Kings and the King of wines'. Today, the famous Champagne houses welcome visitors to underground caverns, perfectly manicured vineyards and exquisite tasting rooms.

BARMALINI/SHUTTERSTOCK ©

Crisp Whites

The Loire Valley produces France's greatest variety of wines, some in troglodyte caves. Light delicate whites from **Pouilly-Fumé**, **Vouvray**, **Sancerre**, **Bourgueil** and **Chinon** are excellent. Muscadet, cabernet franc and chenin blanc grapes contrast with chardonnay grapes that go into Burgundy's great whites. There are also plenty of reds, particularly in Chinon, most made from cabernet franc grapes, aged in caves carved out of *tuffeau*, the soft local limestone, which offers the ideal temperature and humidity.

Pale Rosé

Chilled, fresh pink rosé wines are synonymous with the hot south, and 80% of the wine produced in Provence is rosé. **Côtes de Provence**, with 20 hectares of vineyards between Nice and Aix-en-Provence, is France's sixth-largest appellation. Look for rosés from **Bandol**, **Coteaux d'Aix-en-Provence**, **Palette** and **Coteaux Varois**.

HOW TO

Burgundy Wineries are almost impossible to visit; buy from *négociants* (wine merchants) in specialist wine shops instead.

Champagne Most Champagne houses are in Reims, Épernay or in between the two. Tastings often require reservation and include a tour, and are much more expensive than in other wine regions, starting from €27 per person.

Loire Valley Hundreds of vineyards welcome visitors, although advance reservations are preferred. Visit *vinsdeloire.fr/caves-touristiques* for information and an interactive map.

Provence Many vignerons (growers) open their doors to visitors; taste two or three vintages before buying. In Provence fill your own container with cheap *vin de table* (table wine) at the local wine cooperatives.

Oeno-tourism

E-bike tours are common in areas like Beaujolais, Jura and the Loire; or in the Dordogne and Ardèche, wake up to sunrise yoga sessions among the vines. In the Alps, try heady combinations like snowshoe walks to taste wine in forest tipis, or take blind tasting up a level by combining speleology and wine tasting in the Ardèche's caves. Wine-infused runs are increasingly popular, too. The Marathon du Médoc is now almost 40 years old, and obtaining a place is reminiscent of getting tickets for Glastonbury or Coachella. Bigger and more popular year-on-year, the riotous Marathon du Beaujolais is a popular alternative, but even that sells out well in advance. Look out for smaller wine runs, and prepare to don full fancy dress.

When buying wine from a shop, visit a caviste rather than a supermarket. Often the price difference is nominal, and they'll have a greater selection of wines from small producers.

Places We Love to Stay

€ Budget €€ Midrange €€€ Top end

Paris   MAP p182

Hôtel Chopin € A rare budget hotel in Paris, and in the unique location of one of the city's historical *passages couverts*. This historic hotel originally opened in 1846 and features classic, period-inspired rooms overlooking the Paris rooftops.

People Marais € This modern hostel is built for community, with well-equipped dorms, communal kitchens, and a light-filled sociable cafe and restaurant.

123 Sebastopol €€ A cinema-themed hotel, where each floor is dedicated to a film director or film-music composer, with an entertaining atmosphere. It is family-friendly and conveniently located between Sentier and Le Marais.

Hôtel des Académies et des Arts €€ An effortlessly cool design hotel housed in the building where Modigliani once had his studio (book room 52 if you want to sleep in it). The hotel also has its own art atelier downstairs.

Hotel Dame des Arts €€ This hip hotel is one of St-Germain-des-Prés coolest addresses, with design-led rooms and a rooftop terrace with fantastic views that pulls in locals as well as guests.

Hôtel HoY €€ One of the most restful places to stay; there's a yoga studio and in-room mats. The highlight is the ground-floor flower shop and the excellent MESA, serving up creative plant-based dishes steeped in Latin American flavours.

Mama Shelter Paris East €€ This cool Philippe Starck–designed, 170-room hotel draws a younger, creative crowd to its off-grid location, thanks to its bold industrial decor, rooftop bar and playful touches such as cartoon-mask lampshades.

Mont St-Michel   MAP p196

Chambres d'Hôte Les Bruyères du Mont € Find an enchanted garden and gracious host Nadine in this guesthouse near Mont St-Michel.

Camping La Baie du Mont St-Michel €€ A well-maintained, no-frills campsite with friendly hosts and plenty of hot water for showers.

Auberge Sauvage €€€ Farmhouse chic aesthetic with a garden and tennis courtyards – and a Michelin-starred restaurant.

Annecy

Hôtel du Château €€ Family-run hotel in Annecy with panoramic breakfast terrace and free parking, on a hill across from the château's imposing gatehouse.

Chamonix   MAP p204

Le Chamoniard Volant € Veteran favourite of climbers and ski bums on a budget, with bunk dorms and communal kitchen in a self-catering chalet.

Hôtel Richemond € Third-generation family hotel, with old-school rooms in a grand old building from 1914; exceptional value.

La Folie Douce €€ The famous après-ski brand's only hotel parties hard inside a monumental Belle Époque palace.

Refuge du Montenvers €€ Mourn France's longest but fast-melting glacier at this elegant grand dame, an 1880 vintage with chic retro-styled rooms, restaurant and summer terrace above Mer de Glace.

Lyon   MAP p210

Pilo € Almost too stylish to be a hostel, with oodles of plants, Friday-night DJ sets alfresco, boules pitches and frequent visiting tattoo artists.

Hotel de Verdun 1882 €€ Beautiful rooms in a historic building formerly belonging to the founders of Lyonnais institution Brasserie Georges.

Lyon Country House €€ A breath of fresh air just 15 minutes from the city centre, with lodges, treehouses and suites.

Fourvière Hôtel €€€ Chic, upmarket hotel in a former convent. The old altar and confessional booths spill over with house plants.

Loire Valley

Hôtel de Biencourt € Just 150m from the entrance to Azay-le-Rideau, 17 charming rooms in a one-time school from the 17th and 18th centuries.

Côté Loire-Auberge Ligérienne € Facing the river in Blois, this establishment – an inn since 1675 – has eight spotless rooms, some with 350-year-old beams and/or great Loire views.

Le Bois des Chambres €€ A very classy 39-room hotel, 300m from Chaumont-sur-Loire, that occupies a 19th-century barn and ecofriendly, modern pavilions surrounded by gardens.

Hôtel Le Grand Monarque €€
An 18th-century coaching inn transformed into a charming hotel just five minutes on foot from the château. Rooms are spacious, with a mix of 21st-century mod cons and antique touches.

Relais de Chambord €€€
Chambord's former kennels are now a luxury hotel with an unbeatable château-adjacent location, country-chic rooms, a sensational bar, a spa and a *bistronomique* restaurant.

Nice   MAP p222

Hostel Meyerbeer Beach €
Friendly hostel with a cracking city-centre location, just three minutes from the beach. Dorms are mixed.

Hôtel Rossetti €€ Charming three-star boutique hotel with seven rooms in the shadow of Cathédrale Ste-Réparate in Vieux Nice. The hidden terrace is lovely.

Hôtel La Pérouse €€€ Clinging to the Colline du Château with a hidden pool and sea views, this delightful four-star hotel is one of Nice's finest.

Le Negresco €€€ The grande dame of Nice's hotels, set across from the beach. Each room is unique and styled to a theme. The art collection is priceless.

Marseille   MAP p227

Hotel Peron €€ Wes Anderson–style hotel with views of the corniche and beyond. Art deco from every angle and a friendly reception.

Le Ryad €€ North African–inspired hotel that has a sanctuary of a garden to drink fresh mint tea in after a long day.

La Relève €€ There are only four rooms, so book in advance for this 1950s-inspired guesthouse that is attached to a very cool bar in the 7e.

St-Tropez

Hôtel Ermitage €€ Self-consciously retro, with sweeping views over town.

Hôtel Lou Cagnard €€€ Lovely jasmine-scented garden patios and welcoming feel. Open year-round.

Bordeaux   MAP p233

Jost € A new-gen lifestyle hostel with a Spritz-fuelled bar around a rooftop pool (guests only). Tip-top Italian tapas too.

Chez Dupont €€ B&B-style rooms decorated with vintage furniture and curiosities, on Chartrons' old-world main street.

La Maison du Lierre €€ As serene as its name, the House of Ivy has quaint boutique rooms and serves breakfast in a vine-draped garden.

Hôtel La Zoologie €€€
Four-star luxury in Bordeaux's historic Institute of Zoology, a glorious 1903 mashup of brick, stone and glass.

JUAN ANTONIO ORIHUELA/SHUTTERSTOCK

Hotel Peron, Marseille

Practicalities

MONEY & CURRENCY

The currency in France is the euro (€). Payment by card is widespread and can be contactless up to €50; smaller shops can impose a minimum payment (€10 or €15). In rural France, many B&Bs, *fermes auberges,* produce markets and taxi drivers don't accept cards. You cannot hire a car without a credit card.

BILLION PHOTOS/SHUTTERSTOCK

SMOKING

Smoking in France is illegal in indoor public spaces, summer forests and – since July 2025 – in public parks and gardens, beaches, bus shelters, sports facilities and outdoor spaces around schools.

HEALTHCARE

Pharmacies – an illuminated green cross indicates they're open – sell a wide range of medicines without *ordonnance* (prescription). Details of the closest *pharmacie de garde* open at night and on Sundays are displayed in pharmacy windows. Call 118 or Europe-wide 112 for an ambulance.

LGBTIQ+ TRAVELLERS

The rainbow flag flies high in France. 'Laissez-faire' perfectly sums up France's liberal attitude towards homosexuality and people's private lives in general, in part because of a long tradition of public tolerance towards unconventional lifestyles.

OPENING HOURS

In many French towns and villages, shops close on Monday.
Banks 9am–noon and 2pm–5pm Monday to Friday or Tuesday to Saturday
Bars 7pm–1am
Cafes 7am–11pm
Clubs 10pm–3am, 4am or 5am Thursday to Saturday
Restaurants Noon–2.30pm and 7pm–9pm or later six days a week
Shops 10am–noon and 2pm–7pm Monday to Saturday

ACCESSIBLE TRAVEL

France presents constant challenges for *visiteurs à mobilité réduite* (visitors with reduced mobility) and *visiteurs handicapés* (visitors with disabilities), but inroads are being made into helping them get around more easily. Paris metro is not good for accessibility, but Paris buses are 100% accessible.

PUBLIC HOLIDAYS

New Year's Day 1 January
Easter Sunday & Monday Late March/April
May Day 1 May
WWII Victory Day 8 May
Ascension Thursday May; 40th day after Easter
Pentecost & Whit Monday Mid-May to mid-June; seventh Sunday after Easter

Bastille Day (Fête Nationale) 14 July
Assumption Day 15 August
All Saints' Day 1 November
Remembrance Day 11 November
Christmas Day 25 December

Language

Standard French is taught and spoken throughout France. This said, regional accents and dialects are an important part of identity in certain regions, but you'll have no trouble being understood anywhere if you stick to standard French.

Basics

Hello. Bonjour. *bon-zhoor*
Goodbye. Au revoir. *o-rer-vwa*
Yes. Oui. *wee*
No. Non. *non*
Please. S'il vous plaît. *seel voo play*
Thank you. Merci. *mair-see*
Excuse me. Excusez-moi. *ek-skew-zay-mwa*
Sorry. Pardon. *par-don*
What's your name? Comment vous appelez-vous? *ko-mon voo-za-play voo*
My name is ... Je m'appelle ... *zher ma-pel ...*
Do you speak English? Parlez-vous anglais? *par-lay-voo ong-glay*
I don't understand. Je ne comprends pas. *zher ner kom-pron pa*

Directions

Where's ...? Où est ...? *oo ay ...*
What's the address? Quelle est l'adresse? *kel ay la-dres*
Could you write the address, please? Est-ce que vous pourriez écrire l'adresse, s'il vous plaît? *es-ker voo poo-ryay ay-kreer la-dres seel voo play*
Can you show me (on the map)? Pouvez-vous m'indiquer (sur la carte)? *poo-vay-voo mun-dee-kay (sewr la kart)*

Signs

Entrée Entrance
Fermé Closed
Ouvert Open
Sortie Exit
Toilettes/WC Toilets

Time

What time is it? Quelle heure est-il? *kel er ay til*
It's (8) o'clock. Il est (huit) heures. *il ay (weet) er*
Half past (10). Il est (dix) heures et demie. *il ay (deez) er ay day-mee*
Morning Matin. *ma-tun*
Afternoon Après-midi. *a-pray-mee-dee*
Evening Soir. *swar*
Yesterday Hier. *yair*
Today Aujourd'hui. *o-zhoor-dwee*
Tomorrow Demain. *der-mun*

Emergencies

Help! Au secours! *o skoor*
Leave me alone! Fichez-moi la paix! *fee-shay-mwa la pay*
I'm ill. Je suis malade. *zher swee ma-lad*
Call ... Appelez... *a-play*
   a doctor un médecin. *un mayd-sun*
   the police la police. *la po-lees*

Eating & Drinking

What would you recommend? Qu'est-ce que vous conseillez? *kes-ker voo kon-say-yay*
Cheers! Santé! *son-tay*
That was delicious. C'était délicieux! *say-tay day-lee-syer*

NUMBERS	
1	un *un*
2	deux *der*
3	trois *trwa*
4	quatre *ka-trer*
5	cinq *sungk*
6	six *sees*
7	sept *set*
8	huit *weet*
9	neuf *nerf*
10	dix *dees*

245

TRAVELVIEW/SHUTTERSTOCK

Charles de Gaulle airport

Arriving

For many, touchdown in Paris, at Charles de Gaulle or Orly airports, is their first taste of France, although there are international airports across the country. Trains link much of continental Europe and the UK with France, with many ferry connections joining the UK to northern France, too. Cruises dock on much of the French coast, particularly along the Mediterranean.

By Air

Charles de Gaulle, Paris, is the largest international airport in France, and most flights linking non-European countries arrive here. There are international airports in Lyon-St-Exupéry, Marseille-Provence, Nice-Côte d'Azur, Bordeaux-Mérignac and Toulouse-Blagnac, among others.

By Train

Eurostar (*eurostar.com*) is currently the only trans-Channel service to the UK; book tickets to/from London St Pancras in advance for best rates. Renfe (*renfe. com*) runs France–Spain connections, and Trenitalia (*trenitalia.com*) serves the France–Italy route.

MONEY

Currency Euro (€)

CREDIT & DEBIT CARDS

Some metro systems (including Lyon) accept contactless card payments. In other cities, like Paris, you'll need to buy a rechargeable Navigo card.

ATMS

ATMs – *points d'argent* or *distributeurs automatiques de billets* – are the cheapest and most convenient way to get euros, usually offering the best exchange rates. Cashpoints connected to Visa/MasterCard/Cirrus/Maestro networks are situated in all cities and towns, on central squares, outside banks on main streets and inside large supermarkets.

Getting Around

There's excellent public transport but you'll also want your own wheels to explore deeper. EU nationals don't need a visa to visit France, but by the end of 2026, it is anticipated that arrivals from the UK, US, Canada and New Zealand, among others, will have to fill in a pre-arrival, online form to meet the EU's new electronic vetting system (*etiasvisa.com*).

Train & Bus
France's SNCF rail network has frequent services (both high-speed TGVs and regional TER trains). Principal rail lines radiate out from Paris, making services between towns on different spokes slow or nonexistent. Bus services are reduced weekends and school holidays.

GREGORY_DUBUS/GETTY IMAGES

Bicycle & E-Bike
Dedicated cycling paths are widespread; many skirt canal towpaths or retired railway lines (*voies verts* or greenways). Long-distance itineraries like La Vélodyssée (p236) favour roads with light traffic and are ideal for bike-packing. Bike rental – road and mountain bikes, regular and electric-assisted – is omnipresent.

Hiring a Car
Driving is a delight in backstage France, but a car is a liability in traffic-plagued city centres. Find rental agencies at airports and by train stations; many offer electric cars. Some cities have a public car-sharing scheme, ideal for an out-of-town day flit. Consider car-sharing platforms *ouicar.fr* and *fr.getaround.com*.

Using Motorways
Autoroutes (motorways) command *péages* (tolls). Take a ticket on entering, pay when exiting. Cash payers: drive into a tollbooth displaying a green arrow – booths showing a white card symbol only accept cards. Check traffic conditions, motorway services etc on *bison-fute.gouv.fr*.

Ridesharing
Covoiturage (ridesharing) in France is a national institution. BlaBlaCar (*blablacar.fr*) is the most popular app, connecting passengers with drivers. In towns and cities, hitchhikers can stand in front of an '*Arrêt sur le pouce*' sign to be picked up by a vetted driver in the Rézo Pouce network (*rezopouce.fr*).

DRIVING ESSENTIALS

Any car entering an intersection (including a T-junction) from a road on your right has the right of way unless street signs indicate otherwise.

There's generally a tollbridge, but some motorways have phased this out; pay within 72 hours online at *sanef.com*.

Approx. €1.72/L

For places to stay
in Germany, see
p312

CANADASTOCK/SHUTTERSTOCK

Brandenburger Tor (p254), Berlin

Curated by
Barbara Woolsey

Germany

TRANQUIL LANDSCAPES AND FESTIVE TRADITIONS

Travel in Germany is just like its culture: direct and efficient. In a world of options, Germany is serious about the joy of simple pleasures.

Germany's take on fun and adventure is just like how it brews its beer: an age-old recipe that never wavers from tradition and values good taste. If you're on a roller-coaster, multicountry Eurotrip, what Germany offers is a breath of fresh air (literally) in forests, beer gardens and laid-back cities where parks and nature are a must.

Getting from A to B is efficient on the autobahn, the world's fourth-longest highway system, and a train network where high-speed and wide-spanning regional services tick like clockwork. There's something undeniably artistic in the way scenery unfolds here; the corrugated, dune-fringed coasts of the north; the moody forests, romantic river valleys and vast vineyards of the centre; and the off-the-charts splendour of the Alps, carved into rugged glory by glaciers and the elements. All of these are integral parts of a magical natural matrix that's bound to give your legs a good workout.

Experiencing Germany is all about your belly, too. Local food is so much more than sausages and pretzels. Beyond the clichés awaits a cornucopia of seasonal palate-teasers and ingredients varying greatly from region to region. Dishes are a formidable means of consuming Germany's culture and history, and understanding its regional differences. In many ways, the country is akin to its hodgepodge dinner staples like *Eintopf* (one-pot stew) and *Auflauf* (casserole) – a vibrant mix of flavours and influences offering new surprises in every bite.

THE MAIN AREAS

BERLIN
Germany's nonconformist capital. **p254**

COLOGNE
Energetic yet ancient Roman city. **p267**

DÜSSELDORF
Germany's fashion capital. **p272**

HAMBURG
Northern charms – medieval and maritime. **p275**

MUNICH
World-class beer and museums. **p281**

BAVARIA
Modern fairy-tale landscapes. **p286**

STUTTGART & THE BLACK FOREST
Fast cars and enchanting greenery. **p292**

BREMEN & LOWER SAXONY
Dramatic scenery and architecture. **p296**

DRESDEN & LEIPZIG
Historical elegance, countercultural stride. **p300**

CENTRAL GERMANY
Intellect and innovation on the heartland. **p303**

FRANKFURT AM MAIN
Manhattan vibes on the Maine. **p305**

Find Your Way

Wherever you go in Germany's north, water is a loyal travel buddy. Hop on a car or train for a couple of hours, and landscapes shift from wild nature to quaint countryside and lively small-city life.

Hamburg, p275

Germany's largest port boasts cosmopolitan vibes and urban dwellers with cash to spend. Urban renewal, counterculture and a vibrant nightlife create excitement.

Berlin, p254

Berlin's alternative spirit, eclectic food scene, layered history and anything-goes nightlife enthral. Cavernous museums and industrial nightclubs outnumber rainy days.

CAR

Useful for travelling at your own pace or visiting nature-heavy regions and national parks where public transport is meagre. Frequent rest stops make for comfortable journeys – and the experience of blasting down speed-limit-free autobahn.

TRAIN

An extensive network of long-distance and regional trains have frequent departures. The national operator Deutsche Bahn has a monopoly on tracks and can be fairly expensive; private operators offer some deals. Carriage chaos ensues on weekends and public holidays.

AIR

Only useful for longer distances, such as Hamburg to Munich or Berlin to Munich. It's sometimes cheaper than trains but not necessarily faster when you factor in check-in, security and getting into the city centre; trains drop you right into the downtown action.

Central Germany, p303

Germany's heartland of nature and history. Ancient beech forests, rococo castles atop vine-clad hills, historic redoubts of German culture and lively university towns all await.

Bavaria, p286

Traditional Germany bottled into one region. Intoxicating landscapes – rolling vineyards, storybook forests and alpine peaks – spiked with castles, palaces and breweries along the way.

Munich, p281

Its reputation as the 'City of Art and Beer' is well earned. Attack the art quarter's museums and galleries; drink up beer-garden vibes and brewhouse traditions.

Stuttgart & the Black Forest, p292

Exciting thrills from fast Swabian cars to the outdoor action of Black Forest firs. Hike, swim and ski, then sink into healing thermal waters.

Frankfurt am Main, p305

Europe's de facto financial hub offers fine dining and art museums against an iconic skyline; further out, regional discoveries span mystical villages, castles and forests.

Cologne, p267

Feel your spirits soar in the cathedral's luminous beauty, then come back to earth with a Kölsch beer, fantastic shopping and museums.

0 km 100
0 miles 50

VIENNA

AUSTRIA

Linz
Wels

Prague
CZECHIA
Ústí nad Labem
Plauen
Gera
Zwickau
Zwinger
Nationalmuseum
Dresden
Goethe-Nationalmuseum
Saalfeld

Gedenkstätte Buchenwald
Suhl
Coburg
Hof
Marktredwitz
Bayreuth
Weiden
Amberg
Neumarkt in der Oberpfalz
Regensburg
Deggendorf
Zwiesel
Cham
Passau
Braunau am Inn
A3

Würzburg Residenz
Würzburg
Bamberg
Schweinfurt
Erlangen
Nuremberg
Ansbach
Ingolstadt
Landshut
Mühldorf
Salzburg
Berchtesgaden
Kirchstein

Fulda
Marburg
Giessen
Frankfurt-am-Main
Römerberg
Kaiserdom
Städel
Wiesbaden
Mainz
Aschaffenburg
Darmstadt
Heilbronn
Schwäbisch Hall
Aalen
Nördlingen
Augsburg
Dachau
Englischer Garten
Munich Residenz
Munich
Kunstareal
Rosenheim
Chiemsee
Innsbruck

Aachen
Düren
Römisch-Germanisches Museum
Kölner Dom
Bonn
Siegen
Limburg
Worms
Mannheim
Heidelberg
Pforzheim
Karlsruhe
Baden-Baden
Mercedes-Benz Museum
Stuttgart
Tübingen
Ulm
Biberach
Memmingen
Kempten
Landsberg am Lech
Starnberg
Schloss Neuschwanstein
Zugspitze
Garmisch-Partenkirchen

Liège
BELGIUM
LUXEMBOURG
LUXEMBOURG CITY
Bernkastel-Kues
Koblenz
Cochem
Prüm
Bitburg
Kaiserslautern
Saarbrücken
Saarlouis
Metz
Nancy
Strasbourg
FRANCE
Offenburg
Freudenstadt
Vaihingen
Singen
Konstanz
Friedrichshafen
Ravensburg
Lindau
Bregenz
St Gallen
Lake Constance

Triberger Wasserfälle
Freiburger Münster
Freiburg
Waldshut
Basel
Zürich
SWITZERLAND

Colmar
Mulhouse
Belfort
Besançon
Épinal

251

Plan Your Time

Seeing Germany's different landscapes makes for a special journey. Beyond capitals like Berlin and Munich, countryside and small-city life are worth exploring – especially where scenic rivers run through.

MAJONIT/SHUTTERSTOCK

Kölner Dom (p267), Cologne

Weekend in the Capital

● A few days in **Berlin** (p254) is all it takes for key cultural highlights and a high-level perspective on German history. In Historic Mitte, trace the past against evocative landmarks: sobering WWII commemoration at the **Holocaust Memorial** (p256), Cold War divide at **Checkpoint Charlie** (p256), and finally, celebrating today's reunified Republic of Germany at the **Reichstag** (p256) and **Brandenburger Tor** (p254).

● On the UNESCO-listed **Museumsinsel** (p259), former Prussian palaces are prime for discovering ancient Egyptian history as well as globetrotting ethnology and Asian art at the **Neues Museum** (p259) and **Humboldt Forum** (p260) respectively. On an easy day trip to Potsdam, **Sanssouci Palace** (p266) and **sumptuous gardens** (p266) drive home Prussian glory days.

SEASONAL HIGHLIGHTS

Germany embraces all seasons, with events spread across the year. Weather and even public holidays range wildly across states.

MARCH

Longer-lingering daylight puts a spring in even the most gruff Germans' steps. Fresh **herring** hits coastal menus, and dishes prepared with *Bärlauch* (wild garlic) are all the rage.

APRIL

The Easter Bunny? Pfff. Germany's springtime mascot is the village Asparagus Queen, ushering in the nation's favourite cream-coloured crop. From markets to menus, **white asparagus** is everywhere.

MAY

Surprisingly warm and sunny, May is perfect for clinking in **beer gardens**. It's also packed with public holidays; trains and highways become awfully busy.

A Week's Southerly Quest

● Exploring southern Germany is an odyssey meandering high and low. Over two weeks, make your first impression in **Munich** (p281), Bavaria's cosmopolitan capital, visiting world-class museums of **Kunstareal** (p284) and tipping beer in **Englischer Garten** (p285). Wander from the famous piazza, **Marienplatz** (p281), to the truly urban **Viktualienmarkt** (p283) farmers market.

● Next, chase the superlative and fantastical within the Bavarian Alps: Germany's highest point, the **Zugspitze** (p288), and the Disney-inspiring **Schloss Neuschwanstein** (p288). Along the southern border, continue following fairy tales into the **Black Forest** (p294) and along the **Romantic Road** (p290). Backtrack to **Stuttgart** (p292) to discover further German legends – the **Porsche** (p292) and **Mercedes-Benz** (p293) museums.

A Few Days in the East

● Challenge historical assumptions about eastern Germany, chasing cultural highlights that reveal royal elegance and artsy modern gumption. Spin through **Berlin** (p254), Germany's wild-child capital with its eclectic neighbourhoods, iconic nightlife and GDR history. Hop over to **Dresden** (p300), exploring its baroque elegance and treasure troves of art.

● From there, it's just a zip over to **Leipzig** (p302), dubbed the City of Heroes for its role in razing the Berlin Wall. Immerse yourself in a cultural heritage to a soundtrack by Bach, Mendelssohn and Wagner, as well as today's modern rhythms of industrial nightlife and contemporary art. Some say 'Hypezig' is the better Berlin; go ahead and judge for yourself.

JUNE
it's **festival season** and there's fresh, local produce in supermarkets. Life moves fully outdoors upon summer solstice's blessed 9.30pm sundown.

JULY
School's out, and peak season begins. Pre-book accommodation – mountain or coast. Dip into lakes, rivers and Baltic or North Sea waters.

SEPTEMBER
It's sunny, but not hot. Summer is over but **wine** and autumn festivals (also, **Oktoberfest**) ease the season out. Changing leaves excite.

DECEMBER
Cold, sun-deprived days are brightened by **Advent** festivities, **Christmas markets** and twinkle-light canopies across streets, beer halls and restaurants.

Berlin

WORLD-FAMOUS MUSEUMS | MONUMENTAL HISTORY | GASTRONOMY

☑ TOP TIPS

Today, the site of the **Führerbunker** lies beneath an unremarkable car park, revealing its grim history only by a modest information panel. A diagram outlines the vast bunker network alongside construction data and the site's post-WWII fate. The Soviets blew up the interior in 1947, sealing off one of the darkest chapters of the 20th century.

Berlin is a city built on sand, water and the refusal to sit still. From its orderly Prussian foundations to its roaring industrial boom, through wartime destruction, Cold War division and the euphoric tearing down of the Wall, it's reinvented itself more times than most capitals can fathom. Former French culture minister Jack Lang said it well when he quipped that Paris will always be Paris, but Berlin will never be Berlin. True, although that's the city's magic. It's always becoming.

What keeps Berlin magnetic is sheer variety. Swoon over Nefertiti on Museum Island in the morning, raise your pinkie at afternoon tea at posh Hotel Adlon and sip natural wine in a trendy bar by evening. Street art decorates Berlin's facades like a second skin; weekend flea markets are a citywide ritual. Even club culture still exudes global pull, from marathon Berghain techno sessions to summer raves and sex-positive parties.

Historic Mitte

MAP p255

Symbol of division and unity

Brandenburger Tor (Brandenburg Gate) is Berlin's most famous – and most photographed – landmark. Trapped right behind the Berlin Wall during the Cold War, it symbolised division for decades before becoming an emblem of German reunification when the hated barrier fell in 1989. Today, it's a photogenic backdrop for New Year's Eve parties, concerts, festivals and mega-events, including FIFA World Cup finals.

 GETTING AROUND

Berlin is a sprawling city, but key areas are compact. Most blockbuster sights are found between Alexanderplatz and Zoo Station. Walking around Berlin's *Kieze* (neighbourhoods) is a joy, but to travel between them you'll need the excellent public transport – or a bicycle. Bike lanes, rental stations and app-based bike- and e-scooter-sharing services abound. Bicycles may be taken aboard specially marked U-Bahn, S-Bahn and tram carriages but require a separate *Fahrradkarte* (bike ticket).

Crowned by the Quadriga (Johann Gottfried Schadow's sculpture of the Roman goddess of victory), the Brandenburg Gate looks over **Pariser Platz**, which was completely flattened in WWII. Look around now: the US, French and British embassies and the venerable **Hotel Adlon** once again frame the square.

Beacon of German democracy

It's been burned, bombed, rebuilt, buttressed by the Berlin Wall, wrapped in fabric and finally reimagined by Norman Foster

BEST SHOPPING IN HISTORIC MITTE

Frau Tonis Parfum:
This made-in-Berlin perfume boutique offers scent tests to help you choose a matching fragrance plus bespoke blends.

Ritter Sport Bunte Schokowelt:
Colourful flagship store with classic, limited-edition, vegan, organic and personalised chocolate bars, and a bean-to-bar exhibit.

Dussmann – Das Kulturkaufhaus:
Eldorado for bookworms, with a huge music selection, free concerts and high-profile book readings and signings.

Rausch Schokoladenhaus: Emporium of truffles and pralines with replicas of Berlin landmarks and a cafe with a view of Gendarmenmarkt.

KPM Berlin: Store and outlet for handmade porcelain from the royal KPM manufactory, established by Frederick the Great in 1763.

MICHELANGELOOP/SHUTTERSTOCK

Holocaust Memorial

as the modern seat of Germany's parliament, the Bundestag. Topped with a glistening glass dome, the iconic **Reichstag** *(bundestag.de; free)* now stands as the symbolic and architectural heart of the surrounding Federal Government District, built in the 1990s after German reunification.

Reserve a time slot online for the lift to the rooftop terrace for fabulous views and access to the glass dome. Resembling a giant glass beehive, the glistening cupola is open at the top and bottom, and hovers directly above the plenary chamber, serving as a visual metaphor for political transparency.

Confronting Holocaust history

The **Holocaust Memorial** *(stiftung-denkmal.de; free)* was dedicated in 2005 to commemorate the six million Jewish victims of the Holocaust. Designed by New York architect Peter Eisenman, the football-field-size area is filled with 2711 concrete stelae, rising in sombre silence from undulating ground and inviting quiet reflection on loss, absence and memory.

You're free to access this massive concrete maze at any point and make your individual journey through it. Lose yourself in the narrow passageways and connect with its metaphorical sense of disorientation, claustrophobia and oppression. Remember that this is a space for respectful reflection.

Alfa, Bravo...Checkpoint Charlie

Checkpoint Charlie was the principal Cold War–era border crossing for foreigners and diplomats between the American

EATING IN HISTORIC MITTE: OUR PICKS

MAP p255

India Club: Curries are culinary poetry at this elegant North Indian outpost led by top toque Manish Bahukhandi. *5-11.30pm Wed-Mon* €€€

Crackers: Cosmopolitan gastro-cathedral where the lofty ceiling matches the dishes made with sustainably sourced provisions. *6pm-1am* €€€

Ganymed Brasserie: Paris meets Berlin at this charming and historic all-day riverside spot for French classics and seafood. *9am-midnight* €€€

Zollpackhof: Hearty German fare and Bavarian beer in a riverside beer garden or historic dining room with a crackling fireplace. *noon-11pm* €€

A LEISURELY TIERGARTEN STROLL

Clear your head with a spin around Tiergarten, one of the world's largest inner-city park.

START	END	LENGTH
Potsdamer Platz	Tiergarten S-Bahn station	6km; 2 hours

From **1 Potsdamer Platz**, make your way to **2 Luiseninsel**, an enchanting enclosed garden adorned with statues and flowerbeds. Follow the waterway west to **3 Rousseau-Insel**, a teensy island and memorial to 18th-century French philosopher Jean-Jacques Rousseau.

Continue to the **4 Siegessäule** (Victory Column) to climb up to the skirt hems of its gilded Victoria statue for fabulous city views. Following Spreeweg north takes you past snowy-white **5 Schloss Bellevue**, a palace originally built for Frederick the Great's brother and now the residence of the German president.

Meander along the Spree River, then check out the latest art exhibit at the **6 Akademie der Künste**.

Walk south through the park to reach the Neuer See, a romantic lake fronted by the charming **7 Café am Neuen See** restaurant and beer garden.

Stroll north on Tiergartenufer along the Landwehrkanal until you reach Schleuseninsel to strike see the wacky **8 Rosa Röhre**, a massive piglet-pink pipe snaking around a university research facility painted cornflower-blue.

Then arrive at the magnificent **9 Charlotten-burger Tor**, a counterpart to the Brandenburg Gate. If you're hungry, drop by **10 Capt'n Schillow**, a quirky fish-focused restaurant boat moored below the gate. Otherwise follow Strasse des 17 Juni east to wrap up your tour at **11 Tiergarten S-Bahn station**.

On Sundays you can browse **Berliner Trödelmarkt**, Berlin's oldest flea market, which sets up along Strasse des 17 Juni.

The **Hansaviertel quarter** is a showcase of modernist 1950s buildings designed by Gropius, Niemeyer and other big mid-century architects.

A **memorial** below Lichtenstein Bridge marks where the body of revolutionary Rosa Luxemburg was thrown into the Landwehr Canal after her 1919 murder.

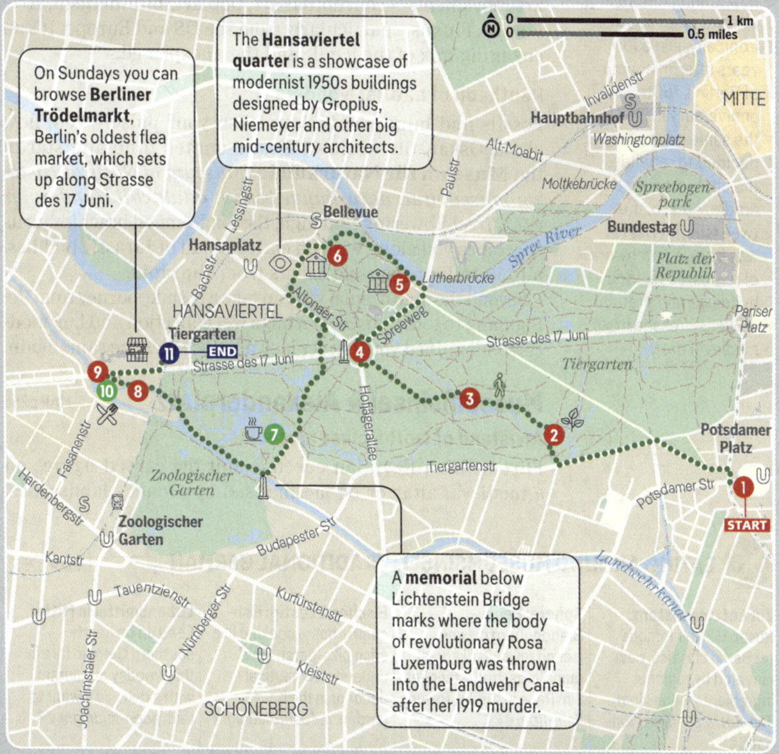

MEDIEVAL REBOOT

The area west and south of the TV Tower was once the bustling heart of medieval Berlin. Back in the 13th century, traders set up shop along the Spree, giving rise to the twin towns of Berlin and Cölln. Many of the old buildings and crooked lanes survived until WWII, but in the aftermath, East German city planners bulldozed most of what remained, sparing only a few token landmarks like the Marienkirche that now stands forlorn in a sea of open space. Ironically, just a few years later, in honour of Berlin's 750th anniversary in 1987, the same government decided to rebuild the city's medieval cradle. And so, the twee **Nikolaiviertel** was born, a patchwork of relocated historic buildings and prefab replicas dressed in medieval drag.

sector in West Berlin and Soviet-controlled East Berlin. It got the name 'Charlie' because it was the third Allied checkpoint to open – hence the third letter in the NATO phonetic alphabet.

These days, the recreated checkpoint, complete with young men in uniform posing for tips, may scream 'tourist trap', but there are a few genuinely worthwhile exhibits that help you connect with this historic site.

For a crash course in Cold War milestones, check out the photos and documents of the free outdoor **Checkpoint Gallery**. Stories of daring escapes across the Wall are at the heart of the **Mauermuseum** (mauermuseum.de; adult/child €18.50/12.50).

Edgy art in a Nazi bunker

Pick up on the vibes of war, vegetables and whips still clinging to the labyrinthine warren now housing the **Sammlung Boros** (Boros Collection; sammlung-boros.de; adult/student €18/10), one of Berlin's most exciting private art spaces. A fresh exhibition rolls out every four years. Tours (also in English) run for 90 minutes and tend to sell out fast, so book early.

All aboard the art train

Housed in a grand old train station, **Hamburger Bahnhof – Nationalgalerie der Gegenwart** (hamburgerbahnhof.de; adult/child €16/free) is one of Germany's top spots for contemporary art. Its collection spans the full arc of post-1960s art movements – conceptual art, pop art, minimalism, Arte Povera, Fluxus – particularly from the US and Europe. It's an engaging mix of the iconic and the unexpected.

Pantheon of natural wonders

Fossils and minerals don't quicken your pulse? Well, how about Oskar, the world's tallest mounted dino and star of the **Museum für Naturkunde** (Museum of Natural History; museumfuernaturkunde.berlin; adult/child/under 6yr €11/5/free). Towering 13m high, the long-limbed brachiosaurus welcomes you along with an entire squad of Jurassic buddies, all 150-million-year-old expats from Tanzania.

Beyond the dino drama, you can take a cosmic journey from the Big Bang to today, discover a huge wet collection and bug models so magnified you'll never look at house flies the same again.

Museumsinsel & Alexanderplatz   MAP p255

An island of world-class museums

Flirt with an Egyptian queen, count the carved figures on a medieval altar or be mesmerised by Monet's landscapes.

EATING AROUND MUSEUMSINSEL: TRADITIONAL GERMAN   MAP p255

Zur Letzten Instanz: Rustic 1621 lair famous for Berlin classics, now elevated by regional ingredients. *noon-3pm Tue-Sat, 5.30-11pm Mon-Sat* €€	**Sphere:** Berlin– Brandenburg cuisine (schnitzel, *soljanka*, veal dumplings) from star chef Tim Raue in the TV Tower. *9am-11pm* €€€	**Fischer & Lustig:** Fish-centric home cooking like crisp pike-perch amid understated nautical decor or in the beer garden. *11.30am-midnight* €€	**Lebensmittel in Mitte:** Load up on hearty southern German fare in this woodsy restaurant with a deli you'll want to raid. *noon-midnight* €€

SEANPAVONEPHOTO/GETTY IMAGES

Fernsehturm (p260)

DOWN INTO THE UNDERBELLY

Berliner Unterwelten *(berliner-unterwelten. de; adult/child from €17/13)*, a nonprofit committed to preserving the city's hidden depths, is your gateway to exploring Berlin's mysterious underbelly on a guided tour. The most popular is 'Dark Worlds', a 90-minute descent into a civilian air-raid shelter beneath Gesundbrunnen U-Bahn station. Inside, you'll pick your way through claustrophobic rooms, narrow corridors and heavy steel doors, and past haunting wartime relics like hospital beds, gas masks and guns. The guides bring alive the chilling reality of ordinary Berliners cooped up here, crammed and scared, as the bombs rained down on the city. The minimum age is seven; children under 14 must be accompanied by an adult. Tickets are only available online.

Welcome to **Museumsinsel** *(Museum Island; smb.museum; day pass adult/child €24/free)*. Berlin's renowned repository of 6000 years of art, artefacts and sculpture from Europe and beyond is spread across five grand buildings.

The grand neoclassical **Old Museum** holds historical antiquities and the **New Museum** has a show-stopping Egyptian collection. The Greek-temple-style **Old National Gallery** is a tribute to 19th-century European art while the palatial **Bode-Museum** brings together several period-spanning collections under one grand roof. Note that the **Pergamonmuseum**, Museum Island's crown jewel, will remain closed for renovation until at least 2027.

Iconic Egyptian collection

For over 60 years, the **Neues Museum** *(New Museum; smb. museum; day pass adult/child €24/free)* sat in ruins. But today it's one of the city's most celebrated attractions and a standout on Museumsinsel.

With her elegant neck and eternal good looks, Egyptian queen Nefertiti is definitely the head-turner of the **Egyptian Museum and Papyrus Collection**. Berlin's world-renowned Egyptian collection shares a roof with the **Museum of Pre- and Early History**, a rather clunky name for a trove of fascinating finds from the Stone Age to the Middle Ages.

The entire museum building was a wartime ruin resurrected by David Chipperfield, who ingeniously incorporated salvaged remnants.

Pantheon-inspired antiquities

The Neues Museum shares top billing on Museumsinsel with the **Altes Museum** *(Old Museum; smb.museum; day pass adult/ child €24/free)*. The first museum to open on Museumsinsel in 1830, its Pantheon-inspired rotunda is the centrepiece. The ground level is home to sculptures, vases, tomb reliefs and jewellery that delve into Greek mythology, daily life in cities and the royal courts, and the importance of theatre. Two sculptures are standouts: the *Praying Boy* behind the rotunda and the *Berlin Goddess* off to the right. Upstairs, the busts of Caesar and Cleopatra are especially striking.

Atop Germany's tallest structure

No matter where you are in Berlin, chances are you'll spot the **Fernsehturm** *(tv-turm.de; adult/child from €29.50/19.50)*. The TV Tower – Germany's tallest structure – is as iconic to the city as the Eiffel Tower is to Paris. It has stretched its slim frame to a dizzying 368m (including the antenna) since its 1969 debut.

Up top, pinpoint city landmarks from the glass-fronted **observation deck** at 203m, complete with a bar and a slow spin (twice an hour). The TV Tower's newest attraction is the rotating restaurant **Sphere** (p258); it's now helmed by Tim Raue, whose two-starred eponymous restaurant, **Restaurant Tim Raue** *(tim-raue.com)*, has long made foodies swoon.

Explore Berlin's royal cathedral

Spirituality meets spectacle at the **Berliner Dom** *(berliner dom.de; adult/student €10/7.50),* which pulls quadruple duty as church, museum, concert hall and royal crypt. Inside, the former royal court church is gilt to the hilt, featuring an altar of marble and onyx, a 7269-pipe Sauer organ and lavish chapels, including one housing the sculpted sarcophagi of Friedrich I and Sophie Charlotte. For more dead royals, albeit in less extravagant coffins, head down to the crypt. There's an optional leg workout: a 270-step climb to the dome for glorious 360-degree views.

Berlin's newest cultural hub

After 20 years of debate, planning, construction and delays, Berlin's newest culture hub finally fully opened in 2022. Housed in a replica of the baroque Prussian city palace, the **Humboldt Forum** *(humboldtforum.org; prices vary, many exhibits free)* was named after Enlightenment-era brothers Wilhelm and Alexander von Humboldt. At its heart lie the dazzling collections of the **Ethnologisches Museum** and the **Museum für Asiatische Kunst** – your ticket to tapping into centuries of culture and creativity from across Africa, Asia, the Americas and Australia. It's open Wednesday to Monday.

Prenzlauer Berg

MAP p261

From death strip to urban living room

No other park in Berlin has pulled quite as radical a transformation as the **Mauerpark** *(mauerpark.info)*. Once part of the Berlin Wall death strip, it now pulses with a free-spirited vibe, especially on Sundays during the outdoor season. That's when thousands of locals, expats, tourists and bleary-eyed clubbers flood in to forage for treasure at the **Flohmarkt**

PRENZLAUER BERG

SIGHTS	**SLEEPING**	9 Prater
1 Gedenkstätte Berliner Mauer	4 Myer's Hotel Berlin	**ENTERTAINMENT**
2 Mauerpark	5 Soho House Berlin	10 Bearpit Karaoke
ACTIVITIES	**DRINKING & NIGHTLIFE**	**SHOPPING**
3 Berliner Unterwelten	6 August Fengler	11 Flohmarkt im Mauerpark
	7 Bryk Bar	12 Trödelmarkt Arkonaplatz
	8 Pluto	

im Mauerpark, snack at street-food stalls, chill in the beer gardens or stake out **Bearpit Karaoke** in the amphitheatre

Legend of a divided city

Though dismantled over 30 years ago, the Berlin Wall continues to capture our collective imagination. You'll find answers to just about any Wall-related question at the **Gedenkstätte Berliner Mauer** *(Berlin Wall Memorial; stiftung-berliner-mauer.de; free)*. Along with the superb 1.4km-long outdoor exhibition, visit the **Documentation Centre**'s exhibition – called '1961/1989. The Berlin Wall' – for a concise, engaging history (it's closed on Mondays).

BUDGET-FRIENDLY SIGHTSEEING

One of Berlin's best bargains is a DIY city tour aboard buses 100, 200 and 300, whose routes pass by many of the capital's greatest hits, all for the price of a standard public transport ticket (tariff AB). You have two hours to ride, hop off or switch lines. Better yet, get the 24-hour ticket to explore without the rush.

Bus 100 travels between Berlin-Zoo station and Alexanderplatz, and provides glimpses of landmarks such as the Gedächtniskirche, the Siegessäule, the Reichstag and the Brandenburg Gate.

Bus 200 also links Berlin-Zoo station and Alexanderplatz through a more southerly route via Potsdamer Platz.

Bus 300 connects the Philharmonie and U-Bahn/S-Bahn station Warschauer Strasse via Alexanderplatz and the East Side Gallery.

DRINKING IN PRENZLAUER BERG: OUR PICKS

MAP p261

Prater: Berlin's oldest beer garden (1837) offers custom pilsner and snacks; also has a woodsy beer hall with a full menu. *noon-11.30pm*

Bryk Bar: Sophisticated neighbourly cocktail lab, with classic and next-gen drinks, some starring the house-made Bryk gin. *7pm-1am Tue-Sat*

Pluto: Unpretentious wine bar with burgundy walls, serving biodynamic European wines and seasonal small plates. *5pm-late Thu-Mon*

August Fengler: The flirty party vibe, wallet-friendly prices and mix of locals and visitors make this 1936-born spot a Berlin classic. *6pm-4am*

BEST MURALS IN KREUZBERG

Astronaut/ Kosmonaut Mural: Victor Ash's monumental stencil-style piece was inspired by the US–Soviet space race.

Pink Man Mural: A lone terrified figure crouches on the finger of Blu's scary creature built from writhing pink bodies.

Rounded Heads Mural: Berlin artist Nomad's faceless figure hugs a hooded character in his signature pictogram style, inspired by punk and hip-hop culture.

Yellow Man Mural: Brazilian twins Os Gemeos painted a yellow-skinned, gender-neutral figure in eccentric attire, blending folklore with social messaging.

Nature Morte: Belgian artist ROA's depiction of animal carcasses reflects on the life-and-death cycle of native species within the urban environment.

Charlottenburg & Western Berlin

MAP p263

Pandas, pythons and piranhas

Zoo Berlin (*zoo-berlin.de; adult/child €25/12.50*), established in 1844, holds the triple crown as Germany's oldest, most species-rich and most visited animal park. Its biggest heart-throbs are panda twins Meng Hao and Meng Tian, born here in 2024, and their parents, on loan from China. To catch the antics of bears, gorillas, hippos, sea lions and other zoo inhabitants, plan your visit around feeding times, posted on-site and online. Special mention goes to the zoo's architecture, in particular the ornate **Elephant Gate** on Budapester Strasse.

Where history and commerce collide

In the 1950s and '60s, as Berlin rebuilt itself, Breitscheidplatz became a hub of modern urban life in the western half of the divided city. Its main landmark is the **Kaiser-Wilhelm-Gedächtniskirche** (*gedaechtniskirche-berlin.de; free*), once a majestic neo-Romanesque church that was crushed by WWII bombs. The ruined west tower has been preserved as an antiwar memorial, with photographs and artefacts in the **Gedenkhalle** (Hall of Remembrance) showcasing the church's former grandeur.

Outside, look down at the golden crack in the steps north of the church: the **Mahnmal am Breitscheidplatz** is a simple, striking memorial to the victims of the 2016 terror attack here.

From Hitler to Hertha BSC

Berlin's monumental **Olympiastadion** (*olympiastadion.berlin; adult/student/under 14yr €11/8/6, tours €17-25*), built by the Nazis for the 1936 Olympic Games, is one of the city's few surviving Third Reich architectural relics. Revamped for the 2006 FIFA World Cup, the coliseum-like venue is now a state-of-the-art space for concerts, sports and major events. It's also the home turf of Berlin soccer team, Hertha BSC.

On non-event days (check the website first), explore the stadium with an optional multimedia guide (*€4*). To see the locker rooms and stadium roof, join a guided tour (some are offered in English).

In the footsteps of Prussian royalty

Schloss Charlottenburg (*spsg.de; day pass to all open buildings adult/student/under 7yr €19/14/free*) is an exquisite palace ensemble and the best place in Berlin to soak up the grandeur of the Hohenzollern clan, who ruled Brandenburg and later Prussia from 1415 to 1918. A visit is especially pleasant in summertime when you can fold a picnic in the palace park into a day of peeking at art, treasures and period rooms. It's closed on Mondays.

DRINKING IN CHARLOTTENBURG: CLASSIC PUBS

MAP p263

Zwiebelfisch: Cosy pub popular with artsy barflies, exemplifying Charlottenburg at its boho best since the 1960s. *noon-2am*

Schleusenkrug: Next to a canal lock, Schleusenkrug has a charming 1950s interior but truly rocks the beer-garden season. *11am-10pm*

Diener Tattersall: Signed stills of celeb patrons decorate this artist pub founded by a heavyweight boxer. *6pm-2am Mon-Sat*

Dicke Wirtin: Stuffed with knick-knacks, this long-standing pub doles out homemade schnapps and hearty local fare. *11am-midnight Wed-Mon*

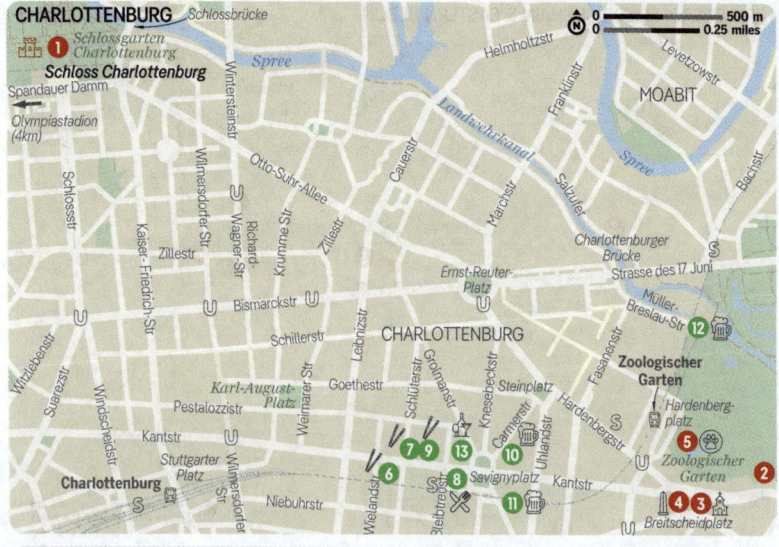

★ HIGHLIGHTS
1 Schloss Charlottenburg

● SIGHTS
2 Elephant Gate – Zoo Berlin Entrance

3 Kaiser-Wilhelm-Gedächtniskirche
4 Mahnmal am Breitscheidplatz
5 Zoo Berlin

● EATING
6 893 Ryōtei
7 Good Friends
8 Lo Fūfu
9 Madame Ngo

● DRINKING & NIGHTLIFE
10 Dicke Wirtin
11 Diener Tattersall
12 Schleusenkrug
13 Zwiebelfisch

Kreuzberg
MAP p264

Beacon of enlightenment

The **Jüdisches Museum** *(jmberlin.de; free)*, Europe's largest Jewish museum, is an eye-opening destination for anyone curious about Jewish history and culture, regardless of background or belief. The building alone is a showstopper: the zigzagging, zinc-clad masterpiece by American-Polish architect Daniel Libeskind stands as a powerful metaphor for the fractured yet enduring journey of the Jewish people in Germany over the past 1700 years.

Street-food pioneers

Berlin has embraced the global street-food frenzy with the fervour of a newfound convert. It all started back in 2013 with

 EATING ON KANTSTRASSE (CHINATOWN): ASIAN RESTAURANTS MAP p263

Lo Fūfu: Bold Italian pairs happily with Japanese precision in this sleek open kitchen. *6-10pm Mon, Thu & Fri, from 1pm Sat & Sun* €€

893 Ryōtei: Glam Japanese den behind a graffiti facade, serving aroma-rich bites with Nikkei influences. Bookings a must. *6-11pm Tue-Sat* €€€

Madame Ngo: This Hanoi-style brasserie makes pho-nomenal soups but also plays with French colonial influences. *noon-10pm* €€

Good Friends: Old-school Chinese-community darling has a long Cantonese menu and great weekday lunch specials. *noon-10.45pm Fri-Wed* €€

KREUZBERG, FRIEDRICHSHAIN & EASTERN BERLIN

⭐ **SIGHTS**	7 Rounded Heads Mural	12 Katerschmaus	17 Galander Kreuzberg
1 Astronaut Mural	8 Tempelhofer Feld	13 Markthalle Neun	18 Limonadier
2 East Side Gallery	9 Yellow Man Mural	14 Michelberger	
3 Jüdisches Museum	⬤ **SLEEPING**	⬤ **DRINKING**	🟥 **SHOPPING**
4 Karl-Marx-Allee	10 Kiez Hostel	**& NIGHTLIFE**	19 Flohmarkt Boxhagener
5 Nature Morte			Platz
6 Pink Man Mural	⬤ **EATING**	15 Apotheken Bar	20 Nowkoelln Flowmarkt
	11 Aleppo Supper Club	16 Bar Franzotti	

the launch of **Street Food Thursday** at **Markthalle Neun** (*markthalleneun.de*), a historic market hall that also hosts a popular farmers market on Friday and Saturday. The weekly Thursday snack-athon, which runs from 5pm to 10pm, remains a solid fixture on Berlin's culinary lineup and has also propelled numerous aspiring chefs to prominence.

Neukölln

MAP p264

Field of freedom

The airfield of **Tempelhofer Feld** (*tempelhoferfeld.de; free*) that so gloriously handled the Berlin Airlift of 1948–49 has been repurposed as one of the world's largest urban parks. In this steadily evolving open-sky adventure playground, cyclists

---

🍸 **DRINKING IN KREUZBERG: COCKTAIL BARS** ——————— MAP p264

Apothekenbar: Get your hands on a potent Penicillin at this charming cocktail bar in a retired 150-year-old pharmacy. *6pm-1am or later*

Limonadier: Top-shelf spirits make for a night of sophisticated drinking at this cocktail cavern with a sensuous 1920s vibe. *7pm-2am Tue-Sat*

Bar Franzotti: Overwhelmed by the 1000+ spirits at this vintage-style bar? Let the bartender whip up a cocktail tailored for you. *7pm-2am Mon-Sat*

Galander Kreuzberg: Leather armchairs and flattering lighting create an intimate ambience for the expert drinks at great prices. *6pm-1am Wed-Sun*

and bladers zip down old runways, while fun zones include barbecue areas, community gardens and basketball courts. In spring, Skudde sheep roll in to serve as natural lawnmowers.

Friedrichshain & Eastern Berlin

MAP p264

Political oppression in East Germany

Thousands of offices across 40 buildings served as the nerve centre of East Germany's most feared institution, the Ministry of State Security, better known as Stasi, until 1989. House 1 is now home to the **Stasimuseum** *(stasimuseum.de; adult/student/under 12yr €12/6/free, tours additional €5)*, where exhibits unpack the organisation's origins, working methods and far-reaching grip on East German society and beyond.

Secrets, cells and fear

Victims of Stasi persecution often ended up at the infamous **Stasi Prison** *(stiftung-hsh.de; adult/concession €9/5)*, now a memorial site called Gedenkstätte Berlin-Hohenschönhausen. Between 1951 and 1989, over 11,000 suspected regime opponents were held in this vast remand facility, about 30 minutes' ride on tram M5 from Alexanderplatz.

Book a time slot online for a punch-in-the-gut tour through this claustrophobic warren, including peeks inside cells and interrogation rooms. Don't be shy to ask questions. For a deeper understanding of prison life and the Stasi surveillance machine, budget some time for the two on-site exhibitions.

Grim history, glorious art

Along Mühlenstrasse, a 1.3km stretch was saved from the Berlin Wall to become the **East Side Gallery** *(eastsidegall eryberlin.de; free)*. Featuring more than 100 paintings by international artists, the world's largest open-air gallery stands as a testament to the peaceful revolution unfurling German reunification.

The East Side Gallery runs between Ostbahnhof and the Oberbaumbrücke; kick off your stroll at either end. Each mural has a QR code you can scan to learn about the artwork and its creator. Also watch out for the shiny information stelae with historical bites. On many weekends, multilingual guides stand by to answer any burning Wall-related questions.

EAST BERLIN'S MONUMENTAL BOULEVARD

Friedrichshain brims with monumental architecture, but nothing quite matches the pomp and scale of **Karl-Marx-Allee**, a 2.3km stretch of socialist showmanship between Frankfurter Tor and Alexanderplatz. Stroll down this 90m-wide boulevard, known until 1961 as 'Stalinallee'. Bilingual information panels unpack the architecture and history. Restaurants, galleries and shops inject contemporary vibrancy.

Living in these monumental 'workers' palaces' was considered a privilege reserved for party loyalists. The apartments featured central heating, lifts, tiled baths and built-in kitchens – serious luxury for the time. The most impressive buildings, riffing on Moscow's wedding-cake style, were constructed from 1952 to 1960 between Strausberger Platz and Frankfurter Tor.

 EATING IN FRIEDRICHSHAIN: OUR PICKS

MAP p264

Michelberger: Locally adored all-day spot with upscale bistro fare made with ingredients from small producers and its own farm. *7am-11pm* €€

Katerschmaus: Light lunches and a meat-focused dinner menu, plus Spree views, at this spot below Holzmarkt. *noon-3pm & 6-10pm Mon-Sat* €€

Aleppo Supper Club: At his pint-sized cafe, Samer Hafez dishes up Syrian soul food enriched with 'secret' spices and made for sharing. *11.30am-11pm* €€

Hafenküche: Marina spot with self-service lunches, modern German dinners and Spreedeck beer-garden snacks. *noon-3pm Sat & Sun, 6-9.30pm Wed-Sun* €€

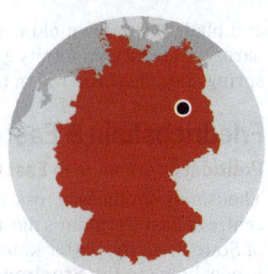

Potsdam

FAIRY-TALE PALACE | COLD WAR HISTORY | LAKESIDE DELIGHTS

GETTING AROUND

Potsdam is about 35km southwest of Berlin. It can be reached in under an hour from central Berlin, on the S-Bahn (S1 or S7). The city lies within Berlin's C fare zone, so you'll need an ABC ticket.

Walking or cycling are the best ways to explore Potsdam; rent a bike from Pedales outside the Hauptbahnhof. Schloss Sanssouci is 3km from the train station and is served by buses 614 and 695.

☑ TOP TIP

The Potsdam tourist office maintains a branch at the Mobiagentur Potsdam in the Hauptbahnhof and another on Alter Markt in the historic centre near Museum Barberini. Sanssouci Park sits west of the Altstadt, while the Neuer Garten with Schloss Cecilienhof is north. Babelsberg is about 4km east of central Potsdam.

Potsdam, the state capital of Brandenburg, is home to magnificent palaces and gardens embraced by lakes and the Havel River. It's an essential stop if you're spending any time in the region at all. Leading the roll call of royal pads is Schloss Sanssouci, a charming mini-Versailles and summer refuge of Frederick the Great with a splendid park. No wonder UNESCO gave World Heritage Status to large parts of the city in 1990.

Most people visit on a day trip from Berlin, but you'll need more time if you don't want to miss out on its many other attractions. Find out why there's a Dutch Quarter, visit the palace that hosted the Potsdam Conference, peer behind the walls of a sinister KGB prison and soak up splendid vistas on a cruise along the tranquil lakes embracing this enticing city.

Stepping into Potsdam's Past

Restored historic centre

Potsdam's biggest stunner is **Schloss Sanssouci** (*Sanssouci Palace; spsg.de; adult/student/under 7yr €22/17/free*). The rococo palace sits daintily above vine-draped terraces with Frederick the Great's grave nearby. Sanssouci's resplendent **park** (*free*), Potsdam's oldest, is dotted with palaces reflecting the Italian obsession of successor Friedrich Wilhelm IV (1795–1861).

Although much of Potsdam's historic town centre fell victim to WWII bombing and socialist town planning, it's been nicely restored for exploring on foot. Potsdam's own **Brandenburger Tor** (*free*), modelled after Rome's Arch of Constantine, is a gateway to the main shopping street, Brandenburger Strasse. The pedestrian drag links with the scenic **Holländisches Viertel** (Dutch Quarter).

Alter Markt, the old market square, is anchored by an obelisk and lorded over by the domed **St Nikolai-Kirche** (*nikolai-potsdam.de*); clamber up 216 steps to the church's viewing **platform** (*€5*). Finally, in **Altstadt**, don't miss exploring Impressionist masterpieces at the **Museum Barberini** (*museum-barberini.de; adult/child €18/free*).

Cologne

GRAND CATHEDRAL | RHENISH JOIE DE VIVRE | ART MUSEUMS

Founded by the Romans, Cologne (Köln) offers a mother lode of attractions, led by its famous cathedral with filigree twin spires dominating the skyline. The museum scene is outstanding when it comes to art, but the city will also inspire fans of chocolate, sports and history.

Cologne's spirited locals are known for their liberal outlook and zest for life. Join them in the Pride celebration (one of Germany's biggest) in July, and in the beer halls of the Altstadt or bars in the student-centric Zülpicher Viertel, trendy Belgisches Viertel or gritty Ehrenfeld. Cologne also has an excellent electronic-music club scene.

Shopping is a popular pastime, with a fun mix of eclectic boutiques, and designer and vintage stores scattered throughout the neighbourhoods. For mainstream shopping, stroll along Hohe Strasse in the city centre, one of Germany's oldest pedestrianised shopping strips. Souvenir hunters should seek out the classic outlets selling the famous eau de cologne.

GETTING AROUND

Cologne is eminently walkable, and places further afield can easily be reached by public transport, bicycle or e-scooter. Radstation behind the Hauptbahnhof rents bikes.

Cologne's Pride & Joy

Uncover endless cathedral treasure

Cologne's geographical and spiritual heart is the magnificent, UNESCO-listed **Kölner Dom** (koelner-dom.de; tower adult/child €8/4). It's a treasure-packed, centuries-long pilgrimage site, home to a powerful diocese centre.

Top billing inside belongs to the jewel-encrusted, gilded **Shrine of the Magi** (main altar). The basilica-shaped sarcophagus allegedly contains the remains of the three kings who followed the celestial star to Bethlehem. The bones were spirited out of Milan in 1164 by Emperor Barbarossa.

The Dom's newest stained-glass window, unveiled in 2007, is the **Richter Fenster** (south transept). The work of Germany's most important living artist, Cologne-based Gerhard Richter, it weaves together 11,500 square glass panes in 72 vibrant hues (a twist on Richter's 1974 work, *4096 Colors*).

☑ **TOP TIP**

The city's excellent website (museenkoeln.de) has information on most of Cologne's museums. The **MuseumsCard** (individual/family €18/30) is good for one-time admission to all municipal museums on two consecutive days and free public transport on the first day. Buy it online, at the tourist office opposite the cathedral or at participating museums.

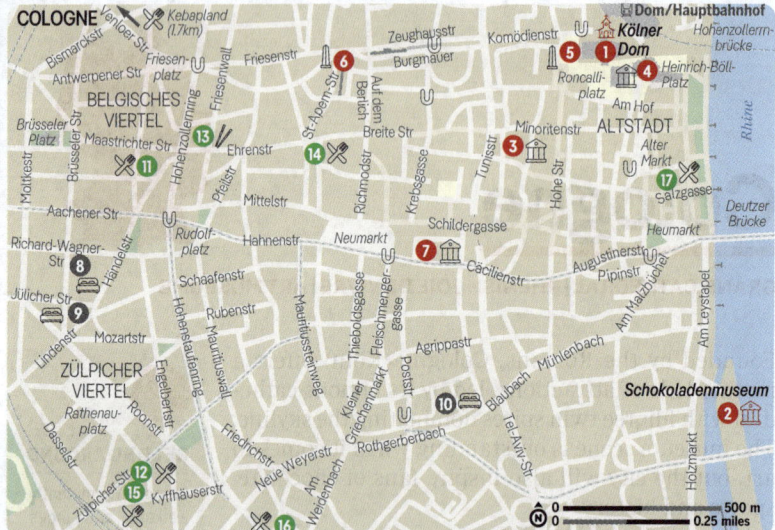

Take the 533 steps up the Dom's **south tower** that dwarfed all European buildings before the Eiffel Tower. En route to the 95m-high viewing platform, admire the 24-tonne **St Peter's Bell**, the world's largest free-swinging working bell.

From the Dom's heights, saunter into the vaulted medieval cellars of the **Domschatzkammer** (treasury), which practically spills over with precious reliquaries, robes, sculptures and liturgical objects.

A Romp Around Western Art

Visit a dazzling art museum

Museum Ludwig (museum-ludwig.de; adult/child €12/free), in a shed-roof building near the Dom, owes its reputation to a sublime collection of global modern art. In light-filled galleries you can binge on Picasso, pop art, Pollock and photography, or linger over German expressionists and the Russian avant-garde. Works rotate regularly because there's only room to show off one-third of the collection at a time, with the rest of the space reserved for temporary exhibitions. These dig into everything from post-colonial critique and identity politics to rising voices in global contemporary art and less well-known chapters of modernism.

TRAVELVIEW/SHUTTERSTOCK

Kölner Dom (p267)

Hail to the Ancient Romans

Tracking down Cologne's origins

Some 2000 years ago, Cologne was a thriving Roman city with temples, paved roads, an aqueduct and stone houses. Nobody knows how much of its ancient history still lurks beneath the modern city, but plenty of what's been dug up already can be admired in the **Römisch-Germanisches Museum** (*roemisch-germanisches-museum.de; adult/child €6/free*).

While its original 1970s home by the Dom is getting a serious facelift until at least 2030, highlights from its vast collection are on view in the Belgisches Haus near Neumarkt (closed Tuesdays). Standouts include a sculpture of Hercules mid-battle with a lion and a delicate marble torso dubbed the 'Kölsche Venus'. There's also remarkably well-preserved glassware and items from daily life like toys, tweezers, lamps and jewellery, the designs of which have changed little over time.

Ancient Roman ruins are scattered all over town. When checking out the dome, stop by the **Roman Arch** on the cathedral plaza, once part of the northern gateway to the Roman colony. Over at Zeughausstrasse 13 is the **Römerturm**

EXPLORING DOM DEEPER

Construction of Cologne's landmark cathedral began in 1248 in the French Gothic style but was suspended in 1560 for lack of money. The half-built church lingered for nearly three centuries and even served as a horse stable and prison during the Napoleonic occupation. A sizeable cash infusion from Prussian king Friedrich Wilhelm IV finally led to its completion in 1880. Miraculously, the cathedral got through WWII bombing raids with nary a shrapnel wound.

Kölner Dom has plenty of delights that must be experienced on guided tours (in English, upon request). Dive into the building's Roman-era roots on an archaeological tour, or climb to lofty heights to study its industrial-era filigree-iron roof truss or to get close-ups of its famous bells. Book on *domfuehrungen-koeln.de*.

EATING IN COLOGNE: OUR PICKS

Neobiota: Michelin-starred lair with breakfast until 3pm and innovative multicourse dinners in a casual setting. *10am-3pm & 7-11pm Tue-Sat* €€€

Bei Oma Kleinmann: Old-school, family-owned restaurant that has fed generations with schnitzel and other German fare. *5pm-midnight Mon-Sat* €€

Chum Chay: First-class plant-based Vietnamese at economy prices in Belgian Quarter; try the curry with rambutan and lychee. *noon-10pm Mon-Sat* €

Bad Ape: Cheerful lunch spot that doles out gourmet salads, low-gluten sandwiches and excellent coffee; lots of vegan options. *10am-6pm Tue-Sat* €

KÖLSCH PRIMER

Cologne has its own style of beer, Kölsch, which is light, hoppy, slightly sweet and served cool in *Stangen* – skinny, straight glasses that only hold 0.2L. In traditional Cologne beer halls and pubs you don't order beer so much as subscribe; the constantly prowling servers, called *Köbes*, will ply you with another round until you indicate you've had enough by placing a beermat on top of your glass.

A ceaseless flow of *Stangen* filled with Kölsch, along with earthy humour and platters of meaty local foods, are the hallmarks of Cologne's famed beer halls. A local speciality served on select days is *Reibekuchen* (or *Rievkooche* in the local dialect), traditional potato pancakes.

Schokoladenmuseum

(Roman Tower) that formed the northwest corner of the 4km-long Roman city wall.

Chocolate Paradise

Sweet museum treat

Cologne's **Schokoladenmuseum** *(schokoladenmuseum.de; adult/student/under 6yr Mon-Fri €15.50/9/free, Sat & Sun €17/10.50/free)* is a sleek, boat-shaped temple to the 'elixir of the gods' (as the Aztecs referred to chocolate), anchored at the tip of the old city port just south of the Altstadt. Its centrepiece is a walk-through **chocolate factory** that lifts the lid on the bean-to-bar process. Watch chocolatiers handcraft truffles and pralines, and find out how hollow bunnies are born. The interactive 'Cocoa's Journey Through Time' exhibition traces 5000 years of the cultural history of chocolate, from its pre-Columbian origins to its rise as a royal indulgence and the dawn of the chocolate vending machine. For an extra €3, you can cap your tour with a 30-minute **tasting session** (also offered in English). Or head straight to the glorious finale: dipping a wafer into the museum's famous 3m-high **fountain** flowing with 200kg of warm melted Lindt chocolate.

Dodge the crowds by visiting on a weekday, and save time by buying your time-slot ticket online.

Cologne's Creative Underbelly

Ehrenfeld street-art exploration

While Cologne is celebrated for its fine-arts scene, the city's streets are just as expressive. Murals, stencils, stickers, graffiti

– it's all out there, especially in Ehrenfeld, a former working-class *Veedel* (Cologne slang for 'neighbourhood') that's evolved into an eclectic cross-cultural cauldron of creativity.

Urban art royalty like Herakut, El Bocho, Stohead and M-City have splashed colour across once drab walls, often as part of the **CityLeaks Urban Art Festival** *(cityleaks-festival.de)*. The festival's been on hiatus since 2021 (a revival is planned) but the CityLeaks crew still runs street-art tours of Ehrenfeld and the Südstadt. Tours are also offered by **Alternative Cologne Tours** *(alternativecolognetours.com)*.

One of the most powerful pieces is right at Ehrenfeld train station: a tribute to local Nazi resistance group Edelweiss-piraten by hometown spraymeisters Captain Borderline. It's on Schönsteinstrasse, right under the railway arch where the SS publicly hanged 13 of the group's members in late 1944.

Christian Art Progressively Staged

Religious museum for the 21st century

Art, history, architecture and spirituality collide brilliantly at **Kolumba** *(kolumba.de; adult/child €8/free)*, the quietly striking art museum of the Archdiocese of Cologne. Designed by renowned Swiss architect Peter Zumthor, the minimalist structure encases the ruins of the late-Gothic church of St Kolumba, destroyed during WWII.

Start in the airy foyer, where an oversized steel door swings open into a cavernous, almost meditative space. A wooden walkway zigzags over exposed archaeological layers going back to Roman times, while soft daylight dancing through the perforated facade creates a sense of calm and mystery.

The actual galleries are up a steep staircase and are changed every September. However, the concept stays the same: modern art juxtaposed with sacral objects, creating a surprising dialogue between old and new. A wood-panelled library with leather chairs invites quiet reading or simply zoning out. Don't skip the **Madonna in the Ruins** chapel, an octagonal structure built from war debris in 1950; its separate entrance is on Brückenstrasse.

CARNIVAL: FOOLS, FLOATS & REVELRY

Called the 'fifth season', **Karneval** *(koelnerkarneval.de)* is one of Cologne's wildest parties, when the city collectively loses the plot over street parades, packed pubs and way too much Kölsch. Festivities peak in the week before Lent, kicking off on **Weiberfastnacht** (Thursday), when women playfully chop off ties and take charge. Over the weekend, parades featuring wacky homemade floats criss-cross the local neighbourhoods. By the time it all comes to a head with the big parade on **Rosenmontag** (Rose Monday), the entire city has come unglued. Swaying and drinking while crammed in a pub, or following other costumed fools behind a huge bass drum leading to who-knows-where, you'll be swept up in one of the world's most unhinged celebrations.

EATING IN COLOGNE: FAST FOOD

Kebapland: Cologne's top kebab: marinated meat, charcoal-grilled and served with local flavour in Ehrenfeld. *11.30am–1am Sun–Thu, to 3am Fri & Sat* €

Freddy Schilling: Burgers in the Zülpicher Viertel student quarter: meaty or plant-based organic patties, home-made sauces, hand-cut fries. *noon–10pm* €

Rievkoochebud: Made-to-order local-style potato pancakes, a perfect preparation for an Altstadt drink-a-thon. *noon–8pm Wed–Sat, to 6pm Sun* €

Curry B: Join the queue for Cologne's *Currywurst* – fried bratwurst, slivered and slathered with house-made spicy curry ketchup. *11am–8pm Mon–Sat* €

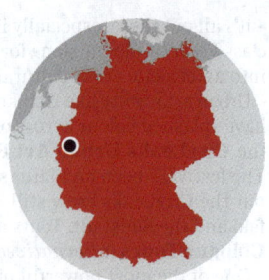

Düsseldorf

ALTBIER BARS | AVANT-GARDE ART | BOLD ARCHITECTURE

GETTING AROUND

Rheinbahn *(rheinbahn.
de)* operates an
extensive network of
U-Bahn trains, trams
and buses throughout
Düsseldorf. Tickets
are available from bus
drivers and vending
machines at U-Bahn
and tram stops, and
must be validated
upon boarding. Tickets
bought inside vehicles
are pre-validated.

☑ **TOP TIP**

The **Düsseldorf tourist
office** *(duesseldorf-
tourismus.de)* in the
Altstadt has a wealth of
printed information and
staff eager to help with
lodging, events tickets
and the Düsseldorf Card. It
also organises well-done
city tours, including an
Urban Art Walk, an Altstadt
Beer Safari and a Sound
of Düsseldorf music
expedition.

Düsseldorf impresses with edgy architecture, nightlife that doesn't quit and an art scene to rival many
flashier cities. At first, the capital of North Rhine–
Westphalia may seem all buttoned-up business:
banking, advertising, fashion and telecoms have
helped make it one of Germany's wealthiest cities.
Yet all it takes is a bar-hop around the Altstadt to
realise that locals have no problem letting their hair
down once they shed those Boss jackets. Nicknamed
the 'longest bar in the world', this historic riverside
quarter is packed with enough energy to keep things
going well into the night. Down by the redeveloped
harbour, Medienhafen is a parade of bold avant-garde
architecture by international design-meisters. Urban
explorers should check out creative and style-savvy
neighbourhoods like Flingern and Unterbilk that
offer fun shopping, laid-back cafes and good people-
watching. For prime ramen and sushi, venture to
Little Tokyo, the hub of Düsseldorf's huge Japanese
community.

The Altstadt Beyond Beer

Hidden wonders, history, culinary delights

Düsseldorf's Altstadt is (in)famous for its 300-plus bars. Beyond partying, museums and historical gems make a case for
visiting during daytime.

The **K20** *(kunstsammlung.de; adult/student/chld €9/5/
free)* is a powerhouse of modern art, from Klee, Picasso and
Mondrian to seminal non-European heavyweights like Etel
Adnan, Lygia Pape and Rasheed Araureen. Veer off Rheinufer-
promenade to the **Hetjens Museum** *(duesseldorf.de/hetjens;
adult/child €5/free)*, covering 8000 years of world ceramic art.

On Burgplatz, the **Schlossturm** *(schifffahrtmuseum.de;
adult/child €3/free)* is all that remains of Düsseldorf's old palace; it houses a small Rhine-focussed **museum**. The **Markt am
Carlsplatz** *(carlsplatz-markt.de)* is a prime foodie playground.

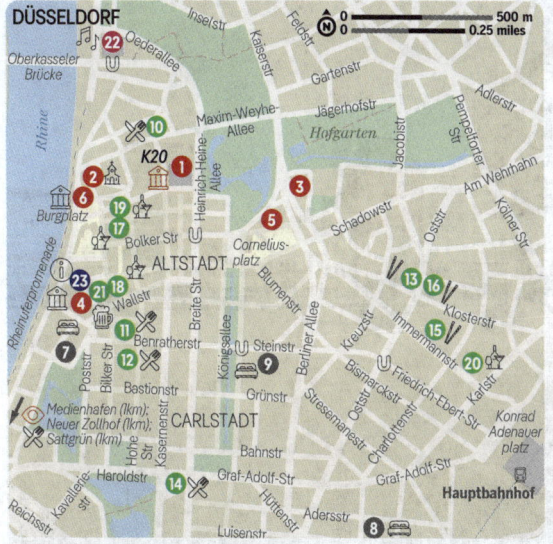

DÜSSELDORF

DÜSSELDORF'S ARCHITECTURAL MARVELS

Kö-Bogen I & II: Daniel Libeskind's Kö-Bogen I caps the Königsallee with angular glass and limestone. Kö-Bogen II is practically a vertical park.

Basilika St Lambertus: The twisted spire of this Gothic church is not a design quirk – warped by a storm, it was deliberately left that way.

Tonhalle: An expressionist 1920s jewel, Düsseldorf's premier concert hall has a ribbed blue dome and started out as a planetarium.

Dreischeibenhaus: This 94m-high tower gets its name from the three offset slim slabs *(Scheiben);* it was a symbol of Germany's postwar economic recovery.

Neuer Zollhof: Stainless steel meets playful asymmetry in a trio of shimmering buildings that turned Medienhafen into a contemporary art piece.

★ **HIGHLIGHTS**
1 K20

● **SIGHTS**
2 Basilika St Lambertus
3 Dreischeibenhaus
4 Hetjens Museum
5 Kö-Bogen I & II
6 Schlossturm & SchifffahrtMuseum

● **SLEEPING**
7 Hotel Orangerie

8 Max Hotel Garni
9 Ruby Coco Hotel

● **EATING**
10 Brauerei im Füchschen
11 Markt am Carlsplatz
12 Münstermann Kontor
13 Naniwa
14 Pelican Fly
15 Takumi
16 Yabase

● **DRINKING & NIGHTLIFE**
17 Elephant Bar
18 Et Kabüffke
19 Melody
20 Sakura Bar
21 Uerige

● **ENTERTAINMENT**
22 Tonhalle

● **INFORMATION**
23 Tourist Office – Altstadt

Industrial Harbour Reimagined

Architectural port of call

Where dockworkers once hauled cargo, creative minds now forge ad campaigns and brainstorm headlines. The **Medienhafen** *(Media Harbour; medienhafen.de)* is Düsseldorf's boldest urban revitalisation project. The old commercial harbour is now a striking lineup of avant-garde buildings by top architects. Frank Gehry's **Neuer Zollhof** draws the most

---

🍸 **DRINKING IN DÜSSELDORF: ALTSTADT FAVES**

Uerige: Traditional Altbier brewpub with hearty snacks, local colour aplenty and a merry crowd that often spills into the street. *10am-midnight*

Et Kabüffke: Chase your Altbier with a shot of Killepitsch (local liqueur blending 90 fruits, herbs and spices) served through the window. *11am-midnight*

Melody: Island of sophistication among the boisterous Altstadt bars, with quality cocktails and eggnog made by the owner. *10pm-late Wed-Sat*

Elephant Bar: Good drinks and good times at this James Bond–style '60s bar with complexion-friendly lighting and mellow sounds. *6pm-late Wed-Sat*

SAIKO3P/SHUTTERSTOCK

Medienhafen (p273)

camera clicks – a trio of warped towers sheathed in stainless steel, red brick and white plaster, respectively.

For a different selfie angle, head to the promontory below the Hyatt Regency Hotel, anchored by a silver-clad, egg-shaped bar that buzzes in summer. From this spot, the full sweep of Medienhafen with the Rheinturm TV tower is Insta-gold. There's also a two-hour **Media Harbour Tour** *(€20)* run by Düsseldorf Tourism.

Japanese Flavours & Culture

Tokyo on the Rhine

Düsseldorf's **Little Tokyo** is the commercial heart of the city's sizeable Japanese expat community. Centred on Immermannstrasse, just outside the Hauptbahnhof, this buzzing strip is chock-a-block with ramen joints, sushi bars, manga shops and Japanese supermarkets. Local faves for slurping ramen include **Takumi** and **Naniwa**, while **Yabase** is tops for sushi and **Sakura Bar** for cocktails.

 EATING IN DÜSSELDORF: OUR PICKS

Münstermann Kontor: Buzzy bistro with seasonal pan-European dishes that are both creative and down-to-earth. *noon-8pm Tue-Fri, from 11am Sat* €€€

Brauerei Im Füchschen: Boisterous and full of local colour – the 'Little Fox' is a true Rhenish beer hall. *11am-midnight Wed-Sun, from 3pm Mon & Tue* €€

Pelican Fly: 'Berlin-style *Imbiss*' (snack bar) reborn as a fries-and-wine bar in a retro-styled pavilion. *noon-3pm & 5pm-midnight Mon-Thu, noon-midnight Fri & Sat* €

Sattgrün: Cheerful vegan self-service buffet with international dishes in three sizes and two branches in the Medienhafen and Flingern. *noon-10pm* €

Hamburg

MARITIME HISTORY | INNOVATIVE ARCHITECTURE | NIGHTLIFE

Hamburg is one of Europe's coolest, most affluent cities, but most people don't know that – the vibe is just that unpretentious. Germany's largest port and second-largest city merits its historic label 'the gateway to the world'. It's been hustling since medieval times, especially in the late 19th and early 20th centuries, cultivating quiet wealth via global trade. Innovative architecture and sustainability shape a stylish, media-savvy modern city, yet Hamburg stays true to its maritime soul – embodied in endless, glimmering blues and squawking gulls. Today's zeniths include vibrant subcultures, lively neighbourhoods, and a performance scene defined by rising stars (which once included the Beatles). No, hamburgers weren't invented here (though patties are inspired by local cooks). And yes, the nightlife extends far beyond the notorious Reeperbahn red-light district. Rest assured, no matter where you drop anchor in Hamburg, it's a safe haven for letting the good times roll.

> ☑ **TOP TIP**
>
> Undeterred by the infamous *Schmuddelwetter* (drizzly weather), Hamburgers have come up with inventive ways to enjoy the Elbe. No matter the weather, **StrandPauli** *(strandpauli. de)*, a sandy beach bar, is a lively favourite. If it's chilly, board the moored party boat **Frau Hedi** *(frauhedi. de)* where disco evenings get sweaty.

From Chambers to Courtyard

Uncover City Hall's hidden features

Hamburg's 1897 **Rathaus** *(hamburg-travel.com; tours adult/ child €5/free)* is a 647-room beehive full of fascinating, beautiful details. Currently the seat of Senate and Parliament, it's

---

 GETTING AROUND

Hamburg's excellent public-transport system (trains, buses, trams) will take you all around the city and into suburban neighbourhoods.

Bikes are free on public trains outside peak hours (6am to 9am and 4pm to 6pm). Download the **StadtRAD** *(stadtrad.hamburg. de)* app for cross-city bike-sharing. Driving is easy, but parking is a pain. Uber vehicles are limited and not worth long pickup waits; rely on taxis instead.

For an authentically local experience, board a **Hadag commuter ferry**. The **St Pauli Piers** is the key hub for seven Elbe lines used primarily by locals. The most important for sightseers is 62 – a seven-minute commute to the **Elbphilharmonie** (p277) pier.

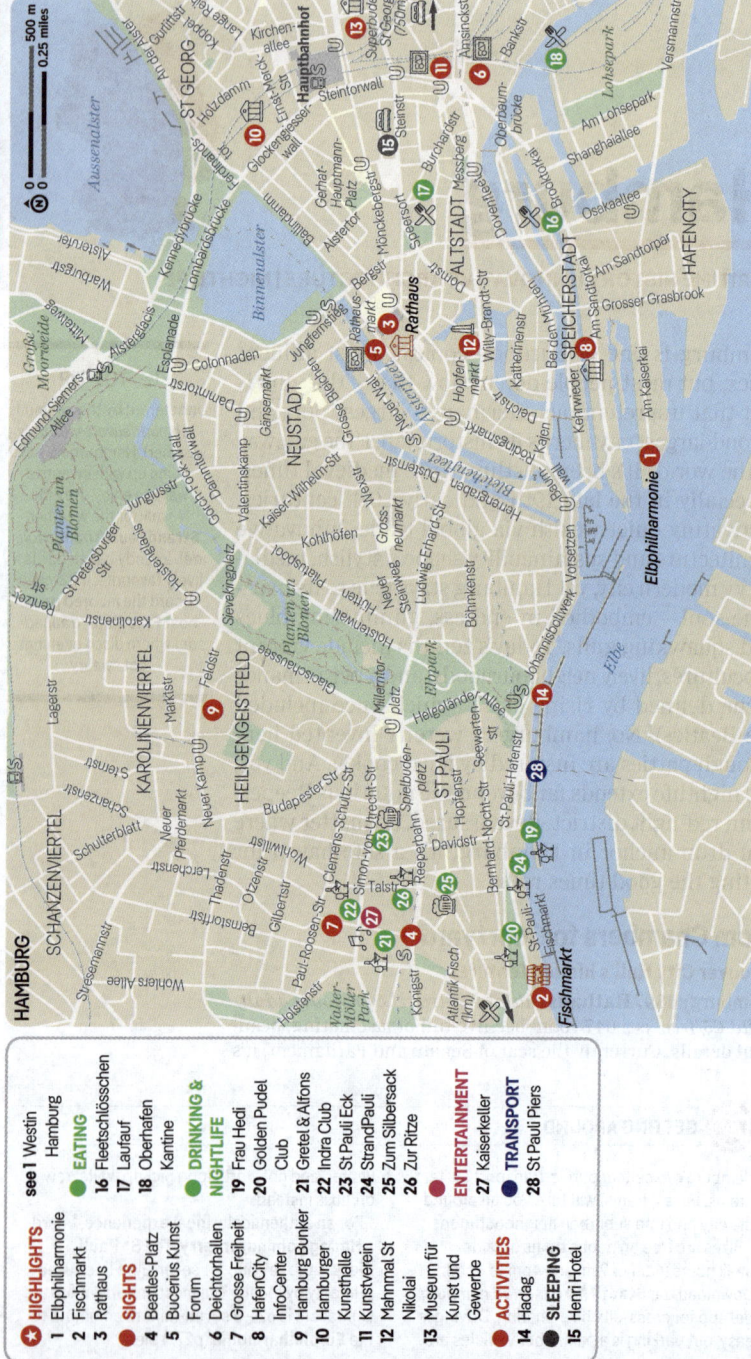

HAMBURG

★ HIGHLIGHTS
1 Elbphilharmonie
2 Fischmarkt
3 Rathaus

● SIGHTS
4 Beatles-Platz
5 Bucerius Kunst
  Forum
6 Deichtorhallen
7 Grosse Freiheit
8 HafenCity
  InfoCenter
9 Hamburg Bunker
10 Hamburger
  Kunsthalle
11 Kunstverein
12 Mahnmal St
  Nikolai
13 Museum für
  Kunst und
  Gewerbe

● ACTIVITIES
14 Hadag

● SLEEPING
15 Henri Hotel

see 1 Westin
  Hamburg

● EATING
16 Fleetschlösschen
17 Laufauf
18 Oberhafen
  Kantine

● DRINKING &
NIGHTLIFE
19 Frau Hedi
20 Golden Pudel
  Club
21 Gretel & Alfons
22 Indra Club
23 St Pauli Eck
24 StrandPauli
25 Zum Silbersack
26 Zur Ritze

● ENTERTAINMENT
27 Kaiserkeller

● TRANSPORT
28 St Pauli Piers

one of Europe's most opulent, still-functioning government buildings.

On a guided tour (see the website for booking information), you'll wind through a fraction of the building's maze of chambers. The most renowned are the **Kaisersaal** (Emperor's Hall), a lavish, neobaroque vision once designed to host Emperor Wilhelm II during visits, and the **Grosser Festsaal** (Great Hall) ceremonial room.

Tours aside, march through the Grand Entrance Hall during opening hours and take in its 'hidden' courtyard. Take breaks on comfy chairs with tables overlooking the eternally gorgeous Hygieia Fountain. The female bronze figure, the Greek goddess of health, commemorates Germany's last major cholera epidemic in 1892.

Historic Fish Sammies

Wake up early for the Fischmarkt

Wake up early on Sunday (or stay up Saturday night) to hit Hamburg's legendary **Fischmarkt** *(fischauktionshalle.com; free),* a port tradition since 1703. Over 70,000 people attend the weekly market, which is open from 5am to 9.30am April to October and from 7am November to March. Whether you're a morning person or not, the Fischmarkt is a truly energising, one-of-a-kind sunrise experience. Get caught up in its signature tidal wave of high-sensory shenanigans, from noisy vendors to smoky fish grilling.

The iconic specialities are the *fischbrötchen* (fish sandwiches) topped with decadent North Sea and Elber River delights. The assortment is incredible: pickled herring, smoked salmon, fried or grilled fish fillets, regional shrimp or crab, you name it.

Breakfast in hand, head to the historic **Fish Auction Hall**, inaugurated in 1896 and a testament to Hamburg's long-standing maritime heritage. While the building once hosted fish auctions, today it's a live-entertainment venue. Consider German *Schlager* (cheesy pop) and rock cover bands your 6am wake-up call.

Musical Heights & Iconic Architecture

Discover the Elbphilharmonie

Perched majestically over the Elbe River, the **Elbphilharmonie** *(elbphilharmonie.de; tickets €20-150)* is one of Europe's most exciting and recent architectural feats.

The landmark 2017-unveiled building harmonises old and new. Striking glass rises high above Hamburg's skyline, framing a

WELCOME TO THE WATERFRONT

The **Speicherstadt** is the largest warehouse district in the world, where the buildings stand on timber-pile foundations – oak logs, in this particular case. The seven-storey red-brick warehouses lining the Speicherstadt archipelago are a famous Hamburg symbol and they're increasingly filled with fine museums.

Meanwhile, the neighbouring **HafenCity** quarter, part of the port area where Speicherstadt is located, is a world seemingly being created before your eyes. Wander around and check out the Kesselhaus (Old Boiler House) where the **HafenCity InfoCenter** *(hafencity. com/infocenter)* is located; the information office is closed on Mondays. A room-sized scale model of Hamburg shows the full vision of HafenCity's expected completion in 2030 (it's only about 50% there).

 EATING IN HAMBURG: NORTHERN GERMAN SPECIALITIES

| **Fleetschlösschen:** Overlook a Speicherstadt canal while eating Northern-style fish dishes with cucumber salad and remoulade. *11am-10pm* €€ | **Laufauf:** North German dishes like *Bratheringe* (fried herring) in Altstadt. Well-priced lunch specials. *11.30am-10pm Mon-Fri, from 1pm Sat* €€ | **Oberhafen Kantine:** Traditional Hamburg fare beneath a HafenCity train bridge. *5-9.30pm Tue, noon-9.30pm Wed-Sat, noon-5.30pm Sun* €€ | **Atlantik Fisch:** Altona-based cafe run by a seafood vendor; offering 20 different *Fischbrötchen* (fish sandwiches). *6am-4pm Mon-Fri, from 7am Sat* €€ |

HAMBURG'S ART MILE

Enjoy Hamburg's five-pack of renowned art institutions, aka the Kunstmeile, with a three-day **Art Mile Pass** *(kunstmeile-hamburg.de; €35).*

Hamburger Kunsthalle: World-renowned museum with a treasure trove of period-spanning masterpieces.

Bucerius Kunst Forum: Private art museum with four annual exhibitions; multimedia links contemporary society and antiquity.

Museum für Kunst und Gewerbe: Europe's foremost, oldest applied arts institution: sculptures, jewellery, ceramics and more.

Deichtorhallen: Two industrial halls – one for modern/documentary photography, another for large-scale contemporary art.

Kunstverein: Long-established local art association for emerging contemporary and conceptual art.

Hamburg Bunker

restored historic brick warehouse. Inside, a one-of-a-kind concert hall has exceptional acoustics and a stunning auditorium orchestrating immersive symphony and musical experiences.

Architects allegedly drew inspiration from the Ancient Greek theatre at Delphi, sport stadiums and tents. The building's glass structure with its wave-like roof is meant to mimic the ethereal, floating quality of a hoisted sail, water wave, iceberg or quartz crystal. It provides contrast to the 1963-built heavy brick warehouse it sits atop.

Catching a concert in the state-of-the-art surrounds here is an unforgettable experience. Don't miss taking Europe's longest escalator up to the viewing platform, a 360-degree wrap-around balcony providing dizzying city and harbour perspectives.

Concrete Rooftop Garden

Scale the Hamburg Bunker

An anomaly on Hamburg's skyline, the brooding WWII concrete structure **Hamburg Bunker** *(hamburgbunker.com;*

🍺 DRINKING IN ST PAULI: PUB CRAWL

Zur Ritze: Pass between the painted legs of this Reeperbahn pub's entrance. Inside, it's a serious drinking den. *hours vary*

Golden Pudel Club: Tiny bar-club in a 19th-century bootleggers' jail. Programming prize underground bands and vinyl DJs. *10pm–6am*

Zum Silbersack: Diverse crowd and cheap drinks make for weird and wild evenings. Down an infamous caraway shot. *5pm–2am Mon–Thu, to 3am Fri & Sat, to 1am Sun*

St Pauli Eck: A quintessential German pub: jukebox, stiff pours and gruff staff behind a cluttered bar. *5pm–late Mon–Sat*

free) – a former air-raid shelter – was transformed in 2024 into a panoramic cultural attraction. Climb the cement-poured 'mountain path' up to a rooftop urban garden for unparalleled, 360-degree views across the city.

Though it's a gargantuan, painful reminder of the Nazi era, demolition was never realistic here. The amount of explosives required for demolition would likely raze the surrounding residential area. Today, it endures as a multi-purpose building holding everything from a hotel to a nightclub and cafe.

The highlight, however, is a 10,000-sq-metre rooftop garden with over 20,000 trees and more flora. Follow a spiralling staircase to get here; the ascent's 300-plus steps provide historical info along the way.

Finding the Fab Four
German Beatlemania

Long before forging rock-and-roll history, the Beatles paid their dues performing in Reeperbahn pubs. On the famous **Grosse Freiheit** party mile, the band set the stage for its meteoric rise. Stand atop the vinyl-record-shaped **Beatles-Platz** next to abstract steel sculptures of the Fab Four (including a hybrid of Ringo Starr and the band's original drummer during Hamburg days, Pete Best).

Down Grosse Freiheit, the band's name is featured outside the **Kaiserkeller** (*docksfreiheit36.de/kaiserkeller*). Meanwhile, a small outside plaque commemorates the Beatles' inaugural German gig at the **Indra** (*indramusikclub.de*). Another plaque at **Gretel & Alfons** claims this particular pub to be the boys' favourite haunt. Legend has it Paul McCartney ran up (and forgot) a considerable tab here. He eventually returned to pay up decades later.

Sacred War Memorial
Take in the views from Mahnmal St Nikolai

Mahnmal St Nikolai (*mahnmal-st-nikolai.de; observation deck & museum adult/child €5/3*) was the world's tallest building from 1874 to 1876, and it remains Hamburg's second-tallest structure (after the TV Tower). Today, the bombed-out remains of St Nikolai Church encompass a war memorial and **crypt history museum**. Take the elevator up to the church's 76.3m-high **observation tower** inside the surviving spire for awesome views. Down below, walk among church remnants in an open-air courtyard.

PATCHWORK CITYSCAPE

Harmonising surviving prewar structures, functionalist feats and seafaring motifs, Hamburg's architecture is a fascinating mishmash. During WWII, Hamburg's city centre – mostly Gothic and neo-Gothic architecture – was destroyed. The Rathaus remains as enduring style icon, while 19th-century Speicherstadt highlights the city's neo-Gothic-influenced era. Mid-20th-century functionalism saw classic architecture razed for unappealing, utilitarian structures. The period's 'high point' is the Fernsehturm (TV Tower), still Hamburg's tallest building. The exception to this architectural 'reset' was the indestructible WWII Hamburg Bunker. Now, city architects are incorporating maritime motifs along the harbour – the Elbphilharmonie and HafenCity are examples.

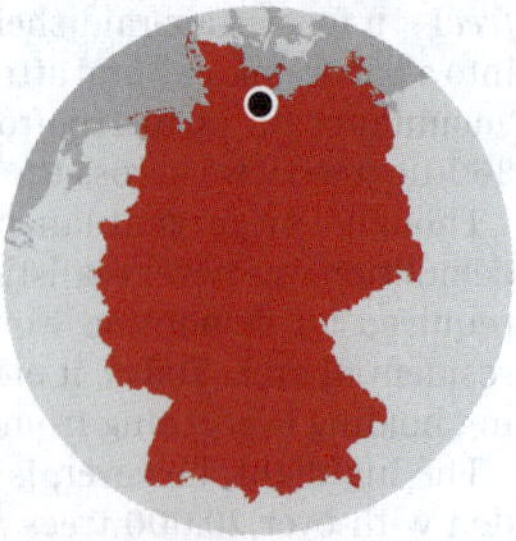

Lübeck

MEDIEVAL ARCHITECTURE | HANSEATIC HISTORY | MARZIPAN CAPITAL

Lübeck's global claim to fame is certainly its Christmas confections – but this Hanseatic city proves to be much sweeter than its marzipan. A 12th-century gem in Germany's northernmost state of Schleswig-Holstein, Lübeck has more than 1000 historic buildings. Picture-book streets are an enduring reminder of its role as the mighty Hanseatic League capital, a status that earned it the nickname 'the Queen of the Hanse'.

Designated a UNESCO World Heritage site in 1987, Lübeck's well-preserved Altstadt (old town) is abundant with delightful ornate facades and narrow cobblestone streets. It offers an alluring silhouette from its waterfront position on the Trave River, which leads towards the Baltic Sea and from there to Scandinavia. Beyond the medieval spires and red-brick buildings, Lübeck is a lively provincial city blending old-world character with urban impulses.

GETTING AROUND

Lübeck's Altstadt is on an island encircled by the canalised Trave River. The Hauptbahnhof and central bus station are 500m west of the Holstentor. Walking around is easy; many streets are pedestrianised and off limits to all but the vehicles of hotel guests. Lübeck is an hour's drive from Hamburg or about 40 minutes by train.

Hanseatic History & Medieval Gems

Tour Lübeck's museums

Lübeck's most impressive treasure, **Holstentor** (Holsten Gate) is among the best-known surviving medieval city gates in Germany. The **Museum Holstentor** *(museum-holstentor.de; adult/child €8/free)* sheds light on the city's mercantile glory days.

Essentially an open-air historical exhibit on Brick Gothic architecture, the cobblestoned **Museumsquartier St Annen** *(museumsquartier-st-annen.de; free)* comprises an old synagogue, church and several medieval buildings. The namesake **St Annen Museum** *(adult/child €8/free)* details the area's history tracing 700 years of art and culture; the adjoining **St Annen Kunstalle** has ecclesiastical and contemporary art.

The **Europäisches Hansemuseum** *(European Hanseatic Museum; hansemuseum.eu; adult/child €16/free, incl guided tour €21)* offers fascinating accounts of Hanse's far-reaching network via high-tech audiovisuals and artefacts. The ticketing system 'personalises' tours according to your interests, bringing interactive experiences to another level. 'Choose your own adventure' across four thematic fields and one of 50 trading sites.

TOP TIP

The **Lübeck Day Pass** *(1/2 days €12/16)* is excellent value. It offers access to all of Lübeck's museums; the **Day Pass Plus** *(1/2 days €18/22)* also includes the St Petri observation deck and St Marien churches.

Munich

WORLD-CLASS ART | BREWING TRADITIONS | METROPOLITAN VIBES

Munich isn't called Germany's secret capital for nothing. Nowhere else in the Bundesrepublik will you find such a lively blend of past and present, in a city that manages to combine Mediterranean flair with alpine flavours, traditional oompah culture with the freakishly modern, and horrible history with eco-tech.

And Munich's nickname isn't 'the City of Art and Beer' for nothing, either. Prepare for an art attack at the world-class museums in the Kunstareal, an entire quarter of the city centre given over to galleries and museums. There are also plenty more throughout the city. Then there's the beer, celebrated nightly in countless beer gardens and beer halls including the world's most famous, the Hofbräuhaus. It's so good that the annual Oktoberfest attracts over six million drinkers – and there are other beer festivals, such as the Starkbierzeit, that draw many an elbow-bender to the Bavarian metropolis.

The Altstadt & Residenz

Meet Munich on Marienplatz

The Altstadt's heart and soul, **Marienplatz** heaves from dawn till dusk and beyond with throngs of tourists, revellers and locals. Save for the 1638 **Mariensäule** (St Mary's Column) and the 1950s **Fischbrunnen** (Fish Fountain), the inventory of the square is limited. Completely dominating its northern side, the neo-Gothic **Neues Rathaus** *(New Town Hall; muenchen. travel; tower adult/child €7/3)* features gargoyles and other statuary. Pinpoint Munich's landmarks while catching the lift up the 85m-tall tower. Upcoming renovations here could last years. Arrive in front of the Neues Rathaus at 11am, noon or at 5pm (March to October) and see the famous Glockenspiel.

How Bavarian royalty lived

Munich's most visited sight, the **Residenz** *(residenz-muenchen. de; adult/child €20/free)* was the family home of the ruling Wittelsbach dynasty for over five centuries, from 1508 until WWI. Generations of big-egoed Bavarian royals shunned their

GETTING AROUND

The airport is around 30km northeast of the city centre. To reach the centre, take the S1 or S8 S-Bahn (around 40 minutes) to the Hauptbahnhof. An Uber costs €60 to €70.

Trams are good for getting around the centre and to the suburbs. The underground railway, the U-Bahn, serves the centre and the inner suburbs. There are eight lines; the main interchanges are at the Hauptbahnhof and the Sendlinger Tor. The S-Bahn lines go outside the city.

☑ TOP TIP

The Hauptbahnhof area has one of the highest concentrations of accommodation options in Munich. This location puts you within walking distance of many sights. However, during Oktoberfest bagging a room anywhere in Munich is almost impossible unless you book a year ahead.

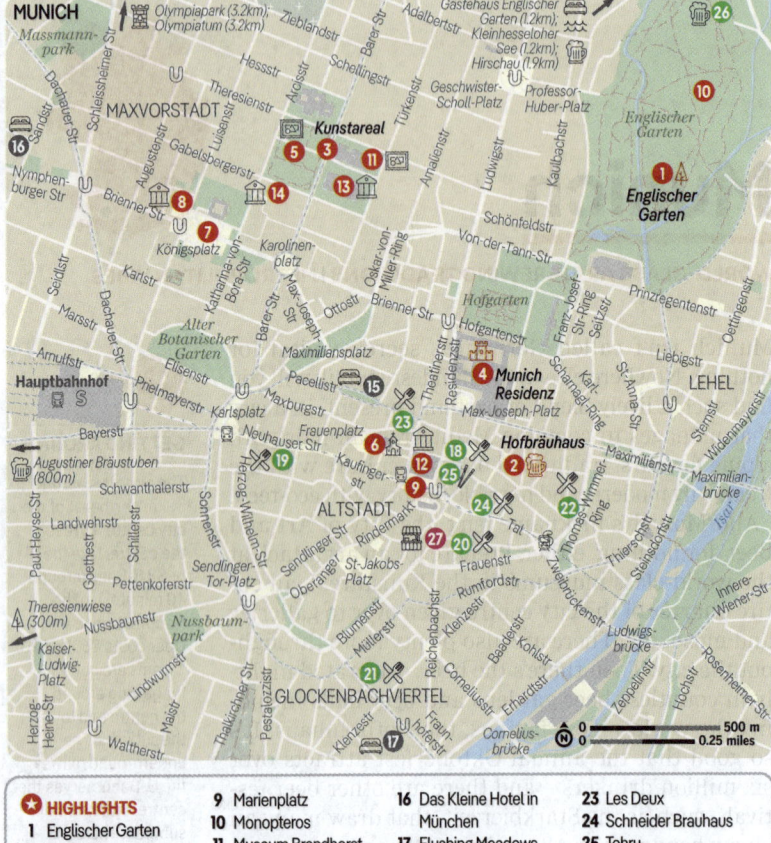

predecessors' living quarters, preferring to commission their own, hence the sheer size and scale. Among several resplendent rococo and gilded rooms, the climax is Ludwig I's **Royal Palace**. The **Schatzkammer**, containing the Wittelsbachs' collections of jewel-encrusted priceless bling, is also not to be missed.

Mother of all Munich churches

Munich's top temple is the **Frauenkirche** (*muenchner-dom. de; south tower adult/child €7.50/5.50*), instantly recognisable on the city's skyline – no building in the Altstadt can stand taller than its 99m. Built in the 15th century but severely damaged during WWII and rebuilt, it has some interesting

Hofbräuhaus

features including the tomb of Ludwig the Bavarian in the **crypt**. The highlight (though a rather pricey one) for most visitors is climbing the 98m **south tower** to peer out the small windows across all of Munich.

Check out the Hofbräuhaus

Even committed teetotallers should at least poke their heads around the door of the **Hofbräuhaus** *(hofbraeuhaus.de)*, Munich institution and the world's most celebrated beer hall. For those into Central European lager, a night on the Hofbräu is like the culmination of a hop-scented pilgrimage. It's a beer hall and tourist attraction rolled into one: take a seat in the main hall or in the horse-chestnut-shaded garden, order a *Mass* (1L tankard) and some Bavarian food and sway with the other tourists to the oompah band. The place is open every day of the year, even Christmas Day.

Feast at Munich's city-centre market

Bio *Weisswurst,* alpine cheese or pickled anything – **Viktualienmarkt** *(viktualienmarkt-muenchen.de)* has it all. Just steps from the Marienplatz, this 200-year-old, open-air market occupies 22,000 sq metres.

This is no ordinary farmers market. Over the past two decades it has become a dining hot spot, with countless stalls

SIGHTSEEING MADE EASY

Don't get your Pinakotheken in a twist while sightseeing in Munich. The city centre's bus route, the 100, aka **Museenlinie**, links over 20 museums and other interesting localities en route. The Königsplatz, Lenbachhaus, the Kunstareal and the English Garden are all linked by this ordinary *Stadtbus* (city bus). Leaving every 10 minutes in both directions (every 20 minutes on weekends), the 100 also serves as a kind of budget hop-on/hop-off route, especially with a day pass. The whole route takes around 25 minutes to complete, connecting to U-Bahn, S-Bahn and trams at both ends.

For the Kunstreal, the official website has an interactive stroll which eases some of the overwhelm here.

 EATING IN THE ALTSTADT: FINE DINING

Alois – Dallmayr Fine Dining: Enjoy the double-Michelin-starred menu at this top-drawer Munich stalwart. *12.30-3pm Thu-Sat, 7pm-midnight Wed-Sat* €€€

Les Deux: The modern French cuisine at this restaurant near the Frauenkirche has earned it a Michelin twinkler. *noon-midnight Mon-Sat* €€€

Tohru: Minimalist Michelin Japanese cuisine in a retro dining room prepared by German-Japanese chef, Tohru Nakamura. *7pm-midnight Tue-Sat* €€€

Le Stollberg: Intimate little restaurant serving Bavarian food with Mediterranean touches. *11.30am-2.30pm & 6pm-midnight Wed-Fri, 4.30-11pm Sat* €€€

TOP EXPERIENCE

Kunstareal

The Kunstareal, Munich's cultural quarter, is made up of two areas. The heart and soul of Maxvorstadt is the Königsplatz, commissioned by Ludwig I as part of his 'German Athens' vision for Munich and resembling a city in the ancient world. The addition of the various Pinakotheken, the area's second focus, over the decades expanded the Kunstareal into today's starring attraction.

Lenbachhaus

TOP TIPS

● On Sundays, try the €1 challenge (expect to be exhausted). Many institutions close Mondays.

● Main works from the closed Neue Pinakothek can be seen at the Sammlung Schack and the Alte Pinakothek.

● The lawns around the Alte Pinakothek are popular for picnics.

PRACTICALITIES

● kunstareal.de
● admission varies ● each institution has one late opening day

On Königsplatz

The **Lenbachhaus** (lenbachhaus.de; adult/child €10/free) specialises in members of the Munich-born modernist group *Der Blaue Reiter* (The Blue Rider) including Wassily Kandinsky and Paul Klee.

Meanwhile, the **State Museum of Egyptian Art** (smaek. de; adult/child €7/free) traces 5000 years of Egyptian and Sudanese history in one of Europe's finest collections.

Kunstareal Museums

With its vast collection of art from the 14th to the 18th centuries, the **Alte Pinakothek** (pinakothek.de; adult/child €9/free) is a world-class art museum. if you're going to choose just one gallery to visit in the Kunstareal, many would say this should be it. Da Vinci, Cranach the Elder, Dürer, Memling, Bruegel the Elder, Rubens, Botticelli, Rafael, Titian, Velázquez, Raphael...the list of big names and priceless masterpieces goes on room after room.

Germany's largest modern-art museum, the cavernous **Pinakothek der Moderne** (pinakothek.de; adult/child €10/free), comprises four museums in one – engaging (and often confusing), but there's something for everyone. The abstract, multi-hued **Museum Brandhorst** (museum-brandhorst.de; adult/child €9/free) showcases art from the 1960s onwards – Warhol, Hirst and co. Temporary exhibitions challenge the art world.

offering tasty gourmet (and not so gourmet) snacks. Put together a (very pricey) picnic or grab lunch. The market has its very own chestnut-shaded beer garden, the Altstadt's best and a Munich institution since 1807. All of Munich's main breweries take turns serving here, but in summer you'll have a long wait for a table.

Schwabing

Endlessly stroll an English Garden

Strolling through the vast meadows of the sprawling city park is how the good folk of Munich escape the stresses of the 21st century. The **Englischer Garten** *(English Garden; free)* is one of the world's largest urban parks. Dodge the joggers and high-speed cyclists to discover a tranquil world of woodland, birdsong and students swotting up in the sun.

In the park's middle, the **Monopteros** (1838) is a Greek temple with city-centre views. A short walk north lies the **Chinesischer Turm** *(Chinese Tower; chinaturm.de),* the unlikely setting for a classic beer garden.

Further north, the English Garden becomes wilder, despite two 'tamed' spots: **Kleinhesseloher See**, a lovely lake for boating around three little islands, and **Hirschau** *(hirschau-muenchen.de)* beer garden, one of Munich's best.

Theresienwiese & Olympiapark

Munich's best beer hall?

The vast, ear-shaped **Theresienwiese**, aka the *Wies'n* (meadow), is the home of Oktoberfest but it's a big, vacant, gravelly space the rest of the year. Just north, another lager-related attraction, the **Augustiner Bräustuben** *(braeustuben.de),* is a smarter stop. The oldest, second-largest of the 'big six', Augustiner is the last Munich brewery storing lager in oak barrels. The atmosphere in the evenings is slightly more authentic than its city-centre cousins.

Exploring Olympian levels

The **Olympiapark** *(olympiapark.de; free)* was the site of Munich's 1972 Summer Olympics – a chance to break with the past and the Nazi-era Berlin Olympics. It became better known for tragedy. Today, you can go up to the 190m-high viewing platform of the **Olympiaturm** *(adult/child €13/10).* The fast lift is nausea-inducing but these are Munich's best views bar none. Sometimes, the Alps are visible.

BEST MUNICH TOURS

Olympiapark Tour: Fascinating stadium experiences include a vertigo-inducing Stadium Roof Tour and zip-lining 35m above the pitch.

Radius Tours: Themed tours of Munich and beyond (Neuschwanstein, Salzburg). Its Third Reich tour is a classic.

Dark History Tours: Themed walks led by local-expert guides specialising in the Third Reich, WWII and medieval gore.

Munich Walk Tours: All kinds of walking tours in English including beer tours, the English Garden and cycling trips.

OzTour Munich: Award-winning city tours, Dachau trips and days out at Schloss Neuschwanstein.

Heart of Munich: Family-run agency offering city walking tours plus interesting Third Reich and Munich Suburbs tours.

EATING IN THE ALTSTADT: TRADITIONAL BAVARIAN PLACES

Augustiner Stammhaus: Monster beer hall with different rooms and a tranquil, old-world courtyard. *10am-midnight* €€

Fraunhofer: Wonderfully characterful, 19th-century Bavarian inn with a tiny theatre at the back. *5pm-1am* €€

Schneider Brauhaus: One of Munich's classic beer halls, with a rabble-rousing oompah band. *9am-10pm* €€

Bratwurstherzl: Sausages are the focus at this old Munich tavern with a Franconian twist. *10am-11pm Mon-Sat* €€

Bavaria

ALPS | STORYBOOK CASTLES | ROMANTIC FOREST

 TOP TIP

Nuremberg's **Christkindlesmarkt** (*christkindlesmarkt.de*) in December is often touted as Germany's best. Fairy-lit stalls proffer Yuletide baubles, roasted chestnuts, toffee and mead bottles against medieval splendour. Famous local bratwurst and *Glühwein* (mulled wine) scent the air. Weekends get busy with locals and Czech tourists – visit on a weekday for a less shuffling experience.

Bavaria packs a lot into its 70,000 sq km, from the glorious Alps and fertile Danube plain to the moody Bavarian Forest and the toytown-medieval Romantic Road. Devouring a vast chunk of Germany's south, Bavaria is like a country unto itself (many locals nostalgically dream it still is), with multilayered diversity and sophistication to match. If you came to Germany to see storybook castles and half-timbered towns, the Free State keeps its promises.

But incredibly varied Bavaria offers much more than the chocolate-box, felt-hat idyll. Descend from the Alps to learn about the rise and fall of the Nazis in Nuremberg, to follow the Wagner trail in Bayreuth or to sample a different local wine in every tavern in Würzburg. Destinations are often described as possessing 'something for everyone', but in Bavaria's case it just happens to be true. The Free State is no bargain, but it's worth every cent to see.

Ettal

Marvel at Ludwig II's alpine escape

A 45-minute drive from Garmisch-Partenkirchen, in a wide valley hemmed by peaks rising over 1700m in places, UNESCO-listed **Schloss Linderhof** (*schlosslinderhof.de; adult/child €10/free*) is the most remote and smallest of all Ludwig II's

---

⊚ GETTING AROUND

Getting around Bavaria is simple, if slightly more expensive than it once was. With its smooth, fast and toll-free autobahn, Bavaria is best explored by car, though in big cities parking can be costly.

The vast majority of medium to large centres are linked by rail. The Bayern Ticket (aka Bayern Regional Day Pass) gives 24-hour access to all of Bavaria's rail system (except high-speed services).

There are no domestic flights within Bavaria.

castles and the only one he lived to see fully built. It's a bizarre yet unforgettable castle experience.

Explore a Benedictine monastery

The definite highlight of the famous, alpine-topped Benedictine monastery **Kloster Ettal** *(kloster-ettal.de; entry free, tour adult/child €5/free)* is a rococo basilica housing the monks' prized possession, a marble Madonna. On guided tours (German only), explore the monastery's architecture, beer brewery and liqueur factory.

Oberammergau

Admire Oberammergau's painted buildings

Any visit to this small town should begin with a wander around the centre to admire the numerous examples of *Lüftlmalerei*. These huge, decorative murals on house facades can be found throughout the Alps, but the style was invented here. Common motifs include biblical stories, and fairy tales are also popular. The **Little Red Riding Hood House** and **Hansel & Gretel House** depicts scenes from the Brothers Grimm's best-known tales.

CLIMBING THE NEUSCHWANSTEIN HILL

There are a number of ways to get up to Neuschwanstein. The cheapest is to walk – it costs nothing, but it's a long and relentless climb. If you want to visit Marienbrücke first, as we suggest you do, follow the signs as you near the top – there's a steep cut-through to the bridge. The other options are to take a horse-drawn carriage, but it takes you directly to the castle, which means you need to climb past Neuschwanstein and then back again. Unless you like the walk up, we recommend taking the shuttle bus up (it drops you at the start of the short trail to Marienbrücke), then walking down to the castle before following the road down on foot.

Zugspitze cable car station, Garmisch-Partenkirchen

Garmisch-Partenkirchen

Ascend Germany's tallest mountain

At 2962m, the **Zugspitze** *(zugspitze.de; adult/child €75/37.50)* is Germany's tallest mountain with the country's only (and shrinking) glacier. Going up is the most magical anywhere in the German Alps; dedicate at least half a day to the experience.

A cogwheel train called the **Zugspitzbahn** chugs up in a 75-minute, valley-viewing journey. At the **Zugspitzplatt**, a plateau below the summit, you can rent skis and snowboards *(skiverleih-garmisch.com)*. A 10-minute cable car takes you up the final vertical metres to the top.

Füssen

A fairy-tale German castle

Rising amid the forested peaks like a fantasy vision, **Schloss Neuschwanstein** *(neuschwanstein.de; adult/child €23.50/2.50)* was the model for Disney's Sleeping Beauty castle. King Ludwig II's fairy-tale Schloss Neuschwanstein is Bavaria's most visited attraction, and as it comes into view from **Marienbrücke**, it's instantly obvious why.

You'll enjoy your visit more if you plan ahead. It can only be visited on guided tours (in German or English, about 35 minutes). Outside the peak summer season, tickets are available on-site, but reserving online is recommended – especially in summer.

 EATING IN FÜSSEN: OUR PICKS

Vinzenzmurr Metzgerei: Sample hearty food like *Leberkäse* (meatloaf) in a bun, goulash soup, bratwurst or schnitzel. *9am-6pm Mon-Fri, 8am-1pm Sat* €

Beim Olivenbauer: Tyrol meets the local Allgäu region at this fun eatery. Try the *Maultaschen* (pork and spinach ravioli) and a mug of local beer. *noon-11pm* €€

Zum Franziskaner: Specialises in *Schweinshaxe* (pork knuckle) and schnitzel as well as other meaty Bavarian and Allgäu staples. *11.30am-10pm Thu-Tue* €€

Zum Hechten: Füssen's best hotel restaurant keeps things regional with Allgäu favourites like schnitzel, noodles and venison goulash. *11am-10pm* €€

Ludwig's childhood palace

You get two for your money visiting Neuschwanstein. The 'other' castle, where King Ludwig II grew up, **Schloss Hohenschwangau** (*hohenschwangau.de; adult/child €26/14.50, incl Neuschwanstein €48.50/17*), is just as interesting, if not as dreamily storybook-ish.

Climb high into the Alps

In summer, the cable car **Tegelbergbahn** (*tegelbergbahn.de; adult one-way/return €20.50/31, child €8.50/13*) ascends Tegelberg (1881m) to a mountain chalet. From the summit, and despite the relatively low altitude, the views seem to extend forever.

Augsburg

Pop into a Renaissance city

Ranking among Germany's oldest towns – its story dates back around 2000 years – Augsburg is worth as much time as you can give it. The city centre's offering is varied, from the fascinating **Fuggerei** (*fugger.de; adult/child €8/4*) settlement's social and architectural history, to memorable churches and great food. Its puppet or marionette theatre, **Augsburger Puppenkiste** (*puppenkiste.de; tickets from €10, museum adult/child €5/3.30*), is one of southern Germany's most underrated museums.

Rothenburg ob der Tauber

Magical medieval streets

Few large villages or small towns in Germany are so impressively medieval as Rothenburg. Painstakingly preserved architecture makes the city centre a period piece of gables, turrets and half-timbered facades encircled by tower-dotted stone walls. A visit here is all about wandering around; the small square of **Plönlein** is a magical evocation of Rothenburg's charm. Arguably the best views are from the **Rathausturm** (*adult/child €4/2*), the tower of the town hall.

Würzburg

Big, baroque and beautiful

The vast UNESCO World Heritage–listed **Residenz** (*residenz-wuerzburg.de; adult/child €10/free*), once the home of local prince-bishops, is one of Germany's most beautiful baroque palaces. Commissioned in 1720 by prince-bishop Johann Philipp Franz von Schönborn, it took almost 60 years to complete. Today the 360 rooms are home to government institutions,

BAVARIA'S MEDIEVAL CITY WALLS

Rothenburg ob der Tauber: Extending over 2.5km, Rothenburg's ancient walls encircle the town – walk their length and admire them from afar.

Dinkelsbühl: Also 2.5km long, the walls at Dinkelsbühl are much quieter than Rothenburg's but just as beautiful.

Nördlingen: Dating back to the 14th century, Nördlingen's walls are almost perfectly circular.

Landsberg am Lech: One of Bavaria's least-known walled cities, Landsberg has fine, 15th-century fortified gates and imposing stone ramparts.

Nuremberg: Beginning opposite the Hauptbahnhof and extending around the Altstadt, Nuremberg's walls are a constant presence in the city.

 EATING IN ROTHENBURG OB DER TAUBER: OUR PICKS

Zur Höll: Medieval wine tavern in Rothenburg's oldest building, offering regional specialities and Franconian wines. *5-11pm Mon-Sat* €€

Gasthof Butz: Family-run inn in a former brewery serving no-nonsense southern German dishes. *11.30am-2pm & 6-9pm Tue, Wed & Fri-Sun* €€

Mittermeier: Savour a finely crafted menu at one of Rothenburg's oldest fine-dining establishments. *6-9pm Tue-Sat* €€€

Weinstube zum Pulverer: Ancient spot serving classic German cooking in a tranquil ambience. *5-11pm Wed-Fri, noon-11pm Sat & Sun* €€€

The Romantic Road

From the vineyards of Würzburg to the foot of the Alps, the almost 400km-long Romantic Road (Romantische Strasse) is by far Germany's most popular tourist route. It passes through more than two dozen cities, towns and villages in a ribbon of half-timbered quaintness. This is the Germany many expect to see, with perfectly conserved towns delivering on all the promises seen pre-trip on Instagram.

KONSTANTIN YOLSHIN/SHUTTERSTOCK

Schloss Weikersheim, Weikersheim

VITAL STATS

Length 460km

Visitors Around 30 million annually

Year created 1950

Number of official stops 29

Number of castles and palaces 22

Number of UNESCO sites 4

Largest city Augsburg (population 301,000)

Smallest stop Röttingen (population 1681)

Number of autobahns 0

Most visited town Rothenburg ob der Tauber

PRACTICALITIES

● romantischestrasse.de

North to South

The Road is designed to be driven north to south. Leaving from Würzburg, the scenery becomes more magnificent. Getting to Würzburg is straightforward via regular trains from Munich (two hours), Bamberg, Frankfurt and Nuremberg (one hour from each). Spend a few days in Würzburg, including an afternoon at **Festung Marienberg** *(schloesser.bayern.de; adult/child €4/free)* with its 800-year-old bastions. The Romantic Road ends in Füssen, where **Schloss Neuschwanstein** (p288) is unmissable. From Füssen, Austria's Alps are nearby.

Romantic Road Coach

For those who aren't driving or cycling the Romantic Road, the **Romantic Road Coach** *(romanticroadcoach.de)* is a seasonal bus service (May to September) connecting towns not serviced by regular rail. The most popular routes are day trips (sometimes with wine tastings) from Würzburg or Frankfurt am Main to Rothenburg ob der Tauber. After Rothenburg, **Deutsche Bahn** *(bahn.de)* trains service 15 stations, including Dinkelsbühl, Harburg, Nördlingen, Donauwörth, Augsburg, Landsberg am Lech, Füssen and Munich. The coach route's midway stop is effectively in Weikersheim, a pretty small town straddling the Tauber River with the finest palace along the entire Road, **Schloss Weikersheim** *(schloss-weikersheim. de; adult 60/80min tour €9/11).*

university faculties and a museum, but the grandest 40 have been restored for visitors to admire.

Nuremberg

Revisit the Nuremberg trials

You can visit the courtroom where the Nazi leaders were tried for crimes against peace and humanity, now the **Memorium Nuremberg Trials** (*memorium-nuremberg.de; adult/child €7.50/2.50*). Courtroom No 600 has been left pretty much as it was back then, and there's a multimedia exhibition telling the story of one of the world's most famous legal processes.

Regensburg

Explore religious Regensburg

The austere **Dom St Peter** (*bistum-regensburg.de; free*), dominating Regenburg's skyline, is a masterpiece of Gothic grandeur in Bavaria. Beyond incredible architectural features, the **Domspatzen** is a boys' choir that has been around for over 1000 years; they accompany the 10am Sunday service during the school year. Attached to the church, the **Domschatzmuseum** (Cathedral Treasury) overflows (and overwhelms) with lavish monstrances, tapestries and other treasures.

Bavarian Forest

Hiking and biking in the Bavarian Forest

Apart from the obvious attractions of the Bavarian Alps, there's no better place in the Free State to pull on hiking boots than the **Bavarian Forest National Park** (*nationalpark-bayerischerwald.de*) and surrounding areas. The park extends for around 24,250 hectares along the Czech border, from Bayerisch Eisenstein in the north to Finsterau in the south. You'll encounter far fewer people on the trails here than in the Alps and there's also more wildlife to spot.

The European long-distance E6 hiking route cuts through the Bavarian Forest, but with over 350km of trails amid thick mountain spruce in the park, there are countless other routes to follow. Popular hikes include those to the summit of **Mt Lusen** (1373m), to the top of **Mt Grosser Arber** (1456m), the park's highest, and along the ridge that divides Bavaria from West Bohemia. Some paths in the national park are out of bounds from November to July.

Other activities include mountain biking, trail running, skiing and snowshoeing. The maps produced by Kompass – sheets 195, 196, 197 and 198 – are invaluable companions. They are available from tourist offices, some bookshops, the park visitor centre and online.

BASES FOR THE BAVARIAN FOREST

The German part of the Bavarian Forest is fringed by villages and small towns, all of which work as bases for exploring the national park. The more accessible ones can be reached via the Waldbahn railway line.

Zwiesel is the largest town just outside the park, with plenty of accommodation, places for eating and provisioning, a well-stocked, helpful **tourist office** (*zwiesel.de*), and a museum about local traditions. Another option for the south of the national park, **Grafenau** has shops, accommodation, a spa and a **tourist office** (*grafenau.de*). And if you're looking to combine the region's glass-making traditions with time spent exploring the park, **Frauenau**, very near the park's boundary, has the **Glasmuseum** (*glasmuseum-frauenau.de; adult/child €5/free, Sun €1*).

Stuttgart & the Black Forest

ENCHANTING WOODLAND | SPAS | INNOVATION

☑️ **TOP TIP**

The money-saving
SchwarzwaldCard
*(schwarzwaldcard.shop;
adult/child from €51/35)* is
good for three days of free
or reduced entry to over 200
attractions, including cable
cars, museums, adventure
parks and swimming pools.
Popular inclusions are the
Triberger Wasserfälle and
Europa-Park.

Welcome to the southwest, known as the sunniest region in Germany. You're in the state of Baden-Württemberg, where locals are renowned for their inventiveness, prosperity and work-hard, play-hard mentality. Stuttgart, the region's capital, has a proud history of engineering that has given the world the automobile, spark plugs and the pretzel. Freiburg, one of the world's greenest cities, is also a gateway to exploring the depths of the Schwarzwald.

The Black Forest (Schwarzwald), a sprawling mass of spruce trees, tight-knit villages and pocket-sized lakes, is a place that both adventure seekers and slow travellers will be captivated by. The name itself casts a mysterious spell over the region, and you wouldn't be blamed for expecting to see a wicked witch straight out of a Brothers Grimm fairy tale cackling in the sky. But with one step into the undergrowth, you'll soon discover the only mystery here is how they make such a delicious cake.

Stuttgart

Rev your engines

There's nothing more synonymous with Stuttgart than fast cars. At the **Porsche Museum** *(porsche.com; adult/child €12/6),* almost 100 Porsche vehicles are on display. There are kids' exhibits, a racing simulator and a comprehensive audio

GETTING AROUND

Covering Germany's southwest corner, the state of Baden-Württemberg is well connected by train, bus and autobahn. Trains run regularly and are your best option for getting around, though driving allows you to see and do more. Towns are best explored on foot.

Even the smallest of towns have dedicated bike paths. However, navigating long distances on two wheels may see you riding in the slip lane a fair bit. Bike routes such as the **Bodensee Radweg** *(bodensee-radweg.com)* are good options.

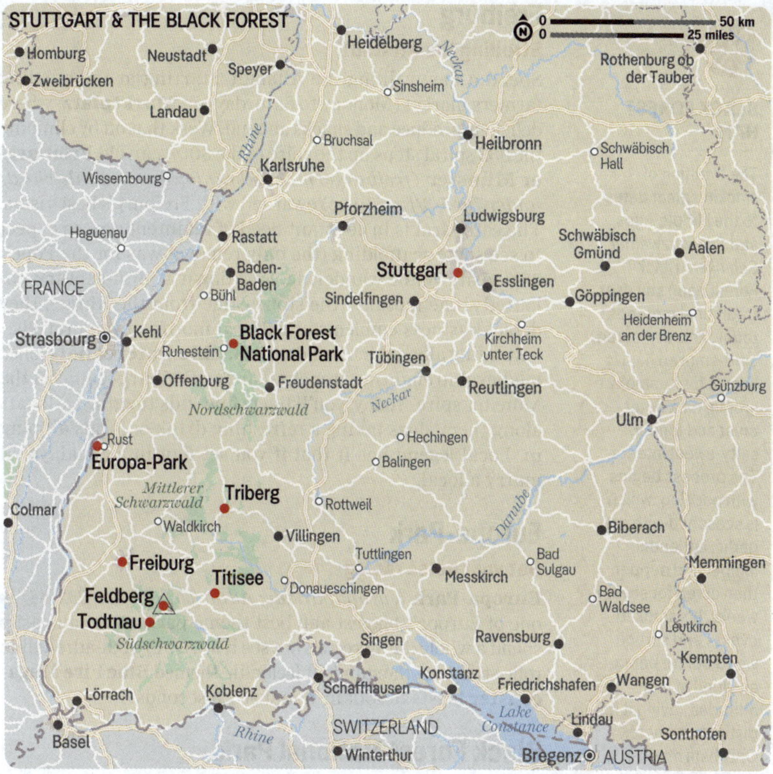

STUTTGART & THE BLACK FOREST

[Map of the Stuttgart and Black Forest region, showing locations including Homburg, Zweibrücken, Neustadt, Speyer, Heidelberg, Rothenburg ob der Tauber, Landau, Sinsheim, Wissembourg, Bruchsal, Heilbronn, Schwäbisch Hall, Karlsruhe, Pforzheim, Ludwigsburg, Schwäbisch Gmünd, Aalen, Haguenau, Rastatt, Stuttgart, Esslingen, Göppingen, Heidenheim an der Brenz, FRANCE, Baden-Baden, Bühl, Sindelfingen, Kirchheim unter Teck, Strasbourg, Kehl, Black Forest National Park, Ruhestein, Tübingen, Reutlingen, Günzburg, Offenburg, Freudenstadt, Nordschwarzwald, Hechingen, Ulm, Rust, Balingen, Europa-Park, Mittlerer Schwarzwald, Triberg, Rottweil, Colmar, Waldkirch, Villingen, Tuttlingen, Bad Sulgau, Biberach, Memmingen, Freiburg, Titisee, Messkirch, Bad Waldsee, Feldberg, Donaueschingen, Todtnau, Südschwarzwald, Singen, Ravensburg, Leutkirch, Kempten, Lörrach, Koblenz, Schaffhausen, Konstanz, Friedrichshafen, Wangen, Basel, Rhine, SWITZERLAND, Lake Constance, Lindau, Sonthofen, Winterthur, Bregenz, AUSTRIA)]

tour. You can even splash out and rent a Porsche for the day from the ticket desk.

Across town lies the 'competition'. The **Mercedes-Benz Museum** *(mercedes-benz.com; adult/child €16/8)* celebrates the evolution of the car over 135 years, contextualised through world history. From the first internal combustion engine to a history-making road trip in 1888 and the Silver Arrows sports-car hall of fame and the Popemobile, the collection is impressive and vast. The museum itself is an architectural marvel earning an entry in the Guinness World Records for the world's biggest artificial tornado – an atrium feature designed to extract smoke in case of fire.

EATING IN FREIBURG: LOCAL CUISINE

Grosser Meyerhof: Altstadt tavern specialising in local Badish dishes such as *Maultaschen* (pork and spinach ravioli). *11.30am-11pm* €€

Heiliggeist Stüble: Dine on local specialities with the sound of church bells at this stylish tavern under the Münster. *11.30am-11pm* €€

Martin's Bräu: Home-brewed ales and meaty snacks like ox-tongue salad, bratwurst or pork knuckle. *11am-11pm Sun-Thu, to midnight Fri & Sat* €€

Schmidt: This is the best place to enjoy a fluffy, rich Black Forest cake and coffee. Big breakfast menu, too. *9am-6pm Mon-Sat* €

BLACK FOREST HAM

The tradition of smoking meat dates to the Middle Ages, and *Schwarzwälder Schinken* (Black Forest ham) still uses traditional methods today. This dry-cured, cold-smoked ham is known for its smoky aroma, dark outer crust and tender, salty-sweet interior. The process begins with pork leg, which is seasoned with salt, garlic, coriander, juniper and pepper, then cured for several weeks. It's smoked over fir and spruce wood before being air-dried at high altitudes, giving it its distinct character. Only ham made in the Black Forest region can carry this name, in efforts to ensure it's made using traditional methods and authentic regional ingredients. It's often enjoyed with thick slices of bread or added to *Flammkuchen* (Alsatian pizza).

Freiburg

Strolling the Altstadt

Spend a day walking the Altstadt, starting at the bustling farmers market (Monday to Saturday) on **Marktplatz**, where delicious produce and snacks abound. Work that off by climbing the 333 spiral steps up the spire of the 800-year-old **Freiburger Münster** *(freiburgermuenster.info; tower adult/child/under 7yr 5/3/free)* to be rewarded with Freiburg's best vistas. The cathedral is in constant need of maintenance, so expect to see some scaffolding (the only removal was for the Pope's 2011 visit). While wandering, look down at 19th-century, coloured stone mosaics (the stone came from the Rhine); they depict business emblems or cultural motifs – even pretzels.

Running along the Altstadt, the **Bächle water canals** (once medieval firefighting trenches) are as Freiburg-iconic as the Münster spire. Today, you'll likely find kids tugging sailboats along them, dogs taking a refreshing drink or locals dipping in. Local legend has it that if you set foot in a canal, you'll marry a local.

Europa-Park

Get your pulse racing

Europa-Park *(europapark.de; adult/child from €52/44)* is one of Europe's biggest and best theme parks. You can easily spend a whole day here and not see it all. Of 13 high-adrenaline roller-coasters, the standout Icelandic-themed **Blue Fire Megacoaster** blasts to 100km/h in just 2.5 seconds.

Black Forest National Park

A wild adventure

The **Nationalpark Schwarzwald** *(nationalpark-schwarzwald.de)* is a 10,000-hectare area best explored on foot. Magnificent flora and fauna abound. For a real adventure, you can even stay a night in the wilderness at a secret nature camp only accessible on foot. The visitors centre at Ruhestein offers maps and an exhibition on the project.

Triberg

Going cuckoo for a waterfall

The busy tourist town's claims to fame are cuckoo clocks and Germany's highest waterfall. **Triberger Wasserfälle** *(triberg.de; adult/child €8/7.50)* is impressive – winding boardwalks

 DRINKING IN THE BLACK FOREST: LOCAL TIPPLES

Rothaus: Visit the Black Forest brewery in Grafenhausen to taste what makes its cult beer, the Tannenzapfle, so special. *11am-6pm*

Alpirsbacher Klosterbrau: Tour the family-owned brewery in Alpirsbach that has been crafting award-winning brews since 1880. *hours vary*

Black Forest Distillers: Pre-book a distillery tour in Lossburg to try Monkey 47, an award-winning dry gin made using 47 botanicals. *noon & 2pm Sat*

Emil Scheibel Schwarzwald-Brennerei: Learn to make great fruit schnapps at this distillery in Kappelrodeck. *9am-5pm Mon-Fri, 10am-1pm Sat*

and scenery-heavy trails abound – and cuckoo clocks less so, with many cheap imports. **Oli's Schnitzstube** (*olisschnitz stube.de*) still produces handcrafted clocks while **Rombach und Haas** (*black-forest-clock.de*) does ultra-modern ones.

Titisee

Make a splash

Titisee's scenic alpine lake is alive in summer with a quaint tourist village and plentiful water activites. The 7km shoreline has plenty of quieter swimming spots; in the town, there are good restaurants and souvenir boutiques. If weather isn't co-operating, the **Badeparadies Schwarzwald** (*badeparadies-schwarzwald.de; adult/child from €23/19*) indoor pool complex is a forest-hidden oasis.

Feldberg

'Tis the ski-son

Ski through the Black Forest mountains on **Feldberg**, the Black Forest's highest peak at 1493m. It's family-friendly and offers ski hire. Cross-country skiing is also popular, with 120km of marked trails winding through snowy enchantment – there's also snowshoeing and toboggan runs. Afterwards, hit the après-ski bars in small resort towns such as Todtnau and Feldberg.

Todtnau

Swing through the trees

From the **Blackforest Line suspension bridge** (*blackforest line.de; adult/child €12/9*), get a bird's-eye view of the multi-tiered **Todtnauer Wasserfall** (*todtnauer-wasserfaelle.de; adult/child/under 6yr €2.50/1.50/free*), one of the highest natural waterfalls in Germany. A combined ticket gets you entry to both the bridge and the waterfall, with a 2.4km circular walk connecting the two.

BEST SHORT HIKES IN THE BLACK FOREST

Uhrwaldpfad Rohrhardsberg: This 8km circular hike through dense forest features over 30 cuckoo clocks along the path from April to October.

Mummelsee to Hornisgrinde: From picturesque Mummelsee, this 4km loop ascends to Hornisgrinde, the highest peak in the northern Black Forest.

Allerheiligen Wasserfälle: This trail near Oppenau leads hikers 4.2km through a series of stunning waterfalls in a lush forest.

Gauchach Gorge Gourmet Trail: Challenging 5.6km trail through the wild Gauchach Gorge with its many waterfalls.

Muggenbrunn Barefoot Path: Feel spruce cones, bark mulch and fresh mountain water underfoot on this 600m-long trail. Great for kids.

WINTER FUN
Check out the ski resorts of **Garmisch-Partenkirchen** (p288) in Bavaria if you're keen on more winter adventures.

Bremen & Lower Saxony

ART MUSEUMS | WWII HISTORY | RICH GREENERY

Map inset showing: Hamburg, Bremerhaven, Oldenburg, Bremen, Lüneburg, Uelzen, Verden, Cloppenburg, Nienburg, Bergen-Belsen, Celle, Wolfsburg, Osnabrück, Minden, Hanover, Herford, Hamelin, Braunschweig, Bielefeld, Hildesheim

GETTING AROUND

Rail connections are excellent and often integrated with bus services. ICE fast trains service main hubs like Bremen and Hanover, and there's an extensive regional network.

To reach Bergen-Belsen Memorial Site, take an ICE or regional train to Celle. Take bus 900 from Schlossplatz and change to bus 110 at 'Küsterdamm, Winsen' stop. It's best to avoid Sunday, as only a *Rufbus* (call bus) completes the journey from Winsen and needs to be booked ahead.

☑ TOP TIP

During trade fairs, hotels and private accommodation in Hanover and nearby towns are booked out, so it's important to always run a quick check online *(visit-hannover.com/ Messen-Kongresse)* before coming. As an alternative, visit Bremen first.

Lower Saxony, spilling northwards to the North Sea and in most parts flat as a pancake, is the largest German state after Bavaria. For the traveller, it's a low-key place with an understated character to its the landscape: wide-open spaces and heath, occasional hilly countryside, and tidal mudflats that submerge and reappear in daily cycles. Hanover, its capital, has several excellent museums, as well as large swathes of green space that invite a stroll. An hour's drive from Hanover, the Bergen-Belsen Memorial Site, a former concentration camp, reveals Lower Saxony's stark contrasts.

Meanwhile, Bremen is a city-state unto itself with its own port, Bremerhaven. Bremen brings together culture, particularly the fine arts, and plenty of nightlife in one small bundle. Within a short space of time, you can wind down medieval streets, duck into another gallery featuring unusual expressionism, stroll along the 'museum mile' and rest up in some great cafes and student places.

Bremen

MAP p297

All about expressionism

Bremen's longstanding ties with expressionism are best reflected in the architecture along **Böttcherstrasse**. Red-brick houses sport unique facades; some are now artisan shops and art museums. The **Paula Modersohn-Becker Museum** *(museen-boettcherstrasse.de; adult/child €12/free)* showcases the early expressionist and member of movement-founding Worpswede artist colony. The adjoining **Roselius-Haus Museum** *(museen-boettcherstrasse.de; adult/child €12/free)*, in a 16th-century patrician house, primarily displays 16th- and 17th-century art. The standout is a section dedicated to Lucas Cranach the Elder.

Works of Gerhard Marcks

Next to Gerhard Marcks' **Town Musicians of Bremen Statue** on the Marktplatz, the same Brothers Grimm fairy tale it's

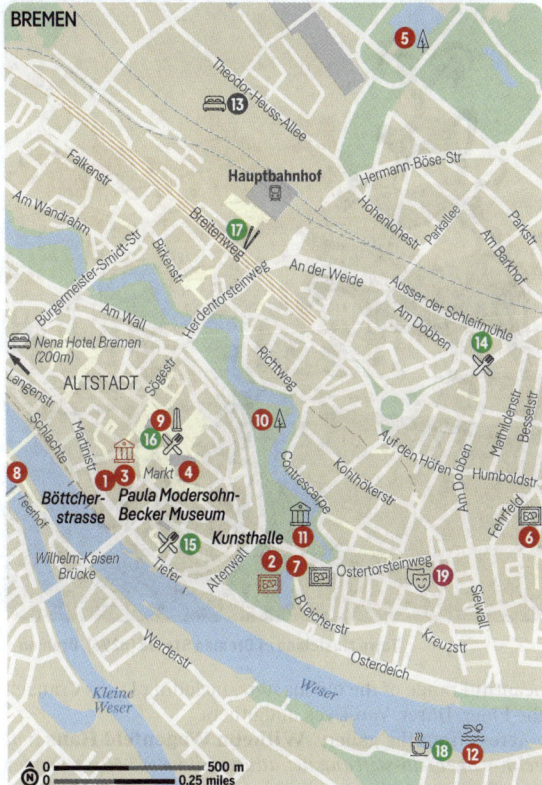

BREMEN

inspired by is charmingly re-enacted at noon from May to September. It's a beautiful, lighthearted performance honouring an artist condemned as 'degenerate' during Nazi times. The excellent **Gerhard Marcks Haus** (*marcks.de; adult/child €5/ free*) exhibits the artist's own donated works.

Bremen's cultural mile

The **Kunsthalle** (*kunsthalle-bremen.de; adult/child €15/ free*) is Bremen's premier art exhibition space with a large, permanent collection of paintings, sculpture and copperplate engravings, spanning medieval to present times. There's a

---

 EATING IN BREMEN: OUR PICKS ──────────── MAP p297

Hanoi Deli: Sushi, Vietnamese dishes and some pan-Asian classics; large servings. *11.30am-10pm Mon & Wed-Fri, from noon Sat & Sun* €€

Bremer Ratskeller: Hearty traditional German cuisine beneath the Rathaus. Gorgeous vaulted ceilings. *noon-9.30pm Sun-Thu, to 10pm Fri & Sat* €€

Argana: Moroccan cooking in the Schnoor quarter. Lots of meat-based tajines, and veg offerings. *noon-3pm & 5.30-10pm Tue-Fri, 2.30-11pm Sat, 5.30-10pm Mon* €€

Al Pappagallo: Delicious Italian dishes prepared in an open kitchen and elegantly presented. *noon-2pm & 6-11pm Mon-Fri, 6-11pm Sat* €€€

BEST BREMEN PARKS & QUIET SPOTS

Wallanlagen: Bremen's town fortifications were converted into parkland in the 19th century, with ponds and meadows.

Teerhof: This quarter on the spit of land in the Weser River has a slightly abandoned feel, despite its gentrified housing. On the same peninsula but reached by ferry from Sielwall, the **Weser Strand** (Weser Beach) is a summer bathing spot, and **Café Sand** a popular retreat.

Bürgerpark Bremen: Northeast of the centre, an enormous stretch of parkland with lakes, trails, forests and meadows. It also has a small animal park, popular with kids.

Bibelgarten: The Bibel Garden is a tranquil yard at the entrance to the Bleikeller crypt.

Town Musicians of Bremen Statue (p296), Bremen

beautiful range of the old masters, including Lucas Cranach the Elder, Dürer, Van Dyck and others.

Across from the gallery, **Wilhelm Wagenfeld Haus** *(wilhelm-wagenfeld-stiftung.de; adult/child €6/3.50),* a former guardhouse and jail, now houses contemporary design from industrial to photography. It's named after a Bauhaus luminary.

Bremen's cultural mile gives way to great cultural venues in **Das Viertel**, such as the **Mensch, Puppe** *(menschpuppe.de; matinee adult/child €10/8, evening incl drink €25/15)* puppet theatre and a handful of galleries including the outstanding **Galerie Kramer** *(galeriekramer.de; free).*

Hanover

Relax in royal parkland

Hanover's highlight is **Herrenhäuser Gärten** *(hannover.de/herrenhausen),* a sprawling constellation of gardens. Start in the **Grosser Garten** *(incl museum & Berggarten adult/child €10/free),* known for baroque golden sculptures, a maze and the beloved Niki de Saint Phalle Grotto. A path leads down to the Grosse Fontäne, one of Europe's tallest fountains jetting to 80m high. In summer, dancing fountain shows, **garden illuminations** *(adult/child €6/free),* concerts and fireworks competitions delight.

The **Museum Schloss Herrenhausen** *(incl Grosser Garten & Berggarten adult/child €10/free)* recounts the grounds' history from the 17th century to their Hanoverian royal creators.

Exploring the old town

Despite severe WWII damage, Hanover's small old town retains much historic character. The most interesting buildings on Am Markte, the central square, are the medieval **Altes Rathaus** *(Old Town Hall; altes-rathaus-events.de)* and the Gothic **Marktkirche** *(Market Church; marktkirche-hannover. de; free)*. **Leibnizhaus** on Holzmarkt was once the home of the renowned mathematician and philosopher Gottfried Wilhelm Leibniz (1646–1716) and has an attractive, reconstructed Renaissance facade. The nearby **Aegidienkirche** soberly recollects wartime horrors; the medieval church remains in bombed-out condition since 1943.

Not to be missed along the river are the voluptuous and fluorescent-coloured **Die Nanas** sculptures. These Venus figures are Hanover's beloved landmarks.

Into the sky, onto a lake

The **Neues Rathaus** *(adult/child €4/3.50)* has an unusually curved lift leading up to its green dome. A glass ceiling and floor make for an ascent that's nerve-tingling and claustrophobic (six-person capacity and busy in summer). Afterwards, stroll through parkland to **Maschsee** for endless splashy fun including rental pedalling and rowing boats. Ferries – some solar-powered – ply the lake from Easter to October (weather depending).

Bergen-Belsen

Visit a Holocaust memorial

Visiting the **Bergen-Belsen Memorial Site** *(bergen-belsen. stiftung-ng.de; free)*, a former concentration camp, takes you to where Anne Frank died in 1945. The modern **Documentation Centre** chronicles the fates of the people who passed through and the grounds' evolution from a forestry workers' barracks to a POW camp.

HANOVER PLANNING PRACTICALITIES

The **Hanover Tourist Office** *(hannover. de/tourismus)* is located opposite the Hauptbahnhof and has an excellent website. Its **HannoverCard** *(1/2/3 days €13/20/26)* gives you free or discount admission to sights and free public transport. There's an accommodation booking service on the website, as well as a telephone booking service that's especially useful for rooms with private hosts during peak trade-fair periods. Also consult the website for information on accessibility and barrier-free offerings.

The Museum Schloss Herrenhausen is closed Mondays. The Herrenhäuser Gärten themselves have reduced winter hours but are open all year, though illuminations are only in summer.

DRINKING IN HANOVER: OUR PICKS

Waterloo: This beer garden is on the way to football club Hanover 96's home ground, with *Wurst* and more on the menu. *hours vary*

Brauhaus Ernst August: Sprawling brewpub with food, parties and live music, serving its own beers. *11am-11pm Mon-Thu, to late Fri & Sat*

Holländische Kakao-Stube: Historic (1895) Dutch coffeehouse with a great selection of pastries and a maritime ambience. *10am-6.30pm Mon-Sat*

Cafe Mezzo: Cafe and bar alongside the Pavillon cultural venue; the latter has live music and lots of events. *9am-midnight Mon-Sat, to 11pm Sun*

Dresden & Leipzig

BAROQUE | ROYAL TREASURES | ART

GETTING AROUND

Both cities are best explored on foot. In Dresden, trams connect the Altstadt and Neustadt and serve every corner of the centre. In Leipzig (1½ hours from Dresden by car or train), the distance between most attractions is walkable. For Plagwitz, KarLi and Connewitz, you'll need to catch a tram from the Hauptbahnhof or Augustusplatz. Install the Nextbike app on your phone to book municipal bicycles available in both cities.

☑ TOP TIP

Sold at tourist information centres, the Leipzig Card allows unlimited travel within one or three days and entitles you to discounts at most of the important museums.

With a colourful history as an independent entity, a quasi-empire at times, Saxony is the most distinctive East German region. It takes pride in speaking a dialect that other Germans – according to regular national opinion surveys – appear to dislike. This might be a secret strategy to keep others away from a land that is truly blessed.

Dresden's 18th-century cultural heyday is evident in the Altstadt's baroque wonders and their precious art collections. Across the river, Dresden's Neustadt has dozens of restaurants and shops and one of the liveliest nightlife scenes in Germany's east. In the north, Leipzig is an energetic and progressive metropolis that rivals Berlin as the country's hippest destination. Leipzig has nurtured some famous composers and scientists as well as important German painters, and has a plethora of fascinating museums and a world-class picture gallery. It's an all-round liveable city, half of which is covered by lakes and wood-like parks.

Dresden

A cityscape to die for

Before anything else, take in marvellous views from **Brühl's Terrace** (aka the Balcony Europe). Dark-green, untamed Neustadt banks juxtaposed against the blackened stones and baroque curves of Altstadt provide an intense visual experience.

Another marvel is the **Frauenkirche** *(frauenkirche-dresden.de)*, a magnificent cathedral resurrected after being reduced to WWII rubble. Next, take in **Residenzschloss** *(skd. museum; adult/child €16/free)*, a Renaissance palace home to Saxony's rulers for around 400 years. Its collections include the unmissable **Historisches Grünes Gewölbe** *(€16, incl other collections €28)*, a real-life Aladdin's cave of precious ivory, silver, diamonds and jewels. Reconstruction on the bombed-out palace began in the 1960s and was finally completed in 2013.

Nearby, the **Albertinum** *(skd.museum; adult/child €14/free)*, a former Renaissance-era arsenal, is the stunning home

Brühl's Terrace and Frauenkirche, Dresden

BEST DRESDEN FESTIVALS

Dixieland Fest: A May parade of Dixieland bands riding retro and steampunk vehicles; concerts are also held aboard steamships.

Filmfest Dresden: Held in April, the international short-film festival takes place in various city locations, including on giant screens in Altstadt.

Flottenparade: The full might of the Saxon navy is displayed in the 1 May parade, with Dresden's famous steamships floating past the Altstadt.

Louisenfest: 'Party, music, food' is the motto of this late-June festival celebrating the city's happening street. Visual arts are also on the menu.

Elbhangfest: A late-June festival organised by people living on the high bank of the Elbe between Pillnitz and Loschwitz.

of the **Galerie Neue Meister** (New Masters Gallery), which has paintings by the likes of Caspar David Friedrich, Claude Monet and Marc Chagall.

Private Eden

At **Zwinger** *(der-dresdner-zwinger.de; adult/child €16/free)* palace, discover an Earthly version of paradise for the chosen – Saxon royals and their guests.

Inside, the **Gemäldegalerie Alte Meister** (Old Masters Gallery) is an astounding collection of 16th- to 18th-century European art including Raphael's famous *Sistine Madonna* (1513), and works by Titian and Cranach.

The extraordinary **Porzellansammlung** brings together 17th- and 18th-century porcelain from China and Meissen. The **Tiersaal** (Animal Hall) is the ultimate highlight with hundreds of porcelain animals. Lastly, the **Mathematisch-Physikalischer Salon**, a collection of scientific implements, will delight anyone interested in the Enlightenment.

Sounds of Dresden

Dresden's opera house, the **Semperoper** *(semperoper.de)*, is another architectural jewel in the Altstadt. Destroyed by Allied air raids, it was resurrected in 1945. Counting premieres of famous works by Strauss and Wagner, it still hosts world-class concerts today (buy tickets well ahead).

Dresden's other top venue for classical music is a strikingly different piece of GDR-era brutalism. The **Dresdner Philharmonie** *(dresdnerphilharmonie.de)* is home to one of Germany's best orchestras.

 ## EATING IN LEIPZIG & DRESDEN: OUR PICKS

Bayerische Bahnhof: Gose beer and stylish food in the intriguing setting of a defunct Leipzig railway station's waiting room. *noon-10pm* €€

Café Puschkin: KarLi's flagship hangout is well past its heyday, but it still draws a merry Leipzig crowd and has an eclectic menu. *9am-2am* €€

Lila Sosse: Intriguing vegan and meaty concoctions served in glass preserve jars inside Dresden's Kunsthof-passage courtyard complex. *4-11pm* €€

PlanWirtschaft: A quiet courtyard setting in the heart of Dresden's Neustadt and a menu alluding to GDR-era culinary standards. *5-11pm Tue-Sun* €€

LEIPZIG MUSIC FESTS

Anna Toropova, a Leipzig-based journalist, recommends the following events.

Bachfest: (May/June) Bach's music in all shapes and forms, from Thomanenchor to jazz-band interpretations.

Wave-Gotik-Treffen: (May/June) A massive Gothic music fest, but it's the costumed audience that rocks most.

Klassik Airleben: (June) Gewandhaus Orchestra picnic performances at the end of the season draw enormous crowds.

A Capella: (May/June) Annual vocal competition held in all kinds of venues, from churches to libraries.

Leipziger Markt Music: (August) Ten eclectic nights with classical orchestras and indie bands at the city's main square.

Leipzig

You want a revolution?

Leipzig's **Nikolaikirche** *(nikolaikirche.de)* is famous for the 'peace prayers' held here every Monday at 5pm since 1982. Starting in September 1989, the prayers kicked off a chain reaction of events leading to East Germany's collapse and Germany's reunification.

The **Zeitgeschichtliches Forum** *(hdg.de; free)* further covers East German political history with an enormous exhibition, while the darker side of Communist times is chillingly documented by the **Stasi Museum** *(runde-ecke-leipzig.de; adult/student €5/4),* located in the former secret police headquarters. English-language audio guides accompany displays (in German) on propaganda, surveillance devices, recruitment and other machinations.

Singing city

The 800-year-old boys' choir **Thomanerchor** still performs at its original base in the Gothic **Thomaskirche** *(thomaskirche. org)*. Bach repertoire honours the composer who led it for 27 years until his death. Bach's remains lie buried beneath a bronze plate afront the altar. The church hosts other musical events – some are free – including **Bachfest** *(bachfestleipzig.de)* in June.

Notes and notables

Walk the footsteps of Leipzig's famous composers along the 5km **Leipziger Notenspur** *(Leipzig Music Trail; notenspur-leipzig. de)*. Each of the 23 stops has information panels and phone numbers to call and listen for music or additional commentary. There are six museums along the route, most doubling as concert venues, including **Mendelssohn-Haus** *(mendelssohn-stiftung. de; adult/child €10/free),* the house where Schumann composed the *Spring Symphony,* Wagner's former school, and apartments Edvard Grieg stayed in. At the interactive **Bach-Museum Leipzig** *(bachmuseumleipzig.de; adult/child €10/free),* learn how to date a Bach manuscript, listen to baroque instruments or treat your ears to any of his compositions.

Treasures of knowledge

Leipzig University is one of the world's oldest, founded in 1409 by scholars fleeing the Hussite uprising in Prague. The list of alumni is stellar – from Goethe and Nietzsche to former German Chancellor Angela Merkel. Located in Augustusplatz, its contemporary home known as **Paulinum** looks like an airport terminal devouring a Gothic cathedral. It's a boldly postmodern tribute to the 13th-century university church, which stood here until East German authorities blew it up in 1968.

Thankfully, the university's treasure trove of scientific collections was left unscathed. The **Museen im Grassi** *(grassi-leipzig.de)* includes the **Musikinstrumenten-Museum** *(adult/child €6/free)* where you can discover five centuries' worth of music in an interactive sound laboratory. There's also the **Museum für Völkerkunde** *(free)* exploring global cultures and the **Museum für Angewandte Kunst** *(free)* flaunting Art Nouveau and Art Deco furniture, porcelain, glass and ceramics.

Central Germany

HISTORY | ANCIENT BEECHWOOD | BROTHERS GRIMM

Central Germany is truly the heart of the country. Plenty of sites in Thuringia, Lower Saxony, Saxony-Anhalt and Hesse have a special historical resonance or even a mythic significance. And so much of the national story has unfolded here – key sites in intellectual, religious and political developments that have shaped modern Germany, Europe and beyond. Look no further for the seedbed of Germany's most revered artists, writers and thinkers from Goethe to Nietzsche and Bach.

Here, beyond the time-worn churches, half-timbered, 16th-century merchants' houses and grim fortresses of tourist brochures, you'll find glowing examples of the German rural ideal. Ancient swaths of beech and conifer forest, the low mountains and farmsteads of Brothers Grimm stories, and broad fields of corn and sunflowers are abundant. There's room to stretch your legs, to cycle, to swim and to get back to basics in some of the largest nature reserves in Central Europe.

Weimar

Discover Goethe's Weimar

Johann Wolfgang von Goethe (1749–1832), the colossus of German letters, spent much of his life in Weimar. He lived in the 18th-century *Wohnhaus* (residence) on Frauenplan square for more than 50 years. The house now houses the **Goethe-Nationalmuseum** *(klassik-stiftung.de; adult/student €10/4)*, the world's largest collection of Goethe manuscripts and artefacts.

Allow several hours to explore the residence and the superbly curated permanent exhibition, **Lebensfluten – Tatensturm** ('Floods of Life – Storm of Action') including where he wrote *Faust*. Meanwhile, the **Goethe Gartenhaus** *(klassik-stiftung. de; adult/student €7/3)* is where he lived prior to the *Wohnhaus*. The lovely cottage, surrounded by the garden that Goethe himself laid out, is within the 58-acre, UNESCO-listed **Park an der Ilm** *(free)*.

GETTING AROUND

This region is most easily explored by car. In the towns, you can mostly get around on foot.
Deutsche Bahn *(bahn.de)* runs most services in Central Germany. The major rail hubs are Kassel and Halle, though there are regular connections throughout. Private operator **FlixTrain** *(flixtrain.com)* runs between Halle and Berlin but comfort is lacking. The region's bus network is efficient and much cheaper than rail.

☑ TOP TIP

In Weimar, head for the tourist office and get a Weimar Card. It's seriously good value – for €32.50 you'll get 48-hour access to the many museums and historic sites of the Klassik Stiftung Weimar ensemble, plus a guided walking tour and free 'iguide'.

MUSEUMS FOR EXPLORING GREAT MINDS

Schiller Museum: Friedrich Schiller's *Wohnhaus* includes a permanent exhibition on the 18th-century author.

Liszt-Haus: Where composer Franz Liszt lived from 1869 until his death in 1886.

Museum Neues: The former Grand Ducal Museum hosts a permanent exhibition on early modernist art spanning the Weimar School to Henry van de Velde.

Haus Hohe Pappeln: An unusual house designed by the Belgian Art Nouveau architect-designer himself.

Nietzsche Archiv: Where the troubled philosopher and nihilist lived out his final years.

House of the Weimar Republic: Exhibit on the story of Germany's short-lived first democracy.

Bauhaus beginnings

The **Bauhaus Museum Weimar** *(klassik-stiftung.de; adult/ student €10/4)* commemorates the Bauhaus (literally 'building house') school founded in Weimar in 1919. The collection here focuses on the early days. To actually see Bauhaus architecture, **Haus Am Horn** *(adult/student €5/2)* is Weimar's only truly Bauhaus building.

The dark history of Buchenwald

Buchenwald concentration camp has been preserved almost untouched as a memorial, the **Gedenkstätte Buchenwald** *(buchenwald.de; tour adult/student €7/3, multimedia guide €5)*. Visitors are encouraged to wander quietly and freely around its numerous structures, including the crematorium.

Kassel

Deep dive into fairy tales

Kassel is an ideal launching pad for exploring the **Märchen-strasse** (Fairy Tale Road), one of Germany's most beguiling tourist routes. The 600km route stretches from Hanau, the birthplace of the Brothers Grimm, to Bremen. Of the 50-odd fairy-tale-associated stops, five are 'life stations' of the brothers: Hanau, Steinau, Marburg, Kassel and Göttingen. All make for excellent day trips or overnight destinations. Before heading off, discover the Brothers' legacy in Kassel at **Grimmwelt** *(grimmwelt.de; adult/student/under 3yr €10/7/ free)*, the world's leading museum and archive on their work.

Dessau

The wonderful world of Bauhaus

Bauhaus, considered the most influential school of design and architecture of the 20th century, reached its creative peak in Dessau. The purpose-built **Bauhaus-Dessau Museum** *(bauhaus-dessau.de; adult/child €10/free)*, home to wonderful exhibitions curated from 49,000 pieces, is the world's second largest after Berlin. Also obligatory is the **Bauhausgebäude** *(adult/child €10/free)*. The iconic modernist building, designed by Gropius himself, is a teaching institution but permits audio guided tours inside.

Wittenberg

Lutheran churches and sights

The Lutherstadt-Wittenberg is UNESCO-recognised for its wealth of Reformation-related sites. Most important is the **Schlosskirche** *(schlosskirche-wittenberg.de; tower €3)* where Martin Luther nailed his *Ninety-Five Theses* to the door. There's also **Stadtkirche Wittenberg** *(stadtkirchengemeinde-wittenberg.de)*, where Luther conducted the world's first Protestant worship services in 1521.

Frankfurt am Main

SKYLINE VIEWS | APPLE WINE | ART MUSEUMS

Glinting with glass, steel and concrete skyscrapers, Frankfurt am Main (pronounced 'mine') is unlike any other German city. 'Mainhattan' is a high-powered finance and business hub, home to one of the world's largest stock exchanges and the gleaming headquarters of the European Central Bank, and it famously hosts some of the world's most important trade fairs, attracting thousands of business travellers. Yet, at its heart, Frankfurt is an unexpectedly traditional and charming city, with half-timbered buildings huddled in its quaint medieval Altstadt (old town), cosy apple-wine taverns serving hearty regional food, village-like neighbourhoods filled with outdoor cafes, boutiques and street art, and beautiful parks, gardens and riverside paths. The city's cache of museums is second in Germany only to Berlin's, and its nightlife and entertainment scenes are bolstered by a spirited student population. The area around the Hauptbahnhof is the red-light and drug district, and while it offers the cheapest accommodation, you should avoid it.

Frankfurt's Historic Heart

Roman market square

The **Römerberg** is Frankfurt's old central square, buzzing with tourists and street performers. Ornately gabled half-timbered buildings, reconstructed in the 1980s after WWII bombings, give an idea of how beautiful the city's medieval core once was. The photogenic **Rathaus** building, with its three step-gabled 15th-century houses, is one such example. In the time of the Holy Roman Empire, it was the site of celebrations during the election and coronation of emperors. Today, it houses the office of Frankfurt's mayor.

GETTING AROUND

Frankfurt is a surprisingly compact, small and navigable city. It is very walkable and the River Main acts as a primary landmark to guide your journey. To get a real feel for the city, try to take it in on foot as much as you can. Public transport is also robust and easy to use, with commuter trains, buses, trams and a subway system. If renting a car, parking can be a bit expensive, so prepare to pay €1 for every 20 minutes in most cases.

☑ TOP TIP

The **Moselle Valley** is especially scenic walking country. Variants of the Mosel Erlebnis Route follow the entire Moselle Valley along both banks of the river. Expect some steep climbs if you venture away from the river, such as on the 185km-long Moselhöhenweg, which sticks to high ground but offers spectacular vistas.

FRANKFURT AM MAIN

BEST FESTIVALS IN FRANKFURT

Christopher Street Day: A colourful Pride parade in mid-July, as well as a *Strassenfest* (street festival) at Konstablerwache.

Rheingauer Weinmarkt: At this 10-day late-summer festival, enjoy a taste of over 600 wine varieties from the surrounding Rheingau region.

Apfelweinfestival: Frankfurt's famous *Apfelwein* is celebrated in August with tastings, music and storytelling in dialect.

Frankfurt Book Fair: The largest annual global book fair, Frankfurter Buchmesse, takes place at Frankfurt Messe in mid-October. Book early to get a hotel room.

Christmas Market: Every December, Frankfurt's Christmas market in the Altstadt brings cheer with choirs, *Glühwein,* stalls and traditional foods.

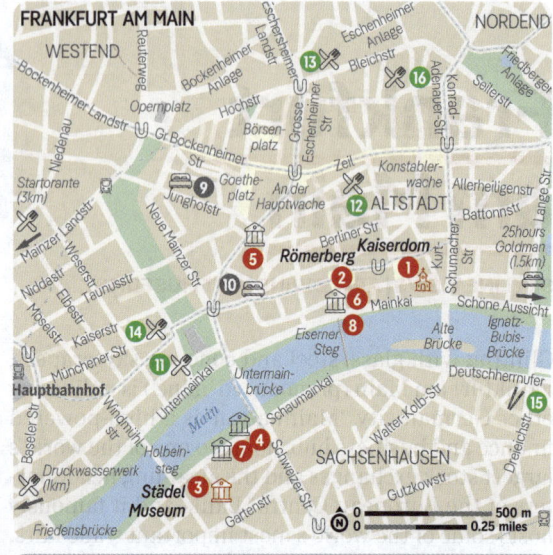

⭐ **HIGHLIGHTS**
1 Kaiserdom
2 Römerberg
3 Städel Museum

🔴 **SIGHTS**
4 Deutsches Filmmuseum
5 Deutsches Romantik-Museum

6 Historisches Museum Frankfurt
7 Museum für Kommunikation

🔴 **ACTIVITIES**
8 Primus Linie

⚫ **SLEEPING**
9 Ruby Louise Hotel

10 Steigenberger Frankfurter Hof

🟢 **EATING**
11 Im Herzen Afrikas
12 Kleinmarkthalle
13 Occhio D'Oro
14 Pizzeria Montana
15 Ramen Muku
16 Zu den 12 Aposteln

Regal History

Climb the Kaiserdom

The red-sandstone Imperial Cathedral of St Bartholomew, aka **Kaiserdom** *(dom-frankfurt.de; tower adult/child €3/1.50)* or Frankfurt Cathedral, is located in the heart of the Altstadt. An unmatched view of the city is your reward if you climb the 328 steps up the cathedral's Gothic tower to the viewing platform at an impressive 66m. The cathedral itself, the construction of which began in the 13th century, houses many regal memories as the German emperors and kings of the Holy Roman Empire were either crowned or elected here. The original chapel where the elections took place is now used only for silent prayer. The cathedral was rebuilt after an 1867 fire and again after the bombings of 1944, which left it a burnt-out shell.

A Soaring Romantic Journey

Learn about German Romanticism

The **Deutsches Romantik-Museum** *(German Romanticism Museum; deutsches-romantik-museum.de; adult/child €12/3)*

SVEN HANSCHE/SHUTTERSTOCK

Kaiserdom

is the very first of its kind in the world, deep-diving into the art and ethos of the German Romantic movement.

The first-level Goethe gallery contains over 5000 paintings from 1750 to 1850. The 2nd-floor gallery broadens the scope to explore Romanticism as a whole, focusing heavily on the literary works from the era. Weave through a maze of mirrors and standing panes with varying definitions of Romanticism imprinted on them; you can even type out your very own ode to love. The 3rd-floor gallery brings the intense feelings of the German Romantics to life. Learn how philosophers, poets, novelists, painters and fine artists throughout Europe began to gain inspiration from the German Romantics.

Down the Main

Relax on a river cruise

The Main River divides the city, with Frankfurt proper on the northern bank, and Sachsenhausen on the southern. You can appreciate the city's many charms while bobbing down the river on a boat. Hour-long sightseeing cruises with **Primus Linie**

EATING IN FRANKFURT: CHEAP EATS

Kleinmarkthalle: Traditional market hall with stalls selling artisan smoked sausages, cheese and pastries, plus espresso bar. *8am-6pm Mon-Fri, to 4pm Sat* €

Pizzeria Montana: Thin-crust pizzas with premium ingredients prepared fresh and cooked in a wood-fired oven. *11.30am-10pm Mon-Fri, from noon Sat & Sun* €

Ramen Muku: One of Frankfurt's excellent Japanese restaurants serves homemade ramen noodles and sashimi. *noon-1.30pm & 6-9.30pm Wed-Sun* €

Startorante: Social enterprise offering hospitality training and apprenticeships to young women; it serves three-course lunches. *11.30am-2pm Tue-Fri* €

THE TASTE OF FRANKFURT

Handkäs mit Musik:
A tangy, sour-milk cheese topped with onions, vinegar, oil and sometimes caraway seeds. *Musik* refers to the onions' after-effect!

Apfelwein (Ebbelwoi):
Frankfurt's famous apple-wine cider, served tart and dry, always in a diamond ribbed glass known as a *Gerippte*.

Grüne Sosse: A green sauce made from seven fresh herbs – chives, parsley, chervil, borage, sorrel, burnet and cress – served with boiled eggs, potatoes or schnitzel.

Frankfurter sausages: Slim, lightly smoked sausages, often served in pairs with mustard horseradish.

Frankfurter Kranz:
A thick buttercream cake shaped like a crown, covered in crunchy caramelised nuts and topped with cherries.

(primus-linie.de) leave hourly from Eiserner Steg, or catch an evening cruise to see the city's glittering skyline as dusk falls.

Longer full-day and multi-day cruises often begin in Frankfurt and float onwards to Mainz where the river meets the Rhine. At the Rhine–Main junction, you can continue on through the spectacular Rhine Valley.

Get Your Culture Fix

Explore Museum Embankment

On the southern bank of the Main River, nine world-class museums line up like dominoes. A further three jostle for position on the opposite side under the name **Museumufer** (Museum Embankment). You'd need weeks to visit them all, so focus on the heavy hitters.

Founded in 1815, **Städel Museum** *(staedelmuseum.de; adult/child €16/free)* is a world-renowned art gallery with an outstanding collection of European art from masters like Rembrandt, Rubens and Cézanne. It also features temporary photography exhibits, included in the ticket price.

Next door is the **Museum für Kommunication** *(mfk-frankfurt.de; adult/child/under 5yr €8/2/free)*, which promises to revive some nostalgia as you trace the history of communication from Mesopotamian writing stones through to today's ultra-connected tech, with engaging, hands-on exhibitions.

Movie buffs will love the **Deutsches Filmmuseum** *(German Film Museum; dff.film; adult/child/under 6yr €8/4/free)*, where you can try your hand at editing, play around with green screens and explore iconic props, costumes and film posters.

Jump back across the river to visit the **Historisches Museum Frankfurt** *(historisches-museum-frankfurt.de; adult/child €8/free)*. This museum focuses specifically on the long and storied history of Frankfurt. Don't miss the giant snow globe on the bottom floor.

EATING IN FRANKFURT: OUR PICKS

Zu den 12 Aposteln:
German food such as Frankfurter schnitzel with *Grüne Sosse* and *Käsespätzle* under dim lamplight. *noon-11pm €€*

Druckwasserwerk:
German cuisine in a beautiful building from 1899. Outside, there's an umbrella-shaded terrace. *5pm-midnight Mon-Sat €€€*

Occhio D'Oro: On the rooftop of the Flemings Hotel, this Italian restaurant with stunning city views serves regional cuisine. *6pm-midnight Mon-Sat €€*

Im Herzen Afrikas:
Eritrean cuisine at a rustic tavern with a sandy floor and colourful murals transporting you to Africa. *4-11pm Mon-Fri, from 1pm Sat €€*

Beyond Frankfurt

Leave behind Frankfurt's towering cityscape to discover quiet charm, Gutenberg's legacy, medieval castles...and, of course, Riesling after Riesling.

Straddling the Rhine, Mainz offers a chance to explore the region's quieter side. The hometown of Johannes Gutenberg, the inventor of the printing press, Mainz has a sizeable university and a rich wine culture. Strolling along the Rhine and sampling local wines in a half-timbered tavern is as much a part of any Mainz visit as its fabulous sightseeing.

Between Rüdesheim and Koblenz, the Rhine cuts deeply through the Rhenish Slate Mountains, meandering between hillside castles and steep fields of wine-producing grapes. This is Germany's landscape at its most dramatic – forested hillsides alternate with craggy cliffs and near-vertical terraced vineyards. Idyllic villages appear around each bend, their half-timbered houses and Gothic church steeples seemingly plucked from the world of fairy tales.

Places
Mainz p309
Heidelberg p311
Rüdesheim am Rhein p311
Koblenz p311

Mainz

TIME FROM FRANKFURT: **50MIN**

Birthplace of the printing press

The **Gutenberg-Museum Mainz** *(mainz.de; adult/child €10/4)* is a proud homage to the history of the printed word and the 15th-century Mainz native who invented it – Johannes Gutenberg. The museum's most incredible exhibits, kept under dim light, are the two copies of the 42-line **Gutenberg Bible**, printed in 1455 and hand-decorated. Don't miss the 20-minute

---

GETTING AROUND

ICE trains run frequently from Frankfurt's Hauptbahnhof via the airport and are the easiest and quickest way to reach Mainz. All main attractions are within walking distance from the train station. The public bus and tram systems are easy to use.

Navigate the Romantic Rhine Valley by renting a car. Only two train lines run along this section of the Rhine. The Linke Rheinstrecke (Left Rhine Line) runs along the west bank from Cologne to Mainz, passing through

Boppard, St Goar, Oberwesel and Bacharach. The Rechte Rheinstrecke (Right Rhine Line) runs along the east bank and passes through Braubach, Kaub, Assmannshausen and Rüdesheim.

KD runs cruises and scheduled services up and down the river between Cologne and Mainz. Travelling end to end takes over 11 hours, or you can opt for shorter sections such as St Goar to Bingen.

SADMAN/SHUTTERSTOCK

Drosselgasse, Rüdesheim am Rhein

demonstrations of Gutenberg's printing press to understand the ingenuity of his invention.

Chagall's blue-hued church

Around 200,000 pilgrims make their way to the **St-Stephan-Kirche** *(bistummainz.de/pfarrei/mainz-st-stephan)* every year. This would be just another Gothic church rebuilt after WWII were it not for the nine brilliant-blue stained-glass windows created by the Jewish artist Marc Chagall in the final years of his life, which serve as a symbol of Jewish–Christian reconciliation. Pick up an audio guide inside the church to learn more about each individual artwork.

Marvel at the Mainz markets

Three times a week year-round, open-air markets fill the pretty squares around **Mainzer Dom** *(bistummainz.de/mainzer-dom),* the city's immense 12th-century cathedral built from deep-red sandstone blocks. Many of the stall-holders have been selling local produce, smoked meats and more at these markets for generations. On Saturdays from March to November, you can enjoy the **Market Breakfast** with Mainz winegrowers. In front of the cathedral, treat yourself to a *Worscht un Woi,* a sausage served with a roll and wine. In December, these markets become even more festive, with Christmas shopping, holiday-themed stalls and carol music.

Heidelberg

TIME FROM FRANKFURT: **1HR**

A majestic hilltop castle

Hit the Romantic Road for Heidelberg's Altstadt and the ruined Renaissance **Schloss Heidelberg** (*schloss-heidelberg.de; adult/child €11/5.50*). The castle gardens are worth strolling for views of the Neckar River and the Altstadt rooftop. The castle cellar is also home to the **Heidelberg Tun (Großes Fass)**, the world's biggest wine barrel. The Schlossticket combines entrance to the castle and a ride on the **Bergbahn** funicular railway (a steep walk up is also an option).

Rüdesheim am Rhein

TIME FROM FRANKFURT: **1HR**

It's wine o'clock

Although Rüdesheim is an unofficial starting point on a journey up the Rhine (day-tripping coach tourists abound), it stays surprisingly small and maintains its old medieval charms. Explore the kitschy, colourful town centre and, especially, the famously narrow medieval alley **Drosselgasse**.

Rüdesheim is primarily a winemaking town and its vineyards are UNESCO-listed. The town has its own delicious white variety, called the Rheingauer Riesling, which you can sample at **RheinWeinWelt** (*rheinweinwelt.de*).

Koblenz

TIME FROM FRANKFURT: **1½HR**

Fall in love with Festung Ehrenbreitstein

Perched 118m above the Rhine, the **Festung Ehrenbreitstein** (*Ehrenbreitstein Fortress; tor-zum-welterbe.de/festung -ehrenbreitstein; adult/child €10/5.50*) was indestructible for decades until Napoleonic troops arrived. To prove a point, the Prussians rebuilt it as one of Europe's mightiest fortifications. Inside, there are several museums and fabulous views from its ramparts and viewing platform, from where you can see the confluence of the Rhine and Moselle rivers. The most fun way to travel up is the **Seilbahn** (*seilbahn-koblenz.de; one-way adult/child €12/6*) cable car.

Where the rivers meet

At the point of confluence of the Moselle and the Rhine, the **Deutsches Eck** (German Corner) is a testament to German unity lost and found. The stone pedestal links up to a grassy promenade for the most perfect riverside stroll.

TASTE THE WINE ROUTE

One of Germany's oldest tour routes, the **Deutsche Weinstrasse** (German Wine Route) traverses the heart of the Palatinate (Pfalz) – a region of vine-covered hillsides, rambling forests, ruined castles, 35 picturesque hamlets and thriving fruit orchards. The drive is especially pretty during spring (March to mid-May) and harvest (September to October). Starting in Schweigen-Rechtenbach, on the French border, the route winds north for 85km to Bockenheim an der Weinstrasse, although it can be driven in either direction. Key stops along the way include the postcard-perfect medieval Riesling villages of **Bacharach** and **Oberwesel**, as well as fairy-tale landmarks in **St Goar**.

Places We Love to Stay

€ Budget €€ Midrange €€€ Top End

Berlin MAP p255, p261 & p264

Generator Berlin Alexanderplatz € Huge and high-energy, this modern designer hostel has cheerfully painted private rooms and dorms, plus industrial-chic public areas.

Kiez Hostel € Central, squeaky-clean base with a welcoming homey vibe and imaginatively designed dorms, but limited check-in hours.

Cosmo Hotel €€ The lobby's extravagant lamps and armchairs set the tone for crisply angular rooms with silvery design accents and floor-to-ceiling windows.

Park Inn by Radisson Berlin Alexanderplatz €€ This sleek tower is honeycombed with 1029 generic but comfy rooms featuring panoramic windows, wooden floors and noiseless air-con.

Myer's Hotel Berlin €€ Feeling like your rich uncle's manor, this 56-room boutique hotel has antique-style rooms, a clubby bar and a cosy cellar spa.

Sly Berlin €€ Modern luxury meets local flair across four revamped factory-era buildings, anchored by a lush atrium and crowned with a rooftop sauna.

Hotel Château Royal €€€ Hip and haute boutique hotel in two listed buildings and a Chipperfield-designed annex features elegant rooms and site-specific art throughout.

Soho House Berlin €€€ This celeb-fave offers vintage-styled rooms in multiple sizes and access to members-only areas like the spa and rooftop pool.

Cologne MAP p268

Hostel die Wohngemeinschaft € This next-gen hostel turned creative space has smartly designed rooms with themes from spaceship to Bollywood.

Hotel Chelsea €€ Originals created by international artists, in exchange for lodging, grace the public areas and 39 rooms, including the eye-catching deconstructivist top floor.

Wasserturm Hotel Cologne €€€ A-list sanctuary in a landmark water tower with quirky-luxe design, top gym and rooftop bar.

Düsseldorf MAP p273

Max Hotel Garni € Modern self-check-in hotel near the Hauptbahnhof is a solid bargain base, with 11 snug but comfortable and quiet rooms.

Ruby Coco Hotel €€ 'Lean luxury' hotel with rooftop terrace, channeling Coco Chanel in rooms with glass-fronted shower cubicles.

Hotel Orangerie €€€ Stylish refuge in a neoclassical mansion in a quiet corner of the Altstadt within staggering distance of pubs, the river and museums.

Hamburg MAP p276

Superbude St Georg € Design hotel-hostel combo with comfy beds, sleek private bathrooms and a 'rock star suite' – another location in St Georg near Central Station.

Henri Hotel €€ Kidney-shaped tables, plush armchairs, vintage typewriters – 1950s chic à la Don Draper. Rooms and studios for urban lifestyle junkies.

Westin Hamburg €€€ Hamburg's premier address, inside the lower half of the Elbphilharmonie. Rooms are stylish and minimalist. Splurge on an upper-floor room with city or harbour views.

Munich MAP p282

Flushing Meadows €€ Up-to-the-minute minimalist design on the top two floors of an industrial building in the hip Glockenbachviertel. There are views, designer styling and a restaurant to enjoy.

Gästehaus Englischer Garten €€ Occupying a 200-year-old ivy-clad mill, this small guesthouse on the edge of the English Garden offers an intimate, pre-millennium experience in individually done-out, antique-speckled rooms.

Das Kleine Hotel in München €€ There's a dearth of accommodation in Maxvorstadt, so this 'little hotel in Munich' with its parquet floors, slightly dated fabrics and art sprinkled throughout is a well-used but welcome place to unpack.

Bayerischer Hof €€€ In a super-central location since 1841, this is one of the grandes dames of the Munich hotel world. Elegant rooms, impeccably regimented staff, antique-dotted public spaces and five fabulous restaurants.

Garmisch-Partenkirchen

Reindl's Partenkirchner Hof €€ Five-star everything here includes wine bar, gourmet restaurant and folk-themed rooms.

Gasthof zum Rassen €€
Behind a 14th-century frescoed facade, this guesthouse has modern rooms, antique public areas and Bavaria's oldest folk theatre.

Rothenburg ob der Tauber

Hotel Herrnschlösschen €€€
Occupying a 900-year-old Rothenburg mansion, this top-class hotel is a blend of ancient and new, Gothic and faux-retro.

Altfränkische Weinstube €€€
This 650-year-old Rothenburg inn has heaps of medieval character and an excellent restaurant.

Würzburg

Hotel Zum Winzermännle €€
Family-run converted winery in the heart of Würzburg with old-fashioned rooms, some with balconies.

Hotel Rebstock €€€
Würzburg's best hotel inhabits a renovated rococo town house, with great facilities, service and Altstadt location.

Bremen

MAP p297

Prizeotel Bremen City €
Good-value hotel, with large rooms in fluorescent colours and soundproofed windows close to the station. Prices vary, but it's great value during quiet times.

Nena Hotel Bremen €€€
Design hotel on the river in the centre, with indoor pool and wellness area.

Dresden

Hostel Mondpalast €
Each playful room is designed to reflect a sign of the zodiac in this out-of-this-world hostel-bar-cafe in Neustadt.

Hotel am Terrassenufer €€
This brutalist GDR-era block looming over Altstadt features large rooms with panoramic views of the river.

Gewandhaus Hotel €€€
In Altstadt, the 18th-century trading house has sleek public areas plus beautiful and bright rooms.

Leipzig

Hostel Five Elements €
Super-central and well-equipped hostel featuring dorms, cheap

private rooms, comfy common spaces and cooking facilities.

Gwuni Mopera €€
No-nonsense rooms and an on-site restaurant-bar in a quiet courtyard across the ring road from Altstadt.

Townhouse €€€
Boutique gem with sound-sculpture lamps, Bach manuscript wallpaper and views of the Thomaskirche.

Weimar

Labyrinth Hostel €
Artist-designed rooms in an extremely friendly and well-run hostel, close to the Weimarhallen Park.

Hotel Alt Weimar €€
Good-value rooms in the former home of 19th-century occultist, archivist and architect Rudolf Steiner.

Frankfurt am Main

MAP p306

25hours Goldman €
Artfully decorated rooms in the east end, a 10-minute tram ride from Römer. Score the best deals and early check-in by booking directly. Paid parking.

Ruby Louise Hotel €€
Find a super-trendy vibe at this designer hotel featuring a rooftop terrace and reception on level 6.

Steigenberger Frankfurter Hof €€€
Luxurious rooms, full spa, bar and restaurant with outdoor dining. Perfect location-wise for exploring the city.

Bayerischer Hof, Munich

Practicalities

BALKANSCAT/SHUTTERSTOCK

HEALTH

Health care in Germany is of a high standard. German *Drogerien* (chemists) do not sell any kind of medication, not even aspirin. Even *rezeptfrei* (over-the-counter) medications for minor health concerns are only available at an *Apotheke* (pharmacy), so bring what you need along with you. Tap water is drinkable.

ELECTRICITY

Germany's electricity supply is 230V, and plugs are of the European two-round-pin type (Type C and Type F). Most sockets accept both. Three-pin sockets are not used, so you'll only need standard European adapters.

PRIVACY

Photographing individuals in public places is not allowed in Germany unless you check with the person first. This is taken very seriously. Do not take photos of children. Many nightlife establishments ban photography completely.

SMOKING

Smoking is legislated differently in every state. Some bars, pubs and cafes allow smoking. Bavaria bans it practically everywhere, while in Berlin and Hamburg smoker-friendly bars abound. Look for a sign out front reading *Raucherkneipe* (smoking bar) to indicate such establishments.

DAYS OF CLOSURE

On Sundays, Germany observes *Ruhetag* (day of rest) when supermarkets, malls and individual retailers are closed. Don't expect to get any shopping done on these days. Some supermarkets are open in major train stations – these are helpful in a pinch, though expect long queues. Museums and restaurants stay open on Sundays but they might close on a Monday and/or Tuesday (check ahead).

OPENING HOURS

Opening hours vary seasonally and between cities and villages.
Banks 9am–4pm weekdays
Bars 8pm–2am
Cafes 10am–6pm
Restaurants 11am–10pm (food until 9pm)
Shops 10am–6pm Monday to Saturday
Supermarkets 8am–8pm Monday to Saturday (earlier in rural areas)

PUBLIC HOLIDAYS

Germany observes 11 national public holidays. Additional holidays vary between states.
New Year's Day 1 January
Easter March/April; Good Friday, Easter Sunday and Easter Monday
Ascension Day 40 days after Easter

Labour Day 1 May
Whit/Pentecost Sunday and Monday 50 days after Easter
Veteran's Day 15 June
German Unity Day 3 October
Christmas Day 25 December
Boxing Day 26 December

Language

German belongs to the West Germanic language family, with English and Dutch as close relatives.

Basics

Hello. Servus. *ser*-vus
Hello. Grüss Gott. grewss-got
Good morning. Guten Morgen. goo-ten *mor*-gen
Goodbye. Auf Wiedersehen. owf vee-der-zay-en
Bye. Tschüss./ Tschau. chüs/chow
Yes. Ja. yah
No. Nein. nain
Please. Bitte. *bi*-te
Thank you. Danke. *dang*-ke
Excuse me. Entschuldigung. ent-*shul*-di-gung
Sorry. Entschuldigung. ent-*shul*-di-gung

What's your name?
Wie ist Ihr Name? (pol) vee ist eer *nah*-me
Wie heißt du? (inf) *vee* haist doo

My name is ...
Mein Name ist ... (pol) main *nah*-me ist ...
Ich heiße ... (inf) ikh *hai*-se ...

Do you speak English?
Sprechen Sie Englisch? (pol) *shpre*-khen zee *eng*-lish
Sprichst du Englisch? (inf) *shprikhst* doo *eng*-lish

I don't understand. Ich verstehe nicht. ikh fer-*shtay*-e nikht

Directions

Where's (the station)?
Wo ist (der Bahnhof). vor ist (der *bahn*-hawf)

What's the address?
Wie ist die Adresse? vee ist dee a-*dre*-se

Could you please write it down?
Könnten Sie das bitte aufschreiben? *kern*-ten zee das *bi*-te owf-shrai-ben

Can you show me (on the map)?
Können Sie es mir (auf der Karte) zeige *ker*-nen zee es meer (owf dair *kar*-te) *tsai*-gen

Signs

Ausgang Exit
Eingang Entrance
Damen Women
Herren Men
Heiß Hot
Kalt Cold
Offen Open
Geschlossen Closed
Kein Zutritt No Entry
Rauchen Verboten No Smoking
Verboten Prohibited

Time

What time is it? Wie spät ist es? vee shpayt ist es
It's (10) o'clock. Es ist (zehn) Uhr. es ist (tsayn) oor
morning Morgen *mor*-gen
afternoon Nachmittag *nahkh*-mi-tahk
evening Abend *ah*-bent
yesterday Gestern *ges*-tern
today Heute *hoy*-te
tomorrow Morgen *mor*-gen

Emergencies

Help! Hilfe! *hil*-fe
Go away! Gehen Sie weg! *gay*-en zee vek
I'm ill. Ich bin krank. ikh bin krangk
Call the police! Rufen Sie die Polizei! *roo*-fen zee dee po-li-*tsai*
Call a doctor! Rufen Sie einen Arzt! *roo*-fen zee *ai*-nen artst

NUMBERS	
1	eins *ains*
2	zwei *tsvai*
3	drei *drai*
4	vier *feer*
5	fünf *fünf*
6	sechs *zeks*
7	sieben *zee*-ben
8	acht *akht*
9	neun *noyn*
10	zehn *tsayn*

NIKADA/GETTY IMAGES

Frankfurt International Airport

Arriving

Most travellers arrive in Germany by air or by rail and road from neighbouring countries. Frankfurt International is Germany's busiest airport (and one of Europe's largest), servicing some 300 destinations; it's the headquarters for Germany's flag carrier, Lufthansa. Non-EU visitors will probably enter into Europe and go through customs here, even if their final stop is elsewhere.

By Air
Most large and many smaller German cities have their own airports, and numerous carriers operate domestic flights within Germany. However, unless you're flying from one end of the country to the other, planes are only marginally quicker than trains.

By Rail
Rail services link Germany with virtually every country in Europe. **Deutsche Bahn** (bahn.de) handles ticketing. In the EU's Schengen (free-movement zone) crossing borders is visa-less; there are no passport controls entering from the Netherlands, Belgium, Austria and Switzerland, among others.

MONEY
Currency: Euro (€)

CASH
Cash is king in Germany. Always carry some and plan to pay cash at places like cafes and pubs. Since the pandemic, e-payments are catching on, but setting aside smaller bills for tips and emergencies is always a good idea. Barkeepers and kiosks may gripe about big notes.

CREDIT CARDS
Plastic is essential for booking hotels and sometimes for reserving tables at high-end restaurants. In Berlin, a small yet rising number of coffee and nightlife joints only take electronic payments, too. Usually Visa and Mastercard are accepted (not American Express or Diners Club). Kiosks usually require a minimum purchase of €10.

TIPPING
Quality of service and setting dictate how Germans tip. Say either the amount you want to pay, or 'Stimmt so' for no change.

Hotels €1 to €2 per bag/cleaning day.

Restaurants Most Germans will tip 5% to 10%.

Cafes and bars Simply round up to the nearest euro.

Getting Around

For speedsters on tight schedules, driving a car on the autobahn's limitless stretches will be deeply satisfying, but parking in cities is a pain. Germany's excellent train system makes for efficient travel too – it's stress-free, you can stretch your legs and mind your carbon footprint. Last-minute bookings can be expensive during busy periods (weekends and holidays).

WERNER SPREMBERG/SHUTTERSTOCK

Public Transport
Germany's cities and larger towns have efficient public transport systems. Bigger cities such as Berlin and Munich integrate buses, trams, U-Bahn (underground) trains and S-Bahn (suburban) trains in one network. Fares are determined by zones or time travelled (sometimes both).

Car
German roads are excellent and no tolls are charged on any public roads. The country's pride and joy is its 13,000km network of autobahns (motorways). Every 40km to 60km, you'll find elaborate service areas with 24-hour petrol stations, toilets and restaurants.

Train
Intercity Express (ICE) trains are high-speed sprinters, and Regional Express (RE) are slower but more affordable public trains. Some private operators offer significantly cheaper fares, though on slower, older (and less comfortable) trains. Reserving seats is always smart.

Ridesharing
In cities, car-share apps like **Miles Mobility** (miles-mobility. com) offer renting cars by short duration or distance. Check out long-distance carpooling (travel in someone's private car in exchange for some petrol money) via **BlaBlaCar** (blablacar.com) and **Mitfahrzentrale** (mifaz.de).

Ferry
Ferries connect Germany's two seas, and provide convenient transport in its lake- and river-filled interior. Frequent ferries connect popular North and Baltic Sea islands; short-distance ferries shuttle passengers and vehicles along the Rhine and Elbe River.

DRIVING ESSENTIALS

Drive on the right

No general speed limits – usually 50km/h in urban areas, 80km/h on secondary roads, 130km/h recommended on motorways

0.05%

Blood alcohol limit is 0.05%

Researched by
Kate Armstrong

Greece

THE PLACE FOR EPIC ADVENTURES

Greece's legendary status is defined by its astonishing ancient civilisations, stunning azure seas, fresh culinary delights and mind-blowing museums.

Greece is a legendary destination in every sense. Literally speaking, it's where many myths of gods and giants originated, and it's not hard to see why. With wide skies, an island-speckled ocean and a varied and stunning terrain, it's made for adventure, relaxation and imagination.

You can evoke the essence of Ancient Greek civilisation at the Acropolis in Athens, consult the oracle at Delphi and reach lofty heights in the monasteries of Meteora in central Greece. Then wander under clear blue skies and white domes of the Cyclades, or even live out your inner knight in Rhodes' medieval Old Town. Eat your way through the local dishes in Crete and wander through fortresses and the ancient Palace of Knossos.

As for Greek cuisine? *Nostimo!* (Delicious!) Greek food is renowned across the globe for its wholesome, hearty dishes and philosophy of simple but superior-quality local ingredients, from mountain meats and coastal seafood to wild herbs and vegetables. And Greeks love eating out, sharing impossibly big meals with family and friends in a drawn-out, convivial way. Whether you're eating octopus at a seaside table or sampling a contemporary lamb recipe under the floodlit Acropolis, dining out in Greece is never just about what you eat but the whole sensory experience.

Finally, whether you're after beaches, ancient sites, mountain walks or city life, Greece has you covered.

IMARZI/SHUTTERSTOCK

THE MAIN AREAS

ATHENS
Greece's riveting, ancient capital.
p324

CENTRAL & NORTHERN GREECE
Full of history, with Greece's coolest city.
p330

PELOPONNESE
Filled with amazing archaeological sites.
p336

CYCLADES
Blue, white, gorgeous and ever popular.
p340

For places to stay in Greece, see p356

MIKHAIL MARKOVSKIY/SHUTTERSTOCK

Left: Grilled octopus; Above: Ancient Delphi (p331)

DODECANESE
A stunning array of
history and beauty.
p343

CORFU
A pearl of the
Ionian Islands.
p348

CRETE
Cretan cuisine, Minoan
civilisation and fun.
p352

0 — 100 km
0 — 50 miles

Central & Northern Greece, p330

The focus is Meteora, famous for its Byzantine monasteries; Delphi, the centre of the ancient world; and Thessaloniki, Greece's creative city-by-the-sea.

Corfu, p340

Stroll atmospheric alleys between two fortresses, and explore world-class museums and gilded churches, all set against Venetian, French and British architecture.

Peloponnese, p336

Home to Nafplio, Greece's first capital, amazing archaeological sites of Mycenae and Epidavros, and Ancient Olympia, the spiritual home of the modern Olympics.

BULGARIA

NORTH MACEDONIA
Prilep
Ohrid
Lake Ohrid
Lake Prespa
Bitola
Gevgelija
Doirani
Kerkini Reservoir
Sidirokastro
Dra
Serres
Kave
Kajmakčalan
Edessa
Kilkis
Strimonas
Florina
Korça
Naoussa
Giannitsa
Thessaloniki
Kastoria
Veria
Alexandria
Vlorë
ALBANIA
Mt Grammos
Ptolemaïda
A2
Katerini
A24
Lecce
Mt Smolikas
Kozani
Thermaic Gulf
ITALY
Otranto
Konitsa
Grevena
Mt Olympus
Saranda
Metsovo
Moni Megalou Meteorou
A1
Corfu
Elassona
Palaio Frourio
Ioannina
Kalambaka
Corfu Town
Mon Repos
Trikala
Larissa
Achilleion Palace
A2
Igoumenitsa
Ionian Sea
Parga
Karditsa
Farsala
Volos
Paxi
Arta
A5
Skiathos
Alonn
Skopelos
Preveza
Karpenisi
A3
A1
Isteia
Skiathos Town
Lefkada Town
Lamia
Lefkada
Agios Konstantinos
Agrinio
Ancient Delphi
Mt Parnassos
A1
Halkida
Kyr
Evia
Fiskardo
Messolongi
Nafpaktos
Itea
Livadia
National Archaeolo Museum
Argostoli
Ithaki
Gulf of Corinth
Egio
Thiva
Sami
Patras
A8
Loutraki
ATHENS
Kefallonia
Xyiokastro
Acropolis
Rafin
Agios Nikolaos
A5
Kyllini
Amaliada
Corinth
A8
Piraeus
La
Zakynthos
Pirgos
Aegina Town
Acropolis Museum
Zakynthos Town
Olympia Archaeological Museum
Argos
PELOPONNESE
A7
Aegina
Poros Town
Ke
Tripoli
Nafplio
Theatre of Epidavros
Hydra Town
Kyth
Megalopoli
Astros
Spetses Town
Hydra
Kyparissia
Kalamata
Sparta
Mt Profitis Ilias
Pylos
Kardamyli
Mediterranean Sea
Gythio
Areopoli
Neapoli
Kythira
Antikythira
Vene Harb
Kissamos
Hania
Paleohora
Ho Sfak
Gavdos

Find Your Way

Given its complex geography, Greece has an extensive network of domestic flights. Ferries link all the islands. Buses run on the larger islands, and a car or motorbike is the best way to explore most islands.

CAR

Given the vastness of mainland Greece, a car is useful as it allows you to get off the beaten track. Your own wheels can be useful on islands, too, where bus services may be limited.

BOAT

Greece's extensive ferry network includes fast modern ferries and overnight boats with cabins. Departures are subject to delay during poor weather. Schedules change annually, and services are greatly reduced between mid-October and Easter. In high season, book ahead. For schedules and tickets, *ferryhopper.com* is reliable.

BUS

The bus network on larger islands and in Athens is comprehensive and fares are cheap; buy tickets at the office (sometimes on board). Corfu (and some other Ionian islands) can be reached from Athens by bus – the fare includes ferry ticket price. Village services can be more limited.

Athens, p324

Ogle world-renowned treasures in one of the cradles of civilisation, from the Acropolis to the historic backstreets.

Cyclades, p352

Be mesmerised by white-and-blue architecture, dramatic cliffs and epic sunsets. The largest island, Naxos, has ancient ruins, mountain hamlets and white-sand beaches.

Dodecanese, p343

The historic centre of the Dodecanese, Rhodes Town is a medieval time capsule, while Kos Town is a charmer, with fabulous ancient ruins and more.

Crete, p348

Explore Minoan culture at the Palace of Knossos, enjoy the best of fresh and local Cretan cuisine, and hike through gorges to open sea.

Evros (Maritsa)
vdiv
Haskovo
Edirne
Kârdzhali
Orestiada
Didymotiho
Xanthi
Komotini
A2
asos
wn
Alexandroupoli
nasos
Samothraki
TURKEY
Keşan

Imvros (Gökçeada)
Limnos
rina
Agios
fstratios
Aegean
Sea
vros
wn
Molyvos
Ayvalık
Lesvos
Mytilini
Town
Psara
Chios
Aliağa
İzmir
Chios Town
Çeşme
Cyclades
Andros
Gavrio
Hora
Tinos (Tinos)
oupoli
vros
Hora
(Mykonos)
Mykonos
Delos
Patmos
Aegean
Sea
ifos
Parikia
Hora
(Naxos)
nos
Paros
Naxos
Antiparos
Amorgos
Sikinos Ios
Museum of
Prehistoric
Thera
legandros
Fira
Anafi
Red
(Kokkini)
Beach
Santorini
(Thira)
Samos
Ikaria
Vathy
(Samos
Town)
Miletus
Kuşadası
Aydın
TURKEY
Milas
Leros
Kalymnos
Bodrum
Asklepieion
Kos Town
Kos
Astypalea
Nisyros
Tilos
Symi
Rhodes Town
Street of
the Knights
Dodecanese
Halki
Rhodes
Lindos
Kastellorizo
(Megiste)
Sea of
Crete
Karpathos
Diafani
Crete
Heraklion
Archaeological
Museum
Kasos
Pigadia
hymno
Iraklio
Agios
Nikolaos
Sitia
as
Mt
Psiloritis
Agia
Galini
Ierapetra
Mediterranean
Sea

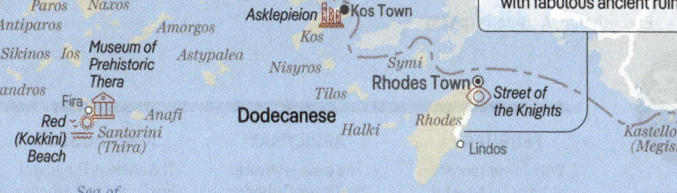

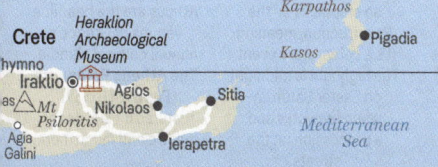

Plan Your Time

You can choose to spend more time in Athens and visit just one (or two) islands, or go crazy and do a ferry-heavy (or flight-focused) whirlwind trip to get a taste beyond the mainland.

Erechtheion, Acropolis (p325)

YASEMIN OZDEMIR/SHUTTERSTOCK

Mainland Greece in a Week

● Spend two days in the Greek capital, meandering around **central Athens** (p324) and visiting the **Acropolis** (p325), the **Acropolis Museum** (p326) and the Plaka district.

● Then catch the bus to **Delphi** (p330) and enjoy the sacred ruins. Alternatively, head to **Meteora** (p332) to visit the monasteries before hiking through the surreal landscape (connections are difficult and time-consuming between Delphi and Meteora).

● Afterwards, catch another bus to **Thessaloniki** (p333) and indulge in the city's restaurants, museums and artistic spaces, before returning to Athens. Another mainland itinerary option is to take the bus from Athens to **Nafplio** (p334). Explore the historic town and surrounding archaeological sites before heading west to **Ancient Olympia** (p339).

SEASONAL HIGHLIGHTS

Greece is a year-round destination. Many islands are 'closed' during winter. What you're looking for should dictate when you go.

FEBRUARY

With fewer tourists, it's a great time for sightseeing – you won't have to push through crowds at the major sights like the Acropolis or Roman Agora in Athens.

APRIL/MAY

The main festival in the Greek Orthodox calendar, **Easter** has an emphasis on the Resurrection, meaning it's a celebratory event. The highlight is midnight on Easter Saturday, when fireworks and a procession hit the streets.

JUNE/AUGUST

The ancient Theatre of Epidavros and Athens' Odeon of Herodes Atticus are the headline venues of Greece's annual cultural shindig. The **Athens Epidaurus Festival** (p339) features music, dance, theatre and much more.

Two Weeks to Explore

● Follow the **Athens** (p324) itinerary, then on day three catch the bus to **Delphi** (p330) for a night to experience the sacred ruins, and return to Athens.

● Next, fly to **Corfu** (p348) and spend several days exploring the Old Town and the **Achilleion Palace** (p351) before enjoying a beach day. Take a one-hour ferry to **Paxi** (p351) where you can relax for a day or two amid the olive groves, seaside villages and beach coves.

● Return to Corfu and take the ferry to Igoumenitsa, where you can catch a bus to Kalambaka (via Ioannina) for **Meteora** (p332). Fill two days with visits to the rock monasteries and outdoor pursuits before heading back to Athens.

Ten Days to Travel Around

● Start on Crete by flying in to **Hania** (p353). Spend a day strolling the Venetian fortifications or people-watching from a cafe by its charming harbour. Enjoy a day trekking the **Samaria Gorge** (p355) and another day at the Minoan ruins of **Knossos** (p355) and the state-of-the-art **Heraklion Archaeological Museum** (p354) in Iraklio.

● From Iraklio, either fly to **Rhodes** (p344) or get the twice-weekly, 11-hour ferry (less time from Sitia). On historic Rhodes, explore its atmospheric medieval **Old Town** (p345).

● To end your journey, take a three- to five-hour ferry ride to the island of **Kos** (p346). Here, experience its own ancient Old Town, before venturing out to beaches and archaeological sites.

SEPTEMBER

In early September, sample widely at the **wine festival** (p338) that celebrates the Nemea region's *agiorgitiko* red grape with tastings, concerts and more.

OCTOBER

A simple 'no' (ohi in Greek) was the famous response when Mussolini demanded passage for his troops on 28 October 1940. Now, **Ohi Day** is a national holiday with remembrance services and parades.

NOVEMBER

Around 150 films are crammed into 11 days of screenings, alongside concerts, exhibitions, talks and theatrical performances at the **Thessaloniki Film Festival** (p335).

DECEMBER/ JANUARY

This season brings joyful, light-festooned harbours, honey cookies and good cheer. New Year's Day brings the **Feast of Agios Vasilios** (St Basil), a church ceremony. This is time for the *vasilopita* (cake with a lucky coin).

Athens

ANCIENT LANDMARKS | ARCHITECTURE | CONTEMPORARY CULTURE

 TOP TIP

You could skip all the sights in Athens and still feel you have the city's pulse just by strolling along the pedestrian Dionysiou Areopagitou street around sundown. Lights glow on the Acropolis above, and the road is filled with tourists, snack vendors, musicians and local couples out for a promenade.

Cradle of European civilisation and democracy, Athens is a master of reinvention, serving a thrilling mashup of architectural gravitas, bodacious street life and inspiring creativity. With both grace and grunge, Athens creates a heady mix of ancient history and contemporary cool. The cultural and social life of the city plays out amid and within ancient landmarks, and the magnificent Acropolis remains the hub around which Athens' neighbourhoods revolve. This citadel crowns a rocky outcrop with ancient temples (including the jewel, the Parthenon) and serves as a daily reminder of Greece's heritage and the city's many transformations.

With a past rooted in mythology, drama, philosophy, Byzantine churches and, more recently, the 2004 Olympic Games, the city continues to pulse with art, community spirit and political debates. It's a must for most visitors to Greece. Athens can be chaotic, but take the pressure off by people-watching at a cafe or retreating to a wooded hilltop.

GETTING AROUND

The transit system uses the **Ath.ena Ticket**, a reloadable card available from metro ticket offices and machines. Load it with credit, rides *(€1.20 each, discount for 5 or 10)* or travel pass *(24 hours/5 days €4.10/8.20)*. These exclude airport transfer. Three-day tourist tickets *(€20)* include airport transfer. Swipe at metro turnstiles or, on buses/trams, validate in the machine. One swipe gives you 90 minutes, including transfers.

The Piraeus port is massive – 12 quays from which ferries and cruises depart to most Greek island groups and the Peloponnese. The metro line 1 (green) and suburban rail line 3 (blue) from Athens terminate at gate E7. A free shuttle bus runs regularly along the northern quays inside the port from gate E7 to E1.

Direct bus X96 to Eleftherios Venizelos International Airport stops outside the metro and along the road outside the port. The T7 tram departs from outside E8. Bus 040 goes to Athens, as does express X80 (May to October).

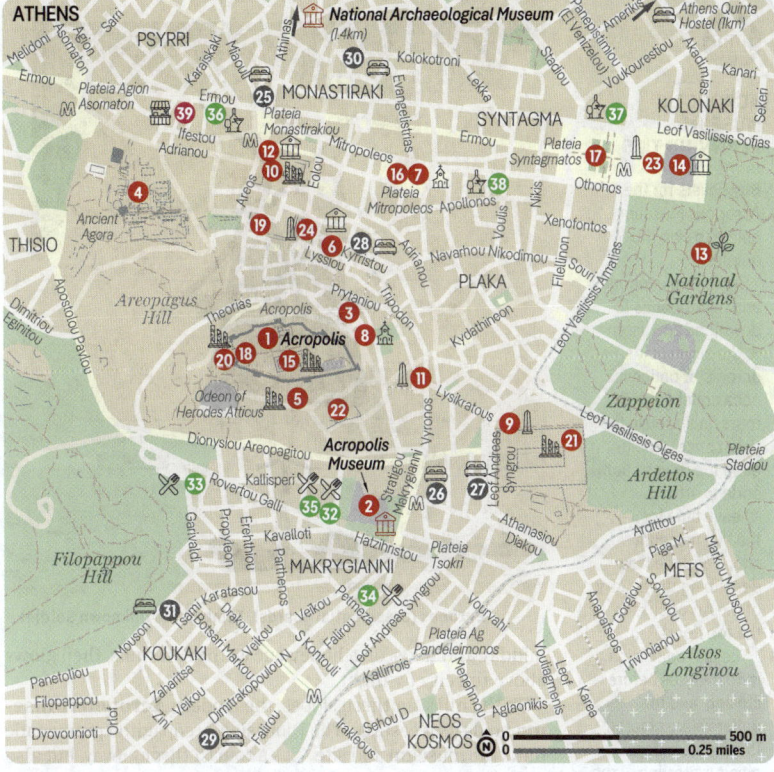

ATHENS

Athens' Crown Jewel

Epic monuments and vistas at the Acropolis

The **Acropolis** (*odysseus.culture.gr; adult/child €30/free*) is the most important ancient site in the Western world, and a glimpse of this magnificent monument cannot fail to exalt your spirit. Crowned by the Parthenon, it's visible from almost everywhere in Athens. Its marble gleams white in the

ACROPOLIS MUSEUM PLANNING TIPS

Buy tickets for the Acropolis Museum online to skip the queue.

Bring a smartphone and headphones to download and listen to the audio guide, or register online for occasional guided tours (included in the ticket price). You'll need the registration code to attend.

Leave time for the fine museum shops and the film describing the history of the Acropolis (on the top floor).

The last admission is 30 minutes before closing, and the galleries are cleared 15 minutes before closing, starting at the top floor.

The ground-floor shop and cafe are accessible without a ticket.

Every Friday and Saturday the 2nd-floor restaurant is open until midnight.

THANASIS F/SHUTTERSTOCK

Evzones (presidential guards), Tomb of the Unknown Soldier

midday and takes on a honey hue as the sun sinks, then glows above the city by night.

On the hill's southern slopes, the modern **Acropolis Museum** holds its treasures. The Dionysiou Areopagitou promenade links the museum and site – it's a tourist throughway, but also a favourite spot for locals to stroll at sundown. Entering from the southeastern entrance (near the museum), you come to the ancient **Theatre of Dionysos** before ascending the stairs towards the **Asclepieion** temple ruins. Continue on the trail and, as you climb the final steps, look up to see the **Temple of Athena Nike**. Then, like so many pilgrims before you, pass through the **Propylaia**, the monumental entrance to the Acropolis. The **Parthenon**, one of the largest Doric temples ever completed in Greece, looms before you.

Ancient Masterpieces

Admire the treasures of the Acropolis Museum

The state-of-the-art **Acropolis Museum** (*theacropolismuseum.gr; adult/child €20/free*) displays the surviving treasures

 EATING AROUND THE ACROPOLIS: STYLISH SPOTS

Mani Mani: i Dig into herb-filled cuisine from the Mani peninsula region in the Peloponnese, like seafood orzo with wild fennel. *2-11pm €€*

GH Attikos: Greek classics in a casual, airy setting with Acropolis views and an open terrace. *noon-4pm & 6-9pm Mon-Sat €€*

Ellevoro: Family-run, decorated with candles and mini-chandeliers and serving trad Greek dishes. *7pm-midnight Wed-Mon, from noon Sun €€*

Point A: Rooftop restaurant of the Herodion Hotel, with stunning Acropolis and Acropolis Museum views. *7pm-midnight €€€*

from the temple hill, with emphasis on the Acropolis as it was in the 5th century BCE, the apotheosis of Greece's artistic achievement. Layers of history are revealed and interpreted: glass floors expose subterranean ruins, and the Acropolis itself is visible through the floor-to-ceiling windows, so the masterpieces are always in context.

As you enter the museum, look down through the glass floor to view the ruins of an ancient Athenian neighbourhood that were uncovered during the museum's construction and had to be preserved and integrated into a new building plan.

The Finest Collection of Greek Antiquities

A pilgrimage to the National Archaeological Museum

Housed in an enormous 19th-century neoclassical building, the 11,000 treasures of the **National Archaeological Museum** *(namuseum.gr; adult/child €12/free)* date from prehistoric to Classical periods – a comprehensive overview of historic Greek art. It's impossible to appreciate all the exquisite sculptures, pottery, jewellery and frescoes in one go, and whatever you see will be a treat. You'll need time here to do it justice or make a beeline for the big-ticket items: the Mask of Agamemnon, Vaphio gold cups, the colossal Sounion Kouros and the Antikythera Mechanism.

Watch the Changing of the Guard

A photo op at the Tomb of the Unknown Soldier

Located on Athens' principal plaza, Plateia Syntagmatos, an essential photo op is of the traditionally costumed *evzones* (presidential guards) flanking the **Tomb of the Unknown Soldier**, a cenotaph dedicated to Greek soldiers killed in war, which stands just below the neoclassical **Parliament** building. Every hour, on the hour, the guard changes. On Sunday at 10.30am, a whole platoon, accompanied by a band, sets off from the Presidential Guard complex on Irodou Attikou, and marches down Vasilissis Sofias to the tomb for the 11am ceremony. The *evzones*' uniform of the fustanella (skirt) and pompom shoes reflects the attire worn by the klephts, the mountain fighters of the War of Independence.

GUIDED TOURS

On Foot: Athens Walking Tours *(athenswalkingtours. gr)* and **Alternative Athens** *(alternative athens.com)* have expert guides. **This is Athens** *(thisisathens. org)* has a free program to team up visitors with locals for themed walks.

By Bike: E-bike tours by **We Bike Athens** *(webikeathens.gr)* in Thisio, **Solebike** *(solebike.eu)* near the Acropolis and **Roll in Athens** *(facebook. com/rollinathens)* near Syntagma take the strain out of pedalling uphill. **Coco-Mat.Bike Tours** *(coco-mat. bike)* in Gazi gains cool points for unique ash-wood-frame bikes (regular and e-bikes). Or rent your own bike at **Funky Ride** *(funkyride.gr)*.

On the Bus: Hop-on, hop-off with **City Sightseeing Athens** *(city-sightseeing.com)* or **Athens Happy Train** *(athenshappy train.com)*.

DRINKING IN MONASTIRAKI & SYNTAGMA: ROOFTOP BARS

| **A for Athens:** The rooftop cafe-bar at this Monastiraki hotel is grand, with sweeping 360-degree views. *4pm-midnight* | **Couleur Locale:** In a Monastiraki arcade, this all-day bar-restaurant has Acropolis views. *10am-2am Sun-Thu, to 3am Fri & Sat* | **Metropolis Roof Garden:** Head to the top of luxe Electra Metropolis Athens Hotel for creative cocktails and inventive cuisine. *1-6pm & 7-11pm* | **GB Roof Garden:** Glam it up on the top of the Grande Bretagne Hotel on Plateia Syntagmatos, with radiant Acropolis views. *1pm-2am* |

THE GUIDE

ATHENS GREECE

Central Athens Meander

Boisterous, monument-packed central Athens is best explored on foot. The historic centre and the main archaeological sites, major landmarks, museums and attractions, are quite close to one another. The main civic hub of Athens, Plateia Syntagmatos, merges into the historic Plaka and Monastiraki neighbourhoods, which mesh one into the next and make for a super stroll (3km, three hours) for soaking up the city-centre history and life.

❶ Plateia Syntagmatos

Plateia Syntagmatos, considered the centre of Athens, has been a favourite place for protests since the rally that led to the granting of a constitution on 3 September 1843. Time your visit with the hourly changing of the guard at the **Tomb of the Unknown Soldier** (p327) in front of Parliament.

❷ Temple of Olympian Zeus

Stroll through the lush **National Gardens**, exiting south to the striking **Temple of Olympian Zeus** or what remains of the largest temple ever built. Teetering on the edge of the traffic alongside the temple, **Hadrian's Arch** is the ornate gateway marking the boundary of Hadrian's Athens.

❸ Lysikrates Monument

Cross Leoforos Vasilissis Amalias and walk up Lysikratous into Plaka. Built in 334 BCE, the **Lysikrates Monument** is the only remaining example of monuments that once lined this street to the **Theatre of Dionysos** (p326), site of dramatic contests.

PIC MEDIA AUS/SHUTTERSTOCK

Temple of Olympian Zeus

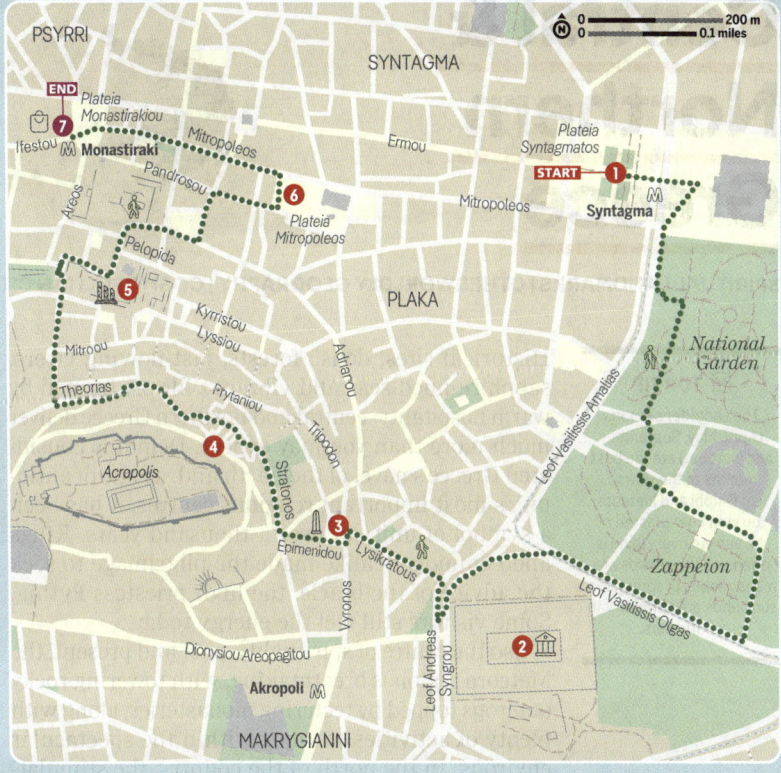

The monument commemorates one chorus' victory.

④ Anafiotika

Ascend the Epimenidou steps, turn right into Stratonos, and **Church of St George of the Rock** marks the entry to **Anafiotika**, a picturesque maze of whitewashed houses. Explore a bit, then emerge at Theorias road, above the old Athens University (1837–41). Descend on pedestrianised Diaskouron for views of the **Ancient Agora**.

⑤ Roman Agora

Descend as far as the ruins of the **Roman Agora** where you can see its **Tower of the Winds**, a classical time-and-weather station. Across the road, duck into **Bath House of the Winds**, a historical Turkish *hammam*. Northeast of the Roman Agora, the ruins of **Hadrian's Library** sit next to 1759 **Mosque of Tzistarakis**.

⑥ Plateia Mitropoleos

Jaunt north to **Plateia Mitropoleos**, where you'll find Athens Cathedral and its smaller, more historically significant neighbour, 12th-century **Church of Agios Eleftherios**, which was built from pieces of ancient temples and earlier Christian monuments.

⑦ Monastiraki Flea Market

Cruise up Mitropoleos and you'll reach colourful, chaotic Plateia Monastirakiou. To the left, down Ifestou, is **Monastiraki Flea Market**, a gateway to shopping throughout the district.

Central & Northern Greece

SPIRITUAL LANDMARKS | OTHERWORLDLY GEOGRAPHY | COSMOPOLITAN CITY

☑ TOP TIP

The shoulder seasons (April, May, September and October) are the best months of the year to visit Delphi and Meteora. You won't get blasted by the sun yet everything is open and the crowds are manageable. In spring, the surrounds are abloom with wildflowers.

Historical sites, dense forests, fast-flowing rivers, sapphire-hued seas and vibrant villages framed by warm hospitality: central and northern Greece deliver much more than you may expect. Delphi is considered Greece's navel of the Earth and, as one of antiquity's most important religious centres, it has been a symbol of unity of over a thousand years. Kings and commoners alike made the pilgrimage to seek the advice of the oracle, the high priestess Pythia. Some visitors still feel the energy today.

Also the centre of spirituality, past and present, the Meteora region is breathtaking, with towering rocky outcrops topped by teetering monasteries, along with plenty of activities to enjoy within the spectacular environs. In the north of the country, the stimulating and stylish city of Thessaloniki always surprises and is considered Greece's most cosmopolitan city (shhh, don't tell the Athenians). Expect excellent cuisine, bars and shopping here, too.

Delphi

Legend has it that Zeus released two eagles from opposing ends of the Earth to locate its centre. They crossed paths above Delphi. In the 8th century BCE, the cult of Apollo was established here. Leaders and commoners alike from the Mediterranean and Asia Minor made the pilgrimage to the oracle of sacred Delphi to consult a mysterious high priestess, Pythia,

 GETTING AROUND

Central Greece is the country's largest region. Meteora (Kalambaka) is easily reached by train from Athens; for Delphi, catch a direct KTEL bus from Athens' Liosion bus terminal. Connections between Delphi and Meteora are surprisingly tricky. There are limited bus services, though these are long and you must change at Trikala, 22km east of Kalambaka. For exploring central Greece, having a car is best as it allows you to reach historical sites, remote mountain villages and far-flung beaches.

CENTRAL & NORTHERN GREECE

who prophesied on everything from matters of the heart to a city-state's decision to go to war. The joy of staying right in the town of Delphi is that you can easily walk to all the ancient sites and museums.

One of Greece's top sights

As you ascend the archaeological site of **Ancient Delphi** *(odysseus.culture.gr; incl museum adult/child €20/free)*, look out across the olive-grove-carpeted valley and Gulf of Corinth below, close your eyes and tap into Delphi's divine energy. Get here early to avoid the crowds, take snacks and water. And time!

Like the original pilgrims, start your visit at the **Sanctuary of Athena Pronaia**, a 20-minute walk east past the region's highlights while taking in the sweeping views down to the Gulf of Corinth. The fenced site is always open. You'll pass the **Castalian Spring**, a sacred source for Delphi.

You can scamper about the hilly site in a sweat-soaked, manic hour, but why? It's better to take it slow, ponder the many individual features and tease out the surviving nuances. Gaze out over the views and find quiet, shady spots to contemplate the deep meaning it has held over the millennia. Just thinking of the countless feet that have trod the **Sacred Way** and who they've belonged to, will give all but the dullest minds pause.

Taking a tour with a local guide is a wonderful way to evoke the sense of place. Try English-speaking **Penny Kolomvotsou** *(kpagona@hotmail.com)*.

Treasures and masterpieces

Save the unmissable **Delphi Archaeological Museum** *(odysseus.culture.gr; incl site adult/child €20/free)* for the afternoon, when the outdoor sites swelter in the midday sun. Entry is by time slot, so reserve ahead. You'll gain a clearer

---

APOLLO'S VOICE: THE ORACLE

Perched in the Temple of Apollo, the Delphic oracle ranked high among the sacred sites of Ancient Greece. Devotees flocked here asking for Apollo's guidance in making decisions. Wars were fought, colonies created, marriages sealed, leaders chosen and journeys begun on the strength of the oracle's advice.

Apollo's instrument of communication, the Pythia (priestess), was usually an older woman who sat on a tripod in the temple. Although there's no evidence for the theory that she inhaled vapours of ethylene from cracks in the rocks below the sanctuary, evidence shows she made her prophesies in a trancelike state.

The Pythia's pronouncements were notorious for their ambiguity, which left the interpretation up to the recipients.

METEORA'S HISTORY

The name Meteora is derived from the Greek adjective *meteoros*, meaning 'suspended in the air' (the word 'meteor' comes from the same root).

Hermit monks began inhabiting the scattered natural caverns of Meteora during the 11th century. By the 14th century, the power of the Byzantine Empire was waning, and with Turkish incursions into Greece on the rise, monks fled the bloodshed for a safe haven here.

Ruins of abandoned communities in sites that now seem utterly inaccessible dot the area. Removable ladders were used at first. Later, windlasses hauled the monks up in nets. When curious visitors asked how frequently the ropes were replaced, the monks' straight-faced reply was 'when the Lord lets them break'.

Sphinx of the Naxians, Delphi Archaeological Museum

understanding of the context of where the treasures were found. You can have a deeply rewarding visit in under two hours and you'll come away with a clearer picture of how lavish Ancient Delphi must have been and the wealth it attracted. Get more info on selected exhibits in 3D via the Digital Delphi phone app or the comprehensive *Delphi Monuments and Museum* by Photios M Petsas.

The collection starts with some impressive bronze works: a bronze figurine believed to depict Apollo, the forerunner of stone-carved *kouros* statues; the **Sphinx of the Naxians** (560 BCE), with the face of a woman, the body of a lion and the wings of a bird; and the crown jewel, the life-size **Bronze Charioteer** (478–474 BCE).

Meteora

Meteora's otherworldly stone pillars rise up vertically from the vast Thessaly plain. This geological marvel came about some 11 million years ago: earthquakes, wind and rain gradually sculpted a mass of rocks, sand and sediment. It's hard to comprehend how monasteries were built atop these precipitous cliffs and into rockfaces.

Has a fabulous beer menu of regional brews!

 EATING IN DELPHI: OUR PICKS

Taverna Gargadoyas: Welcoming, no-frills traditional taverna at the west end of town, serving great grilled meats. *1-11pm* €

Dion Tavern: Classic Greek dishes, like rice-stuffed tomatoes and souvlaki, are well executed. Tables inside and out; stark decor. *noon-11pm* €

Taverna Vakhos: Well-crafted Greek fare, including vegan dishes; seasonal artichokes and mountain herbs from the garden. *noon-10.30pm* €

To Patriko Mas: Elevated views to go with the elevated Mediterranean fare. Game casseroles are a speciality. *noon-3pm & 6-10pm* €€

Free-climbing, cave-dwelling ascetics were the first to make Meteora home in the 11th century. Deemed a holy place, Meteora was where the first Orthodox monastic communities formed in the 12th century. At its peak, 24 monasteries were hosted here; today, six remain active and open to visitors in this UNESCO-listed destination.

Moseying about monasteries

There's enough variation between the opening hours of Meteora's monasteries that crafting an itinerary is a bit like a jigsaw puzzle. As always, try to hit top sights such as Moni Megalou Meteorou as early as possible.

All six of Meteora's monasteries – **Moni Megalou Meteorou**, **Moni Varlaam**, **Moni Agiou Stefanou**, **Moni Agias Varvaras Rousanou**, **Moni Agias Triadas** and **Moni Agiou Nikolaou Anapafsa** – are impressive in their own way. With precision planning, you might see four in one day, but this would be a stunt. To enter the monasteries, visitors are required to cover their shoulders and legs; shawls are available to buy or borrow at most monasteries. Be prepared to scale between 140 and 300 steps at all but the accessible Moni Agiou Stefanou.

Each monastery charges the same admission *(adult/child €5/free)*. Good sources of information include **Visit Meteora** *(visitmeteora.travel)* and the **Kalambaka Tourist Office** *(infotouristmeteora.gr)*.

Thessaloniki

Map p334

It's easy to fall in love with Thessaloniki. Greece's second-largest (and arguably coolest) city is built along the water, and the view over the Aegean Sea to snowcapped Mt Olympus is superb. Old and new coexist in architectural anarchy: here, the ruins of Byzantine churches give way to 1960s apartment blocks, and Ottoman-era *hammams* and historic buildings have been repurposed into art spaces, cafes, bars and shops.

Boardwalk empire and people-watching

Walking along the waterfront promenade is a way of life in Thessaloniki. It even has its own word in Greek: *volta*. Start walking the Nea Paralia from the port, where a crop of new cafes and restaurants have opened up in this once seedy area. Head towards the 15th-century **White Tower** *(lpth.gr; adult/child €6/free)*, Thessaloniki's most iconic image, and continue to the strikingly contemporary **Thessaloniki Concert Hall**. The total distance is 3.5km.

BEST ACTIVITIES IN METEORA

To arrange these, see visitmeteora.travel.

Hike to hermit caves: Trace the routes of the earliest monks on a trek to cave hermitages and chapels. Guides offer more options.

Mountain biking: Fly along oak-forest trails, across rockfaces and through a verdant valley, all while glimpsing stellar views.

Rock climbing: Navigate adventurous climbing routes with local experts. Residents hit the rocks in April on the feast day of St George.

Paragliding: Soar above Meteora's towering columns of rock on a tandem or motorised paragliding flight.

Meteora Photo Tour: Venture to out-of-the-way spots that capture the colossal rock columns and monasteries in their best light.

EATING & DRINKING IN KASTRAKI & KALAMBAKA: OUR PICKS

Taverna Gardenia: Kastraki taverna with a huge front patio and snug old-fashioned interior. Open-air grill/spit-roast mains. *12.30-11pm* €

Qastiro: Stylish wine bar in Kastraki serving Med-accented meals from a short menu. Enjoy quality coffee on the stone terrace. *10am-midnight* €€

Fortounis Tsipouradiko: Long-standing Kalambaka *ouzerie* (place serving ouzo and food) that gets a lively, late crowd. *11am-midnight* €

Ambrosia Taverna: Modern Greek place in Kalambaka that does creative fresh fare served with aplomb. Fine wine list. *noon-11pm* €€

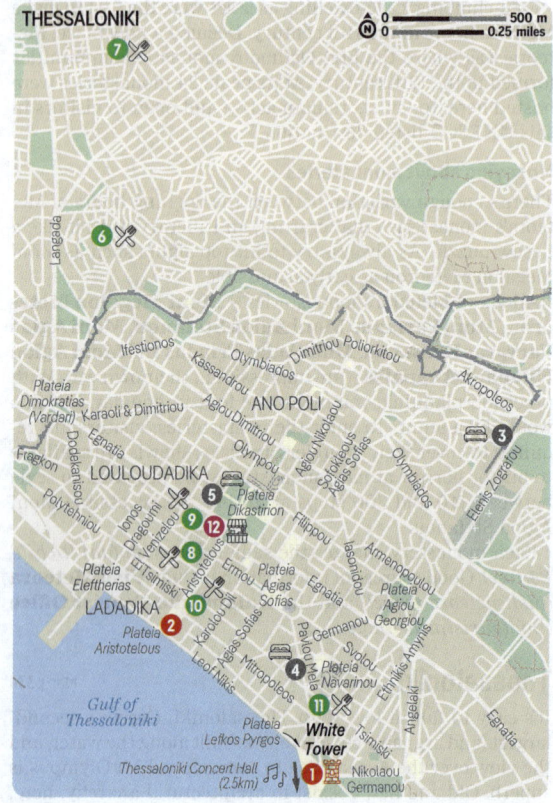

THESSALONIKI

HIGHLIGHTS
1 White Tower

SIGHTS
2 Plateia Aristotelous

SLEEPING
3 Little Big House
4 Trilogy House
5 Zeus is Loose

EATING
6 Bougatsa Bantis
7 Milano Bakery
8 Modiano Market
9 Stou Mitsou
10 Terkenlis
11 Trigona Elenidis

SHOPPING
12 Kapani Markete

Afterwards, relax in **Plateia Aristotelous**, Thessaloniki's heartbeat. It's a cross between a Parisian boulevard, Bologna's covered arcades and Venice's Piazza San Marco, with an unmistakably Greek flair. Elsewhere, the port of Thessaloniki is the city's hotbed for contemporary art. Just up from the port is the **Ladadika** neighbourhood, where former brick warehouses have been converted into tavernas, cafes and bars.

Thessaloniki's markets

Rich in both history and culinary delights, Thessaloniki is a city that can be best appreciated through its markets.

 EATING IN THESSALONIKI: BEST PASTRY SHOPS   MAP p334

Milano: Hands down the city's best *tiropita* (cheese pie) can be found at this bakery in the Neapoli neighbourhood. *8am-7pm* €

Trigona Elenidis: A flaky triangle stuffed with custard and dripping in sweet syrup, the *trigona* found here is a hallmark Thessaloniki dessert. *9am-11pm* €

Bougatsa Bantis: Salty cheese or sweet custard is layered in filo, cut in squares and served warm. It's the ideal breakfast. *6.30am-2.30pm* €

Terkenlis: *Tsoureki* is a slightly sweet, yeasted loaf with a mastic flavour; try it covered in chocolate and stuffed with chestnut puree. *7am-11pm* €

AIVITA ARIKA/SHUTTERSTOCK

White Tower (p333), Thessaloniki

The **Modiano Market** (_agoramodiano.com_) was originally built in 1930 by renowned local Jewish architect Eli Modiano, and quickly became the centre of daily life for Thessalonikians. Today, the revamped, cavernous, glass-and-brick structure is home to dozens of stalls, divided into 'neighborhoods' by food type. From fruits and veg to syrupy pastries to third-wave coffee, you can find almost anything here. The space is now also used for events and concerts.

Food lovers should make a beeline for the **Kapani Market** (_kapani.gr_). Located in the city centre, this is the place to stock up on Greek products like mountain tea, mastic from Chios and pine-tree honey. In addition to non-perishables, you can stroll through the fresh fish and meat sections. Grab lunch at **Stou Mitsou**, a _tsipouradiko_ selling delicious grilled and fried dishes between the market stalls.

LIGHTS, CAMERA, ACTION

Each year, Thessaloniki hosts its **international film festival**, the most important silver-screen event in the country. First launched in 1960 as a national film festival, it has adapted to the times: in its earliest years, it focused on New Greek Cinema, and then, following the end of Greece's military dictatorship, the festival promoted much more political cinema. These days, the focus is still on arthouse cinema, with an emphasis on voices from the Balkans. For 11 days each November, the city is awash in screenings, premieres, lively talks and discussions. It's an event cinephiles shouldn't miss. See _filmfestival.gr_ for more info.

Peloponnese

ARCHAEOLOGICAL WONDERS | ANCIENT OLYMPIA | MYTHICAL MOMENTS

☑ **TOP TIP**

Nafplio is a good base from which to explore the sites of Mycenae and Epidavros; for Ancient Olympia, it's best to spend a night or two in Olympia.

With secluded beach coves, bucolic cypress forests, lofty peaks and concealed villages, mainland Peloponnese has the charm of a seasonal island all year round. The region is legendary – fables are central to its culture and landscape. It's where many a Greek god and human hero performed their deeds in historical sites, classical temples, Mycenaean palaces, Byzantine cities and Venetian fortresses. You can commune with the ghost of Agamemnon at Mycenae, a once-great civilisation, or test your sprinting skills at Ancient Olympia, spiritual home of the Olympics. Or recite the lines of Oedipus at the Theatre of Epidavros and be captivated by Mystras where the Byzantine civilisation ended in the 14th century. If 'ancient' isn't your thing, explore the natural surroundings instead. The region's cuisine is among the best in Greece thanks to its fresh seafood, mountain meats and wild greens. The Peloponnese has the best of everything.

Nafplio

Explore the Old Town Nafplio

Nafplio is one of Greece's prettiest towns and admirers revel in its knockout waterside location. The town is a sum of its

GETTING AROUND

The Peloponnese is one of Greece's largests region with distinct sub-areas and varied topography. Various KTEL bus networks link main towns and remote villages throughout the region. Buses run from Athens to both Nafplio and Ancient Olympia. For the former, you can take a direct bus or, if you're in or near the Peloponnese, you can change at the interchange known as KTEL Isthmus, located near the Corinth Canal and gateway to the

region. Similarly, to get to Ancient Olympia from Nafplio, you'll need to head first to KTEL Isthmus and change buses at Pyrgos, from where you can get a small train or bus to Olympia. Apart from this train, the main train network no longer operates in the region, except for the *proastiako*, a handy suburban network that runs between Athens Airport and Kiato, on the outskirts of Corinth (town). For remote regions, having your own wheels allows you more access.

PELOPONNESE

Nafpaktos
Patra
Kato Achaia
Kyllini
Vardha
Amaliada
Pyrgos
Ancient Olympia
Zacharo
Kyparissia
Filiatra
Meligalas
Marathopoli
Kalamata
Methoni
Schiza
Egio
Gulf of Corinth
Aigeira
Xylokastro Kiato
Loutraki
Megara
Corinth
Nemea Ancient Mycenae
Argos
Ligourio
Tripoli
Nafplio Epidavros
Astros Argolic Gulf
Megalopoli Kranidi
Sparta
Mt Profitis Ilias
Gythio Molai
Plitra
Lakonian Gulf
Neapoli
Ionian Sea
Messinian Gulf
Elefsina (Eleusis)
Piraeus
Aegina Town Saronic Gulf
Aegina
Galatas
Ermioni
Hydra
Spetses
Myrtoön Sea
Kopanaki

50 km
25 miles

parts: enchanting narrow streets, elegant Venetian houses and neoclassical mansions.

All alleys seem to lead to the bustling **Plateia Syntagma**, the heart of the Old Town. Here, the cafes afford views of the **Trianon**, a former mosque, the handsome former **National Bank building** (1932) and the **Archaeological Museum** *(odysseus.culture.gr; adult/child €10/free)*, a former Venetian warehouse. The outstanding collection includes bronze armour from near Mycenae.

The **Peloponnesian Folklore Foundation Museum** *(bpf. gr; adult/child €5/free)* displays Greek cultural items. Further on is **Plateia Kapodistrias**, named after Ioannis Kapodistrias, the first governor of the modern Greek state, who was murdered outside the church of Aghios Spiridonas. A block south of here is the **Land Gate**, identifiable by the lion carving. In the first Venetian occupation it was the only entrance to the city by land.

Power to the fortresses

Nafplio's imposing landmark, the citadel known as **Palamidi** *(odysseus.culture.gr; adult/child €20/free)*, stands on a 216m-high outcrop of rock. An hour or so within its walls will give you time to wander the grounds and enjoy bird's-eye views over the sea and landscape. Built by the Venetians between 1711 and 1714, the fortress is regarded as a masterpiece of military architecture. To get there, you can go by road via taxi or tackle the 911 steps that begin southeast of the bus station. Climb early or towards sunset.

Back on the waterfront, boats run the five-minute journey (half-hourly) between the waterfront and the **Bourtzi** *(incl boat ride €12)*, an islet fortress about 500m off the port. A

THE WINE ROUTES OF NEMEA

The rolling hills 37km northwest of Nafplio are part of the Nemea region, one of Greece's premier wine-producing areas that's particularly famous for its *agioritiko* grape and full-bodied reds. Look out also for wine made from *roditis*, a local variety of white grape. Nemea has been known for its fine wines since Mycenaean times, when nearby Phlius supplied the wine for the royal court at Mycenae.

There are dozens of wineries in the region. Many of these are open to the public; for tastings, most – but not all – require bookings. Visits usually include a winery tour and a tasting, sometimes with accompanying nibbles. To hop between vineyards, you'll need your own transport.

A **wine festival** in early September marks the beginning of the vintage.

MATYAS REHAK/SHUTTERSTOCK

Lion Gate, Ancient Mycenae

half-hour or so allows time to 'recreate' the events of the fortress 'of the rock'. Constructed between 1471 and 1472 by the Venetians, it helped defend the city for 350 years under different conquerors. Explanatory signs are in English.

Ancient Mycenae

Where myth and history are linked

The region's must-see historical attraction is **Ancient Mycenae** (*odysseus.culture.gr; adult/child €20/free*), 24km northwest of Nafplio, in the barren foothills of Mt Agios Ilia and Mt Zara. Ancient Mycenae was the home of the legendary King Agamemnon, ruler of the Greeks during the Trojan War. It was, for four centuries in the second millennium, the most powerful kingdom in Greece. One of Greece's most impressive ancient sites, it provides context to understanding Mycenaean influence over Ancient Greece.

KTEL buses from Athens and Nafplio drop you at Fichti village; it's an uphill slog for 3.5km to the site. It's easiest to have your own wheels.

EATING IN NAFPLIO: OUR PICKS

Pidalio: A 10-minute walk west of the Od Town, Pidalio prepares some of the best mezedhes around. Just ask locals. *1.45-11.15pm Wed-Mon* €€

I Gonia Tou Kavalari: Some of the best contemporary Greek mezedhes around, from *spetsofaï* (sausage) to *apaki* (fried pork). *noon-late* €€

To Omorfo Tavernaki: Modern twist to traditional cuisine: creative salads and excellent meats, plus tasty starters. Always busy. *11.30am-late Fri-Wed* €€

Antica Gelateria di Roma: Nafplio's original gelateria, run by Italians – as genuine as they come. Handmade on premises, any flavour is good. *9am-1am* €

Epidavros

The stage of ancient dramas

Built of limestone, yet one of the best-preserved Ancient Greek structures in existence, the late-4th-century-BCE **Theatre of Epidavros** (*argolisculture.gr; incl Sanctuary of Asclepius adult/child €20/free*) will have you singing. Part of the Sanctuary of Asclepius (an ancient health sanctuary), and considered to have played an important role in the cultural life of ancient times, it's renowned for its symmetry and amazing acoustics; a coin dropped in the theatre's centre can be heard from the highest seat. The theatre is now used for performances during the annual **Athens Epidaurus Festival** (*aefestival.gr*).

In high season, buses head here from Nafplio. If visiting by car, follow the signs to Ancient Theatre (not to P Epidavros or A Epidavros).

Ancient Olympia

In the footsteps of glory

It's worth the energy to reach Olympia, if only for one impressive site. This is **Ancient Olympia** (*odysseus.culture.gr; adult/child €20/free*), birthplace of the modern Olympic Games, where states come together for the sake of friendly competition just as they did here some 2800 years ago. This atmospheric site is also fun: sprint the 192.27m in the stadium and the ghosts of cheering crowds are guaranteed to make your skin prickle. At the ruins of the gymnasium, conjure up an aroma of sweat and oil (athletes smeared their bodies with this).

There's no right way to approach the site; the QR code at the entrance helps recreate the buildings in 3D, thereby revealing the sanctuary's former glory, and there are good information panels in Greek, English and German. But you'll need at least half a day for the site and Archaeological Museum. Archaeological or sports buffs might like one to two days to visit all museums. A guide will bring the site alive.

One ticket includes access for one day to the **Archaeological Site of Olympia**, **Olympia Archaeological Museum**, the **Museum of the History of the Olympic Games in Antiquity**, and the **Museum of the History of the Excavations in Olympia**. These are located within walking distance of the site, on the way to Olympia village.

ANCIENT OLYMPIA TIPS

Niki Vlachou is a guide and owner of **Niki Olympic Tours** (*olympictours.gr*).

What's the 'must visit' at the site? The stadium. Close your eyes and feel the energy as you imagine the young men who were trying to fulfil their dreams to become Olympic champions. You can almost 'hear' the roar of the crowds.

And the 'must see' at the museum? The East and West pediments of the temple of Zeus, like an ancient movie theatre where the statues are like actors conveying the tales.

Something people might not know about the site? When the Roman Emperor Nero competed in the games (around 67 CE), he made his own rules. In a chariot race, he fell off the chariot, yet declared himself the winner!

 DRINKING IN NAFPLIO: OUR PICKS

Allotino: The place to be seen for daytime coffee and evening cocktails. Also serves salads and club sandwiches. *8am–3am*

Mavros Gatos: Nafplio's popular hangout, especially the young and trendy, with music and good drinks. *8am–3am*

A!Ladokampos Gold: Olive oil and wine tastings (think organic wine) in this store-cum-bar run by a Greek-American. *10am–12.30am Wed–Mon*

3Sixty: A posh wine bar in a hotel of the same name, it has a more international feel, a snob factor and high-end cocktails. *9am–midnight*

Cyclades

INCREDIBLE VISTAS | BEACHES | BLUE-AND-WHITE DOMES

☑ TOP TIP

If flying, give yourself extra time when leaving from Santorini Airport as the small terminal can be mayhem. Fira can become crammed with people, especially when the cruise ships are in port.

What do you think of when you think of the perfect Greek island? Why, one of the Cyclades, of course. This circular archipelago is Greece from central casting: rugged, sun-drenched outcrops of rock anchored in turquoise waters and strewn with gleaming white hamlets and blue-domed churches. Add to that a fabulous set of culinary flavours, fantastic hiking, plentiful beaches and a good dose of sophistication, and you really get the best of Greece's ample charms.

Of all of the Cyclades, one island seems to be the principal actor. Santorini (Thira) exudes in-your-face charm, including sheer cliffs and a snowdrift of white Cycladic houses. But beauty brings admirers and the island is slammed by them in peak season (so much so that the strain on the infrastructure is a huge concern). The more relaxed alternative, Naxos, has an entrancing variety of attractions including grand beaches, mountains and a lovely historic town.

GETTING AROUND

Conventional and fast ferries connect both Santorini and Naxos with Athens' Piraeus and Rafina ports. Ferries also link the two islands (two to three hours). In Santorini, Athinios port sits at the cliff base; buses and taxis meet ferries and cart passengers up to Fira. Consult **KTEL Santorini Buses** *(ktel-santorini.gr)* for schedules and prices. May to September buses are overcrowded. Having a car is the best way to explore the island, but traffic in high season is a menace. Fira's taxi stand is on Dekigala, near the bus station.

Naxos' small airport has several daily flights to/from Athens. Buses leave from the end of the ferry quay in Hora; timetables are posted outside the bus information office. While there are frequent buses to the villages, they can take a long time to get there and back. Buy tickets from the office or the machine outside (not from the bus driver). For larger exploration, get your own wheels; taxis are useful only for short hops.

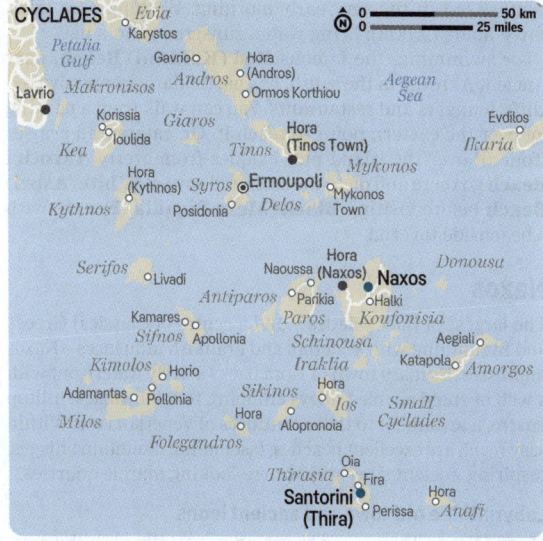

CYCLADES

Santorini (Thira)

Booming caldera town and more

Santorini's main town, **Fira**, is a busy place, its caldera edge
layered with swish cave hotels, infinity pools and restaurants.
It's backed by narrow streets packed with shops, and more
bars and restaurants. Sitting 220m below Fira – three minutes
by cable car, or 587 steps on foot – the **Old Port** (Fira Skala)
is mainly used by cruise-ship passengers visiting for a day.
Santorini Cable Car (*scc.gr; adult/child €10/5*) is swamped
with those same passengers, especially in the morning and
afternoon. Views over the multicoloured cliffs are breathtaking, and come sunset, crowds gather at the caldera edge.

Fira merges into two more villages: **Firostefani** (about a
15-minute walk north) and posher **Imerovigli** (about a half-
hour walk from Fira). All are loaded with stores – browse for
original art, ceramics, woodwork, local foodstuffs, high-end
fashion and junk. Fira is also the island's nightlife hot spot.
Nine kilometres further on, with white dwellings hewn into
the volcanic rock, **Oia** is a gleaming gem and a famous place
to watch a sunset. It, too, gets packed – your only hope is to

BEST ANCIENT SITES & MUSEUMS ON SANTORINI

Ancient Thera:
Perched on a
mountaintop, the
town was first settled
by the Dorians in the
9th century BCE and
remains a maze of
Hellenistic, Roman
and Byzantine ruins.

Ancient Akrotiri: In
1967, excavations in
Santorini's southwest
uncovered this
ancient Minoan
city buried beneath
volcanic ash from the
eruption of 1613 BCE.

**Museum of
Prehistoric Thera:**
Fira's standout has
extraordinary finds
excavated from
Akrotiri, a wealth of
Minoan frescoes,
ceramics and a
17th-century-BCE
gold ibex figurine.

Gyzi Megaron:
Displays fascinating
photographs of the
1956 earthquake,
centuries-old maps
of the Cyclades
and medieval
manuscripts.

**Archaeological
Museum:** Impressive
artefacts and marble
statues excavated
from Akrotiri and
Ancient Thera.

 EATING IN SANTORINI: OUR PICKS

Aroma Avlis: Part of the
Artemis Karamolegos
winery, this terrific
restaurant does brilliant
things with local
ingredients. *1-11pm €€*

Fistikies: Head to this
restaurant in an elegant
courtyard in Kamari for
seafood, pasta and Greek
fare. *2-11pm €€*

Pelican Kipos: Gorgeous
garden and good food in
central Fira, plus a good
selection of wines. *8am-
11.30pm €€*

To Krinaki: Superb, all-
fresh, all-local ingredients
are paired with local beer
and Santorini-grape wine;
just east of Oia. *noon-11pm
€€€*

BEST BEACHES ON NAXOS

Agios Prokopios: Sandy and shallow beach set in a sheltered bay south of Cape Mougkri.

Agia Anna: Merging with Agios Prokopios, this is a stretch of crowded white sand, with development along its length.

Glyfada and Plaka: Sandy beaches and turquoise waters, with accommodation and restaurants, perfect for a chilled-out stay.

Mikri Vigla: Golden granite boulders divide the beach into two; it's big on the kitesurfing scene, with reliable wind conditions.

Pyrgaki: Windsurfing and kitesurfing spot reachable via an unpaved road past the Aliko promontory.

Hawaii Beach: Shines with calm, limpid blue waters just north of the promontory.

venture out in the very early morning. Walking here takes three hours (9.1km); bring water, sunscreen and a hat.

For swimming, the famous **Red (Kokkini) Beach**, near Ancient Akrotiri in the south, has particularly impressive red cliffs, loungers and restaurants. You can walk from a parking lot over the eastern point to reach it. Or, catamaran cruises from all over the island plus caïques from pretty **Akrotiri Beach** go there and on to the sheltered cove of **White (Aspri) Beach** before visiting **Black (Mesa Pigadia) Beach**, with a beachside taverna.

Naxos

The largest of the Cyclades – and a centre of Classical Greece and Byzantium, with Venetian and Frankish influences – Naxos impresses. Its main town of Hora backs a lively waterfront with a web of steep cobbled alleys climbing to its dramatic hilltop *kastro*, a testament to three centuries of Venetian rule. Within easy reach are excellent beaches, fascinating mountain villages, inspiring ancient sites and bizarre-looking marble quarries.

Labyrinthine old town and ancient icons

Hora (Naxos Town) is enchanting, especially with the remnants of the fortified Venetian **kastro** looming above the waterfront. This was the seat of power for Marco Sanudo, the 13th-century Venetian who founded the town and made Naxos the heart of the Duchy of the Aegean. The tangle of steep footpaths is divided into two historic Venetian neighbourhoods: Bourgos, where the Greeks lived, and the hilltop Kastro, where the Roman Catholics lived.

Hora is easily managed on foot, though it's almost impossible not to get lost in the old town, but it's just as easy to find your way again. And that's half the fun. Within the *kastro*, the remnants of Sanudo's castle, the **Tower of Sanoudos**, is surrounded by gorgeous Venetian mansions.

Reach the two marble columns with a crowning lintel of the **Temple of Apollo** via a causeway to Palatia islet.

EATING IN HORA: OUR PICKS

Avaton 1739: Atop Hora's *kastro*, don't miss the exalted panorama – a favourite for sunset cocktails and creative cuisine. *8.30am-2am €€*

O Apostolis: Occupying a tiny plaza right at the heart of labyrinthine Bourgos, with good traditional dishes in a pretty courtyard. *7pm-midnight €€*

Doukato: Magical setting in a former monastery, with top Naxian specialities like *kalogeras* (beef, eggplant and cheese). *6pm-midnight €€*

Kamaraki: Excellent taverna frequented by locals, with traditional dishes such as *horta* and fried fish, and tables in a pretty alley. *noon-11.30pm €*

Dodecanese

STUNNING COVES | VARIED LANDSCAPES | ANCIENT CULTURES

Timeless charm and natural beauty, historic ruins and tranquil beaches – welcome to the Dodecanese, which has all that epitomises old Greece. Meaning '12 islands' (these are the main ones, though there are more), the archipelago curves through the southeastern Aegean parallel to the ever-visible shoreline of Türkiye. The footprints of everyone from Greeks and Romans to crusading medieval knights and Byzantine and Ottoman potentates to 20th-century Italian bureaucrats are found here.

Admittedly, Rhodes and Kos are magnets for package tourism and cruise-ship crowds, but you can find your own corners on each of these islands. They offer two very different experiences, so you can commune with the ghosts of the knights over one or two nights in Rhodes, and the ghost of Hippocrates in the Asklepieion, an ancient healing centre in Kos, the next. Both islands also have beautiful beaches that are perfect for swimming.

☑ **TOP TIP**

If you're only visiting Rhodes for a short time, perhaps as part of an island-hopping itinerary, there's plenty to see in Rhodes' Old Town without venturing further afield. Beware that in high season, the Old Town gets terribly crowded with tourists.

 GETTING AROUND

Direct ferries connect Rhodes with Kos (between two and four hours, depending on the service).

Rhodes has an excellent bus network. Buses leave from the urban bus stop on Mandraki Harbour; buy tickets on board. If you're based in Rhodes Old Town, you can't drive into that district, so it makes sense to rent a car only for the actual day(s) you'll use it. Rhodes Town's main taxi rank is on the northern edge of the Old Town, just east of

Plateia Rimini; a board displays set fares for specific destinations.

In Kos, cycling is very popular, with plenty of bicycles for hire, and it's a great way to get around. Cycle lanes thread all through Kos Town, with the busiest route running along the waterfront to connect the town with Lambi to the north and Psalidi to the south. Taxis congregate on the south side of the port. The line of boats moored in Kos Town offer excursions around Kos and to nearby islands.

RHODES' HISTORY

The Minoans and Mycenaeans established early outposts on Rhodes, around the 16th century BCE, followed by the Dorians. Over the next centuries, Rhodes switched allegiances like a pendulum between Athens, Persia, Sparta and Alexander the Great; the island was assimilated into the Roman Empire in 70 CE, then the Byzantine province of the Dodecanese. When the Crusaders seized Constantinople, it was granted independence. Later, the Genoese gained control followed by the Knights of St John, who ruled Rhodes for 213 years from 1309. They were ousted after two sieges by the Ottomans, who were kicked out by the Italians nearly four centuries later. In 1947, after 35 years of Italian occupation, Rhodes, along with the Dodecanese Islands, became part of Greece.

Rhodes Town

Rhodes Town sits at the island's northern peak and is made up of the Old and New Towns, each its own entity. Sealed like a medieval time capsule behind a double ring of high walls and a deep moat, the Old Town is a magical labyrinth. The New Town is a modern Mediterranean resort, with busy beaches, nightlife and waterfront bars.

Trace the history of the knights

An easy walk down the somewhat forbidding **Street of the Knights** is the quintessential Rhodes Town experience, not least because its architecture speaks of the various historical

 EATING IN RHODES TOWN: BEST RESTAURANTS

Paradosiako Kafeneio I Symi: Rhodes' cutest terrace and some of the best seafood and fish you're likely to taste. *1-11pm Mon-Sat* €€

Romios Restaurant: Traditional, elegantly presented Rhodian dishes in a tree-canopied Old Town courtyard. *noon-midnight* €€

Kelari Pantieras: Taste the meze and listen to live bouzouki music in this gorgeous neighbourhood taverna. *5pm-midnight Mon-Sat* €

4 Rodies: Eat perfectly prepared Rhodian dishes in the leafy garden of this locally loved, family-run restaurant. *1.30-11pm Wed-Mon* €€

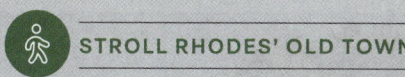

STROLL RHODES' OLD TOWN

A walk around the historical capsule of Rhodes' Old Town will take you through millennia of history.

START	END	LENGTH
D'Amboise Gate	Jewish Museum of Rhodes	2.5km; 2–3 hours

Start from the 16th-century ❶ **D'Amboise Gate**, one of the most impressive of the nine approaches to the Old Town; it's protected by two massive concentric towers. Go down Orfeos and turn into the Street of the Knights. The austere mansions (known as inns) that line the arrow-straight streets of the ❷ **Knights' Quarter** were home to the medieval occupying army of the Knights of St John.

From the outside, the 14th-century castle-like ❸ **Palace of the Grand Master** looks much as it did when erected by the Knights Hospitaller, though it has fascist-style interiors. Walk to Apellou street and the ❹ **Archaeological Museum**, located inside the magnificent 15th-century Knights' Hospital.

Carry on south down Apellou, and you'll reach Sokratous street and ❺ **Hora**, the so-called Turkish Quarter that occupies the central bulk of the Old Town. Look out for the ❻ **Mosque of Suleyman**, built in 1522 to commemorate the Ottoman defeat of the knights, and renovated in 1808 (not open to visitors). The peaceful ❼ **Muslim Library**, founded in 1793, sits in an inviting little garden courtyard opposite the mosque.

Head back down Sokratous to the Old Town's southeast corner and the ❽ **Jewish Quarter**, once home to a population of 5500 Jewish people. End the walk at the ❾ **Jewish Museum of Rhodes**, entered via the 1577 Kahal Shalom Synagogue.

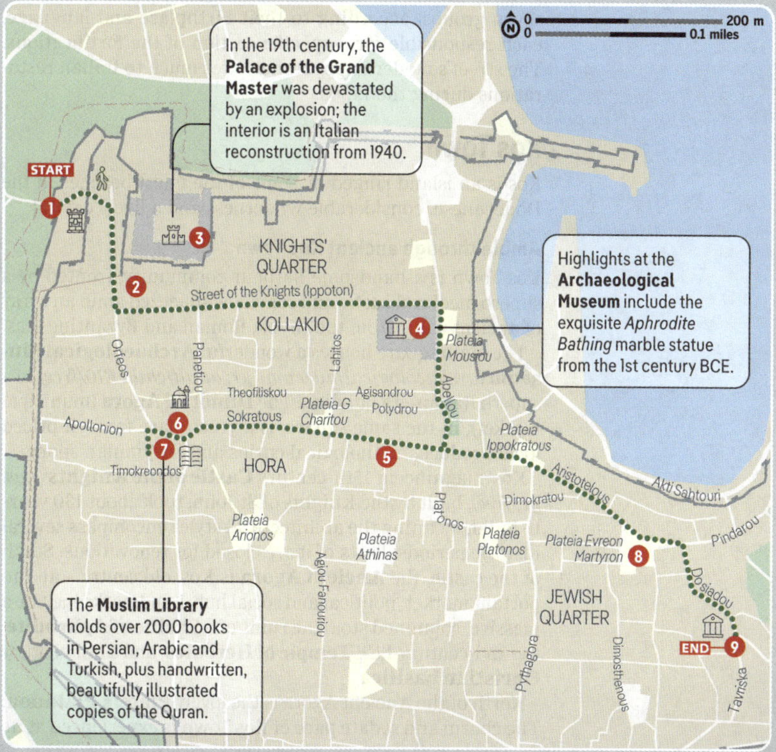

In the 19th century, the **Palace of the Grand Master** was devastated by an explosion; the interior is an Italian reconstruction from 1940.

Highlights at the **Archaeological Museum** include the exquisite *Aphrodite Bathing* marble statue from the 1st century BCE.

The **Muslim Library** holds over 2000 books in Persian, Arabic and Turkish, plus handwritten, beautifully illustrated copies of the Quran.

0 — 200 m
0 — 0.1 miles

START
KNIGHTS' QUARTER
Street of the Knights (Ippoton)
KOLLAKIO
Orfeos
Panetiou
Theofiliskou
Sokratous
Apollonion
Timokreontos
Lahitos
Plateia G Charitou
Agisandrou Polydrou
Plateia Mousiou
Apellou
Plateia Ippokratous
Platonos
Plateia Arionos
Plateia Athinas
Agiou Fanouriou
Plateia Platonos
Dimokratou
Aristoteleous
Akti Sahtouri
Plateia Evreon Martyron
Pindarou
Dosiadou
HORA
JEWISH QUARTER
Pythagora
Dimosthenous
END
Tavriska

rulers of this Mediterranean island. It should take you no more than 20 minutes.

From the 14th century, this was home to the Knights Hospitaller who ruled Rhodes. The knights were divided into seven groups, according to their birthplace and language, each responsible for a specific section of the fortifications. The street's modern appearance owes much to Italian restorations during the 1930s.

Kos Town

Kos is an island ringed by some of the finest beaches in the Dodecanese, considerable wilderness and a lively capital.

Amble through ancient Kos Town

Kos Town is a handsome harbour community, fronted by a superb medieval castle and somehow squeezed amid an array of ancient ruins from the Greek, Roman and Byzantine eras.

The main square houses a wonderful **Archaeological Museum** *(archaeologicalmuseums.gr; adult/child €10/free)* in a superb Italian-era building. The **Dimotiki Agora** (municipal market), in the same square, is a great place for well-priced local produce, mythological curios and Kalymnian sponges.

Kos' magnificent 15th-century **Castle of the Knights** *(kos. gr; free),* built by the Knights of St John, took about 130 years to build, meaning the architectural styles encompass several historic periods. Parts of it are closed for renovations. South of the castle, the **Ancient Agora** is Kos' old centre – an important market, political and social hub. Landmarks include a massive, columned stoa, the ruins of a **Shrine of Aphrodite**, the 2nd-century-BCE **Temple of Hercules**, and a 5th-century **Christian basilica**.

North of the Ancient Agora is the lovely **Plateia Platanou**. The charm and sedate pace of Kos Town is experienced at its

TRABANTOS/SHUTTERSTOCK

Asklepieion, Kos

best in this lovely cobblestone square. Sitting in a cafe here, you can pay your respects to **Hippocrates' plane tree**. Hippocrates himself is said to have taught his pupils in its shade – though this is legend, since plane trees don't usually live for more than 200 years.

Discover the ancient site of healing

The island's most important ancient site, **Asklepieion** (kos. gr; adult/child €15/free) stands on a pine-covered hill 3km southwest of Kos Town, commanding lovely views towards Türkiye. A religious sanctuary devoted to Asclepius, the god of healing, it was also a healing centre and a school of medicine. It was founded in the 3rd century BCE, according to legend by Hippocrates himself, the Kos-born 'father' of modern medicine. He was already dead by then, though, and the training here simply followed his teachings. Bus 3 runs hourly from Kos Town to the site. It's also a pleasant, if uphill, bike ride.

BEST BEACHES ON KOS

Magic Beach: Great spot for a nature-based experience with few(er) resources, in the island's southwest.

Exotic Beach: If you like to get into your birthday suit, this spot near Magic Beach is the nudist option.

Lagada Beach: Lovely and simple, also referred to as Banana Beach.

Agios Stefanos Beach: Sadly, this beach has been ruined by a massive resort behind it. Nevertheless, the small beachfront promontory has the photogenic islet of Kastri, topped with a tiny church, within swimming distance offshore.

Agios Theologos Beach: On the west coast, backed by meadow bluffs carpeted in olive groves, it feels far removed from the resort bustle.

EATING ON KOS: OUR PICKS

Haihoutes: In a ghost village, this tastefully restored cafe serves history, traditional food and good coffee. *3pm-midnight* €

O Makis: In Mastihari, this is a genuine Greek experience with friendly Makis, serving seafood and grills at incredible prices. *10am-midnight* €

Oria Taverna: Walk up for 15 minutes to this idyllic taverna, near old Pyli Castle, for the best views on Kos and traditional food. *9am-9pm* €

Restaurant Agios Theologos: Set above Agios Theologos Beach, this much-loved seafood taverna enjoys the best sunsets in Kos. *10am-9pm* €€

Corfu

COSMOPOLITAN VIBE | MIGHTY FORTRESSES | REGAL REFUGE

☑ TOP TIP

Parking and car congestion can be a nightmare in Corfu Town. It's best to find a space where you can leave your car; the centre is largely pedestrianised and you won't need it while you're in town.

Still recognisable as the idyllic refuge where the ship-wrecked Odysseus was soothed and sent on his way home, Corfu – one of the seven main Ionian Islands – continues to attract travellers with its lush scenery, bountiful produce and pristine beaches. While certain parts of the island have succumbed to overdevelopment, it's possible to escape the crowds.

Imbued with Venetian elegance, historic Corfu Town (Kerkyra) stands halfway down the island's east coast. Located between two strongholds (each topped by a fortress built to withstand Ottoman sieges), the UNESCO-listed Old Town unfolds as a tight-packed car-free warren of cobbled lanes. Some are lined with fine restaurants, lively bars and intriguing shops; others exude a timeless charm, with flowery side alleys and weathered facades. The Old Town's majestic architecture includes the splendid Liston arcade, high-class museums, and many churches.

By day, streets buzz with cruise-ship passengers and day-trippers; come evening, the atmosphere thrives around teeming bars.

🧭 GETTING AROUND

Corfu's Old Town is compact and mostly pedestrianised, so getting around is best done on foot.

Corfu City Bus (*astikoktelkerkyras.gr*) serves points around Corfu Town and the nearby communities in central Corfu; most lines depart from the main local bus station near San Rocco Sq (aka Plateia Theotoki). Line 15 goes to the airport and the port, New Limani. Buy tickets at vending machines or kiosks; tickets bought from bus drivers are more expensive.

Buses to destinations in northern and southern Corfu leave from the **Green Buses** (*ktelkerkyras.gr*) terminal in the New Town, a 15-minute walk south of the centre. Green Buses has frequent services to major beaches and island communities, the port and airport. Services are reduced on weekends and outside peak season.

To thoroughly explore the island, you'll need your own transport. Car and motorbike rentals are widely available at the airport, in Corfu Town and at the resorts. Prebook in summer.

CORFU

0 ——— 200 m
0 ——— 0.1 miles

Ionian Cruises (700m);
Manessis Apartments
(35km)

Arseniou

Donzelot

Proseleindou

Plateia
Paleo Limani

3

Plateia
Taxiarchis

16

17

15

6

OLD TOWN

Youhirotou

Kapodistriou

8

Solomou

13

Nikiforou Theotoki

M Theotoki

14

Ag
Spyridonos

5

7

Old
Cricket
Ground

4

12

Bosketo

EVRAIKI

Velisariou

Paleologou

Voulgareos

Plateia
Dimarchio

Eleftherias

Plateia
G Theotoki
(Plateia San
Rocco)

S Padova

9

Idromenon
Moustoxidou

11

The
Spianada

Agnisiton Polytechniou

1

Palaio
Frourio

Gerasimou Markora

Mitropoliti Methodiou

Samara

N Mantzarou

Gulford

Kapodistriou

Dimodokou

Achilleion
Palace
(8.8km);
Rolling Stone
(13km)

Rizospaston Vouleftori

Lefkimis

Akadimias

10

G Aspioti

P Vraila

18

NEW TOWN

2

Dimokratias

Bay of
Garitsa

Mon Repos (1.3km);
Museum of Palaeopolis
(1.5km)

★ **HIGHLIGHTS**
1 Palaio Frourio
● **SIGHTS**
2 Archaeological
   Museum
3 Byzantine Museum of
   Antivouniotissa
4 Casa Parlante
5 Church of Agios
   Spyridon
6 Corfu Museum of
   Asian Art

7 Liston
8 Neo Frourio
see 6 Palace of St
   Michael & St
   George
9 Spianada
● **SLEEPING**
10 Bella Venezia
11 Locandiera
● **EATING**
12 Chrisomalis

13 Marina's Taverna
14 Papagiorgis
15 Tsipouradiko
16 Venetian Well
● **DRINKING &**
NIGHTLIFE
17 Imabari Seaside
   Lounge
● **INFORMATION**
18 Aperghi Travel

THE GUIDE

GREECE CORFU

**BEST ORGANISED
TOURS**

**Corfu Walking &
Food Tours:** Guided
tours of Corfu's Old
Town, plus island
coach tours, including
a Durrell-themed one.
*(corfuwalkingtours.
com)*

**Corfu Perspectives
Guided Tours:**
Insightful tours
focus on Corfu's
lesser-known sides,
personalities and
locations. *(corfu
guidedtours.com)*

Aperghi Travel:
Island hikes, from
guided one-day treks
up Mt Pantokrator
to two-week
self-guided Corfu
Trail expeditions.
(aperghitravel.gr)

S-Bikes & Cycle:
Acharavi-based
company leads
guided mountain-bike
tours around northern
Corfu and e-bike
tours of Corfu Town.
(cyclecorfu.com)

Ionian Cruises: Day
cruises to Paxi and
Antipaxi, to Parga and
Syvota islands and
across to Albania.
(ionian-cruises.com)

A Stroll Through History

Explore Corfu's Old Town

A Corfu Town landmark, the elegant **Liston** is an arcaded building dating back to Corfu's Napoleonic occupation
(1807–14). These days, it houses see-and-be-seen cafes. Across
the grassy expanse known as the **Spianada**, the imposing
Palaio Frourio *(odysseus.culture.gr; adult/child €10/free)*
fortress was built in the 14th century by the Venetians to

TRABANTOS/SHUTTERSTOCK

Neo Frourio

defend against Ottoman attacks. Previously, it enclosed the entire Byzantine city within massive stone walls; spend half an hour clambering up to the viewpoints.

After a sightseeing respite at **Imabari Seaside Lounge** on Faliraki Beach, follow the waterfront to reach a pale-yellow 15th-century church that houses the **Byzantine Museum of Antivouniotissa** *(odysseus.culture.gr; adult/child €5/3)*. Then wander through a web of lanes and alleyways, where bougainvillea plants blaze in pink and red across pastel-painted walls.

The **Church of Agios Spyridon** shelters the remains of Corfu's patron saint. Cross the pretty Plateia Agios Spyridon for an ice cream at **Papagiorgis** *(papagiorgis.gr),* an old-school patisserie from 1924, before popping into **Casa Parlante** *(casaparlante.gr; adult/child €10/6)* to gain the sense of the lifestyle of a 19th-century merchant family.

On the other side of town looms the **Neo Frourio** *(odysseus. culture.gr; adult/child €5/free),* or New Fort, another Venetian masterpiece of military engineering built in the 16th century. The bastion can be accessed via the stairway at the western end of Solomou. It's open from April to October.

Eastern Masterpieces

Greece's only collection of Asian art

Looming over the northern end of the Spianada is the neo-classical **Palace of St Michael and St George**. Built by the British as a residence for the high commissioner, it also served as the seat of the Ionian Parliament and summer palace of the Greek royal family. Today, it's home to the prestigious **Corfu Museum of Asian Art** *(matk.gr; adult/child €10/free),* which features 15,000 artefacts, mostly from Japan and China, donated by private collectors.

Archaeological Treasure Chest
Catch a glimpse of Corfu's distant past

South of the city centre, the **Archaeological Museum of Corfu** *(adult/child €10/free)* should be on the to-do list of anyone interested in Ancient Greek history and art. Its fine collection of pieces unearthed around the island provides an insightful survey of Corfu's rich archaeological heritage, from prehistoric to Roman times.

Forest, Royals & Ruins
Discover Corfu's regal connections at Mon Repos

The rambling wooded estate of **Mon Repos** sits partly on top of Palaeopolis, an ancient settlement dating back to the 8th century BCE. The park's centrepiece is a neoclassical mansion, showcased as the **Museum of Palaeopolis** *(odysseus. culture.gr; adult/child €10/free)*. It was built in 1830 as the summer retreat of Corfu's British governors and used as a residence by Greek royals from 1864 until 1967. Perhaps its biggest claim to fame is as the place where Prince Philip of Greece, later Duke of Edinburgh and husband of Queen Elizabeth II, was born in 1921.

Mon Repos is about 2km south of the Old Town and served by bus 2a from the Spianada or San Rocco Sq. Pack a picnic and water, as there are no cafes or shops on the grounds or nearby.

Royal fans, garden lovers and mythology buffs should make the 10km trip south to **Achilleion Palace** *(achillion-corfu. gr; adult/child €7/5)*, the splendid summer retreat of Empress Elisabeth of Austria, aka Sissi. It was completed in 1892, and Sissi only got to enjoy a few years here before her tragic assassination in 1898. To get here, hop on Blue Bus 10 at San Rocco Sq.

PAXI & ANTIPAXI

A mere 10km off the south of Corfu island, and measuring 13km from tip to toe, Paxi packs a lot of punch in its pint-sized frame. Its sublime beaches are bound to bring a smile to your face. Facilities are concentrated in three peaceful harbour villages on its eastern shores – Lakka, Loggos and the ferry port of Gaios. The vibe is laid-back but sophisticated. From Gaios, it's a short hop to sister island Antipaxi, a wonderful day-trip destination for its beach coves.

Paxi does not have an airport. Passenger-only ferries operated by Joy Cruises, Lefkada Palace and Kerkyra Lines serve Paxi from Corfu Town, while Kamelia Lines leaves from Lefkimmi in southern Corfu (free bus shuttle from Corfu Town). Kerkyra Lines and Kerkyra Seaways link Paxi with Igoumenitsa.

EATING IN CORFU TOWN: OUR PICKS

Tsipouradiko: Pick from plenty of mezedhes at this rustic old mansion with tables under a tree and occasional live music. *6.30pm–midnight* €€

Chrisomalis: Going strong since 1904, this little taverna was a Durrell family fave. Warm service and good people-watching. *12.30pm–midnight* €€

Marina's Taverna: Tables strewn around a cobbled square, and home-cooked dishes made from tried-and-true family recipes. *noon–midnight* €€

Venetian Well: Local recipes elevated with contemporary techniques and cosmopolitan flair. It's tucked on a romantic square. *7–11.30pm* €€€

Crete

STUNNING COASTS | VIBRANT CULTURE | HISTORIC WONDERS

☑ **TOP TIP**

Hania is known for having some of the best food on the island, from prized meats to seasonal vegetables. Be sure to try cheeses, preserves and olive oil.

Crete is a treasure chest of splendid beaches, ancient marvels and striking landscapes, weaving in entrancing cities and throwback villages where residents share uniquely Cretan traditions. There's something undeniably artistic in the way Crete's landscape unfolds, from the sun-drenched beaches in the north to the rugged canyons spilling out at the cliff- and cove-lined southern coast. In between, valleys cradle moody villages, and round-shouldered hills are the overture to often snow-dabbed mountains.

Crete's natural wonders are equalled only by the richness of its history. The Palace of Knossos is but one of many vestiges of the mysterious ancient Minoan civilisation (as seen in the unmissable Archaeological Museum in Iraklio). Then there are Venetian fortresses, Turkish mosques and Byzantine churches – Hania and Rethymno showcase these spectacularly. The island's beauty is rivalled by its food, with rural tavernas often producing their own ingredients and catching their own seafood.

 GETTING AROUND

KTEL buses serve the island and link Iraklio, Hania and Rethymno. Local buses head from Iraklio to the Palace of Knossos.

If you're driving to Hania, park on the periphery (there are car parks to the south) and walk to the Old Town. From the airport, insist to your driver that they stick to the posted fixed price before setting off.

The historic quarter of Rethymno is mostly car-free and best enjoyed on foot. Parking is always a problem; try the huge car park east of the Municipal Park or the paid parking on Kriari. The bus station is at the western edge of the commercial centre.

Most places of interest in Iraklio are within the city centre, which is largely pedestrianised. Leave the car in your hotel garage, a 24/7 car park or use the free parking at the Cultural Centre on Giannikou. The airport is 4km east of the centre; access is a breeze. The ferry port is even closer.

CRETE

Sea of
Crete

0 ——— 50 km
0 ——— 25 miles

Kolymbari   Stavros
Kissamos   ● Hania
           Georgioupolis Rethymno Panormo Bali   *Dia*
Samaria Gorge   Plakias   Perama   **Iraklio** **Palace of**
        Sougia △ *Mt Pahnes*   Anogia   **Knossos** Malia
Paleohora   Agia   Hora *Mt Psiloritis* △ Arhanes Kastelli Neapoli Agios Sitia Palekastro
          Roumeli   Sfakion   Spili   Zaros Agia Varvara   Nikolaos   Mohlos
                Agia Galini Tymbaki   Arkalokhorion △ *Mt*   Istron Makrygialos Zakros
                       Mires   Pyrgos *Dikti* Myrtos   Xerokampos
                              Arvi   **Ierapetra**

Gavdos   *Gaidouronisi*   *Koufonisi*
                           (Hrysi)

                  *Libyan
                  Sea*

Hania

Hania (also spelt Chania) is Crete's most evocative city. Wandering its tangle of alleys and lanes is one of the island's pleasures. It was historically the seat of Venetian, Turkish and then Cretan rule, and remnants of Venetian and Turkish architecture abound, with ancient synagogues, plus old townhouses now transformed into atmospheric restaurants and boutique hotels.

Explore the Venetian Harbour

There are few places where Hania's historic charm and grandeur are more palpable than in the **Venetian Harbour**. Lined by pastel-coloured buildings that punctuate a maze of narrow lanes lined with shops and tavernas, its oldest parts date to the 15th century. The eastern side is dominated by the domed **Mosque of Kioutsouk Hasan**, now an exhibition hall. On the west side, short and steep streets lead up to the remains of the Venetian fortifications. (It's worth ascending the steps for the somewhat hidden high Venetian-era terrace, to enjoy views across the city and harbour.)

Heading east around the harbour, the restored **Grand Arsenal** houses the **KAM Centre of Mediterranean Architecture**. Continuing on, the somewhat dilapidated, 15th-century **Neoria**, or **Venetian shipyards**, are a historic treasure hiding in plain sight.

Following the waterfront out onto the 14th-century **breakwater**, you can clamber over the huge blocks of stone as you take in captivating views back to the Old Town. Imagine the port filled with Venetian sailing ships laden with valuable cargo. Parts of the magnificent 21m-high **lighthouse** date to 1595. It was rebuilt by the Egyptians in the 1820s in the shape of a minaret.

HANIA TOURS & INFO

Boats of every shape and size tour Hania's harbour and coast, especially at sunset. Touts offer a choice of glass-bottom, vintage or sailing boats and more. Some tours are all-day affairs and visit the remote beaches on the Rodopou Peninsula and **Balos Beach** on the Gramvousa Peninsula, which are difficult to reach via land.

Tours on land cover much of Western Crete. Check durations carefully – for instance, the trip for the hike in the **Samaria Gorge** lasts from dawn until after dusk.

Hania's **municipal tourist office** (explorechania.gr) has limited hours but is an excellent resource for special events and getting around the region without a rental car. Check its official website and phone app.

Heraklion Archaeological Museum, Iraklio

Treasures in the Archaeological Museum of Chania

For greater historical insight, don't miss the **Archaeological Museum of Chania** (amch.gr; adult/child €15/free) where artefacts from across the island are displayed in two light-filled galleries, with plenty of signage offering details and context. For time out, relax in the breezy cafe with views from the deck to the Aegean. The museum is 1.5km east of the Old Town. Come in the afternoon, and after the visit walk back along the shoreline for pre-sunset views plus glimpses of hidden beaches below a tiny park and the remains of waterfront tanneries that were a major Hania industry 100 years ago.

Iraklio

Minoan culture at the Heraklion Archaeological Museum

Snake goddesses, bull leapers and the Prince of the Lilies are among the intriguing characters you'll encounter in the unmissable **Heraklion Archaeological Museum** (heraklion museum.gr; adult/child €12/free). This is the world's premier museum of the Minoan culture, widely considered the first civilisation in Europe. Reaching a peak of development beginning in 2000 BCE, their art, architecture and culture are celebrated in the 27 rooms of this visitor-friendly museum.

A two-hour spin around here will greatly enhance your understanding of Cretan history, help put any archaeological site on Crete in context, and shine a spotlight on aspects of daily life and the development of Cretan societies. It's best to visit after 3pm in summer when it's less busy. The simple

EATING IN HANIA: BEST TAVERNAS

Pinaleon Fine Kitchen: A menu of the greatest hits of Greek classics is served in this spiffy yet unpretentious corner taverna. *1-10pm* €€

Kouzina Epe: Stylish cafe on a relaxed square serving an appealing mix of modern Greek fare and daily specials. *noon-7.30pm* €€

Christostomos: Behind the harbour, popular for its classic Cretan cuisine cooked over wood or in a pot with homegrown ingredients. *1-11pm* €€

Kalderimi: A traditional, busy taverna in Topanas. Cretan standards cooked with creative flair, plus dishes from around the Med. *8.30am-11pm* €€

cafe is good for refreshments and has shady outdoor seating overlooking architectural digs.

Palace of Knossos

The grand capital of Minoan Crete

Crete's must-see attraction is the **Palace of Knossos** (*knossos-palace.gr; adult/child €26/free*), just 5km south of Iraklio. Combining a visit here with Iraklio's excellent Archaeological Museum is highly recommended and will give unparalleled insight into Crete's Minoan civilisation. The setting is awe-inspiring and the ruins and recreations impressive, incorporating an immense palace, courtyards, private apartments, baths, lively frescoes and more. To beat the crowds and avoid the heat, get to Knossos either at 8am or after 3pm. Skip ticket-booth queues by buying timed-admission tickets online. Plan on spending at least two hours to do the place justice.

Samaria Gorge

Crete's world-class hiking

Samaria Gorge (*samaria-gorge.gr; adult/child €10/free*) is one of Europe's top geological wonders. The best way to experience the gorge is by hiking its 18km length from the starting point in the hillside village of **Xyloskalo** near Omalos. You begin at an elevation of 1230m and end at sea level. The national park ends at the 13km mark just north of the almost abandoned village of **Palea Agia Roumeli**, from where it's a further 3km to the sea. All along the route stay alert for *kri-kri*, a mountain goat that's native to Crete, and enjoy the wildflowers blooming in profusion.

Day trips to the gorge are heavily marketed to tourists across Crete and it gets crowded in summer. Start as early as you can manage to get ahead of the crowds. The park's main entrance is open from 7am to 1pm May to October. After closing, visitors are not permitted to walk on the entire trail, as everyone needs to be out of the park by 4pm. Sturdy shoes are a must. Day trips to Samaria Gorge start at the park entrance and include a pick-up from either Sougia or Hora Sfakion, after a ferry ride from Agia Roumeli. The Samaria Gorge website has excellent details on the hike and how to get there.

BEST WINERIES BEYOND IRAKLIO

Boutari Winery: One of Greece's largest wine producers has a vast, airy tasting room in Skalani.

Stilianou Winery: Rustic and down-to-earth, it specialises in organic wines made with local varietals only; in Kounavi.

Titakis Wines: Huge facility and garden in Kounavi, with sample plots of 11 Cretan varietals.

Digenakis Winery: In Peza, with an artful tasting room and unusual vintages.

Agelakis Winery: In a bare-bones facility around a Peza courtyard. Vines cover just 4.5 hectares.

Domain Paterianakis: This organic specialist has views as big as its tasting room off the main road in Alagni.

 EATING IN IRAKLIO: OUR PICKS

Peskesi: Culinary magic forged from family-farm ingredients and served amid unpretentious sophistication in a Venetian mansion. *1pm-1am* €€

Thigaterra: This rustic-elegant slow-food champion at Ammoudara Beach gives traditional Greek dishes the next-gen workout. *4pm-midnight* €€

Vourvouladiko: Turkish-infused Cretan cuisine in an enchanted Lakkos garden with historic photographs. A genteel retreat. *7pm-1am* €€

Apiri: Stylish but relaxed corner bistro with a tightly curated menu of modern Greek cuisine, cocktails and craft beer. *noon-midnight* €€

Places We Love to Stay

THE GUIDE

PLACES WE LOVE TO STAY GREECE

Athens

MAP p325

Athens Backpackers € Aussie-run backpackers near the Acropolis, with spotless dorms, a courtyard, well-stocked kitchen and busy social scene. Also has Athens Studios.

Athens Quinta Hostel € Friendly hostel in an old Exarhia mansion, furnished with velvet sofas and patterned tile floors.

Marble House Pension € In a quiet cul-de-sac in Koukaki, this pension offers well-maintained rooms and one apartment; some have small balconies. Air-con is extra.

Athens Gate €€ Stunning views over the Temple of Olympian Zeus from the spacious front rooms, and a central (if busy) location.

Athens Muses Suites €€ Renovated townhouse up on the slopes of Plaka with small, well-kept rooms.

Mosaikon €€ One in a cluster of high-end, reasonably priced suite hotels in the heart of Monastiraki.

Neoma €€€ Light and airy, with sensational Acropolis views from the rooftop bar and pool, on the edge of Filopappou Hill.

Delphi

Fedriades Hotel € Attractive, value-for-money three-star hotel with comfortable, family-friendly rooms and terrific mountain views. Breakfast features homemade food. Free bikes.

Hotel Tholos € Minimalist (not to say humdrum), central and great value. Has sea-view balconies and caring owners.

Meteora

Meteora Central Hostel € Well-managed spot in Kalambaka and one of Greece's best hostels. Dorm rooms are spotless, with good lockers; also private doubles.

Doupiani House €€ Breakfast in a carefully tended garden with uninterrupted Meteora views at this warmly welcoming family-run Kastraki hotel.

Thessaloniki

MAP p334

Zeus is Loose € Hostel (or rather, poshtel) with a muted colour scheme, big windows, sleek furniture and a rooftop bar.

Little Big House € Choose from private doubles or small dorms in this cute and eclectic hostel in charming Ano Poli.

Olganos VL €€ Lovely, family-run boutique hotel in the old Jewish quarter of Veria, close to all the archaelogical sites.

Trilogy House €€ Design buffs will feel at home in this restored 1920s building, where modern fixtures mix with neoclassical lines.

Nafplio

Pension Marianna €€ Vibrant place with convivial owners, Greek *filoxenia* (hospitality) and wide-vista setting – you can't get better for value. Organic breakfasts.

Aetoma €€€ Intimate yet comfortable, the five rooms in a classic mansion have dark, heavy and stylish furnishings. Generous traditional breakfast.

Grand Sarai €€€ This renovated pink mansion is sleek and modern on the inside, with stylish rooms. Most have marvellous views; some have balconies.

Olympia

Hotel Pelops €€ Our pick for Olympia's most welcoming lodgings, with comfortable rooms and a delightful, sunny lounge. Greek-Australian Suzanne is a fount of knowledge.

Pension-Tavern Bacchus €€ Located only a few kilometres from the ancient site in the village of Ancient Pissa, this pleasant spot has wonderful valley views, a swimming pool and a decent tavern.

Santorini (Thira)

Spiros & Hiroko Hotel €€ Behind a huge bloom of geraniums on Perissa's main street, Japanese-Greek couple Hiroko and Spiros run an immaculate 10-room hotel. No kids.

Aroma Suites €€ Overlooking the caldera at the quieter southern end of Fira, this boutique hotel has charming service and six cave-house rooms and suites.

Chelidonia Traditional Villas €€€ Traditional Oia cliffside dwellings that have been in the owner's family for generations. It has beds in cosy alcoves, and private patios with caldera views.

Villa Blanca €€€ A superb option away from the crowds amid Megalohori's vineyards, this luxury villa is built in traditional Cycladic style with a hot tub and ocean view.

Naxos

Hotel Grotta €€ Located on high ground overlooking the *kastro* and Hora, this excellent family-run hotel has immaculate rooms, great sea views, and a cool indoor hot tub.

Hotel Glaros €€ A well-run and immaculate 13-room boutique hotel with an indoor hot tub. The beach is only a few steps away. Adults only.

Rhodes Town

S Nikolis Hotel €€ Set across several restored buildings and a flowery courtyard, the stylish, split-level rooms feature four-poster beds, marble floors and stone walls. Breakfast is superb.

Marco Polo Mansion €€ This 15th-century pasha's house lovingly recreates an Ottoman ambience. Some rooms are in the mansion itself; the rest open onto the stunning garden.

Spirit of the Knights €€€ With their thick rugs, dark woods, stained-glass windows and sense of tranquillity, the six opulent suites in this gorgeous boutique hotel ooze medieval atmosphere.

Kos Town

Hotel Afendoulis € There may be plusher hotels in Kos, but none with such spirit. Clean rooms with small balconies, a homely lounge area and delicious breakfasts.

Kos Aktis Art Hotel €€€ Bedrooms are minimalist affairs of glass, light and wood. The view of the Aegean and, by night, Bodrum glittering like a giant chandelier is romantic.

Corfu   MAP p349

Locandiera €€ This stylish guesthouse in a historic building in Corfu Town is a standout for its superb breakfasts and rooms with a subtly artsy vibe.

Manessis Apartments €€ Lovely two-bedroom apartments with balconies facing Kassiopi's harbour, framed by flower-filled gardens and managed by a caring owner who ensures everything goes smoothly.

Rolling Stone €€ Indie travellers' favourite on Kontogialos (Pelekas) Beach, with a shared outdoor kitchen and hosts who organise barbecue evenings and boat rides to hidden caves.

Bella Venezia €€€ This city hotel in a neoclassical villa on a peaceful street features compact but well-equipped rooms and a flowery breakfast terrace.

Hania

Kumba Hostel € Restored, hip hostel east of the centre. Bright cafe–bar, spacious and modern dorms, and rooms that are quiet and comfortable.

Ionas Boutique Hotel €€ Historic building with nine contemporary rooms and a rooftop terrace, located in the labyrinth old Splantzia quarter.

Malmo Historic Hotel €€ Beautifully restored hotel arching over the pedestrianised street in Splantzia. Rooftop deck; nightlife is right outside the door.

Iraklio

Intra Muros Boutique Hostel € Family-run and central, with a fully equipped communal kitchen and a veranda for socialising.

Olive Green Hotel €€ Contemporary hotel with minimalist white and olive-green decor. It gets eco-cred from solar panels and sustainable building materials.

Lato Boutique Hotel €€ Iraklio goes Hollywood – with all the sass but sans the attitude – at this mod boutique hotel overlooking the old harbour.

JAYSKYLAND IMAGES/ALAMY

Hotel Grotta, Naxos

Practicalities

FAMILY TRAVEL

Greeks love children, and yours will be fussed over wherever you go. While there may not be specific tourist infrastructure for families, the country is crammed with fascinating history, thrilling ferry rides and sandy beaches. Children receive discounted admission at nearly all museums and sights.

SVEN HANSCHE/SHUTTERSTOCK

SMOKING

Be aware: while smoking is prohibited in all enclosed public spaces, including restaurants and bars, enforcement can be lax. And outdoors (including restaurant/bar terraces) is another matter – it's permitted (and enjoyed) by many.

HEALTH & SAFE TRAVEL

Probably the biggest danger travelling in Greece is heatstroke; much of Greece experiences seaside breezes, so it's easy to become overexposed to the sun without realising it. Be careful, too, at isolated swimming spots that may have powerful currents. Mosquito repellent can be hard to find; bring some with you. Cannabis is illegal and brings heavy fines and/or imprisonment.

VISAS

Visitors from the UK, Canada, New Zealand, the US and Australia are among nationalities that can stay for up to 90 days in any six-month period without a visa.

OPENING HOURS

Opening hours vary throughout the year, the following are high-season hours.
Banks 8.30am–2.30pm Monday to Thursday, 8am–2pm Friday
Restaurants 11am–11pm
Cafes 9am–midnight
Bars 8pm–late
Shops 8am–3pm Monday, Wednesday and Saturday; 9am–2pm and 5.30pm–9pm Tuesday, Thursday and Friday

LGBTIQ+ TRAVELLERS

Same-sex marriage was legalised in Greece in 2024; attitudes to the LGBTIQ+ community have grown more liberal across Greece. However, the Orthodox Church plays a prominent role in shaping society's views, so attitudes outside major cities and gay-friendly islands are more conservative.

PUBLIC HOLIDAYS

New Year's Day 1 January
Epiphany 6 January
Lent First Sunday in February
Greek Independence Day 25 March
Good Friday April/May
Orthodox Easter Sunday April/May
May Day (Protomagia) 1 May
Whit Monday (Agiou Pnevmatos) 50 days after Easter Sunday
Feast of the Dormition 15 August
Ohi Day 28 October
Christmas Day 25 December
St Stephen's Day 26 December

Language

With just a little Modern Greek under your belt, you'll have a richer understanding of this language's impact on contemporary Western culture; and even if you learn only the very basics, your travel experience will be the better for it.

Basics

Hello. Γειά σας. ya·sas (polite/plural)
Γειά σου. ya·su (informal/singular)
Good morning. Καλημέρα. ka·li·me·ra
Good evening. Καλησπέρα. ka·li·spe·ra
Goodbye. Αντίο. an·di·o
Yes./No. Ναι./Οχι. ne/o·hi
Please. Παρακαλώ. pa·ra·ka·lo
Thank you. Ευχαριστώ. ef·ha·ri·sto
Sorry. Συγγνώμη. sig·no·mi
My name is ... Με λένε ...
me le·ne ...
Do you speak English?
Μιλάτε αγγλικά mi·la·te an·gli·ka
I (don't) understand.
(Δεν) καταλαβαίνω.
(dhen) ka·ta·la·ve·no

Directions

Where is ...? Πού είναι ...;
pu i·ne ...
What's the address?
Ποια είναι η διεύθυνση
pia i·ne i dhi·ef·thin·si
Can you show me (on the map)?
Μπορείς να μου δείξεις
(στον χάρτη)
bo·ris na mu dhik·sis (ston har·ti)

Signs

ΕΙΣΟΔΟΣ Entry
ΕΞΟΔΟΣ Exit
ΠΛΗΡΟΦΟΡΙΕΣ Information
ΑΝΟΙΧΤΟ Open
ΚΛΕΙΣΤΟ Closed
ΓΥΝΑΙΚΩΝ Toilets (Women)
ΑΝΔΡΩΝ Toilets (Men)

Time

What time is it? Τι ώρα είναι;
ti o·ra i·ne
It's (2 o'clock).
Είναι (δύο η ώρα). i·ne (dhi·o i o·ra)
It's half past (10).
Είναι (δέκα) και μισή. (dhe·ka) ke mi·si
today σήμερα si·me·ra
tomorrow αύριο av·ri·o
yesterday χθες hthes
morning πρωί pro·i
(this) afternoon
(αυτό το) απόγευμα
(af·to to) a·po·yev·ma
evening βράδυ vra·dhi

Emergencies

Help! Βοήθεια! vo·i·thya
Go away! Φύγε! fi·ye
I'm lost. Εχω χαθεί. e·kho kha·thi
There's been an accident.
Έγινε ατύχημα. e·yi·ne a·ti·hi·ma
I'm ill.
Είμαι άρρωστος. i·me a·ro·stos (m)
Είμαι άρρωστη. i·me a·ro·st (f)
I'm allergic to (antibiotics).
Είμαι αλλεργικός/αλλεργική
(στα αντιβιωτικά).
i·me a·ler·yi·kos/a·ler·yi·ki (m/f)
(sta an·di·vi·o·ti·ka)

Eating & Drinking

What would you recommend?
Τι θα συνιστούσες;
ti tha si·ni·stu·ses
That was delicious.
Ηταν νοστιμότατο!
i·tan no·sti·mo·ta·to
Cheers! Εις υγείαν! is i·yi·an

NUMBERS

1
ένα e·na
2
δύο dhi·o
3
τρία tri·a
4
τέσσερα te·se·ra
5
πέντε pen·de
6
έξι e·xi
7
επτά ep·ta
8
οκτώ ok·to
9
εννέα e·ne·a
10
δέκα dhe·ka

MARCUS MAINKA/SHUTTERSTOCK

Eleftherios Venizelos International Airport

Arriving

While it's possible to drive south via the Balkans, many visitors arrive by air into Eleftherios Venizelos International Airport (Athens) or one of the four other international airports. Visitors from the UK, Canada, New Zealand, the US and Australia are among nationalities that can stay for up to 90 days in any six-month period without a visa.

By Air
Greece is easy to reach by air, particularly in summer. There are five main international airports: Athens and Thessaloniki, as well as two on Crete and one on Rhodes. Kos and Corfu receive year-round flights and these increase in high season.

By Boat
Ferries reach Greece from ports in Italy (Ancona, Bari, Brindisi). Services to Patras are useful for the Peloponnese (specifically Ancient Olympia), while those that head to Igoumenitsa are handy for ongoing journeys to Kalambaka (Meteora) or Delphi. See *ferryhopper.com*.

MONEY

Currency: Euro (€)

CREDIT & DEBIT CARDS

Big resorts and hotels accept payments by credit and debit card, but family-owned properties often don't. MasterCard and Visa are the most widely accepted.

CASH

Cash is accepted everywhere and helps businesses avoid extra fees from banks (and in some cases, the tax office). ATMs are found at banks in cities and towns.

TIPPING

Hotels Tip porters €1 per bag and housekeepers €1 per night.

Restaurants Even if a service charge is included, a small tip is customary for good service. Round up the bill or tip around 10%.

Taxis Not expected but rounding up to nearest euro is a welcome gesture.

Getting Around

Given its complex geography, Greece has an extensive network of domestic flights and ferries. Intercity buses (KTEL network) are frequent, cheap and air-conditioned; services to remote villages are limited though not impossible. A car remains the best way to explore off-the-beaten track locations, but roads can be narrow and winding, especially in mountainous terrain and mountain villages.

LYDIAREI/SHUTTERSTOCK

Boat
Greece's network of ferries includes fast modern ferries and overnight boats with cabins. For safety, departures are subject to delay during poor weather. Schedules change annually, and services are greatly reduced between mid-October and Easter. In high season, book ahead.

Bus
The bus network is comprehensive and fares are cheap. It's mostly run by public companies under the **KTEL** (ktelbus.com) umbrella. Towns on the mainland have frequent connections to Athens. The island of Corfu can also be reached from Athens by bus (ferry ticket may be included).

Taxi
Taxis are widely available in Greece. They are reasonably priced by European standards, making them a viable alternative to hiring a car if you aren't exploring much. Beware of meter scams. In Athens, useful apps to avoid rip-offs include Beat and Uber.

Car Hire
Hire cars are available on all but the smallest of islands; local firms often have the best rates. Some islands are becoming jammed with hire vehicles, and parking can be challenging in summer. You'll need a good dose of road smarts.

Driving Conditions
Main highways in Greece are in good condition. However, some island roads aren't paved. Road surfaces are also prone to weathering and subsidence, and roads passing through mountainous areas can be littered with rocks (or, in winter, ice and snow).

DRIVING ESSENTIALS

Drive on the right

 50   **120**

Speed limit is 50km/h in urban areas, 90km/h on secondary roads and 120km/h on highways

0.05

Blood alcohol limit is 0.05%

For places to stay in Ireland, see p390

PATRYK KOSMIDER/SHUTTERSTOCK

Above: Cliffs of Moher (p385); Right: General Post Office (p369), Dublin

THE MAIN AREAS

DUBLIN
Ireland's characterful capital. **p366**

KILKENNY
Medieval heritage, arts, crafts and design.
p371

CORK
Urban buzz, artisan producers, wild coastline.
p374

Researched by
Catherine Le Nevez

Ireland

ANCIENT HISTORY, SPELLBINDING SCENERY AND SPIRITED CULTURE

The wild Atlantic coastline, misty mountains, monastic ruins, medieval castles, colourfully painted villages and cities teeming with culture enchant visitors to Ireland.

For a small island at Europe's western edge, Ireland's history is immense. Forged by glacial events during the last ice age that formed its mountains, valleys and drumlins, and laid the foundations for its waterways and bogs, it has had a human presence stretching back to the pre-Celts, Celts and early Christians. Following St Patrick's arrival in 433 CE, some of Europe's most significant – often mystical – ancient and monastic sites are scattered across the Irish landscape. Marauding Vikings plundered Irish monasteries from 795 to 841, establishing settlements throughout the country, including economic powerhouse Dublin.

The battle between the forces of the high king, Brian Ború, and king of Leinster, Máelmorda mac Murchada, in 1014

set in motion events that have reverberated ever since. Helped by MacMurrough, in 1169 Welsh and Norman barons captured areas in Ireland's southeast, beginning an 800-year occupation by Britain.

A centuries-long struggle – including the Great Famine that led to a worldwide diaspora, and revolutionary period in the early 20th century – resulted in the 1922 formation of the Irish Free State, with six Northern Ireland counties gaining legislative and executive authority under 1998's Good Friday Agreement.

These events have shaped this thriving contemporary country today, but haven't altered the cultural expression spanning storytelling to trad-music sessions and the revival of ancient festivities such as Samhain (Halloween), and warmth and spirit at Ireland's heart.

KERRY	GALWAY	BELFAST
The jewel in Ireland's scenic crown.	Vibrant festivals, trad music, rugged landscapes.	Revitalised port city filled with history.
p378	**p382**	**p387**

Find Your Way

The Emerald Isle covers just 84,421 sq km in the Republic of Ireland and 13,843 sq km in Northern Ireland, but plan ahead as backroads can be slow going and there's a lot to see.

Belfast, p387
Belfast's enduring links to the *Titanic* and its recent history are explored throughout this engaging and revitalised city.

Galway, p382
Home to evocative landscapes including Connemara National Park, as well as a creative city with a fabulous trad-music scene.

Dublin, p366
Georgian architecture, distilleries and breweries, sights celebrating a rich literary heritage and legendary nightlife infuse Ireland's absorbing capital.

Kerry, p378
Spectacular scenery spans Ireland's highest mountains, two national parks, charming peninsulas and remote islands including the remarkable Skellig Michael.

Map labels

Portrush, Coleraine, Letterkenny, Derry, Ballymena, A26, Dungloe, Strabane, A6, A5, Larne, Bangor, N15, Donegal, Omagh, NORTHERN IRELAND, Lough Neagh, **BELFAST**, Bundoran, Dungannon, Enniskillen, A4, A3, A1, Sligo, Armagh, N2, Newry, Belmullet, Ballina, N4, Carrick-on-Shannon, Cavan, Dundalk, Castlebar, N5, Carrickmacross, M1, Westport, Ballyhaunis, N3, Longford, Navan, Drogheda, N17, Roscommon, Clifden, Lough Corrib, Tuam, Mullingar, M3, **DUBLIN**, Athlone, M4, **Galway**, M6, Tullamore, IRELAND, M7, Naas, Wicklow, Lahinch, M18, Roscrea, Portlaoise, Ennis, Nenagh, M9, Carlow, M11, Kilkee, M7, M8, **Kilkenny**, Gorey, Shannon, Limerick, Cashel, New Ross, Enniscorthy, Listowel, Clonmel, Wexford, Tralee, N20, M8, Waterford, Dingle, Killarney, Mallow, Tramore, Carrantuohil, Macroom, Dungarvan, Waterville, **Kerry**, Kenmare, **Cork**, Kinsale, Cobh, Bantry, Clonakilty, Skibbereen

North Channel, *Irish Sea*, *Isle of Man*, Douglas, Dumfries, SCOTLAND, *Atlantic Ocean*, *Aran Islands*, *St George's Channel*, Fishguard, WALES, Carmarthen, Swansea

N
0 ——— 100 km
0 ——— 50 miles

CAR
A car gives you the most freedom and is essential in out-of-the-way areas. Get off the main roads when you can: narrow, winding secondary or tertiary roads lead to some of Ireland's most magical scenery.

BUS & TRAIN
Ireland's extensive network of public and private buses is the most cost-effective way to get around, with services to and from most inhabited areas. A limited rail network links Dublin to all major urban centres.

Guinness Storehouse (p370), Dublin

Plan Your Time

Quality, not quantity, should be your goal: instead of a hair-raising race to see everything, narrow down destinations and give yourself time to linger for the most memorable Irish experiences.

If Time Is Tight

● Start in Ireland's dynamic capital, **Dublin** (p366), visiting its collection of Georgian showpieces, history museums, literary sites, **Guinness Storehouse** (p370) and whiskey distilleries, and legendary music venues and pubs. Then explore **Kilkenny city** (p371) along its medieval mile, linking its landmark cathedral and castle. Browse Irish crafts and design in the castle stables, or stroll the riverbanks into the green countryside.

Two Weeks to Explore

● After Dublin and Kilkenny, make your way to the Republic's buzzing second city, **Cork** (p374). Detour to picturesque harbours **Cobh** (p377) and **Kinsale** (p377), then see majestic scenery in **Killarney National Park** (p378), the **Cliffs of Moher** (p385) and Galway's **Connemara** (p385). Save a night for **Galway city** (p382) for live music at its rollicking pubs, before finishing with *Titanic* history in **Belfast** (p387).

SEASONAL HIGHLIGHTS

SPRING
St Patrick's Day festivities liven up often-chilly March. April and May can be glorious times to visit before the crowds descend.

SUMMER
From June to August, days are at their longest, everything is open and **beaches** get busy. Activities take place both indoors and out.

AUTUMN
Outdoor adventures are prime amid September/ October's blazing colours. Parades celebrate ancient Celtic **Samhain** (Halloween).

WINTER
Christmas brightens up December. In January and February, pubs with roaring turf fires, trad sessions and craic are cosy refuges.

Dublin

HISTORY | FOOD & DRINK | LITERATURE

☑ **TOP TIP**

Dublin's thriving food scene means it's often tricky to nab a dinner reservation, particularly around the Grafton St area and especially on weekends. Check for last-minute cancellations, follow @lastminutetabledublin on Instagram, or try **EarlyTable** *(earlytable.ie)*, which gets you up to 50% off your bill if you book an early sitting.

A small city with a huge reputation, Dublin exudes an irresistible mix of heritage and hedonism. Dublin has been making noise since around 500 BCE, when Celtic settlers set up camp at a crossing on the River Liffey. They called it Áth Cliath – the 'Ford of the Hurdles' – and the name lives on today as the Irish for Dublin, Baile Átha Cliath. It's still Ireland's busiest hub, with over a quarter of the country's population living in or around the capital. While the city centre is fairly small, Dublin spreads wide: it's a city of neighbourhoods, each with its own personality. It's not the prettiest capital, and Dubliners won't pretend otherwise. But they'll also tell you that charm beats beauty, and they'll point you towards show-stopping Georgian squares or Victorian shopfronts and remind you that it's easy to love a city that's lovely, but real affection is rooted in character.

Academic Grandeur

Roam the hallowed Trinity College

All elegant courtyards and ivy-clad buildings, Ireland's most prestigious university, **Trinity College Dublin** *(visittrinity. ie; €16-33.50)* is home to the twin treasures of the **Old Library's** vaulted, oak-scented Long Room and the *Book of Kells;* created around 800 CE by monks on the island of Iona,

 GETTING AROUND

Dublin is compact and flat, with most major sights within walking distance. The city has a rent-and-ride Dublinbikes scheme, a two-line light-rail system called the Luas, a suburban DART train that runs along the coast, and an extensive bus network for getting beyond the centre. The easiest way to pay for public transport is with a Leap Visitor Card (p393).

Daily **Mary Gibbons' Tours** *(newgrange tours.com; per person €75)* from Dublin visit Newgrange and the Hill of Tara. **St Kevins Bus Service** *(glendaloughbus.com; adult/ child return €23/14)* departs from St Stephen's Green North (stop 181) for Glendalough. Otherwise, both are easily reached by car.

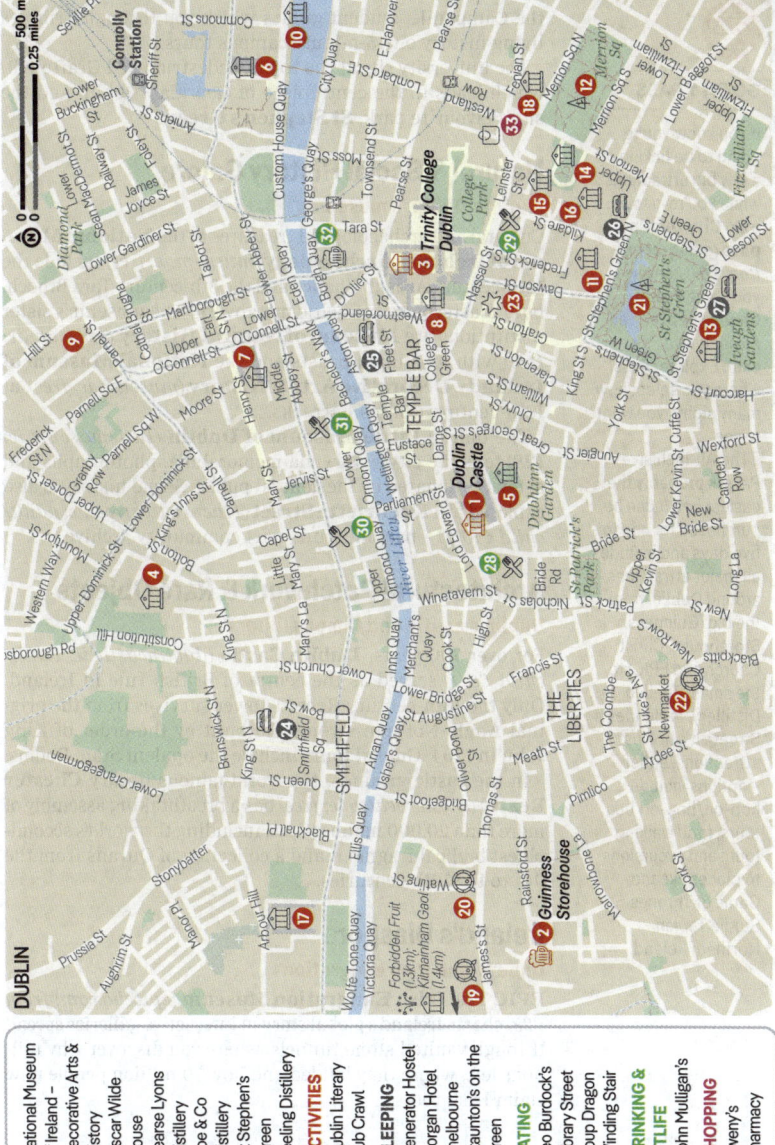

DUBLIN

★ **HIGHLIGHTS**
1 Dublin Castle
2 Guinness Storehouse
3 Trinity College Dublin

● **SIGHTS**
4 14 Henrietta Street
5 Chester Beatty
6 EPIC The Irish Emigration Museum
7 General Post Office
  see 7 GPO Museum
8 Irish Whiskey Museum
9 James Joyce Centre
10 Jeanie Johnston
11 Little Museum of Dublin
12 Merrion Square
13 Museum of Literature Ireland
14 Museum of Natural History
15 National Library of Ireland
16 National Museum of Ireland – Archaeology
17 National Museum of Ireland – Decorative Arts & History
18 Oscar Wilde House
19 Pearse Lyons Distillery
20 Roe & Co Distillery
21 St Stephen's Green
22 Teeling Distillery

● **ACTIVITIES**
23 Dublin Literary Pub Crawl

● **SLEEPING**
24 Generator Hostel
25 Morgan Hotel
26 Shelbourne
27 Staunton's on the Green

● **EATING**
28 Leo Burdock's
29 Library Street
30 Soup Dragon
31 Winding Stair

● **DRINKING & NIGHTLIFE**
32 John Mulligan's

● **SHOPPING**
33 Sweny's Pharmacy

it's the world's most famous illuminated manuscript. Beneath the Campanile, student guides whisk you through Trinity's living history on 45-minute campus tours.

The university sits at the top of pedestrianised Grafton St, which leads to the centrepiece of Georgian Dublin and the city's favourite park, **St Stephen's Green**.

Natural & Social History Galore

Explore Dublin's museums

Cultural and archaeological treasures at the **National Museum of Ireland – Archaeology** *(museum.ie; free)* include the 12th-century Ardagh Chalice and the 8th-century Tara Brooch, both masterpieces of Celtic metalwork. The museum's sister institutions are **Museum of Natural History** *(museum.ie; free)* with its stuffed beasts and the **National Museum of Ireland – Decorative Arts & History** *(museum.ie; free)*, at 18th-century Collins Barracks.

The quirky **Little Museum of Dublin** *(littlemuseum.ie; €18)* tells the city's story via memorabilia, photographs and artefacts donated by the general public. Social history is also explored at **14 Henrietta Street** *(14henriettastreet.ie; adult/child €10/6)* – part museum, part community archive.

Architectural Patchwork & Rare Objects

Dublin's castle and famous library

For over 700 years, **Dublin Castle** *(dublincastle.ie; adult/child €8/4)* served as the centre of British rule in Ireland. Only the 13th-century Record Tower survives from the original Anglo-Norman stronghold built by the order of King John in 1204. Guided tours include the opulent State Rooms.

In the castle grounds, the world-famous library **Chester Beatty** *(chesterbeatty.ie; free)* has a breathtaking assembly of more than 20,000 manuscripts, including the world's second-oldest biblical fragment and a collection of Qurans from the 9th to the 19th centuries.

Ireland's Diaspora

Understand Irish emigration

EPIC The Irish Emigration Museum *(epicchq.com; from €28)* charts Ireland's global story in interactive galleries spread through vaulted stone tunnels, where you discover why millions left, where they landed and how 70 million people now claim Irish roots.

GO CITY PASS

If you know you're going to be ticking off a few big attractions while you're in town, a **Go City Dublin pass** *(gocity.com; from €69)* can save you some cash. Choose between an All-Inclusive Pass or an Explorer Pass, where you select how many sights you want to see.

The All-Inclusive Pass is probably the easiest bet. It can be purchased for one to five days and includes all major attractions around Dublin, from the big (Guinness Storehouse, Christ Church and EPIC) to the small (Teeling Distillery, 14 Henrietta Street). It's not just attractions, either – options include hop-on/hop-off bus tours, food walking tours and excursions to places like the Game of Thrones Studio Tour in Northern Ireland.

 EATING IN DUBLIN: OUR PICKS

Leo Burdock's: Dublin's most famous fish-and-chip shop is a rite of passage for many. *11.30am-midnight Sun-Thu, to 1am Fri & Sat €*

Soup Dragon: This cafe has been a budget favourite for years. The daily soup, bread and fruit deal is a bargain. *8am-5pm Mon-Fri €*

Winding Stair: Contemporary Irish cuisine in an elegant 1st-floor dining room. *noon-3.30pm & 5.30-10.30pm €€*

Library Street: Sophisticated, superb sharing plates from Michelin-trained Kevin Burke. *5-11.30pm Tue-Thu, from 2.30pm Fri & Sat €€*

EPIC The Irish Emigration Museum

Combination tickets are available with the **Jeanie Johnston** *(jeaniejohnston.ie; adult/child €15/10),* a replica 19th-century 'coffin ship' that carried starving Irish emigrants across the Atlantic during the 1845–52 Great Famine.

The Struggle for Nationhood

Learn about Irish independence

A quintessential Dublin landmark, the **General Post Office** served as command HQ for the rebels during the 1916 Easter Rising; you can still see the pockmarks of the struggle in the Doric columns outside. Its interactive visitor centre, **GPO Museum** *(gpomuseum.ie; adult/child €15/7.50),* serves as a fitting tribute to its role in the creation of the Irish state, exploring the Rising's origins to its aftermath.

Grim prison **Kilmainham Gaol** *(kilmainhamgaolmuseum. ie; adult/child €8/4),* built in 1796 and closed in 1924, played a pivotal role in nearly every chapter of the country's long resistance to British rule.

City of Literature

Leaf through literary Dublin

A UNESCO City of Literature, Dublin is the vanguard for Irish writing, superbly covered at the **Museum of Literature Ireland** *(moli.ie; adult/child €14.50/12).* The **James Joyce Centre** *(jamesjoyce.ie; adult/child €7/5)* has evocative exhibits and also leads walking tours of his novels' settings. Overlooking elegant **Merrion Square**, the childhood home of Oscar Wilde is now the **Oscar Wilde House** *(oscarwildehouse.com; tour €25)* with guided tours. And on a two-hour **Dublin Literary Pub Crawl** *(dublinpubcrawl.com; adult/ student €20/18),* actors lead you on a jaunt between pubs associated with famous Dublin writers.

BEST FESTIVALS IN DUBLIN

Dublin International Film Festival: Two weeks of screenings, premieres and celebrities around the city in February/ March.

St Patrick's Festival: Apart from the parade, in March the Festival Quarter is the hub of live music, DJs and comedy, usually held at Collins Barracks.

Pride: Pride is a big deal in Dublin, and the LGBTIQ+ festival in June is only growing. Expect gigs, parties and one hell of a parade.

Forbidden Fruit: The city's foremost music festival, with huge acts playing on the grounds of Royal Hospital Kilmainham in June.

Dublin International Literature Festival: Merrion Sq goes literary for 10 days in May, with food trucks between tents hosting readings and interviews.

Sláinte! (Cheers)

Dublin's brewing and distilling history

Dublin's most popular attraction is the **Guinness Storehouse** (*guinness-storehouse.com; experiences €26-350*). Seven floors of foam, folklore and flawless pours, it's part brewery, part immersive brand shrine. Toast your visit at the rooftop Gravity Bar, pint in hand, city skyline laid out before you.

Distilling has been revived in the surrounding Liberties neighbourhood in recent years, with **Teeling Distillery** (*teelingwhiskey.com; tours €20-35*), **Pearse Lyons Distillery** (*pearselyonsdistillery.com; tours €22-32*) and **Roe & Co** (*roeandcowhiskey.com; from €25*) in the art deco Guinness Power Station all offering tours and tastings.

If you want to taste a few different spirits and not just one brand, head to the **Irish Whiskey Museum** (*irishwhiskeymuseum.ie; tours €23-35*) near Trinity College.

Testament to Prehistoric Humankind

Day trip to Newgrange

Located 54km north of central Dublin in County Meath, the vast Neolithic necropolis known as **Brú na Bóinne** (*heritageireland.ie; tour & Newgrange chamber adult/child €18/12*) is one of the most extraordinary sites in Europe. A thousand years older than Stonehenge and a UNESCO World Heritage site, the complex's tombs were the largest artificial structures in Ireland until the construction of the Anglo-Norman castles 4000 years later. The area consists of many different sites; a startling 80m in diameter and 13m high, **Newgrange's** circular stone ramparts, topped by a grassy dome and fronted by a wall of blazing white quartz, look eerily futuristic. Underneath lies the finest Stone Age passage tomb in Ireland.

Magical Mountain Monastery Ruins

Day trip to Glendalough

Tucked into a narrow valley in the Wicklow Mountains 51km south of central Dublin, **Glendalough** (*glendalough.ie; car park €4*) is one of Ireland's most important early Christian sites. With its stone ruins scattered amid forest and misty lakes, it's not difficult to see why monks came seeking solitude and pine-scented silence. In the late 5th century, St Kevin, a bishop, established a monastery here. The most fascinating ancient structures lie in the lower part of the valley east of the Lower Lake; the Upper Lake has the best scenery. Bring walking boots for its trails.

Kilkenny

HISTORY | ARCHITECTURE | FESTIVALS

County Kilkenny's centrepiece is its namesake city. Known as the Marble City for its dark, fossil-speckled limestone, it bewitches visitors with medieval alleys winding between a historic cathedral and an imposing castle that fulfils every storybook fantasy of what one should look like, along with craft studios, traditional pubs and glorious riverside walks and cycle trails. Surrounding it, the county too is a delight, a place of rolling hills where tiny roads navigate the valleys alongside trout-filled rivers, moss-covered stone walls, idyllic towns and villages, and relics of centuries of Irish religious history.

Across the border in County Tipperary, Cashel was once the seat of the high kings of the province of Munster. Among the country's most majestic religious sites, the extraordinary Rock of Cashel emerges out of the craggy landscape on a limestone bluff above the Golden Vale. This is one of the most enchanting corners of Ireland's Ancient East.

☑ **TOP TIP**

Guided tours give a great insight into Kilkenny city. Options span historian-led **Pat Tynan Kilkenny Walking Tours** *(kilkennywalkingtours.ie)*, craic-filled **Shenanigans** *(shenaniganswalks.com)*, 'Spooktacular' tours of haunted sights with **Kilkenny Ghost Tours** *(kilkennyghosttours. com)*, sunset tours with **Kilkenny Cycling Tours** *(kilkennycyclingtours. com)* and castle-view river cruises with **Boat Trips Kilkenny** *(boattrips.ie)*.

Kilkenny City

Sightseeing along the medieval mile

Kilkenny city's medieval mile connects its major historic sites. Marking its southern end beside the River Nore is **Kilkenny Castle** *(kilkennycastle.ie; self-guided tours adult/child €8/4,*

⊚ GETTING AROUND

Kilkenny city's centre is easily walkable, though its narrow streets can get crowded. Cycling is an enjoyable option; **Bolt** *(bolt.eu)* has app-based e-bikes, or rent bikes from **Kilkenny Cycling Tours** *(kilkennycyclingtours.com).*

Located 1.2km northeast of Kilkenny Castle (around a 15-minute walk) across the River

Nore, **MacDonagh Train Station** is on the line from Dublin Heuston south via Thomastown to Waterford city. Cashel is just 60km southwest of Kilkenny city, but there's no direct public transport; you'll need a car, or catch a bus from Cork city (1¾ hours).

KILKENNY'S WITCHCRAFT TRIAL

Several sights along the medieval mile have connections to the infamous witchcraft trial of Dame Alice Kyteler. In medieval Kilkenny, Dame Alice established **Kytelers Inn** *(kytelersinn. com)* on St Kieran's St in the early 14th century (it's still full of atmospheric spaces for a pint). After Dame Alice's four wealthy husbands died in mysterious circumstances, she fled Ireland to avoid conviction for witchcraft; in her absence, her maid, Petronella de Meath, was burned at the stake in 1324 just north of St Mary's Church, where Kilkenny's Tholsel (City Hall) was built in 1761. The central tower of St Canice's Cathedral collapsed in 1332 after Dame Alice's son, William, was made to carry out roof repairs as penance.

St Canice's Cathedral, Kilkenny City

guided tours €12/6); book tickets up to a week ahead. Dating back to the Anglo-Norman conquest, it was built in stone in 1192 and over the centuries it has undergone successive adaptations; three of its four round towers survive. Strolling its richly decorated rooms, gardens and 21 hectares of public parkland evokes its past. The castle's former stables and coach houses, Castle Yard, is now the **National Design & Craft Gallery** *(dcci.ie; free).*

Early-13th-century St Mary's Church houses the **Medieval Mile Museum** *(medievalmilemuseum.ie; audio tour adult/ child €7/3, guided tour €10/5),* putting 800 years of city history into context. Artefacts include maces, sceptres, keys, coins, civic records and skeletons. Works are underway to combine it with the adjacent **Tholsel** (City Hall) to create the Museum of Medieval Kilkenny.

Accessed via an arched entry and stone steps, **Butter Slip** is a dark, narrow walkway built in 1616 and once lined with the stalls of butter vendors. To the north, **Rothe House & Garden** *(rothehouse.com; self-guided tours adult/child €8.50/4, guided tours €10/6),* a Tudor merchant's house, dates from 1594.

St Canice's Cathedral *(stcanicescathedral.ie; adult/child €7.50/5, incl guided tour & tower climb €16/9)* was built between 1202 and 1285. Rising 30m outside, the remarkably preserved round tower dates from the 9th century. Heading southwest on Abbey St through the **Black Freren Gate** (the medieval

EATING IN KILKENNY CITY: OUR PICKS

Arán Deli & Bakery: This deli/bakery uses great sourdoughs in its gourmet sandwiches, plus savoury and sweet pastries. *7am-3pm Wed-Mon* €

Foodworks: In a restored bank, with all-day brunch dishes that incorporate the owners' vegetables, herbs and reared pigs. *8.30am-4pm Wed-Sun* €€

Petronella: Modern Irish cuisine in a stone-walled, oak-beamed building on the medieval Butter Slip. *noon-2.30pm & 4-9.30pm Tue-Sat, noon-5pm Sun* €€€

Campagne: Michelin-starred chef Garrett Byrne creates regional French cuisine from seasonal Irish produce. *5.30-9pm Wed-Sat, 12.30-2.30pm Sun* €€€

NO LIMIT PICTURES/GETTY IMAGES

city walls' only surviving arch), you'll reach the **Black Abbey** *(dominicans.ie; by donation)*, a Dominican priory built in 1225.

Thomastown
Unearth architectural treasures
Thomastown (Baile Mhic Andáin; historically known as Grennan), 17km southeast of Kilkenny city, centres on a quadrant of streets lined by colourfully painted buildings and enticing galleries and cafes. One of the most complete Cistercian abbey ruins in Ireland, the 12th-century **Jerpoint Abbey** *(heritageireland.ie; adult/child €5/3)* lies 2.5km southwest.

Sprawling across a hectare of pastoral landscapes 9km northwest of Jerpoint Abbey, **Kells Priory** *(heritageireland.ie; free)* was founded in 1193. Extensive ruins of this fortified Augustinian monastery remain, including a nave, chancel, chapel, bread oven and mill.

Inistioge
Fall for Inistioge's charms
With its 18th-century, 10-arch stone bridge and central green ringed by churches, cafes and pubs, Inistioge (Inis Tíog), 26km southeast of Kilkenny, is one of Ireland's prettiest villages. Just outside, 1.5km south at **Woodstock Gardens & Arboretum** *(woodstock.ie; per car €5)*, 20 hectares of formal and informal gardens have been restored to the Victorian era of 1840 to 1890, with long avenues lined with noble fir and monkey puzzle trees. Foxgloves, lavender and cornflowers on the terraced flower garden are linked to the rose garden by the yew walk.

Cashel
Explore ecclesiastical history
Bristling with medieval towers on a limestone outcrop above green fields, the **Rock of Cashel** *(heritageireland.ie; adult/child €8/6)* is one of Ireland's most spectacular sights. Sturdy 15th-century walls surround an enclosure containing a 13th-century Gothic cathedral, early-12th-century 28m-tall round tower, and 15th-century choristers' kitchen and dining hall. The highlight is **Cormac's Chapel**, with its beautifully carved doorways and Ireland's only surviving Romanesque frescoes. The best photo opportunities are from the hauntingly beautiful ruins of **Hore Abbey**, 1km west.

KILKENNY FESTIVALS

St Patrick's Festival Kilkenny: Celebrations over four days in March include marching bands, a funfair, fireworks and parade.

Kilkenny Tradfest: This four-day mid-March event has gigs, sessions, workshops and a trad-music trail.

Kilkenny Roots Festival: Bluegrass, swing, folk and Cajun music play during May's four-day fest.

Cat Laughs Comedy Festival: Uproariously funny Irish and international comedians perform over four days in June.

Kilkenny Arts Festival: Over 250 artists perform in more than 150 events at historic venues during August.

Savour Kilkenny: Harvest celebrations in October include cookery demonstrations, market stalls and a craft brewery and distillery marquee.

Yulefest: Winter cheer warms the city from late November to late December.

DRINKING IN KILKENNY CITY: OUR PICKS

Sullivan's Taproom: Reviving local brewing with its Black Marble Stout, Maltings Red Ale and Irish Gold. Huge beer garden. *noon-11pm Sun-Thu, to 12.30am Fri & Sat*

Tynans Bridge House Bar: Charming former grocery/pub with original timber cabinetry opposite St John's Bridge. *10.30am-11.30pm Sun-Thu, to 12.30am Fri & Sat*

Dylan Whisky Bar: Cosy snugs, old advert-etched mirrors, open turf fire and tasting flights from its 200-strong whiskey collection. *5pm-midnight Mon-Fri, from 3pm Sat & Sun*

Left Bank: In an 1870s Bank of Ireland building, with nine bars, regular live music, a heated courtyard and 1st-floor nightclub. *noon-11pm Sun-Thu, to 2am Fri & Sat*

Cork

FOOD & DRINK | HISTORY | WILD COASTLINE

Ireland's second city, Cork – a thriving metropolis made glorious by location and its almost Rabelaisian devotion to the finer things in life – has an understated confidence grounded in its plethora of food markets and an ever-evolving cast of creative eateries, and in its selection of pubs, entertainment and cultural pursuits including copious festivals.

Surrounding it is an undulating landscape dotted with charming villages. The country's largest county, Cork can fairly lay claim to being the nation's food and drink capital, with lush pastures and coastal fishing fleets, as well as 60% of the country's artisan producers located here – traditional cheesemakers, craft bakers, boutique coffee roasters... Seafood-famed Kinsale is the gateway to the 2500km-long Wild Atlantic Way; heading west, narrow roads wind around rugged, rock-girt coastlines and pass through a dozen or more old fishing villages where boats bob at their moorings and harbourside bars entice you in for a pint.

Cork City

Enter a Victorian prison

Behind towering walls dating from 1818, the imposing **Cork City Gaol** *(corkcitygaol.com; adult/child €11/7, audio guide or guided tour extra €2)* received its first inmates in 1824. Poverty was the most common crime, especially during the desperate

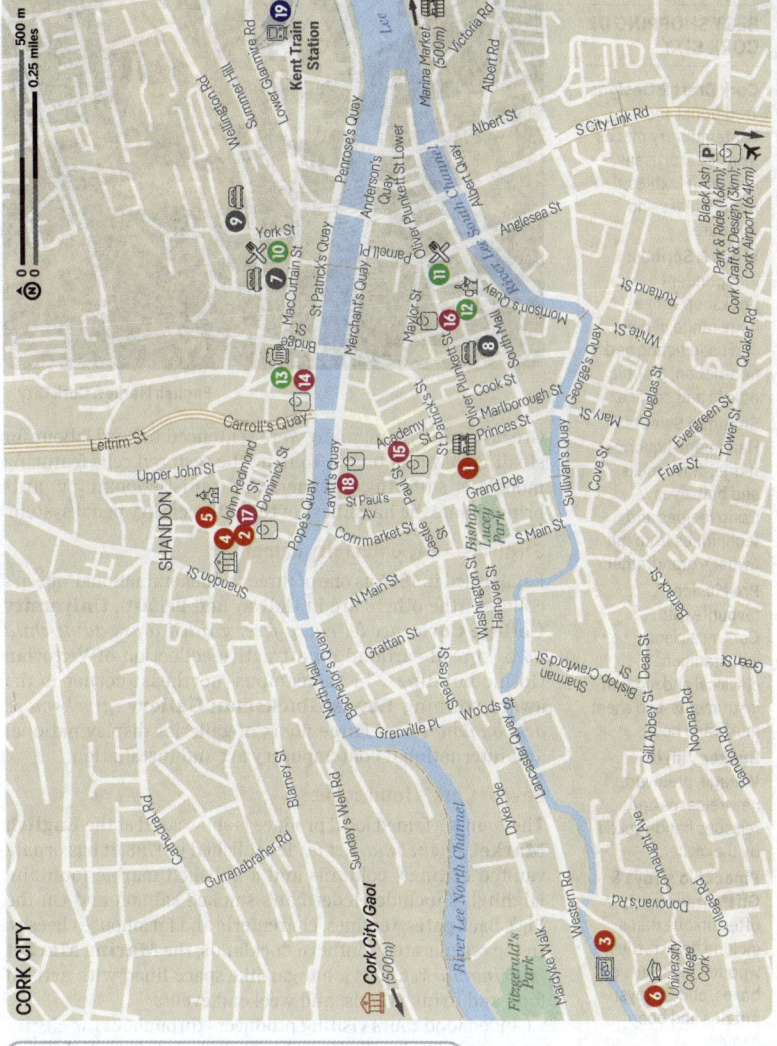

CORK CITY

SIGHTS
see 4 Cork Butter Museum
1 English Market
2 Firkin Crane
3 Lewis Glucksman Gallery
4 Old Butter Market
5 St Anne's Church
6 University College Cork

SLEEPING
7 Hotel Isaacs
8 Imperial Hotel
9 Sheila's Hostel

EATING
10 Glass Curtain
11 Market Lane

DRINKING & NIGHTLIFE
12 Crane Lane Theatre
13 Sin É

SHOPPING
14 Bunker Vinyl
15 Pinocchio's Toys & Gifts
16 Pro Musica
17 Shandon Sweets
18 Vibes & Scribes

TRANSPORT
19 Kent Train Station

BEST SHOPPING IN CORK CITY

Cork Craft & Design: Traditional and contemporary pieces from local artisans including textiles, framed glass and furniture.

Vibes & Scribes: Independent bookshop with a huge range of new and used fiction and non-fiction, graphic novels and comics.

Shandon Sweets: Handmade liquorice, fudge, clove rocks and bullseyes using recipes and techniques from the owner's grandfather.

Pro Musica: A favourite with Cork musicians, with traditional, classical and modern instruments, and sheet music and books.

Bunker Vinyl: Vintage, preloved, new releases and reissues hand-picked by the owner.

Pinocchio's Toys & Gifts: Traditional, often unique items include baby rattles, wooden toys, music boxes, cuddly toys, puzzles and board games.

D. RIBEIRO/SHUTTERSTOCK

English Market, Cork City

Great Famine years; many were sentenced to hard labour for stealing loaves of bread. Touring the restored cells featuring models of suffering prisoners and sadistic-looking guards brings home the harshness of the 19th-century penal system.

Stroll a stately university campus

Established in 1845 as one of three nondenominational 'queen's colleges' (the others are in Galway and Belfast), **University College Cork** (*ucc.ie; entry free; guided tours adult/child €5/3*) spreads around an attractive collection of Victorian Gothic buildings. In the campus' northeast corner is the award-winning **Lewis Glucksman Gallery** (*glucksman. org; by donation*). Three floors of galleries display national and international contemporary art and installation.

Savour Cork's food scene

The county's famed local produce is showcased at the **English Market** (*englishmarket.ie*). Established in 1788, it has ornate vaulted ceilings, columns and a polished marble fountain. Highlights include Hederman's smoked salmon and On the Pig's Back patés, terrines, charcuterie and farmhouse cheeses. In the regenerated southern docklands, the **Marina Market** (*marinamarket.ie*) is a hangar-like space lined with artisan food and drink stands, and weekend events.

Guided food tours visiting producers throughout the city include Cork Tasting Trails (2½ to three hours) from **Fab Food Trails** (*fabfoodtrails.ie; €80*) and the Cork Culinary Tour (three hours) from **Bonner Travel** (*bonner-travel.com; €130*).

 EATING & DRINKING IN CORK CITY: OUR PICKS

Market Lane: Bright bistro with a hearty menu reflecting what's fresh at the English Market. *noon-9.30pm Sun-Wed, to 10pm Thu & Fri, to 10.30pm Sat €€*

Glass Curtain: Contemporary Irish cuisine like lamb belly with black garlic and whey, in a 19th-century bakery. *5.30-10.30pm Tue-Thu, from 5pm Fri & Sat €€€*

Crane Lane Theatre: Three bars, a covered laneway beer garden, roaring 1920s decor, live bands from jazz and bluegrass to rock plus DJ sets. *4pm-2.30am*

Sin É: A true craic-filled pub, long on atmosphere and short on pretension, with live music almost every night. *12.30-11.30pm Sun-Thu, to 12.30am Fri & Sat*

In Cork pubs, locally brewed Murphy's and Beamish stouts, not Guinness, are the preferred pints.

Ring the Shandon bells

Overlooking the city centre, hillside Shandon (from the Irish Sean Dún, meaning 'old fort') is an atmospheric spot to wander. Built in 1855, the large, circular **Firkin Crane** (*firkincrane. ie*) is where Cork's butter was weighed and packed for export; it now houses a dance centre. Neoclassical columns adorn the facade of the **Old Butter Market**; the trade's history is told at the adjacent **Cork Butter Museum** (*thebuttermuseum. com; adult/child €5/1.50*).

Shandon is dominated by the 1722 **St Anne's Church** (*stanneshandon.ie; church €3, incl tower climb adult/child €9/5*); on the tower's 1st floor, aspiring campanologists can ring the **Shandon Bells** then continue up the 132 steps to the top for 360-degree views of the city.

Kinsale

Tour Kinsale's picturesque harbour

Kinsale (Cionn tSáile), 25km south of Cork city, is one of many colourful gems strung along County Cork's coastline. Guarded by a huge 17th-century fortress, the star-shaped artillery **Charles Fort** (*heritageireland.ie; adult/child €5/3*), its narrow, winding streets are lined with galleries, lively bars and superb seafood eateries.

Discover the history of the town by joining Dermot Ryan of **Kinsale Heritage Town Walks** (*kinsaleheritage.com; adult/child €5/free*) for a one-hour walking tour. To get out on the water, take a one-hour boat trip of the harbour with **Kinsale Harbour Cruises** (*kinsaleharbourcruises.com; adult/child €15/7*) or a two-hour open-topped adventure boat trip with **Kinsale Sea Safari** (*kinsaleseasafari.ie; €53*).

Cobh

Contemplate Cobh's Titanic heritage

Cobh (pronounced 'cove'), 23km east of Cork city, is dotted with brightly coloured houses and overlooked by the single-spire, Gothic Revival–style **St Colman's Cathedral** (*cobhcathedralparish.ie; by donation*).

This was the final port of call for RMS *Titanic* in 1912. The original White Star Line offices on Cobh's waterfront, where passengers embarked, now house the poignant **Titanic Experience Cobh** (*titanicexperiencecobh.ie; adult/child €13/9*); guided tours provide an insight into the ill-fated liner's first and final voyage.

Sail to a prison island

Clearly visible offshore, **Spike Island** (*spikeislandcork.ie; adult/child incl ferry & guided tour €27.95/14.95*) lies low and green in Cork Harbour, topped by a huge 18th-century artillery fort that commanded the harbour entrance. During the Irish War of Independence and from 1984 to 2004, it served as a prison, gaining the nickname 'Ireland's Alcatraz'.

THE GREAT FAMINE

The Great Famine of 1845–52 remains Ireland's greatest national tragedy. With farmers already crippled by repressive Penal Laws, when a blight hit potato crops, prices soared. Most tenants fell into arrears and were evicted or sent to the dire conditions of the workhouses. Yet Ireland was forced to export its food to Britain. Lord Dufferin and GF Boyle, who journeyed from Oxford to Skibbereen in 1847 to see if reports of the Famine were true, reported: 'The accounts are not exaggerated – they cannot be exaggerated – nothing more frightful can be conceived'. The Poor Law deemed landlords responsible for the maintenance of their poor and encouraged many to 'remove' tenants from their estates by paying their way to America aboard the scourged 'coffin ships'.

Kerry

SCENERY | OUTDOOR ACTIVITIES | HISTORY

 TOP TIP

Kerry's standout sight, Skellig Michael, needs to be booked well in advance but sea crossings can be cancelled at short notice due to bad weather, so have a plan B just in case.

County Kerry (Irish: Chiarraí) contains some of Ireland's most iconic scenery: surf-pounded sea cliffs, soft golden strands, emerald-green farmland stitched by stone walls, mist-shrouded bogs and mountain peaks. Offshore, the jagged, improbable outpost of Skellig Michael is one of the Republic's two UNESCO World Heritage sites.

With one of the country's finest national parks as its backyard, the lively tourism hub of Killarney spills over with colourful shops, restaurants and pubs with spirited trad music. The town is the jumping-off point for the famed Ring of Kerry driving route, which skirts the Iveragh Peninsula, with photo-worthy views at every twist and turn.

To Killarney's north, the Dingle Peninsula is like a condensed version of its southern neighbour, with the Slea Head Drive linking ancient prehistoric ring forts, beehive huts, Christian sites and sandy beaches looping from the charming fishing port of Dingle, renowned for its seafood, traditional culture and music-filled pubs.

Killarney National Park

Clip-clop in a jaunting car

Traditional horse-drawn jaunting cars provide tours from Killarney town to Ross Castle and Muckross Estate, complete

---

GETTING AROUND

County Kerry covers a large area, much of it mountainous and remote, with narrow winding roads. Rail is more useful for getting to Kerry from Dublin or Cork than getting around. Regular bus services run from Killarney to Kerry Airport, and from Killarney to Dingle town.

Local minibuses serve the Ring of Kerry and Dingle Peninsula though services can be infrequent, so a car is preferable. Find car rental outlets in Killarney and at Kerry Airport. Bicycles are ideal for exploring the Killarney region; try your accommodation or **Killarney Rent A Bike** (killarneyrentabike.com).

Gap of Dunloe (p381), Killarney National Park

KILLARNEY TOWN'S TOURISM EVOLUTION

Set amid lakes, waterfalls and woodland beneath heather-clad peaks, Killarney town is the natural base camp for excursions into the neighbouring national park. In the business of welcoming visitors since 1747, when Thomas Browne (fourth Viscount Kenmare) tapped into its tourism potential, followed by the railway's arrival in 1853 and the 2014 launch of the Wild Atlantic Way, the town is a well-oiled tourism machine, with competition keeping standards high. Green initiatives, such as the 2023 ban on single-use coffee cups (BYO or pay a €2 deposit for a reusable 2GoCup), and the Killarney Hotels Sustainability Charter (eliminating single-use items, reducing properties' carbon footprints, minimising food waste and using local suppliers) are paving the way for its sustainable future.

with amusing commentary from the 'jarvey' (driver). Cars typically fit up to four people; expect to pay around €20 per person for a one-hour tour. Pick them up at Kenmare Pl or book tours online with companies such as fifth-generation-run **Killarney Jaunting Cars** *(killarneyjauntingcars.com).*

Explore Muckross Estate

The impressive Victorian mansion of **Muckross House** *(muck ross-house.ie; adult/child house & farms €16/10, house or farms only €9/6)* was built as a hunting and fishing lodge for the Herbert family in 1843. Sloping down to the Middle Lake, beautiful **Muckross Gardens** are free to explore. Also here are three recreations of 1930s **Muckross Traditional Farms** (closed November to February).

Visit Ross Castle

A lovely 2.6km walk or bike ride southwest of Killarney town's St Mary's Cathedral pedestrian entrance through the park (you might spot deer along the way), **Ross Castle** *(heritageireland. ie; adult/child €5/3)* is a traditional tower house and keep from the 15th century, when it's thought to have been built by Irish chieftain O'Donoghue Mór. Entertaining 45-minute guided tours provide an easily digested medieval history lesson.

 EATING IN KILLARNEY TOWN: OUR PICKS

Lir Café: Brews some of Killarney's best coffee; the food spans toasties, pastries, cakes and handmade chocolates. *7am-7pm* €

Mad Monk: Fresh seafood from its own fishing fleet with hand-cut chips in a bright, bare-brick space. *12.30-8.30pm Sun-Thu, to 9pm Fri & Sat* €€

Cronin's Restaurant: Kerry produce includes Skellig prawns, Kenmare salmon and MacGillycuddy Reeks venison. *4-9.30pm Mon-Fri, from 3pm Sat & Sun* €€

Brícín: Charmer with antique lamps, stained glass and vintage art; try the house-speciality boxty (potato pancake). *6-9.30pm Tue-Sat* €€

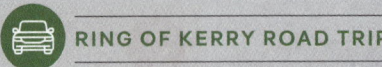

RING OF KERRY ROAD TRIP

This circuit of the Iveragh Peninsula winds past pretty villages, pristine beaches, craggy mountains and sparkling loughs, with views of the island-dotted Atlantic.

START	END	LENGTH
Killarney	Killarney	170km; 1 day

South of Killarney, the summit of the narrow pass known as ❶ **Moll's Gap** is worth a stop for the great views towards the Gap of Dunloe and breakfast at Avoca Cafe. The N71 road descends via swooping bends to ❷ **Kenmare**, with a neat triangle of streets lined with craft shops, art galleries and cafes. West on the N70, the pretty village of ❸ **Sneem** is split by a river, with a picturesque waterfall tumbling below the old stone bridge.

The coastal scenery ramps into overdrive as the road winds over the hill to tiny ❹ **Caherdaniel**, hidden among the trees at Derrynane Bay. A short detour leads to beautiful Derrynane Beach.

The N70 now climbs high above the sea, passing Beenarourke viewpoint, with grandstand views over scattered islands, before descending to the old-fashioned seaside (and golf) resort of ❺ **Waterville**. Stay on the N70 (or detour via the Skellig Ring before continuing north) to ❻ **Cahersiveen**, the main town on the Ring and home to the excellent Old Barracks heritage centre.

Follow the N70 to the family-favourite, recreated 19th-century ❼ **Kerry Bog Village** museum, with the thatched homes of the turfcutter, blacksmith, thatcher and labourer, and a dairy, and meet Kerry bog ponies. Continue on the N70 to Killorglin, then the N72 back to Killarney.

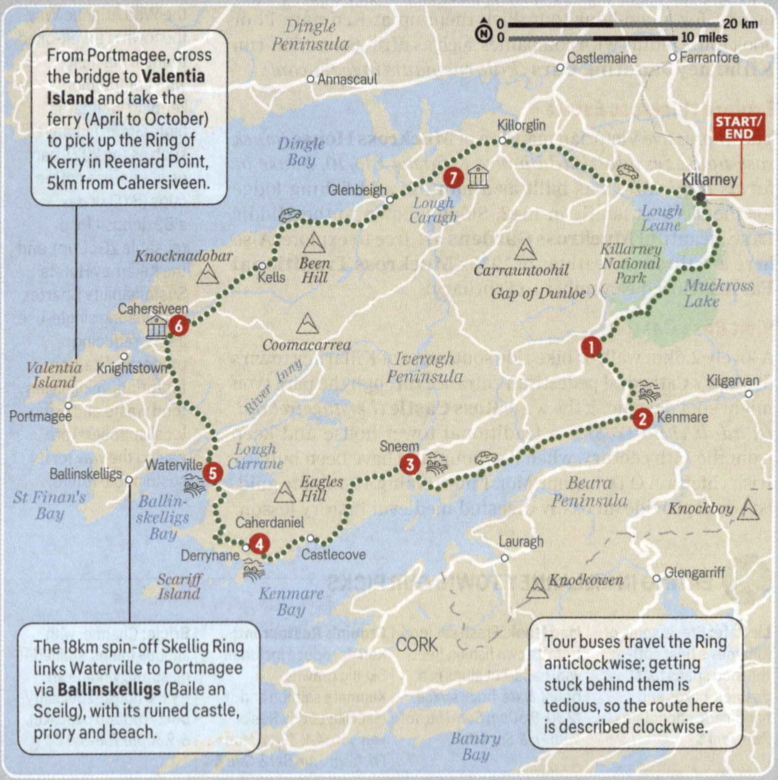

From Portmagee, cross the bridge to **Valentia Island** and take the ferry (April to October) to pick up the Ring of Kerry in Reenard Point, 5km from Cahersiveen.

The 18km spin-off Skellig Ring links Waterville to Portmagee via **Ballinskelligs** (Baile an Sceilg), with its ruined castle, priory and beach.

Tour buses travel the Ring anticlockwise; getting stuck behind them is tedious, so the route here is described clockwise.

0 20 km
0 10 miles

Dingle Peninsula · Annascaul · Castlemaine · Farranfore · Killorglin · Dingle Bay · Glenbeigh · Lough Caragh · Killarney · START/END · Lough Leane · Knocknadobar · Kells · Been Hill · Carrauntoohil · Killarney National Park · Gap of Dunloe · Muckross Lake · Cahersiveen · Coomacarrea · Iveragh Peninsula · Kilgarvan · Valentia Island · Knightstown · River Inny · Kenmare · Portmagee · Lough Currane · Sneem · Beara Peninsula · Knockboy · Ballinskelligs · Waterville · Eagles Hill · St Finan's Bay · Ballinskelligs Bay · Caherdaniel · Lauragh · Knockowen · Glengarriff · Derrynane · Castlecove · Scariff Island · Kenmare Bay · CORK · Bantry Bay

Killarney Lake Tours (*killarneylaketours.ie; waterbus adult/child €15/10*) departs out front, and traditional **open boats** (*€15/10*) nearby at **Reen Pier**.

The Gap of Dunloe by boat and bike

A boat trip across the lakes followed by a bike ride through the mountain scenery of the **Gap of Dunloe** is the classic Killarney experience; organise it with your accommodation or book online at **Gap of Dunloe Tours** (*gapofdunloetours.com*). Boats depart from Reen Pier at 11am, with bikes propped in the bow for the 1½-hour cruise. Disembarking at 19th-century hunting lodge **Lord Brandon's Cottage**, the cycling section begins with a 4.5km climb to the head of the Gap; at the summit, you're rewarded with stunning views back to the Upper Lake and forward into the narrow pass of the Gap itself, a wild and scenic glaciated valley. The total distance cycled is 23km. Allowing for stops, you should be back in Killarney by 3.30pm.

Skellig Islands

Voyage to a remote island monastery

The jagged, 217m-high rock of **Skellig Michael** (*Sceilg Mhichíl; heritageireland.ie; landing tour/non-landing ecotour per person from €130/50*) rises dramatically out of the sea 11.5km off the coast, topped with the remains of an early Christian monastery that famously featured in two *Star Wars* movies. Reached by 618 steps cut into the steep rockface (no handrails), the 6th-century monastery is a miracle of masonry, set on platforms built on the vertiginous slope using nothing more than drystone walls and earth. Birdlife includes puffins from around April to early August.

Landing tours (around five hours) usually run from mid-May to September, weather permitting; dates and tour-boat permits are announced each year. Most boats depart from Portmagee. Numbers are limited, so book well ahead (landings are still subject to conditions on the day). Children must be over 12.

Dingle

Discover the Slea Head Drive

Beyond Dingle town, the peninsula's scenery goes into overdrive. The 42km **Slea Head Drive** passes through the villages of Ventry, Dunquin and Ballyferriter, taking in a host of superbly preserved structures from the ancient past including beehive huts, ring forts, inscribed stones and early Christian sites. Allow at least half a day.

PÁIRC NÁISIÚNTA NA MARA, CIARRAÍ

Known by its Irish name **Páirc Náisiúnta na Mara, Ciarraí** (*nationalparks.ie/mara-ciarrai*), the **Kerry Seas National Park** became Ireland's first marine national park when it was officially designated in April 2024. Centred around the Dingle Peninsula, its 290 sq km take in islands off the Kerry coast (including Skellig Michael), offshore marine reefs (notably the deep limestone Kerry Head Shoal), and coastal mainland sites such as the fore dunes and fixed dunes at **Inch** (both a Special Area of Conservation and a Special Protection Area), **Mt Brandon** uplands and the peninsula's spectacular **Connor Pass**. The park's coast is home to seabird colonies including puffins, storm petrels and Manx shearwaters, with other bird species including gannets, fulmars, kittiwakes, guillemots and razorbills.

DRINKING IN DINGLE TOWN: OUR PICKS

Foxy John's: This classic Dingle shop-pub stocks stout and whiskey. *10.30am-11.30pm Mon-Thu, to 12.30am Fri & Sat, noon-11.30pm Sun*	**Dick Mack's:** Snugs inside, tables in the courtyard, plus the pub's own craft beers from its restored 19th-century brewhouse. *noon-11pm*	**Curran's:** Shop-pub with original stained-glass snugs; regular spontaneous trad sessions. *noon-11.30pm Sun-Thu, to 12.30am Fri & Sat*	**John Benny's:** Local musos pour in most nights for trad sessions at this stone-floored pub. *11.30am-11.30pm Tue-Thu & Sun, to 12.30am Fri & Sat*

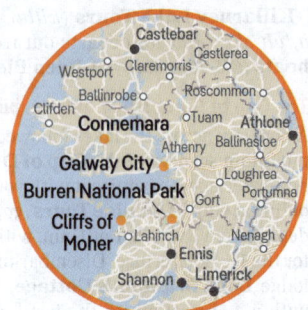

Galway

MUSIC | FOOD & DRINK | SCENERY

 TOP TIP

Numerous companies offer day trips from Galway city to highlights of Galway's Connemara region like Kylemore Abbey, Clare's Cliffs of Moher and Burren National Park in Clare, and the ancient, starkly beautiful Aran Islands (a geological extension of the Burren), off the coast of both counties. Try **Lally Tours** (lallytours.com).

The halfway point of the weaving 2500km Wild Atlantic Way, County Galway's exuberant namesake city is a swirl of colourful shop-lined streets filled with buskers and performance artists and enticing old pubs that hum with trad-music sessions, hosting some 120 festivals held throughout the year.

Some of Ireland's most spellbinding scenery fans out from Galway's city limits, particularly in the breathtaking Connemara region, where tiny roads wander along a coastline studded with islands, dazzling white-sand beaches and intriguing villages; the interior shelters heath-strewn boglands, glassy lakes, looming mountains and isolated valleys. Stone walls and sheep are always on the horizon.

To Galway's south are the windswept landscapes of County Clare, including the ocean-pounded coast, eroding rock into fantastic formations, sea stacks and sheer precipices including those at the Cliffs of Moher and the moonscape-like bare limestone Burren, together forming a UNESCO Global Geopark.

Galway City

Take a traditional music pub crawl

For the best of Galway's toe-tapping tunes, head to the **Latin Quarter**, named for the city's historic trading links with Spain and Portugal.

GETTING AROUND

Galway city is well connected with other major towns by both bus and train. Bus Éireann has limited services in most of Connemara. Driving is the best way to explore, getting you to remote spots. Fuel up in larger towns when you can. If you're driving from County Kerry, stop off in Clare en route to Galway.

Galway's city centre is easily explored on foot. Buy a Visitor Leap Card to save up to 30% on fares. Use the Coca-Cola bike-share scheme to get around the city. A bus connects Shannon Airport to Galway city.

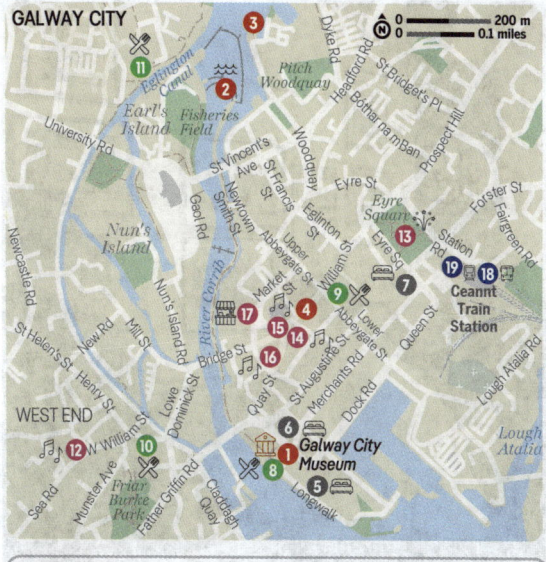

GALWAY CITY

0 — 200 m
0 — 0.1 miles

GALWAY CITY'S BEST FESTIVALS

Cúirt International Festival of Literature: April sees one of Ireland's premier literary festivals, featuring a week of talks, interviews, poetry sessions and readings.

Blas na Bealtaine: 'A Taste of May' is a month-long celebration of Galway's culinary scene including farm tours, foraging, cookery demos and more.

Galway International Arts Festival: The biggest event on the calendar is held in late July, a two-week fiesta of theatre, comedy, music and art.

Galway Races: A week of horse racing begins on the last Monday in July, drawing tens of thousands of punters.

Galway International Oyster & Seafood Festival: Going strong since 1954, the world's oldest oyster festival takes place over the last weekend in September.

● **HIGHLIGHTS**
1 Galway City Museum

● **SIGHTS**
2 Salmon Weir

● **ACTIVITIES**
3 Corrib Princess
4 Galway Food Tours

● **SLEEPING**
5 Heron's Rest

6 House Hotel
7 Kinlay Hostel

● **EATING**
8 Ard Bia at Nimmo's
9 Food for Thought
10 Oscars Seafood Bistro
11 Sult

● **ENTERTAINMENT**
12 Crane Bar

13 Galway Christmas Market
14 Taaffes Bar
15 Tig Cóilí
16 Tigh Neachtain

● **SHOPPING**
17 Galway Market

● **TRANSPORT**
18 Bus Éireann
19 Train Station

The fire-engine-red **Tig Cóilí** (*tigchoiligalway.com*) is a favourite among local musicians. This atmospheric gem hosts two evening trad sessions, usually around 6pm and 9.30pm. **Taaffe's** (*taaffesbar.ie*) is across the road, popular with locals and GAA sports fans. Heading down to Quay St, you'll find family-run **Tigh Neachtain** (*tighneachtain.com*), founded in 1894, the heart of the Galway music scene.

Cross the Wolfe Tone Bridge to the West End, where the **Crane Bar** (*thecranebar.com*) holds nightly Irish music sessions.

Board a boat for Lough Corrib

Join a 90-minute cruise aboard the open-top **Corrib Princess** (*corribprincess.ie*; adult/child €20/10) passing ruined castles along the River Corrib en route to the Republic's largest lake – Lough Corrib, the haunt of herons, swans and, if you're lucky, leaping salmon. From May to September, there are two or three departures daily from Woodquay, just north of the **Salmon Weir**.

ROBERT ORMEROD/LONELY PLANET

Crane Bar (p383), Galway City

Dip into Galway's colourful past

Exhibits at the modern **Galway City Museum** *(galwaycity museum.ie; free),* by the Spanish Arch, engagingly convey the city's archaeological, political, cultural and social history. Look out for the Galway hooker fishing boat suspended from the ceiling, and gold Claddagh ring dating from around 1700.

Catch the weekend markets

Galway's bohemian spirit comes alive at its **markets**. Saturdays and Sundays from 8am to 6pm are the standout for food, when farmers and fisherfolk sell fresh produce alongside stalls selling flowers, arts, crafts and street food; buskers add to the festive atmosphere. Additional markets take place from noon to 6pm daily in July and August, and there's an atmospheric **Christmas Market** from 14 to 24 December.

Galway's gastronomic delights

From Michelin-star dining to the freshest fish and chips, Galway's food scene runs the gamut. Book an outing with

 EATING IN GALWAY CITY: OUR PICKS

Ard Bia at Nimmo's: Long-established cafe-restaurant beside the Spanish Arch, working with local producers. *10am-3pm daily, 6-9pm Tue-Sun* €€

Food for Thought: Good-value organic, vegetarian and vegan sandwiches and wholesome lunch dishes. *8am-5pm Mon-Sat, noon-3.30pm Sun* €

Oscars Seafood Bistro: Outstanding West End restaurant helmed by cookbook author Michael O'Meara. *6-9pm Tue-Thu, to 9.30pm Fri & Sat* €€€

Sult: Riverside cafe-bar-restaurant on Galway University campus, with prices half of those in city centre. *8.30am-8pm Mon-Fri* €

Galway Food Tours *(galwayfoodtours.com; per person €90)* to sample everything from local oysters and craft beers to artisan cheese and chocolate.

Connemara

Ramble in Connemara National Park

Connemara National Park, once part of the privately owned Kylemore Estate, opened to the public in 1980. Set in the northern part of County Galway, near the village of Letterfrack, it encompasses 20 sq km of mountain, bog, heath and woodland, showing off the region's wild, rugged landscape at its best, and is home to rare plant species, wild red deer and Connemara ponies. Park rangers lead free guided walks from the **Connemara National Park Visitor Centre** *(nationalparks.ie; free)*. Pick up free trail maps here and check out the exhibits describing the peatland landscape and conservation projects.

Tour postcard-perfect Kylemore Abbey

Perched photogenically on the shores of Pollacappall Lough, 4km east of Letterfrack, the crenelated neo-Gothic **Kylemore Abbey** *(kylemoreabbey.com; adult/child €18/free)* looks like a scene from a fairy tale. Mitchell Henry, the son of a wealthy cotton merchant, originally built this 19th-century structure as a country house, then called Kylemore Castle. In 1920, the castle was purchased by a community of Benedictine nuns, becoming the first Benedictine abbey in Ireland. A pleasant 20-minute walk or a free shuttle-bus ride west, past little Maladrolaun Lake, is an extravagant Victorian walled garden.

Cruise Killary Harbour

Slicing 16km inland and more than 45m deep in the centre, Killary Harbour is strikingly scenic and often referred to as Ireland's only fjord. The small village of Leenane sits on its southern shore, nestled among the Mweelrea, Devilsmother and Maamturk Mountains. Hop aboard the catamaran operated by **Killary Fjord Boat Tours** *(killaryfjord.ie; adult/child €27/free)* for a 90-minute cruise along the harbour to Barna island and back; keep your eyes peeled for dolphins.

Set out on Clifden's Sky Road

A definitive stop on any tour of Connemara, Clifden (An Clochán, meaning 'stepping stone') is an appealingly picturesque Victorian-era market town presiding over the head of the narrow bay where the River Owenglin tumbles into the sea. Its triangle of central streets is home to a colourful collection of craft shops, galleries, designer boutiques and lively pubs. The 20km scenic **Sky Road** loop drive starts and ends here.

Cliffs of Moher

Feel the sea spray from Ireland's famous cliffs

Rising to a height of 203m in a series of receding headlands, the Cliffs of Moher are the most popular sight outside Dublin (with crowds to match). One of Ireland's most important

BURREN & CLIFFS OF MOHER GEOPARK

The geology that underlies the rugged scenery of the Burren and the Cliffs of Moher is protected as a UNESCO **Global Geopark** *(burrengeopark. ie)*. During the Carboniferous period 350 million years ago, this whole area lay at the bottom of a warm, shallow sea. The remains of coral and shells fell to the sea bed, then coastal river deltas dumped sand, silt and mud on top. Time and pressure turned the sediments to stone, with fossil-rich limestone below and stratified shale and sandstone above, while continental collisions tilted and folded the rock layers. As you travel south, you move from the limestone landscapes of the Burren into the overlying shale and siltstones exposed in the Cliffs of Moher.

CLADDAGH RINGS

Proudly adorning fingers around the world, the Claddagh ring is traditionally a symbol of love. The two open hands represent friendship and hold a heart that signifies love. They're topped by a crown of loyalty. Traditionally, how you wore the ring would indicate your relationship status.

Single: On your right hand, with the point of the heart facing your fingers and away from your heart.

In a relationship: On your right hand, with the point of the heart pointing at your wrist and heart.

Engaged: On your left hand, with the point of the heart facing your fingers.

Married: On your left hand, with the point of the heart facing your wrist.

Burren National Park

seabird-nesting sites, the vertical, west-facing cliffs are home to more than 35 species including the mainland's largest colony of puffins on the grass-topped promontory below O'Brien's Tower viewpoint. Sunsets are spectacular.

Cut into the hillside, the state-of-the-art **Cliffs of Moher Visitor Centre** *(cliffsofmoher.ie; parking at gate/booked online €15/8, cyclists & pedestrians free)* has engaging exhibitions on the cliffs' fauna, flora, geology and climate.

Burren National Park

Hike in the Burren National Park

The Burren National Park protects 15 sq km of limestone landscapes centred on the small hills of Mullaghmore (191m) and Slieve Roe, whose dramatic scenery and rare flora are emblematic of the greater Burren region that covers some 360 sq km. Hiking details and a free shuttle bus to the trailhead are available from the **National Park Information Point** *(nationalparks.ie)* in Corofin.

No matter when you visit the Burren, wildflowers are in bloom. The region supports an incredibly diverse range of flora, with more than 70% of Ireland's 900 native species and many of the country's native orchids.

Belfast

HISTORY | CULTURE | LANDSCAPES

The capital of Northern Ireland and gateway to its spectacular landscapes, beaches and dramatic natural features, Belfast has transformed into a modern city with a thriving cultural life and arts scene. Belfast today is a different city from the Belfast of the Troubles (from the late 1960s until the signing of the Good Friday Agreement of 1998). Though political tensions remain, the years of paramilitary campaigns and sectarian violence have been left in the past. Over recent years, Belfast has also emerged as a major film and TV production destination, beginning with blockbuster series *Game of Thrones*. Since then, the filming of further productions has helped rebrand Belfast as a 21st-century city. But history is rarely far from mind here. The murals of West Belfast reflect issues of national identity at the root of the conflict. Meanwhile, no visitor to Belfast leaves without learning about the Belfast-built liner *Titanic*.

> ☑ **TOP TIP**
>
> For a scenic walk or bike ride from Belfast's leafy Queen's Quarter, stroll or cycle through the Botanic Gardens to Stranmillis Embankment, then follow the path north for 3km along the west bank of the Lagan to reach Queen's Bridge, just east of the city centre.

Historic Landmarks

Public buildings, public house and markets

Opposite the 1895-built **Grand Opera House** *(goh.co.uk)*, the **Crown Liquor Saloon** *(nicholsonspubs.co.uk)* is a historical monument decorated with ornate tiles and a crown mosaic at the entrance.

Belfast's architectural centrepiece is the council's domed, Renaissance-style **City Hall** *(belfastcity.gov.uk; tours adult/*

 GETTING AROUND

Belfast is small and easy to navigate. The city centre, Cathedral Quarter and Titanic Quarter are best tackled on foot, while buses and trains link the centre with neighbourhoods further afield. The city's cycling network includes a number of traffic-free stretches;

bikes can be rented through the Belfast Bikes bike-share scheme.

From the Laganside Bus Centre, Goldliner bus 221 runs via the world's oldest whiskey distillery at **Bushmills** to the Giant's Causeway (1½ hours).

CAVE HILL HISTORY

Evidence suggests that people lived on **Cave Hill** as far back as the Stone Age: a stone cairn on the summit dates from the Neolithic period (4500–2500 BCE). Flint arrowheads from the period have also been discovered nearby; they can be seen in **Belfast Castle**.

There are several *ráths* (defensive earthen ring forts) dating from early Christian times (400–1200 CE), including **McArt's Fort**, on a high rocky outcrop. It was here that members of the United Irishmen looked down over the city in 1795 and pledged to fight for Irish independence.

Between 1840 and 1896, limestone was extracted from Cave Hill for use in the shipping industry. You can see the remains of a limestone quarry on the hills southern slopes.

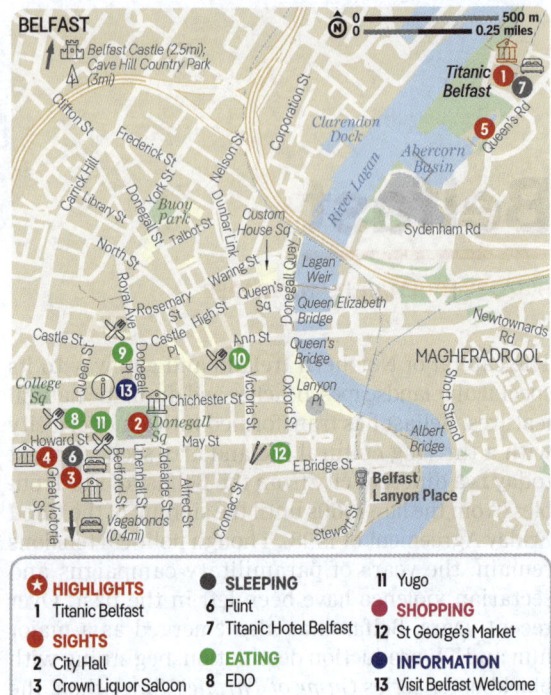

BELFAST

☆ HIGHLIGHTS	● SLEEPING	11 Yugo
1 Titanic Belfast	6 Flint	● SHOPPING
● SIGHTS	7 Titanic Hotel Belfast	12 St George's Market
2 City Hall	● EATING	● INFORMATION
3 Crown Liquor Saloon	8 EDO	13 Visit Belfast Welcome
4 Grand Opera House	9 Jumon	Centre
5 SS Nomadic	10 Pocket	

child £6/free), with stained-glass windows, Greek columns and Italian marble, visitable on 45-minute tours.

Housed in a Victorian-era building with sandstone porticos and a glazed roof, **St George's Market** *(belfastcity.gov.uk)* has live music and food, drink, antiques and craft stalls on market days (Friday to Sunday).

Titanic Quarter Icon

Learn about the Titanic

The shipyards where the *Titanic* was built are now part of the redeveloped Titanic Quarter. At the head of the slipway is **Titanic Belfast** *(titanicbelfast.com; incl SS Nomadic adult/child £26.95/13),* a state-of-the-art multimedia exhibition that charts the liner's history from its construction to its launch, fit-out and ill-fated maiden voyage. Highlights include a high-tech ride through a noisy, smells-and-all recreation of the city's shipyard, and the Belfast-built **SS Nomadic** *(nomadicbelfast.com),* the last remaining vessel of the White Star Line.

Belfast Backstories

Political murals and a Victorian prison

West Belfast developed with the linen mills that propelled the city into late-19th-century prosperity. It was an area of

Titanic Belfast

low-cost, working-class housing where sectarian divisions became yet more entrenched from the early 1970s, as paramilitary groups ramped up their campaigns. These days the area is safe and visitors are welcome.

Black taxi tours of West Belfast's murals stop to see the Solidarity Wall, the Bobby Sands mural and the murals of the Shankill. The **Visit Belfast** (*visitbelfast.com*) tourist information office on Donegall Sq can arrange a one- to two-hour **black taxi tour** (*for 2 people around £70*) with local cabbies.

In the Footsteps of Giants

Explore a geological phenomenon

Equally exhilarating when cloaked in mist or bathed in sunshine, the **Giant's Causeway** (*nationaltrust.org.uk; causeway free, visitor centre incl parking adult/child £15/7.50*) is a UNESCO World Heritage wonder. Uneven stacks of over 40,000 hexagonal basalt columns along the water's edge form a causeway that inspired the legend that the stones were put in place by a giant. From the **visitor centre**, it's a gentle 10- to 15-minute walk (or £1 shuttle-bus ride) downhill to the Causeway itself, where you can walk out onto the stones.

 EATING IN BELFAST: BRUNCH & SMALL PLATES

Yugo: Asian fusion dishes in an industrial-style dining room. Sit at the counter to watch the chefs at work. *5-9pm Tue, noon-2.45pm & 5-9.30pm Wed-Sat* ££

Pocket: Creative brunch dishes (like the excellent Ulster Fry), speciality coffee and booze. *8am-3pm Mon-Thu, to 4pm Fri & Sat, 8.30am-4pm Sun* ££

Jumon: Vegan/vegetarian Southeast Asian fusion; has an upbeat atmosphere and wall murals. *5-10pm Mon-Thu, noon-3pm & 5-10pm Fri & Sat* ££

EDO: Modern European tapas, perfect for sharing. Dishes are cooked over apple and pear wood in a Bertha oven. *noon-9.30pm Tue-Sat* ££

Places We Love to Stay

€ Budget €€ Midrange €€€ Top End

Dublin
MAP p367

Generator Hostel € Bright hostel on Smithfield Sq with a fun design, comfy dorms and a lively social scene.

Staunton's on the Green €€ This handsome Georgian house has charming bedrooms and a beautiful garden.

Morgan Hotel €€ Temple Bar hotel right in the middle of the action; some rooms have balconies.

Shelbourne €€€ Dublin's most famous hotel was founded in 1824 and is the height of old-school luxury.

Kilkenny City

Langton's Hotel Kilkenny €€ Kilkenny empire with historic and modern rooms, gardens, multiple restaurants and bars, and nightly live music.

Hibernian Hotel €€ Central 18th-century Georgian bank now housing 46 contemporary guest rooms, a brasserie restaurant and bar.

Butler House €€€ In private gardens with an entrance to Castle Yard, this 1786 mansion has 17 sumptuous period-furnished rooms.

Cork City
MAP p375

Sheila's Hostel € Popular backpacker's hostel in a handy location for exploring the city, with great facilities including a cinema room and sauna.

Hotel Isaacs €€ Housed in a Victorian furniture warehouse in a buzzing central location, with spacious, well-decorated rooms.

Imperial Hotel €€€ History-filled, two-century-old landmark in the heart of Cork with lavish rooms and contemporary amenities and spa.

Kinsale

Giles Norman Townhouse €€ Stylish guest rooms with elegant bathrooms, espresso machines and a discount at the downstairs gallery.

Old Presbytery €€€ Luxury self-catering apartments set in a gorgeously refurbished 18th-century Georgian property.

Killarney

Black Sheep Hostel € Eco-focused, traveller-designed hostel with custom-made bunks and built-in lockers, free breakfast and attached coffee shack.

Fleming's White Bridge Caravan & Camping Park € Lovely, sheltered family-run campsite on the banks of the River Flesk 2.5km southeast of town.

Crystal Springs €€ Wonderfully relaxing B&B just outside the centre, with a glass-enclosed breakfast room overlooking the river. Two-night minimum.

Cahernane House Hotel €€€ Grand manor dating from 1877, with antique-furnished rooms (some with a claw-foot bath or Jacuzzi).

Killarney Plaza Hotel €€€ Central 198-room modern hotel channelling art-deco-era style, with a lavishly tiled pool, sauna, steam room and spa.

Dingle Town

Rainbow Hostel & Camping € Set in large gardens 1.5km northwest of town, this bright, fresh bungalow is also the nearest place to town you can pitch a tent.

Base Dingle €€ Contemporary lodgings in Dingle's heart, offering 30 sleek rooms that can sleep two to five people (no breakfast).

Castlewood House €€€ A haven of country-house quiet and sophistication 10 minutes' stroll from town.

Galway City
MAP p383

Kinlay Hostel € Centrally located hostel just off Eyre Sq, a stroll away from the traditional pubs of Shop St.

House Hotel €€ Boutique hotel in a converted warehouse with an amazing location in the Latin Quarter.

Heron's Rest €€€ Boutique B&B in a lovely row of houses on the banks of the Corrib; sit outside and enjoy the views. Breakfast hampers include organic local produce.

Belfast
MAP p388

Vagabonds £ Within walking distance of the city centre, this popular, well-run hostel has dorms, private rooms and common areas for socialising.

Flint ££ Suites here have a small kitchen and a table for eating or working. Located right by City Hall.

Titanic Hotel Belfast £££ Located in the Harland & Wolff shipping company's old headquarters; the hotel's interior design references the city's shipbuilding past.

Practicalities

INSURANCE

Travel insurance is not required to enter Ireland, but comprehensive insurance is highly recommended to cover theft and loss as well as any medical problems. EU citizens carrying a free European Health Insurance Card (EHIC) are covered for most emergency medical care but not for emergency repatriation.

ALANHORRIS/SHUTTERSTOCK

LANGUAGE

Irish (Gaeilge) is the country's official language. In 2003, the government introduced the Official Languages Act, whereby all official documents, street signs and official titles must be either in Irish or in both Irish and English.

BEACH SAFETY

Rip currents are the leading hazard for beachgoers. If lifeguards aren't present, ask locals whether the water is suitable to enter. For more advice on keeping safe in and around the water, see *watersafety.ie*.

OPENING HOURS

Pubs 10.30am–11.30pm Monday to Thursday, 10.30am–12.30am Friday and Saturday, noon–11pm Sunday
Restaurants noon–10.30pm
Shops 9.30am–6pm Monday to Saturday (to 8pm Thursday in cities), noon–6pm Sunday

REPUBLIC OF IRELAND ENTRY REQUIREMENTS

Ireland and Britain are part of the Common Travel Area (CTA). No UK ETA is required for the Republic. The Republic is in the EU but isn't a member of Schengen, and isn't planning to implement ETIAS (European Travel Information and Authorisation System) launching in late 2026.

NORTHERN IRELAND ENTRY REQUIREMENTS

Northern Ireland, as part of the UK (and no longer the EU post-Brexit), requires visa-exempt visitors to obtain a UK ETA (Electronic Travel Authorisation; *gov.uk/eta*), whether arriving directly or from the Republic. While the 'soft' border between the Republic and Northern Ireland means there are no passport controls, visitors still require a UK ETA for Northern Ireland.

PUBLIC HOLIDAYS

New Year's Day 1 January
St Brigid's Day 1st Monday in February (Republic of Ireland)
St Patrick's Day 17 March
Easter Monday March/April
Easter Tuesday March/April (Northern Ireland)
May Holiday 1st Monday in May
Spring Bank Holiday Last Monday in May (Northern Ireland)
June Holiday 1st Monday in June

The Twelfth 12 July (Northern Ireland)
August Holiday 1st Monday in August (Republic of Ireland)
Summer Bank Holiday Last Monday in August (Northern Ireland)
October Holiday Last Monday in October (Republic of Ireland)
Christmas Day 25 December
St Stephen's Day (Boxing Day) 26 December

391

TUPUNGATO/SHUTTERSTOCK

Ryanair planes, Dublin Airport

Arriving

Dublin is the main point of entry for most travellers to Ireland. Flights arrive at Dublin Airport, 10km north of the city centre, which has two interconnected terminals with ATMs, restaurants and convenience stores. Buses connect Dublin Airport with towns and cities across Ireland. You can also fly to Belfast, Shannon and Cork, and smaller airports including Kerry (near Killarney).

US Preclearance
When travelling from Dublin or Shannon airports to the US, passport and immigration formalities are handled before boarding at US Preclearance; allow extra time. When you arrive in the US, the flight is treated as a domestic arrival.

Ferry
Car ferries from Liverpool in England, Holyhead in Wales and Cherbourg in France arrive at Dublin ferry port, 5km east of the city centre. Belfast has ferry links with Scotland and England. Ferries sail between Rosslare in County Wexford and Britain, France and Spain.

MONEY
Currency: Euro (€) – Republic of Ireland; Pound sterling (£) – Northern Ireland

TIPPING
Accommodation Hotel porters €1–2/£1–2 per bag; cleaning staff at your discretion. Not expected in small B&Bs.

Pubs Not expected unless table service is provided, then €1–2/£1–2 for a round of drinks.

Restaurants Check whether your bill includes a service charge. For decent service 10%; up to 15% in more expensive places.

Cafes Not expected; many have an optional tip jar on the counter.

Taxis Round up to an even amount.

Toilet attendants Loose change; no more than 50c/50p.

MONEY-SAVING TIPS
Many attractions offer discounted rates if you buy tickets online in advance. You can also buy visitor passes that include entry to a number of attractions, such as the Dublin Pass. The Heritage Card includes free entry to all Office of Public Works–managed sites; it can be a good deal depending on how many spots you plan to visit.

Getting Around

Transport in Ireland by bus and train is efficient and reasonably priced to and from major urban centres; smaller towns and villages along those routes are well served. Service to destinations not on major routes is less frequent and often impractical. Exploring Ireland's wildest and most beautiful corners is easiest by car.

Leap Visitor Card
In Dublin, the Leap Visitor Card includes all Dublin Bus, Luas tram, DART and commuter train travel (though not Aircoach and Dublin Express airport bus services) for one, three or seven days. It's easiest to buy it in Dublin (online purchases require postage); points of sale include Dublin Airport.

4KCLIPS/SHUTTERSTOCK

Irish Explorer Rail Pass
If you're travelling around Ireland by train, the Irish Explorer rail pass includes five days of unlimited rail travel in the Republic within 15 consecutive days. It's sold at larger train stations (not from ticket machines or online).

TFI Live App
Download Transport for Ireland's TFI Live app *(transportforireland.ie/ available-apps/tfi-live)* to plan bus, train and tram trips using real-time departure information.

Toll Roads
Ireland currently has 11 toll roads; 10 have barrier toll plazas where you pay at the cashier's booth. Dublin's M50 toll plaza is barrier-free; pay online *(eflow.ie)* before 8pm the following day. Peak rates are charged on weekday mornings and evenings at the Dublin Tunnel.

Rural Road Hazards
Ireland's rural roads can be steep, narrow and winding. Single-track roads with blind bends can be challenging; if you see an oncoming vehicle, the etiquette is for the car nearest to a passing place to reverse; thank the driver with a wave.

DRIVING ESSENTIALS

Drive on the left-hand side

Speed limits are in kilometres per hour in the Republic and miles per hour in Northern Ireland

0.05

Blood alcohol limit is 0.05%

Curated by
Cristian Bonetto

Italy

EUROPE'S CULTURAL AND CULINARY PARADISE

World-famous art, architecture, food and passion, wrapped up in some of Europe's most magnificent natural landscapes.

A favourite destination since the days of the 18th-century Grand Tour, Italy may appear to hold few surprises. Its iconic monuments and masterpieces are known the world over, while cities like Rome, Florence and Venice need no introduction.

Yet Italy is far more than the sum of its sights. Its fiercely proud regions maintain centuries-old customs and culinary traditions, making the country feel more like a collection of mini nations – each with its distinct identity, specialities, architecture and festivals. After all, Milan and Turin are closer to Paris and Munich than they are to Palermo, while the latter's souk-like markets and Arabesque flourishes serve as a constant reminder that Tunis is much closer than Rome.

The extraordinary contrasts extend beyond the lively streets and piazzas, spilling into the very landscapes that frame them. Italy offers an amazing suite of natural backdrops: icy northern Alps and glacial lakes, gentle Tuscan hills, vertiginous Campanian coastlines and spitting Sicilian volcanoes. Few countries can claim such breadth and beauty in such a compact area.

Then, Italy has always had a knack for superlatives – from ancient glories and Renaissance masterpieces to fashion, design, food and wine. No other country matches its number of UNESCO World Heritage Sites, and few others seduce with such effortless style and heart-on-sleeve charm. *Benvenuti* to Europe's most intoxicating, theatrical stage.

RAUL JICHICI/SHUTTERSTOCK

THE MAIN AREAS

ROME	**NORTHERN ITALY**	**FLORENCE & TUSCANY**	**NAPLES & THE AMALFI COAST**	**SICILY**
Italy's ancient, eternal capital. **p400**	High fashion, lakeside villas, gondolas. **p412**	Renaissance masterpieces and a lopsided icon. **p433**	Hyperactive street life, coastal beauty. **p444**	A Greek, Arab and Norman melting pot. **p455**

For places to stay
in Italy, see p464

SERGEY NOVIKOV/SHUTTERSTOCK

Left: Tuscany (p433); Above: Cattedrale di Santa Maria del Fiore (p437), Florence

TRAIN & BUS

Fast, efficient and well connected, Italy's train network is best for travelling between major cities and along the coast. It works in conjunction with an efficient regionalised bus network, which can be useful for reaching smaller towns.

CAR

Cars aren't needed for getting around Italian cities and major towns, where historic centres are walkable and public transport is generally reliable. Beyond urban areas, a car offers flexibility to explore rural, off-the-beaten-track locations at your own pace.

FERRY

Ferry and hydrofoil services connect the Italian mainland to various islands, including regular overnight services between Naples and Sicily. Regular high-speed hydrofoils run year-round between Naples, Capri and other islands in the Bay of Naples, with seasonal services connecting Amalfi Coast towns.

Northern Italy, p412

Operatic encores in Milan, glittering mosaics in Venice, the plunging Cinque Terre: Italy's well-heeled north isn't short of blockbuster moments.

Florence & Tuscany, p433

Birthplace of the Renaissance, Florence is Italy's preeminent city of art. Hop between masterpieces, then detour to a Tuscan town or an infamously crooked tower.

Sicily, p455

A heady, cross-cultural mash-up: wander Palermo's Arab-Norman landmarks, go baroque in Catania, soak up Taormina's *White Lotus* vibes and lose yourself in Syracuse's luminous, labyrinthine streets.

Naples & the Amalfi Coast, p444

Dive into Naples' churches, palaces and catacombs, snoop around ghostly Herculaneum and Pompeii, then live your best life along Italy's most glamorous coastline.

Rome, p400

Trace the footsteps of Roman emperors, lose yourself in Michelangelo's frescoes, and hang with Trastevere *bon vivants* in the city of *la dolce vita*.

Find Your Way

We've zoomed in on some of Italy's top offerings, from ancient ruins in Rome, Naples and Sicily to art-slung palaces in Florence, Venice and Milan. Speckled in between – spectacular natural highs and some lesser-known treasures.

0   100 miles
0   200 km

397

Plan Your Time

It's tempting to cram as many must-sees as you can into a single trip. High-speed trains make hopping between highlights easy, but also consider focusing on a smaller corner of the country. You won't be disappointed.

ARCADY/SHUTTERSTOCK

Villa Rufolo (p454), Ravello

Two-Week Grand Tour

● Start with a couple of days in **Venice** (p425), losing yourself in its Byzantine mosaics and art-slung palace, then whistle-stop in bookish **Bologna** (p423) for crooked towers and proper *bolognese*. A couple of days in **Florence** (p433) lets you skim the cream of its Renaissance treasures, among them Michelangelo's brawny *David*, while a day in **Siena** (p440) means lounging in its world-famous, Palio-hosting piazza.

● Three days in **Rome** (p400) lets you catch headline sights like the **Colosseum** (p401), while also having time to explore atmospheric **Trastevere** (p410). In **Naples** (p444), hit the **MANN** (Museo Archeologico Nazionale di Napoli; p447) in preparation for a day exploring ancient **Pompeii** (p449). Wrap up on the Amalfi Coast, boating in **Positano** (p453) and wandering sky-high gardens in impossibly romantic **Ravello** (p454).

SEASONAL HIGHLIGHTS

Spring and autumn are ideal for sightseeing. Summer heat packs the coasts, while winter snows fuel alpine skiing.

JANUARY
January is ideal for rugging up and strapping on skis in the Alps: the snow is generally solid, and the slopes are a little calmer after the Christmas and New Year's holiday rush.

APRIL
Springtime blooms across the country, with mild temperatures perfect for sightseeing and hikes among the wildflowers. Crowds are generally lighter than summer, though Easter brings busy streets and higher prices.

MAY
Coastal hot spots like the Amalfi Coast and Taormina are buzzing as shoulder season brings longer days and pleasant temperatures without the sweltering summer crush. Epicureans hit local markets for prime-time asparagus.

Six Northern Days

● Strut straight into Italy's fashion-and-finance capital, **Milan** (p417), for a couple of days. Scale its spindly **Duomo** (p419), take in Leonardo da Vinci's **The Last Supper** (p420) and dive into the Navigli's canal-side **aperitivo scene** (p420). Book ahead to catch a show at the world-famous opera house **La Scala** (p417).

● Head west for a few days in Italy's former capital, **Turin** (p415) – elegant, faintly French and home to royal palaces, grand cafes and the **Museo Egizio** (p417), Europe's greatest repository of Egyptian antiquities. Then, trade the city's stately arcades for the dramatic coast of the **Cinque Terre** (p412). Spend another two days or so hiking between its pastel villages, take a dip in turquoise coves and linger over Liguria's famous seafood, pesto and focaccia.

Sicily in Short

● Time-poor? Sicily's Ionian Coast delivers easy-to-reach thrills, from ancient Graeco-Roman ruins and jaw-dropping coastal towns to baroque splendour and vibrant street life. Start with two days in **Syracuse** (p461), indulging in Ortigia's island charm and roaming the vast **Parco Archeologico della Neapolis** (p463).

● Then continue up the coast to **Catania** (p458), Sicily's second-largest city, where UNESCO-listed piazzas, stuccoed churches and a raucous fish market make light work of a couple of days. The dining is sensational and its youthful, student energy invigorating. Then slow down with a day or so in polished **Taormina** (p460). Stroll old-world alleys, savour clifftop views of moody Mt Etna, and catch a moonlit show at the resort town's spectacular, millennia-old **Teatro Greco** (p461).

JUNE
School is out and the summer holidays begin, with tourist numbers increasing significantly across the country. Warm days and evenings herald outdoor festivals, from opera and theatre to Pride parades.

JULY
Hot days, packed beaches, and wild blueberries in full bloom. Outdoor festivals continue and Siena's Piazza del Campo hosts the thrilling horse race **Palio** (p442) on 2 July (a second edition is held on 16 August).

OCTOBER
While central and southern Italy still enjoy mild days, northern regions may see the season's first snow. Leaves are ablaze and autumn produce shines, from pumpkin-filled tortellini to roasted chestnuts.

NOVEMBER
Truffle season hits its peak in northern Italy, especially for the prized white Alba truffle. Gourmands flock to truffle festivals and waiters shave it fresh over steaks, pastas and warming risottos.

Rome

ROMAN ARCHITECTURE | BAROQUE LANDMARKS | LA DOLCE VITA

 TOP TIP

Trastevere's riverfront is the place to be in summer as the Lungo il Tevere street carnival revs into action. Stalls, pop-up bars, restaurants and even dance floors set up on the waterfront between Ponte Sisto and Ponte Sublicio between June and September.

Ever since its golden age as the ancient *caput mundi* (world capital), Rome has been seducing visitors. Its thrilling cityscape, piled high with martial ruins and monuments, is achingly beautiful, and its museums and churches harbour some of Europe's finest masterpieces.

Managing the twin demands of tourism and modern civic life has increasingly become a reality of governing Rome, a city whose population of 2.7 million is dwarfed by the annual influx of Italian and foreign visitors. The result of all this is a city that can sometimes appear to be living on the edge of perpetual chaos. And while Rome is undeniably busy, and is often scruffy and noisy, it's not the giant free-for-all it's occasionally portrayed as. Look closer and you'll see most drivers are wearing their seatbelts, and that few people are smoking in banned public places. In Rome, first impressions can be gloriously misleading.

Ancient Rome

Just to the south of the city centre, Ancient Rome is a thrilling mix of ancient treasures, iconic monuments and mesmerising views. This is where you'll find Rome's most celebrated ruins and showstopping landmarks: the Colosseum, Palatino (where

continued on p404

GETTING AROUND

Rome is best explored on foot: the main sights are clustered in and around the *centro storico* (historic centre), the centre is relatively flat, and traffic is restricted in many areas. Driving is stressful, parking scarce and scooters better left to locals. Public transport fills the gaps: the metro (lines A and B) links Termini to the Colosseum and the Vatican. There are no metro stations in the *centro storico*, but you can walk from Barberini, Spagna and Flaminio stations. Spagna is also useful for Villa Borghese. Buses cover much of the *centro storico* and trams run to Trastevere. Tickets are easy to buy at stations and kiosks.

TOP EXPERIENCE

Colosseum

The Colosseum is the most thrilling of Rome's ancient monuments, an electrifying, spine-tingling sight commissioned by Vespasian in 72 CE and inaugurated by Titus in 80 CE. This is where gladiators met in mortal combat and prisoners fought off wild beasts in front of baying, bloodthirsty crowds. Two thousand years on and it remains the city's most popular attraction.

VIACHESLAV LOPATIN/SHUTTERSTOCK

Making the Most of Your Visit

Even without a ticket, the outer walls – originally covered in travertine and with statues in the niches – impress. The upper level, punctuated by square window openings and slender Corinthian pilasters, had supports for 240 masts, which held a giant awning over the arena.

Once you make it inside, steep steps lead to the first and second tiers. From here you can look over the partially rebuilt arena floor and down into the underground areas. On the 2nd floor you'll also find the small **Museo del Colosseo** illustrating the Colosseum's history. You'll need a Full Experience ticket (€24) to gain access to the upper floors, where women spectators would have sat. The Full Experience ticket also allows you to walk on the arena floor and explore the subterranean sections, which once served as the stadium's backstage.

Demand for all tickets is high, so book well in advance, even a month ahead for peak periods; check the website for details. You can buy same-day tickets (subject to availability) at ticket offices on Piazza del Colosseo (credit/debit cards only) and Largo della Salara Vecchia.

TOP TIPS

● Tickets include the holder's name, so bring photo ID to enter.

● Reckon on about an hour inside the Colosseum. Try to visit first thing or late afternoon, when it's cooler, less crowded and there's better lighting.

● Free interactive audio guides are available on the official MyColosseum app.

PRACTICALITIES

● colosseo.it ● adult/ reduced €18/2 ● 8.30am-1hr before sunset, last entry 1hr before closing

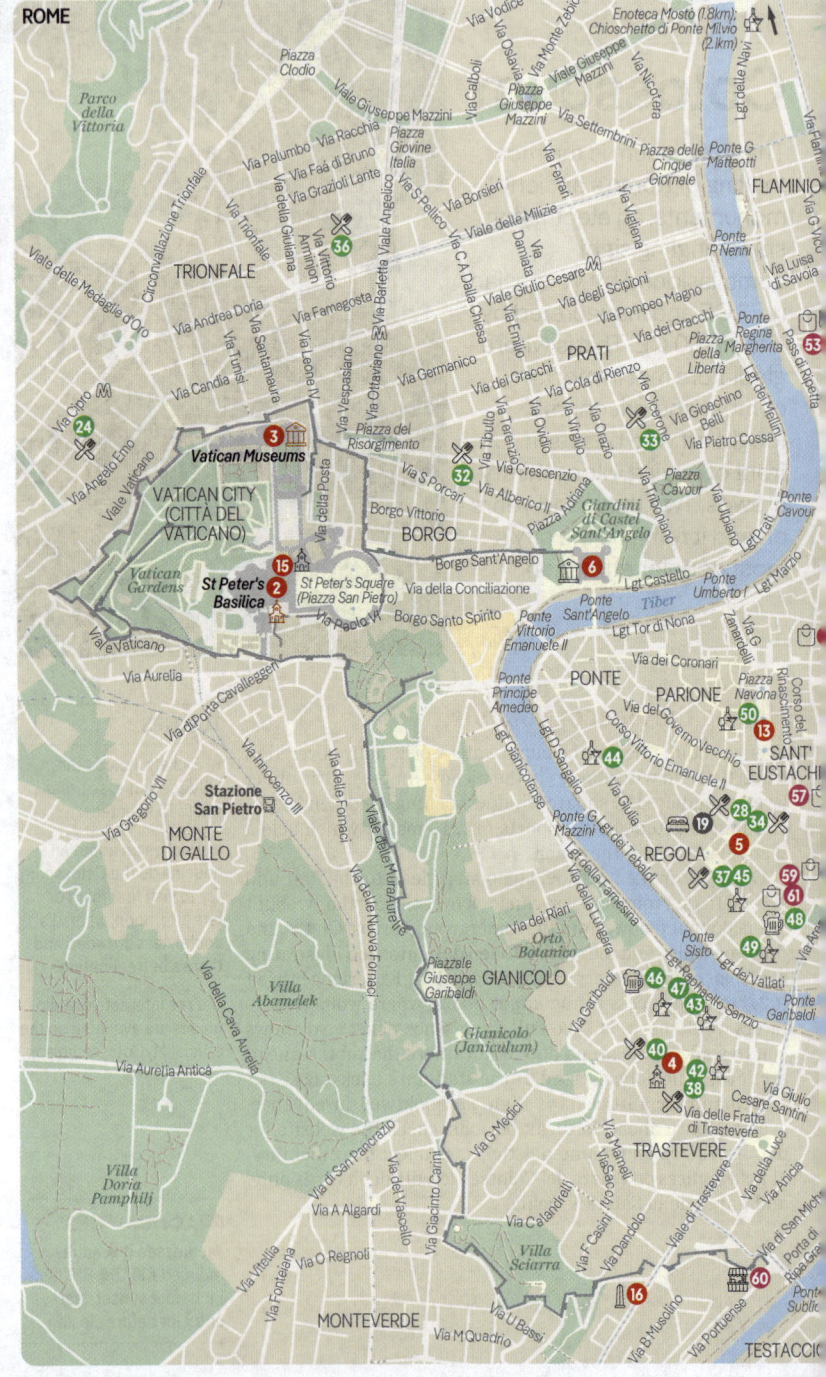

THE GUIDE

ROME ITALY

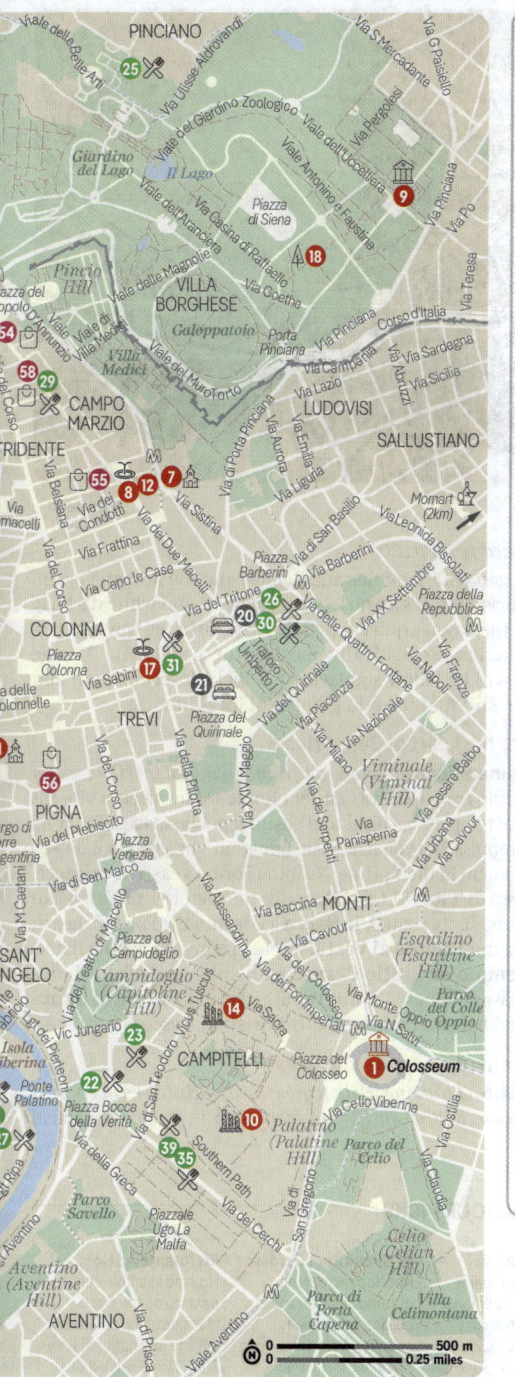

ANCIENT HIGHLIGHTS

Darius Arya, a Rome-based archaeologist, highlights some must-sees. *@dariusaryadigs; ancientromelive.org*

The Forum and Palatino are the real heart of Rome's history. You'll want to get the Super pass to have access to the 'secret' sites and monuments like Santa Maria Antiqua and the Curia Iulia. Due to new openings, everyone should walk up Domitian's ramp (which once connected to the palace on top) and through the substructures of the Domus Tiberiana.

For the Colosseum, try to take the elevator ride to the top or the hypogeum (underground chambers). They are both wonderful experiences that bring you closer to the Colosseum's history.

RESUL MUSLU/SHUTTERSTOCK

Pantheon

continued from p400

it all began with Romulus and Remus) and the Roman Forum. Unsurprisingly, it's a touristy part of town and while it's busy during the day, it's quiet at night with little in the way of after-hours action. Realistically, most of the people you'll come across will be fellow sightseers but look closely enough and you can still find the odd glimpse of local life.

Explore the heart of Caput Mundi

The **Roman Forum** *(colosseo.it; adult/reduced incl Colosseum & Palatino from €18)* was ancient Rome's showpiece, a vibrant centre of temples, basilicas and bustling public spaces. Today its ruins impress, but you'll need imagination – or a good guide – to picture them in their prime. Near the Forum's eastern entrance, the **Arco di Tito** (81 CE) celebrates the victories of Vespasian and Titus. To its right, **Via Sacra** leads into the Forum's heart, passing the **Tempio di Vesta**, where virgins tended the flame. The **Tempio di Giulio Cesare** marks the spot where Julius Caesar was cremated, while the 6th-century **Chiesa di Santa Maria Antiqua** harbours early Christian frescoes.

Roam where emperors slumbered

Palatino *(Palatine Hill; colosseo.it; adult/reduced incl Colosseum & Roman Forum from €18)* is Rome's mythical

 EATING IN ANCIENT ROME: OUR PICKS

Alimentari Pannella Carmela: A workaday food store ideal for sandwiches. *8.30am-2.30pm Mon-Sat, 5-8pm Mon-Fri* €

Osteria Circo: This Circo Massimo *osteria* specialises in traditional Italian fare and hearty Roman pastas. *12.30-3.30pm & 7.30-11.30pm* €€

47 Circus Roof Garden: Rooftop restaurant offering Mediterranean cuisine and sunset *aperitivi* (from 4pm). *noon-3.30pm & 7-10.30pm* €€€

Ristorante Ad Hoc: Housed in a 16th-century *palazzo* on the Circo Massimo. Modern Italian cuisine and national wines. *7-10.30pm Fri-Wed* €€€

birthplace, where Romulus supposedly founded the city in 753 BCE. Archaeology reveals Iron Age huts from the 9th century BCE. Later, emperors lived in palatial luxury, most notably in Domitian's 1st-century palace, divided into the public **Domus Flavia**, private **Domus Augustana**, and sunken **stadio**. Highlights include Augustus' frescoed **Casa di Augusto**, the **Orti Farnesiani** gardens with stunning Forum views, and the towering **Domus Tiberiana**, the Palatino's first palace. The **Museo Palatino** chronicles the hill's development, though you'll need a Forum Pass Super (€18) or Full Experience (€24) ticket to access the museum, as well as the Aula Isiaca and Loggia Mattei, Casa di Augusto and Domus Tiberiana. Allow about three hours to explore the Palatino and adjoining Forum.

Centro Storico

A tangled knot of cobbled alleyways, Renaissance palaces and baroque piazzas, Rome's *centro storico* (historic centre) is the city many visitors come to find. The Pantheon and Piazza Navona are the star turns, but walk around and without even trying you'll come across a whole host of monuments, museums and churches, many containing masterpieces. But it's not all high culture. There's plenty of fun to be had just strolling the area's theatrical streets, taking in its romantic nooks and enjoying the many boutiques, cafes, *trattorias* and bars. Just make sure to bring some comfortable shoes for the uneven cobbles.

Admire an engineering marvel

Built by Hadrian around 125 CE on the site of Marcus Agrippa's earlier temple, the 2000-year-old **Pantheon** (pantheon roma.com) is the best-preserved of Rome's ancient monuments. Step through its immense bronze doors and you're met with the largest unreinforced concrete dome ever built – a feat so breathtaking it inspired Michelangelo before he designed the dome of St Peter's Basilica. The temple-turned-church, whose tombs include that of Raphael, is best visited early to avoid the biggest crowds, and it's wise to book **tickets** (portale.mu seiitaliani.it; adult/reduced €5/2) online in advance to skip long queues. Return at night to see it illuminated.

Pose on a perfect piazza

A cinematic sweep of fountains and baroque *palazzi* (mansions), **Piazza Navona** has long been a hub of city life. For close on 300

WATER FOUNTAINS

Sightseeing can be thirsty work in Rome. Fortunately, you can get free drinking water throughout the city, courtesy of 2500 or so fountains known as *nasoni* (or 'big noses'). First introduced in the 1870s, these cast-iron fountains supply a constant flow of safe, refreshingly cool, *acqua potabile* (drinking water), which you can use to fill up your bottles or drink directly. To do so, block the main spout and cup the water as it spurts through the hole in the top of the nozzle. You'll find *nasoni* in Piazza della Rotonda and Piazza Navona, among other places. To locate the nearest one to you, check out the free app Acea Waidy Wow.

A hip trattoria with piazza seating.

EATING & DRINKING IN THE CENTRO STORICO: OUR PICKS

Osteria La Quercia: On a charming square near Piazza Farnese eat Lazio regional classics. *noon-3.30pm & 7-11.30pm* €€

Ditirambo: Central location, informal vibe and seasonal, organic cuisine. Roman pastas to thoughtful vegetarian offerings. *12.30-3pm & 6.30-11pm* €€

Rimessa Roscioli: Gourmets adore this place, with its wine-pairing dinners, tastings, tours and classes. Book ahead. *5-11pm Mon-Sun* €€

Luciano Cucina Italiana: Near Campo de' Fiori, this spot serves renowned carbonara and inventive mains. *12.15-3pm & 7.15-11pm* €€€

BEST SHOPS FOR SOUVENIR HUNTING

Aldo Fefè: Pick out a beautifully hand-painted notebook or picture album created by master craftsman Aldo Fefè.

Salumeria Roscioli: Rome's most celebrated deli, with a range of cured hams, cheeses, wines, olive oils and balsamic vinegars.

Confetteria Moriondo & Gariglio: A historic confectioner's specialising in delicious handmade chocolates, many prepared according to original 19th-century recipes.

Emporio Centrale: Choose from a 500-strong range of vintage Italian household goods and products made by artisans and long-standing Italian companies.

Ibiz – Artigianato in Cuoio: For wallets, bags, belts and sandals hand-crafted at this family-run leather workshop.

years it hosted Rome's main market, and still today it attracts a daily circus of street artists, hawkers and tourists. It stands on the 1st-century **Stadio di Domiziano**, whose underground remains can be visited from Via di Tor Sanguigna. The piazza's centrepiece is Bernini's 1651 **Fontana dei Quattro Fiumi**, featuring four river gods. Dominating the square's western flank, the domed **Chiesa di Sant'Agnese** in Agone was designed by the revered baroque architect Francesco Borromini. To catch the piazza at its most alluring, come first thing in the morning before the crowds or after dark when the fountains are illuminated.

Browse on the Campo

Hanging out on a busy piazza is a quintessential Roman experience. And nowhere does piazza life quite like **Campo de' Fiori**. Colourful, noisy and always busy, the square hosts a well-known market during the day and teems with life at night as visitors and young locals pack its restaurants and brash bars.

Amid the piazza's hurly-burly, you'll see a statue of a hooded monk. This is the philosopher Giordano Bruno, who was burned here for heresy in 1600.

Tridente & Trevi

Tridente, named after the three streets that form a trident as they lance off Piazza del Popolo, is a glamorous district, full of old money, fashionable bars and swish hotels. It's also Rome's premier shopping district, home to luxury designer boutiques and flagship stores. But once the shops close, the area quietens, leaving few after-hours distractions.

To the south, the Trevi Fountain stands out in a knot of dark, narrow streets, which teem throughout the day as crowds stop off to toss their coins into the *Dolce Vita* fountain.

Climb some famous steps

Few spots in Rome are as iconic (or romantic) as **Piazza di Spagna**, especially in April or May, when its famous Steps are adorned with azaleas. Once dubbed *'il salotto di Roma'* (Rome's parlour), the square takes its name from the 17th-century Spanish embassy still standing here. At its heart is Pietro and Gian Lorenzo Bernini's **Fontana della Barcaccia**, which depicts a seemingly sinking boat. Rising above, the 1725 Scalinata della Trinità dei Monti – better known as the **Spanish Steps** – links the piazza to the 16th-century **Chiesa della Trinità dei Monti** and its striking frescoes. Make sure not to sit on the Steps as hefty fines apply.

DRINKING IN THE CENTRO STORICO: OUR PICKS

L'Angolo Divino: Near Campo de' Fiori, this snug wine bar serves interesting Italian wines and tasty dishes. *11am-3pm Tue-Sat & 5pm-1am Mon-Fri*

Open Baladin: Modern pub near Campo de' Fiori with 40 craft beers on tap and up to 100 bottled brews. *noon-1am, to 2am Fri & Sat*

Il Goccetto: An old-school *vino e olio* (wine and oil) shop with a bottle-lined interior and a fabulous wine list. *noon-midnight Tue-Sat, from 5pm Mon*

Terrazza Borromini: Bask in sunset views over Piazza Navona from this rooftop bar atop a 17th-century *palazzo*. Reservations recommended. *noon-midnight*

Spanish Steps, Piazza di Spagna

Relive a Fellini scene

The **Trevi Fountain** is Rome's most famous, and most flamboyant, baroque masterpiece. Designed by Nicola Salvi in 1732, it fills an entire piazza, with Oceanus riding a shell chariot, tritons and seahorses symbolising the sea's moods. Fed by the Aqua Virgo aqueduct, it will be forever tied to Fellini's *La Dolce Vita,* in which a glamorous Anita Ekberg wades through its waters (don't try it – bathing is banned). Spot the odd stone urn on the right, rumoured to have been placed there by Salvo to block the view of a rude, meddling barber during construction. And don't skip the ritual: back turned, eyes closed, coin tossed with your right hand over your left shoulder.

Vatican City & Borgo

The Vatican City sits across the river to the northwest of the historic centre. Officially it's an independent sovereign state – the world's smallest, with an area of 44 hectares – but in practice it's more like a city neighbourhood. It's also one of Rome's most visited areas, home to priceless treasures and revered masterpieces, many housed in St Peter's Basilica, the Vatican Museums and Sistine Chapel.

A short walk from St Peter's Square, Castel Sant'Angelo looms over the quaint Borgo district. Originally, this was a much larger medieval quarter, but much of it was destroyed in 1936 to make way for Via della Conciliazione.

TRIDENTE'S BEST SHOPS

Bomba: Designer Cristina Bomba's atelier creates gorgeous pieces that hit the wallet hard but are oh so worth it.

Artisanal Cornucopia: Jewellery, handbags and homeware are for sale at this stylish independent boutique on Via dell'Oca.

Borsalino: On Piazza del Popolo, Borsalino showcases headwear for both men and women, selling classic and newer models.

Fabriano: Fabriano stocks stylish stationery, including delightful leather-bound journals and notebooks, at its store in Via del Babuino.

c.u.c.i.n.a.: If you've always dreamed of owning a *caffettiera* and other Italian kitchen essentials, then this is the place for you.

 EATING AROUND TRIDENTE & TREVI: OUR PICKS

Colline Emiliane: Regional delicacies of Emilia-Romagna, according to what's in season. *12.45-2.45pm & 7.30-10.45pm Tue-Sat* €€

Hostaria Romana: A textbook Italian *trattoria* serving up delicious Roman classics. *12.30-3pm & 7.15-11pm, closed Sun & Mon lunch* €€

Il Chianti: Enjoy Tuscan classics, from soups to steaks, or select pizzas at this ivy-clad location. *noon-1am* €€

Da Edy: A chic restaurant, with high-ceilinged interiors and painting-covered walls. *noon-3pm & 6.30-11pm Mon-Sat* €€

Vatican Museums

The Vatican Museums claim more masterpieces than some countries, and with 7km of exhibition halls, they are rightly considered one of the world's greatest art museums. While exploring the entire complex would take several days, even a single visit is sure to leave you star-struck as you take in its never-ending collection of world-famous artworks, culminating in Michelangelo's frescoes in the Sistine Chapel.

ANTON_IVANOV/SHUTTERSTOCK

Galleria delle Carte Geografiche

TOP TIPS

● Save time by booking tickets online (for a small surcharge) or joining a guided tour.

● Rainy days are busiest and afternoons tend to be quieter than mornings.

● The museums are free (and very busy) on the last Sunday of the month.

PRACTICALITIES

● museivaticani.va
● adult/reduced €20/8, free last Sun of the month
● 8am-8pm Mon-Sat, 9am-2pm last Sun of month

Must-See Treasures

Start your explorations by heading to the **Pinacoteca**, often overlooked but full of treasures, among them a trio of works by Raphael, Leonardo da Vinci's *San Gerolamo* and Caravaggio's moving *Deposizione*.

The ground-floor **Museo Pio-Clementino** houses classical sculptures, and many top pieces are found in the Cortile Ottagono, including the *Laocoön* and *Apollo Belvedere*. Elsewhere, the Sala delle Muse houses the famous *Torso Belvedere*, while the Sala Rotonda displays the towering bronze *Hercules*.

The Simonetti staircase leads up to the popular **Galleria delle Carte Geografiche**, a 120m-long corridor adorned with Renaissance topographic maps. The so-called **Stanze di Raffaello**, once part of Pope Julius II's private apartments, astounds, with its frescoes by Raphael and his pupils, including *La Scuola di Atene* and scenes of Constantine.

They're a fitting prelude to the grand finale – the inimitable **Sistine Chapel**. Start by gazing at Michelangelo's ceiling from the east wall, then take in the *Last Judgement* on the western wall and the side frescoes of Moses and Christ. Just remember photography is strictly forbidden in the Sistine Chapel. Time wise, allow at least three hours to cover the Vatican Museum's highlights.

BEBOY/SHUTTERSTOCK

Vatican City (p407)

Make a pilgrimage to St Peter's

St Peter's Basilica *(basilicasanpietro.va)* is the pinnacle of Rome's artistic and architectural brilliance. Built over St Peter's supposed burial site, Constantine's 4th-century church gave way to the current basilica, consecrated in 1626. Inside lies Michelangelo's hauntingly beautiful *Pietà,* a red floor disc marking Charlemagne's coronation spot, and Bernini's towering baldachin, soaring beneath Michelangelo's 133m-tall dome. Don't miss the bronze statue of St Peter, its foot worn smooth by centuries of pilgrims' caresses. Dress modestly (cover shoulders and knees), and plan to visit at lunch or late afternoon to avoid the longest lines. To the right of the main portico is entry to the dome, which offers magnificent views of the city.

Scale a mighty fortress

With its distinctive round keep, **Castel Sant'Angelo** *(castel santangelo.beniculturali.it; adult/reduced €16/2)* is an immediately recognisable landmark. Built as a mausoleum for Emperor Hadrian, it was converted into a papal fortress in the 6th century. Nowadays it houses a fascinating collection of paintings, sculpture, military memorabilia and medieval firearms. Many of these weapons were used by soldiers fighting to protect the castle, which is linked to the Vatican by a 13th-century passageway, the Passetto di Borgo.

VATICAN CURIOSITIES

The Vatican is quite the curious place, besides being a repository for some of the world's greatest artworks. It might be a tiny pocket of Rome, but officially it's an independent state, the world's smallest, complete with its own flag, army (the Swiss Guards), postage stamps, licence plates and, of course, head of state (the pope). And another thing – while Italian is widely spoken throughout the Vatican, Latin is technically the official state language. That means that if you want to withdraw some money at a Vatican ATM, you will find Latin among the possible language options.

EATING IN VATICAN CITY, BORGO & AROUND: OUR PICKS

Bonci Pizzarium: Some of Rome's best sliced pizza, served with tonnes of creative toppings. *11am-11pm Tue-Sat, 11am-3pm & 5-11pm Sun* €

Il Sorpasso: A popular spot in Prati, serving everything from salads to pizza to *trapizzini* (pizza pockets). *9am-1am Mon-Fri, 9.30am-1am Sat* €€

Osteria dell'Angelo: Authentic neighbourhood *trattoria* offering fixed-price menus. *12.30-2.30pm & 7.30-11pm Mon-Fri, 7.30-11pm Sat* €€

L'Arcangelo: Treading the line between informal and chic, this restaurant enjoys a stellar local reputation. *7.15-10.45pm Mon-Sat* €€€

COBBLESTONES & PIETRE D'INCIAMPO

It pays to look down as you're walking your way through Trastevere, and not just because its oh-so-picturesque cobblestones can be notoriously treacherous and slippery, especially when wet. But among the regular cobblestones, you will sometimes find gilded *pietre d'inciampo* (stumbling stones). Every single one of these bronze squares is engraved with the name of a Jewish Roman citizen and marks the spot where he or she was rounded up by Nazi troops during WWII and deported to one of the Reich's concentration camps. More than 1000 Jewish residents were forcibly removed from their homes, and many of the stones appear in a group with several others – marking where entire families were taken.

LACHRIST7/GETTY IMAGES

Pincio Hill, Villa Borghese

Museum highlights include the papal apartments on level five and the terrace, immortalised by Puccini in his opera *Tosca,* from where you can enjoy a truly spectacular view over Rome.

Trastevere

On the left bank of the Tiber – hence the name *trans Tevere,* 'across the Tiber' – Trastevere is one of Rome's most attractive areas, an endlessly photogenic pocket of cobbled lanes, medieval piazzas and ochre, ivy-clad *palazzi*. It's beautiful any time of day but really comes into its own at night when street sellers set up camp on its picturesque alleyways and crowds swarm to its many restaurants, bars and cafes.

This beauty and carnival-like atmosphere has made it popular with visiting students and foreign home buyers. But while gentrification has undeniably changed the area, it hasn't eradicated its unique character.

Ponder medieval mosaics

The **Basilica di Santa Maria in Trastevere** is one of Rome's oldest churches dedicated to the Virgin Mary. Tradition places its founding in the 3rd century, though the current building

Located right in the heart of Trastevere.

 EATING IN TRASTEVERE: OUR PICKS

Tonnarello: Always packed but rightfully so, since it serves up all the delicious staples of Roman cuisine. *11am-11pm* €€

Da Enzo: Tiny *trattoria* with a menu made from locally sourced Lazio ingredients. *12.15-3pm & 7-11pm Mon-Sat* €€

Osteria Nannarella: A great place to sit down and enjoy everything from carbonara to fried artichokes. *11.30am-11.30pm* €€

Trattoria da Teo: A textbook *trattoria* that's perfect for digging into platefuls of Roman standards. *12.30-3pm & 7.30-11.30pm Mon-Sat* €€

– featuring 24 Roman columns from the Baths of Caracalla and stunning medieval mosaics – is a 12th-century rebuild. The portico was added at the beginning of the 18th century, with various pieces of Roman marble forming another informal mosaic to echo those found inside. Legend holds the basilica stands atop a miraculous oil fountain, marked inside near the altar, though scholars suggest it may have been a polluted water source. To catch the mosaics in the best light, visit early morning or late afternoon.

Treasure-hunt at a flea market

Every city needs its own giant flea market, and the **Mercato di Porta Portese** fills that role for Rome. With more than 500 stalls selling everything from secondhand clothes and everyday home stuff to antiques, paintings, books and picture frames, the sprawling open-air market takes over the area around Porta Portese every Sunday morning. While undoubtedly chaotic, it's the perfect way to truly immerse yourself in the local atmosphere of Trastevere.

Villa Borghese

For a leisurely stroll, a family bike ride or an outdoor yoga class, **Villa Borghese** is the place. The gateway to Rome's affluent northern suburbs, it's the city's central park – an 80-hectare oasis of shadowy glades, gardens and grassy banks. Among its attractions is a small boating lake, the Giardino del Lago; a panoramic viewing terrace on the Pincio Hill; and several excellent museums, including the superlative Museo e Galleria Borghese.

Schmooze with the masters

Set in a lavishly decorated villa, the **Museo e Galleria Borghese** (*galleriaborghese.beniculturali.it; adult/reduced €17/4*) boasts some of the city's greatest Renaissance and baroque masterpieces. Among them are Bernini's *Apollo e Dafne* and *Ratto di Proserpina,* not to mention Canova's daring depiction of Napoleon's sister, Paolina Bonaparte Borghese, as *Venere vincitrice.* Caravaggio dominates Sala VIII with six intense canvases, including his much-loved *Giovane col Canestro di Frutta.* Upstairs, Titian's early masterpiece *Amor Sacro e Amor Profano* is one of the museum's most prized works. Tickets must be booked in advance, with timed-entry ensuring you can savour the highlights sans the hordes. Bring photo ID.

GOFFREDO MAMELI

The Palazzo Corsini was the theatre of one of the most violent battles of the Siege of Rome of 1849 – and among the many soldiers who were fatally wounded was a poet and patriot named Goffredo Mameli, barely in his early 20s. His compositions included the 1847 'Canto degli Italiani', literally 'Song of the Italians'. His fellow patriot Michele Novaro arranged it into music, and that song is now known as the 'Inno di Mameli', or 'Hymn of Mameli' – Italy's national anthem, recognised as provisional in 1946 and made official in 2017. While Mameli's original text includes six verses and a refrain, the anthem is performed by repeating the first verse twice and adding the refrain at the end of the second repetition.

DRINKING IN TRASTEVERE: OUR PICKS

Ma Che Siete Venuti a Fà: A paradise for beer lovers, with a wide selection of beers on tap and by the bottle. *11am-2am*

Meccanismo: Cool, hip and good at any time of day, from morning coffee to afternoon tea or late-evening cocktails. *8am-2am*

Freni e Frizioni: Cool, lively and with a young crowd. Ideal for an afternoon *aperitivo* or post-dinner cocktail. *6.30pm-2am*

Bar San Calisto: Packed with locals at every hour of the day and night. Come here for a taste of authentic Trastevere. *6am-2am*

Northern Italy

ICONIC CHURCHES | OPULENT PALACES | STUNNING HIKES

☑ TOP TIP

If you plan on buying Murano glass, beware of foreign-made imposters. As a rule of thumb, if it's not expensive, it's probably not made locally (expect to pay upwards of €35 for a single handblown tumbler). Certified artisans are listed on *muranoglass.com* and display 'Vetro Artistico Murano' labels.

Italy's well-heeled north is the country at its most powerful and creatively charged. Home to names like Missoni, Maserati and Kartell, it's here that Italian style, creativity and flair reach their enviable zenith, shaping trends across the world. Its biggest city, Milan, is the country at its sharpest and chicest – a place where past and future collide with spectacular effect. Celebs and mere mortals sigh collectively over villa-flanked Lago di Como, while others fall madly for Liguria's wilder, equally stunning Cinque Terre. Do you feast in mouthwatering Bologna, museum hop in orderly Turin, or catch a summer opera in Verona's ancient Roman arena? Then, of course, there's the fairest of them all: Venice. The world's most improbable masterpiece, no city quite blurs the line between reality and fantasy like this one. Tread lightly and respectfully, and it promises to reward you with its own extraordinary treasures.

Cinque Terre

Clinging like timeworn citadels to Liguria's precipitous coast, Cinque Terre – namely Riomaggiore, Manarola, Corniglia, Vernazza and Monterosso al Mare – are five diminutive fishing villages linked by a network of ancient cliff-side footpaths that are

---

⊚ GETTING AROUND

Spanning several regions – including Lombardy, Piedmont, Liguria and the Veneto – northern Italy is well served by trains, buses and tolled *autostrade* (freeways). Frequent high-speed services link Turin and Milan with Verona, Venice, Bologna and cities further south, while *regionale* (regional) trains and buses connect smaller towns.

Milan and Venice are major international gateways, with airports offering domestic

and global connections. Outside urban areas, driving can be rewarding, but Liguria's cliffside roads are not for the faint-hearted, especially in summer.

Within cities, public transport – including buses, metro lines, trams, and in Venice, *vaporetti* (passenger ferries) – makes getting around easy. For short distances, walking remains the most convenient option.

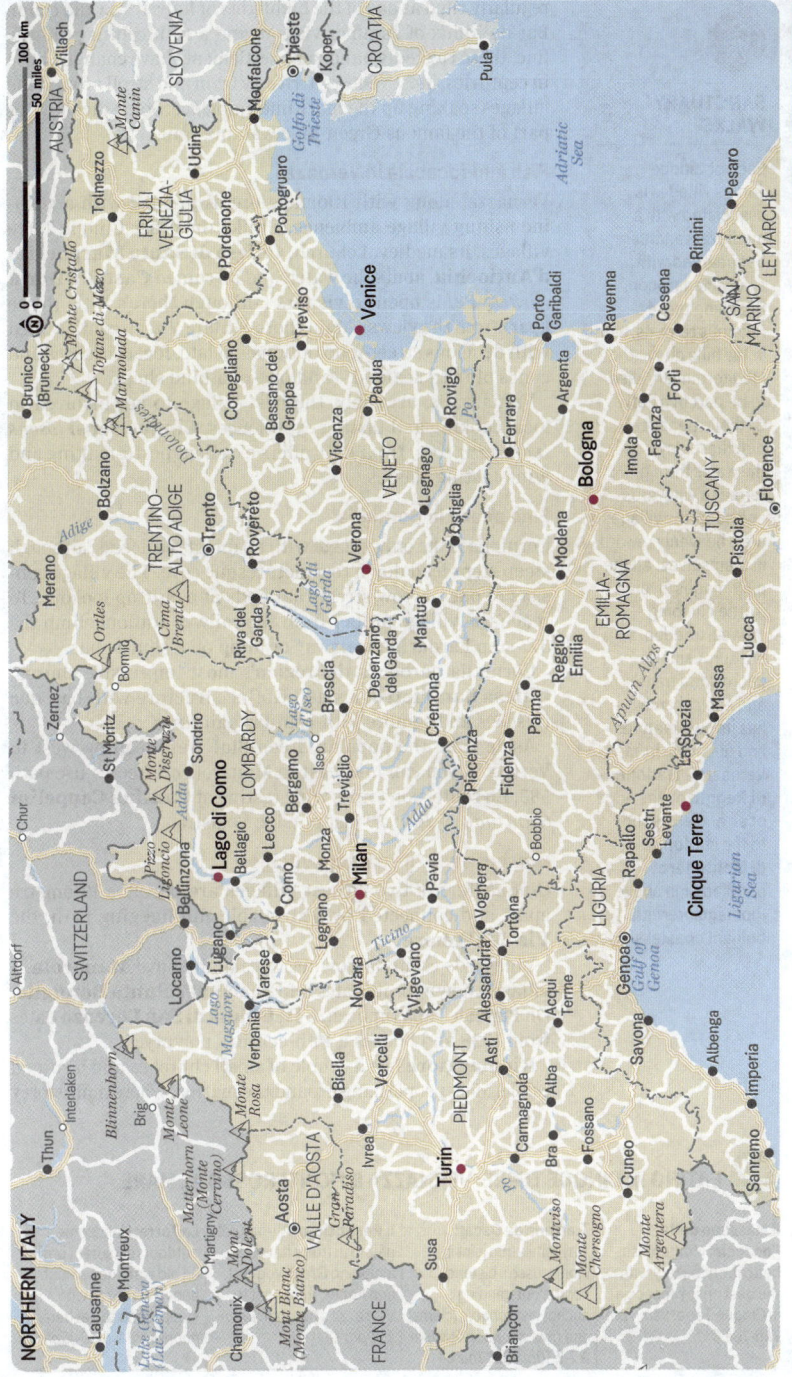

NORTHERN ITALY

100 km
50 miles

413

SANCTUARY WALKS

Each of Cinque Terre's villages is associated with a medieval sanctuary bequeathed with a holy Marian icon. Reaching these religious retreats, high in the hills above the Mediterranean, used to be part of a hefty Catholic penance but, these days, the walks through terraced vineyards and soporific villages are a heavenly reward in themselves. All the pilgrimages involve a little climbing on well-trodden but surprisingly uncrowded trails and each church has its own features and nuances, from Vernazza's **Madonna di Reggio** on the edge of an ancient wood, to the **Madonna di Montenero** perched high above Riomaggiore with brilliant coastal views.

regularly cited as one of the highlights of Italy. It's a valid claim. Bar an influx of summer visitors and a 19th-century railway line, these ruggedly handsome settlements have changed little in centuries. Most visitors arrive by train and stroll around the villages soaking up the maritime ambience. Some tackle all or part of the famous Green-Blue walking trail.

Fish and focaccia in Vernazza

Vernazza, along with Riomaggiore, is imbued with a genuine fishing village ambience. Unlike the other Cinque Terre villages, its medieval church, **Chiesa di Santa Margherita d'Antiochia**, abuts the water, and its ruined **Castello Doria** *(tickets €2)* is open to visitors (although there's little to see apart from the views). Main thoroughfare Via Visconti is lined with delicious street-food options – gelato, focaccia slices and cones of fried seafood – and one-of-a-kind shops.

Vernazza is, arguably, the best village to get involved in local cooking and tasting experiences. **Cinque Sensi** *(5sensivernazza.com; from €50)* offers excellent pesto-making and wine-tasting classes.

Find peace in Corniglia

Corniglia is the only village with no direct sea access, although steep steps lead down to a picturesque cove. The village consists of one narrow street that ends at a clifftop lookout. To reach the village proper from the railway station, climb the 377-step Lardarina stairway or jump on a shuttle bus.

Corniglia harbours the region's most impressive church, **Chiesa San Pietro**, a small Gothic structure with baroque frescoes and sombre 18th-century paintings.

Aside from the popular Green-Blue trail heading west to Vernazza, you can hike east to Manarola on free-to-use path 583. En route, don't miss wine tasting at **Cantina Cappellini** *(cantinacapellini.it)* just outside Volastra.

Hop between the eastern villages

Cinque Terre's two closest villages are barely a kilometre apart and connected by a strollable cliff-hugging path, the **Via dell'Amore**.

Vineyards cram narrow terraces high above **Manarola**, a village known for its cafes and panoramic **Punta Bonfiglio**. On Piazzale Papa Innocenzo IV, **Chiesa di San Lorenzo** dates from 1338 and houses a 15th-century polyptych.

Riomaggiore has a couple of small churches and a ruined castle. Most people hang around the marina, where multistorey

EATING IN CINQUE TERRE: VERNAZZA & MONTEROSSO AL MARE

Il Massimo della Focaccia: Monterosso beachfront bakery with the best crispy focaccia in Cinque Terre. *9am-7pm Thu-Tue* €

Trattoria da Oscar: Tiny family-run joint in Monterosso's historic centre; outstanding anchovies, *vongole* (clams) and gnocchi. *noon-2.30pm & 7-9.30pm Sat-Thu* €€

Il Porticciolo: All-natural gelato in fruity flavours, including Greek yoghurt and honey, right next to Vernazza's harbour. *10am-7.30pm* €

La Torre: Handsome outdoor restaurant beside an old watchtower high above Vernazza with a steep climb to get here. *noon-4pm & 6.30-10pm* €€

Chiesa di Santa Margherita d'Antiochia, Vernazza

pastel houses glow romantically at sunset. This is the best place in Cinque Terre to rent a kayak or organise a diving or snorkelling excursion. A short walk to the east brings you to pebbly, wave-battered **Spiaggia di Fossola**.

Kayak the coast

Laced with caves and beaches, some of them only accessible by boat, Cinque Terre lends itself to the pulse-raising pursuit of sea-kayaking. When the weather is cooperating, it's possible to paddle into the harbours of all five towns in one day. Riomaggiore is the best launch point and has a reliable rental point, **Cinque Terre Adventure** (*cinqueterreadventure.com; kayak rental 1/2hr €10/20),* in the marina. For extra safety and insider knowledge, join a guided trip.

Turin

Turin has abundant history moving through its streets and sailing down its river, the mighty Po. What was once a small settlement of the Taurini people in the 3rd century BCE became a Roman colony first and a Renaissance duchy after. But most of Turin's current look comes from the 19th and 20th centuries: grand royal palaces in the city centre, which speak to its former status as a capital of the Kingdom of Italy and seat of the country's royal family, and industrial suburbs

PARCO NAZIONALE DELLE CINQUE TERRE INFO

The whole Cinque Terre area is part of the **Parco Nazionale delle Cinque Terre** *(parconazionale 5terre.it).* Park authorities maintain the various hiking trails that surround the five villages and preserve the surrounding seas, which are included in a protected marine area. The park's useful website is worth visiting when you are planning your trip, and there are also information points at each Cinque Terre train station and in La Spezia. Check out the two options for the Cinque Terre Card ahead of your visit. Opt for the Trekking Card if you just want to hike on the SVA between the villages, and the Treno MS Card if you want to also include unlimited train travel.

 EATING IN CINQUE TERRE: CORNIGLIA

Ristorante Cecio: Large portions of risotto, pasta and fish served by charismatic staff who treat you like family. *noon-3pm & 6.30-10pm* €€

Alberto Gelateria: Often touted as offering the best ice cream in the five villages, using local herbs to augment its fruity flavours. *9am-10pm* €

Pan e Vin: Friendly staff serve hearty breakfasts, focaccia sandwiches, wine and the best Nutella cake on the Riviera. *7am-8pm Fri-Wed* €

Enoteca Il Pirun: Spread across two floors of an old village house, this trad *trattoria* offers earthy Cinque Terre classics. *noon-3pm & 7-10pm* €€

THE HOLY SHROUD

Don't expect to see the Holy Shroud when you visit the **Cattedrale di San Giovanni Battista** – it's usually kept locked inside a very specific case to prevent any damage, and pilgrims can only stop in front of the chapel that houses it. The Shroud is, however, exhibited to the public at irregular intervals – with years potentially separating them, considering the last ones were in 2013, 2015, 2020 and 2021, with some of the viewings only being via TV. These are always announced beforehand on its official website *(sindone.org)*. If you happen to visit around the time of an *ostensione* (showing) and want to take advantage, prepare for some considerable queues.

TARA VAN DER LINDEN PHOTO/SHUTTERSTOCK

Palazzo Reale, Turin

dating back to when Turin was one of the engines behind Italy's modernisation process.

Tap into the city of kings

The **Palazzo Reale** *(museireali.beniculturali.it; full/reduced €15/2)* was once the official residence of the House of Savoy. Close by is **Palazzo Madama**, also used by members of the royal family as a residence. Both palaces are museums in their own right, but also host exhibitions. Passing through the Palazzo Reale's courtyards will lead you to the relaxing **Giardini Reali**.

Just off the side of the Palazzo Reale, the **Cattedrale di San Giovanni Battista** contains the **Chapel of the Holy Shroud**, which houses the famous Shroud of Turin, believed to be the cloth used to wrap the body of Jesus Christ after his crucifixion.

Piazza-hop *alla torinese*

The quickest way to gain a sense of Turin's atmosphere is to get lost in the perfectly parallel, grid-like streets of its city centre. Linger in its piazzas, like **Piazza Statuto** – not too far from the Porta Susa railway station – or the sprawling

EATING IN TURIN: OUR PICKS

Barbagusto: Tiny, cosy and featuring a menu bursting with all the delicacies the Piedmontese culinary tradition has to offer. *12.30-3.30pm & 7.30-10pm Wed-Sat, 7.30-10pm Sun* €

Osteria Antiche Sere: Your textbook Turin restaurant in both looks and food, on a quiet street away from the most beaten tourist tracks. *7.30-10.30pm Mon-Sat* €€

Pasticceria Ghigo: This incredibly *torinese* cafe is perfect for sitting under the Via Po porticoes. Try their *nuvola*, a little *pandoro* (sweet bread) that's renowned throughout the city. *7.30am-8pm* €€

Vintage 1997: Enjoy a Michelin-starred meal at this elegant place. Tasting menus include local dishes and quirkier creations. *12.30-2.30pm & 8-11pm Mon-Thu, 12.30-2.30pm & 7.30-11pm Fri, 7.30-11pm Sat* €€€

Piazza Vittorio Veneto, or the tiny **Piazza Carlo Emanuele II**, which locals know as 'Piazza Carlina'.

Getting from one to the other is simple, thanks to Turin's porticoes. When put together, the city's monumental porticoes are almost 20km long, lining the major avenues of its centre and allowing people to be outside even when the weather isn't the nicest.

Enjoy a museum day

Rainy days are the perfect occasion to explore one of Turin's many museums. History buffs can head to the **Museo Nazionale del Risorgimento Italiano** *(museorisorgimento torino.it; full/reduced €10/8),* housed inside the magnificent **Palazzo Carignano**, or the nearby **Museo Egizio** *(museo egizio.it; full/reduced €18/3),* which hosts the second-largest collection of Egyptian antiquities after the one in Cairo. If you prefer cinema, then head to the **Museo Nazionale del Cinema** *(museocinema.it; full/reduced €16/14),* located inside the skyline-defining **Mole Antonelliana**.

For something a little different, car lovers should try the **Museo Nazionale dell'Automobile** *(museoauto.com; full/ reduced €15/12)* a few kilometres outside the city centre.

Milan

MAP p418

Milan is an industrial powerhouse, a fashion capital and global trendsetter in architecture and design. The birthplace of Prada and Alfa Romeo, Italy's wealthiest city continues to nurture innovation, but for many residents its finest attributes have nothing at all to do with financial clout or iconic labels. This is a place of countless, only-in-Milan experiences. It's sinking into a red velvet chair and waiting for the curtain to rise at La Scala. Or enjoying a balmy summer evening at a canal-side cafe while watching the world stroll past, wandering through a provocative art installation or happening upon a glowing Duomo at sunset.

Watch the curtain rise at La Scala

One of the most famous opera stages in the world, **La Scala** *(teatroallascala.org)* is where Maria Callas made her debut, Verdi triumphed and Toscanini established his legacy as a virtuoso conductor. Sitting in the crimson and gilt boxes of Teatro alla Scala among the Milanese dressed to impress is one of those moments you won't forget. The opera season kicks off on 7 December, the day of Sant'Ambrose – Milan's patron saint – and it typically runs until mid-July. If you're not a fan

LOCAL DRINKS

If you want to truly take a sip of Turin, then you can't leave the city without having tried two of its most typical drinks. First up is the *bicerin* (quite literally 'small glass' in the local dialect), a shot of espresso carefully layered with chocolate and milk. Try it at **Caffè al Bicerin**, where it was supposedly invented at the beginning of the 18th century. Then there's vermouth, an aromatised and fortified wine whose modern version was first produced right here in Turin around the same time the *bicerin* was invented. It's usually drunk as an *aperitivo*, even though you'll find that a good number of the city's cafes serve it around the clock.

EATING NEAR MILAN'S DUOMO: OUR PICKS

MAP p418

Trattoria Milanese: Generous goblets of wine, hearty servings of traditional Milanese (try pan-fried risotto). *noon-2.30pm & 7-10.30pm Mon-Fri* €€

Peck: Restaurant and deli; Milanese specialities like *osso buco* (veal and vegetables in broth) and *mondeghili* (meatballs) with chicory. *9am-7.30pm Tue-Sat, from 3pm Mon* €€

Rinascente Food Hall: On the 7th floor of Rinascente department store; excellent options include Il Bar, with Duomo views. *10am-midnight* €€

Il Marchese: A beautiful courtyard and photogenic bar, with decadent dining on Roman specialities like pasta carbonara. *12.30pm-2am* €€€

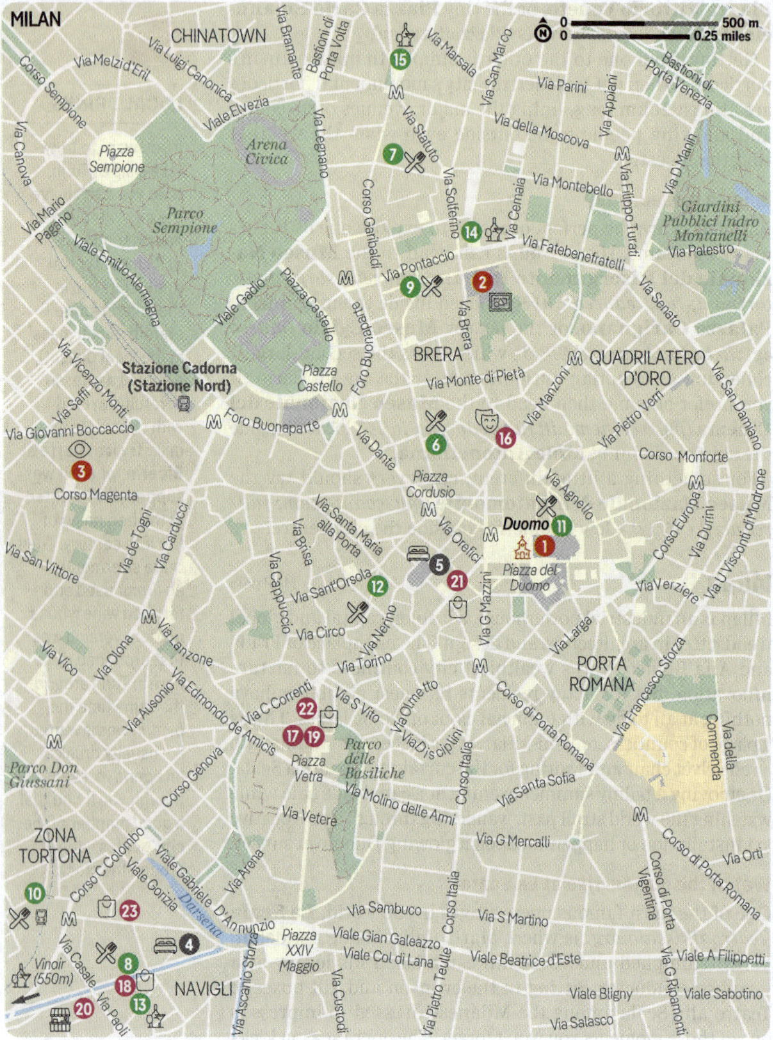
MILAN
CHINATOWN
Via Bramante
Bastioni di Porta Volta
Via Marsala
Via San Marco
0 500 m
0 0.25 miles
Bastioni di Porta Venezia
Corso Sempione
Via Melzi d'Eril
Via Luigi Canonica
Viale Elvezia
Via Statuto
Via Parini
Via della Moscova
Via Appiani
Via Canova
Piazza Sempione
Arena Civica
Via Legnano
Corso Garibaldi
Via Solferino
Via Cernaia
Via Montebello
Via Filippo Turati
Via D Manin
Giardini Pubblici Indro Montanelli
Via Palestro
Via Mario Pagano
Parco Sempione
Viale Emilio Alemagna
Via Pontaccio
Via Fatebenefratelli
Via Senato
Viale Gadio
Piazza Castello
Foro Buonaparte
Via Brera
BRERA
QUADRILATERO D'ORO
Via Vicenzo Monti
Via Saffi
Stazione Cadorna (Stazione Nord)
Piazza Castello
Via Monte di Pietà
Via Manzoni
Via Pietro Verri
Via San Damiano
Via Giovanni Boccaccio
Foro Buonaparte
Via Dante
Corso Monforte
Corso Magenta
Piazza Cordusio
Via Agnello
Via Santa Maria alla Porta
Via Brisa
Via Orefici
Duomo
Corso Europa
Via Durini
Via U Visconti di Modrone
Via de Togni
Via Carducci
Via San Vittore
Via Cappuccio
Via Sant'Orsola
Piazza del Duomo
Via Verziere
Via G Mazzini
Via Circo
Via Nerino
Via Lanzone
Via Torino
Via Larga
Via Vico
Via Olona
PORTA ROMANA
Via Ausonio
Via Edmondo de Amicis
Via C Correnti
Via S Vito
Via Olmetto
Corso di Porta Romana
Via Francesco Sforza
Via della Commenda
Parco Don Giussani
Corso Genova
Piazza Vetra
Parco delle Basiliche
Via Disciplini
Corso Italia
Via Molino delle Armi
Via Santa Sofia
Via Vetere
ZONA TORTONA
Corso C Colombo
Viale Gorizia
Viale Gabriele D'Annunzio
Darsena
Via Arena
Via G Mercalli
Corso di Porta Romana
Via Orti
Via Sambuco
Corso Italia
Via S Martino
Corso di Porta Vigentina
Piazza XXIV Maggio
Viale Gian Galeazzo
Viale Col di Lana
Viale Beatrice d'Este
Via Casale
Vinair (550m)
Via Ascanio Sforza
Via Custodi
Via Pietro Teulie
Via G Ripamonti
Viale A Filippetti
NAVIGLI
Via Paoli
Viale Bligny
Viale Sabotino
Via Salasco

HIGHLIGHTS
1 Duomo

SIGHTS
2 Pinacoteca di Brera
3 The Last Supper

SLEEPING
4 Maison Borella
5 Spadari al Duomo

EATING
6 Il Marchese
7 Le Tre Regioni
8 Luca & Andrea
9 Osteria da Fortunata
10 Osteria del Binari
11 Rinascente Food Hall
12 Trattoria Milanese

DRINKING & NIGHTLIFE
13 Mag Cafè
14 N'Ombra de Vin
15 Radetzky Cafe

ENTERTAINMENT
16 Teatro alla Scala

SHOPPING
17 Cavalli e Nastri Uomo
18 Dischivolanti
19 Frip
20 Mercatone dell'Antiquariato
21 Peck
22 Scout
23 Tenoha

ARTEM EVDOKIMOV/SHUTTERSTOCK

Duomo, Milan

LA SCALA TICKETS

Tickets with a full view of the stage typically cost from €65 to €320. Buy tickets online or from the box office up to four months before the performance. The box office also sells discounted same-day tickets, available online two hours before the performance or from the box office one hour before opening.

Keep in mind that the cheapest seats (which can start at €10) may be partial or no view. Located in the highest galleries, you'll either be forced to stand or crane your neck just to put a face to those angelic voices. But you'll still get to revel in the butterflies-inducing energy of a performance at La Scala – at an unbeatable price.

of operatic glory, you can also see theatre, ballet and classical-music concerts here year-round (except during August).

Swoon over the Duomo

Milan's pink-marble **Duomo** (*duomomilano.it*) was begun by Giangaleazzo Visconti in 1387. Canals were dug to transport the vast quantities of marble, and new technologies invented to cater for the never-before-attempted scale. During his stint as king of Italy, Napoleon offered to fund its completion in 1805. Neo-Gothic details were piled on – the petrified pinnacles, cusps, buttresses, arches and more than 3000 statues are almost all 19th-century additions.

Inside, stare up, and up, to the enormous stained-glass windows, with 144 panes illuminating stories from the Bible. Climbing to the roof terraces, you'll be within touching distance of the elaborate 135 spires and their forest of flying buttresses. The good-value €22 combination ticket covers the cathedral, roof terraces and more.

Trawl the Pinacoteca

Upstairs from Brera Academy, the **Pinacoteca di Brera** (*pinacotecabrera.org*) houses Milan's impressive collection of old masters, much of it 'lifted' by Napoleon during his Italian campaigns.

🍴 EATING & DRINKING IN BRERA: OUR PICKS

MAP p418

Le Tre Regioni: Tiny family-run deli – compile a delicious sandwich from quality cold cuts and Lombard cheeses. *7.30am-8pm Mon-Sat* €

Radetzky Cafe: Fabulous banquette and window seating on a stylish, pedestrianised strip make it popular for an *aperitivo*. *8am-2am* €€

N'Ombra de Vin: Atmospheric former Augustine refectory with top wines, meat boards and tapas-style dishes. *10am-midnight Mon-Wed, to 1am Thu-Sat, 6pm-midnight Sun* €€

Osteria da Fortunata: Go early to beat the long lines at this perennially popular spot, famed for its homemade pasta. *noon-12.30am* €€

BOUTIQUES & INDIE SHOPS

Running directly south of the Duomo, the Via Torino chain shops gradually morph into the city's hippest streetwear strip, Corso di Porta Ticinese.

Frip: The small boutique is a showcase for avant-garde fashion, from cutting-edge to more subtle designs.

Cavalli e Nastri Uomo: A beautifully curated collection of vintage menswear. The women's store is across the street.

Dischivolanti: This canal-side shop is a must for vinyl lovers, with a great selection of classic and hard-to-find LPs.

Tenoha: Direct from Tokyo, this Japanese concept store features beautiful objects for home and wardrobe, plus a stylish restaurant and bar.

Scout: Affordable, attractive and well-made basics by the well-known Italian retailer.

Rembrandt, Goya and van Dyck are included, but you're here to see the Italians: Titian, Tintoretto, Veronese and the Bellini brothers. Much of the work has tremendous emotional clout, notably Mantegna's brutal *Lamentation over the Dead Christ.* Allow several hours to cover 38 rooms at a reasonable pace. Among the highlights is Room IX, a showcase of Venetian Renaissance masters. Don't miss Caravaggio's *Cena in Emmaus* (Supper at Emmaus) in Room XXVIII, or the Rubens, Van Dyck and Jan Fyt paintings in Rooms XXXI and XXXIII.

Attend the Last Supper

Milan's most famous painting, Leonardo da Vinci's **The Last Supper** *(cenacolovinciano.org/en),* is hidden away on a wall of the refectory adjoining the Basilica di Santa Maria delle Grazie. Depicting the moment when Jesus drops the bomb of his impending betrayal, the mixed reactions of his disciples rendered through their gestures and expressions – what da Vinci described as 'motions of the soul' – are utterly enthralling. The illusion of a 3D space created by various tricks of perspective only adds to the image's realism. Online reservations are released quarterly (mid-March for June, July or August visits); tickets go quickly. If sold out, book a **Viator city tour** *(from €80),* which guarantees a visit.

Hang out by the canals

Milan was once laced with waterways that da Vinci himself had a hand in developing. Sadly, in the 1930s the fascist regime closed them for supposed hygiene reasons and to accommodate the increasing number of cars. Now you can have a drink on the photogenic **Naviglio Grande** and **Naviglio Pavese**, and imagine what might have been. Naviglio Grande is *the* place for *aperitivo* and on Saturday nights it feels like the whole city is here. On the last Sunday of the month, it hosts the **Mercatone dell'Antiquariato** *(navigliogrande.mi.it),* a sprawling antiques market.

Lago di Como

Set in the shadow of the snow-covered Rhaetian Alps and hemmed in on both sides by steep, verdant hillsides, Lago di Como (aka Lake Lario) is spectacular. Shaped like an upside-down Y, the lake is littered with villages, including exquisite Bellagio. Where the southern and western shores converge is the lake's main town, Como, an elegant, prosperous city that was once a powerful rival of Milan. Among the area's siren

EATING & DRINKING IN NAVIGLI: OUR PICKS ———————— MAP p418

Luca & Andrea: Tiny place overlooking the canal. Chalkboard menu of classic fare with standouts like *osso buco* and summer pastas. *8am-2am €€*

Osteria del Binari: Bedrock of quality Milanese fare with a Liberty Style design interior and garden terrace. *7am-3pm & 7.30pm-1am €€*

MAG Cafe: Canal-side cocktails crafted with curious herbs and syrups, served in vintage glassware by knowledgeable barkeeps. *9am-2am*

Vinoir: Small, spare bar at Navigli Grande's quieter end, harbouring unusual natural wines and delicious small plates. *noon-3pm & 5pm-midnight*

Bellagio and Lago di Como

Alberto Trombetta, founder of Lake Como Adventures. *@lakeco moadventures*

The *via ferrata* is basically a system of steel cables and ladders secured to a rockface that allows you to safely travel up a steep mountain. Nowadays, there are 15 or so *via ferrata* around Lake Como that provide the next big challenge when it comes to hiking. You'll find all different levels – easy, medium and hard – and *via ferrata* are free and open to all. The only gear you need are the harness and clip system, a helmet and decent hiking shoes. Those who aren't ready to go alone can hire a guide, who can help you find the perfect *via ferrata* for your fitness level.

calls are extraordinarily sumptuous villas, often graced with gardens bursting with plant and animal life. The mountainous terrain provides numerous opportunities for bird's-eye views of the lake. Prepare to swoon.

Ride the cable car to Brunate

The 1894 **Funicolare Como–Brunate** *(funicolarecomo.it; one way €3.60)* takes seven minutes to trundle up to the quiet hilltop village of **Brunate** (720m), revealing a memorable perspective of mountains and lakes. Once at the Brunate funicular stop, continue to nearby baroque **Chiesa di San Andrea**. With its faded pink exterior and giant bell peeking out of the tower, it's hard to miss. If you want to keep going, allow another 30 minutes or so for the steep walk (1.3km) up to **San Maurizio**. There you can scale 143 steps to the base of **Faro di Volta**, a lighthouse built in 1927 to mark the centenary of the physicist Alessandro Volta's death.

Fall in love with Bellagio

Flanked by blue waters and lined with villas, cypress groves, oleanders and lime trees, **Bellagio** lives up to its moniker as the 'pearl' of Lago di Como. From the port, wander up the stony stairs of Salita Serbelloni, stopping to peruse the wine and silk shops. At Via Garibaldi, if you turn left and walk for

 EATING & DRINKING IN BELLAGIO: OUR PICKS

Enoteca Cava Turacciolo: Bellagio's most charming wine bar is in a candlelit, stonewalled space down a lane near the waterfront. *noon-11pm Thu-Tue* €

Trattoria San Giacomo: Cosy spot in the heart of town, with reasonably priced homemade pasta and lake fish. *noon-2.30pm & 7-9.30pm Wed-Mon* €€

La Grotta: Satisfying pizzas, pastas and seafood in an understated dining room with vaulted ceilings. *noon-2.30pm & 7-9.30pm Tue-Sun* €€

Dispensa 63: Small, creative, seasonally inspired menu with hits like risotto with scallops and roe. *noon-2pm Thu-Sat & 7-9pm Tue-Sat* €€€

VERONA VERITÀ

Alice Ronconi, former craft-beer publican, is a barista at Amaro. @alice_beerland

When she isn't pursuing hops, her perfect Verona day goes something like this:

I recommend starting your morning with a *risino* (shortcrust pastry filled with rice and custard) at **Pasticceria Scapini** and a nice walk to Castel San Pietro for the best view of the city; nearby there's the archaeological museum of Teatro Romano. Weather permitting, you can continue walking to one of the greenest places in the centre of Verona, **Parco delle Mura**, where you can have a picnic or simply relax. The perfect day in Verona ends with an Americano *aperitivo* at **Archivio** and a tasty plate of *bigoli* with donkey *ragù* at **Osteria al Duca**.

10 minutes you'll hit **Punta Spartivento**, the northernmost tip of the town where there's a swath of green and pretty views. You'll pass the town's brick Romanesque church en route, worth ducking into for its stark simplicity. But the real stars of Bellagio are its **villa gardens**.

Hike Menaggio's ancient pathways

A narrow cobblestone lane that was once part of a Roman road along the western side of Lago di Como has been preserved in sections. The **Antica Strada Regina** traverses wooded greenery, passes through age-old villages and offers fine views over the shoreline – at times from 150m heights. One of the best sections to walk is the 7km stretch (about a three-hour walk) between Menaggio and Rezzonico. If you don't want to walk back, return on the C10 bus (22 minutes).

Verona

Best known for its Shakespeare associations, Verona attracts a multinational gaggle of tourists to its pretty piazzas and knot of lanes, most in search of Romeo and Juliet. But beyond the heart-shaped kitsch and Renaissance romance, it's a bustling city whose centre is dominated by a mammoth, remarkably well-preserved 1st-century amphitheatre, the venue for an annual summer opera festival. Add to that countless churches, a couple of architecturally fascinating bridges, regional wine and food from the Veneto hinterland and some impressive art, and Verona shapes up as one of northern Italy's most attractive cities.

Beyond Romeo and Juliet

Avoid the crowds leaving lovelorn graffiti at **Casa di Giulietta** *(adult/reduced €22/13)* – which some might say is...ahem... much ado about nothing.

Verona's actual teen lovers climb up to the hilltop terraces of **Castel San Pietro** for spectacular views. Art lovers shouldn't miss the **Galleria d'Arte Moderna Achille Forti** *(gam.comune.verona.it; adult/reduced €6/4),* nor the extraordinary **Palazzo Maffei** *(palazzomaffeiverona.com; adult/reduced €15/13),* overlooking wonderful **Piazza delle Erbe**.

Veronetta, on the right bank of the Adige, is the authentic part of the city. It's home to the beautiful Renaissance garden **Giardino Giusti** *(giardinogiusti.com; adult/reduced €13/9)* and the striking **Teatro Romano e Museo Archeologico**

 EATING IN VERONA: OUR PICKS

Café Carducci: Storied 1920s-style bistro in classic surrounds (mirror-lined interior, linen-topped tables with candles). Exquisite for charcuterie and local cheeses. *8am-3pm & 6-10pm Tue-Sat* €

Hostaria la Vecchia Fontanina: The tables at this historic eatery fill mostly with Italians – a good sign. Excellent food at easy-to-digest prices. *noon-2.30pm & 7-10.30pm Mon-Sat* €

Osteria da Ugo: Back-alley *osteria* with a wonderful courtyard; Veronese specialities are executed with creative flair and smart service. *noon-2.30pm & 7.30-10.30pm Mon & Wed-Sat, noon-2.30pm Sun* €€

Casa Perbellini: World-class, three-star Michelin dining, such as warm spaghetti, lemon, anchovy, chicken and spring-onion emulsion (tasting menus from €220). *12.30-2pm & 7.30-9pm Tue-Fri, 12.30-2pm Sat* €€€

(museoarcheologico.comune.verona.it; adult/reduced €9/6), both worthwhile pit stops.

An arena of arias

The eighth-biggest amphitheatre in the Roman Empire and predating the Colosseum in Rome, the 1st-century **Arena di Verona** *(arena.it; adult/reduced €12/9)* is an engineering marvel. Book tickets online to avoid long queues, then pass through its ancient corridors to re-emerge into the massive, sunlit stone arena (head to the top!).

The arena is at its best during the **Arena di Verona Opera Festival** *(arena.it; tickets €30-365)*, which runs from June to September and draws international stars. There's no need to spring for top-end tickets – the numbered stone steps are fine. Rent a cushion and prepare for an unforgettable evening.

Bologna

Bologna is a city of two intriguing halves. One side is a high-tech city located in the super-rich Po valley, where opera-goers waltz out of regal theatres and into some of Italy's finest restaurants. The other is a bolshie, politically edgy city that hosts the world's oldest university and is famous for its graffiti-embellished piazzas filled with tipsy students.

No wonder Bologna has earned so many historical monikers: *La Grassa* (The Fat One) for its rich food legacy, *La Dotta* (The Learned One) for its university, and *La Rossa* (The Red One), a nod to its medieval terracotta and long-standing penchant for left-wing politics.

A medieval marvel

The foundations of Bologna's forward-thinking ethos were laid in the Middle Ages. Home to the world's oldest continually operating university, founded in 1088, the city welcomed everyone from Dante to Petrarch.

On this day-long sojourn, all roads lead to 13th-century **Piazza Maggiore**, dominated by **Basilica di San Petronio** *(basilicadisanpetronio.org)*. On the western flank is **Palazzo Comunale (Palazzo d'Accursio)**, home to the Bologna city council since 1336 and the **Collezioni Comunali d'Arte** *(museibologna.it; adult/reduced €6/4)*, a collection of 13th- to 19th-century paintings, sculptures and furniture. Head up the attached 13th-century **Torre dell'Orologio** *(Clock Tower; bolognawelcome.com)* for panoramic views, including of the

A DAY OFF IN BOLOGNA

Daniele Bendanti, chef at **Oltre**, one of the city's top modern *trattorias*, shares some insights from his days off in the city. *@d.bendanti*

You can't miss a great breakfast at **Gino Fabbri Pasticcere** *(ginofabbri.com)* in La Caramella, a bit outside Bologna but worth it. Take a nice walk at **Giardini Margherita**, the city park that raised me. Eat something from Alessandro, my meat supplier at **Macelleria Con Cucina Agnoletto Bignami** *(facebook .com/Macelleria .Agnoletto.Bignami)*, and stop for a glass of wine or two at the **Osteria del Sole**. Towards evening, cuddle up with a nice plate of *tagliatelle* at **All'Osteria Bottega** *(osteriabottega.com)*, where I worked as a chef for five years and to which I'm very attached.

 EATING IN BOLOGNA: OUR PICKS

I Panini di Mirò: Friendly Mirò holds court at this glorified food stall with over 50 versions of great-value gourmet *panino* (roast pork, caramelised onions, pecorino). *noon-11pm* €

Delizie Bolognesi: Forging incredible, seasonally driven gelato, often with surprising local ingredients. Try Nettuno (Cervia salt, Bourbon vanilla, Sorrento lemon, orange-scented pistachio brittle). *11am-midnight Tue-Sun* €

Al Sangiovese: A convivial husband-and-wife team as generous with their portions as they are with their hospitality runs this somewhat off-the-beaten-path *trattoria*. *12.15-2.30pm & 7-10.30pm Mon-Sat* €€

Oltre: Trendy Oltre bucks tradition with creative nightly specials, without foregoing outstanding modern takes on classics. *12.30-2.30pm & 7.30-11pm Mon, Sat & Sun, 7.30-11pm Thu & Fri* €€€

SAN MARCO'S BEST SHOPPING

Piedàterre: Stylish, colourful *furlane* (Venetian slippers), hand-stitched by Italian artisans.

Merchant of Venice: Locally inspired perfumes, toiletries and home fragrances sold in a neo-Gothic pharmacy.

Giuliana Longo: A milliner and living institution, crafting everything from fascinators to classic Panamas.

Rubelli: Silk foulards and lavish handbags from a world-renowned textile house.

Chiarastella Cattana: Elegant, understated tablecloths, napkins, tea towels, cushions, robes and more from Venetian textile designer Chiarastella Cattana.

Libreria Linea d'Acqua: A high-end treasure trove of antiquarian books, first editions, maps, sculptures and engravings driven by a genuine love of Venice.

Torre degli Asinelli and Torre Garisenda, Bologna

leaning 97.2m-high **Torre degli Asinelli** and its neighbour, **Torre Garisenda**. Finally, there's **Basilica di Santo Stefano** (*santostefanobologna.it*)*,* a labyrinth of interlocking ecclesiastical structures dating to the 11th century.

Taste-test the city

A misnomer, spaghetti *bolognese* is about as Bolognese as Yorkshire pudding, and Bologna's fiercely traditional *trattorias* don't serve it. Instead, the city prides itself on a vastly superior meat-based sauce called *ragù,* which sees slow-cooked minced beef and pork added to a *soffritto* (sautéed onions, celery and carrots), enlivened with a liberal dash of red wine and simmered for hours.

Ragù is one of a long list of renowned specialities birthed in the kitchens of what is arguably Italy's culinary capital, Emilia-Romagna. Lasagne, tortellini, *mortadella* and *passatelli* (pasta made with breadcrumbs, eggs and Parmesan) all hail from here.

It's generally difficult to eat badly in Bologna (though you'll need reservations at the best places, at least a week in advance). At **Trattoria Bertozzi** (*trattoriabertozzibologna.it; meals €30-45),* locals in the know indulge in authentic local

DRINKING IN BOLOGNA: OUR PICKS

Enoteca Storica Faccioli: This storied – if somewhat touristy – *enoteca* features Italy's best natural, organic and biodynamic juice. *4-10pm Mon-Wed, from noon Thu-Sat*

Ruggine: Locally driven craft mixology down a serene alleyway near Piazza Maggiore: house-made shrubs, Venetian aperitifs, Romagnan brandies. *6pm-1am*

Le Serre dei Giardini Margherita: Bologna's unique alfresco bar; a part co-working/event space and vegetarian restaurant immersed in greenery. *8am-midnight Mon-Fri, from 9am Sat & Sun*

Il Punto: Bologna's best and most Italian-focused craft-beer bar, with eight taps and 150 choices by the bottle. *6pm-12.30am Tue & Sun, to 1am Wed-Thu, to 2.30am Fri & Sat*

speciality. And at richly traditional **Al Cambio** (*ristorante al cambio.it; meals €42-55*) the incredible lasagne is the pinnacle by which all others are judged. Make these your can't-miss meals in Bologna (reservations mandatory).

Walk it all off around the city's old food market, a squared grid of narrow lanes just off the southeast corner of Piazza Maggiore known as the **Quadrilatero**. For a deeper dive into local kitchens, get cooking with **Cesarine** (*cesarine. com; per person €65-214*).

Venice

MAP p426

The French novelist Marcel Proust famously declared: 'When I went to Venice, I discovered that my dream had become – incredibly but quite simply – my address'. In this city of masks, storybook palaces and ghostly winter fogs, the line between reality and fantasy can be very thin indeed.

For over 1000 years, Venice was the capital of the Republic of Venice, a sovereign state which, at its peak, ruled lands as far away as the Peloponnese, Crete and Cyprus. Trading with Asia Minor, Persia and the Mongol Empire, La Serenissima was also one of the world's most cosmopolitan commercial hubs, its *calli* (streets) graced with the silks, spices and languages of distant lands. This melting pot would leave an indelible mark on the city's architecture, cuisine and culture. To this day, these worldly influences are palpable, whether it be in the Islamic flourishes of its Palazzo Ducale or the sweet-and-sour flavour of the city's signature *sarde in saor* (deep-fried sardines).

Eye-up Venice's keepsakes

Taking up most of the Procuratie Nuove and Procuratie Nuovissime (Ala Napoleonica) wings of Piazza San Marco, **Museo Correr** (*correr.visitmuve.it; adult/reduced €14/11*) offers a crash course in Venetian history, with an inventory that includes Doge Francesco Morosini's buff coat and sword.

Part of the 1st floor houses the **Museo Archeologico Nazionale** and its Graeco-Roman relics. If you're pressed for time, skim it and focus instead on Museo Correr's old globes and maps, its extraordinary cache of weapons and trophies from Venetian battles, and the magnificent reading room of the 16th-century **Biblioteca Nazionale Marciana**. Upstairs, the **Pinacoteca** explodes with four centuries of masterpieces, including works by Paolo Veronese.

continued on p429

THE CAPPELLA MARCIANA CHOIR

Marco Bellussi, director and composer. *@bellussiteatro*
Attend Sunday morning mass at the **Basilica di San Marco** (p428) to hear the magnificent Cappella Marciana choir, which has performed at the church for more than 700 years. Occasionally the choir performs works in the Venetian polychoral style, a Renaissance-era technique that sees it split into two 'competing' formations *(cori battenti)*. The architecture is perfectly suited to this stereophonic sound, turning the basilica itself into an instrument. In my opinion, Cappella Marciana performs the most interesting music on normal, non-festive Sundays. This might mean works by Andrea Gabrieli, Giovanni Pierluigi da Palestrina, Baldassare Galuppi or Antonio Lotti. You might even hear contemporary works composed by the choir's current director, Marco Germani.

🍴 EATING IN SAN MARCO: OUR PICKS

MAP p426

Rosticceria Gislon: Historic, canteen-style joint famous for deep-fried street food, including croquettes and deep-fried mozzarella. *9am-9.30pm* €

Ai Mercanti: Top chefs and sommeliers dine here for the modern, produce-driven dishes and artisanal wines. *1-2pm & 7-10pm Tue-Sat* €€

Rossopomodoro: Neapolitan chain serving decent pizzas, pasta dishes and grazing platters in upbeat, modern digs. *11.30am-11.30pm* €€

Chat Qui Rit: Refined, creative cooking celebrating top-tier Italian produce and subtle Asian accents. *noon-3pm & 6-10pm Tue-Sat* €€€

⭐ **HIGHLIGHTS**
1 Basilica di San Marco
2 Gallerie dell'Accademia

🔴 **SIGHTS**
3 Basilica dei Santi Maria e Donato
4 Basilica di Santa Maria della Salute
5 Basilica di Santa Maria Gloriosa dei Frari
6 Burano
7 Chiesa di San Martino Vescovo
8 Murano
9 Museo Correr
10 Museo del Merletto
11 Museo del Vetro
12 Palazzo Ducale
13 Peggy Guggenheim Collection
14 Piazza Baldassare Galuppi
15 Ponte di Rialto

⚫ **SLEEPING**
16 3749 Ponte Chiodo
17 Giò & Giò
18 Gritti Palace

🟢 **EATING**
19 Ai Mercanti
20 Alla Maddalena
21 All'Arco
22 Antiche Carampane
23 Chat Qui Rit
24 Crema Gelato
25 Osteria Acquastanca
26 Osteria Ai Bisatei
27 Osteria al Duomo
28 Osteria La Zucca
29 Panificio Pasticceria Marangon

30 Rossopomodoro	**37** Experimental Cocktail Club	**43** Chiarastella Cattana	● **INFORMATION**
31 Rosticceria Gislon	**38** Il Caravellino	**44** De Biasi	**53** Ateneo San Basso Left Luggage Office
32 Trattoria al Gatto Nero	**39** Library Bar at Nolinski Venezia	**45** Fornace Mian	
33 Venissa Osteria		**46** Giuliana Longo	
● **DRINKING & NIGHTLIFE**	**40** Malvasia all'Adriatico Mar	**47** Libreria Linea d'Acqua	
	41 Osteria ai Pugni	**48** Merchant of Venice	
34 Arts Bar	● **SHOPPING**	**49** Piedàterre	
see 18 Bar Longhi		**50** Rubelli	
35 Café Noir	**42** Cesare Toffolo	**51** Venini	
36 Cantina Do Mori		**52** Wave Murano Glass	

TOP EXPERIENCE

Basilica di San Marco

In a city packed with architectural wonders, nothing trumps the Basilica di San Marco for sheer spectacle. In 828 CE, wily Venetian merchants allegedly smuggled St Mark's corpse out of Egypt in a barrel of pork fat to avoid inspection by Muslim authorities. Venice built a basilica around its stolen saint in keeping with the city's own sense of supreme self-importance.

PAOLO GALLO/SHUTTERSTOCK

TOP TIPS

● Dress modestly, covering knees and shoulders.

● Arrive early to avoid queues or purchase 'Skip the Line' tickets online; leave large bags at **Ateneo San Basso Left Luggage**.

● The **Campanile** *(adult/ under 7yr €10/free)* offers 360-degree lagoon views, but book 'Skip the Line' tickets in high season.

PRACTICALITIES

● basilicasanmarco.it
● admission from €3
● 9.30am-5.15pm, museum & loggia only 9am-2pm Sun

Unmissable Highlights

Church authorities in Rome disapproved of Venice's self-glorification, but the city defiantly created a private chapel for its Doge that outshone the official cathedral. After the original St Mark's burned, the basilica was rebuilt twice, with the current incarnation completed in 1094.

Its facade ripples like a wave, with five portals capped by mosaics and arches, and four bronze horses prancing above the central doorway. Enter beneath the ornate triple arch of porphyry columns and reliefs from the 13th to 14th centuries. The oldest mosaic (1270) sits above the far-left portal, showing St Mark's stolen body arriving here.

Inside, 8500 sq metres of mosaics – many with 24-carat gold leaf – glitter with divine light. The narthex holds the oldest mosaics of apostles with the Madonna, standing sentry by the main door for more than 950 years.

Treasures abound: the **Pala d'Oro** *(€5),* studded with 2000 gems; the **Tesoro** *(€3)* with Crusader booty, a Byzantine chalice and Archangel Michael icon; and the **Museo** *(€7),* with close-ups of the mosaics and piazza views from the Loggia dei Cavalli. The most unforgettable experience? An **After Hours tour** *(walksofitaly.com; from €139),* which includes the crypt.

continued from p425

The Doge's palace

For over seven centuries, Venice's spectacular **Palazzo Ducale** *(palazzoducale.visitmuve.it; adult/reduced incl Museo Correr from €25/13)* was the city's seat of government, enduring storms, fires, conspiracies – and even Casanova, who famously escaped the attic prison. The site likely became the Doge's residence in the 10th century, but the current palace began taking shape around 1340. The 1443 **Porta della Carta**, facing the Piazzetta, welcomed dignitaries into the **colonnaded courtyard**. Today, entry is from the waterfront side of the building, which leads into its colonnaded courtyard. From it, the **Scala d'Oro** leads to Palladio's **Sala delle Quattro Porte**, while the **Sala Consiglio dei Dieci** is where Venice's star chamber plotted under a Veronese ceiling. The vast **Grand Council Chamber**, with Tintoretto's gigantic *Paradise,* once hosted elections and ducal audiences, while the **Armoury** displays weapons and fragments of frescoes. Cross the **Bridge of Sighs** to the eerie **Prigioni Nove**, complete with graffitied cells.

The worthy, 60-minute **Secret Itineraries Tour** *(adult/reduced €32/20)* uncovers the **Pozzi** wells, top-secret **Chancellery**, and the **Piombi** attic prison where Casanova was imprisoned in 1756. Book both standard entry tickets and Secret Itinerary Tours online in advance to avoid queues.

Ponder Titian's masterpiece

Built for the Franciscans in the 14th and 15th centuries, the **Basilica di Santa Maria Gloriosa dei Frari** *(basilicadei frari.it; adult/reduced €5/2)* has none of the flying buttresses, pinnacles and gargoyles typical of international Gothic – but its vaulted ceilings and broad, triple-nave, Latin-cross floor plan give this minor basilica a grandeur befitting the masterpieces it contains.

Its undisputed star is Titian's restored 1518 altarpiece *Assunta* (Assumption), one of Italy's greatest Renaissance artworks and also the world's largest wood-panel painting.

The church harbours works by other Venetian greats as well, among them Bellini and Donatello, not to mention a rare Monks' Choir area dating from 1468. Among the numerous monumental tombs is that of Antonio Canova, designed by the sculptor himself and home to his heart.

Cross the Rialto at dawn

The best time to experience Venice's world-famous **Ponte di Rialto** is early in the morning (before 8.15am). Uncluttered

---

VENICE FROM THE WATER

Steven Moore, TV presenter, *Antiques Roadshow* judge. @mrstevenmoore

Some visitors think gondola rides are tacky, but they're actually a fabulous experience. Many gondoliers know Venice intimately, so instead of asking them to sing you 'O Sole Mio', ask them to point out any interesting details about the buildings. Golden hour, when the sun is beginning to set, is especially magical. Evening rides are also wonderful: look up and you might catch a glimpse of a chandelier or a ceiling fresco.

If you've got an hour to kill, take the *vaporetto* up or down the Grand Canal. From tip to toe it's around 40 minutes. I prefer the number 2 *vaporetto* over the 1: it's generally quieter and has less stops.

🍸 **DRINKING IN SAN MARCO: OUR PICKS** — MAP p426

Bar Longhi: Superlative martinis and bellinis in sumptuous surrounds on the Grand Canal. Expensive but magical. *11am-1am*	**Il Caravellino:** Historic restaurant bar with handsome wood panelling, leather armchairs and classic drinks. *8.30am-11pm*	**Library Bar at Nolinski Venezia:** Posh hideaway, with floor-to-ceiling bookshelves, Simon Buret ceiling art and creative libations. *5pm-12.30am*	**Arts Bar:** Cocktail den inside the St Regis Hotel serving clever libations inspired by Venetian artworks and architecture. *6.30pm-12.30am Tue-Sat*

THE GUIDE

ITALY NORTHERN ITALY

GUGGENHEIM

Karole PB Vail, Director Peggy Guggenheim Collection, granddaughter of Peggy Guggenheim. When visiting the Peggy Guggenheim Collection, get up close to the paintings to appreciate their superb execution. Note the thickness of the paint in Jackson Pollock's *Alchemy* and the meticulousness of Leonora Carrington's *Oink (They Shall Behold Thine Eyes)*. Joan Miró's wonderful Dutch *Interior II* is a bit of a riff on Jan Steen's 17th-century painting *The Dancing Lesson*, but Miró made it all his own in a very entertaining, surreal way. I also love the work of Yves Tanguy, who painted surreal, dreamlike landscapes. The collection is very rich in sculpture; look for Jean Arp's *Head and Shell*, the first sculpture Peggy Guggenheim bought.

KIEV.VICTOR/SHUTTERSTOCK

Ponte di Rialto (p429), Venice

by tourists and awnings, you'll be able to fully appreciate its elegant Renaissance lines and the superb view from its balustraded decks. Below you, the city prepares for another busy day: sharply dressed commuters spill out of *vaporetti* (small passenger ferries) and delivery workers unload restaurant supplies from bobbing boats. Costing 250,000 gold ducats and completed in 1592, the Istrian-stone bridge is the work of Antonio da Ponte, whose nephew Antonio Contino would go on to design San Marco's Bridge of Sighs.

Admire Venetian greats

Tracing the development of Venetian art from the 14th to 19th centuries, the unmissable **Gallerie dell'Accademia** (*gallerieaccademia.it; adult/reduced €15/2*) contains more murderous intrigue, forbidden romance and shameless politicking than the most outrageous Venetian parties. Room 5 harbours Giovanni Bellini's sublime *Madonna and Child between Saints Catherine and Mary Magdalene* while Room 8 claims two Giorgione masterpieces: *Old Woman* and *The Tempest*. Even more commanding is Paolo Veronese's monumental *Feast in the House of Levi* in Room 10, condemned by Inquisition leaders for depicting dogs, drunkards, dwarves, Muslims and

---

 EATING IN SAN POLO & SANTA CROCE: OUR PICKS ──────── MAP p426

All'Arco: Epicureans relish All'Arco's market-fresh seafood *cicchetti* (Venetian tapas) and in-the-know wines by the glass. *10am-2.30pm €*

Cantina Do Mori: Venice's oldest *bacaro* (bar), with interesting pan-Italian wines and tasty *cicchetti* and cheeses. *8am-7.30pm Mon-Sat €*

Osteria La Zucca: Daily changing menu of delicious vegetarian and meat dishes; book ahead. *noon-2.30pm & 7-10.30pm Mon-Sat €€*

Antiche Carampane: Book ahead for market-driven Venetian classics. Near Ponte de le Tette. *12.30-2.30pm & 7.30-10pm Tue-Sat €€€*

Reformation-minded Germans cavorting with apostles. Another highlight is Gentile Bellini's recently restored *Miracle of the Reliquary of the Cross at San Lorenzo Bridge* in Room 20. Allow at least 1½ hours for a visit, and avoid high-season queues by arriving at opening time or after 4pm.

Picasso, Pollock and Peggy

Set aside a couple of hours for the **Peggy Guggenheim Collection** *(guggenheim-venice.it; adult/reduced €16/9)*, one of Italy's finest modern-art museums. Occupying an unfinished 18th-century Grand Canal *palazzo*, it was once home to American arts doyenne Peggy Guggenheim.

Works on display rotate, but look out for early works by Picasso and Mondrian – among them Picasso's *A Poet* (1911) and Mondrian's *Ocean 5* (1915) – as well as Magritte's enigmatic *Empire of Light* (1953–54). Another highlight: *Alchemy* (1947), one of Jackson Pollock's first revolutionary 'poured' paintings. A spirited advocate for contemporary Italian art, Guggenheim also influenced the reappraisal of artists such as Umberto Boccioni, Giacomo Balla and Giorgio de Chirico.

The gallery's **Nasher Sculpture Garden** includes works by Henry Moore, Alberto Giacometti and Isamu Noguchi.

Ponder a mystical basilica

Sitting on over a million tree trunks at the mouth of the Grand Canal, Baldassare Longhena's **Basilica di Santa Maria della Salute** *(basilicasalutevenezia.it; church free, sacristy adult/reduced €6/4)* is the Senate's *grazie* to the Madonna for saving the city from the plague of 1630–31. Inside, the lines of the building converge beneath the dome to form a vortex on the inlaid marble floors: esoteric types believe that the central black dot radiates healing energy. The **sacristy** houses Titian's self-portrait in the guise of St Matthew and Tintoretto's made-to-measure *Wedding Feast of Cana*. For a divine view, climb the basilica's iconic **dome** *(adult/reduced €8/6)*.

Observe master glassblowers

The interlinked islands of **Murano** have been synonymous with glassmaking since the 13th century, and despite being extremely touristy, some of its furnaces offer fascinating glassblowing demonstrations. Among these is certified traditional furnace **Wave Murano Glass** *(wavemuranoglass.com)*, where you can watch the blowers from the entry to the factory for free, join an in-depth tour (€29 for 45 minutes) or take a two-hour beginners' course (€245).

MURANO'S BEST IN GLASS

Venini: Even if you don't have the cash to buy a Venini, pop by to see Murano glass at its finest.

De Biasi: These certified Murano artisans design their own jewellery, picture frames, bottle stoppers and even chopsticks.

Cesare Toffolo: Mind-boggling miniatures are the trademark here, along with featherlight drinking glasses and glossy black candlesticks.

Fornace Mian: Shuffle past the typical Murano kitsch and you'll find one of the best ranges of classic stemware on the islands.

Wave Murano Glass: This team of young artisans offers a modern take on ancient traditions.

 DRINKING IN DORSODURO: OUR PICKS — MAP p426

| **Malvasia all'Adriatico Mar:** Waterside spot offering natural, small-scale wines from the Adriatic region. *5-10pm Mon & Tue, from 11am Wed-Sun* | **Osteria ai Pugni:** Hefty selection of wines by the glass plus *aperitivo*-friendly nibbles by Ponte dei Pugni. *10am-10.30pm Mon-Sat* | **Experimental Cocktail Club:** Seriously curated cocktail menus at the Zattere's old Adriatic Naval Company. *6.30pm-1am Sun, Mon & Thu, to 2am Fri & Sat* | **Café Noir:** Gritty, friendly, boho-spirited bar with a long list of cocktails and a faithful student following. *7am-2am* |

You'll need about an hour to explore the excellent **Museo del Vetro** (museovetro.visitmuve.it; adult/reduced €10/7.50), which recounts the backstory of glassmaking.

A short walk away is the remarkable, 12th-century **Basilica dei Santi Maria e Donato** (adult/reduced €3.50/1.50), lavished with intricate mosaics.

See where Venice began

Torcello is one of the lagoon's most tranquil islands. But 1500 years ago, it was a different story. The first lagoon island to have been settled, it was once the site of a major city, with nine churches, two abbeys and its own bishop. The Byzantine-Romanesque **Basilica di Santa Maria Assunta** (adult/child €6/5) served as his cathedral. The oldest parts of the building date from 639, making it by far the oldest church on the lagoon.

Inside, grab an audio guide to decode the basilica's astonishing 12th-century mosaics, and make time for the **Museo di Torcello** (adult/reduced €3/1.50) across the square, which outlines the island's history.

Combine your Torcello trip with Burano, and avoid Mondays when the museum is closed.

Slow the pace

Famed for its lace and technicolour buildings, **Burano** has become a popular destination for social-media hacks seeking a bright backdrop for posing purposes. After you've snapped a trillion photos of the multihued houses of the outer canals, inevitably you'll find yourself on bustling **Piazza Baldassare Galuppi**.

Here, call inside the 16th-century **Chiesa di San Martino Vescovo** (parrocchiadiburano.weebly.com; admission free) to see Giambattista Tiepolo's 1725 La Crocifissione and the Madonna di Kazan, a 19th-century Russian icon considered a masterpiece of enamelwork.

Across the square, give yourself an hour to explore the **Museo del Merletto** (museomerletto.visitmuve.it; adult/reduced €5/3.50), which tells the story of Burano's revered lace industry.

From Burano, a bridge reaches tiny **Mazzorbo**, perfect for a mind-clearing walk or a feast at vine-flanked **Venissa Osteria** (venissa.it).

VINE REVIVAL

If you were ever invited to dinner with the Doge, chances are you would have been served dorona, a local varietal that was golden hued and highly prized.

Venice's devastating 1966 flood was thought to have wiped out the remaining dorona vines, meaning the wine of the Doges was lost for ever. That is, until 2002 when winemaker Gianluca Bisol stumbled across golden grapes growing on Torcello. He subsequently tracked down another 88 vines and used them to revive an ancient vineyard enclosed by medieval walls on Mazzorbo.

Venissa now sells bottles of the liquid gold in handblown Murano glass bottles embossed with gold leaf. Tours and tastings are available.

EATING ON MURANO: OUR PICKS

MAP p426

Panificio Pasticceria Marangon: Grab a morning pastry from this local bakery. 6.30am-1pm Mon-Sat, plus 5-7pm Mon, Tue & Thu-Sat €	**Osteria Ai Bisatei:** Glassblowers come here for plates of fried fish, seafood risotto and spaghetti vongole. 11.30am-2.30pm Thu-Tue €	**Osteria al Duomo:** Dishes up bowls of pasta and excellent pizza within a walled garden. noon-2.30pm & 6.30-9pm Fri-Wed €€	**Osteria Acquastanca:** The best restaurant on Murano serves mainly seafood dishes. noon-3pm Mon-Sat, plus 7-9.30pm Mon & Fri €€€

Florence & Tuscany

ICONIC LANDMARKS | RENAISSANCE ART | MEDIEVAL TOWNSCAPES

Stretching along the Tyrrhenian Sea below Liguria and Emilia-Romagna, Tuscany beckons with its wealth of historic sites scattered on the changing landscapes that slope down from the Apennines to the coast. Fortified palaces and ancient *case-torri,* the tower houses erected by wealthy pre-Renaissance families, define skylines, as do the stone-built bell towers of Gothic and Romanesque churches continuously visited by long-distance pilgrims for nearly a millennium.

The region's capital and undisputed headliner is Florence (Firenze), cradle of the Renaissance and home to an embarrassing wealth of cultural riches (even by Italy's inimitable standards). While it's easy enough to stay put in Florence, Tuscany's cypress-lined countryside rewards the curious. Of all the region's hilltop towns, few match Siena, where winding medieval streets lead to an extraordinary cathedral and storybook square. Closer to the coast, scholarly Pisa beckons with more than just its vertically challenged tower.

☑ **TOP TIP**

Summers can be scorching hot in Florence. If you're climbing the Duomo, Giotto's Campanile or the Torre di Arnolfo, keep in mind that hundreds of narrow steps await. People have fainted in the past – avoid the middle of the day when booking your tickets.

Florence

MAP p436

Few cities are so compact in size or so packed with extraordinary art and architectural masterpieces at every turn. The

---

 GETTING AROUND

Frequent high-speed trains connect Florence to other major Italian cities, including Rome, Bologna and Milan. High-speed and *regionale* (regional) trains connect Florence to Pisa, while a reasonably extensive regional bus network includes *corse rapide* (express services) between Florence and Siena. Other bus routes in Tuscany can involve long trips.

Florence itself is small and best navigated on foot; most major sights are within easy walking distance. Nonresident traffic is banned from the historic centre, and parking is an absolute headache and best avoided. Trams run between Florence Airport and the city's main train station, Firenze Santa Maria Novella.

TUSCANY

LIGURIA
Pontremoli
Fivizzano
Aulla
Monte Cusna
Carrara
Monte Pisanino
La Spezia
Massa
Castelnuovo di Garfagnana
Apuan Alps
Pescia
Pistoia
Viareggio
Prato
Lucca
Pisa
Arno
Florence
Empoli
Pontedera
Livorno
Castelfiorentino
Greve in Chianti
Figline Valdarno
San Gimignano
Poggibonsi
Volterra
Colle di Val d'Elsa
Siena
Asciano
TUSCANY
Massa Marittima
Montalcino
Pienza
Montepulciano
Chianciano Terme
Piombino
Follonica
Monte Amiata
Abbadia San Salvatore
Portoferraio
Castiglione della Pescaia
Grosseto
Pitigliano
Orvieto
Porto Santo Stefano
Orbetello
LAZIO

Bologna
Pavullo nel Frignano
EMILIA-ROMAGNA
Imola
Ravenna
Faenza
Forlì
Adriatic Sea
Cesena
Borgo San Lorenzo
Rimini
Monte Falterona
SAN MARINO
Urbino
Bibbiena
LE MARCHE
Montevarchi
Sansepolcro
Arezzo
Città di Castello
Gubbio
Castiglion Fiorentino
Cortona
Umbertide
Sinalunga
Lago Trasimeno
Perugia
Marsciano
Foligno
UMBRIA
Bolsena
Terni
Lago di Bolsena
Viterbo

Ligurian Sea
Gorgona
Castiglioncello
Cecina
San Vincenzo
Capraia
Pianosa
Elba
Tyrrhenian Sea
Montecristo
Giglio

0   50 km
0   25 miles

urban fabric of this small city, on the banks of the Arno river in northeastern Tuscany, has hardly changed since the Renaissance and its narrow cobbled streets are a cinematic feast of elegant 15th- and 16th-century *palazzi,* medieval candlelit chapels, fresco-decorated churches, marble basilicas and world-class art museums brimming with paintings and sculptures by Botticelli, Michelangelo et al. Unsurprisingly, the entire city centre is a UNESCO World Heritage Site.

Florence's centre of power

For over 700 years, **Palazzo Vecchio** has housed Florence's government, and it's still home to the mayor's office today. Built in 1299 above a Roman theatre, the fortress-like palace was designed by Arnolfo di Cambio and later expanded by the Medici.

Buy a **ticket** (*bigliettimusei.comune.fi.it; adult/reduced €12.50/10*) to see the vast Salone dei Cinquecento, begun in 1494 under preacher Savonarola and later transformed by Vasari with grand scenes of Florentine victories and a ceiling celebrating Cosimo I de' Medici.

Snoop around the private quarters, including Duchess Eleonora di Toledo's chapel by Bronzino and the Sala delle Udienze, awash with frescoes by Furio Camillo. Also, don't miss

T PHOTOGRAPHY/SHUTTERSTOCK

Salone dei Cinquecento, Palazzo Vecchio, Florence

Donatello's *Judith and Holofernes* and Ghirlandaio's *Apoteosi di San Zanobi*. The **Secret Passages tour** *(musefirenze.it/en/attivita/percorsi-segreti; €5)* reveals Francesco I's hidden Studiolo of rare and curious treasures.

Cross the Ponte Vecchio

Built in 1345, Florence's **Ponte Vecchio** is one the city's best-known symbols, both because of its unusual architecture and its convoluted past. Originally, the bridge was mainly populated by *beccai* (butchers), but in 1593 Grand Duke Ferdinando I, who could not stand the smell of meat and the insalubrious state of the market, evicted all businesses involved in 'vile arts', allowing only goldsmiths and jewellers to trade on the bridge. The 48 jewellery stores perched on the bridge survived the 1944 bombing of the city – all other bridges in central Florence were destroyed – and the major flood that hit the city in 1966.

Feast on masterpieces

The **Galleria degli Uffizi** *(uffizi.it; adult/reduced €25/2)* is one of the world's greatest museums, home to masterpieces from Giotto to Caravaggio. Commissioned in 1560 by Cosimo I

continued on p438

THE 1993 BOMBING OF THE UFFIZI

In 2021 the 4.4m-tall **Albero della Pace** (Peace Tree) – a bronze olive tree created by sculptor Andrea Roggi – was placed in Via dei Georgofili, behind the Uffizi, to commemorate one of the darkest days in Italy's recent history. In the early hours of 27 May 1993, a car bomb exploded, killing five people and injuring 48. Besides the loss of human life, the detonation devastated the Torre dei Pulci housing the Accademia dei Georgofili and the Uffizi. The bomb had been placed in a parked car and detonated by remote control by the Mafia, which had escalated its tactics in response to the tightening of prison laws for those involved in organised crime.

Beloved eatery near Dante's museum.

 EATING IN DUOMO & SIGNORIA: OUR PICKS ⎯⎯⎯⎯⎯ MAP p436

Osteria Nuvoli: People spill onto the sidewalk with vino in hand, or enjoy authentic Tuscan fare at a table in the cellar. *8am-9.30pm Mon-Sat* €

I Buongustai: The sisters running this historic *trattoria* on Via dei Cerchi serve homemade Tuscan pastas. *noon-3.30pm Mon-Sat* €

Da' Vinattieri: Traditional Florentine street food, with 18 different fillings for your *schiacciata* (flat bread) – or try the Florentine tripe. *11.30am-7.30pm Mon-Sat* €

Maledetti Toscani: The 'cursed Tuscans' are far from blasphemous when it comes to food – enjoy one of their rustic sandwiches on the go. *8.30am-7pm Mon-Sat, 10am-5pm Sun* €

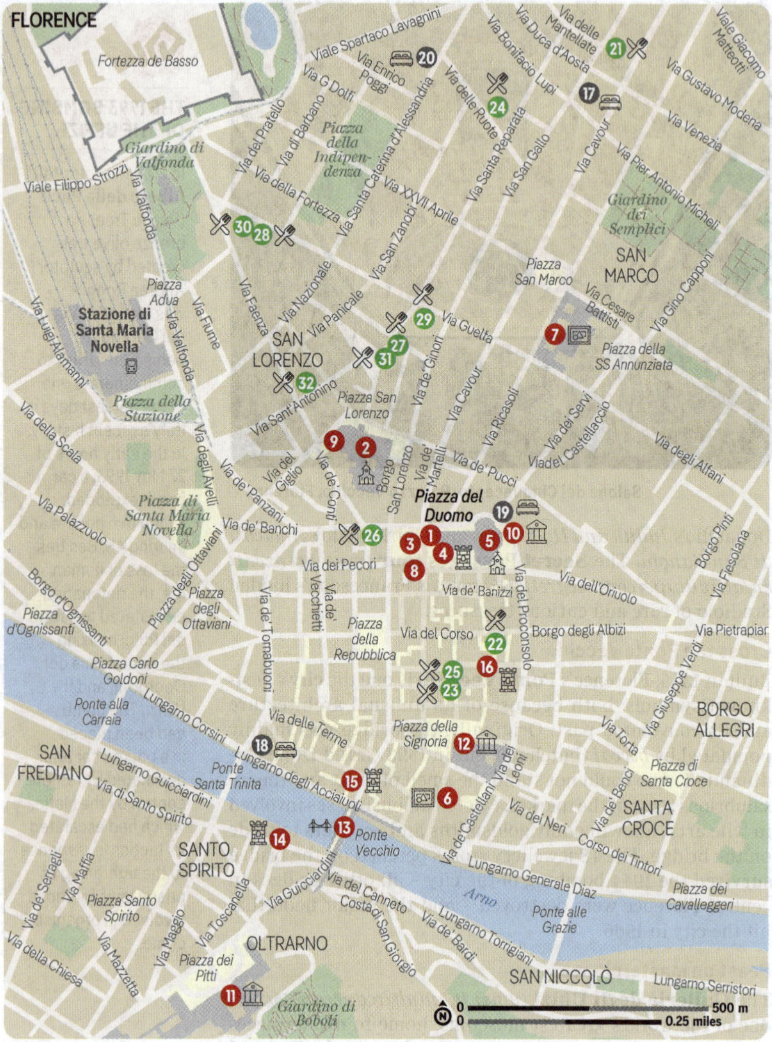

Fortezza de Basso

FLORENCE

Giardino di Valfonda

Viale Filippo Strozzi

Piazza Adua

Stazione di Santa Maria Novella

Piazza della Stazione

Piazza di Santa Maria Novella

Piazza Carlo Goldoni

Ponte alla Carraia

SAN FREDIANO

Piazza d'Ognissanti

Piazza degli Ottaviani

Piazza della Repubblica

Piazza della Signoria

SANTO SPIRITO

Piazza Santo Spirito

Piazza dei Pitti

OLTRARNO

Giardino di Boboli

Ponte Vecchio

Ponte Santa Trinita

Ponte alle Grazie

Arno

SAN NICCOLÒ

Piazza della Indipendenza

SAN MARCO

Piazza San Marco

Piazza della SS Annunziata

Giardino dei Semplici

Piazza San Lorenzo

SAN LORENZO

Piazza del Duomo

BORGO ALLEGRI

SANTA CROCE

Piazza di Santa Croce

Piazza dei Cavalleggeri

0   500 m
0   0.25 miles

TOP EXPERIENCE

Piazza del Duomo

Nearly six centuries have passed since Filippo Brunelleschi completed the cupola topping the Cattedrale di Santa Maria del Fiore, providing Florence with an architectural landmark that would be revered for centuries. But the octagonal dome is only the most visible of the many treasures on Piazza del Duomo, where Gothic and Renaissance masters left an indelible mark on the city's identity.

Cattedrale di Santa Maria del Fiore

Designed by Arnolfo di Cambio and consecrated in 1436, the **Cattedrale di Santa Maria del Fiore** is crowned by Brunelleschi's revolutionary dome, inspired by Rome's Pantheon. Highlights include Ghiberti's stained-glass windows, a vast marble floor by Pollaiolo, and Vasari and Zuccari's *Last Judgement* fresco, best admired while climbing the 463 steps to the cupola's rooftop. The current neo-Gothic facade was added in the 19th century.

Giotto's Campanile

The 85m-tall bell tower of Santa Maria del Fiore was initiated by Giotto in 1334 and completed by Andrea Pisano and Francesco Talenti after Pisano died in 1337. The **Campanile di Giotto** encloses a narrow 414-step staircase leading to the panoramic platform Talenti added in 1359.

Battistero di San Giovanni

A prime example of Florentine Romanesque architecture, the piazza's octagonal **baptistery** was consecrated in 1059. Andrea Pisano and Lorenzo Ghiberti created its monumental bronze doors. Inside, stunning 13th-century mosaics are being restored and are viewable on scaffolding **tours** *(duomo.firenze.it; €65)*.

Museo dell'Opera del Duomo

Many original sculptures from Piazza del Duomo now reside in the **Museo dell'Opera del Duomo**. Highlights include baptistery doors by Pisano and Ghiberti, and a reproduction of Arnolfo di Cambio's 1296 facade.

TOP TIPS

● The cathedral's ground floor is free, but a ticket is required for the cupola.

● Three passes are available: Ghiberti, Giotto and the all-inclusive Brunelleschi. Purchase online in advance.

● Before leaving Piazza del Duomo through Via dei Calzaiouli take a moment to admire the 1358 Gothic **Loggia del Bigallo**.

PRACTICALITIES
● duomo.firenze.it
● adult/reduced from €15/5 ● hours vary

BELOW THE DUOMO

What is commonly referred to as the 'crypt' was in fact a welcome centre for pilgrims travelling along the ancient Via Francigena, the 3000km medieval route between Canterbury and Rome. Pilgrims would descend into the rooms below the cathedral to admire the vivid 13th-century cycle of biblical frescoes decorating the walls – well-earned spiritual wonder and respite to weary, faith-filled travellers. Hidden for centuries beneath layers of history, the rooms were only rediscovered in 1999, revealing a breathtaking visual narrative of faith and artistry. The frescoes' vibrant colours remain remarkably intact, their preservation owed to the absence of sunlight and humidity. Today they stand as an essential piece of the city's rich medieval heritage.

continued from p435

and designed by Vasari, the U-shaped palace once housed government offices before becoming a gallery under Francesco I. Admire its symmetrical facade from Piazza della Signoria before ascending to the 2nd floor via the Scalone Granducale. Highlights include Botticelli's *Nascita di Venere* (1485), the octagonal Tribuna degli Uffizi, and Michelangelo's *Tondo Doni* (1504–06), his only existing panel painting.

Don't miss the restored **Terrazzo delle Carte Geografiche**, covered in handpainted 16th-century maps. Later, encounter Leonardo, Raphael, and Roman sculptures in the **Sala della Niobe**. On the 1st floor, the Collezione degli Autoritratti showcases 250 self-portraits, while the final stretch includes Caravaggio's chilling *Giuditta che Decapita Oloferne* (1620). Book tickets in advance online.

Where the powerful prayed

Built over a 4th-century church, the **Basilica di San Lorenzo** *(sanlorenzofirenze.it; adult €9)* became the Medici family church in the 15th century. In 1425, Cosimo the Elder commissioned Brunelleschi's elegant redesign; his tomb now lies in the crypt-turned-museum, Museo del Tesoro di San Lorenzo. Nearly a century later, Pope Leone X, son of Lorenzo the Magnificent, asked Michelangelo to revamp the facade – but the Carrara-marble plan was never realised, leaving the exterior bare. Inside, *pietra serena* columns frame masterpieces like Filippo Lippi's *Annunciazione Martelli* (1440), Rosso Fiorentino's *Sposalizio della Vergine* (1523) and Donatello's sculpted pulpits (1460). Brunelleschi's *Sagrestia Vecchia* (Old Sacristy), left of the altar, is a highlight, decorated with Donatello's sculptural details. Before exiting, look up to the **Tribuna delle Reliquie** above the main portal, designed by Michelangelo.

Mingle with the Medicis

Matching their opulent palaces, the Medicis' final resting place is a grandiose masterpiece. Enter the **Museo delle Cappelle Medicee** *(bargellomusei.it/musei/cappelle-medicee; adult €9)* from the rear end of the Basilica di San Lorenzo in Piazza di Madonna degli Aldobrandini to find yourself under the 59m-high cupola of the Cappella dei Principi, where the Cosimo I, Francesco I and Cosimo III tombs are surrounded by the city's Florentine mosaic, or *commesso*. Continue to the **Sagrestia Nuova**, the marble hall designed by Michelangelo, where Lorenzo the Magnificent and his brother Giuliano are

Cooking up Tuscan classics for over a century.

EATING IN SAN LORENZO & SAN MARCO: OUR PICKS

Trattoria Guelfa: Select a first and second course from the hand-written menu that changes daily. *noon-2.45pm & 7-10.45pm* €

Trattoria Mario: Bustling *trattoria* serving authentic Tuscan cuisine. No reservations. *noon-3pm Mon-Sat, 7.30-10pm Thu & Fri* €

Il Vegetariano: Vegetarian dishes, freshly made savoury cakes and a variety of teas. *12.30-2.30pm Mon-Fri, 7.30-10.30pm Mon-Sun* €

Antica Trattoria da Tito: The walls are covered in scrawled messages testifying from past customers testifying to its popularity. Book ahead. *12.30-3pm & 7-11pm Mon-Sat* €€

TODAMO/SHUTTERSTOCK

Michelangelo's *David*, Galleria dell'Accademia

buried. This smaller room, built between 1520 and 1534, is adorned with monumental sculptures whose details are elevated by two carefully constructed sources of natural light, which Michelangelo viewed as an essential element of his design.

Make a date with David

Michelangelo's iconic *David* is one of hundreds of artworks at the **Galleria dell'Accademia** (*galleriaaccademiafirenze. it; adult/reduced €16/2),* from 13th-century gilded panels to Bartolini's neoclassical busts. Originally a Medici drawing academy (1563), it became a public museum in 1784. At the heart of the Sala del Colosso stands Giambologna's dynamic plaster *Ratto delle Sabine* (1581), surrounded with works by Lippi, Perugino and Botticelli. Before reaching *David,* pause at Michelangelo's four intentionally unfinished *Prigioni* (1519–34), marble figures straining to escape their stone prisons. Waiting at the end of the gallery is *David* (1504) himself, a 5m marble icon of freedom and beauty sculpted by Michelangelo at just 29. Book tickets on the website (there's a €4 reservation fee). Entry is free on the first Sunday of the month, but expect queues.

FLORENCE'S TOWER HOUSES

The stone-built *case-torri* (tower houses) that dot Florence's heart are a fascinating architectural remnant of the Middle Ages. These residential structures rise above the city's red rooftops, taking you back to an era when powerful families erected hermetic homes to protect themselves from enemy attacks and show off their wealth. The towers generally had a rectangular or square base and could have up to six or seven storeys. About 50 *case-torri* still stand. The best-preserved ones are the **Torre della Castagna**, the **Torre degli Amidei** and the **Torre de' Barbadori**. You can even sleep in one – the hotel **Antica Torre di Via Tornabuoni 1**, offering spectacular 360-degree views over the city from its crenellated rooftop.

MAP p436

Trattoria Palle D'Oro: Ideal lunch break, with simple Tuscan dishes. *noon-3pm & 7-10.30pm* €

Ristorante Cafaggi: Local favourite offering changing seasonal classics in an old-school atmosphere. *12.30-3pm & 7-10pm Mon-Sat* €

Osteria Pepó: Book ahead to secure a spot at this popular place serving generous portions of pastas and meats. *noon-2.30pm & 7-10.30pm* €€

Osteria Vecchio Cancello: This quirkily decorated *osteria* is known for its calm atmosphere and its steaks. *noon-2pm & 7-10pm Wed-Mon* €€

As you stroll through San Lorenzo, you'll inevitably spot the Medicis' emblem hanging on many of the neighbourhood's buildings. The shield adorned with six or seven spheres continues to loom over Palazzo Medici Riccardi, the Biblioteca Medicea Laurenziana and the ceiling of the Basilica di San Lorenzo. No one knows exactly what the balls of the Medicis' emblem mean. One hypothesis suggests that they represent the marks left by the Mugello Giant on the shield of Averardo, an ancestor of the Florentine rulers. A more worldly take on the story says that the spheres are simply coins, linking the family with their banking activities.

Trawl treasures at the Pitti

Dominating its namesake piazza, stately **Palazzo Pitti** *(uffizi .it/en/pitti-palace; adult €16)* became the Medici residence in 1549 and was later expanded by court architect Bartolomeo Ammannati. Start in the Galleria Palatina to explore the Sala di Ulisse, with works by Raphael and Vasari, then continue to the Sala dell'Iliade, where paintings by Andrea del Sarto surround Bartolini's *La Carità* under a Homeric ceiling. In the Sala di Apollo, meet Cosimo I's court jester Morgante, painted nude by Bronzino. Upstairs, the Galleria d'Arte Moderna showcases neoclassical sculptures by Canova, as well as Romantic and Macchiaioli works. Don't miss the Museo della Moda e del Costume, tracing Italian fashion from Eleonora di Toledo to Prada. Back on the ground floor, the dazzling Sala di Giovanni da San Giovanni, frescoed in 1635, celebrates a Medici wedding with trompe l'oeil splendour.

Siena

MAP p441

Unlike other major medieval powers, Siena could not rely on access to rivers or seas for transport and trade. Still, the city, nestled on three hills, flourished during the 13th century, developing a political system that would guarantee a period of peace prolonged enough to allow the development of one of Italy's most influential universities and one of Europe's richest art collections. Traces of this legacy are still visible today, starting from the architecture of the enchanting Piazza del Campo, the city's main square, to the Duomo, one of Tuscany's most impressive cathedrals.

Explore a theatrical square

Siena's shell-shaped **Piazza del Campo** has been the city's civic and political heart since the 12th century. Its transformation began with the 13th-century construction of the Gothic Palazzo Pubblico. Strict urban planning laws ensured architectural harmony, with double- or triple-arched windows and no balconies. The square, divided into nine segments, hosts December's **Mercato del Campo** *(mercatonelcampo.it)* and, most famously, the Palio horse race (p442). A 19th-century copy of Jacopo della Quercia's **Fonte Gaia** (1419) stands at its northern edge. Originally topped with a Venus statue, the fountain was altered after the Black Death, when religious authorities blamed pagan imagery for the plague. The statue's remains were reportedly buried in Florentine lands to wish the enemy an equal misfortune.

Art for the powerful

Flanked by the 88m **Torre del Mangia**, Siena's iconic **Palazzo Pubblico** was built between 1288 and 1342 as the seat of the Government of the Nine. Today, it houses the extraordinary **Museo Civico** *(museocivico.comune.siena.it),* showcasing centuries of Sienese art. Highlights include Martino Bartolomeo's *Sixteen Virtues* fresco and Spinello Aretino's *Storie di Alessandro III* in the Sala di Balìa, and Simone

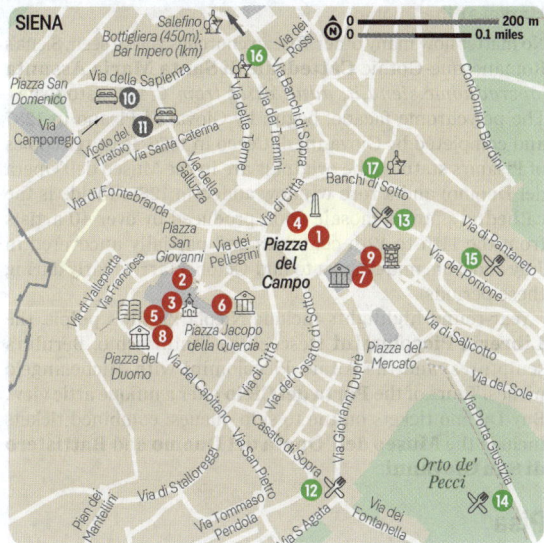

SIENA

Salefino
Bottigliera (450m);
Bar Impero (1km)

Piazza San Domenico

Via Camporegio

Piazza San Giovanni

Piazza del Campo

Piazza Jacopo della Quercia

Piazza del Duomo

Banchi di Sotto

Piazza del Mercato

Orto de' Pecci

Martini's *Maestà* (1312) in the Sala del Mappamondo. The star attraction is Ambrogio Lorenzetti's *Buon Governo* fresco cycle (1337–39) in the Sala della Pace, a powerful allegory of good government in city and rural life. And if the message wasn't clear enough, opposite the fresco you can see the *Effetti del Cattivo Governo,* the effects of a bad government.

✏️ **MICHELANGELO'S DRAWING ROOM**

In 1975 a series of wall drawings was discovered behind a layer of plaster in a storage room below the New Sacristy of the **Cappelle Medicee** (p438). The sketches were attributed to Michelangelo, who's believed to have hidden in this room in 1530, fearing retaliation from Pope Clement VII, a member of the Medici family, due to work done for the republican government during the brief period when the Medici were ousted from Florence. Fifty years after the discovery, Michelangelo's drawing room has opened to the public for the first time. A test run of guided tours was held in 2024 – tickets were sold out immediately and new dates have yet to be announced. Keep an eye on *bargellomusei.beniculturali.it* for updates.

🍴 **EATING IN SIENA: OUR PICKS**
MAP p441

Ristorante Gallo Nero: Named after the black rooster icon of Chianti, Gallo Nero is worth visiting for its truffle *pappardelle* alone. *noon-2.30pm Thu-Sat, 7-9.30pm Mon-Sat* €€

Ristorante All'Orto de' Pecci: Behind the Torre del Mangia, this garden-restaurant is run by a co-op serving seasonal dishes made from ingredients grown on-site. *12.30-2.30pm & 7.30-10.30pm Tue-Sun* €€

La Taverna di San Giuseppe: Prepare for a Tuscan-flavours overload in this historic spot inside a 12th-century building with an Etruscan foundation. *noon-2.30pm & 7-9.30pm Mon-Sat* €€€

Osteria Le Logge: This Sienese institution breathes tradition from every pore, starting from the in-house underground cellar. *noon-2.30pm & 7-10.15pm Mon-Sat* €€€

SIENA'S PALIO: A HEARTFELT HORSE RACE

Piazza del Campo has been the heart of Siena since the Middle Ages. Today it remains the focal point during the **Palio**, a traditional horse race held on 2 July and 16 August, where Siena's *contrade* (districts) compete to win the *drappellone,* a painting displayed in the winning district's museum. Leading up to the race, centuries-old rituals are observed, including neighbourhood decorations, horse assignments, open-air dinners and horse blessings in local churches. Originating from 1633 Assumption celebrations, the Palio involves a historical parade, jockeys in traditional costumes and three laps around the sand-covered piazza. The event is deeply rooted in local culture – this is not a tourist attraction but a heartfelt celebration for all communities involved.

Marvel at the Duomo

No matter how many other Tuscan churches you've seen, Siena's Romanesque-Gothic **Cattedrale di Santa Maria Assunta** (*operaduomo.siena.it; adult/child from €14/3*) astonishes. The polychrome facade, begun by Giovanni Pisano in 1287 and completed by Giovanni di Cecco in 1376, features copies of Pisano's statues (the originals are in the Museo dell'Opera del Duomo) and a rose window added in 1288. Inside is the cathedral's famed mosaic floor, produced by over 40 artists from the 14th to 19th centuries and partially uncovered in July and from mid-August to mid-October (arrive early during these periods).

Year-round highlights include Nicola Pisano's pulpit, the **Libreria Piccolomini** frescoed by Pinturicchio, Bernini's sculptures, and the Altare Piccolomini with Michelangelo niches. Tours of the **Porta del Cielo** offer a unique attic view. Buy Duomo tickets online to skip queues; combined tickets include the **Museo dell'Opera del Duomo** and **Battistero di San Giovanni**.

Pisa

Once a maritime power to rival Genoa and Venice, modern Pisa is best known for an architectural project gone terribly wrong. But the world-famous Leaning Tower is just one of many noteworthy sights in this compelling city. Education has fuelled the local economy since the 1400s, and students from across Italy compete for places in its elite university. This endows the centre of town with a vibrant cafe and bar scene, balancing an enviable portfolio of well-maintained Romanesque buildings, Gothic churches and Renaissance piazzas with a lively street life dominated by locals rather than tourists.

Piazza dei Miracoli's sights

Piazza dei Miracoli is far more than the **Leaning Tower**, though its 251 steps and iconic tilt remain a must-see. Completed in 1370 but only stabilised in the late 20th century, the *torre pendente* is a medieval marvel. The adjacent **Duomo di Pisa**, built from 1063 with a dome added in 1380, incorporates materials looted during Pisa's Sicilian campaign, while the **Museo dell'Opera del Duomo** houses sculptures by Nicola and Giovanni Pisano and Bonanno Pisano's bronze Porta di San Ranieri. The piazza's **Battistero di San Giovanni** is the world's largest baptistery and home to Nicola Pisano's Carrara marble pulpit. Make time also for **Camposanto cemetery** to

DRINKING IN SIENA: OUR PICKS

MAP p441

Salefino Bottiglieria: An extension of the homonymous restaurant, this natural-wine-focused *enoteca* is an ideal spot for discovering new labels. *6pm-1am Mon-Sat*

Bar Impero: Excellent cocktails are served under the tall, vaulted ceilings of this historic bar near Porta Camollia. *7am-midnight*

Trefilari Wine Bar: Get the evening going with a couple of glasses of wine sourced from small regional producers. *4pm-2am Tue-Thu, 2pm-2am Fri-Sun*

Gastronomia Morbidi: The artisanal products displayed at this deli-bar will make your mouth water. *9am-7.30pm Mon, 8am-8pm Tue-Thu, to 9pm Fri, to 7.30pm Sat, to 3pm Sun*

Duomo di Pisa and the Leaning Tower, Pisa

view Buffalmacco's impressive fresco *Il Trionfo della Morte*, and for the **Museo delle Sinopie**, to eye-up rare preparatory sketches for Renaissance frescoes.

Five centuries of Tuscan art

Despite housing one of Italy's most valuable collections of medieval art, the **Museo Nazionale di San Matteo** (*adult/ reduced €5/2*) doesn't receive much attention from visitors. The precious collection of paintings and sculptures produced between the 12th and 16th centuries includes works by Masaccio, Beato Angelico, Benozzo Gozzoli, Nicola and Giovanni Pisano, Donatello and Michelozzo. It's contained in a former Benedictine convent founded in the 11th century overlooking the Arno.

SOLVING THE TILT

After its completion in 1370, Pisa's bell tower continued to slowly tilt southward for over six centuries, defying gravity and baffling architects through the ages. Only in the 1990s did engineers finally find a solution to stabilise its fragile foundation, through a pioneering technique known as 'controlled sub-excavation', which involved the careful removal of small quantities of soil from beneath the north side of the structure. Over the past three decades the tower has straightened by as much as 4cm, and is now tilted by 'only' 3.97° – and, remarkably, it's now considered as stable as it has ever been, secure for generations of future visitors to take a dubious photo of themselves pretending to prop it up.

EATING IN PISA: OUR PICKS

Numeroundici: No reservations, no frills. Order at the counter, sit at a wooden table and enjoy one of the daily specials. *noon-10pm Mon-Fri, from 7pm Sat* €

Trattoria Sant'Omobono: Walk past the market stalls into this *trattoria* that seems sustained by a Corinthian column in the middle of the room. *12.30-2.30pm & 7.30-10pm* €€

Osteria di Culegna: With exquisite ravioli and a wide selection of meaty mains, this family-run *osteria* offers up authentic Tuscan flavours. *12.30-2.30pm & 7.30-10pm* €€

Trattoria da Stelio: Stelio has spent most of his life serving loyal returning customers after half a century of cooking simple, traditional classics. *noon-3pm Mon-Fri* €€

443

Naples & the Amalfi Coast

STREET LIFE | ARCHAEOLOGY | SPECTACULAR COASTLINES

 TOP TIP

The popularity of Naples' Quartieri Spagnoli has seen holiday accommodation proliferate in recent years, making housing increasingly scarce or too expensive for residents. Consider staying in an adjacent neighbourhood and then heading in for meals or experiences. It really helps.

If you picture Italy, much of it is likely infused with the lore of Campania. Perhaps it's the holy chaos of Naples, Vespas buzzing down ancient alleys while women hang laundry above, chatting animatedly with neighbours. Or the glittering island of Capri, playground of the rich, powerful and artistic for millennia. Then, you might be conjuring the plunging seascapes of the Amalfi Coast: vertical towns crossed by lemon-coated zigzag alleys that seem to rise straight out of the Mediterranean. Yes, any one of these things might well be on your mood board. The good news? It's all real, all waiting for you. Of course, the reason it will feel familiar is because much of it has been discovered already, so prepare yourself for high-season crowds. But there's plenty left to explore and still more than a few corners that will seem like a delicious secret. No matter where you go, there will be magic.

Naples

MAP p446

Italians sometimes joke that there's Italy and then there's Napoli – so singular is its character, so potent its historical legacy. And yet so few visitors are prepared for its uniqueness and capacity to surprise.

Its story begins with the Greek colony of Neapolis, founded in 474 BCE. Norman, Spanish and Bourbon rulers made

GETTING AROUND

Frequent high-speed trains connect Naples to Rome and other major Italian cities. Circumvesuviana trains connect Naples to Herculaneum, Pompeii and Sorrento.

Frequent ferries connect Naples to its bay islands, including Capri, where buses traverse the island. Ferries sail between Capri and Sorrento, while the extensive SITA bus network covers the Amalfi Coast. In Naples itself, the dense city centre is best explored by foot, though use a little more caution in crowded places and at night. Mass transport – buses, funiculars, the metro – is essential for making it up to hilltop areas like Capodimonte and Vomero. Driving in Naples is unnecessary and highly discouraged, as is driving along the Amalfi Coast in high season.

NAPLES & THE AMALFI COAST

Avellino

Monte Vergine

Avella

Nola

Marigliano

Acerra

Pomigliano d'Arco

San Gennaro Vesuviano

Somma Vesuviana

Sarno

Palma Campania

Nocera

Tramonti

Cava

Mt Finestra

Salerno

Vietri sul Mare

Cetara

Golfo di Salerno

10 km

5 miles

Riserva Statale Valle delle Ferriere

Ravello

Minori

Maiori

Atrani

Amalfi

Conca dei Marini

Amalfi Coast

Agerola

Bomerano

Pimonte

Mt Sant'Angelo a Tre Pizzi

Nocelle

Praiano

Positano

Moiano

Colli di Fontanelle

Caivano

Casavatore

Casoria

Giugliano in Campania

Marano di Napoli

Pompeii

Tezigno

Mt Vesuvius (Vesuvio)

Torre Annunziata

Castellammare di Stabia

Vico Equense

Piano di Sorrento

Sant'Agata sui Due Golfi

Marina del Cantone

Termini

Mt San Costanzo

Sorrento

Massa Lubrense

Naples

Portici

Herculaneum

Torre del Greco

Golfo di Napoli

Capri

Marina Grande

Anacapri

Mt Solaro

Capri Town

Bagnoli

Pozzuoli

Campi Flegrei

Aversa

Qualiano

Baia

Bacoli

Lago d'Averno

Lago d'Fusaro

Torregaveta

Lido di Licola

Villaggio Coppola

Golfo di Gaeta

Procida

Procida

Ischia

Casamicciola

Lacco Ameno

Forio

Mt Epomeo

Ischia

Sant'Angelo

Tyrrhenian Sea

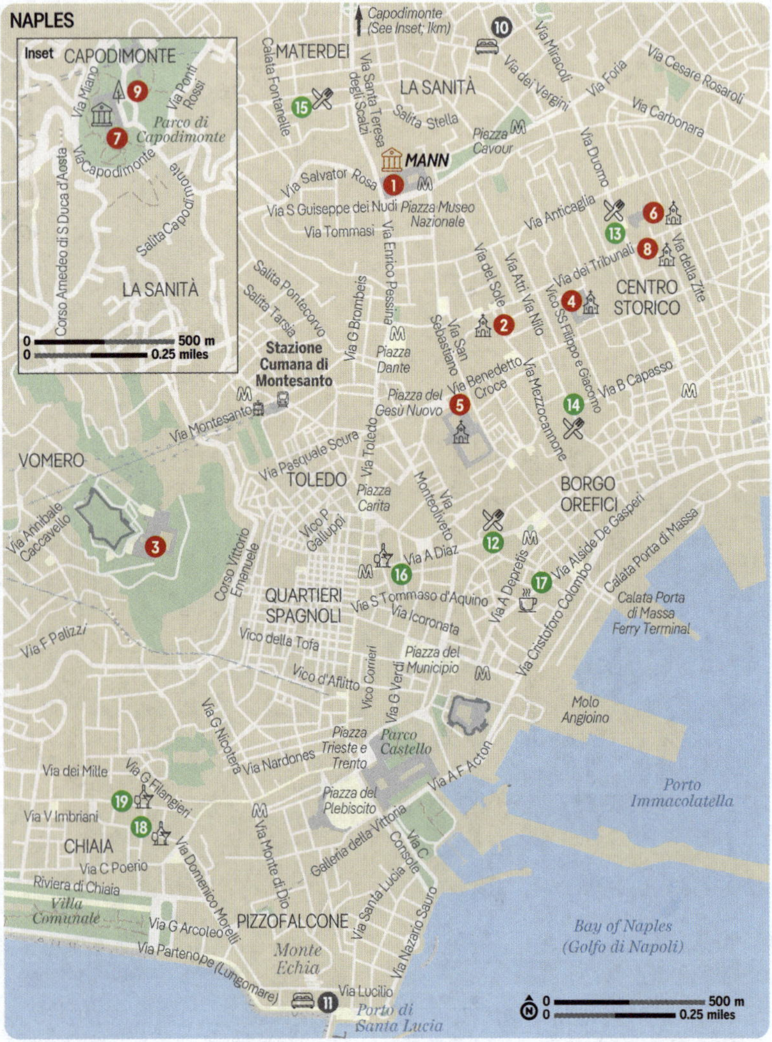

NAPLES

Inset CAPODIMONTE

MATERDEI

LA SANITÀ

Parco di Capodimonte

Piazza Museo Nazionale

MANN

CENTRO STORICO

Stazione Cumana di Montesanto

Piazza Dante

Piazza del Gesù Nuovo

BORGO OREFICI

VOMERO

TOLEDO

Piazza Carità

QUARTIERI SPAGNOLI

Piazza del Municipio

Calata Porta di Massa Ferry Terminal

Molo Angioino

Piazza Trieste e Trento

Parco Castello

Piazza del Plebiscito

CHIAIA

PIZZOFALCONE

Monte Echia

Villa Comunale

Porto Immacolatella

Bay of Naples (Golfo di Napoli)

Porto di Santa Lucia

★ **HIGHLIGHTS**

1 MANN

● **SIGHTS**

2 Cappella Sansevero
3 Certosa e Museo di San Martino
4 Chiesa e Chiostro di San Gregorio Armeno

5 Complesso Monumentale di Santa Chiara
6 Duomo di Napoli
7 Museo di Capodimonte
8 Pio Monte della Misericordia
9 Real Bosco di Capodimonte

● **SLEEPING**

10 Atelier Inès
11 Grand Hotel Vesuvio

● **EATING**

12 Aria Restaurant
13 Januaris
14 La Locanda Gesù Vecchio

15 Pizzeria Starita

● **DRINKING & NIGHTLIFE**

16 Astronomia Bar Segreto
17 Bar Mexico
18 Chandelier
19 Enoteca Belledonne

Naples wealthy, leaving behind architectural splendours like the imposing Castel Sant'Elmo and the Palazzo Reale. Today, it's a deliciously layered, always surprising beast – gritty yet aristocratic, unrelenting yet deeply humane, a maze of glittering ballrooms and bellowing street life.

Indeed, Naples is exactly what you expect while being not what you expect at all.

Witness a miracle

San Gennaro's blood – reputedly saved by a devotee after his rather gruesome death in 305 – has become famous for its miraculous liquefaction on the first Saturday in May, 19 September and 16 December. On these days, thousands flock to the **Duomo di Napoli** *(free) t*o witness this miraculous event. Whether it's truly the blood of San Gennaro (or whether it's blood at all) is impossible to say: the Catholic Church prohibits anyone from opening the two hermetically sealed ampoules. Besides, it hardly matters. Those who gather do so out of reverence for their city as much as for their saint.

On any day, the Duomo is worth a visit for its artistic treasures, among them a breathtakingly frescoed **Chapel of San Gennaro**.

Wander the Museo Archeologico Nazionale di Napoli

The largest museum in central Naples, **MANN** *(mann-napoli.it; adult/reduced €20/2; closed Tue)* is also one of Italy's most important archaeological repositories. Its vast collection of Greek and Roman antiquities includes the monumental Farnese Bull, priceless Roman bronzes, and exquisite mosaics recovered from the ruins of Herculaneum and Pompeii. MANN also houses the second-largest collection of Egyptian artefacts in the country, spanning seven rooms and six centuries. Then there's the museum's blush-inducing Secret Room, home to over 250 pieces of erotica (gathered mainly from excavations at Pompeii and Herculaneum) that once titillated the Bourbon monarchy.

Escape to a hilltop palace and wood

The Royal Palace of Capodimonte began life in 1738 when Charles III originally planned to build himself a hunting lodge on the hill above Naples but pivoted to a palace that could accommodate both his expanding court and the priceless art he'd inherited from his mother, Elisabetta Farnese.

That palace is now the **Museo di Capodimonte** *(capodimonte.cultura.gov.it; adult/under 18 €15/free),* whose magnificent

BEST SACRED ART IN THE CENTRE

Cappella Sansevero: Houses the iconic *Cristo Velato* statue, whose realistic marble folds and delicate contours have attracted admirers for centuries. *(museosansevero.it; adult/reduced €12/8)*

Pio Monte della Misericordia: Contains Caravaggio's *Sette Opere della Misericordia*. *(piomontedellamisericordia.it; €10)*

Chiesa e Chiostro di San Gregorio Armeno: The frescoes of San Gregorio Armeno here are among the best examples of Luca Giordano's intricate work in central Naples. *(free)*

Complesso Monumentale di Santa Chiara: An explosion of colourful majolica tilework set over 72 octagonal columns that connect to similarly decorated benches framing a lush private garden. *(Chiostro di Santa Chiara; monastero disantachiara.it; adult/reduced €7/5)*

EATING IN NAPLES: OUR PICKS

MAP p446

Pizzeria Starita: A constant contender for best in the city, and even if it's franchised, it's still stellar. *noon-3.30pm & 7pm-midnight Tue-Sun* €€

La Locanda Gesù Vecchio: Traditional recipes, local ingredients and a broad selection of wines. *2-3.30pm & 7-11pm Tue-Sun* €€

Aria Restaurant: This intimate Michelin-star restaurant elevates Neapolitan street food. *7.30-11pm Mon-Sat* €€€

Januarius: The cuisine is classical Neapolitan with down-to-earth products, but the fresco ceilings are out of this world. *1-3pm & 7.30-11pm Wed-Mon* €€€

collection includes a Caravaggio in situ, where it was meant to be, as well as contemporary works from artists like Mimmo Paladino and Umberto Manzo.

Done, get some fresh air at the **Real Bosco di Capodimonte**, the palace's 124-hectare former royal forest.

Explore a panoramic charterhouse

The paradoxical density and splendour of central Naples is hard to grasp when you're amid it, so spend a few hours surveying it from the hilltop **Certosa e Museo di San Martino** *(adult/reduced €6/2)*. Originally a Carthusian monastery built between 1325 and 1368, it's now home to priceless frescoes and paintings by Neapolitan baroque masters such as Jusepe de Ribera and Cosimo Fanzago. The cloisters here are among the most beautiful in Italy, adorned and altered over the centuries by some of the country's finest artists, most importantly architect Giovanni Antonio Dosio in the 16th century and baroque sculptor Cosimo Fanzago a century later.

Herculaneum

Head back to 79 CE

The same eruption that destroyed Pompeii in 79 CE buried **Herculaneum** *(coopculture.it/en/poi/archaeological-park-of-Herculaneum)* under a volcanic mudslide. This site is more manageable than Pompeii and has an incredible array of artefacts. Among the highlights is the **Casa dei Cervi**, a two-storey villa that belonged to a noble family with a twisted sense of humour: cross the courtyard to see marble deer attacked by dogs and a drunkenly inappropriate Hercules. The **Casa Sannitica**, built in the 2nd century BCE by the Samnites, is a portal into Herculaneum's pre-Roman past, with wooden lattice fences, an impluvium and a fresco of the rape of Europa, while the vaulted rooms of **L'Antica Spiaggia**, likely port warehouses, became a refuge during the eruption. Equally intriguing is the **Terme Suburbane**, featuring intricate mosaics, and the **Casa del Tramezzo di Legno**, which preserves a folding wooden screen and bedframe.

Capri

Encounter the magical Blue Grotto

The world-famous **Grotta Azzurra** (Blue Grotto) is a spectacular natural phenomenon, although – fair warning – the tourist crush and breakneck pace of the experience may taint

---

HELP KEEP COMMUNITIES ALIVE

Naples' Quartieri Spagnoli has been synonymous with social decline for many years. However, thanks to the grassroots work of cultural associations, artists and residents, the neighbourhood has become a unique heritage site, a place that welcomes visitors with pride. Yet many people are forced to live on meagre incomes, and life remains difficult. It often means that they adapt in creative ways, and this might look charming to the outside eye. But these are real people living real lives – something to keep in mind when visiting. If you want to take a picture of someone or their home, ask first. If they say no, don't take it personally. The difference between gawking and engaging begins with our approach to delicate situations.

DRINKING IN NAPLES: OUR PICKS ⸻ MAP p446

Bar Mexico: This 1960s relic in Piazza Garibaldi serves a thick, sugary rocket fuel that will remind you why you're here. *5.30am-8pm Mon-Sat*

Astronomia Bar Segreto: A speakeasy that'll take a moment to find but is worth the search for its inspired drinks and service. *8pm-2am Thu-Tue*

Enoteca Belledonne: Stellar wine bar with a great selection of finger foods and a cosy setting. *hours vary*

Chandelier: You'd best reserve a table. Your reward is incredible drinks and abundant snacks. *8am-3pm*

TOP EXPERIENCE

Pompeii

The once-thriving city of Pompeii was buried under a layer of lapilli (burning fragments of pumice stone) by the eruption of Vesuvius in 79 CE. The result is a remarkably well-preserved slice of ancient life, where visitors can walk down Roman streets and snoop around millennia-old houses, temples, shops, cafes, amphitheatres and a brothel.

Top Sights

The Romans were nothing if not entertainers, and the 20,000-seat **Anfiteatro** (Amphitheatre) at the park's eastern end is proof of their love for the stage.

Pompeii's main piazza, the **Foro**, was the seat of religious, commercial and political life. It's best to end your day here because even when it's not summer the sun can be punishing.

The restored 90-room **Villa dei Misteri** dates to the 2nd century BCE. The Dionysiac frieze spans the walls of the large dining room and is one of the biggest and most arresting paintings from the ancient world.

The site of **Insula dei Casti Amanti** was first uncovered in 1912 and has since been discovered to include a room decorated with mythological figures, charcoal drawings made by children in a service courtyard, and an entrance hall where the skeletons of two eruption victims were found. You can watch the process of bringing Pompeii to life, as well as an innovative effort to bring photovoltaic panels onto the site, which was designed as part of the Pompeii for All initiative and has access for travellers with disabilities.

TOP TIPS

● Always enter the park via the less-crowded Amphitheatre entrance. Crowds are thickest in the morning; take the afternoon to explore.

● You should only buy your tickets directly through the Pompeii website.

● The excellent audio guides are multilingual.

PRACTICALITIES

● pompeiisites.org
● adult/reduced from €18/2 ● 9am-7pm Apr-Oct, to 5pm Nov-Mar

HERCULANEUM'S FRESCOES & MOSAICS

Pompeii may have more frescoes and mosaics, but Herculaneum is no slouch in the art department. Check them out in these fascinating dwellings and temples.

Casa dello Scheletro: Spectacular *lararium* (shrine) inlaid with impossibly tiny mosaic tiles.

Casa di Nettuno e Anfitrite: Intricate and vivid mosaic depicting Neptune and Aphrodite.

Colegio degli Augustali: Frescoes of Hercules fighting the good fight.

Casa dell'Atrio a Mosaico: This sea-view villa's floor is entirely covered in floral and geometric mosaics.

Casa del Gran Portale: Beautiful brick lintel entrance, and fascinating wall decorations of birds and bizarre designs.

RUI VALE SOUSA/SHUTTERSTOCK

your buzz. The grotto opens at 9am, but try to get here as early as possible to (slightly) shorten your wait. A ticket to the grotto costs €18 for a five-minute tour; duck as the gondolier ushers the boat inside, lest you crack your head open on the rock. Inside, the waters glow electric blue and the gondoliers serenade you with Neapolitan classics.

Ride a heavenly chairlift

From **Anacapri**'s Piazza Vittoria, the chairlift **Seggiovia del Monte Solaro** (*montesolarocapri.it; one way/return €11/14*) whisks riders up to **Monte Solaro**, Capri's highest peak. The 13-minute 589m ride up provides unforgettable views of terraced vineyards, white houses and lemon groves, with the Gulf of Naples and the Amalfi Coast winking in the distance.

Vertigo? You can also get to the top on foot by following Via Axel Munthe to Via Salita per il Solaro. Go right, then look for the iron crucifix marking La Crocetta pass. A left turn will take you to the hermitage of **Santa Maria a Cetrella**; turning right will get you to the summit. The hike takes about an hour each way.

 EATING & DRINKING NEAR POMPEII: OUR PICKS

Melius: Gourmet deli-restaurant offering dishes made with local ingredients such as Graniano pasta or anchovies from Cetara. *9am-2pm Tue-Sun, 5.30-10pm Tue-Sat* €€

Zi'Caterina: Spacious old-school restaurant that looks touristy but serves delicious traditional southern Italian food. *noon-midnight* €€

La Bettola del Gusto: Highly innovative Italian food such as seared-octopus couscous, made with proudly artisanal ingredients. *12.30-3pm & 7.30-11pm Tue-Thu & Sun, to midnight Fri & Sat* €€

Na' Pasta: Excellent pastas and a magical parmigiana makes the tight seating entirely worth it, especially after a few glasses of local wine. *12.15-7pm Tue-Sat, to 8pm Sun* €€

Seggiovia del Monte Solaro, Capri

Live it up in Capri Town

Capri Town's beauty is iconic. It's no wonder. Its white-washed labyrinthine streets – with their tiled courtyards and hand-painted ceramic street signs, shaded by purple blooms – are the ultimate Italian island dreamscape.

Your first port of call is **Piazza Umberto I**, called La Piazzetta by locals. It's perfect for people-watching, though your nosiness will cost you – an espresso can set you back €8. Wander side streets like **Via Le Botteghe**, peppered with luxe boutiques and restaurants. In Via Vittorio Emanuele, a queue leads to **Gelateria Buonocore**, famous for its freshly pressed waffle cones. Continue on to **Via Camerelle**, Capri's bougainvillea-strung haute couture street.

Escape to the gardens

For a break from Capri Town's bustling centre, escape to the tranquil **Giardini di Augusto** and nearby **Certosa di San Giacomo**. Built in 1371, the *certosa* (Carthusian monastery) houses 17th-century frescoes in its church and revolving modern-art exhibits. Meanwhile, the Giardini di Augusto

EATING ON CAPRI: OUR PICKS

Salumeria da Aldo: A well-stocked Marina Grande minimart with a delicatessen where you can get a freshly made *panino* (sandwich). 7am-9pm €

Pescheria Le Botteghe: Fish market with a raw bar and restaurant serving fishburgers and seafood pastas. *8am-3pm & 7-11pm, to 1pm Mon* €€€

Gennaro Amitrano: Michelin-star seafood restaurant at Marina Piccola, with elegant farm-to-table fare. *12.30-2.30pm & 7.30-10.30pm* €€€

La Capannina: A family-run traditional restaurant (established 1931) for dinner or drinks. Book ahead. *12.15-3pm & 7.15-11.30pm* €€€

THE BEST BEACHES ON CAPRI

Bagni di Tiberio: Take a *gozzetto* (dinghy) to this chic pebble beach (entry €20), once Emperor Tiberius' bathing grounds – next to the ruins of one of his villas.

Marina Grande Beach: Free beach popular with day-trippers for its proximity to the port; large, boisterous stretch of pebbles and *lidos* (stretches of sand) with lots of families.

Marina Piccola: Petite (free) pebble beach with views of the Faraglioni and water that's always warm and still. Enjoy lunch and snacks at the various *lidos*.

Isole Faraglioni: This cliff 'beach' and diving point is stunning, but its beach clubs Da Luigi and La Fontelina are reservation only. Shuttle-boat service.

Spiaggia del Faro (Anacapri): Luscious cliff beach with views of the historic lighthouse; enjoy light lunches and *aperitivi* at the beach's *lidos*. Spectacular sunsets.

Bagni Regina Giovanna, Amalfi Coast

rewards with soaring views of Marina Piccola and the Faraglioni. Time your visit for the spring bloom for a particularly beautiful experience. Just outside the gardens, you'll find the entrance to **Via Krupp**, a 1.5km paved hairpin path leading down to **Marina Piccola** and a refreshing dip in the sea (the bus will take you back up).

Amalfi Coast

If you're looking for a secret corner of paradise, you're 1000 years too late to the Amalfi Coast. But who cares? It remains transformatively beautiful. Stretching 50km along the southern side of the Sorrentine Peninsula, the UNESCO-protected Costiera Amalfitana is a postcard-perfect vision of shimmering blue water fringed by vertiginous cliffs on which cling whitewashed and pastel-hued villages and terraced lemon groves. You won't be able to see it all, and you'll ruin your time trying. But choose wisely and you'll find yourself grinning like a fool at your luck.

Go beyond the souvenirs

Sorrento's historic centre offers much more than kitschy souvenirs. At the edge of town lies haunting **Il Vallone dei**

 DRINKING ON CAPRI: OUR PICKS

Giardino Mediterraneo: Chic outdoor cocktail lounge in a historic lemon grove. Enjoy tranquil views and lemon cocktails. *10am-midnight, to 8pm Sun & Mon*	**Bianca by La Palma Hotel:** Super luxe cocktail lounge in the new La Palma hotel, with bespoke cocktails, a restaurant and a rooftop view. 'Island chic' dress code. *7pm-1am*	**Taverna Anema e Core:** Bar with live music, DJ sets and a full menu of cocktails on Via Sella Orta. No dress code. A Capri institution. *11pm-4.30am*	**Hangout Capri:** Capri Town gastropub serving steaks plus classic and inventive cocktails in a cool, relaxed atmosphere. *11.30am-4pm & 6.30pm-2am*

Mulini and its ruins of ancient wheat mills. A short walk away, **Piazza Tasso** is the city's convivial living room. From here, follow Via Luigi de Maio to the **Chiesa and Chiostro di San Francesco**, where pagan, Roman and medieval architecture make an evocative backdrop for art exhibitions. Make a stop at the nearby **Sedile Dominova**, a fresco-covered 14th-century nook that once served as a place for nobles to congregate, and check out the tiny **Chiesa dei Santi Felice e Baccolo**, home to *intarsio* (inlaid wood) master Giuseppe Rocco.

Swim like a queen

When Queen Giovanna II of Anjou-Durazzo wanted to escape the 14th-century bustle, she came to the dazzling natural pools beside a vast Roman villa outside Sorrento. Known today as **Bagni Regina Giovanna**, they can get crowded in summer but they're free, almost surreal in beauty, and worth the hike. Spend half a day and picnic at the ruins of the Pollio Felice villa above the pools. To reach them, take Via Capo from Sorrento to Traversa Punta Capo. Stop at the *alimentari* (deli) for a sandwich and water, then continue down the Traversa until it becomes a footpath that leads to a steep staircase.

Take to the sea

The best way to enjoy **Positano** may be from the sea, but ferries and group tours can be crowded and private tours can be exorbitant. Family-run **Bluestar Positano** *(bluestar positano.it)* offers a range of tours for every budget and timeframe. Early-bird and sunset tours offer a 1½-hour ride around the coast. The best part? Many of the boats are traditional wooden *gozze*.

The boat ride to **Adolfo** *(daadolfo.com)* might be short, but this throwback beach club and restaurant is one of the greatest reminders of how life used to be in Positano. You can only make reservations by telephone, and their distinctive boat is the only ride available from Positano town. Make sure you reserve sunloungers as well as lunch.

Hike the Path of the Gods

In the 1980s hikers christened an ancient, panoramic shepherd's trail the **Sentiero degli Dei** (Path of the Gods). Stretching 6km each way, it is indeed heavenly – running from Agerola (Bomerano) to Nocelle above Positano, and taking three to five hours to tackle. It's moderately challenging, with several route options; the most popular is Bomerano to Nocelle (mostly downhill), reachable by bus from Amalfi.

SONGS OF SORRENTO

It's not just the Sirens who composed intoxicating odes to Sorrento. Throughout the years some of Italy's most famous songs have been written in or about the city. 'Torna a Surriento', composed in 1894 by the De Curtis brothers, is one of the most famous examples of the *canzone napoletana* and has been recorded by singers all over the world. There are few songs so well known (and heartbreaking) to Italians as Lucio Dalla's 'Caruso', a tribute to the great opera singer and his lover. Indeed, the Bologna-born Dalla is considered by many to be an honorary citizen of the town, in honour of the song.

 EATING & DRINKING IN AMALFI: OUR PICKS

Pasticceria Pansa: More than just morning coffee and *cornetti* (croissants), with plenty of non-alcoholic options. *7.30am-11pm* €

Trattoria dei Cartari: Head towards the paper museum for a locals-approved meal with the freshest catch in town. *noon-3.30pm & 7-10.30pm Tue-Sun* €€

Donna Stella: Pizzeria in an atmospheric lemon grove that serves delicious pizza plus salads. *11am-4pm & 5.30-10pm Wed-Mon* €€

Ristorante La Caravella: Michelin-starred restaurant with tasting menus featuring local specialities. *noon-2pm & 7-10pm Wed-Mon* €€€

BEST AMALFI SHOPPING

Dalla Carta alla Cartolina: Magical paper shop with art exhibits, near the famous Museo della Carta. Drop postcards in a mailbox and see its beautiful story come to life.

JP Boutique: Signature Amalfi designs, gauzy fabrics and unique accessories from an Amalfi-born artist and illustrator with a flair for the dramatic.

L'Altra Costiera: The best place in Amalfi for locally sourced ceramics from up-and-coming and established artists, many from Vietri sul Mare.

La Scuderia del Duca: Tucked behind the Terminal restaurant at the port, this place is full of great antiques and funky paper crafts that make excellent gifts.

Continue to Positano or return by public transport. The trail is well signposted, but consider getting a guide to explain the surrounding area and make sure you're OK. Also, wear good shoes, carry water, a windbreaker and prepare for crowds. With care, it's an unforgettable experience.

Dig deeper in Amalfi

Amalfi has always been a central point on the coast, and it remains so today. Pass through the vaulted arches to Piazza Duomo, dotted with historic coffee bars and dominated by the Arabic-Norman **Cattedrale di Sant'Andrea**.

The town centre was constructed in the 10th and 11th centuries, when Amalfi was a powerful maritime republic and the natural landscape lent itself to a fortification in the hills. Neighbourhoods followed suit and almost disappear into the stone, so sticking to the main drags means you'll likely miss them. So wander just a bit and you'll find yourself in a very local world of covered walkways and ancient alleys.

Find romance in Ravello

High above the coast, **Villa Rufolo**, just off Ravello's Piazza Duomo, was founded in the 13th century. In its 700 years, it's been the residence of King Robert of Anjou and several popes. Its history is evident in the 14th-century entrance tower, Gothic gateway, Moorish courtyard and 19th-century cascading gardens and lavish sitting rooms with sweeping Gulf views. It's not hard to see how it inspired Wagner in the second act of his opera *Parsifal*.

A 10-minute walk away is **Villa Cimbrone** and its gasp-inducing Terrace of Infinity, 280m above sea level. Both villas are swank hotels. If you're looking for somewhere to splash out, you could do worse. Otherwise, sip at Villa Cimbrone's **Grotto di Eva** garden bar.

DRINKING IN POSITANO: OUR PICKS

Franco's Bar: It would be criminal not to try to get here, even though the prices might magically swallow your wallet. *5pm-midnight*

Il San Pietro di Positano: You can't get much higher up and you won't get much more dramatic; worth the hike and the prices. *Apr-Oct*

Fly: Come on, when's the last time you had it large? Start here and continue below at Music on the Rocks. *6pm-2am*

Bar Internazionale: The closest you'll get to no frills in town, with locals stopping in for their own *aperitivo. 7am-11pm Thu-Tue*

Sicily

GRAECO-ROMAN RUINS | GOLDEN MOSAICS | STREET MARKETS

Everything about the Mediterranean's largest island is extreme, from the beauty of its rugged landscape to its hybrid cuisine and flamboyant architecture. Sicily is intense, ancient and contradictory, and every corner reveals the same incongruous mash-up of old and new, chaos and calm.

Now an autonomous region in Italy, the island was hotly contested for centuries – the ancient Greeks, Carthaginians and Romans all fell into its devilishly handsome lair. Later rule by Byzantines, Saracens, Normans, Germans, Angevins and Spanish blessed Sicily with artistic and architectural riches that remain star attractions.

The rich Sicilian kitchen, crafted from multiple cuisines, only intensifies the sensory feast. Island produce – sun-spun capers and cherry tomatoes, olives, creamy almonds and pistachios, pomegranates, wild saffron, farm-churned ricotta, shellfish, tuna and swordfish – has been the magic ingredient ever since Bacchus planted vines near Taormina and the Greek god of blacksmiths fired up his forge inside Mt Etna. Come curious. Come hungry.

☑ **TOP TIP**

Late spring and early autumn are ideal times to visit Sicily; temperatures are warm but not extreme, prices are lower and crowds much more manageable than they are in July and August.

 GETTING AROUND

Regular car-passenger ferries cross the Strait of Messina from the Italian mainland to Sicily. Once on the island a flurry of high-speed hydrofoils and slower *traghetti* (ferries) sail to Sicily's offshore Aeolian and Egadi islands. Boats run year-round, with reduced schedules in winter.

Driving in traffic-busy Palermo and Catania is a headache, but motoring along the coast and inland is pleasurable and scenic. The A18 and A20 *autostrade* (motorways) are toll roads. Away from towns, electric-vehicle charging stations are scarce. Trains and buses link Ionian coastal cities; buses offer faster links than trains between Palermo and Catania. Private operator **Ferrovia Circumetnea** (*circumetnea.it*) runs trains around Mt Etna villages. Island-wide, Sunday services are limited.

SICILY

Tyrrhenian Sea

Aeolian Islands

Stromboli

Ustica

Filicudi   Salina   Panarea

Alicudi

Lipari Town   Lipari
Vulcano

San Vito Lo Capo   Castellammare del Golfo
Terrasini
Capo d'Orlando   Patti   Milazzo   Messina
Trapani   **Palermo**   Bagheria   Cefalù   Santo Stefano di Camastra   Sant'Agata di Militello   Barcellona   Reggio di Calabria
Partinico   Termini Imerese   Castelbuono   Randazzo   **Taormina**
Alcamo
Favignana   Salemi   Pizzo Carbonara   Troina   Bronte   Naxos
Marsala   Corleone   Petralia Soprana   Nicosia   Adrano   Mt Etna   Giarre
Castelvetrano   Agira   Acireale
Mazara del Vallo   Menfi   Mussomeli   Enna   Paternò   **Catania**
Sciacca   Ribera   Caltanissetta   Ionian Sea
Raffadali   Canicattì   Barrafranca   Piazza Armerina
Agrigento   Favara   Mazzarino   Scordia   Lentini   Augusta
Ravanusa   Caltagirone
Niscemi   Vizzini   Palazzolo Acreide   **Syracuse**
Mediterranean Sea   Licata   Gela   Comiso   Ragusa   Noto   Avola
Vittoria   Scoglitti   Modica   Rosolini
Mediterranean Sea   Marina di Ragusa   Scicli   Ispica   Pachino
Pozzallo

0 ——— 50 km
0 ——— 25 miles

Palermo

Nearly 3000 years old, Palermo was conquered by the Arabs
in 831 CE and, when the Normans invaded in 1072, Roger I
(1031–1101) made the old Greek port the seat of his enlightened
'kingdom of the sun', encouraging resident Arabs, Byzantines,
Greeks and Italians to remain.

Contemporary Palermo is stitched from rebellion, bravery,
squalor and solidarity. It's a place where roving street vendors sell *pani ca meusa* (Sicilian bread roll stuffed with sautéed beef spleen) from hand-pushed carts, and locals chat in
Italian, Albanian and Arabic. Be inquisitive. Peek into every
citrus-filled cloister, cherub-spun chapel or trash-strewn back
alley. You'll be astonished by what you find.

Royal tombs and a rooftop walk

The 13th-century **Cattedrale di Palermo** (*cattedrale.pal
ermo.it; adult/child €12/6*) is a larger-than-life example of
Sicily's unique Arab-Norman architectural style. Its interior
safeguards royal Norman tombs containing two of Sicily's
greatest rulers – Roger II and Frederick II of Hohenstaufen.

Save the best for last: the cinematic spiral up 110 steep stone
steps to the cathedral's expansive roof terraces (open until

ELESI/SHUTTERSTOCK

Cappella Palatina, Palermo

DARE-TO-TRY STIGGHIOLA

At quick glance it looks like an ordinary sausage. It's not. Introduced to the city by the Greeks 2000 years ago, Palermo's beloved *stigghiola* sees veal, lamb or goat intestines wrapped around a spring onion or leek, seasoned with parsley and flamed to a crisp on a charcoal- or wood-fired grill. It's deemed both a delicacy and an icon of Palermo's sizzling street-food scene.

Several market stalls and *trattorie* or fast-food joints with street kitchens at Palermo's oldest street market – **Mercato di Ballarò** – grill *stigghiola* on home barbecues in the street. The snack is always served chopped in chunks, salted and doled out on a plastic plate with a wedge of lime.

midnight once-weekly in summer), with an unmatched city panorama. Visit at the end of the day to savour the setting sun recasting the city in spectacular pink.

Save cents with a **combined ticket** *(adult/child €15/8)* covering the cathedral (the tombs, crypt, apse, treasury and rooftop) and 15th- to 18th-century art in the neighbouring **Museo Diocesana di Palermo**.

Explore an Arab-Norman wonder

Norman Sicily's cultural complexity is beautifully evoked at Palermo's star attraction: **Cappella Palatina**, awash in gold mosaics from 1130. It's squirrelled away like a jewel inside **Palazzo dei Normanni** *(federicosecondo.org; adult/child €19/11)*, built by conquering Arabs in the 9th century.

Wind up the stone staircase in the 17th-century Maqueda courtyard to the 2nd floor, where treasures include the Hall of Viceroys, lit up in Murano glass; the Hall of Mosaics, decorated with secular mosaics; and the soaring square tower of the Hall of Winds.

Visit Friday to Monday when the Royal Apartments are also open, and cover up – short skirts, shorts and bare shoulders are forbidden in the chapel.

 EATING & DRINKING IN PALERMO: OUR PICKS

Da Mimì di Guglielmo Damiano: Locals claim this Il Capo icon fries up the city's finest arancini (stuffed rice balls). *7.15am-10pm Mon-Sat, from 10am Sun* €

Moltivolti: You'll be hard-pushed to find a cooler co-working space, cafe, kitchen cooking up world cuisine (vegan included) and late-night bar. *9am-midnight* €

Ciccio in Pentola: Creative fish and seafood dishes paired with excellent service make this elegant *ristorante* a local foodie favourite. *noon-3.30pm & 7-11pm* €€

Gagini: Experience gourmet heaven at the contemporary kitchen of Italian-Brazilian chef Mauricio Zillo – Palermo's only Michelin-starred address. *12.30-2.30pm Wed-Sun, 7.30-10pm Tue-Sun* €€€

BEST SHOPPING: SLOW DESIGN ON VIA VITTORIO EMANUELE

Angela Tripi: Teeny terracotta *presepi* (crib figurines) in a 15th-century *palazzo* courtyard at Via Vittorio Emanuele 452.

Naná Aristova Jewels: Sicilian volcanoes inspire the contemporary jewellery by a Siberia-born Palermo-adopted jeweller at No 314.

Barbisio: Palermo's spiffiest hat shop at No 286 is a 1949 vintage. Buy a Sicilian *còppola* (flat cap).

Sicilia Inspired: Modern art, including drawings in Etna lava pigments, at No 292.

Rogato: 'Bags with history' are crafted from recycled materials at this boutique at No 130.

La Cittàcotte di Vincenzo Vizzari: Purchase a terracotta miniature of a Palermo church, palace or orange tree; No 120.

Fontana dell'Amenano, Catania

Sunset drinks at the Fountain of Shame

So scandalised were Sicilian churchgoers by the flagrant nudity of cheek-baring nymphs and frolicking river gods on Piazza Pretoria's monumental **Fontana Pretoria** that they dubbed it Fontana della Vergogna (Fountain of Shame). Designed by Florentine sculptor Francesco Camilliani between 1554 and 1555 for the Tuscan villa of Don Pedro di Toledo, it was bought by Palermo in 1573 in a bid to outshine Messina's newly crafted Fontana di Orione.

The play of light on the nudes posing in the fountain's tiered basins is theatrical any time of day – and never the same twice. Come sunset, enjoy it from above over alfresco drinks at rooftop bar **Le Terrazze del Sole** *(6pm-midnight Mar-Oct).*

Catania

The days when travellers avoided Sicily's second-largest city are long gone. Despite first-glance chaos and scruffiness, Catania has magnetic pull, brimming with youthful energy and earthy spirit. A smart base for Ionian coast trips or Mt Etna climbs, it delivers both convenience and intrigue.

UNESCO-listed, Catania rose from two disasters: Etna's 1669 lava flow and the 1693 earthquake that killed 12,000. baroque

DRINKING IN PALERMO: OUR PICKS

Altrove Bar: Italian craft beer, cocktails and killer margaritas lure a local crowd to this hip bar on Via Discesa dei Giudici. *5.30pm-1.30am Mon, to 2am Tue-Thu, 10am-1am Fri-Sun*

Tatum Art: Jazz lovers enjoy the intimacy of this small venue; reserve tables online. In summer concerts shift to seaside Mondello. *7pm-1am Tue-Sat, to midnight Sun*

Malox Cult: Don't miss the house Negroni (mixing Bulldog gin with Cinzano 1757 and Bèrto Bitter) at this cult bar with terrace on Piazzetta della Canna. *5.30pm-2am*

Botanico: Late-night music and cocktails down an alley festooned with greenery and street art. *6.30pm-2am Tue-Sun*

palazzi and churches, designed by Giovanni Vaccarini, sprouted from volcanic rock. Roman ruins sit beneath ornate facades, street art enlivens bohemian alleys, and *pasta alla Norma* (pasta with eggplant and ricotta) is served in ancient lava tubes – urban discovery here is intoxicating and richly layered.

Trawl a mouthwatering market

Tables groan under the weight of all manner of sea life at Catania's open-air fish market, **La Pescheria** *(closed Sun)*. Visit early morning – it opens at 7am and is being hosed down by 1pm. Access to the market, through a passageway by the side of gushing **Fontana dell'Amenano** (1867) on Piazza del Duomo, only adds to the theatre.

Grab a pew at **Scirocco Sicilian Fish Lab** *(sciroccolab.com)*, with a terrace overlooking the market on Piazza Alonzo di Benedetto, and enjoy the show over a paper cone of battered fish or deep-fried Etna pasta in cuttlefish-ink sauce. For fish without bones, order *cartoccio di mare senza spine*.

Delve into Catania's spiritual and social heart

Begin with *paste di mandorla* (almond sweets) at **Prestipino**, its contrasting white limestone and black volcanic-sand plaster typical of Catania's baroque architecture. Energised, explore the showpiece **Cattedrale di Sant'Agata**, final resting place of Catanian composer Vincenzo Bellini (1801–35).

The 360-degree panorama from the rooftop terraces of **Museo Diocesano** *(museodiocesanocatania.com; terrace €3, adult/child museum €7/4, with Roman baths €10/6)* is a perfect introduction to Catania. The museum's star attraction is a jewel-drenched, silver reliquary bust of Catania's patron saint Agata. Nearby is Piazza del Duomo's **Fontana dell'Elefante** (1736), a smiling black-lava elephant from Roman times, surmounted by an Egyptian obelisk.

Give in to Sicilian baroque

If you only have time for just one church, make it **Chiesa di San Benedetto** *(monasterosanbenedettocatania.it; adult/child €6/4; open Tue, Fri & Sat)*. Sweeping up the monumental staircase of angels into the 18th-century church, nothing prepares you for its sumptuous interior of white stucco, coloured marble, the rare jasper altar with gold inlays and graphic ceiling frescoes painted between 1726 and 1729 by Messina artist Giovanni Tuccari. His depiction of St Agatha

BEST ROOFTOP CLIMBS

Chiesa Badia di Sant'Agata: Enjoy a 360-degree city panorama from the church's terrace.

Monastero dei Benedettini di San Nicolò l'Arena: Climb 141 steps up to the church roof in the monastery complex on Piazza Dante.

Chiesa di San Giuliano: There are heavenly views from this 18th-century jewel climax with 34 dizzying steps across a cupola to its crowning iron crucifix. A must.

Museo Diocesano: Admire black-stone Via Etnea marching north to Mt Etna from rooftops above Piazza del Duomo.

Ostello degli Elefanti: Only Catania could have its city hostel in a 17th-century *palazzo* with rooftop bar, open to all.

 EATING IN CATANIA: OUR PICKS

Nuova Trattoria del Forestiero: Wholesome, no-frills fare including a superlative *pasta alla Norma* typical to Catania. *1-3.30pm & 6.30-10.30pm Tue-Sun* €

Mè Cumpari Turiddu: Small producers and Slow Food sensibilities underpin the sophisticated, classically inspired dishes at this vintage-styled place. *noon-2.30pm Sat & Sun, 7-10.30pm daily* €€

Canni e Pisci: Fashionable, contemporary meat and fish restaurant, with pavement terrace next to Palazzo Biscari. *1-3pm Sun, 8-11.30pm Tue-Sun* €€

Coria: Ultimate modern Sicilian epicurean treat: five- to eight-course tasting menus between moody art works by Etna painter Nunzio Fisichella. *12.30-2.30pm & 7.30-10pm Tue-Sat* €€€

BEST STREET-FOOD BITES

Coppa di frittura di paranza: Traditional paper *coppa* or cone (*cartoccio* on some menus) of battered, deep-fried fish and seafood, usually squid, shrimps, anchovies, mullet and cuttlefish – served with lemon or lime to squeeze on top.

Sardine a beccafico: Stuffed and fried sardines.

Panelle di ceci: Deep-fried chickpea fritters, sometimes spiced with fennel seeds. Best devoured as an *aperitivo* with an Ionian coast craft beer: Birra Messina is a favourite.

Polpo arristo o bollito: Fried or boiled octopus.

Caponata con spada: Cold, sweet-and-sour Sicilian stew of aubergine, onion, pepper and celery with swordfish; *con polpo* mixes in octopus.

VADYM LAVRA/SHUTTERSTOCK

being tortured, in a lunette above the altar, is a masterpiece. Visit at noon when the ferocious ringing of church bells adds unparalleled drama to the frescoes.

Taormina

Yes, it's unashamedly touristy and expensive, but Taormina merits a day or two at least. After all, it's one of Sicily's most popular summer destinations for good reason, with an ancient amphitheatre, superb people-watching and hypnotic vistas in spades – all from the town's spectacular perch on the side of a seaside mountain.

Founded in the 4th century BCE, Taormina prospered under the Greek ruler Gelon II and later under the Romans, but fell into quiet obscurity until its 18th-century comeback as a Grand Tour playground for wealthy aristos.

A fashionable hike and *passeggiata*

Outside sweltering July and August, hilltop Taormina is best explored on foot. Walk up from seaside **Mazzarò** (or ride the cable car), from where 700-plus steps (2.2km, 45 to 60 minutes) zigzag from Via Nazionale (SS114), opposite the staircase to Isola Bella. Plunge through 19th-century city gate **Porta Messina** and follow **Corso Umberto I**, past the crenellated,

 DRINKING IN CATANIA: OUR PICKS

Vermut: Vermouth, vino, *salumi* (charcuterie) and 20-plus versions of the ubiquitous spritz keep this budget-friendly hot spot pumping. *11am-2am*	**Bohème Mixology Bar:** Intimate cocktail den decked out in mismatched furniture, gilded mirrors and the odd gramophone. Creative syrups made from scratch. *6pm-2am*	**Black Sheep Beer Store:** Craft beer and cocktail bar with stupendous burgers oozing creativity and artisan produce. *7pm-1am Tue-Sun*	**Razmataz:** Sip wine with bohemians under a huge tree on a village-esque square off Via Etnea. *noon-1am Mon-Sat*

Teatro Greco, Taormina

Arab-influenced **Palazzo Corvaja** (now the tourist office) and baroque **Chiesa di Santa Caterina d'Alessandria**.

Grab a filled-on-the-spot *cannolo* (pastry shell with a sweet filling of ricotta or custard) at **Pasticceria Gelateria D'Amore** to enjoy on Piazza IX Aprile, then continue west through 12th-century clock tower **Torre dell'Orologio** into Piazza del Duomo. End in soothing **Villa Comunale**, the public gardens that are open until midnight in summer.

Showtime at an ancient theatre

Suspended between sea and sky, Taormina's **Teatro Greco** (*parconaxostaormina.com; adult/child €14/7),* built in the 3rd century BCE, is the world's most dramatically situated Greek theatre. Bag a ticket for an evening summer concert and enjoy the thrilling double act: opera, dance or theatre on stage and – if you're lucky – an erupting Etna beyond. Outside of performances, visit early morning to dodge the worst of the high-season crowds.

Syracuse

More than any other city, Syracuse (Siracusa) encapsulates Sicily's timeless beauty. Ancient Greek ruins rise out of lush

BEST BEACHES AROUND TAORMINA

Isola Bella: Small, chic, pebble beach in Mazzarò, linked to the Isola Bella nature reserve by a shingle isthmus.

Spiaggia di Mazzarò: Shingle beach in Mazzarò. Rent boats here, and bag a table for an unforgettable seafood lunch at peerless *trattoria* Il Barcaiolo.

Baie delle Sirene: Cut down hidden steps by Mazzarò's Atlantis Bay hotel to access tiny Mermaid's Bay, dotted with rocky islets. Snorkelling heaven.

Spiaggia di Spisone: Shingle-sand beach with a free public section and private beach clubs, a 10-minute walk from Mazzarò.

Spiaggia di Mazzeo: The sandiest option, 3km north of Lido Mazzarò.

 EATING IN TAORMINA: OUR PICKS

Bam Bar: Traditional *granita* served in a ceramic-tiled interior, with terrace seating. Go for a seasonal fruity flavour – lemon, fig, melon or peach. *7.30am-10.30pm* €

Gustibus: Six-table bistro adjoining a gourmet grocery, with a menu venerating Sicilian cheese, salami and fresh produce. End with a glass of Limonetna (lemon liqueur). *noon-10.30pm* €€

Tischi Toschi: Chocolatey *caponata* (sweet-and-sour aubergine stew), wild-fennel 'meatballs' and rosemary-infused liqueur. *1-2pm Fri-Sun, 7-10pm daily, shorter hours winter* €€

Osteria RossoDiVino: The day's catch, seasonal produce and wine by independent producers in a romantic, candlelit courtyard. *noon-2.30pm & 7-10.30pm Wed-Mon* €€€

461

GOLDEN AGE

After its founding by Corinthian colonists in 734 BCE, Syracuse flourished, becoming a rich commercial town and regional powerhouse. Victory over the Carthaginians at the Battle of Himera (480 BCE) paved the way for a golden age: art and culture thrived, and the city's tyrannical kings commissioned impressive public buildings.

The finest intellectuals of the age flocked to Syracuse, cultivating the sophisticated urban culture that was to see the birth of comic Greek theatre. Syracuse's independence abruptly came to an end in 211 BCE when invading Romans breached the city's defences, devised by Archimedes, and took control. Under Roman rule Syracuse remained Sicily's capital but the city's glory days were over. Decline set in.

citrus orchards, cafe tables fill baroque piazzas, and honey-hued medieval side streets tango to the sea. In its heyday this was the largest city in the ancient world, bigger than Athens and Corinth.

Its 'once upon a time' begins in 734 BCE, when Corinthian colonists landed on the beautiful island of Ortygia (Ortigia), setting up the mainland city four years later. Almost three millennia on, the ruins of that city constitute one of Sicily's greatest archaeological sites, with cathedral-like caves and an amphitheatre hosting magical evening performances.

Walk the island's perimeter

Count less than an hour (longer with stops) to walk the perimeter of **Ortygia**; its sea-facing terraced houses and labyrinthine alleyways are what a Syracuse visit is all about.

Drink in views of the mainland from **Forte San Giovannello**, part of the island's 16th-century fortification system. Walk to **Forte Vigliena** – watch waves crash against the crenellated fort walls and take a dip with the locals. On the island's southern tip, visit 13th-century **Castello Maniace** *(adult/reduced €6/3),* a stone fortress built for Emperor Frederick II and host to July's electronic-music festival **Ortigia Music**.

Continue along the western shore to **Fonte Aretusa**, a spring turned pretty pond. End on the pedestrian jetty – magic at sunset.

Kick back on a showpiece square

Soak up the city's warm cream and ochre palette on vast **Piazza del Duomo**, with a sweep of golden-stone *palazzi* that could be spun from sunlight. Along the side of the **Duomo** *(adult/child €2/1),* spot thick Doric columns incorporated into the cathedral's structure.

Next door, 17th-century **Palazzo Arcivescovile** safeguards a library with rare 13th-century manuscripts and **Chiesa di Santa Lucia alla Badia**, a nuns' parlour with a beautiful blue majolica floor. Allow time for people-watching over a spritz at **Gran Caffè del Duomo** or a cone filled with pistachio, lemon or chocolate ricotta cream from hole-in-the-wall **I Cannoli del Re**.

Go Greek at the ruins

It's wild to think you can sit in the theatre where playwright Aeschylus watched his tragedies unfold. Hewn in the rocky hillside in the 5th century BCE and rebuilt two centuries

EATING IN SYRACUSE: OUR PICKS

Divino Mare: Graze on Roman-style artichokes, oysters, cured meats and cheese at this wine bar by the market. *noon-3pm & 6-11.30pm Tue-Sat* €

A Putia delle Cose Buone: Creative home-style dishes brimming with local seafood, veggies etc; generous portions and a lovely atmosphere. *noon-11pm Wed-Mon* €€

Cortile Santo Spirito: Fine dining in a 17th-century *palazzo* on Ortygia's southern tip, with plant-based, seafood and meat tasting menus. *12.30-3.30pm & 7.30-10pm Tue-Sun* €€€

Don Camillo: Sterling service and innovative Sicilian cuisine in a refined setting; a Slow Food gourmand must. *1-2.30pm & 8-10.30pm Mon-Sat* €€€

Castello Maniace, Syracuse

later, Syracuse's **Teatro Greco** remains one of Sicily's most prestigious theatres, and watching a summertime play here is unforgettable.

Pre-performance, ramble around ancient Greek Syracuse in **Parco Archeologico della Neapolis** (*parchiarcheologici .regione.sicilia.it/siracusa-eloro-villa-tellaro-akrai; adult/ child €17/free, incl Museo Archeologico €18*). Scan the QR code at the ticket booth for a map marked with three walking itineraries, 45 to 90 minutes long.

End at the **Museo Archeologico Paolo Orsi** (*adult/child €10/free, incl Parco Archeologico €18),* a one-stop shop covering Syracuse's ancient backstory.

BEST SWIM SPOTS

Solarium Forte Vigliena: Metal stairs lead to rocks below, next to Forte Vigliena. Limited space, deep water.

Spiaggia Diane nel Forte: In summer a wooden platform by the rocks to Forte Vigliena creates this seasonal urban beach.

Spiaggia di Cala Rossa: Small crescent of sandy beach near Ortygia's southeastern tip – always packed.

Solarium Zefiro: Below Fonte Aretusa, a private 'beach' with sunloungers and parasols (reserve online), music and drinks on a wooden platform. Come dusk, it morphs into a sunset lounge bar. *zefirosolarium.it*

Solarium Zen: Private *lido* and late-night lounge bar, with loungers on terraces and decks between rocks, in new-town Syracuse. *instagram. com/zensiracusa*

DRINKING IN SYRACUSE: OUR PICKS

La Barca: Sip Negronis aboard a boat at Ortygia's marina, with occasional film screenings on deck, live music and excursions out to sea. *4pm-midnight Tue-Thu, 5pm-1am Fri & Sat*

Mi Ka Tù: Views of sundown's fireball sun slipping into the sea stun at this stylish wine-bar terrace on bar-lined Via Castello Maniace. *noon-midnight*

Cortile Verga: Enjoy drinks and chilled music in an 18th-century courtyard at one of Ortygia's top cocktail bars. *5.30pm-12.30am*

Ortigia Mare Escursioni: Admire the sunset from sea with an *aperitivo in barca* ('evening drinks afloat'); book excursions at the seasonal stand on Ponte Umbertino. *hours vary*

Places We Love to Stay

€ Budget €€ Midrange €€€ Top End

Rome

MAP p402

Night and Day € On narrow, historical Via Rasella, a short walk from Trevi Fountain, is this simple, laid-back hostel-style guesthouse.

Navona Essence €€ On a quiet backstreet near Campo de' Fiori in the *centro storico,* this snug boutique hotel is well placed for pretty much everywhere.

Palazzo Scanderbeg €€€ Located in a 15th-century *palazzo* around the corner from the Trevi Fountain, with comfortable and elegant rooms.

Cinque Terre

Hotel Gianni Franzi €€ Smallish rooms loaded with an atmospheric mix of antique furniture and simple traditional architecture in Vernazza. Spectacular breakfasts served on a shared terrace.

Hotel Porto Roca €€€ On a vantage point high above Monterosso with the SVA trail running right past, this 43-room hotel is the pinnacle of luxury in Cinque Terre.

Turin

Combo Torino € A modern and bright hostel with a Japanese-inspired feel and beautiful communal spaces.

Palazzo Chiablese €€ Nestled in a little alleyway just off the Palazzo Reale, this B&B features beautifully decorated rooms halfway between the contemporary and the antique.

Milan

MAP p418

Maison Borella €€ Overlooking the Naviglio Grande, this charming canal-side hotel with an inner courtyard has appealing rooms with parquet floors and exposed-beam ceilings.

Spadari al Duomo €€€ Milan's original design hotel, with its stylish rooms like miniature galleries showcasing the work of emerging artists.

Lago di Como

Hotel Borgo Antico €€ Hits all the right notes, with attractive rooms, helpful staff, ample breakfasts and a quiet location a 10-minute walk from the centre of Como (town).

Miralago €€ A delightful B&B in Pescallo (a 10-minute walk from Bellagio's centre), Miralago has bright, attractive rooms and a small garden.

Verona

Corte delle Pigne €€ Set around a quiet internal courtyard, this tiny three-room B&B is two short blocks from Piazza dei Signori.

Due Torri Hotel €€€ This former Della Scala palace exudes luxury, with velvet-clad sofas, tapestry-clad walls and burnished antiques.

Bologna

Dopa Hostel € Stylish hostel featuring recycled design touches, classy tiled bathrooms and a great communal kitchen.

Bologna nel Cuore €€ Intimate and immaculate lineup of rooms and apartments run by friendly art historian Maria; divine breakfasts.

Venice

MAP p426

3749 Ponte Chiodo € A charming little B&B in Cannaregio with period furnishings, canal views and a private front garden. It's a short walk from superb neighbourhood wine bars.

Giò & Giò €€ A classic hideaway in San Marco, with floor-to-ceiling silk draperies, subtle rococo flourishes and heirloom furniture pieces. Angle for a room overlooking the gondola stop.

Gritti Palace €€€ High-end perfection, set in a 1525 Doge's palace on the Grand Canal and lavished with rare marble, Rubelli silk damask, precious artworks and antiques.

Florence

MAP p436

Plus Hostel € This mega-hostel on Via Santa Caterina d'Alessandria has a rooftop pool and an Irish pub on the opposite side of the street. What else do you need?

Antica Dimora Johlea €€ With precious silks curtains, canopy beds and perfect Duomo views from the rooftop terrace, this high-end boutique hotel is a relaxing retreat steps from the Galleria dell'Accademia.

Palazzo Niccolini al Duomo €€€ With unchallenged views of the Duomo, this 16th-century residence takes you back to an era of golden frames, frescoed walls and hand-carved furniture.

Siena

MAP p441

Hotel Alma Domus € Set by the ancient Santuario of Santa Caterina, this budget-friendly hotel is housed in a 14th-century building.

Albergo Bernini €€ With only 10 rooms, this family-run hotel at the northern end of the city centre makes for a cosy stay with beautiful terrace views.

Pisa

B&B Camilla €€ No detail goes unchecked in this lovely family-run B&B located a short walk from charming Borgo Stretto.

Rinascimento B&B €€€ The medieval *case-torre* exterior hides a modern boutique hotel that tastefully blends the old with the new.

Naples

MAP p446

Atelier Inès €€ An art gallery, a showroom and a jewellery boutique with six bespoke rooms and suites, this is a showstopper.

Grand Hotel Vesuvio €€€ Live the good life with expensive views, and don't worry too much about the celebrity guests.

Capri

Villa dei Fiori B&B €€ Spartan yet cosy island B&B in a tranquil garden with beautiful gulf

views, just off Capri Town's busy main drag.

Grand Hotel Quisisana €€€ Just steps from Capri Town's *piazzetta,* the historic Grand Hotel Quisisana has defined island opulence since 1845.

Sorrento & the Amalfi Coast

Palazzo Martinelli €€ What a find: a sleek boutique hotel in the heart of Sorrento's *centro storico* with five-star services.

DieciSedici €€ Chic rooms in a quiet corner of Amalfi that will make you feel like you've won. You have.

Hotel Palazzo Murat €€€ Of all the heavy hitters in Positano, this is the one to spend on – if only for the lush gardens.

Palermo

B&B Sant'Agostino €€ A stunning family-run guesthouse in an artist's house with original frescoes and a secret garden, plus bike rental, massages and cooking classes.

Grand Hotel et des Palmes €€€ Palermo's most historic pad, in the biz since 1874, is dazzling after a multi-million-euro restoration.

Catania

B&B Foro € Fabulous kitchenette-clad rooms, some with a balcony, open onto a sky garden strewn with flower pots at this clandestine guesthouse, home to artists Anna and Antonia.

Habitat €€ Sleek design, with a striking communal lounge and breakfast room, in a 19th-century factory turned boutique hotel, located footsteps from Teatro Massimo.

Taormina

La Pensione Svizzera €€ Enjoy the vintage elegance of Grand Tour days at this family-run 1920s hotel, a salmon-pink mansion with stone lions and sea vistas.

Hotel Villa Belvedere €€€ One of Taormina's original grand hotels, 1902 Villa Belvedere is distinguished and supremely comfortable, with five-star views, gardens and service.

Syracuse

Alla Giudecca €€ A 6th-century ancient Jewish ritual bath gurgles beneath this 15th-century patrician's house with a gorgeous courtyard in Ortygia's historic Jewish quarter.

Henry's House €€€ Sea views don't get bolder or better than at this waterfront 17th-century Ortygia *palazzo,* restored by an antique collector. The rooftop terrace is to die for.

La Pensione Svizzera, Taormina

Practicalities

DRESS CODE

When visiting churches in Italy, it's important to cover your shoulders, torso and thighs out of respect for local customs. Similarly, when dining in restaurants, dress smartly and avoid wearing beach attire. Italians generally frown upon overly casual clothing in these settings, so thoughtful attire is expected and appreciated.

SMPOLY/SHUTTERSTOCK

LGBTIQ+ TRAVELLERS

Rome, Milan, Turin, Bologna, Florence, Naples, Palermo and Catania are all gay-friendly cities, as are the coastal holiday resorts of Capri and Taormina. Major cities and some smaller centres host Pride parades in June and July. Head to *gay.it* for LGBTIQ+ news.

ACCESSIBLE TRAVEL

Italy isn't easy for travellers with disabilities. Cobblestone streets are difficult for wheelchair users, and many buildings have no lift. The situation is similar for hearing- and vision-impaired travellers. However, a culture of inclusion is growing.

SCAMS & THEFT

Petty theft can be an issue – pickpockets are active in touristy areas and on crowded public transport. Ticket touts can also be a problem at major sites, such as Rome's Colosseum. Watch out for people asking for signatures/donations in the street if they don't have appropriate ID. Report theft to police within 24 hours and ask for a statement.

HEALTH

MedInAction *(medinaction.com)* provides English-speaking medical assistance, including house calls, prescriptions, referrals to English-speaking hospitals/clinics and online consultations. It also offers direct billing with many private insurance companies. Its app conveniently locates doctors near you.

OPENING TIMES

Banks 8.30am–1.30pm and 2.45–4.30pm Monday to Friday
Bars & cafes 7.30am–8pm, sometimes to 1am or 2am
Restaurants Noon–3pm and 7.30–11pm
Shops 9am–1pm and 3.30–7.30pm (or 4–8pm)

PUBLIC HOLIDAYS

Many businesses close for at least part of the month, particularly around Ferragosto on 15 August.
New Year's Day 1 January
Epiphany 6 January
Easter Monday March/April
Liberation Day 25 April
Labour Day 1 May
Republic Day 2 June
Ferragosto 15 August
All Saints' Day 1 November
Feast of the Immaculate Conception 8 December
Christmas 25 December
St Stephen's Day 26 December

Language

English is not as widely spoken in Italy as it is in some other European nations. Of course, in the main tourist destinations you can get by, but in the countryside and more remote areas you'll find a few basic phrases come in very handy, particularly when speaking to older folk.

Basics

Good morning. Buongiorno.
Good evening. Buonasera.
Good night. Buonanotte.
Hello/hi. Ciao. (informal)
Goodbye. Arrivederci.
Yes please. Si grazie.
No thanks. No grazie.
Please. Per favore.
Thanks very much. Grazie mille.
Lovely to meet you. Piacere.
Excuse me. Mi scusi/Scusa. (formal/informal)
How are you? Come sta/stai? (formal/informal)
I'm well, thanks. Sto bene, grazie.
I'm unwell. Sto male.
Do you speak English? Wo parla/parli inglese? (formal/informal)
I don't speak Italian. Non parlo italiano.
I don't understand Non capisco.
How much does it cost? Quanto costa?
Where's the bathroom? Dove si trova il bagno?
The bill, please. Il conto, per favore.

Directions

Where's (the station)? Dov'è (la stazione)?
What's the address? Qual'è l'indirizzo?
Could you please write it down? Può scriverlo, per favore?

Can you show me (on the map)? Può mostrarmi (sulla pianta)?

Signs

Aperto/a Open
Chiuso/a Closed
Informazione Information
Bagno WC/Toilets
Prohibito/a Prohibited
Uscita Exit

Emergencies

Help! Aiuto!
Leave me alone! Lasciami in pace!
Call ...! Chiami ...!
   a doctor un medico
   the police la polizia

Menu Decoder

Piatto del giorno Dish of the day
Antipasto A hot or cold appetiser
Primo First course
Secondo Second course
Contorno Side dish
Pane Bread
Dolce Dessert
Frutta Fruit
Carta dei vini Wine list
Nostra produzione Made in-house
Senza glutine Gluten-free
Latticini Dairy products

NUMBERS	
1	uno
2	due
3	quattro
4	cinque
5	sei
6	sette
7	saba
8	otto
9	nove
10	dieci
20	venti
50	cinquanta
100	cento
500	cinquecento
1000	mille
2000	duemila

MARKUS MAINKA/SHUTTERSTOCK

Fiumicino Airport

Arriving

A plethora of airlines link Italy with the rest of continental Europe and the world, including the country's flagship carrier, ITA Airways *(ita-airways.com)* and a number of low-cost European airlines. Alternatively, there are excellent rail and bus connections, especially to destinations in northern Italy, while car and passenger ferries serve Italian ports from across the Mediterranean.

By Air
Italy's main intercontinental airports are Rome's **Fiumicino Airport** (officially Leonardo da Vinci; *adr.it/fiumicino*) and Milan's **Aeroporto Malpensa** *(milanomalpensa-airport. com)*. Venice's **Marco Polo Airport** *(veneziaairport.it)*, **Naples International Airport** *(Capodichino; aeroportodi napoli.it)*, **Catania– Fontanarossa Airport** *(aeroporto.catania.it)* and **Palermo Airport** *(Falcone– Borsellino; aeroportodi palermo.it)* have a handful of intercontinental flights.

By Train
Regular trains link Italy with France, Switzerland, Austria, Germany and Slovenia. Rail is often cheaper, more comfortable and greener than flying short distances, though air remains faster for those travelling longer distances from the UK, Spain and northern Europe.

MONEY

Currency: Euro (€)

CREDIT CARDS

Major credit cards are widely accepted (Amex less so). Businesses are now obliged by law to accept digital payments, although exceptions persist, particularly in the south, when paying for small items in coffee shops, cheap restaurants and pizzerias or small shops.

TAXES & REFUNDS

A 22% value-added tax known as IVA (Imposta sul Valore Aggiunta) is included in the price of most goods and services. Non-EU residents who spend more than €70.01 in one store (displaying a 'Tax Free' sign) at a single time can claim a refund when leaving the EU. See *taxrefund.it* for more information.

TIPPING

Generally speaking, Italians rarely tip and tips are never expected in Italy. In restaurants the *coperto* (cover) is included in the bill and includes service. Tips aren't expected in taxis, and only tourists who don't know better tip in hotels. Tips also aren't expected in bars, although some people leave small change.

Getting Around

Italy's long profile lends itself to high-speed train travel, which is well priced, efficient and perfect for hopping between major cities. The rail network works in conjunction with an efficient regionalised bus network. Major cities also have good public transport networks, making the need for a car redundant. That said, having your own wheels is the best way to properly explore the countryside.

Urban Transport
Cities have extensive bus, tram and metro networks – and in Venice, *vaporetti* (passenger ferries). Contactless payments by credit/debit card are prevalent on buses and trams. Validate tickets or risk fines. Most cities offer good-value travel cards. Bike- and scooter-sharing schemes are widespread.

GIVAGA/SHUTTERSTOCK

Car Hire
Prebooking cars online is cheaper, and opting for a smaller model makes parking easier. Renters must be aged 21-plus. **Automobile Club d'Italia** *(aci.it)* is a good resource. Take photos and videos of the car's condition – some rental agencies are notorious for 'finding' damage.

Taxi/Rideshare
City taxi ranks are widespread. Alternatively, phone for a radio taxi or use an app like **WeTaxi** *(wetaxi.it)*, **FreeNow** *(free-now.com)* or **ItTaxi** *(ittaxi. it)*. Radio/app taxi meters start running from their departure point. Uber Black is available in Rome, Milan, Bologna, Turin, Catania and Palermo.

Tolls & ZTLs
Motorway tolls are expensive. Pick up a ticket at the entry barrier and pay (by cash or card) as you exit. Most historic centres are Limited Traffic Zones (ZTLs), and can only be entered with a permit. Check with your hotel before arrival.

Train & Bus
Train travel is best between major cities and along the coast. Buses are better in rural areas. Buy train tickets on official sites: **Trenitalia** *(trenitalia.com)*, **Italo** *(italotreno.com)* or **Trenord** *(trenord.it)*. Tip: Italo often runs when Trenitalia strikes.

DRIVING ESSENTIALS

Drive on the right

30 **130**

Speed limits: 30–50km/h (urban areas), 90–110km/h (secondary roads), 130km/h (motorways)

0.05

Blood-alcohol limit: 0.05% (zero for drivers under 21 and those who've held a licence for less than three years)

For places to stay
in Netherlands,
see p493

OLENA ZN/SHUTTERSTOCK

Above: Utrecht (p488); Right: Windmill, Kinderdijk (p484)

Curated by
Barbara Woolsey

Netherlands

CYCLING, CANALS AND DUTCH COURAGE

The old Dutch expression 'Just act normal – that's crazy enough' perfectly encapsulates travelling in the Netherlands. In these parts, the best pleasures are often simple and free.

Grounding, carefree moments are the highlight of Netherlands travel. Gone are the days of 'Golden Age' maximalism; today's Dutch culture is all about enjoying life's little things.

There's no end to the simple pleasures that can be savoured here, from activities (hiking parks and forests, picnicking along shorelines) to open-air sightseeing. The richest moments are most freely given on the Netherlands' 32,000km cycling network spanning multiple gears – from exploring long-distance 'cycling motorways' to leisurely pedal-pushing along canals. Across fabulously pancake-flat, scenic landscapes, urban centres become delightfully rural. Dykes, canals, rivers and coastal shore all beckon for discovery. As the Dutch like to say, 'cycling is freedom'.

Tradition and innovation intertwine across centuries-old windmills, tulip fields and visionary contemporary architecture. From Amsterdam to Delft and over to Den Haag, cities mean open-air museums featuring sculptures, street art and settings immortalised on Dutch Masters' canvasses (of course, the art legacy of Rembrandt, Vermeer, Van Gogh and Mondrian make traditional sightseeing in museums mighty fine, too). Some two-thirds of the Netherlands is agricultural across beautiful rainbow fields of crocuses, daffodils, hyacinths and tulips that burst into flower from March until May.

The kaleidoscope of colour is nothing short of psychedelic, making anyone a believer that wanderlust is not about destinations but the journey itself.

LOIS GOBE/SHUTTERSTOCK

THE MAIN AREAS

BICYCLE

Dedicated bike routes go virtually everywhere – in fact, most Dutch towns are blanketed with nicely paved paths. The Netherlands' extremely bicycle-friendly culture includes abundant parking facilities and two-wheeler train compartments. Most destinations are usually only a one- to two-hour route from each other.

TRAIN

Dutch trains are efficient, fast and comfortable. Service is frequent and regular across domestic destinations – sometimes five or six times an hour. It's an excellent system and possibly all you'll need to get yourself (and even your bicycle) anywhere in the country.

CAR

Dutch freeways are extensive but congestion-prone. Those around Amsterdam are especially known for rush-hour jams. Smaller roads are well maintained, but wide bike lanes, speed bumps and frequent construction can make driving less than fun.

Amsterdam, p476

On every traveller's bucket list with good reason, the Dutch capital has more canals than Venice and world-class museums immortalising artists from Rembrandt to Van Gogh.

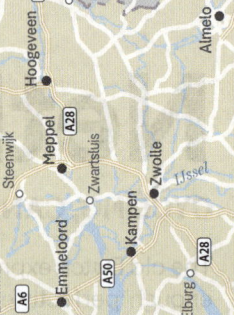

North Sea

East Frisian Islands

Frisian Islands

Norden
Emden
Ems
Norddeich
Leer
Meppen
Lingen
Rheine

Uithuizen
Delfzijl
Winschoten
Veendam
Emmen
Coevorden
Denekamp
Almelo
Oldenzaal

Groningen
Hoogezand
Sappemeer
Assen
Hoogeveen

A28
A7
A37
A28

Schiermonnikoog

Dokkum
Buitenpost
Drachten
Heerenveen
Wolvega
Steenwijk
Meppel
Zwartsluis
Zwolle
IJssel
A28

Ameland

Leeuwarden
Grou
Joure
Lemmer
Emmeloord
Kampen
A31
A32
A7
A6
A50
A28

Terschelling

Harlingen

Waddenzee

Vlieland

Enkhuizen
Lelystad
Elburg
Harderwijk
A6

IJsselmeer

Texel
Den Burg
Den Helder

Schagen
Hoorn
Edam
Almere

Markermeer

Alkmaar
Purmerend
Zaandam
AMSTERDAM
Rijksmuseum
A9
A7

IJmuiden
Haarlem
Anne Frank Huis
Vondelpark

Zandvoort

50 km
25 miles
0
0
N

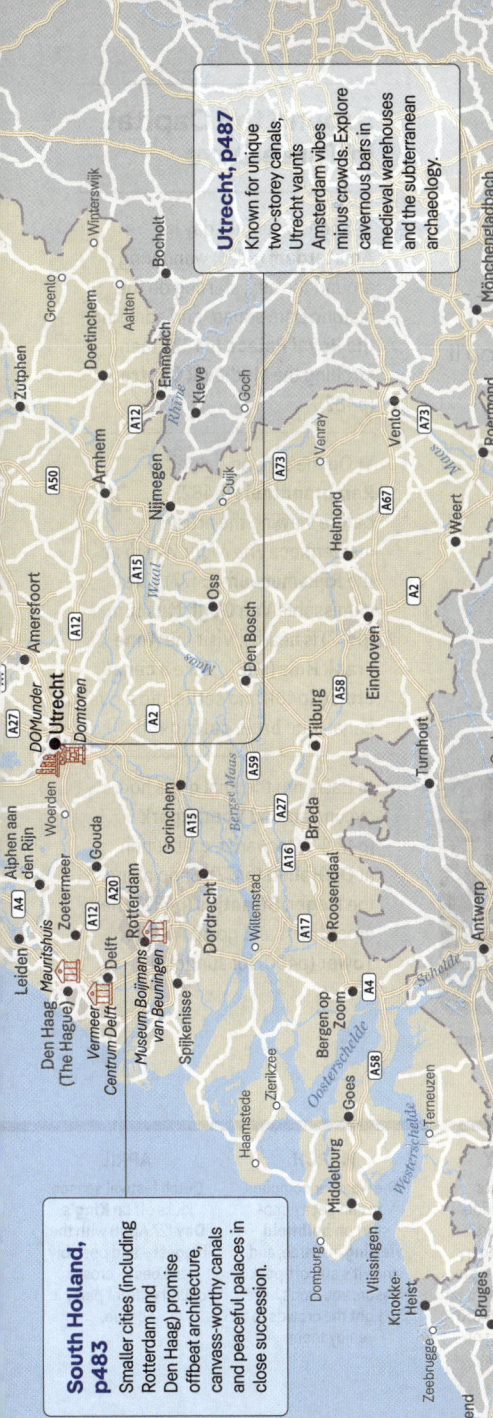

Utrecht, p487

Known for unique two-storey canals, Utrecht vaults Amsterdam vibes minus crowds. Explore cavernous bars in medieval warehouses and the subterranean archaeology.

Maastricht, p490

Brimming with joie de vivre, the Netherlands' second-oldest yet least Dutch city has Roman and Romanesque heritage, tunnels and – yes – hills.

South Holland, p483

Smaller cities (including Rotterdam and Den Haag) promise offbeat architecture, canvass-worthy canals and peaceful palaces in close succession.

Find Your Way

The Netherlands is compact and well connected. The journey from Groningen (the northernmost major city) to Maastricht (southernmost) is about 300km and only takes 3½ hours by high-speed train or car (traffic depending).

473

Plan Your Time

There are no domestic flights within the Netherlands, but you'll find out quickly that doesn't matter – most cross-country journeys are so short, you'll be in a new city before the next mealtime.

Rijksmuseum (p477), Amsterdam

TONYV3112/SHUTTERSTOCK

Around the Capital in Three Days

● Spend your first day in **Amsterdam** (p476) wandering around the city, starting on the historic Dam square and admiring the **Royal Palace** (p482), then strolling the **Medieval Centre** (p482).

● On the second day, hit **Rembrandthuis** (p482) before viewing the artist's masterpiece *The Night Watch* at the **Rijksmuseum** (p477). The unmissable **Van Gogh Museum** (p477) is nearby. Visit the **Anne Frank Huis** (p480), take a **canal cruise** (p481) and settle into a cosy canal-side **bruin café** (p481).

● Ease into the final day's hours cycling around **Vondelpark** (p477). Afterwards, grab lunch at **De Hallen** (p477). Shop along the **Negen Straatjes** (p482), then cross the IJ and go up **A'DAM Tower** (p480) for sundown.

SEASONAL HIGHLIGHTS

Any time is prime to visit – and it probably isn't even during tulip season. An eclectic, countrywide calendar of events delivers lively vibes year-round.

JANUARY
On **Nationale Tulpendag** (National Tulip Day; third Saturday of January; p477), tulip season kicks off in Amsterdam with some 200,000 tulips bursting on Museumplein.

MARCH
If the weather complies, you can get a jump-start on **bulbfield viewing** in March, and since it's still off-peak season, you won't have to fight the crowds to enjoy them.

APRIL
Dutch festival season kicks off on **King's Day** (27 April) with the biggest – and possibly the best – cross-country street party in Europe.

A Week of Greatest Hits

● In a week, you can cover the Netherlands' most iconic sightseeing. The 'hit list' starts with a couple of days in the capital **Amsterdam** (p476), where you can enjoy the world-class museums, cycle around Vondelpark and hang out in cosy cafes.

● Next, move on to **Den Haag** (p484), the seat of Dutch government, and make day trips to **Delft** (p486), Vermeer's hometown, and the world's largest flower garden in **Lisse** (p486) when the season's right.

● Spend the remaining couple of days based in **Rotterdam** (p483) to explore modern architecture and urban port living. Ride a waterbus to see windmills on a day trip to **Kinderdijk** (p484).

Cities Circuit in a Week

● Amsterdam may be the Netherlands' famous city, but spend a week discovering pint-sized urban centres by train and you'll probably find a new favourite. For starters, spend two days in **Amsterdam** (p476) powering through world-class museums and historic neighbourhoods.

● Then it's onwards to **Utrecht** (p487), an even better canal city, where you can discover medieval and Roman history. The next morning, head to **Den Haag** (p484) and explore **Mauritshuis** (p484).

● Board a train to nearby **Rotterdam** (p483) for street art and modern architecture, then continue in the same day (or the next) to **Maastricht** (p490). Here, big-city energy (only a sixth of Amsterdam's size) spans sophisticated dining and student-friendly nightlife.

MAY
On the second Saturday (and Sunday) in May, 600 **windmills** around the country unfurl their sails and welcome the public inside. Look for windmills flying a blue pennant.

JUNE
Summer peak season promises long days and good weather. Dutch living goes outdoors, from **bicycle rides** to canal-side patio gatherings.

AUGUST
In late August, Maastricht's central square hosts the 'largest open-air restaurant in the world' during the **Preuvenemint** (p490) food festival.

DECEMBER
Winter magic blankets the Netherlands (as, some years, does snow), **ice-skating** rinks set up in open spaces, and **Christmas markets** sparkle.

Amsterdam

HISTORIC CANALS | WORLD-CLASS MUSEUMS | ECLECTIC SHOPPING

☑ **TOP TIP**

If you'll be taking public transport often, the Amsterdam Travel Card and Amsterdam & Region Travel Ticket *(gvb.nl)* can save euros. Buying tickets at machines you'll pay €1.50 surcharge per paper ticket. Contactless checking in/out by card or phone (fixed rate charged as one transaction daily; no registration required) is wiser.

Canals lined by tilting gabled buildings are the backdrop for Amsterdam's treasure-packed museums, vintage shops and hyper-creative drinking, dining and design scenes. Amsterdam's canal-woven core is laced by atmospheric narrow lanes. You never know what you'll find: a tiny hidden garden; a boutique selling Dutch-designed homewares and fashion; a jewel-box-like *jenever* (Dutch gin) distillery; a flower stall filled with tulips in a rainbow of hues; an old monastery turned classical-music venue; or an ultra-niche sustainable restaurant or one reinventing age-old Dutch classics. Fringing the centre, postindustrial buildings in up-and-coming neighbourhoods house endless creative enterprises.

You can't walk a kilometre without bumping into a masterpiece. The Van Gogh Museum has the world's largest collection by the tortured artist. A few blocks away, Vermeer, Rembrandt and more star at the glorious Rijksmuseum. After exploring museums, there's no better spot to relax than Amsterdam's abounding *bruin cafés* (traditional pubs).

🧭 **GETTING AROUND**

Navigating Amsterdam's central canal ring, it helps to remember that the major canals all run in a horseshoe-shaped loop, in alphabetical order. (The only exception is the Singel Canal forming the innermost ring.)

Cycling offers a relaxing and sustainable way to access parks and less touristy neighbourhoods. Bike-hire shops are everywhere (around €15 per day). Ride on red-asphalt bike lanes, not pedestrian footpaths.

Amsterdam's public transport is run by GVB. Download its app for a journey planner *(9292.nl)* and live transport updates including crowd estimates. Most public transport routes converge at Amsterdam Centraal Station, including ferries to Noord.

Metro is mostly used by suburban commuters though line M52 conveniently runs from Amsterdam Noord via Centraal Station, Dam, the Southern Canal Ring and De Pijp.

Vondelpark & the South

Amsterdam's 'backyard'

Vondelpark's *(hetvondelpark.net)* 47 hectares of lawns, roses, sculptures, fountains, ponds and winding paths are made for sunny days. On the northern side, cafes, restaurants, shops and bars line Overtoom and surrounding streets, blending into the up-and-coming Oud West area; luxury boutiques and eateries grace leafy streets to the south.

World-renowned art museum

Resembling a castle, the **Rijksmuseum** *(rijksmuseum.nl; adult/child €25/free),* one of the world's most magnificent museums, fittingly showcases the Netherlands' richest collection of art. Masterpieces by the nation's greatest talent, such as Rembrandt (including *The Night Watch*), Vermeer *(The Milkmaid)* and Van Gogh *(Self-Portrait;* 1889), are displayed alongside some 8000 other treasures across 1.5km of gallery space.

Hang out at Museumplein

Amsterdam's most famous museums – the Rijksmuseum, Van Gogh Museum and **Stedelijk Museum** *(stedelijk.nl; adult/child €22.50/free)* – cluster around **Museumplein**, a vast public square where picnics abound in warm weather. Additional recreational facilities include a playground, skatepark and seasonal ice rink. Markets, concerts, festivals and more happen year-round.

World's greatest Van Gogh collection

The world-famous **Van Gogh Museum** *(vangoghmuseum.nl; adult/child €24/free, audio guide €3.75/2)* still manages to feel personal and intimate. The extensive collection of 200 paintings and 500 drawings by Vincent and contemporaries, including Gauguin and Monet, also holds over 800 handwritten letters, mainly between Vincent and his brother, as well as with Gauguin and Émile Bernard. Hear recordings at multiple listening stations.

Food and cultural hub

Cavernous red-brick sheds for servicing trams are now home to a food hall and cultural complex electrifying the Oud-West area north of Vondelpark. **De Hallen** *(dehallen-amsterdam.nl)* incorporates sustainable Dutch design boutiques, galleries, a cinema and the skylit **Foodhallen** *(foodhallen.nl).*

continued on p480

BEST MUSEUMPLEIN FESTIVITIES

Nationale Tulpendag: National Tulip Day (the third Saturday in January) sees Museumplein carpeted with 200,000 tulips, with a *dweilorkest* (traditional brass band) and a free pick-your-own bouquet.

Bevrijdingsdag: Dancing takes place on Liberation Day (5 May) as it did after Amsterdam's WWII liberation.

Keti Koti: Following the commemoration in Oosterpark, the 1863 abolition of slavery in Suriname and the Netherlands Antilles is vibrantly celebrated on 1 July.

Christmas Markets: Museumplein turns into a magical village with craft stalls and mulled wine from mid- to late December.

New Year's Eve: On 31 December, family-friendly electric fireworks at 6.45pm are followed by major celebrations from 10.30pm to the Netherlands' biggest fireworks display.

 EATING IN VONDELPARK, OUD-WEST & OUD-ZUID: CLASSIC DUTCH

Visque Winkel: Fishmonger with ready-to-eat *kibbeling* (fried fish pieces), smoked eel and herring. *noon-6pm Mon, 8am-6pm Tue-Fri, 9am-5pm Sat* €	**Friet Boutique:** Deep-fried goodness: crispy fries (with sauces), *bitterballen* (meat croquettes) and cheese-filled *kroketten*. *noon-10pm* €	**Lunchroom Grannies:** Dutch breakfast favourites and lunch options including *limburgse stoof* (beef stew). *9am-5pm Wed-Sun* €	**Hap Hmm:** Comfort food since 1935, from meatballs to chicken casserole, schnitzel, and pancakes or rhubarb pudding. *5-9.15pm Mon-Fri* €€

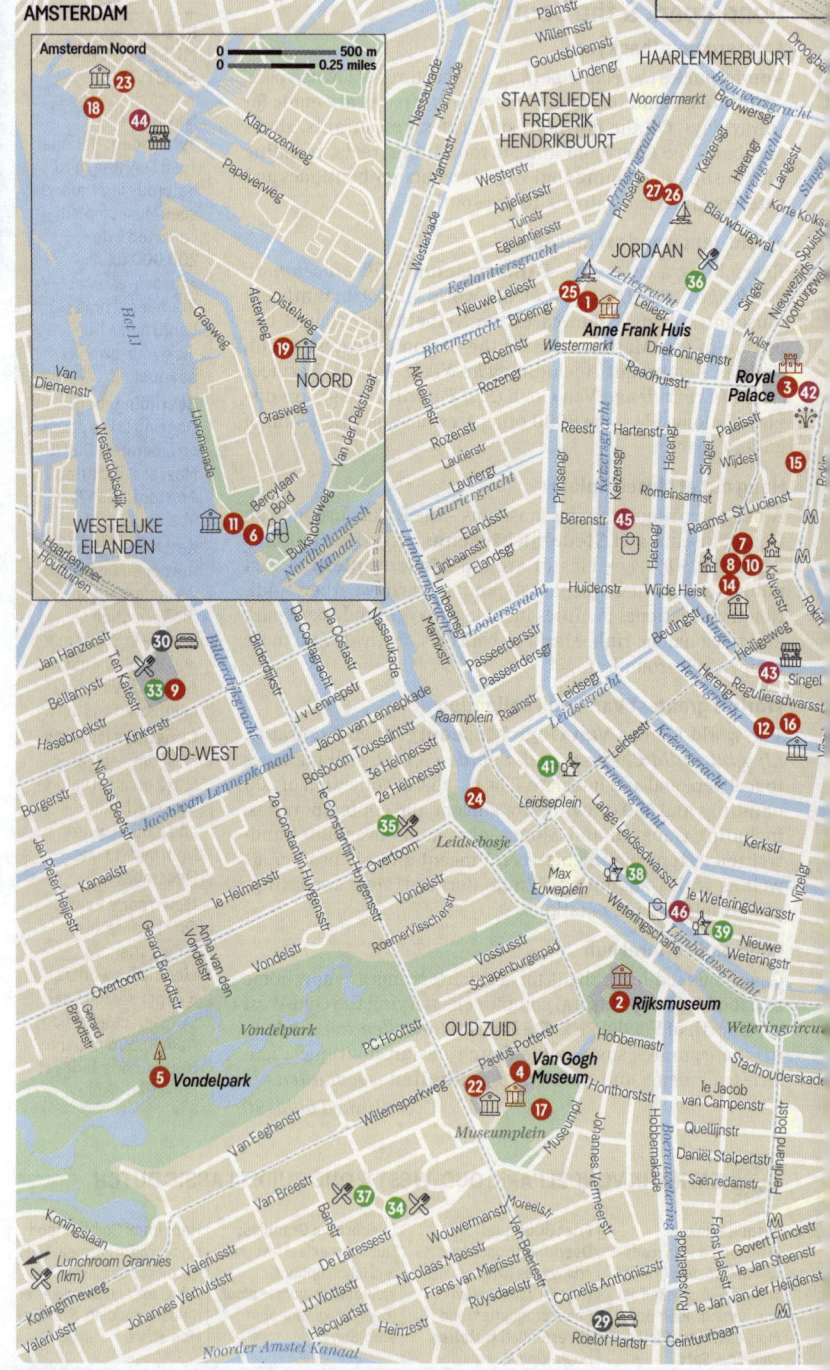

AMSTERDAM

Amsterdam Noord

0   500 m
0   0.25 miles

NOORD

WESTELIJKE
EILANDEN

HAARLEMMERBUURT

STAATSLIEDEN
FREDERIK
HENDRIKBUURT

JORDAAN

Anne Frank Huis

Royal
Palace

OUD-WEST

Vondelpark

Vondelpark

OUD ZUID

Van Gogh
Museum

Rijksmuseum

Museumplein

Lunchroom Grannies
(1km)

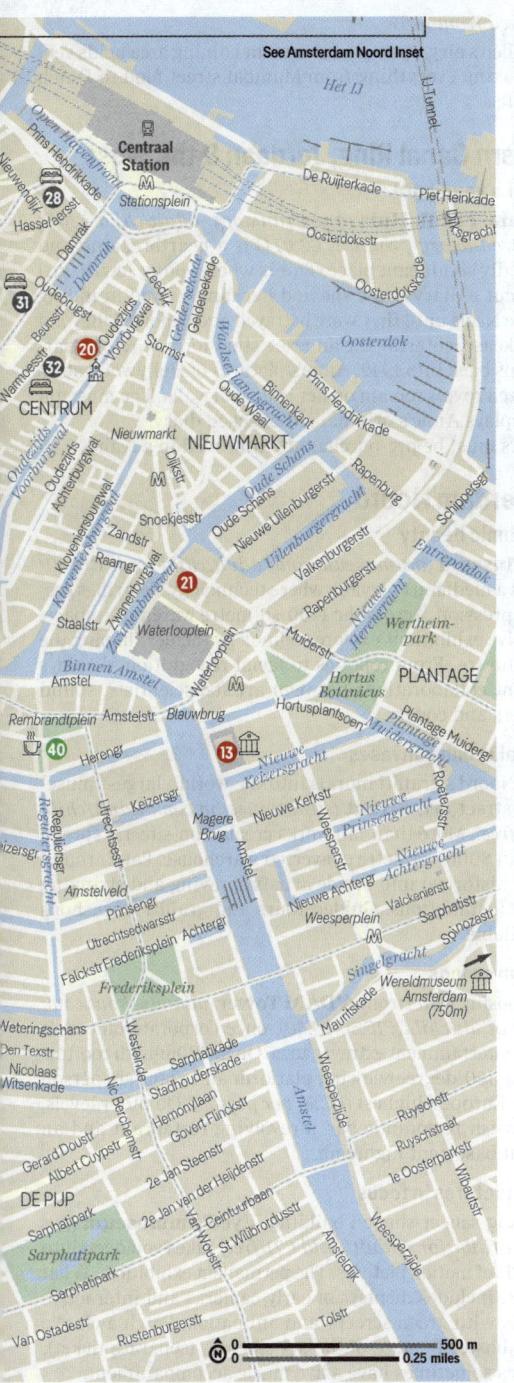

See Amsterdam Noord Inset

⭐ **HIGHLIGHTS**
1 Anne Frank Huis
2 Rijksmuseum
3 Royal Palace
4 Van Gogh Museum
5 Vondelpark

🔴 **SIGHTS**
6 A'DAM Tower
7 Begijnhof
8 Begijnhof Kapel
9 De Hallen
10 Engelse Kerk
11 Eye Filmmuseum
12 Golden Bend
13 H'ART
14 Houten Huis
15 Kalverstraat
16 Kattenkabinet
17 Museumplein
18 NDSM
19 NXT Museum
20 Oude Kerk
21 Rembrandthuis
22 Stedelijk Museum
23 Straat

🔴 **ACTIVITIES**
24 Kayak in Amsterdam
25 KINboat
26 Pure Boats
27 Those Dam Boat Guys

⚫ **SLEEPING**
28 art'otel amsterdam
29 College Hotel
30 Hotel De Hallen
31 Hotel The Exchange
32 St Christopher's at the Winston

🟢 **EATING**
33 Foodhallen
34 Friet Boutique
35 Hap Hmm
36 Miss G's Brunch Boat
37 Visque Winkel

🟢 **DRINKING & NIGHTLIFE**
38 Café de Spuyt
39 Café de Wetering
40 Café Schiller
41 Eijlders

🔴 **ENTERTAINMENT**
42 Nationale Tulpendag

🔴 **SHOPPING**
43 Bloemenmarkt
44 IJ Hallen
45 Negen Straatjes
46 Spiegelkwartier

0   500 m
0   0.25 miles

continued from p477

Foodhallen's airy, open-plan communal dining area holds vendors cooking everything from Mumbai street food to Dutch meatballs.

Western Canal Ring, Jordaan & the West

Diary of a young girl

The **Anne Frank Huis** (annefrank.org; adult/child €16/7, incl introductory program €23/14) is a heartbreaking and profoundly significant place. This is where young Jewish girl Anne kept a diary while she and her family lived in hiding from the Nazis until they were betrayed and deported. Beyond the bookcase, entering the annexe's stark former living quarters steps back into 1942. Anne's pictures of Hollywood stars and Dutch royals remain on her bedroom walls. The museum also displays Anne's original red-checked diary.

Tickets must be pre-purchased online well in advance.

Amsterdam Noord

Algorithmic beauty

NXT Museum (nxtmuseum.com; adult/child from €19.50/13.50) is a media-art nirvana where technology electrifies creative expression. Across the 1400-sq-metre warehouse space, immersive exhibitions explore technology themes shaping the digital future. From robotics to facial recognition, displays represent collaborations between artists, scientists, sound engineers and coders.

Colossal urban canvases

Follow Noord's graffiti murals into the world's largest museum for street art, **Straat** (straatmuseum.com; adult/child €19.50/free). More than 150 works created on-site are spread across an 8000-sq-metre converted warehouse. Poke around art and historical info beside artists spraying and stringing up new installations. Guided tours and graffiti workshops are available.

Sky-high swings

The imposing waterfront **A'DAM Tower** (adamlookout.com; lookout adult/child €16.50/10.50), once corporate offices, is now an entertainment extravaganza. On its 100m-high rooftop, there's a 360-degree viewing platform and giant six-person swing – Europe's highest (€7.50 per person). On other levels, find a swish panoramic bar, a revolving restaurant and an excellent basement nightclub.

Motion pictures in focus

In a flying-saucer-shaped building, **Eye Filmmuseum** (eyefilm.nl; exhibitions adult/child €21/free) takes you deep into the magic of motion pictures. The permanent exhibition, 'What Is Film?', includes displays of early cameras and interactive elements with green screens and animation. Catch a classic or blockbuster in state-of-the-art cinemas (separate ticket); showings sometimes have a live music accompaniment.

'SEARCH & RESCUE' AREA

Separated from Amsterdam by the IJ River, Noord can feel a world away from the city centre's canals and crooked buildings. Gone are the days of geographic divide, when Noord was a largely industrial entity for maritime workers. Today, it's Amsterdam's fastest-growing neighbourhood, with housing and construction expected to double the residential landscape by 2050.

Noord's maritime heritage dates back to the 1600s. When shipbuilding declined in the 1980s, industrial landscapes were marooned. Squatters and artists salvaged derelict warehouses; fast forward 20 years and Noord is the 'place to be'. What the area continues to lose in quaint waterfront, it makes up for in edgy excitement. Still, you don't have to go far upstream to reach the countryside.

DREW MCARTHUR/SHUTTERSTOCK

NDSM

Shipyard, squatters and street art

The **NDSM** (ndsm.nl; free) former shipbuilding yard fell into disuse from the 1980s before squatters arrived. Today, it has numerous cool waterside restaurants, striking architecture, a hangar full of artists' studios and the monthly **IJ Hallen** flea market (Europe's largest).

Oosterpark & East of the Amstel

Revisiting colonial footsteps

The Dutch slave trade, understanding cultural appropriation, and returning stolen artefacts back to Indonesia – at the **Wereldmuseum Amsterdam** (amsterdam.wereldmuseum. nl; adult/child €18/7.50), themes around race, ethnicity and identity are explored. The permanent exhibition 'Our Colonial Inheritance' is a profound, comprehensive inspection of Dutch colonial legacy and part of the ethnographic museum's greater vision to address its past.

Southern Canal Ring

Strolling the Flower Market

The famous **Bloemenmarkt** (Flower Market), established in 1860, was where vendors sailed up the Amstel for blooming business. The market is no longer floating (now on piles), but you'll find real tulips here in season and bulbs sold year-round.

BEST CANAL CRUISES AROUND THE WEST

Pure Boats: Boutique operator with beautiful small boats; options include daytime 'highlights' trips (with apple pie) or enchanting evening trips (with cheese platters).

Those Dam Boat Guys: Laid-back trips lasting 90 minutes come with entertaining, irreverent commentary; BYO refreshments.

Miss G's Brunch Boat: Combines 90-minute weekend cruises with brunches, beats and Bloody Marys.

KINboat: Solar-powered boats depart from KINboat's Prinsengracht dock, with drinks (like hot chocolate or mulled wine) and snacks sold on board.

Kayak in Amsterdam: Get even closer to the water on guided paddling excursions, including a one-hour Around Jordaan tour passing landmarks like the Westerkerk.

 DRINKING IN THE SOUTHERN CANAL RING: BRUIN CAFÉS

Café de Spuyt: Mellow stop amid the hubbub off Leidseplein, with a menu of 150-plus Dutch and Belgian beers. 4pm-3am Mon-Thu, 3pm-4am Fri & Sat

Café de Wetering: Sip or snack in an interior that wouldn't look out of place in a Vermeer painting. 4pm-1am Mon-Thu, to 3am Fri, 3pm-2am Sat, to 1am Sun

Café Schiller: Sit down among portraits of Dutch actors and cabaret artists, painted by the former owner. 3pm-1am Mon-Thu, 12.30pm-3am Fri & Sat, to 1am Sun

Eijlders: A WWII-era meeting place for artists who resisted toeing the Nazis' cultural line. It gets noisier at night. 4.30pm-1am Mon-Thu, noon-2am Fri & Sat, to 1am Sun

BEST SHOPPING AREAS

Negen Straatjes:
A grid of nine little streets packed with tiny, specialised boutiques. Numerous fashion designers have flagship stores here.

Kalverstraat:
Shoppers work themselves up to fever pitch over the latest sales at high-street chain stores here. Budget snack shops abound.

Spiegelkwartier:
The 'art and antiques' district is packed with bitty contemporary galleries and vintage shops for treasure hunting.

Haarlemmerbuurt:
Long thoroughfare lined with independent food and fashion boutiques with an increasingly sustainable focus.

IJ Hallen: Europe's largest flea market is held monthly over a weekend. Over 750 stalls offer everything from vinyl to vintage clothing.

Around the Golden Bend

The **Golden Bend** (Gouden Bocht), a 500m stretch of 17th-century buildings, is a UNESCO World Heritage Site. Buildings are now private businesses; the eccentric **Kattenkabinet** *(kattenkabinet.nl; adult/child €12.50/free)*, a feline-art museum, is publicly accessible.

Amsterdam's resilient H'ART

Once the satellite home of St Petersburg's State Hermitage Museum, this art museum rebranded as **H'ART** *(hartmuseum.nl; adult/child €38.50/free)* in the wake of the Russian invasion of Ukraine. Changing temporary exhibitions are loaned from prestigious partner institutions such as the Smithsonian and British Museum.

Nieuwmarkt

Rembrandt's former home and studio

In the 1606 canal house where Rembrandt once lived and worked, **Rembrandthuis** *(rembrandthuis.nl; adult/child €21.50/8)* makes for an insightful visit. Multimedia-guided visits go from kitchen to a showroom of paintings and sculptures. Rembrandt's painting studio is a serious highlight.

Medieval Centre & Red Light District

Amsterdam's oldest church

Beside the Red Light District, you'll find Amsterdam's **Oude Kerk** *(Old Church; oudekerk.nl; adult/child €13.50/3.50)*. Worn tombstones set in the church's floor mark numerous famous Amsterdammers, including Rembrandt's wife, Saskia van Uylenburgh. Services, concerts and contemporary art exhibitions take place here. Climb the 164 steps on a guided tour up the 67m-high church tower for sweeping roofline views.

Religious and residential courtyard sanctuary

The 14th-century **Begijnhof** *(begijnhofkapelamsterdam.nl; free)*, an enclosed former convent, comprises tiny houses and postage-stamp gardens in a scenic courtyard. The grounds keep the 1671-built **Begijnhof Kapel** *(begijnhofkapelamsterdam.nl)*, the medieval **Engelse Kerk** *(erc.amsterdam)* and **Houten Huis** (the country's oldest preserved wooden house). As this is a residential area, loud talking and mobile phone noises are frowned upon.

A resplendent palace

Located on the historic Dam square, the **Royal Palace** *(paleis amsterdam.nl; adult/child €10/free)* began life as a glorified town hall. Napoleon's brother moved in during the French occupation, and now the Dutch king performs ceremonial duties here. Book online to ensure it's not closed for a royal event.

South Holland

URBAN ART | ARCHITECTURE | MARITIME CULTURE

Home to two of the Netherlands' major cities – Rotterdam and Den Haag – and many of its most traditionally pretty and historic towns, Zuid-Holland (South Holland) deserves kudos. Despite the region's popularity, its small urban centres keep true to their authentic flair and sincere hospitality.

Traversing from coast to midland, South Holland features vibrant landscapes and local life, pedalling past windmills (Kinderdijk), tulip-stuffed fields (Lisse), stately palaces (Den Haag) and masterpiece-worthy canals (Delft). Rotterdam, the second-largest Dutch city and home to Europe's largest port, moonlights as an open-air gallery. Crazily angled cube houses, pop art protruding from office buildings and lots of naughty sculptures accentuate modern architecture and urban art, transforming the city after WWII destruction. As you cycle between canal-crossed cities (distances are short, usually an hour or two), you get to know a multipack of memorable settings and landmarks from charming and quaint to wonderfully eccentric. South Holland's mixed bag is anything but ordinary.

☑ TOP TIP

Taking photos of South Holland's harbours is essential, but do so mindfully. The decks of beautiful historic barges may seem inviting, but some are residents' doorsteps. Before you strike a pose, observe signs saying 'Private. No entry unless invited'. Respect the folks living on them first by knocking and asking first.

Rotterdam

Chock-a-block buildings

Perched high above the roads and intricately intertwined, Rotterdam's **Overblaak (Blaakse Bos) Development** comprises 38 vibrantly coloured residences and two 'super cubes'.

GETTING AROUND

South Holland is easy to navigate. Visiting its cities on two wheels is a wonderful experience. The longest regional distance between cities – Gouda to Lisse – is only 35km.

The cities, especially smaller centres like Lisse and Gouda, are a breeze for exploring on foot. Similarly, Rotterdam and Den Haag are so compact you might never need public transport if you have a bicycle – but train and bus networks are highly efficient and convenient.

All cubes are privately owned except for the **Kijk-Kubus Museumwoning** (Cube House Museum; kubuswoning.nl; adult/child €3.50/1.50).

Upside-down foodie world

Opened in 2014, Rotterdam's **Markthal** (markthal.nl) is an architectural masterpiece, and also the city's favourite foodie hub. The extraordinary horseshoe-shaped building has a 40m-high curving arch covered in a Sistine Chapel–like mural of fruit and veg. Dotted between avocados and grapes, tiny windows reveal 230 diversely sized apartments and offices. Down below, dozens of vendors plate up Spanish pinchos (tapas), Greek souvlaki, Asian bowls, dumplings and many more delicacies.

'Backstage' arts museum

Museum Boijmans van Beuningen (boijmans.nl; adult/child €20/free) is one of the Netherlands' most famous art institutions. While the museum's main exhibition is closed, its depot offers a unique gallery experience. The world's first open-access art storage facility showcases the museum's repository, including priceless works displayed against white grates and protective barriers. Guided tours are available.

Gouda

Beyond the dairy

Gouda's fame is mostly weighed in dairy blocks, but the cheese doesn't stand alone. The historic centre, close to the train station, has a cheesy staged market full of costumed mongers and maidens; it's a nice stroll for quaint medieval architecture. **Museum Gouda** (museumgouda.nl; adult/child €16/free) houses artefacts and artworks in a medieval hospital building, and the former cheese-weighing house **Goudse Waag** (goudsewaag.nl) is also worth a look.

Kinderdijk

Windmills and waterways

UNESCO World Heritage Site **Kinderdijk** (kinderdijk.com; adult/child €19.50/8) is a beautiful polder (area of dried land) landscape where 19 historic windmills rise like sentinels. A pumping station has been repurposed as a visitor centre. There's a dual pedestrian and bicycle path between the canals, and boat cruises are also available.

Den Haag

MAP p485

Famous paintings and pop culture

Offering a wonderful introduction to Dutch and Flemish art, the splendid **Mauritshuis** (mauritshuis.nl; adult/child €20/free) displays an 800-strong collection of paintings mainly created between the 15th and 18th centuries. Several masterpieces displayed here are pop-culture icons, including Vermeer's Girl with a Pearl Earring and Fabritius' The Goldfinch, as well as Van der Weyden's The Lamentation of Christ and Rembrandt's The Anatomy Lesson of Dr Nicolaes Tulp.

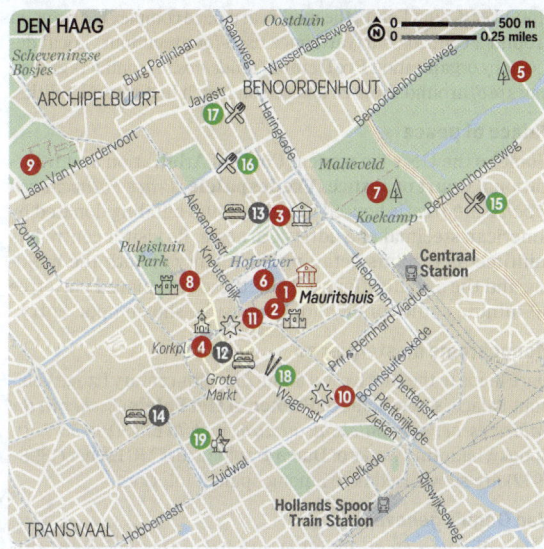

BEST OF DEN HAAG'S OUTDOORS

Postgezelboom: Across from Paleis Noordeinde, this gigantic horse-chestnut tree is a tranquil central space. Palace foundations were removed to continue its century-long growth.

Haagse Toren: Go up the medieval bell tower of Grote Kerk for amazing panoramas.

Hofvijver: Scenic public pondside seating. Stroll waterside Lange Vijverberg; sometimes, there's a market.

Paleistuin: Behind Paleis Noordeinde, this 20-hectare urban park is a flowery paradise.

De Ooievaart: See Den Haag's most interesting sights from a waterborne perspective during a canal cruise.

★ HIGHLIGHTS
1 Mauritshuis

● SIGHTS
2 Binnenhof
3 Escher in Het Paleis
4 Grote Kerk
5 Haagse Bos
6 Hofvijver
7 Koekamp

8 Paleis Noordeinde
9 Vredespaleis

● ACTIVITIES
10 De Ooievaart
11 ProDemos

● SLEEPING
12 Collector Hotel
13 Hotel des Indes
14 Will & Tate City Stay

● EATING
15 Baardman
16 Dekxels
17 Fouquet
18 Little V

● DRINKING & NIGHTLIFE
19 Van Kleef

Urban national park

Unveiled in 2024, **Koekamp** is the perfect city park. Ponds, pathside canals and a deer enclosure create countryside vibes in the heart of the city centre. Koekamp is a green gateway to the adjacent **Haagse Bos** (Hague Forest). Here, 100 hectares of ancient woodlands have excellent cycling paths, wildlife and towering, shady trees. Together, both areas comprise the new national park, **Hollandse Duinen** (*nationaalparkhollandseduinen.nl*).

Palace of politics

Home to both houses of the Dutch government, the **Binnenhof** is one of Den Haag's most beautiful settings. Overlooking the

---

EATING IN DEN HAAG: OUR PICKS — MAP p485

Little V: Trendy Vietnamese restaurant decked to the nines in Dutch *kabinet* (cabinet of curiosities) style. *noon-10.30pm Tue-Thu, to 11pm Fri & Sat* €€

Dekxels: Asian small plates with Mediterranean twists. The well-priced wine list trawls the globe. *5-10pm Sun-Thu, to 11pm Fri & Sat* €€

Fouquet: Multicourse market-fresh daily menus in an elegant restaurant with impressive service. *11am-6pm Wed, Sat & Sun, to 1.30pm Thu & Fri* €€

Baardman: Beautiful, minimalist bistro with a Mediterranean-inspired menu. Mains swim in decadent sauces. *11am-11pm Tue-Sat* €€

EAT HERRING LIKE THE DUTCH

The Dutch have a traditional way of enjoying raw herring called *Hollandse Nieuwe,* or *haringtje eten aan de staart* (eating herring by the tail). Grab the herring by the tail, tilt your head back, and let the fish slide into your mouth all in one bite. The method comes from the days when street vendors sold the fish whole. A firm tail grip ensured a bulls-eye of slippery, oily snack to mouth – no utensils or cleanup necessary (napkins weren't a thing back then, anyway). The raw herring is freshly caught, lightly salted, and often served with finely chopped onions and sometimes pickles. Traditionally, the 'chaser' is a throat-searing shot of *jenever* (Dutch gin). For a slightly less daring approach, order a *broodje haring* (herring in a bun), but don't expect to impress any locals.

Hofvijver (Court Pond), the medieval palace complex is arranged around a central courtyard once used for executions. Local democracy organisation **ProDemos** (*prodemos.nl*) conducts guided tours (€6) around the area focused on Dutch history and politics.

Palace of peace

Home to the UN's Permanent Court of Arbitration and International Court of Justice, **Vredespaleis** (*Peace Palace; vredespaleis.nl; free*) is housed in a grand 1913 building donated by American steelmaker Andrew Carnegie. Its visitor centre has multimedia exhibits detailing the history of both the building and the organisations within; these are enjoyed via a free 30-minute audio-guide tour. ID must be shown upon entry.

Monochrome masterpieces

Once home to the Dutch royal family, the 18th-century Lange Voorhout Palace is now home to **Escher in Het Paleis** (*Escher in the Palace; escherinhetpaleis.nl; adult/teen/child €13.50/10.50/7.50*). Spooky, haunting works of Dutch graphic artist MC Escher (1898–1972) are showcased here among opulent interiors.

Van Gogh's *genever*

Allegedly, Van Gogh found creativity in the barrels of this *genever* (Dutch gin) distiller. **Van Kleef** (*museumvankleef.nl; tastings Sat & Sun €26.50*), Den Haag's only surviving *genever* producer, offers an introduction to *genever* at its former production site. Displayed artefacts include *drankorgels* ('liquor organs'), barrels tapped by patrons, and Den Haag's first telephone book – drinkers (maybe even Vincent himself) dialled '1' for the distillery's 'moonshine hotline'.

Lisse

Seven million flower bulbs

Keukenhof Gardens (*keukenhof.nl; adult/child €20/9; round-trip shuttle bus from Amsterdam €32*), the world's biggest tulip show, hosts over a million annual visitors during the short bloom season (March to May). A springtime trip (preferably April) is a Netherlands' highlight.

Delft

Vermeer's legacy and famous porcelain

Delft's canals are worth aimlessly exploring – the scenery here feels much more quaint and laid-back than in Amsterdam. Delft remains remarkably unchanged since Johannes Vermeer painted *View of Delft* (c 1660–61) as a heartfelt expression of his birthplace. **Vermeer Centrum Delft** (*vermeerdelft.nl; adult/child €12/free*) provides insights into his life and work here.

Delft's **Markt**, one of Europe's oldest squares, has the impressive **Nieuwe Kerk** (*New Church; oudeennieuwekerkdelft.nl; adult/child €8.50/4*). The 109m-high church tower (steps only) promises panoramic views. Also on the square, shop authentic Delftware at the **outlet store** of the most famous Dutch porcelain manufactory. The independent boutique **De Blauwe Tulp** (*blue tulip.nl*) also paints and sells Delftware in a nearby studio-shop.

Utrecht

HIGHEST BELFRY | CRUISING CANALS | BUZZY PUBS

Petite but packing a punch, Utrecht Province has a fine selection of evocative castles and green nature. Utrecht city is a cultural hub in its own right, loaded with entertainment, great museums and throngs of young people. It's hard not to fall in love with one of the Netherlands' oldest urban centres and, for centuries, its religious heart. Historic Utrecht is also the Netherlands' top university city, with some 70,000 students in term time and a plethora of fun bars and cafes to match. Its 'waterline' location on what was then a major course of the Rhine was both blessing and curse, as two fabulous out-of-town archaeology museums explain. Visually, the city's central axis is the soaring Domtoren (belfry), especially at night when cloaked in imaginatively creative illuminations.

The Stormy Void
Roman remains and an invisible nave

Domtoren *(domtoren.nl)* is the city's iconic belfry tower and, at 112m, the Netherlands' tallest. It forms a visual axis for viewings in any direction. Hour-long guided **belfry tours** *(adult/child €14.50/8.50)* climb steps to the highest accessible point (95m).

Across the square is the **Domkerk** *(St Martin's Cathedral; domkerk.nl; entry by donation).* If you think its shape seems odd, that's because only half the original size remains. Beneath the **Domplein** square, the fascinating archaeological site of **DOMunder** *(domunder.nl; tour adult/child €14.50/10)* goes

☑ TOP TIP

Listen to great stories linked to the central sights on one of the entertaining **'Free' Walking Tours** *(freewalkingtourutrecht. com)* at 1.30pm daily, plus some days at 10.30am. The tours aren't actually free; the guide relies on your tips, and there's a €2 booking fee if you reserve a slot online.

 GETTING AROUND

Utrecht's small historic core is a 10-minute walk from Utrecht Centraal station via the Hoog Catharijne shopping mall. Some buses stop centrally at Neude (p489); others depart from the station's west side. Trams access P&R

sites where you'd be wise to leave a car. Diesel cars are banned altogether from the centre.

Het Zwarte Fietsenplan *(black-bikes.com)* hires out bicycles (from €18/72 per day/week). Subterranean bike-parking garages are free for stays of under 24 hours.

UTRECHT

⭐ **HIGHLIGHTS**
1 Domtoren
2 DOMunder

🔴 **SIGHTS**
3 Domkerk
4 Domplein
5 Museum
   Catharijneconvent
6 Museum Speelklok
7 Neude

8 Nieuwegracht
9 Nijntje Museum
10 Oudegracht
11 Paleis Lofen
12 Sonnenborgh Museum
   & Observatory

🔴 **ACTIVITIES**
13 Pedal Boats
14 Schuttevaer Canal
   Tours

⚫ **SLEEPING**
15 Bunk Hotel Utrecht
16 Grand Hotel Karel V
17 Hotel Beijers
18 Mother Goose Hotel

🟢 **EATING**
19 Heron
20 Stadskasteel Oudaen
21 Vegitalian
22 Zala's

🟢 **DRINKING & NIGHTLIFE**
23 Club Poema
24 Hofman
25 Jans Bar

🔴 **SHOPPING**
26 Hoog Catharijne Mall

🔵 **TRANSPORT**
27 Het Zwarte Fietsenplan

back to the Roman period; lantern-lit tours reveal 2000 years of artefacts left lying where they were found.

Romanesque history is also explored on a visit to **Paleis Lofen** (*paleislofen.nl; adult/child €12.50/10*). The 12th-century residence for Holy Roman Emperors is partly built from recycled Roman wall-stone.

Double-Decker Canals

Kelders and canoes

The city's two most charming canals – buzzy **Oudegracht** and peaceful **Nieuwegracht** – cut right through the historic

Nieuwegracht

GREAT UTRECHT MUSEUMS

Museum Speelklok: A former church full of self-playing organs, musical boxes and assorted mechanised noise-makers from the 18th century onwards. *(museum speelkluk.nl)*

Museum Catharijneconvent: Medieval religious art in a Gothic former convent complex. *(catharijneconvent.nl)*

Sonnenborgh Museum & Observatory: A 19th-century observatory on the city ramparts. *(sonnenborgh.nl)*

Nijntje Museum: Aimed at preschool-age children, this interactive museum is based on the cartoon characters created by local artist Dick Bruna (1927–2017), notably Nintje, known in English as Miffy. *(nijntjemuseum.nl)*

quarter. Both are unusual for their double-decker towpaths. Before Amsterdam was of any importance, Utrecht was a major river-trading hub, and merchants offloaded goods into *kelders* (storerooms) at water level. Roadways built above create the canals' special appearance. Glide canal waters on a kayak, canoe (several providers) or **pedal boat** *(stromma.com)*. **Schuttevaer Canal Tours** *(schuttevaer.com; adult/child from €17.50/12.50)* runs two loop routes several times daily.

Party Time
Weekends in Utrecht

On warm evenings, the restaurants on the twin-level canal sides are full to bursting around Bakkerbrug by about 6pm. Groups of friends fill the terraces of **Neude** and Stadhuisplein, which stay rammed until well after midnight. A gaggle of cafes in Domplein's northwest corner are popular party starters. By midnight, many have drifted to Janskerkhof, where **Jans Bar** *(dejansbar.nl)* and **Hofman** *(hofman-utrecht.nl)* become clubs for dancing until 4am. Another small knot of bars on Drieharingstraat feeds the merry into **Club Poema** *(clubpoema.nl)*, a popular student nightclub.

The savoury grilled veggie bowl has great flavours and textures.

 EATING IN UTRECHT: OUR PICKS

Zala's: Low-key yet gourmet multicourse surprise dinners at fair prices in a classy historic-house setting. *6pm-1am Wed-Sun* €€

Stadskasteel Oudaen: Restaurant, grand cafe and microbrewery in a 13th-century 'troubadour's castle'. *11am-late* €€

Heron: Turns 100% locally sourced fare into seasonal and imaginative dinners. *6-8pm Tue-Sat* €€€

Vegitalian: Two very different rooms for small-plate vegetarian dishes designed to share. *8.30am-10pm* €

Maastricht

ROMANESQUE CHURCHES | TUNNELS | FEASTING

GETTING AROUND

The train station and bus station are across the river from the old centre in the Wyck district. Bus 4 links the stations and Vrijthof.

When taking a train, check in/out using the correct pillar: yellow is for NS trains, blue for private Arriva services. International buses to Hasselt (Belgium) and Aachen (Germany) leave from the station's west side. Long-distance Flixbus services and Flibco buses to Charleroi Airport use the International bus stop, east of the rail tracks.

☑ TOP TIP

The concerts of André Rieu's Strauss Orchestra put intense pressure on Maastricht hotel beds for much of July. If you're not here for the waltzes, avoid the city at that time because there's no room at the inn.

Highly attractive Maastricht has Roman roots as a fort that guarded the Maas (Meuse) River crossing between Cologne and Gaul. It retains religious and historical buildings aplenty and brings a Burgundian sophistication to its dining and a bacchanalian delight to its drinking culture. People here are seen as irreverent by the standards of the Dutch, who struggle to follow 'Mestreechs', the impenetrable local dialect.

The fact that the city is Dutch at all is because of military commander Bernardus Dibbets, who in 1830 refused to accept an ultimatum to let Maastricht become part of Belgium. The city withstood a siege and, for nine years, was a disconnected exclave before the Netherlands reclaimed connecting land (the 'Limburg appendix'). It remains hemmed in on three sides by Belgium and Germany, perhaps explaining why Maastricht was chosen for the signing of the February 1992 treaty that paved the way for the EU and the euro as a common currency.

Saints & Sinners

History and revelry on the Vrijthof

The **Vrijthof** is Maastricht's finest square, with many attractive facades, pollarded plane trees, a grand **theatre** *(theater aanhetvrijthof.nl)* and the small **Fotomuseum Aan Het Vrijthof** *(fotomuseumaanhetvrijthof.nl; adult/child €14/7).*

During **Carnaval** in February or March, the clog-footed *Moosweif* (Cabbage Woman) is hoisted here at 12.11pm on the Sunday before Lent, and the open-air finale party on Tuesday night is again on Vrijthof. For much of July, local-born waltz king André Rieu fills the square with wildly popular orchestral concerts of light classical music. In late August, the square becomes one vast dinner party during **Preuvenemint** *(preu venemint.nl),* the Netherlands' biggest food festival.

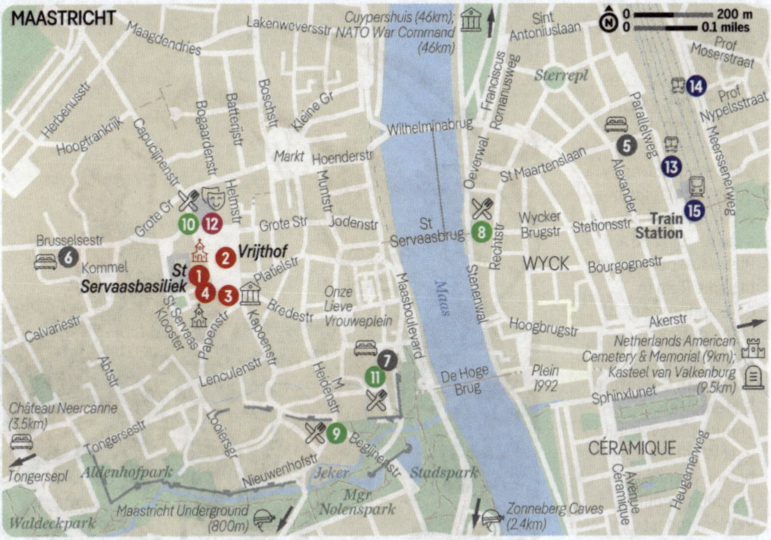

MAASTRICHT

Map legend:

★ HIGHLIGHTS
1 St Servaasbasiliek
2 Vrijthof

● SIGHTS
3 Fotomuseum Aan Het Vrijthof

4 St Janskerk

● SLEEPING
5 Green Elephant
6 Kruisherenhotel
7 Zenden

● EATING
8 Bouchon d'en Face
9 Café Sjiek
10 Pitology
11 Witloof

● ENTERTAINMENT
12 Theater aan het Vrijthof

● TRANSPORT
13 Bus Station
14 International Bus Stop
15 Train Station

At calmer times, come to enjoy the square's cafe-terraces or to survey its gaggle of towers. Painted ox-blood red to prevent erosion, the tower of Protestant **St Janskerk** (*stjanskerk maastricht.nl; adult/child €4/2*) can be climbed for godly city views. Next door, the Romanesque **St Servaasbasiliek** (*sintservaas.nl; adult/child €7/free*) is a basilica museum built over the tomb of Armenian-born bishop St Servatius. His skull is encased in an eerily human-looking gilt reliquary.

Getting Deep

Don't wander off underground

Over the centuries, some 230km of quarry tunnels were dug into the hills south of Maastricht; about 80km still exist.

EATING IN MAASTRICHT: OUR PICKS

Pitology: Grand mansion turned mellow stop for hot Greek wraps; of 15 varieties, five are veggie. Linden-shaded terrace. *noon-9pm Wed-Mon* €

Witloof: Classic Belgian dining: great mussels, rabbit with wine sauce and ham-wrapped chicory. What a beer cellar! *5.30-9.30pm Wed-Sun* €€

Bouchon d'en Face: Old-world place for traditional French cooking, with a good-value set menu. *5.30-10pm daily & noon-4pm Fri & Sat* €€

Café Sjiek: The place to go for *zuurflees* (sour horsemeat stew). Summer tables on the grass opposite. *5-9.30pm Wed-Mon* €€

DAY TRIPS FROM MAASTRICHT

Valkenburg: Gently quaint tourist town with forested hills, a castle ruin and a Pierre Cuypers replica of some Roman catacombs in an old limestone mine.

Netherlands American Cemetery & Memorial: Thought-provokingly vast WWII cemetery behind a white chapel-monolith, 9km southeast of Maastricht.

Roermond: Hometown of architect Pierre Cuypers, whose former home and workshop form a fascinating museum, the Cuypershuis. Munsterkerk and Sint-Christoffelkathedraal are fine churches restored after WWII.

Thorn: Picturesque village that was once the smallest principality of the Holy Roman Empire – and run by women. Almost every house is painted white and has been since the 1790s.

Moosweif (Cabbage Woman), Carnaval (p490)

Various tours run by **Maastricht Underground** *(explore maastricht.nl/en/maastricht-underground; tours adult/child from €11.75/9.25)* visit different sections uncovering charcoal murals linked to the tunnels' creation, Napoleonic history and hiding populations during WWII bombardments. One daily **North Caves** tour includes a visit to the 'secret' vaults in which a trove of the nation's art treasures (including Rembrandt's *The Night Watch*) was squirrelled away for three war years. Another is a once top-secret **NATO War Command**. The **Zonneberg Caves** are wide enough to visit by scooter!

 # Places We Love to Stay

€ Budget €€ Midrange €€€ Top End

Amsterdam
MAP p478

St Christopher's at the Winston € Rock 'n' roll rooms, a busy nightclub with live bands nightly, a bar and restaurant, a beer garden and a smoking deck downstairs. En-suite dorms are designed by artists (some are kinda out-there).

Hotel De Hallen €€ Housed in a former tram depot, this designer hotel has 58 industrial-chic rooms and six loft-style apartments, plus cool art and sculptures in its lobby, lounge areas, restaurant, bar and wraparound terrace.

Hotel The Exchange €€ Eye-popping rooms designed by students from the Amsterdam Fashion Institute. Rooms range from one- to five-star (with concept-driven designs); all have en-suite bathrooms.

College Hotel €€€ Originally a 19th-century school, the impressive-looking College Hotel has 40 stylish rooms you'd never think were former classrooms. It's a celebrity favourite situated 1km from Museumplein.

art'otel amsterdam €€€ Rooms have original artwork and there's a basement public gallery with changing exhibitions; the lobby features a fireplace and library. Located directly opposite Centraal Station.

Rotterdam

CitizenM € A new-generation hostel encompassing modern capsule-like rooms and super-stylish common spaces and coworking areas.

King Kong Hostel € Hip hostel in Rotterdam's party precinct, with female and mixed-sex dorms and great facilities including laundry and communal kitchen.

SS Rotterdam € On a retired 1950s ocean liner, pint-sized cabins restored with kitschy decor are fun (at least, for a couple of nights). The water-taxi station here is convenient.

Pincoffs €€ In an 1879-built customs house, Rotterdam's only truly boutique hotel has generations-spanning art and cosy comfort.

Den Haag
MAP p485

Will & Tate City Stay € Boutique hostel mixing dorms (including one for women only) and a few private rooms – all adorned with different murals. Close to Paard and the Grote Markt.

Collector Hotel €€ Central hotel fully delivering on old-world charm. Elegant decor extends into a lovely Renaissance courtyard.

Hotel des Indes €€€ Built as a residence in 1858, and a luxury hotel since 1881, this is Den Haag's sleekest accommodation.

Delft

Casa Julia € Boutique B&B in a 1920s building. Stylish, comfy and conveniently located rooms, though small, are well-priced.

Hotel Arsenaal €€€ Delft's classiest address, a former artillery warehouse transformed into stylish modern rooms.

Utrecht
MAP p488

Bunk Hotel Utrecht € Luxurious hostel with curtained pod-capsules, digital lockers and towels included, set in a stylishly converted church that's part bar-cafe and part occasional music venue.

Hotel Beijers €€ Beautifully appointed 17th-century mansion with period fittings tucked away in a quiet street a stone's throw from the belfry.

Mother Goose Hotel €€ Highly personable staff add to the considerable appeal of this sensitively reworked 13th-century mansion. The nightlife square right outside can get noisy.

Grand Hotel Karel V €€€ Five-star luxury in a converted historic hospital and former monastery that was visited by Holy Roman Emperor Charles (Karel) V in 1543.

Maastricht
MAP p491

Green Elephant € Choose a 'tiny dream house' to pay hostel prices but receive a degree of privacy in a keypad-lockable box-room with air-con.

Zenden €€ Boutique rooms spread over three city-centre houses, giving a bleached sense of otherworldliness, which is either stylish or antiseptic depending on your taste.

Kruisherenhotel €€€ A 1483 monastery complex converted into a design-statement hotel. Each room is unique, and some are a little small, but the overall ambience is a delight.

Château Neercanne €€€ Majestic 17th-century castle with baroque gardens, a cellar event room, Michelin-star restaurant and five-star luxury suites, 5km south of the centre.

Practicalities

SAMIRA KAFALA/LONELY PLANET

SMOKING

Smoking any substance in bars or restaurants (not coffee shops) is illegal. Since 2024, supermarkets cannot sell tobacco, restricting sales to speciality shops. The government aims for a smoke-free future, with a ban on tobacco sales in shops and supermarkets from 2032.

PUBLIC TOILETS

Public toilets are uncommon, apart from Amsterdam's so-called 'pee curls' (freestanding public urinals) in high-traffic areas. Plan to duck into cafes, pubs or shops (ask first!). Standard fee is €1.

HEALTH

Over-the-counter medications like aspirin are available in pharmacies and supermarkets (which sometimes have their own pharmacies too). Pharmacies and drugstores are widely available in cities and towns. For prescription medications, you'll generally need to get one by visiting a local healthcare provider. Pharmacies only fill medications; they don't write them.

TIPPING

With the demise of cash, it's now normal in restaurants for the credit card terminal to offer guests a choice of tip amounts: 5% is fine, 10% generous. Rounding up your taxi fare is common.

OPENING HOURS

Banks 9am–4pm Monday to Friday
Cafes/Bars Noon–1am Sunday to Thursday, to 3am Friday and Saturday
Museums 10am–5pm daily, some close Monday
Restaurants Lunch 11am–2.30pm, dinner 6–10pm
Shops 10am or noon–6pm Tuesday to Friday, 10am–5pm Saturday and Sunday, 1–5pm Monday (if at all)
Supermarkets 8am–8pm

BIKE SAFETY

In the Netherlands, letting faster riders pass is an important part of cycling etiquette, especially on busy bike paths. Avoid accidents by staying left, signalling when turning or slowing and ringing your bell before overtaking.

PUBLIC HOLIDAYS

Most museums adopt Sunday hours on public holidays (except Christmas and New Year).
Remembrance Day (4 May) is often a day off.
New Year's Day 1 January
Good Friday Before Easter
Easter March/April

Easter Monday Following Easter Sunday
King's Day 27 April
Ascension Day 40th day after Easter Sunday
Whit Sunday/Monday 50th day after Easter Sunday/Monday
Christmas Day 25 December

Language

The pronunciation of Dutch is fairly straightforward. If you read our pronunciation guides as if they were English, you'll be understood just fine. Note that öy is pronounced as the 'er y' (without the 'r') in 'her year', and kh is a throaty sound, similar to the 'ch' in the Scottish loch.

Basics

Hello. Dag./Hallo. *dakh/ha·loh*

Goodbye. Dag. *dakh*

Yes. Ja. *yaa*

No. Nee. *ney*

Please. Alstublieft/Alsjeblieft. (pol/inf) *al·stew·bleeft/a·shuh·bleeft*

Thank you. Dank u/je. (pol/inf) *dangk ew/yuh*

Excuse me. Excuseer mij. *eks·kew·zeyr mey*

How are you? Hoe gaat het met u/jou? (pol/inf) *hoo khaat huht met ew/yaw*

Fine. And you? Goed. En met u/jou? (pol/inf) *khoot en met ew/yaw*

Do you speak English? Spreekt u Engels? *spreykt ew eng·uhls*

I don't understand. Ik begrijp het niet. *ik buh·khreyp huht neet*

Directions

Where's the ...? Waar is ...? *waar is ...*

How far is it? Hoe ver is het? *hoo ver is huht*

What's the address? Wat is het adres? *wat is huht a·dres*

Can you show me (on the map)? Kunt u het mij tonen (op de kaart)? *kunt ew huht mey toh·nuhn (op duh kaart)*

A ticket to ..., please. Een kaartje naar ..., graag. *uhn kaar·chuh naar ... khraakh*

Please take me to ... Breng me alstublieft naar ... *breng muh al·stew·bleeft naar ...*

Does it stop at ...? Stopt het in ...? *stopt huht in ...*

I'd like to get off at ... Ik wil graag in ... uitstappen. *ik wil khraak in ... öyt·sta·puhn*

Can we get there by bike? Kunnen we er met de fiets heen? *ku·nuhn wuh uhr met duh feets heyn*

Time

What time is it? Hoe laat is het? *hoo laat is huht*

It's (10) o'clock. Het is (tien) uur. *huht is (teen) ewr*

Half past (10). Half (elf). *half (elf)* (lit: half eleven)

Morning 's ochtends *sokh·tuhns*

Afternoon 's middags *smi·dakhs*

Evening 's avonds *saa·vonts*

Yesterday gisteren *khis·tuh·ruhn*

Today vandaag *van·daakh*

Tomorrow morgen *mor·khuhn*

Emergencies

Help! Help! *help*

Call a doctor! Bel een dokter! *bel uhn dok·tuhr*

Call the police! Bel de politie! *bel duh poh·leet·see*

I'm sick. Ik ben ziek. *ik ben zeek*

I'm lost. Ik ben verdwaald. *ik ben vuhr·dwaalt*

Where are the toilets? Waar zijn de toiletten? *waar zeyn duh twa·le·tuhn*

NUMBERS

1 één *eyn*
2 twee *twey*
3 drie *dree*
4 vier *veer*
5 vijf *veyf*
6 zes *zes*
7 zeven *zey·vuhn*
8 acht *akht*
9 negen *ney·khuhn*
10 tien *teen*

NIGEL WIGGINS/SHUTTERSTOCK

Schiphol International Airport

Arriving

Located near Amsterdam, Schiphol International Airport – the Netherlands' main airport and the second-busiest in the EU – is serviced by most major airlines. Frequent high-speed trains from the airport's connecting station will have you in Amsterdam in under 20 minutes, Rotterdam and Utrecht in half an hour and Den Haag in just over an hour.

By Land

High-speed trains and a plethora of international buses connect the Netherlands with neighbouring countries. Arriving by car, train or bus is straightforward, with few to no border controls coming from Schengen neighbours. Local trains enter the Netherlands from Belgium and Germany.

By Sea

Several companies operate car/passenger ferries and train-ferry-train packages between the Netherlands and the UK. Routes include Harwich to Hoek van Holland, Hull to Europoort (Rotterdam) and Newcastle to IJmuiden (near Amsterdam). Reservations are essential for cars in high season.

MONEY

Currency: Euro (€)

CONTACTLESS PAYMENT

Increasingly, businesses such as trendier cafes and restaurants in Amsterdam accept digital payments (including credit cards) only. Make sure your credit card or mobile phone are set up for 'tap to pay'.

PAYING FOR PUBLIC TRANSPORT

Tap payments are the most convenient means of purchasing NS (nationwide) and GVB (Amsterdam) public transport tickets. Using OVpay, simply check in and out at the turnstiles into stations or wagons – just tap your contactless debit or credit card or phone on the card reader. Journeys are billed as a single transaction at the end of each day.

MISSED-CHECKOUT FARES

Remember to check in on each ride (each new transport leg in a single journey) by tapping your card to the reader. Tap again on exiting to check out. Failing to do so, you'll be charged a 'missed checkout' or 'incomplete journey' fare (up to €25 for NS transport; up to €5 for GVB transport).

Getting Around

Compact size, flat terrain and excellent rail infrastructure make the Netherlands one of Europe's easiest countries to get around. Train services are frequent and high-speed sprinters keep distances short; regional and national service is well integrated. Local and long-distance cycling paths straightforwardly connect cities and countryside. Endless day-tripping possibilities, whether to neighbouring cities or further out, are standard across Dutch destinations.

DMITRY RUKHLENKO/SHUTTERSTOCK

Commuting Peak Times
The Netherlands is a nation of commuters. Many citizens live in one city (say, Haarlem) and work in another (such as Amsterdam). Cycling long-distance trails or hopping on sprinter trains is a daily routine – plan travel times accordingly for rush-hour crowds.

Cycling
Approximately 35,000km of bike routes across the country make for joyful *fiets* (bicycle) adventures. Routes across cities – and between them – fabulously connect coasts and borders. Most cities are only a one- to two-hour cycling journey from the next.

Train
Trains are frequent and serve domestic destinations at regular intervals, sometimes five or six times an hour. First-class tickets usually aren't worth the extra cost. Consider them, though, during busy periods when seats in 2nd class might be overbooked.

LF Routes
Landelijke fietsroutes (long-distance routes), or LF routes, are the Dutch 'Ventura Highway'. Some are mapped by sightseeing themes across coast, midland and historical attractions. Go your own way, whatever that may be, via the LF app's excellent route planner *(nederlandfietsland.nl)*.

Driving & Rideshare
Peak-time traffic congestion and roadworks make driving a pain. Locals rely on trains and bicycles for every situation apart from missing the last train (midnight to 6am). In this case, taking an Uber from Amsterdam to Rotterdam isn't even uncommon.

DRIVING ESSENTIALS

Drive on the right

 50 **120**

Speed limits range from 50km/h (cities) to 120km/h (freeways)

0.05

Blood alcohol limit is 0.05%

Researched by
Joana Taborda

Portugal

A LAND SHAPED BY THE ATLANTIC

A coastline brimming with beaches and seafood, vineyards
spread across terraced hills, creative cities warm people
welcome you to Portugal.

Portugal's story is one of looking both outwards and inwards. There were times when navigators set sail to colonise other lands, times when the country shut itself to the world, marked by a dictatorship that lasted nearly 50 years, and times when the doors opened to all craving a slice of year-round sunshine, quality surf and a slow-living lifestyle. Tourism drives the Portuguese economy today, and it's easy to see why this Atlantic-facing nation has become so popular in recent years.

Some are drawn to Lisbon's golden light, cast over the capital's hills and cobblestone streets. Others prefer the allure of Porto, with its dreamy riverside promenade, Port wine cellars and end-less tile facades. Some head straight to the coast, to bask on the shores of the Algarve or chase the waves along the wild west coast. Few brave inland, to witness ancient villages, meet the people tending the fields of oaks, olives and vines, or simply disconnect and gaze at the stars. But that's the beauty of Portugal – you get to choose. One day, you could be toasting the sunset at one of Lisbon's numerous viewpoints and rooftops, the the next, hopping on a train from Porto to the Douro Valley for a wine tasting, or driving along the Costa Vicentina, stopping for a seafood feast wherever you feel like. Around here, it's all about going with the flow.

APROPOS IMAGES/SHUTTERSTOCK

THE MAIN AREAS

LISBON
The cool and
laid-back capital.
p504

PORTO
Romantic city
to sip Port wine.
p511

**FARO & THE
ALGARVE**
Beaches, seafood
and coastal trails.
p516

COIMBRA
Home to
Portugal's oldest
university. **p521**

**ÉVORA & THE
ALENTEJO**
Ancient crafts,
vineyards and
rural flavours.
p526

For places to stay in Portugal, see p530

CAIO PEDERNEIRAS/SHUTTERSTOCK

Left: Douro Valley wine (p515); Above: Praia do Camilo (p520), Lagos

Find Your Way

Standing strong on Europe's western border, where the land meets the Atlantic, Portugal's coastline stretches for 560km, but just beyond the dramatic sandy shores lie rugged mountains, schist villages and rolling vineyards.

Porto, p511

Porto captivates with its artistic vibe and riverside setting. Taste the world's best ports or follow the Rio Douro east to discover vineyards and ancient towns.

Coimbra, p521

Home to Portugal's oldest university, Coimbra is perhaps the most visited place in the Beiras, a region of highlands, schist villages and river beaches.

Atlantic Ocean

SPAIN

0   50 km
0   25 miles

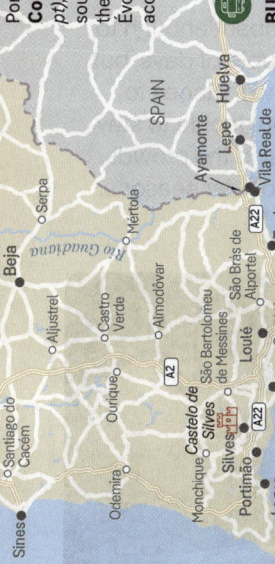

CAR

A car will give you more freedom to explore different regions in a single trip, from beach-hopping along the coastline to touring hidden vineyards, hilltop villages and natural parks.

TRAIN

Portugal's railway system, **Comboios de Portugal** (*cp. pt*), mostly covers the west and south coast, but some areas like the Douro Valley and cities like Évora and Coimbra can also be accessed by train.

BUS

If you're not planning on driving, buses are a great alternative, especially if you want to veer off the coast. **Rede Expressos** (*rede-expressos.pt*) and **FlixBus** (*flixbus. pt*) operate regular trips between major cities and smaller towns.

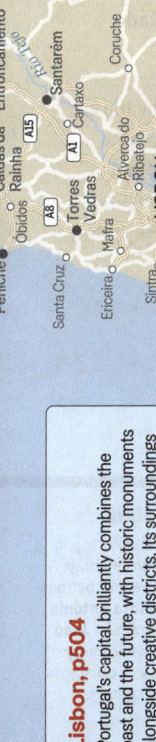

Lisbon, p504

Portugal's capital brilliantly combines the past and the future, with historic monuments alongside creative districts. Its surroundings house romantic palaces and beaches.

Évora & the Alentejo, p526

It's all about slowing down in the Alentejo. Start in Évora, before driving off to explore wineries, meet local artisans or take on the wild coastline.

Faro & the Algarve, p516

Every summer, people flock to the Algarve for a beach holiday. Those flying in will land in Faro, but it's worth venturing further to find other shores, wildlife and seafood.

Plan Your Time

Portugal is compact enough to explore in a couple of days, but there are plenty of places to linger, too, if you decide to stay for a while. To skip the crowds, come in the shoulder seasons.

MAZUR TRAVEL/SHUTTERSTOCK

Mosteiro dos Jerónimos (p504), Lisbon

A Capital Roundup

● Begin your trip in **Lisbon** (p504), taking in the capital's sights. Choose between historic monuments including the **Mosteiro dos Jerónimos** (p504) or modern art hubs such as the **Fundação Calouste Gulbenkian** (p507), but don't miss a chance to sample a *pastel de nata* (custard tart) at a local **pastelaria** (p506).

● As the sun sets, head to the riverside or brave the hills to capture the pink-hued skies from one of the city's numerous *miradouros* (viewpoints; p506) before settling down for a **fado show** (p507).

● A day or two later, end the trip in style by hopping on a train to the city's outskirts, opting between **Sintra**'s (p508) romantic palaces and the urban beaches of **Cascais** (p508).

SEASONAL HIGHLIGHTS

Summers are the busiest here, and there are plenty of beaches, but spring and autumn can be just as nice for wine tasting, hikes and quirky folk festivals.

FEBRUARY

Portugal's **Carnaval** features much merrymaking. Places such as Loulé and Torres Vedras have the largest parades, but villages like Podence have quirkier ancient rites, with devilish-looking characters taking over their streets.

MAY

University students in Coimbra celebrate graduation with a bang by throwing a nine-day-long street party for **Queima das Fitas** (p521).

JUNE

Lisbon and Porto join forces to celebrate their respective patron saints, **Santo António** (p504) and **São João** (p511), while music festivals kick off across the country.

A Week of Highlights

● When you feel like you've seen it all in Lisbon, take the train or bus to **Coimbra** (p521), where students roam the streets in black capes. Visit the country's oldest university, **Universidade de Coimbra** (p522), wander between **monasteries** (p521) and, if you can, stick around to hear the city's **unique fado style** (p523).

● Then continue north on the railway towards **Aveiro** (p524). Art Nouveau buildings line this city's canals, which can be explored on a *moliceiro* boat.

● End your trip in **Porto** (p511), admiring tile facades, touring Port wine cellars along the river, and tucking into a hearty forkful of *francesinha* sandwich. Take a short day trip to the **Douro Valley** (p515), then return to Porto to fly back home.

Slow-Paced Adventure

● From Lisbon, travel down south, following the west coast. Stop at **Vila Nova de Milfontes** (p529) for a swim or a surf lesson, before continuing towards **Lagos** (p519), a small town in the Algarve famous for its caves and award-winning beaches. Then drive east to **Faro** (p516), taking time to explore its surroundings, which include the **Parque Natural da Ria Formosa** (p517), a haven for flamingos and dolphins.

● Next, head to **Mértola** (p529), a riverside town where Islamic ruins stand alongside a medieval castle. Spend an evening around **Barragem de Alqueva** (p527), swimming in river beaches, sipping wine and gazing at the stars, before making your way to **Évora** (p526), home to a Roman temple and an eerie bone chapel. The city is less than two hours from the capital, making it easy to close the loop.

AUGUST
The Minho's most spectacular festival, **Romaria de Nossa Senhora d'Agonia** (p515) in Viana do Castelo, brings fireworks and lively parades with people dressed in folk costumes or sporting giant papier-mâché heads.

SEPTEMBER
The **grape harvest** begins, and the country's major wine regions, the Douro Valley and the Alentejo, offer plenty of opportunities to get in on the action.

NOVEMBER
The smell of roasted chestnuts lingers in the air as the rainy days start to creep in. Marvão celebrates with a **chestnut festival** (p526), and around Vidigueira, *vinho de talha* is poured during the **Amphora Wine Day** (p526).

DECEMBER
With **Christmas** around the corner, towns light up with holiday decorations, and Óbidos' castle becomes even more magical. Fireworks usher in the new year and snow begins to fall around Serra da Estrela.

Lisbon

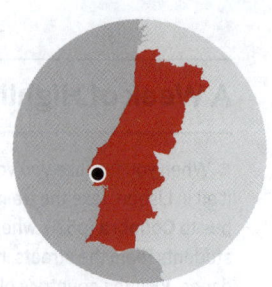

ANCIENT HISTORY | MAGICAL SUNSETS | CREATIVE EDGE

GETTING AROUND

You can explore most of Lisbon on foot, but be ready to encounter a number of hills (some of which you can skip by tram or funicular). The metro *(metrolisboa.pt)* links the city's main districts, with buses *(carrismetropolitana. pt)* covering the remaining outskirts, so there's no need for a car. Trains *(cp. pt)* whisk you up to the coast, and ferries *(ttsl.pt)* cover the river districts. Cycling is best in flatter areas like Belém and Parque das Nações.

☑ **TOP TIP**

From film festivals and book fairs to art exhibits and outdoor concerts, Lisbon is a living cultural hub. June is the busiest month, with locals hitting the streets to celebrate **Santo António**. The whole city is in party mode, with the highlight being the evening of 13 June.

Lisbon may look effortlessly charming today, with its photo-worthy tiled facades, viewpoints scattered across its hills, and flaky custard tarts that melt in the mouth. But it wasn't always like this. The Portuguese capital has seen the rise and fall of empires like the Romans and the Moors, withstood a tragic earthquake that ravaged much of its city centre, and suffered a dictatorship that shook people to their core. It's an emotional backlash that's still heard in the lyrics of fado, the city's traditional melancholic song. However popular Lisbon has become, its roots remain humble. This is a city where past and future coexist, artisans share space with young, up-and-coming designers, and the remaining century-old *pastelarias* (pastry and cake shops) are joined by modern fine-dining halls. In Lisbon, simple pleasures like witnessing the sunset are always worthy of a toast.

A City of Layers

Uncover 2500-plus years of history

As one of the oldest cities in Europe, Lisbon has been through a lot. For a quick history recap, visit **Lisboa Story Centre** *(lisboastorycentre.pt; adult/child €7.50/3.50)*. If you'd rather see what's left today, head to Alfama to find the ruins of a 1st-century-CE outdoor theatre at the **Museu do Teatro Romano** *(ruins free, museum €3)*, before wandering through the district's narrow lanes leading to **Sé de Lisboa** *(sedelisboa.pt; adult/child €7/5)*, a church built in 1150 on the site of a mosque and restored in the 1930s, or hike to **Castelo de São Jorge** *(castelodesaojorge.pt; adult/child €15/free)*, a partly restored mid-11th-century fortress with superb views over the city.

Then jump forward to the 1600s, when Portugal was at the height of its colonial rule, erecting monumental buildings like the **Mosteiro dos Jerónimos** *(museusemonumentos. pt; adult/child €18/free)* and **Torre de Belém** (closed for renovations at the time of writing), now UNESCO-listed sites. But perhaps the most memorable event in Lisbon's history is

LISBON

HIGHLIGHTS
1 Castelo de São Jorge
2 Sé de Lisboa

SIGHTS
3 Convento do Carmo & Museu Arqueológico
4 Largo das Portas do Sol
5 Lisboa Story Centre
6 Miradouro da Graça
7 Miradouro de Santa Catarina
8 Mosteiro dos Jerónimos
9 Museu de Arte Contemporânea MAC/CCB
10 Museu de Arte, Arquitetura e Tecnologia (MAAT)
11 Museu do Fado
12 Museu do Teatro Romano
13 Pink Street
14 Quake
15 Torre de Belém

SLEEPING
16 Home Lisbon Hostel
17 Patio São Vicente Guest Houses

EATING
18 Canalha
19 Confeitaria Nacional
20 É Um Restaurante
21 Manteigaria
22 O Trevo
23 Pastéis de Belém
24 Tasca Zé dos Cornos

DRINKING & NIGHTLIFE
25 Finalmente

ENTERTAINMENT
26 O Corrido

SHOPPING
27 Casa Pereira da Conceição
28 Chapelaria Azevedo Rua
29 Livraria Bertrand
30 Luvaria Ulisses
31 Manteigaria Silva

RIDING LISBON'S TRAMS WITH MINIMAL IMPACT

Carris' yellow trams are ubiquitous in Lisbon's historic centre. Riding them has become such a must-do that travellers often mistake them for tourist rides. **28E** is the most popular, but it's also the locals' only public transport for getting across town from Alfama. Hop on the 28E outside the rush hour or later in the evening – the route is just as enchanting at nightfall. If your time to travel around is tight, look for alternatives – same experience, but slightly different itineraries. Tram **12E** travels to and from Martim Moniz via Alfama's viewpoints and the Sé cathedral, while tram **25E** connects Praça da Figueira to Campo de Ourique (Prazeres) via Cais do Sodré and Santos.

Pastéis de Belém

the Great Earthquake of 1755. Feel the earth shake beneath you again in the immersive room at **Quake** (*lisbonquake. com; adult/child €29/21*), or stand beneath the roofless Gothic church, **Convento do Carmo** (*museuarqueologicodocarmo.pt; adult/child €7/free*) for a quiet reminder of that shocking day.

Sweet Tooth, Much?

Pastries and sweet liquor

Even in the alternative Lisbon of Yorgos Lanthimos' film *Poor Things*, eating a *pastel de nata* (custard tart) is a must-have experience. **Pastéis de Belém** (*pasteisdebelem.pt*) has held the original (and very secret) recipe since its creation in 1837 by monks at Mosteiro dos Jerónimos. But modern versions like **Manteigaria** (*manteigaria.com*) are a close contender. For a bigger sweet spread, hit the city's famous *pastelarias* like **Pastelaria Versailles** (*grupoversailles.pt*) or **Confeitaria Nacional** (*confeitarianacional.com*). And if you want a post-meal tipple, don't miss the *ginjinha* (sour-cherry liqueur) bars around Rossio.

A View to Remember

Capture Lisbon's magical sunsets

More than a lookout, *miradouros* are Lisbon's official gathering spots. Just before the sun sets, you'll see people flock to **Miradouro de Santa Catarina** near Bairro Alto to toast the day away or up to **Miradouro da Graça** (reached via a funicular) for a drink at the neighbourhood's kiosk. Meanwhile, Alfama's viewpoints are more like photo-ops, with **Largo das Portas do Sol** earning you that typical postcard view of terracotta roofs backed by the shimmering Rio Tejo while tram 28 whisks past on the opposite side.

Painting the Town Red
Popular nightlife districts

Kick off your night out in Lisbon at **Bairro Alto**, the city's party district. Space is tight, so you'll most likely wind up standing outside with a drink in hand, hopping from door to door. Alternatively, head to **Cais do Sodré**, where you'll find the infamous **Pink Street** (officially Rua Nova do Carvalho), flanked by several bars, and hit the remaining clubs here or around **Cais do Gás**. If you're looking for a drag show, try **Finalmente** *(finalmenteclub.com; daily shows 3am)* near Príncipe Real – the city's first gay nightclub, open since 1976.

The Calling of Fado
Learn about Portugal's popular urban song

Fado's roots run deep in Lisbon's old quarters, Alfama and Mouraria. This sorrowful music genre went from working-class entertainment to a famous world-music genre in what feels like a heartbeat. Learn about its nuanced history at the **Museu do Fado** *(museudofado.pt; adult/child €5/free)*, catch a live show at **O Corrido** *(ocorrido.com)* or watch the queen of fado, Amália Rodrigues (1920–99), resurrected on stage at **Ah Amália** *(ah-amalia.pt; adult/child €20/17)* through a life-size hologram.

Where Art Lives On
Ancient crafts and modern-art hubs

You could spend a whole day hopping between the city's end-less art spaces, from the classic **Museu Nacional de Arte Antiga** *(museudearteantiga.pt; adult/child €10/free)*, holding Hieronymus Bosch's *Temptations of St Anthony*, to Belém's contemporary-focused museums, including the **MAC/CCB** *(ccb.pt/macccb; adult/child €15/12)*, with a permanent 20th-century collection, and the **MAAT** *(maat.pt; adult/child €15/free)*, with rotating art-meets-tech exhibits.

Street art thrives in districts like **Graça** and **Marvila**, but also underground across the city's metro stations. Contemporary architecture stands out in places like the **Fundação Calouste Gulbenkian** *(gulbenkian.pt; adult/child from €8/free)*, home to two art museums and a beloved free urban park.

LISBON'S BEST HISTORIC SHOPS

Chapelaria Azevedo Rua: The oldest hat-maker in Portugal, in business since 1886.

Luvaria Ulisses: This shop sells custom-made gloves at Rua do Carmo. Its tiny space welcomes one client at a time.

Casa Pereira da Conceição: Go for the decor and architecture, stay for the scent of freshly ground coffee. For both connoisseurs and first-timers.

Livraria Bertrand: The world's oldest in-business bookshop, in Rua Garrett since 1773, is a must-stop for bookworms and history buffs.

Manteigaria Silva: A family-owned grocery shop and one of the top places to buy *bacalhau* (salted cod) and other delicacies.

 EATING IN LISBON: OUR PICKS

É um Restaurante: A project by Crescer, this casual fine-dining restaurant trains and hires unhoused people. *12.30-3pm & 7-10pm Tue-Sat* €€

Tasca Zé dos Cornos: Family-owned Portuguese *tasca* (tavern), where space is tight and sharing tables is the norm. Walk-ins only. *noon-4pm Tue-Sat* €

Canalha: Award-winning chef João Rodrigues mixes the homely environment of a traditional *tasca* with a modern-cuisine menu. *12.30-11pm* €€

O Trevo: Home to Lisbon's (allegedly) best *bifana* (pork sandwich), this corner spot has a mix of tourists and regulars. *7am-10pm Mon-Sat* €

Beyond Lisbon

Travel beyond the capital and you'll stumble upon picturesque coastal towns, World Heritage–listed monasteries and medieval villages.

Places

Cascais p508
Sintra p508
Setúbal p509

GETTING AROUND

Trains whisk you from Lisbon's Cais do Sodré station to Estoril and Cascais, and from Rossio station to Sintra. Check **Comboios de Portugal** *(cp.pt)* for schedules. Tomar can also be reached by rail via Santa Apolónia. For places around Setúbal, you're best off getting a bus from Sete Rios station run by **Carris Metropolitana** *(carrismetropolitana. pt)* or **Rede Expressos** *(rede-expressos.pt)*.

Set off on a day trip or pack up for a week-long adventure across Lisbon's outskirts. You could hit the Portuguese Riviera, a trio of coastal towns to the west of the city stretching from Estoril and Cascais to Sintra, where pristine golden beaches meet romantic palaces less than an hour away. Alternatively, head south across the Rio Tejo to find wilder sandy stretches, hiking trails and wildlife-spotting opportunities, or venture further north where ancient Knights Templar routes and world-famous pilgrimage spots merge with modern surfing hubs, including Nazaré with its record-breaking waves. Whichever direction you choose, you're bound to find something that will captivate you.

Cascais · TIME FROM LISBON: 40MIN

Seaside promenade, beaches and gelato

Portuguese royalty set the trend of holidaying in Cascais long ago. Today, this coastal town remains pretty posh with its seaside manors (some turned into hotels), and curated museums clustered around the **Bairro dos Museus** *(bairrodosmuseus. cascais.pt; from €5, 24hr pass €15)*, the museum quarter. It's the last stop on the train line from Cais do Sodré, with a string of beaches to choose from.

Hot summer days call for ice cream at **Santini** *(santini.pt)*, before riding the seaside promenade towards the dramatic cliff formation of **Boca do Inferno** (Mouth of Hell). You can rent electric scooters or bikes at the **Mobi Cascais** *(mobi.cascais .pt/geral/quiosques-mobicascais)* kiosk inside the train station. If you stick around for lunch, Rua Afonso Sanches (aka **Rua Amarela**) has a stretch of restaurants to pick from.

Sintra · TIME FROM LISBON: 40MIN

Romantic monuments and misty trails

Most of Sintra's romantic palaces and the top-of-the-hill Moorish castle are shrouded in urban legends and ghost stories. A guided full-moon hike with **O Caminheiro de Sintra** *(miguelboim.com; from €14)* reveals the town's mystical charm. If, however, you're here at daylight, you have time to wander through its monuments.

Palácio Nacional da Pena, Sintra

From Sintra's train station, follow the trail along Volta do Duche towards **Palácio Nacional de Sintra** *(parquesdesintra. pt; adult/child €13/10)*. Visit this former royal palace recognised by its striking conical chimneys, then stop by **Casa Piriquita** *(piriquita.pt)* for a mandatory pastry – the pillow-shaped *travesseiros,* filled with egg and almond cream, are the speciality – and finish with a tour around **Quinta da Regaleira** *(regaleira.pt; adult/child €15/10),* a neo-Manueline villa and gardens where a 27m initiation well draws the crowds. Alternatively, tick off the big-hitters, the **Palácio Nacional da Pena** *(adult/child €20/18),* which looks straight out of a fairy tale with its bright yellow walls emerging from the mountains, and the 10th-century **Castelo dos Mouros** *(adult/child €12/10),* with battlements high enough to take in the whole town. You can reach both via bus 434 or by hailing a taxi/tuk-tuk from the station to the top of the hill. Buy tickets at *bilheteira.parquesdesintra.pt.*

Setúbal

TIME FROM LISBON: **1HR**

Market feasts, dolphins and sandy shores

The greasy aroma of *choco frito* (deep-fried cuttlefish), Setúbal's signature dish, lingers through the streets at lunchtime. Many restaurants pick their fresh catch from **Mercado do Livramento** *(mornings only, closed Mon),* where you can also stock up on the region's creamy cheese and sweet Moscatel wine. A small estuary surrounds the city, where you can spot dolphins (boat trips depart from the marina). Further west is **Serra da Arrábida**, home to paradisiacal beaches and numerous mountain trails *(arrabidatrails.com).*

BEST BEACHES NEAR LISBON

Praia do Meco: Between Sesimbra and Costa da Caparica, this beach comes with a separate nudist area.

Praia da Adraga: A secluded beach on Sintra's coast with its own seafood restaurant.

Praia Tróia-Mar: Take the ferry from Setúbal to Tróia to reach this sandy stretch.

Portinho da Arrábida: Crystal-clear waters, a quiet bay and nearby restaurants make this one of Arrábida's best beaches.

Praia da Foz do Arelho: A lagoon meets the sea at this beach near Óbidos, popular with families and windsurfers.

Praia de Carcavelos: Surfers love this beach along the Cascais line.

Praia da Morena: There's sand as far as the eye can see at this Costa da Caparica favourite.

EATING AROUND LISBON: BEST SEAFOOD

Azenhas do Mar: Restaurant perched above Azenhas do Mar saltwater pool, with plenty of seafood dishes and local wines. *12.30-10pm* €€

Casa Santiago: Busy restaurant famous for Setúbal's signature dish, *choco frito. 11.30am-3pm & 6-9.45pm Mon-Sat* €€

Casa Mateus: Restaurant in the centre of Sesimbra for seafood aficionados. Make reservations. *12.30-3pm & 7-10pm Tue-Sun (dinner only Tue)* €€

Taberna do Ganhão: Go for the appetisers with a cold beer and look out on lovely Prainha beach in Baleal. *3-10pm Mon-Sat* €€

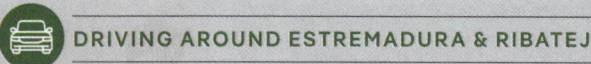

DRIVING AROUND ESTREMADURA & RIBATEJO

Take on medieval castles, sacred landmarks and a surfing hot spot on this road trip around Estremadura and Ribatejo.

START	END	LENGTH
Óbidos	Tomar	127km; 5 hours

Drive along the west coast, beginning in the medieval town of ❶ **Óbidos**, where bookshops take over every corner and sour-cherry liqueur is poured in a chocolate cup. While Rua Direita gets all the traction, especially during festive seasons, it's worth climbing up the battlements to look over the maze of whitewashed houses.

Continue to ❷ **Nazaré**, where surfers have broken records riding waves up to 30m high at Praia do Norte. Watch it all from Forte de São Miguel Arcanjo in winter, or stick to the shore at Praia da Nazaré, where fish sellers showcase racks of dried fish and octopus.

Heading inland, you'll encounter three sacred landmarks. The ❸ **Mosteiro de Alcobaça**,

the stage of one of Portugal's most tragic love stories, is followed by the ❹ **Mosteiro da Batalha**, which steals the show with its stained-glass windows and intricate Gothic facade. Then comes ❺ **Fátima**, home to one of the world's largest Christian shrines. The huge Santuário de Fátima draws thousands of pilgrims on 13 May and 13 October, with celebrations of the apparitions of Our Lady.

End the trip in ❻ **Tomar**, following in the footsteps of the Knights Templar. The Convento de Cristo is the main attraction, with its striking mix of Gothic and Renaissance elements, but there's also a medieval synagogue, a quirky matchbox museum and forest trails to explore.

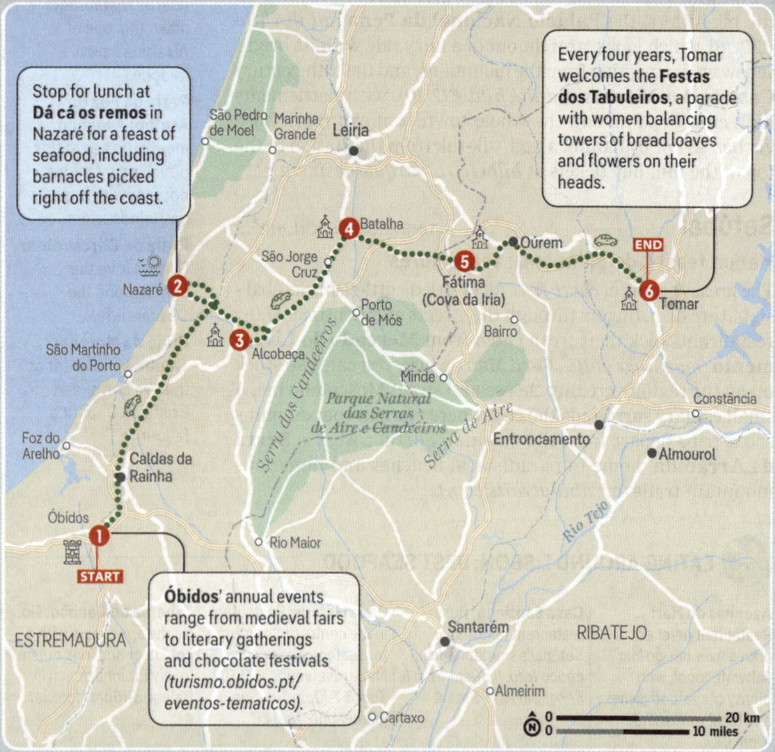

Stop for lunch at **Dá cá os remos** in Nazaré for a feast of seafood, including barnacles picked right off the coast.

Every four years, Tomar welcomes the **Festas dos Tabuleiros**, a parade with women balancing towers of bread loaves and flowers on their heads.

Óbidos' annual events range from medieval fairs to literary gatherings and chocolate festivals (*turismo.obidos.pt/ eventos-tematicos*).

São Pedro de Moel · Marinha Grande · Leiria

Nazaré ❷ · São Jorge · Cruz · ❹ Batalha · Ourém · END · ❻ Tomar

São Martinho do Porto · ❸ Alcobaça · Porto de Mós · Fátima (Cova da Iria) · Bairro

Foz do Arelho · Caldas da Rainha · Parque Natural das Serras de Aire e Candeeiros · Serra dos Candeeiros · Serra de Aire · Minde · Constância · Entroncamento · Almourol

Óbidos · ❶ · START · Rio Maior · Santarém · RIBATEJO

ESTREMADURA · Cartaxo · Almeirim

Rio Tejo

0 — 20 km
0 — 10 miles

BEYOND LISBON **PORTUGAL**

THE GUIDE

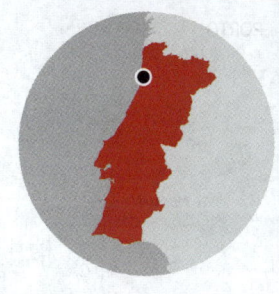

Porto

PORT WINE | ARTISTIC ROOTS | HEARTY CUISINE

Porto is the city that gave Portugal its name and so much more. Its proximity to the river and the ocean made it an attractive place for various peoples to settle, including Celts, Iberians, Romans and Moors. The city grew from the ancient Morro da Sé hilltop neighbourhood to the riverfront district of Ribeira and expanded in multiple waves. By the 19th century, Porto had become a hub for the liberal movement, stuck in a brotherly dispute between Dom Miguel (absolutist) and Dom Pedro IV (liberalist). Eventually, liberalism won, earning Porto the nickname of 'Invicta' (Invincible), which is still thrown about today. This northern city has since forged its own artistic expression and architecture. Locals are known for their distinct accent and hospitality, and for not mincing their words. The University of Porto, among the largest in the country, contributes to perpetually renewing the city's youthful and rebellious spirit.

Hunting for Tiles

Capture Porto's iconic *azulejos*

With its eye-popping blue-and-white tiled facades, Porto makes the perfect backdrop for a photoshoot. The best part is that it's free: stand in front of the **Capela das Almas** with its 16,000-tile facade or step into **São Bento train station** to witness Portugal's history told in a series of panels.

Design lovers can pop into the **Banco de Materiais** *(museu doporto.pt; free; closed Mon),* a pioneering project responsible for safeguarding elements of Porto's architecture, like its iconic *azulejos* (tiles). Or try painting your own by joining a workshop at **Gazete Azulejos** *(gazeteazulejos.com; €38).*

A Trip Back in Time

Explore the city's major historic sites

Wandering through **Cais da Ribeira**, a UNESCO-listed district, you'll encounter some of Porto's oldest sights. Start with

GETTING AROUND

Walking is the best way to get around the city centre, though there are several steep hills. From Porto airport, the metro *(metrodoporto.pt)* goes straight to the city centre. If you're arriving by bus or train, you'll likely end up at the Campanhã station. From there, it's a short metro or taxi ride to the city centre. Trams take you along parts of the coast; buses connect you to the outskirts, like Serralves. Both are run by **STCP** *(stcp.pt).*

☑ TOP TIP

Once a year, Porto celebrates its patron saint, **São João**, by throwing a big party on the evening of 23 June. Locals set up impromptu barbecues outside, paper lamps are launched into the skies, and everyone dances to their favourite tunes, hitting passersby with a squeaky plastic hammer until the midnight fireworks.

PORTO

★ **HIGHLIGHTS**
1 Igreja de São Francisco
2 Museu Nacional Soares dos Reis
3 Palácio da Bolsa

● **SIGHTS**
4 Banco de Materiais
5 Cais da Ribeira
6 Capela das Almas

7 Centro Português de Fotografia
8 Igreja dos Clérigos
9 Livraria Lello
10 Niepoort
11 Porto Augusto's
12 Rua de Miguel Bombarda
13 São Bento Train Station
14 Sé do Porto

15 Torre dos Clérigos

● **ACTIVITIES**
16 Gazeta Azulejos

● **SLEEPING**
17 Mo House
18 Passenger Hostel
19 Yeatman

● **EATING**
20 Borboleta

21 Café Santiago
22 Flor dos Congregados
23 Kind Kitchen
24 Taberna Folias do Baco
see 19 Yeatman

● **DRINKING & NIGHTLIFE**
25 Churchill's 1982 Garden Bar

a visit to the 12th-century Romanesque cathedral **Sé do Porto** (*church free, cloister & treasury adult/child €3/free*), then make your way to the **Igreja de São Francisco** (*ordemsaofrancisco porto.pt; adult/child €10/3*), a church hiding a spectacular baroque interior with carved gilded altarpieces. Next door is the **Palácio da Bolsa** (*palaciodabolsa.com; adult/child €14/free*), where 18kg of gold leaf covers a neo-Moorish-style room. More baroque gems include the **Igreja dos Clérigos** (*free*) with its gilded altar and the adjoining 76m-high **tower** (*torredosclerigos.pt; adult/child €10/free*). While you're here, you might as well pop into **Livraria Lello** (*livrarialello.pt; €10*), one of Portugal's most beautiful bookshops.

Francesinha

Mad for Port & Francesinha

Dive into Porto's culinary obsessions

Porto's most famous delicacy, beyond the namesake Port wine, is the *francesinha*. Some call it a sandwich, but really, it's a knife-and-fork job to tuck into the multiple layers of meat squished inside slices of bread drenched with melted cheese and a thick tomato sauce. Try it at **Café Santiago** (*cafesantiago.pt*) or head to **Kind Kitchen** (*kindkitchen.pt*) for a vegan version.

If you want to sip that sweet fortified wine, go across the Douro to Vila Nova de Gaia, where you'll find a row of cellars offering regular tours. **Porto Augusto's** (*portoaugustos.pt; €15*) does a quick 20-minute rundown of Port styles, **Niepoort** (*niepoort.pt; from €45*) offers more exclusive tastings, and **Churchill's 1982 Garden Bar** (*drinkchurchills.com*) has the perfect views to pair with a glass of Port tonic.

PORTO'S BEST ART SPACES

Museu Nacional Soares dos Reis: Portugal's first public art museum, featuring a mix of sculptures, ceramics, paintings and antique furniture.

Centro Português de Fotografia: This free museum housed in a former political prison displays old cameras and stages temporary photo exhibits.

Rua de Miguel Bombarda: Art galleries line this street in the Cedofeita district.

Casa da Música: Concert hall with an irregular polyhedron structure designed by Dutch architect Rem Koolhaas; guided tours on Monday, Wednesday and Friday.

Serralves: See contemporary art shows in this large estate featuring an Art Deco building, a sculpture park and a museum envisioned by architect Siza Vieira.

 EATING IN PORTO: OUR PICKS

Flor dos Congregados: The smell of roasted pork tenderloin will lure you into this cosy tavern. *7-10pm Mon-Wed, noon-3pm & 7-10pm Thu-Sat* €€

Taberna Folias do Baco: Douro winery set up in Porto to showcase its natural wines paired with delish snacks. *6pm-midnight Thu-Mon* €€

Borboleta: Escape from the city bustle to the terrace of this veggie-friendly restaurant. *noon-4pm & 7-11pm Wed-Fri, noon-11pm Sat & Sun* €€

Yeatman: Chef Ricardo Costa's two-Michelin-star restaurant at the Yeatman resort in Vila Nova de Gaia. *seating at 6.30pm, 7.30pm & 8.30pm Tue-Sat* €€€

Beyond Porto

Terraced vineyards rising above the Douro, lush natural parks and ancient folk rituals await a short hop from Porto.

Places

Braga p514
Guimarães p514
Viana do Castelo p515
Douro Valley p515
Bragança p515

GETTING AROUND

Trains *(cp.pt)* run along the coast towards Viana do Castelo and into the Douro Valley with stops at Régua and Pinhão. Guimarães and Braga are also accessible by rail; the latter is a great base to explore Gerês. While buses take you close to this national park, a car will give you more freedom to reach its wilder sections. Driving is also the best way to cover Trás-os-Montes.

You can spend days lingering in Porto, posing against tile facades and drinking Port tonics at sunset, but there's a whole world to see just outside the city. A train whisks you through the middle of the Douro Valley, where vineyards grow in steep terraces, to the heart of medieval towns like Guimarães, the country's first official capital, and up the coast, where windswept beaches await in Viana do Castelo. Driving further inland, you'll reach the likes of Gerês, home to waterfalls and lush hiking trails, and the region of Trás-os-Montes, where you can still witness ancient carnivals like the Caretos de Podence, wander through remote villages and occasionally hear a different tongue, influenced by its proximity to neighbouring Spain.

Braga

TIME FROM PORTO: 1HR

A sanctuary of churches and coffee

When Holy Week comes around, Braga becomes a magnet for pilgrims. After all, the city has the biggest church collection in Portugal. Even if you're not a devotee, it's worth visiting the **Santuário do Bom Jesus do Monte** *(bomjesus. pt),* a striking baroque sanctuary sitting atop 500-plus stairs (take a funicular). The city also has a laid-back coffee culture. From the century-old **Café A Brasileira** *(abrasileirabraga. pt)* to the bookshop cafe of **Centésima Página** *(centesima. com),* there are plenty of spots to hunker down with a brew – or switch things up with a local craft beer from **Letraria** *(cervejaletra.pt).*

Guimarães

TIME FROM PORTO: 1HR

Meet Portugal's medieval core

Guimarães was the country's first official capital. Today, this UNESCO-listed medieval town still feels kind of frozen in time with its maze of stone houses and a crenellated **castle** looming on a hill. The **Paço dos Duques de Bragança** *(pacodosduques.gov.pt; adult/child €8/free incl castle)* offers a glimpse of what would have been a rich royal residence, complete with Flemish tapestries, porcelain and antique furniture. Later, splurge on modern fine dining at **A Cozinha** *(restauranteacozinha.pt)* or **Le Babachris** *(lebabachris.com),* or kick back at **Taberna Trovador** *(tabernatrovador.eatbu. com)* with wine and a round of *petiscos* (tapas).

Viana do Castelo
TIME FROM PORTO: 1HR

Pilgrimage sites and folk parades

Head north along the coast and you'll reach Viana do Castelo, a city of fishers, sailors and surfers. Every summer, they share their sandy shores with the thousands of visitors who come to partake in pilgrimages like the **Romaria de Nossa Senhora d'Agonia** *(festasdagonia.com)* in August. In the backdrop of nearly every photo of the city is the iconic neo-Byzantine church **Santuário do Sagrado Coração de Jesus** *(templosantaluzia.org).* Drive or hike up the hill, or take the **Elevador de Santa Luzia** *(adult/child €2/1).*

Douro Valley
TIME FROM PORTO: 2½HR, 1½HR

Scenic journeys and terraced vineyards

There are many ways to reach the Douro Valley, including aboard a steam train or driving along the N222. Its steeply terraced vineyards are a sight to behold, whether you're sailing the river on a quiet **solar boat** *(daurum.pt; from €15)* or enjoying the views from a *quinta* (estate) over a glass of wine. A visit to the **Museu do Douro** *(museudodouro.pt; adult/child €8/free)* in **Peso da Régua** is a must if you want to learn more about the history of the region, or you can picture the wine's journey through the tiles at **Pinhão**'s **railway station**. There are outstanding viewpoints here like **Miradouro Casal de Loivos**.

To see a different side of the Douro, head east to **Parque Arqueológico do Vale do Côa** *(arte-coa.pt; tours from €16),* to discover Europe's largest open-air gallery of Palaeolithic rock art on a hike or kayak trip.

Bragança
TIME FROM PORTO: 3HR, 2HR

Medieval walls and carnival masks

Strategically located to deter any curious Spaniard, Bragança's 12th-century **Cidadela** still stands strong today. Step inside its medieval walls to find the **Domus Municipalis**, a rare Romanesque building, the original **Castelo de Bragança** *(castelo-braganca.pt; adult/child €3/free),* and the **Museu Ibérico da Máscara e do Traje** *(museudamascara.cm-braganca.pt; adult/child €1.21/free),* where you can spot a collection of folk-style masks worn in festivals like the **Podence carnival** in February.

Faro & the Algarve

WILDLIFE | BEACHES | SEAFOOD FEASTS

☑️ **TOP TIP**

Consider the Vamus bus tourist pass, including the inter-city Aerobus (from €35 online) or CP Trains Algarve Pass (from €21.90 in ticket offices) if you're planning multiple trips or to travel the Algarve's breadth.

Flourishing as Roman Ossónoba, remembered as the Moors' last stronghold and conquered by King Afonso III in 1249, Faro doesn't lack historical credentials. Yet for many visitors to the Algarve, Faro is little more than a fleeting glimpse through a plane window before being whisked further along the coast. Stick around, though, and you'll find a majestic cathedral, marina-facing rooftop bars and an estuary abounding with wildlife and island beaches.

Doubling as a city and a district, Faro is the best year-round base to explore the Algarve. Whether you're heading east to Tavira, where churches meet oyster farms, to the big resorts in the west including Albufeira, or inland, where small towns like Loulé are proud of their ancient crafts, sweet delicacies and wine heritage, you can reach every part of the region from Faro in little more than an hour.

Faro

Ancient sites and ferry rides

Meander through Faro's old town by passing through **Arco da Vila**, a neoclassical gate. Inside, surrounded by orange trees, you'll find the cathedral, **Sé** *(adult/child €5/free)*, whose bell tower has sweeping views of Ria Formosa. Outside the medieval walls, 18th-century **Igreja de Nossa Senhora do Carmo** *(€2)* hides a creepy yet bewitching chapel built with over 1000 exhumed skulls and bones of Carmelite monks. A

GETTING AROUND

Faro Airport is under 20 minutes from the centre; taxis are usually plentiful. Próximo, Faro's main bus operator, has regular services on line 16 *(€2.80)* between the beach, airport and city centre; buy tickets onboard. Vamus' Aerobus links towns to the west (bus-stop ticket machine). Faro train station, Próximo's bus terminal and the Vamus/long-distance bus station are clustered near the walkable city centre. A large free car park at Largo de São Francisco backs the old town's walls.

loop back brings you to the marina, where you can hop on a ferry *(adult/child from €2.35/1.15 one way)* to **Praia de Faro**, the city's main beach.

Parque Natural da Ria Formosa

An island haven

Encompassing flamingo-visited salt pans, birdlife-rich wetlands, swirling inlets and a handful of barrier islands, the **Parque Natural da Ria Formosa** *(icnf.pt)* is phenomenal. Accessible from Faro, Olhão and Tavira, this nature reserve

COSTA VICENTINA

Ocean-shaved sheer cliffs, footprint-free sands, dune-blotted beaches and surf-pounded shores are only a fragment of Algarve's windswept west coast known as Costa Vicentina. Stretching from Burgau to Odeceixe's regional-border-slicing Ribeira de Seixe, this protected landscape is also a prime spot for hiking. The Rota Vicentina's *(rotavicentina.com)* **Fishermen's Trail** stretches for 227km and has eight one-day sections between Odeceixe and Lagos. All are excellent day hikes, but the final leg between Luz and Lagos is the easiest both in intensity and for public transport. Following a well-marked track, the route ambles atop **Rocha Negra**, a volcanic and sandstone cliff packed with fossils and traces of the Middle Cretaceous period.

is best explored by boat. Ferries take you to the island's sandy beaches in Barreta (aka Deserta), Culatra, Armona, Tavira and Cabanas. Dolphin pods can also be spotted across the waters, with tours led by marine biologists like **Ocean Vibes** *(ocean vibesalgarve.com; €55)*. For birdwatching, join solar-boat tours with **Lands** *(lands.pt; from €45)* or follow the 2.5km trail through the protected area of **Quinta de Marim** *(icnf. pt; €3)*. The salt pans are birdlife havens too, and some are still used for salt production, including **Salinas do Grelha** *(salinasdogrelha.pt; from €9),* where you can float in a mini Dead Sea between May and October.

Loulé

The artisan town

A 30-minute drive west from Faro takes you to Loulé, where you can wander around artisan workshops like **Casa da Empreita**, specialised in palm weaving, or watch *cataplanas* (cooking pots) being hammered at the **Oficina de Caldeireiros**. If you fancy learning the crafts yourself, sign up for a workshop with **Loulé Criativo** *(loulecriativo.pt)*. Other attractions include the **Banhos Islâmicos de Loulé** *(museudeloule.pt; free),* the only (known) example of Islamic baths in Portugal, and the **Mercado Municipal**, with its striking arched Moorish doorways and red onion-dome towers. The town comes alive during the carnival in February or March and **Festival MED** *(festivalmed.cm-loule.pt),* a celebration of world music in June.

Albufeira

The soul of the party

As one of the Algarve's most developed resort towns, Albu-feira has everything you can imagine: all-inclusive hotels, vast sandy stretches and a busy nightlife strip. But there are ways to escape the crowds. Veer off the old town to find wilder beaches like **Praia dos Arrifes** and **Praia da Galé**, hire a kayak or SUP to reach secret coves with **Albufeira Surf Sup** *(albufeirasurfsup.com; from €35)*, or dive under-water with **Easy Divers** *(easydivers.pt; €100)* to discover the **EDP Art Reef**, an artificial-reef-cum-art-gallery filled with sculptures by Portuguese artist Vhils. And if you do decide to have that nightcap on the Strip, there are quieter options like **Connection** *(connectiongaybar.com),* Albufeira's main gay bar, or the tree-shaded cocktail garden at **Libertos** *(liber tosclub.com)* – before midnight, at least.

 EATING IN THE ALGARVE: OUR PICKS

O Recife: Long-standing *churrasqueira* (grill restaurant) in Faro serving chicken piri-piri by the half or whole. *noon-3pm & 7-10pm Thu-Tue €*

A Sereia: Atop Sagres' fish market with a window looking down at the catch arriving, seafood doesn't get fresher. *noon-6pm Mon-Fri €*

Tasca do Kiko: Behind Lagos' boatyard, this tucked-away tapas restaurant has sharing plates crammed with flavour. *12.30-3pm & 6-10pm Mon-Sat €€*

Windmill: Splurge on the three-course Mediterranean menu served inside this romantic windmill in Albufeira. Reservations required. *6.30-10pm €€€*

Castelo de Silves

BEST REGIONAL SEAFOOD DISHES

Cataplana: Arguably the Algarve's most distinctive dish, this seafood stew is cooked in a special pan shaped like a clam.

Conquilhas à Algarvia: *Conquilhas* are small clams pulled from the sand at low tide, cooked with garlic, coriander, lemon and oil.

Arroz de lingueirão: *Arroz de marisco* (seafood rice stew) is plentiful, but this traditional razor-clam version takes top billing.

Muxama: This salt-cured tuna speciality is a delicious, hard-to-find appetiser.

Xerém de conquilhas: Moorish-influenced cornflour dish comparable to porridge; Olhão's clam recipe is most celebrated.

Sardinhas assadas: Charcoal-grilled, salt-seasoned sardines are a summer favourite, especially during celebrations.

Silves

Among vineyards and citrus trails

At Silves' hulking sandstone **castle** *(cm-silves.pt; €2.80),* do as Moorish kings would have done centuries ago: peer through the crenellated russet walls and survey the citrus-scented scene. Sweet oranges can be picked here from November until August in farms such as **Quinta de Santo Estevão** *(quinta-santo-estevao.pt; from €15).* Almond trees are also part of the landscape, with the dried fruit making its way to traditional treats like *doce fino* (almond sweets) sold at **Doçaria do Sul** *(docariadosul.pt).* The surrounding vines, first planted by the Phoenicians, invite you for a wine tasting in estates like **Morgado do Quintão** *(morgadodoquintao.pt; from €42.50)* or **Quinta dos Santos** *(quintadossantos.com; from €45).* Every August, you can travel to another era during **Silves' Medieval Fair** *(feiramedievaldesilves.pt).*

Lagos

Chasing caves, dolphins and sunsets

In the 15th century, caravels embarked from Lagos on colonising missions and returned with enslaved Africans, giving

GUAXNINI/SHUTTERSTOCK

Kayaking, Lagos

rise to Europe's first slave market. Today, boats depart from Lagos' marina seeking dolphins and caves rather than discoveries. Kayaks offer even better access with tours like **Kayak Explorers** *(lagoskayakexplores.com; €35),* often including a stop for snorkelling. And when the crimson sun sinks into the deep blue beyond, there's no better place to be than the wave-chiselled headland of **Ponta da Piedade**. There are also plenty of beaches around, from sweeping **Meia Praia**, a popular kitesurfing spot, to pocket-sized **Praia do Camilo** and **Praia de Porto de Mós**, favoured among surfers.

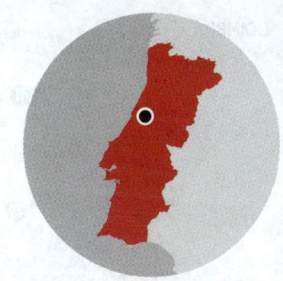

Coimbra

REGAL LEGACY | GRANDIOSE ARCHITECTURE | UNIVERSITY CULTURE

Located along the Rio Mondego (Portugal's longest river at 234km), Coimbra is one of Portugal's most ancient and important cities. Formerly known as Aeminium, back when the town was a centre for Roman commerce, Coimbra went on to become a capital city and residence of the royal family after Dom Afonso Henriques declared himself king. Later, the city found itself at the heart of the Portuguese Renaissance, where baroque art and architecture thrived during the 16th and 17th centuries – the famous Joanina Library is a prime example. Coimbra has no greater claim to fame, however, than its UNESCO-listed university, one of the oldest and most prestigious in the world. The intellectual culture, which has prevailed in the city since the mid-1500s, gave a start to a number of Portugal's best-known literary, music, artistic and scientific geniuses across the decades – and continues to do so to this day.

Sacred Art

Religious sites old and new

Coimbra is one of Portugal's intellectual epicentres, and much of its history began in monasteries like the **Mosteiro de Santa Cruz** *(church free, sacristy, chapter house & cloisters €4)*. This 12th-century Manueline structure was once home to the country's most renowned medieval schools. Come to see the 4000-pipe organ and marvel at the tile paintings and elaborate cloister. On the west bank of the river are the 14th-century **Mosteiro de Santa Clara-a-Velha** *(adult/child €4/ free)*, founded by the saintly Queen Isabel and left in ruins after frequent flooding, and the 17th-century **Mosteiro de Santa Clara-a-Nova** *(adult/child €6/3)*, built nearby to replace it as a tribute to the queen. Near the university is the **Sé Velha** *(€2.50)*, the only Romanesque cathedral still standing in the country, although it's more reminiscent of a small castle than a church, with some clear Islamic influences. A bit further

GETTING AROUND

The city is easily explored on foot, but the old town has some steep hills. On the public bus system, the electric blue line connects the city's upper and lower parts, while the Linha do Botânico goes past the Botanical Garden. You can also opt for the tourist Coimbra Yellow Bus; newspaper kiosks sell daily and single-use tickets. Long-distance trains arrive at Coimbra-B station, while short-distance trains arrive at Coimbra-A station near the city centre.

☑ **TOP TIP**

For a true feel of the city, visit while the university is in session – much of the city's atmosphere is thanks to the student population. If you're into *festas* (parties), plan your trip for **Queima das Fitas** in May or **Festas das Latas** in October.

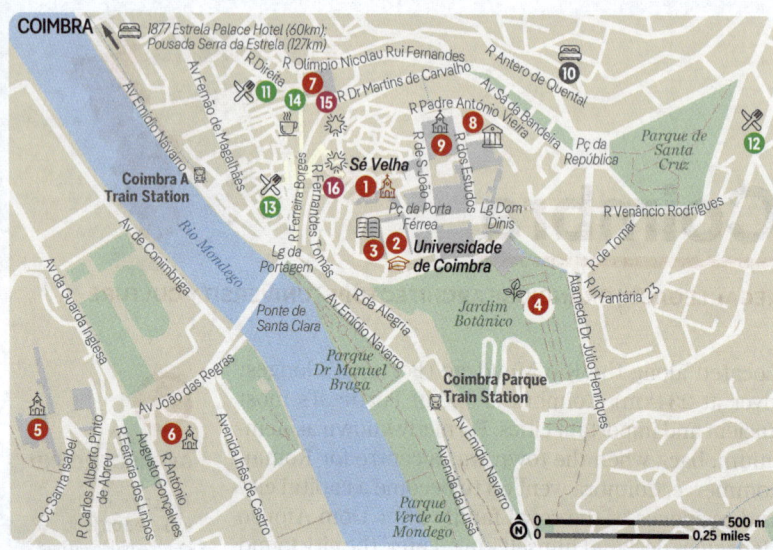

COIMBRA

1877 Estrela Palace Hotel (60km);
Pousada Serra da Estrela (127km)

HIGHLIGHTS
1 Sé Velha
2 Universidade de Coimbra

SIGHTS
3 Biblioteca Joanina
4 Jardim Botânico

5 Mosteiro de Santa Clara-a-Nova
6 Mosteiro de Santa Clara-a-Velha
7 Mosteiro de Santa Cruz
8 Museu da Ciência
9 Sé Nova

SLEEPING
10 AQ 188 Guest House

EATING
11 No Tacho
12 O Palco
13 Zé Manel dos Ossos

DRINKING & NIGHTLIFE
14 Café Santa Cruz

ENTERTAINMENT
15 àCapella
16 Fado ao Centro

away is the **Sé Nova** *(€1),* a 16th-century baroque and neoclassical cathedral that was originally the city's Jesuit College.

A City of Students

Tour Portugal's oldest university

Founded in 1290, the **Universidade de Coimbra** *(visit.uc.pt; adult/child €16.50/free)* is among the oldest universities in the world. While the university got its start in Lisbon, the faculty was moved to Coimbra in 1537 to the grounds of the former royal palace, now a UNESCO World Heritage Site still occupied by the university. The former **Throne Room** is now the Great Hall of Acts, featuring 17th-century *azulejo* walls

 EATING & DRINKING IN COIMBRA: OUR PICKS

Café Santa Cruz: A Coimbra institution, set in a 1264 chapel, perfect for a drink and a pastry and afternoon fado. *8am-midnight Mon-Sat, to 8pm Sun* €

Zé Manel dos Ossos: Tiny *tasca* serving local cuisine in a room wallpapered in hand-written notes. *12.30-3pm & 8-10.30pm Mon-Fri* €

No Tacho: This family-run *tasca* with traditional dishes is a favourite among locals. *7.30-10pm Mon & Tue, 12.30-3pm & 7.30-10pm Wed-Sun* €€

O Palco: Top-tier eatery where everything served is produced within 100km of Coimbra. *12.30-3pm & 7-10pm* €€€

BENNY MARTY/SHUTTERSTOCK

Biblioteca Joanina, Universidade de Coimbra

and gargoyle motifs on the wooden ceiling. The **Armoury** that once stored the weapons of the Academic Royal Guard is now primarily used for academic ceremonies. And the king's private quarters were used as the private examination hall until the age of the Enlightenment.

Tickets also give you access to the **Museu da Ciência**, housing the country's oldest collection of Portuguese natural history and antique scientific instruments; and the **Biblioteca Joanina**, one of the most beautiful baroque libraries in the world, with 60,000 books dating back as far as the 16th century. The library itself is designed to preserve the works, with 2m-thick walls, oak shelves and two resident colonies of bats 'employed' to eat insects that could potentially damage the pages. When you're done exploring the interiors, rest up at the 13-hectare **Jardim Botânico** located nearby.

A MUSICAL LEGACY

Lisbon may claim the origins of fado, but Coimbra also has its own version of this soulful music genre, called *fado de estudante* (student fado). Sung by groups of students dressed in their black capes, the lyrics are typically more hopeful than the *lisboeta* style, covering love, longing and their beloved university, while the guitar is tuned lower to better fit the outdoors where these performances often take place. But if you want to catch a regular session, check out **àCapella** *(acapella.com.pt)* or **Fado ao Centro** *(fadoaocentro.com)*. Some say it was Coimbra's student wear that inspired the Hogwarts look in JK Rowling's *Harry Potter* series.

Beyond
Coimbra

Mountain peaks, ancient cities and lost villages make up the landscape around the Beiras' largest city.

Places

The area around Coimbra is exceptionally varied, so there's a perfect city side trip for every taste. A short train ride takes you to Aveiro, a city of canals, Art Nouveau buildings and sweet delicacies – plus a few beaches not far away. Head inland to find Viseu, where Renaissance art lives on in museums and churches. The city also marks the start of Portugal's longest cycling lane. And if it's the mountains you crave for, drive off to Serra da Estrela, where you can try anything from skiing and hiking to swimming in river beaches, depending on the season. Wool factories and delicate sheep's-milk cheese are also part of the region's appeal.

GETTING AROUND

Trains or buses link Coimbra to Aveiro, while Viseu is accessible by bus only. To reach Serra da Estrela, it's best to rent a car or spend a day in Viseu or Castelo Branco before hopping on a bus to Covilhã, one of the park's gateways. The journey can vary from 2½ to three hours.

Aveiro

TIME FROM COIMBRA: **30MIN**

Canals, dunes and sweet treats

The canals that run through the historic heart of Aveiro have earned it the nickname of 'Portuguese Venice'. Take a ride on the colourful *moliceiro* boats – once used to collect a type of seaweed called *moliço* and now a tourist attraction – past Art Nouveau buildings, salt flats and lagoons. Tours from the **Cais dos Moliceiros** typically run 45 minutes to an hour. Aveiro is equally known for its freshly caught oysters – try them at **Ostraveiro** (*ostraveiro.com*) – and *ovos moles,* a sweet delicacy combining egg yolk and sugar wrapped in wafer-like cases with sea motifs. **Confeitaria Peixinho** (*loja.confeitaria peixinho.pt*) has been dishing out boxes of these since 1856.

With a bit more time, you can tour the ceramic factory at **Museu Vista Alegre** (*vistaalegre.com; adult/child €6/free);* venture further to **Costa Nova**, a beach enclave famous for its row of colourful striped cottages; or hike along the dunes of **São Jacinto** nature reserve, a great place to spot the pink flamingo.

Viseu

TIME FROM COIMBRA: **1½HR**

Historic sites and Renaissance art

Like many great cities, Viseu's story starts with a hero. The city was once the home of Viriato, the chief of the Lusitani tribe, who valiantly defended his people during the Roman invasion. While he lost the battle, the town's Romanisation

ACONGAR/SHUTTERSTOCK

Moliceiro boats, Aveiro

VILLAGE NETWORKS

The **Aldeias Históricas de Portugal** *(aldeias historicasdeportugal. com)*, or Historic Villages of Portugal, is a network of small towns in the Beiras region joined together in a tourism and development project for their unique cultural patrimony. The majority of the villages are fortified, situated on high ground and have a history dating back to at least the Roman period. Among the highlights are Monsanto, Belmonte, Linhares da Beira and Piódão villages. Meanwhile, the **Aldeias do Xisto** *(aldeiasdoxisto.pt),* or Schist Villages, joins together 27 villages built of schist across the Serra do Açor, Zêzere and Tejo-Ocreza regions. This ecotourism initiative allows an immersion into local living, along with access to myriad hiking and mountain-biking trails, regional cuisine, river beaches and more. **Cerdeira** stands out for its creative community.

brought fast development, turning it into an important economic centre. The city's centrepiece today is the **Sé de Viseu**, the 12th-century cathedral sitting imposingly in Viseu's main square, sporting a Romanesque-Gothic portal and a vaulted Manueline ceiling. Next to it, in the old bishop's palace, is the **Museu Nacional Grão Vasco** *(museunacionalgraovasco.gov. pt; adult/child €10/free)*, where you can admire paintings by Portuguese Renaissance artist Vasco Fernandes (c 1475–1542), better known as Grão Vasco.

A countryside cycle

After exploring the city centre, set off on a cycling adventure by following the **Ecopista do Dão**, a 49km trail that connects Santa Comba Dão and Viseu. Rent bikes from **Abelenda Bike Rental** *(quintadoriodao.com; from €14.50)* and look out for the Rio Nagozela beach and the Rio Paiva valley along the way.

Serra da Estrela

TIME FROM COIMBRA: 2½HR 🚗

Winter sports and river beaches

Some 65 million years ago, the Eurasian and African tectonic plates collided, creating the Serra da Estrela, the tallest mountain range in continental Portugal; its highest point is **Torre** at 1993m. When the Portuguese want to see snow, this is where they go. The ski (sledging) season runs from December to April, although your best chances for consistent snowfall are in January and February. Hiking is also popular, with paths like the **Passadiços do Mondego** *(passadic osdomondego.pt)*, a 12km route following the Rio Mondego. Summer is ideal for a swim in the river, with beaches like **Praia Fluvial de Loriga** and **Poço da Broca da Barriosa**, as well as **Cascata do Poço do Inferno** (more famous for the waterfalls and a popular spot for canyoning).

Évora & the Alentejo

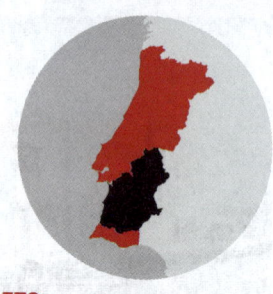

RURAL HEARTLAND | STARGAZING | ANCIENT CRAFTS

GETTING AROUND

Évora is easily accessible from Lisbon by bus and rail. Once there, you can cover the city centre on foot. Surrounding towns like Estremoz can be reached by bus with **Rede Expressos** *(rede-expressos.pt)*, while other places may require two transfers. Having a car can help shorten the distances, and most towns offer free parking.

☑ **TOP TIP**

Summer can be scorching hot, but it's also the time of many festivals. September and October are harvest seasons for grapes and olives, while November is reserved for chestnut and *talha* wine tastings, around Marvão's **chestnut festival** and Vidigueira's **Amphora Wine Day**. Check *visitalentejo.pt* for other popular annual events.

Three rivers flow through the Alentejo, Portugal's largest region: the Tejo, the Sado and the Guadiana. At the heart of their confluence is Évora. The city's strategic position has made it a coveted spot for communities since prehistoric times. The Neolithic people erected menhirs and dolmens across Évora's hills, the Romans built roads and introduced winemaking, while the medieval palaces recall a time when the city was a retreat for the Portuguese crown. It's these historical chapters that have made Évora a UNESCO World Heritage Site. From here, you can set off on endless adventures, taking in the starry skies around Alqueva Lake, the beaches along the coast or the castles dotted across the mountains up north. Take your time to soak in the oak-covered landscape, savour the wine, cheese and black pork, and watch artisans carefully craft textiles, ceramics and all things cork.

Évora

The historic gateway to Alentejo

Évora's iconic site is the **Templo Romano**, a ruined Roman temple dating back to the 1st century BCE, featuring imposing Corinthian columns capped with Estremoz marble. From here, you can access a number of sites: **Convento dos Lóios** *(adult/child €5/free; closed Mon & Tue),* a striking 15th-century church adorned with blue-and-white tiles; **Paço de São Miguel** *(free; open weekends only),* a former palace filled with stunning fresco ceilings; and **Museu Nacional Frei Manuel do Cenáculo** *(museusemonumentos.pt; adult/child €10/free; closed Mon),* displaying the archaeological artefacts uncovered near this ancient city. The striking Gothic cathedral, **Sé** *(evoracathedral.com; adult/child €5/free),* offers incredible views from its rooftop, while the **Igreja de São Francisco** *(https://igrejadesaofrancisco.pt; adult/child €6/free)* has an eerie chapel covered with thousands of bones.

THE ALENTEJO CRAFTS

Portugal is famous for its handmade crafts, some of which are produced in the heart of Alentejo. Arraiolos, Mértola and Reguengos de Monsaraz are known for their intricate rugs and blankets. In **Portalegre**, weavers have become masters in turning paintings into stunning hand-woven tapestries, which can be admired at the **Museu da Tapeçaria de Portalegre Guy Fino** (*cm-portalegre. pt*). Lost crafts like *chocalos* (metal rattles) are produced near **Viana do Alentejo**. For ceramics, head to **São Pedro do Corval**, the country's largest ceramic hub – it seems every door here leads to a ceramic workshop. And if you're just sticking around Évora, don't miss **O Cesto** (*ocesto.com. pt*), which sells a mix of pottery and cork-based souvenirs.

Estremoz

Hunting for art and souvenirs

Travel 40 minutes northeast to Estremoz on a Saturday morning to catch the **weekly market**. The free car park fills up quickly as vendors gather around the surrounding streets to sell anything from fresh produce to leather goods and cork items. From here, it's a short walk to the **Museu Berardo Estremoz** (*museuberardoestremoz.pt; adult/child €3.50/free*), which holds one of Portugal's largest private tile collections. The nearby **Museu Municipal** (*cm-estremoz.pt; adult/child €1.50/free*) traces the origins of Estremoz' UNESCO-listed ceramic figurines known as *bonecos de Estremoz,* while the **Centro Interpretativo do Boneco de Estremoz** (*€1.50*) focuses on more modern interpretations.

Barragem de Alqueva

River beaches, boat rides and stargazing

When it opened in 2002, Barragem de Alqueva changed Alentejo's landscape forever, creating Europe's largest artificial lake.

AROXOPT/SHUTTERSTOCK

Marvão

Just one hour south of Évora, the area has endless draws. Take in the immense landscape from medieval villages like **Monsaraz**, hop on a boat or kayak from **Centro Naútico de Monsaraz** *(sem-fim.com/centro-nautico; from €15),* or dip your toes in idyllic river beaches (with temperatures reaching up to 30°C) like **Praia Fluvial da Amieira** or **Praia de Azenhas d'El Rei**. At night, your eyes will inevitably turn to the stars. The lack of light pollution has made this area one of Europe's first Starlight Tourism Destinations. Two observatories provide regular stargazing sessions *(from €20):* the **Observatório do Lago Alqueva** *(olagoalqueva.pt)* and the **Dark Sky Alqueva** *(darkskyalqueva.com).*

Comporta to Zambujeira do Mar

Surf, beaches and coastal trails

If you miss the sight of the sea, travel west to find a coast sprinkled with secluded beaches and fishing towns. **Praia da Comporta** is the closest to Évora, and its shores can

 EATING IN THE ALENTEJO: OUR PICKS

PREC: This food hub in Mértola doubles as a shop and restaurant serving top-notch vegetarian meals. *9am-4pm Mon-Fri* €

Taberna Sal Grosso: Choose from a range of tasty *petiscos* on the chalkboard of this lively Évora tavern. *noon-3.30pm & 7-10.30pm Thu-Mon* €€

Venda Azul: Waiters rush between tables with trays of Alentejo pork at this friendly restaurant in Estremoz. *noon-3pm & 7-10pm Tue-Sat* €€

Fago: A creative seasonal menu and local *ginjinha* await within Marvão's castle walls. *7.30-11pm Thu-Sat, 12.30-3pm Sat & Sun* €€€

be explored barefoot or on a horse with **Cavalos na Areia** *(cavalosnaareia.com; from €70)*. Further down, the nature reserve of **Santo André** is a prime spot for birdwatching, **Porto Covo** is famous for its small coves, while **Praia do Malhão** near **Vila Nova de Milfontes** is ideal for beginner surfers. **SurfMilfontes** *(surfmilfontes.pt; from €50)* offers lessons and vacation packages with accommodation. And if you feel like escaping the crowds, the beaches of **Almograve** and **Zambujeira do Mar** are great alternatives. You can also explore the entire coastline in one fell swoop by hiking the **Fishermen's Trail** (p518).

Serra de São Mamede
Tracking medieval gems

Most people think of the Alentejo as a region of dry flatlands. But head north, and you'll encounter the mountains of Serra de São Mamede. Here, nature thrives, with lush fields lining the roads with oak, ash and chestnut trees, the fruit of which is melded into local sweets. History is visible in the remains of medieval strongholds like **Marvão**, with its striking castle clinging to a rocky ridge, and **Castelo de Vide**, where a synagogue recalls the town's former Jewish community. The old train tracks that once connected the two villages have been converted into the **Rail Bike Marvão** *(railbikemarvao.com; from €25)* route, allowing visitors to pedal through the middle of the mountains, while **Caballos Marvão** *(caballosmarvao. com; from €30)* takes you across on a horse.

Mértola
The Museum Village

Just before the Alentejo meets the Algarve, you'll pass through a sea of whitewashed villages, rural farms and vineyards. Occasionally, you'll hear the sound of *cante alentejano,* the region's polyphonic song, echoing through old taverns. Among the highlights is riverside Mértola, nicknamed the Museum Village after the network of free museums *(museudemerto la.pt)* spread across town, including a Roman house and the remains of an Islamic neighbourhood.

BEST ALENTEJO WINERIES

Fitapreta: António Maçanita and Alexandra Leroy are reinstating forgotten grape varieties at this innovative winery on Évora's outskirts.

Quinta do Quetzal: Whether you're standing outside or atop the panoramic terrace, you can expect fine views of sloping vineyards.

Herdade do Cebolal: After a tour of his family's vineyards, Luís will produce an assortment of cheeses and charcuteries, all showcasing local producers.

Herdade do Esporão: Wine and olive-oil tastings come together at this Reguengos de Monsaraz winery that houses Alentejo's only Michelin-star restaurant.

Herdade dos Outeiros Altos: With sustainable agriculture practices, this Estremoz winery strives to use indigenous varieties for its organic wines – some aged in *talhas* (clay amphorae).

Places We Love to Stay

€ Budget €€ Midrange €€€ Top End

Lisbon & Around

MAP p505

Home Lisbon Hostel € One of the city's oldest hostels, this affordable option in the heart of Baixa was rated the best in the world for four years straight.

Patio São Vicente Guest Houses €€ Refurbished, independent cottage houses in Alfama with a private interior courtyard.

Chalet Saudade €€ This classic 19th-century manor in Sintra's historic centre has been transformed into a vintage guesthouse.

Wine & Books Hotel €€€ Culture-driven five-star hotel in Belém near Mosteiro dos Jerónimos. One for bookworms and wine lovers.

Porto

MAP p512

Passenger Hostel € Dorms and private rooms above the iconic São Bento train station.

Mo House €€ Tastefully decorated guesthouse that provides breakfast and a kitchenette to cook your own meals.

Yeatman €€€ A two-Michelin-star restaurant and a spa make this one of the most luxurious options in Vila Nova de Gaia.

Douro Valley & Minho

Hostel Douro Backpackers € Owners Pedro and Sara will tell you everything you need to know about Pinhão while handing you a glass of wine on arrival.

Pousada Caniçada-Gerês €€ Exceptionally comfortable, modern guesthouse with mesmerising mountain views and an inviting pool for summer visits.

Ventozelo Hotel & Quinta €€€ Splurge a little and stay amid the vineyards of this estate near São João da Pesqueira.

Feel Viana €€€ Overlooking Praia do Cabedelo, this hotel features sustainably built luxury cabins, good food and a spa to make up for the Minho's unpredictable weather.

Faro & the Algarve

Olive Hostel € Laid-back dorms and private rooms in Lagos with colourful decor, welcoming hosts and a sociable terrace.

São Paulo Boutique Hotel €€€ Five soothing suites, with a peaceful private patio and small pool, make this converted historic home in Tavira a central bolthole.

Vila Origens €€€ Set in Albufeira's old town, this luxurious, Moorish-inspired, adult-only hotel is personality-packed with patterns, tiles and cabanas around the inviting pool.

3HB Faro €€€ Modern, comfortable and upscale, this Faro hideaway has an indulgent spa, rooftop pool and quality restaurant.

Coimbra & Around

MAP p522

AQ 188 Guest House €€ Renovated historical home turned guesthouse with light-filled spaces, comfy beds and an inviting back patio, near the university.

Pousada Serra da Estrela €€ This classic, mountain hotel has been fully modernised, and while its pool and restaurant are great, the views are the winner.

1877 Estrela Palace Hotel €€€ This elegant, carefully restored palace in Aveiro has nice modern decor, rooftop canal views and excellent staff.

Évora & the Alentejo

Heaven Inn Évora Hostel € Choose between a double room with a terrace or shared dorms at this friendly hostel with a cosy lounge facing the Igreja de São Francisco.

Três Marias €€ Between Vila Nova de Milfontes and Porto Covo is this serene country house with 15 rooms, a swimming pool and sauna; also offers bike rentals.

Montimerso Skyscape €€€ Sleep under the starry skies at this sustainable property on the outskirts of Monsaraz. Cycling and hiking trails take you along the lake.

Hotel Albergaria do Calvário €€€ Custom-made wool headboards, exposed stone walls and old millstones dot this central Évora hotel with 22 rooms and an apartment with a fully equipped kitchen.

Practicalities

TRAVEL INSURANCE

Insurance is not mandatory to travel to Portugal, but it's good to have. Consider one that covers flight cancellation and medical care. EU travellers can apply for the European Health Insurance Card (GHIC for UK residents) that covers emergency medical treatment free of charge.

K I PHOTOGRAPHY/SHUTTERSTOCK

ELECTRICITY

Portugal uses 230V/50Hz European-style plugs with two round pins. Don't forget to pack an adaptor if travelling from outside the region.

LGBTIQ+ TRAVELLERS

In 2025, Portugal ranked fourth in the Spartacus Gay Travel Index of the world's best LGBTIQ+ friendly countries. For a country that has spent decades under a dictatorship, liberal ideals are something of a novelty, and negative attitudes may prevail outside the big cities.

VISAS

EU nationals don't need a visa for any length of stay. Visitors from the UK, Canada, the US, Australia and New Zealand can stay for up to 90 days in any six months without a visa.

OPENING HOURS

Banks 8.30am–3pm Monday to Friday
Bars 7pm–2am
Cafes 9am–7pm
Clubs 11pm–4am Thursday to Saturday
Museums 10am–6pm Tuesday to Sunday
Restaurants noon–3pm and 7–10pm
Shopping malls 10am–10pm
Shops 9.30am–noon and 2–7pm Monday to Friday, 10am–1pm Saturday

WILDFIRES

Emerging heatwaves, lack of rain and neglected rural lands have all contributed to the rise of wildfires in Portugal. Check the latest report on wildfire risk at IPMA *(ipma.pt/en/riscoincendio/rcm.pt)* to avoid getting caught off guard.

PUBLIC HOLIDAYS

New Year's Day 1 January
Carnaval Tuesday February/March
Good Friday March/April
Liberty Day 25 April
Labour Day 1 May
Corpus Christi May/June
Portugal Day (Camões and Communities Day) 10 June

Feast of the Assumption 15 August
Republic Day 5 October
All Saints' Day 1 November
Independence Day 1 December
Feast of the Immaculate Conception 8 December
Christmas Day 25 December

Language

Portuguese comes from the Romance language family and is closely related to Spanish, French and Italian. It's descended from the colloquial Latin spoken by Roman soldiers.

Basics

Hello. Olá. *o-laa*
Goodbye. Adeus. *a-de-oosh*
Yes. Sim. *seeng*
No. Não. *nowng*
Please. Por favor. *poor fa-vor*
Thank you. Obrigado/a (m/f). *o-bree-gaa-doo/a*
Excuse me. Faz favor! *faash fa-vor*
Sorry. Desculpe. *desh-kool-pe*
What's your name? Qual é o seu nome? *kwaal e oo se-oo no-me*
My name is ... O meu nome é ... *oo me-oo no-me e ...*
Do you speak English? Fala inglês? *faa-la eeng-glesh*
I (don't) understand. (Não) Entendo. *(nowng) eng-teng-doo*

Directions

Where's the ...? Onde é ...? *ong-de e ...*
Could you please write it down? Podia escrever isso, por favor? *poo-dee-ashkre-ver ee-soo poor fa-vor*
Can you show me (on the map)? Pode-me mostrar (no mapa)? *po-de-me moosh-traar (noo maa-pa)*

Signs

Entrada/Saída Entrance/Exit
Aberto/Fechado Open/Closed
Há Vaga Rooms Available
Não Há Vaga No Vacancies
Informação Information
Esquadra da Polícia Police Station
Proibido Prohibited
Casa de Banho Toilets
Homens Men
Mulheres Women
Quente/Frio Hot/Cold

Time

What time is it? Que horas são? *kee o-rash sowng*
It's (10) o'clock. São (dez) horas. *sowng (desh) o-rash*
Half past (10). (Dez) e meia. *(desh) e may-a*
in the morning. da manhã. *da ma-nyang*
in the afternoon. da tarde. *da taar-de*
in the evening. da noite. *da noy-te*
yesterday. ontem. *ong-teng*
tomorrow. amanhã. *aa-ma-nyang*

Emergencies

Help! Socorro! *soo-ko-rroo*
Go away! Vá-se embora! *vaa-se eng-bo-ra*
Call ...! Chame ...! *shaa-me ...*
　a doctor. um médico. *oong me-dee-koo*
　the police. a polícia *a poo-lee-sya*

NUMBERS

1
um *oong*
2
dois *doysh*
3
três *tresh*
4
quatro *kwaa-troo*
5
cinco *seeng-koo*
6
seis *saysh*
7
sete *se-te*
8
oito *oy too*
9
nove *no ve*
10
dez *desh*

RADU BERCAN/SHUTTERSTOCK

Gare do Oriente train station, Lisbon

Arriving & Getting Around

Lisbon is the country's main entry point. Domestic and international flights arrive at Terminal 1. Terminal 2 is used by low-cost carriers for departing flights. It's also possible to fly directly to Porto or Faro.

City Sightseeing

While you can explore Porto and Lisbon on foot, the metro system makes it easier to travel between districts. Lisbon has a handful of accessible stations, but Porto is better equipped as most platforms are lower.

Watch the Cobblestones

Rainy days can make Portugal's famous stone pavements pretty slippery, so watch your step. If you're travelling with kids, bring a light pram with thicker wheels and pack a baby carrier just in case.

Hitting the Road

Buses and trains take you on a slow journey around the country, but renting a car is ideal for setting off at your own pace. Most cars are manual; automatic transmission cars are typically more expensive.

Driving Essentials

The Portuguese drive on the right. Paid-toll *autoestradas* (motorways) and high-traffic secondary roads (IPs and ICs) are generally in good condition. Smaller, toll-free roads (N or EN) are usually narrow and curvy in mountainous areas, and poorly lit at night. The speed limit is 50km/h in urban areas, 90km/h on secondary roads and 120km/h on motorways.

PANDO HALL/GETTY IMAGES

MONEY

Currency: Euro (€)

CARDS & DIGITAL PAYMENTS

Most hotels and smarter restaurants accept credit cards; smaller guesthouses and some *tascas* might not. Restaurants will usually display a sign outside with the cards they accept. Tap-and-pay is becoming ubiquitous, though some places may only accept Portuguese cards or require a minimum payment.

CASH

Always carry a bit of cash and loose change with you. You might need it for that coffee and *pastel de nata* later on.

TIPPING

While it's not mandatory, some places have started to include a tipping charge. If there's no prior notice, 10% is usually fine, but few Portuguese ever leave more than a round-up to the nearest euro.

533

For places to stay in Spain, see p596

SAIKO3P/SHUTTERSTOCK

Above: Donostia-San Sebastián (p571); Right: Park Güell (p558), Barcelona

THE MAIN AREAS

MADRID
The elegant
Spanish capital.
p540

BARCELONA
Catalonia's boundless
Mediterranean-side capital.
p555

NORTHERN SPAIN
Surf-whipped coast, buzzing
cities, majestic mountains.
p569

Researched by
Isabella Noble

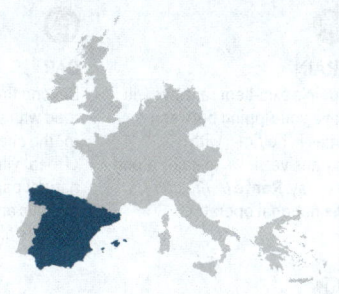

Spain

A SOULFUL, SUNNY, FIESTA-LOVING LAND

Passionate, sophisticated and devoted to living the good life, Spain is at once a stereotype come to life and a country more diverse than you ever imagined.

One of the globe's most-loved travel destinations, Spain proudly combines entrancingly diverse landscapes with bold cultural, arts and gastronomy scenes. Its cities march to their own beguiling beats with cutting-edge architecture spanning the centuries, unrivalled nightlife that goes on until the early hours, and neighbourhood plazas that burst with energetic tapas bars. At the same time, ancient villages – often spectacularly located on hilltops – serve as beautiful signposts to old Spain while often also breaking new ground.

Spain's landscapes stir the soul, from the jagged Pyrenees and the wildly beautiful cliffs of the Atlantic northwest to the charming Mediterranean *calas* (coves) and pine forests. Vast expanses of the country are protected as national parks and nature reserves, where emblematic wildlife prowls the hills and valleys.

Above all, Spain lives very much in the present and every day here is something to celebrate. Perhaps you'll sense it along a crowded after-midnight street when all the world has come out to play. Or maybe that moment will come when a flamenco performer touches something deep in your soul. A sunset stroll along a flour-soft strand as the Mediterranean glows on the horizon could well be the time. And Spain's world of food counts among Europe's finest, whether you're lingering over a *café con leche* with a morning *tostada* or diving into an innovative multicourse tasting menu. Whenever it happens, you'll nod in recognition: this is Spain.

JEFF WHYTE/SHUTTERSTOCK

VALENCIA & AROUND
Spain's culture-rich, arts-packed third-largest city.
p576

BALEARIC ISLANDS
Beachy beauties of the Med.
p580

SEVILLE
Flamenco-loving southern gateway to Andalucía.
p585

TRAIN

Spain's excellent railways will have you zipping between cities in no time, with expansive views to enjoy along the way. **Renfe** *(renfe.com)* is the national operator.

CAR

Beyond the big cities, hit the road with your own wheels for the chance to weave past offbeat villages, explore wild natural parks, road-trip into the hills and discover secluded pockets of coastline.

BUS & FERRY

Buses are often the easiest way to reach smaller destinations without driving. There are few places buses don't go in Spain, but plan ahead and factor in flexibility to accommodate local schedules. Ferries zip to/ between the Balearics plus smaller places like Galicia's Illas Cíes.

Northern Spain, p569

Colourful fishing towns, beautifully green valleys and surf-pounded beaches mingle with mountainous majesty, arts-rich cities and Camino de Santiago heritage.

Madrid, p540

The Spanish capital is one of Europe's liveliest, friendliest and most engaging cities. Come for the show-stopping galleries and architecture, stay for the buzzing *barrios* (districts), festivals and nightlife.

Seville, p585

Andalucía's fun-packed capital is the gateway to fiery flamenco, timeworn white villages, historical cities, fabulous food and beaches both wild and classic.

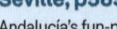

0   200 km
0   100 miles

Find Your Way

Extending almost 1000km from north to south, Spain is one of Europe's largest countries. It's also hugely varied, with regions showcasing distinctive cultures, identities and even languages. Major hubs are well connected; more offbeat destinations reward those who make the effort.

Barcelona, p555

In this unstoppable, richly multicultural city, centuries of Catalan culture and tradition meet creative new energy, Modernista architecture, dazzling museums and a superb food scene.

Balearic Islands, p580

Beautiful beaches draw sun-seekers to the seductive Balearics, where turquoise waves wash onto golden-white shores. But there's much more to discover.

Valencia & Around, p576

Sunny Valencia ranks among Spain's most captivating cities, with Roman ruins, divine dining, regenerated green spaces and an exquisite surrounding coastline.

Plan Your Time

Spain is a richly varied country that rewards slow explorations and (many) repeat visits. The country is a year-round delight, though fewer crowds and usually pleasant weather make shoulder season the sweet spot.

La Sagrada Família (p555), Barcelona

RICHIE CHAN/SHUTTERSTOCK

A Long Weekend

● With just a few days to play with, you'll want to hit Spain's two major cities (linked by high-speed train). You're bound to dine and drink well the entire time.

● Head straight for **Barcelona** (p555) to take in the Mediterranean air on arrival, before digging into Modernista masterpieces like Gaudí's **La Sagrada Família** (p555) and **Casa Batlló** (p558) and picking from an array of top-tier museums. Also spend time simply wandering between neighbourhoods, stopping for coffee or vermouth on the plazas.

● Next, hop on the train to reach the Spanish capital **Madrid** (p540) in under three hours. A couple of days allows time for the **Palacio Real** (p541) and a major gallery or two (perhaps the **Museo del Prado**, p546), as well as a taste of Madrid's famous nightlife, **El Rastro** (p545) market and some flamenco.

SEASONAL HIGHLIGHTS

Summer and spring bring town *ferias* (fairs), but even in winter there's plenty of fun, from flamenco fiestas to ancient cultural events.

FEBRUARY
Riotous Carnaval celebrations light up winter. Sunny Cádiz hosts Spain's most famous **Carnaval** (p592), rivalled only by Tenerife in the Canaries. Badajoz, Sitges, Ciudad Rodrigo and the Balearics also go mad for Carnaval.

MARCH
Teams of local artists create giant papier-mâché sculptures for Valencia's unmissable **Las Fallas de San José**, which involves street parties, fireworks, concerts, cooking competitions and, finally, the burning of the *fallas* (statues).

APRIL
A more sombre celebration takes over during **Semana Santa** (Holy Week), which sees elaborate *pasos* (holy figures) paraded. It's big everywhere, but especially in Seville (p587), Málaga, Lorca, Cuenca, Zamora and Ávila. Sometimes falls in March.

Ten Days to Travel Around

● A slightly longer trip allows you to combine Barcelona and Madrid with another major city, while still freeing up the odd day for adventures further afield. Follow the long-weekend itinerary, then pick from heading south to the Andalucian capital **Seville** (p585; 2¾ hours by train from Madrid) or zipping southeast to lovely **Valencia** (p576) on Spain's east coast (two hours by train).

● In Seville, wander the **Gothic cathedral** (p587) and take in the Islamic-Christian wonders of the **Real Alcázar** (p587), perhaps with a side trip to Córdoba to see the spectacular **Mezquita** (p590) or to Granada for the unmatched **Alhambra** (p593). In Valencia, spend a couple of days wandering the markets, biking to the beach and exploring **La Albufera**'s (p579) waterways. There's wonderful food at every turn on this itinerary, too.

With More Time

● If you're lucky enough to have an extra week (or a few) in Spain, or if you've visited before, pick one of its less obvious regions. Exploring at a slow pace means time for dipping into tiny villages, seeking out secret coves and lingering over lunches.

● Northern Spain is a road-tripping treat. Take in one of Europe's most dramatic coastlines on a spin west from **San Sebastián** (p571), with stops in **Bilbao** (p570), for the don't-miss **Guggenheim** (p570); the **Picos de Europa** (p572), for astonishing mountain hiking; and **Santiago de Compostela** (p573), home to the spectacular, ancient **cathedral** (p573) marking the main end of the Camino de Santiago. Alternatively, combine Catalonia's **Costa Brava** (p566) with the Pyrenees, or meander through Castilla y León's cities, like **Salamanca** (p550).

MAY	JUNE	AUGUST	SEPTEMBER
Madrid's festival calendar is jam-packed, and the major **Fiestas de San Isidro** (p541) celebrates the city's patron saint with parades, live music, *chotis* dancing and all-night fun.	Spain's major pilgrimage sees up to a million devotees join the **Romería del Rocío** (p589) in Andalucía on Pentecost (Whitsunday) weekend; it's sometimes in May. June/July is also the time for **Pride celebrations** in Madrid (p547), Barcelona and beyond.	Visit in August or, depending on regions, September for the start of the **vendimia** (grape harvest). From sherry-making Jerez to famous La Rioja and Galicia's *albariño* bodegas (p575), many wine regions throw a big fiesta.	Barcelona puts on a mesmerising show of Catalan culture in honour of one of the city's two patron saints during the **Festes de La Mercè** (p559) – from *castells* (human towers) to *correfocs* (fire-running).

Madrid

OUTSTANDING MUSEUMS | GASTRONOMY SCENE | NIGHTLIFE CULTURE

 TOP TIP

Grabbing a table on a plaza and watching *barrio* life roll by is one of Madrid's great joys. End your day with sunset and Sierra de Guadarrama panoramas from the viewpoint near **Templo de Debod**, an actual Egyptian temple. Many top museums have specific free-admission days; check ahead.

No one can agree on what exactly the phrase *de Madrid al cielo* (from Madrid to the skies) means. Most likely, the meaning is akin to 'the sky's the limit', a feeling many visitors get waking up to Madrid's crisp mornings. Ask any *madrileño* and they'll proudly tell you it's the best city in the world. They have good reason for this – Madrid has some of the world's best art museums, two enormous parks in its centre, and Europe's largest palace.

But it's the friendliness of its citizens that really makes Spain's capital stand out. This inclusivity has also given Madrid a reputation as one of the world's most LGBTIQ+ friendly cities. *Madrileños* love a good party and Pride is among many fiestas that shake the city till the wee hours. And when the sun rises again in the clear blue sky and the mountain air rushes in from the sierra, the possibilities for the day ahead seem limitless.

Madrid's Historic Heart

Soak up the grand Plaza Mayor

Plaza Mayor sits at the heart of what locals call 'Madrid de los Austrias', which refers to the period of Habsburg rule. From 1619 to 1700, this was the beating commercial and cultural

---

⊚ GETTING AROUND

Central Madrid is mostly flat, compact and walkable, though Lavapiés, Malasaña and Calle de las Huertas are steep. Puerta del Sol is a great place to orient yourself.

You can access just about anywhere within central Madrid by the extremely efficient and cheap metro *(metromadrid.es)*. If you're travelling the long main road that runs from Atocha station to the Prado, it's easier to take the bus. Try to avoid the roads during rush hour between 6pm and 8pm.

From Terminal 4 at Madrid's Barajas airport, the *cercanías* (local train) to central Atocha station takes 29 minutes *(renfe.com)*. From other terminals, you can take the slightly faster metro to Nuevos Ministerios and change or take the bus to Atocha. A taxi from Barajas airport to central Madrid costs €30.

FLORENTINO AR G/SHUTTERSTOCK

Fiestas de San Isidro

MADRID WALKING TOURS

GuruWalk: Platform that recommends curated free walking tours around Madrid's neighbourhoods. (*guruwalk.com*)

Madrid Museum Tours: Tours by licensed art historian Hernan Satt, tailored for art and history lovers and enriched with historical tidbits. (*madridmuseumtours. com*)

Devour Tours: Discover Madrid's fabulous food scene on a neighbourhood walk taking in tapas bars, vermouth spots and local markets. (*devourtours.com*)

Cuadros de la Calle: This free tour takes you around Lavapiés and La Latina to see their best street murals and graffiti. Book through GuruWalk.

La Cara Oculta de Madrid: A macabre-themed free tour explores Madrid's blood-soaked hotspots, from Inquisition tribunals to crime scenes. (*tourstilla.com*)

heart of the city. It still retains its original character with centennial shops located under stone arcades. Five floors up with 377 balconies, this handsome arena was completed in 1619 under head architect Juan Gómez de Mora. While three major fires have ravaged the square – the last in 1790 destroying three-quarters of the space – Juan de Villanueva's reconstruction remained mostly faithful to the original design.

The square is still a major venue for festivities, including the **Fiestas de San Isidro** in mid-May. While it's fun to people-watch at one of the many *terrazas,* you'll pay more for the location. Just north of the square, 1894-founded landmark **Chocolatería de San Ginés** (*chocolateriasangines. com*) serves some of Madrid's finest chocolate and churros, 24 hours a day.

A Royal Palace & Other Treasures

Exploring the Palacio Real and Galería de las Colecciones Reales

A testament to the enormous wealth of Spain's royal family, the **Palacio Real** (*patrimonionacional.es; adult/child €20/13*) is the largest in Europe at 135,000 sq metres. Home to the succeeding Bourbon dynasty, it's a vast baroque Christmas

continued on p544

 EATING AROUND PLAZA MAYOR: OUR PICKS

La Campana: Perhaps the most famous place for *bocadillos de calamares* (squid sandwiches) in Madrid; the queue generally moves quickly. *10am-11pm Tue-Sun* €

Rollo Ocho: Eat Spanish seasonal fare outdoors on a cobbled *terraza* with gorgeous views of Madrid's viaduct. *6pm-2am Mon-Thu, from 12.30pm Fri-Sun* €€

Taberna La Bola: Much-loved bastion of traditional Madrid famed for its *cocido* (meat-and-chickpea) stew. Always busy and very noisy! *1-4pm Sun-Wed, noon-9.30pm Thu-Sat* €€

Mercado de San Miguel: A 19th-century market turned gastronomic hub, with faves like La Casa del Bacalao. *10am-midnight Sun-Thu, to 1am Fri & Sat* €€

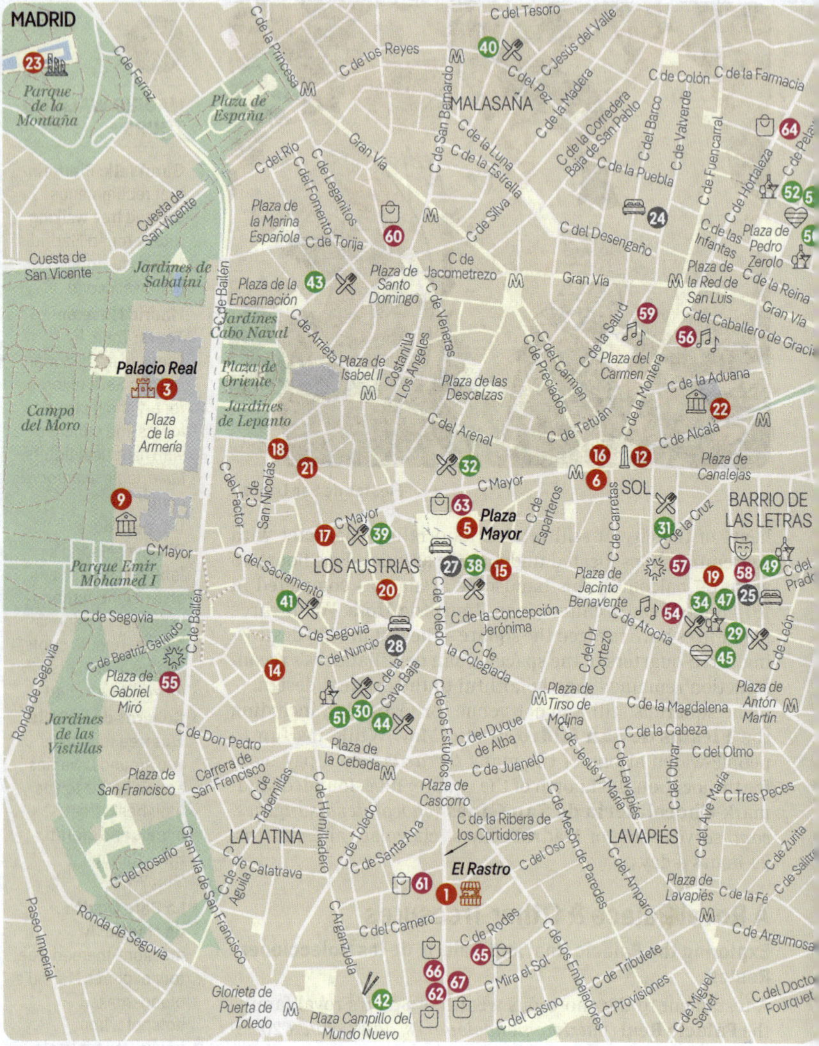

MADRID

El Rastro

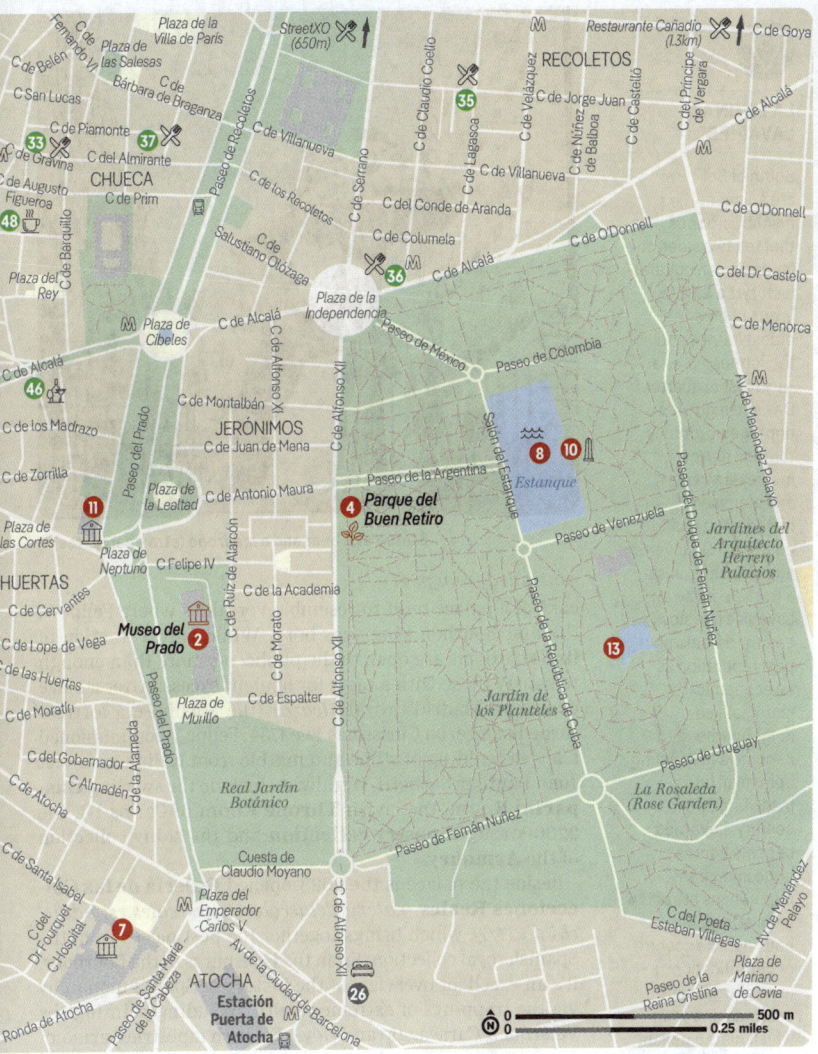

31 Casa Toni	**41** Rollo Ocho	**50** Studio 54	🔴 **SHOPPING**
32 Chocolatería de San Ginés	**42** Shibari Sushi & Grill	**51** Taberna El Tempranillo	**60** Antigua Casa Talavera
33 El Cisne Azul	**43** Taberna La Bola	**52** Why Not?	**61** Antigüedades Palacios
34 El Lateral	**44** Trèsde	**53** YOU&ME	**62** Antonio Martínez Muebles
35 El Paraguas	🟢 **DRINKING & NIGHTLIFE**	🔴 **ENTERTAINMENT**	**63** Casa Yustas
36 El Perro y La Galleta	**45** Axel Hotel Sky Bar	**54** Café Central	**64** Librería Berkana
37 Hermanas Arce	**46** Azotea del Círculo	**55** Corral de la Morería	**65** Siglo 20
38 La Campana	**47** Cervecería Alemana	**56** Sala El Sol	**66** Talleres H. García
39 Mercado de San Miguel	**48** Diurno	**57** Tablao Flamenco 1911	**67** Tienda Hípica El Valenciano
40 Pez Tortilla	**49** Salmón Gurú	**58** Teatro Español	
		59 Wurlitzer Ballroom	

LA LATINA & LAVAPIÉS

South of Sol are adjacent neighbourhoods that tell two sides of Madrid's rich cultural history. **La Latina** is one of Madrid's oldest *barrios* and the former *morería* – its Muslim quarter. Day and night, it's a photogenic journey through narrow medieval streets and stairways, historic plazas and centuries-old taverns and churches. Just a few streets away, Lavapiés has slowly emerged from its past reputation as an economically marginalised neighbourhood to become a fascinating bohemian hub. In the late 20th century, **Lavapiés** became home to large immigrant populations attracted to its affordable housing. The spectre of gentrification looms larger with each passing year, which fuels a defiant community spirit and a progressive arts and culture scene.

ALEXANDRA LANDE/SHUTTERSTOCK

Statue of a bear and a *madroño* (strawberry tree)

continued from p541

cake of a palace built to resemble Versailles where Felipe V, the first Bourbon king, was born. While only a fraction of its 3418 rooms are open to the public, it's more than enough to satisfy those with a taste for opulent excess. After a blaze destroyed Madrid's royal *alcázar* (the Muslim-era fortress turned palace) on Christmas Eve 1734, Felipe V commissioned a lavish building of stone and marble from Italian architect Juan Bautista Sachetti. Highlights include the swirling **Gasparini Room**, the lavish **Throne Room** of Carlos III, the 2200-strong **tapestry collection** and the shiny collection of the **Armoury**.

Beside the palace is the 2023-opened **Galería de las Colecciones Reales** (*galeriadelascoleccionesreales.es; adult/child €14/7)*, which brings together the best pieces from the Spanish royal collection. From the Habsburgs to the Bourbons, it's an excellent overview of the history of Spain's monarchy via the trappings of extreme wealth, including paintings by Velázquez, Caravaggio and Goya, Flemish tapestries, armour, fabulous furniture and ornate carriages. Also here is a section of the city's original 9th-century wall, built by Mohamed I of Córdoba to protect the kingdom of Al-Andalus from Christian

EATING & DRINKING IN LA LATINA & LAVAPIÉS: OUR PICKS

Casa Lucio: Iconic Spanish restaurant on Cava Baja known for oxtail and hearty stews. Ask for its dish of the day. *1-4pm & 8.30-11.30pm €€*

Trèsde: Cava Alta star partnering with sustainable producers. Seasonal Mediterranean menu and wine pairing. *1.30-3.30pm & 6.30-10.30pm €€*

Shibari Sushi & Grill: Manchego chef Jordan makes excellent Japanese fare, to go with selected wines from local bodegas. *1-4pm & 8-11pm Wed-Sat, 1-4pm Sun €€*

Taberna El Tempranillo: Outstanding *vinoteca* (wine cellar) on Cava Baja, with an entire wall of excellent wines, and Spanish tapas. *8pm-midnight Mon, 1-4pm & 8pm-midnight Tue-Sun*

invaders. A combined ticket *(adult/child €24/12)* covers both attractions.

A Four-Centuries-Old Flea Market

Shopping at El Rastro

Every Sunday and on public holidays, Madrid's oldest and largest flea market sets up along La Latina's Plaza de Cascorro, Calle de la Ribera de los Curtidores and Ronda de Toledo. Open from 9am to 3pm, vibrant **El Rastro** features a labyrinth of open-air stalls peddling clothes, souvenirs, handicrafts, antiques and every bric-a-brac under the sun. Come earlier to experience the frenetic atmosphere, or kick back with a cold *caña* (small draught beer) in one of the historic taverns surrounding the market. Several vendors only accept *efectivo* (cash). Start at the top from La Latina metro and work your way down.

Stroll in Spain's Epicentre

Puerta del Sol to Plaza de Santa Ana

Sol, Santa Ana and Huertas are the boisterous heart of Madrid, tightly packed with fabulous shopping, eating and entertainment options. Begin in the **Puerta del Sol**, the official centre point of Spain and a perennially busy crossroads. Now a gracious pedestrianised hemisphere of elegant facades, in Madrid's earliest days this was the eastern gate of the city. The **Casa de Correos** houses the regional government of the Comunidad de Madrid and was built as the city's main post office in 1768. Facing it from the rooftops opposite is the towering **Tío Pepe** sign, long a city landmark. Look out for the **statue of a bear** nuzzling a *madroño* (strawberry tree) at the plaza's eastern end; this is the official symbol of Madrid. Right nearby is the **Real Academia de Bellas Artes de San Fernando** *(realacademiabellasartessanfernando. com; adult/child €10/free; closed Mon),* which has works by Goya, Rubens and Zurbarán.

From here, move over to **Plaza de Santa Ana** in Huertas, where the streets tumble down the hillside to the east. A delightful confluence of elegant architecture and irresistible energy, the square presides over the upper reaches of the Barrio de las Letras. Dating from 1810, it became a focal point for intellectual life. A statue of poet and playwright Federico García Lorca stands right by the **Teatro Español** *(teatroesp anol.es),* where Lorca had his biggest theatrical success with

VINTAGE SHOPS & HOME DECOR

Artisanal and antique shops branch out near El Rastro. The Plaza Mayor area has some intriguing specialist shops.

Antonio Martínez Muebles: Rustic tables and chairs for gardens, restaurants and terraces.

Antigüedades Palacios: Mid-century wood cabinets, tables, porcelain and decorative lamps.

Talleres H. García: Iron and aluminium housewares and wrought-iron lamps.

Siglo 20: Antique lamps, Murano glassware and crystal figurines.

Tienda Hípica El Valenciano: Equestrian shop specialising in riding accessories, customised boots and leathers.

Antigua Casa Talavera: Artisanal tiles and plates from Talavera de la Reina and other centres famed for their ceramics.

Casa Yustas: From traditional flat caps to stylish Panama hats.

EATING & DRINKING IN HUERTAS: OUR PICKS

Casa Toni: One of Madrid's best old-school Spanish bars. Specialities include cuttlefish, gazpacho and offal. *12.30-4pm & 7.30-11.30pm Wed-Mon* €

Casa Alberto: Atmospheric old tavern, where Cervantes is believed to have written *Don Quijote. noon-11pm Tue-Sat, to 4pm Sun* €€

Azotea del Círculo: Order a cocktail, then lie down on the cushions and admire the vista from this fabulous rooftop terrace. *10am-2am*

Salmón Gurú: One of Madrid's best cocktail maestros, Diego Cabrera, serves masterful drinks at this excellent space. *6pm-late*

Yerma in 1934. Stop at 1904-opened **Cervecería Alemana** *(cerveceriaalemana.com),* one of Ernest Hemingway's haunts, or at **El Lateral** *(lateral.com)* for creative tapas.

Golden Triangle of Art

Take in Paseo del Prado's splendid galleries

Acting as the city's cultural hub and green oasis, Paseo del Prado (with its three top-tier art museums) and the leafy Parque del Buen Retiro were granted World Heritage status in 2021. The best time to visit the Prado, Thyssen-Bornemisza and Reina Sofía galleries is straight after opening or in the last hour before closing, when it's typically quieter. The Paseo del Arte pass (€32.80) includes admission to all three galleries.

The **Museo del Prado** *(museodelprado.es; adult/child €15/ free)* is one of the world's most dazzling art galleries. From the medieval to early modern, its vast collection of European paintings includes big draws such as Rubens, El Greco, Bruegel, Dürer, Bosch and Rembrandt. But it's the Spanish masters that really steal the show – Velázquez' enigmatic *Las meninas* and Goya's chilling *Pinturas negras* herald the dawn of modern art. Other unmissable highlights include Titian's *Emperor Carlos V on Horseback,* Rubens' *The Three Graces,* El Greco's *Nobleman,* and the shimmering light of Joaquín Sorolla. While the work of female artists is almost completely absent, one notable exception is Sofonisba Anguissola's portrait of Felipe II.

Baron Thyssen-Bornemisza's collection has occupied a mansion set back from the Paseo del Prado since 1992. Featuring Dürer, Caravaggio, Degas and Roy Lichtenstein among its many treasures, the **Museo Thyssen-Bornemisza** *(museo thyssen.org; adult/child €14/free)* will satisfy the most fickle of art connoisseurs. Works are (mostly) arranged top-down in chronological order. Look for standouts such as Dalí's *Dream Caused by the Flight of a Bee Around a Pomegranate,* Caravaggio's *Portrait of Saint Catherine of Alexandria,* Degas' *Swaying Dancer,* Francis Bacon's *George Dyer in a Mirror,* Dürer's *Jesus Among the Doctors,* Picasso's *Harlequin with a Mirror* and Edward Hopper's *Hotel Room.* Don't miss the Baroness' Collection, which includes works by Canaletto, Van Gogh, Gauguin, Toulouse-Lautrec, O'Keeffe, Matisse and Munch.

The third star of Madrid's 'golden triangle of art', the **Centro de Arte Reina Sofía** *(museoreinasofia.es; adult/child €12/free)* is home to a modern collection mainly focusing on Spanish artists, with figures such as Dalí, Miró and Picasso

FLAMENCO & LIVE MUSIC

Café Central: Renowned Art Deco bar where you'll hear everything from Latin jazz and fusion to tango and classical jazz.

Tablao Flamenco 1911: Previously known as Villa Rosa, this well-regarded flamenco venue featured in Almodóvar's *Tacones lejanos* (High Heels).

Sala El Sol: Madrid institutions don't come any more beloved than this terrific venue for rock, pop, techno, funk and soul.

Corral de la Morería: One of Madrid's most renowned flamenco *tablaos,* with over 60 years of history and top-tier performances.

Wurlitzer Ballroom: Just off Gran Vía, this small but consistently good venue is a real indie music gem – a haven for late-night music fans.

EATING IN SALAMANCA: OUR PICKS

El Perro y La Galleta: Chic, cosy spot across from Retiro park, with Spanish and American breakfasts plus homemade pastries and desserts. *hours vary* €€

El Paraguas: Asturian dishes like bean stew or fried veal with ham and cheese, in an elegant setting with a patio for streetside dining. *12.30pm-2am* €€€

Restaurante Cañadío: Cantabrian restaurant with *pintxos* (Basque tapas) bar that opens before dinner service, and outdoor seating. *hours vary* €€

StreetXO: Fiery, edgy younger sibling of Madrid's famous Michelin-starred restaurant, DiverXO, led by Spanish chef Dabiz Muñoz. *noon-midnight* €€€

Palacio de Cristal, Parque del Buen Retiro

Plaza de la Villa: In the heart of the city, this was Madrid's main square in medieval times and still has some of the oldest architecture.

Plaza del Conde de Barajas: Charming square near Calle Mayor. Unless the Sunday art market is on, it's a relatively serene spot.

Plaza de Ramales: Near the Palacio Real, here you can rest in peace – just like Velázquez, whose bones are scattered somewhere nearby!

Plaza de la Provincia: Just off Plaza Mayor, its lovely fountain depicts the evolution of Madrid's coat of arms.

Plazuela de Santiago: A starting point for the Camino de Santiago, so you might see eager pilgrims outside the church.

Plaza de la Paja: One of Madrid's oldest and prettiest squares, in La Latina.

looming large. Its star attraction is indisputably *Guernica*. A harrowing reflection on the atrocities committed during the Spanish Civil War, Picasso's masterpiece stuns crowds to this day.

Madrid's Beloved Green Lung

Relaxing in El Retiro

Once the exclusive preserve of kings, the **Parque del Buen Retiro** is now open for everyone to enjoy its vast grounds. The park is particularly lovely in summer, when it acts as a green oasis for the city's heat-frazzled population, and in autumn when its trees put on a beautiful burnished display.

The oldest surviving part is the large **Estanque Grande**, where visitors can hire rowboats and admire the huge **monument to Alfonso XII** on the east side of the lake. The beautiful cast-iron and glass **Palacio de Cristal** was built to house flora and fauna for the 1887 Philippines exhibition, and its curved glass roof was a marvel of engineering at the time. It's now an annexe of the Reina Sofía museum and regularly hosts modern art exhibitions along with the nearby Palacio Velázquez.

Join the Festivities at Madrid Orgullo

The largest Pride festival in Europe

On the weekend following International Pride Day, the city rolls out the red carpet to welcome LGBTIQ+ tourists from all over the world for Europe's largest Pride festival, **Madrid Orgullo** *(madridorgullo.com)*, held annually in July. In earlier years, bars were allowed to set up impromptu discos outside, but now outdoor music is restricted to Plaza de Pedro

MALASAÑA & CHUECA

There's no question that Malasaña and Chueca are where the party's at. The bohemian hangout and LGBTIQ+ quarter lie side by side, bisected by Calle de Fuencarral, with the boundary between the two becoming ever more fuzzy. All this is a little exhausting for locals, who have complained about the constant noise and high rents. The noise has been a problem ever since *la movida madrileña* got underway in Malasaña in the early 1980s following the transition to democracy. In a reaction against years of repression, a group of artists, who dubbed themselves *raros* (weirdos), were keen to break with tradition. The most famous figures to emerge from this scene are film director Pedro Almodóvar and singer Alaska.

UNAI HUIZI PHOTOGRAPHY/SHUTTERSTOCK

Madrid Orgullo parade (p547)

Zerolo, Plaza del Rey, Plaza de Callao and Plaza de España. Saturday's **parade**, which runs down Paseo del Prado and Paseo de Recoletos, tends to be heaving. You can avoid the worst of the crowds by taking the *cercanías* (local train) to Recoletos and viewing it from there. Another event not to be missed is the **Carrera de Tacones** (High Heels Race) down Calle de Pelayo; if you want to take part, email *carrerataco nespelayo@gmail.com*.

At any time of year, tap into Madrid's LGBTIQ+ scene at the outstanding **Librería Berkana** (*libreriaberkana.com*) bookshop and at beloved nightlife venues like **Why Not?**, **YOU&ME**, **Axel Hotel Sky Bar** (*axelhotels.com*) and **Studio 54** (*studio54madrid.com*).

EATING & DRINKING IN MALASAÑA & CHUECA: OUR PICKS

Hermanas Arce: Clean Nordic lines, home-cooked food, incredible desserts and beautiful breakfasts. *9am-4pm Mon-Fri* €€

El Cisne Azul: Renowned for seasonal produce used in innovative dishes incorporating wild mushrooms. *1-4pm & 8-11.30pm Tue-Sat, 1-4.30pm Sun* €€

Pez Tortilla: Usually packed out with customers clamouring for its superior Spanish omelette and craft beers. *noon-midnight* €

Diurno: One of the most important hubs of *barrio* life in Chueca. It's always full with a fun local crowd relaxing amid the greenery. *hours vary*

Beyond Madrid

Sparkling cities, monumental cathedrals, quiet trails and vast natural expanses await in the *comunidades autónomas* surrounding the capital.

Endless historical, cultural, natural and culinary riches tempt visitors to Spain's great, rolling centre. Stretching across the Iberian Peninsula's interior plateau, Castilla y León is home to historic cities that were already mighty two millennia ago when the Romans ruled Hispania. Within easy reach of Madrid, the Castilian jewels of Salamanca, Segovia, Ávila, León, Burgos and Astorga draw plenty of visitors (especially at weekends), but their buzzing old towns retain a timeless beauty. West of Madrid, little-visited Extremadura is a journey into the heart of old Spain, with the beautifully preserved cities of Mérida, Cáceres and Trujillo. Closer to the capital lie the palatial monastery of San Lorenzo de El Escorial and the 2000-year-old imperial city of Toledo.

San Lorenzo de El Escorial   TIME FROM MADRID: 1HR

A royal residence

Around 50km northwest of Madrid, in the Sierra de Guadarrama, the monumental World Heritage–listed **Real Monasterio de San Lorenzo de El Escorial** (*patrimonionacional. es; adult/child €14/7*) is among the Comunidad de Madrid's most worthwhile excursions. Filled with art and surrounded by glorious gardens, King Felipe II's 16th-century home is both a royal residence and mausoleum. The complex was designed by architect Juan Bautista de Toledo; after his death, Juan de Herrera, a towering figure of the Spanish Renaissance, oversaw its completion. Among endless highlights is the 17th-century **Panteón de los Reyes** (Crypt of the Kings), where almost all Spain's monarchs since Carlos I are interred. Felipe II's marble-and-gold-trimmed coffin lies in the royal crypt. The bright **Salas Capitulares** (Chapter Houses), whose ceilings are richly frescoed, contain a treasure chest of works by El Greco, Titian, Tintoretto, José de Ribera and Hieronymus Bosch (known as El Bosco to Spaniards).

The complex closes on Mondays, though the gardens open every day. For a pause, enjoy a picnic in the gardens or head towards pretty Calle Floridablanca, where standouts include grilled or roasted meats at **Restaurante Charolés** (*charoles restaurante.com*).

GETTING AROUND

This sprawling area is ideal for exploring by car, combining walkable cities with wide-open countryside and villages. That said, most major cities and towns in Castilla y León, Castilla-La Mancha and the Comunidad de Madrid have good **Renfe** (*renfe.com*) train links, making for easy day/overnight trips from the capital. Regular buses fill the gaps. For Extremadura, trains link Madrid and Cáceres, with bus options for other destinations.

Toledo

TIME FROM MADRID: **50MIN**

City of three cultures

Spain's capital until 1561, Toledo has lived through many incarnations since it was first conquered by the Romans in 193 BCE. After the fall of the Roman Empire, it successively became the capital of the Visigothic kingdom, a stronghold of the Córdoba Emirate, and the seat of power of the Holy Roman Emperor and King of Spain, Charles V. Vestiges of a multilayered past give this UNESCO-listed fortified city its unique character today – a rich cultural fusion of Moorish, Christian and Jewish influences, earning it the nickname 'The City of Three Cultures'.

Begin at the **Catedral de Toledo** (*catedralprimada.es; adult/child €12/6*), Toledo's architectural magnum opus featuring lavishly carved baroque chapels, massive murals and intricate frescoes. Its cloister retains some Mudéjar-style elements, hinting at its previous incarnation as a mosque. Make your way to the 14th-century **Sinagoga del Tránsito** (*cultura.gob.es; adult/child €3/free*), with painstakingly detailed carved walls blending seamlessly with Mudéjar design. The whitewashed **Sinagoga de Santa María La Blanca** (*turismo.toledo.es; €4*) could easily be mistaken for a mosque with its horseshoe-shaped Mudéjar arches and ornate carvings. The nearby 15th-century **Monasterio de San Juan de los Reyes** (*toledomonumental.com; adult/child €4/3*), with elaborately carved marble altars, was built by the Catholic Monarchs Isabel and Fernando to be their final resting place. A 10-minute stroll brings you to the **Iglesia de San Román** (*closed Mon*). Finish at the **Mezquita del Cristo de la Luz** (*toledomonumental.com; adult/child €4/3*), constructed in 999 and later transformed into a church.

Salamanca

TIME FROM MADRID: 1¾–2¼HR

Plazas, cathedrals and architecture

There are few places where such a wealth of architectural treasures have been packed into such a small area as in Salamanca. What's often described as Spain's most perfect square is actually an 'irregular quadrilateral', but in simple terms Salamanca's **Plaza Mayor** is absolute perfection. For almost three centuries it has served more like the auditorium of a grand opera house than an administrative centre (and occasional bullring). When the lights go on at dusk, it's worthy of a standing ovation.

EL GRECO IN TOLEDO

Doménikos Theotokópoulos, better known by his Spanish nickname El Greco, moved to Toledo in 1577. Toledo has immortalised his art, with many large commissions gracing its churches.

Iglesia de Santo Tomé: Home to El Greco's 1585 masterpiece *El entierro del Conde de Orgaz*.

Museo del Greco: Impressive collection of El Greco's works from the 16th and 17th centuries.

Museo de Santa Cruz: Formerly a hospital and orphanage, it exhibits several of El Greco's paintings.

Convento de Santo Domingo El Antiguo: El Greco's final resting place houses his earliest canvases created in Toledo.

Mirador del Valle: Spectacular viewpoint portrayed by El Greco's famous masterpiece *Vista de Toledo*.

 EATING & DRINKING IN TOLEDO: OUR PICKS

La Malquerida de la Trinidad: Known for its good breakfast menu and traditional dishes. *10am-1.30am Sun-Thu, to 2.30am Fri & Sat* €€

Bar Ludeña: Charming tavern founded in 1955; its star dish is *carcamusas* (pork stew). *11am-4pm Mon-Sat & 8-11pm Thu-Sat, noon-4pm Sun* €

Bar Santa Fe: No-frills tapas bar near Plaza de Zocodover, with a wide selection of traditional local fare. *7am-midnight* €

Restaurante La Clandestina: Traditional tapas and game with a modern twist, on a tree-shaded terrace. *1-3.45pm Wed-Sun, 8pm-midnight Tue-Sun* €

Plaza Mayor, Salamanca

Guided-tour groups passing among this city's historical riches invariably pause to try to spot the fabled 'lucky' frog on the ornate 16th-century facade of the 1218-founded **Universidad de Salamanca** (usal.es; adult/child €10/free), just 500m southwest of Plaza Mayor. But a stroll through one of the world's great temples of academia is an insight into what made Salamanca great.

Immediately east of the university, Salamanca's two majestic cathedrals can get crowded but, at opening time (10am), savvy visitors who make a beeline directly for the **Catedral Vieja** (catedralsalamanca.org; adult/child €10/7) tend to have the luxury of soaking up 900 years of history in almost complete solitude. Then backtrack to begin the tour 'from the beginning' in the **Catedral Nueva** (dating back a mere five centuries!).

Segovia & Ávila

TIME FROM MADRID: **30–90MIN**

Segovia's fairy tale palace and Roman aqueduct

Segovia's whimsical **Alcázar** (alcazardesegovia.com; adult/child €10/8) is said to have inspired Walt Disney's design of the Sleeping Beauty castle. Built on Roman foundations and taking its name from the Arabic al qasr (fortress), it dates back to the 12th century. With its steeply pitched roofs, like witches' hats, and crenellated battlements, the Alcázar is one

SIERRA DE GREDOS

The great granite slabs of the Sierra de Gredos, rising like whale-backs 150km west of Madrid, are spectacular hiking terrain. Mountain villages are seeing a resurgence after years of accelerating depopulation, as madrileño hikers awaken to the fact that this spectacular wilderness lies within day-tripping distance (a scenic two-hour drive from the capital). We love it here in summer when the highlands, rising to 2592m, bring a respite from the soaring temperatures down below. It's gorgeous in winter too, when the peaks are sifted with snow and wild ibex descend by their hundreds into the valleys. Then comes spring – the best season of all – when the meltwater booms down the hillsides in crystal cascades and the cliffs are laced with waterfalls.

 EATING IN SALAMANCA: BEST TAPAS

Bambú Tapas y Brasa: Pincho moruno (steak skewer) and the award-winning truffled duck-egg are major crowd-pullers. 1-3.30pm & 8-11.30pm Wed-Sun €€€

Cuzco Bodega: Tiny spot popular for great wine and irresistible tapas (including mini-burgers). It's often standing room only. 1-4pm Tue-Sat & 8-11.30pm Mon-Sat €€

El Bardo Centro: Hearty tapas stews are what this backstreet favourite is all about. Also popular for the menú del día (daily set menu). 10am-5pm & 7-11.30pm €€

Bar La Fragua: Amazing value for money. A speciality is the ever-changing cazuela del día (stew of the day). 8am-noon & 4pm-midnight €

551

CAMINO CULTURE

Bisected by the ancient Via de la Plata trade route and the **Camino Francés**, the area around Astorga and León is excellent hiking country. The classic Camino Francés has been pounded by a millennia of boot prints. Almost halfway between Astorga and Ponferrada, **Cruz de Ferro** (Iron Cross), at 1504m above sea level, is the highest point on the Camino Francés. Less famously, Astorga is also the northern extreme of the Via de la Plata.

You don't have to be a dedicated pilgrim to experience the Camino. For something truly memorable, consider spending a day (or two) tackling the mountain passes between Astorga and Ponferrada (a total of about 52km). Breathtaking scenery, pilgrimage camaraderie and hearty local food are all part of the experience.

SCSTOCK/SHUTTERSTOCK

Acueducto, Segovia

of Spain's instantly recognisable national treasures. From the parade ground outside, it's a spectacular sight, but cross the drawbridge over the moat to enter a magical realm that surpasses any movie.

The mind-boggling spectacle of 24,000 blocks of airborne granite that makes up Segovia's **Acueducto** (Roman aqueduct) is impossible to appreciate at a single glance. Fortunately, there are several ways to view the 165 looping arches that constitute one of the finest feats of 1st-century Roman engineering. Our favourite is to climb the steps to the northern end of the main set of arches. The aqueduct is at its best when the setting sun throws looping shadows across Plaza Oriental.

While in town, don't miss the Gothic gem that is Segovia's hilltop **cathedral** *(catedralsegovia.es; adult/child €4/3),* best known for its rare collection of tapestries.

Patrolling Ávila's city walls

Ávila rises from the plains like a monumental granite island, with convents, churches and mansions barely daring to peek above the cliff-like battlements. Broken only by nine main gates, these **murallas** *(murallabeavila.com; adult/child €8/5)* are among the best-preserved medieval ramparts in the world. Climb up from **Puerta del Alcázar** *(10am–8pm)* for a swallow's-eye view of the city as you walk 1km around the top of

EATING IN SEGOVIA & ÁVILA: OUR PICKS

Mesón de Cándido: In a 300-year-old building, the same family has been serving Segovia's best *cochinillo* (suckling pig) for generations. *1-4.30pm & 8-11pm* €€

Casa Duque: Founded in 1895, this historical tavern is known for its garlic soup, roast kid and *cochinillo. 12.30-11pm* €€€

Pastelería Muñoz Iselma: Family-run Ávila business producing delicious almond slices known as Jesuitas. *9.30am-2pm & 4-8pm Mon-Fri, 9.30am-8pm Sat & Sun* €

La Bruja: A rustic wood-beam dining room serving all the Ávila specialities, along with Argentine-style charcoal grilled steak. *1-4.45pm & 8-11.30pm* €€

the battlements to exit near one of the city's 88 watchtowers at **Puerta del Carmen**. For a fuller appreciation, you can walk around the outside from here, enjoying incredible views over the plains and the Sierra de Gredos as you circle the southern ramparts to **Mirador de Ávila** (at the southeastern corner).

Burgos, León & Astorga

TIME FROM MADRID: 2¼–4HR

A tale of three cathedrals

One of Spain's finest Gothic gems awaits discovery in Burgos, 250km north of Madrid. Step into the city's spectacular 13th-century **Catedral** (catedraldeburgos.es; adult/child €10/2) and see the tomb of Rodrigo Díaz (aka El Cid), one of Spain's greatest national heroes. He died in 1099 but his legend reached a crescendo about a century later with the epic poem *Cantar de Mío Cid* ('Song of My Cid').

West from Burgos, León has made an art form out of its plazas. On Plaza de la Regla, the **Catedral de León** (leon. es; adult/child €6/free) dazzles in Gothic splendour and the glint from 125 stained-glass windows.

Equally evocative is the **Catedral de Astorga** (catedralastorga.com; adult/child €10/8), 45km further west from León. It's one of the most important religious sites on the Camino Francés pilgrim route, with three spectacular towers like rocket-ships tethered together with stone bridges and flying buttresses. A visit includes a free virtual-reality tour in which you have the incredibly realistic sensation of flying through the building.

Cáceres & Mérida

TIME FROM MADRID: 3HR

Strolling through a magical old city

One of the thrilling cities of Extremadura, Cáceres is defined by its glowing, UNESCO-listed **Ciudad Monumental** (turismocaceres.org), which has survived almost intact from its 16th-century period of splendour. Signs of the city's flourishing Jewish and Muslim periods create a harmonious mix with its more recent Catholic past and present – so picturesque it has starred in big-screen productions like *Game of Thrones*.

From **Plaza Mayor**, hemmed by elegant houses with elaborate Renaissance facades, a stairway leads underneath the **Arco de la Estrella** arch to the superb Renaissance-style **Plaza de Santa María** and the Gothic **Concatedral de Santa María de Cáceres** (concatedralcaceres.com; adult/child €7/5).

FLAVOURS OF CASTILLA Y LEÓN

Castilla y León has 26 Denominaciones de Origen (DO), and many of these marks of gastronomic distinction hail from southern pastures. Salamanca's Morucha beef, Ávila's Negra Ibérica cow and Guijuelo's *jamón* (ham) are all prized nationally. Distinct dishes from Salamanca include *farinato* (a lard, bread and flour sausage flavoured with paprika, anise and brandy) and *hornazo* (a pork pie with chorizo and boiled eggs). While meat dominates the cuisine, flat green lentils from La Armuña and seven varieties of bean from Ávila are staples in stews. *Segovianos* take *cochinillo* (suckling pig) seriously; traditionally it should be slow-roasted in a clay pot. For something sweet, try the cylindrical *bollo maimón* and egg-yolk *yemas de Santa Teresa*.

EATING IN BURGOS & ASTORGA: OUR PICKS

El Patio: A huge local favourite (but rarely frequented by tourists), this large Astorga bar fills up quickly with tapas-eaters at weekends. *8am-1am Fri-Tue* €€

La Quinta del Monje: Popular for tapas, including *morcilla* (the blood sausage for which Burgos is so famous). *hours vary* €

La Lorencita: A perennial old-Burgos favourite and prize-winner for the regional Tapas y Pincho awards in 2020. *noon-midnight Tue-Sat, to 5pm Sun* €€€

Café Pasaje: Overlooking Astorga's Plaza España, with tables heaped with Maragato meat and vegetables, this place is hard to beat. *8am-11pm* €€

ROBALTO/SHUTTERSTOCK

Templo de Diana, Mérida

EXTREMADURA JEWELS

Many regional highlights are easily visited en route to/ from Cáceres or Mérida.

Trujillo: Dazzling small city, with ancient walls, a hilltop 13th-century castle and a monumental Plaza Mayor.

Parque Nacional de Monfragüe: A dramatic, hilly 180-sq-km paradise for birdwatchers and other nature lovers, just north of Cáceres.

Guadalupe: The UNESCO World Heritage Site of Real Monasterio de Santa María de Guadalupe is Spain's most important monastery.

Medellín: Around 40km northeast of Mérida, little-known Medellín was a major town in Roman times and has its own beautiful Roman Theatre.

Valle de la Vera: One of the remotest parts of Spain, home to small hamlets and delightful hill and mountain country.

Stroll the street to Plaza de los Golfines, and then to **Plaza de San Mateo**, with the **church** of the same name. Follow the unmissable white towers to the imposing **Iglesia de San Francisco Javier**. Continue to the **Judería Vieja**, in the Barrio de San Antonio, the old Jewish district.

Fans of contemporary art will also want to dip into the **Museo de Arte Contemporáneo Helga de Alvear** (*museo helgadealvear.com; free; closed Mon*).

Echoes of Roman times

Born Augusta Emerita, once the capital of the Roman province of Lusitania, today Mérida's spectacular ruins lie sprinkled around town. Admission to most sites is by combined ticket (*adult/child €17.50/8.50*).

At the very heart of Mérida lies an unusual plaza with the **Templo de Diana**, an original ancient Roman temple, flanked by modern buildings. Among many other highlights is the spectacular, 60-arch **Puente Romano** (Roman Bridge) on the broad Río Guadiana. But the main event is Mérida's **Teatro Romano** (*teatroromanomerida.com*). One of the world's best-preserved Roman theatres, it was built around 15 BCE by the will of Marcus Vipsanius Agrippa, Augustus' right-hand man, to seat 6000 spectators – and still hosts summer performances. Before entering, visit the superb **Museo Nacional de Arte Romano** (*turismomerida.org; adult/child €3/free; closed Mon*) next door.

EATING IN CÁCERES & MÉRIDA: OUR PICKS

La Cacharrería: Exclusive and cosy, taking classic Cáceres cuisine and making it even more refined. *2-3.30pm & 8.30pm-midnight Thu-Mon* €€

Tapería 8a Arte: Popular with a young Cáceres crowd for its wide array of local tapas and gluten-free and vegan options. *noon-11.30pm Thu-Tue* €

La Carbonería Restaurante: Perfect place in Mérida for those serious about their meat, with a delicious tapas bar next door. *hours vary* €€

Agallas Gastro & Food: Trendy Mérida restaurant with extravagant dishes and great quality/price ratio. *1-5pm & 8.15pm-midnight Tue-Sat* €

Barcelona

ART & ARCHITECTURE | CATALAN CULTURE | FOOD-AND-DRINK SCENE

Catalonia's capital is one of Europe's most desirable cities – a sunny, Mediterranean-hugging hub that breezily combines its rich cultural traditions with a forward-thinking, environmentally aware attitude.

During Barcelona's medieval Golden Age, great churches and mansions were built across the Ciutat Vella (Old City), shaping today's Barri Gòtic, La Ribera and El Raval neighbourhoods, where creative tapas and vermouth bars and boundary-pushing galleries now sit between centuries-old walls. Then came the industrial boom, with areas like El Poblenou, Gràcia and Sants taking centre stage, and the creation of an entirely new district, L'Eixample, where otherworldly Modernista buildings still command attention. Ever since the late 19th century, the city has been breaking ground in art and style as well as architecture.

Barcelona has experienced an astonishing boom since hosting the 1992 Olympics. With tourism now a key part of the local economy, the city is pushing forward ambitious plans to balance the needs of local residents and the tourism industry.

> ☑ **TOP TIP**
>
> Barri Gòtic and La Ribera (especially El Born) are the busiest, most overtourited neighbourhoods. Head out early to explore, book museum tickets ahead and keep an eye on belongings. Gràcia, Sant Antoni and Poble Sec have few 'official' sights, but offer wonderful restaurants and bars. For wheelchair-accessible tours, see *disabledaccessibletravel. com.*

Gaudí Galore

Best of the Modernista architect

Dominating Barcelona's skyline, Antoni Gaudí's **La Sagrada Família** (*sagradafamilia.org; adult/child €26/free*)
continued on p558

 GETTING AROUND

Much of Barcelona is flat and walkable. The city has over 250km of bike lanes; bike-hire outlets are everywhere (*€12 per day*).

The excellent TMB metro system has eight lines; buy a 10-journey **T-Casual pass** (*tmb. cat; €12.55*). The main exceptions are Tibidabo/

Collserola (funicular or train) and Montjuïc (funicular, bus and cable car).

For the airport, the frequent, 24-hour **Aerobús** (*aerobusbarcelona.es; €7.45*) takes 30 to 40 minutes; alternatively, take a taxi (around €30), train (R2 Nord line) or metro (L9 Sud).

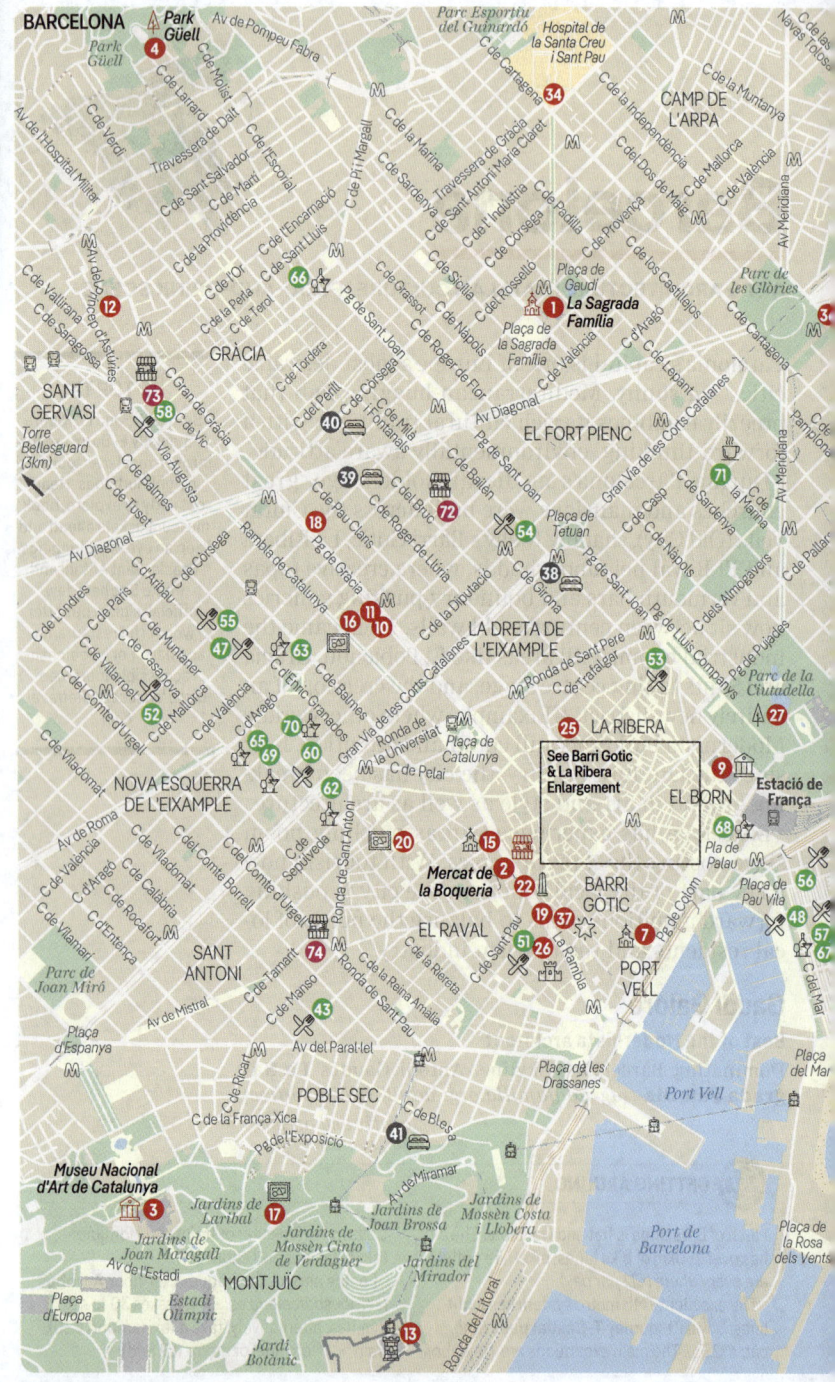

BARCELONA

Park Güell — 4

La Sagrada Família — 1

Museu Nacional d'Art de Catalunya — 3

Mercat de la Boqueria — 2

See Barri Gotic & La Ribera Enlargement

GRÀCIA

SANT GERVASI

Torre Bellesguard (3km)

EL FORT PIENC

LA DRETA DE L'EIXAMPLE

LA RIBERA

EL BORN

Estació de França

NOVA ESQUERRA DE L'EIXAMPLE

SANT ANTONI

EL RAVAL

BARRI GÒTIC

PORT VELL

Parc de Joan Miró

Plaça d'Espanya

POBLE SEC

MONTJUÏC

Jardins de Laribal

Jardins de Joan Maragall

Estadi Olímpic

Jardi Botànic

Jardins de Mossèn Cinto de Verdaguer

Jardins de Joan Brossa

Jardins del Mirador

Jardins de Mossèn Costa i Llobera

Port Vell

Port de Barcelona

Plaça del Mar

Plaça de la Rosa dels Vents

CAMP DE L'ARPA

Parc de les Glòries

Parc de la Ciutadella

Hospital de la Santa Creu i Sant Pau

Parc Esportiu del Guinardó

⭐ HIGHLIGHTS

1 La Sagrada Família
2 Mercat de la Boqueria
3 Museu Nacional d'Art de Catalunya
4 Park Güell
5 Platja de la Barceloneta

🔴 SIGHTS

6 Ajuntament
7 Basílica de la Mercè
8 Basílica de Santa Maria del Mar
9 Born Centre de Cultura i Memòria
10 Casa Amatller
11 Casa Batlló
12 Casa Vicens
13 Castell de Montjuïc
14 Catedral de Barcelona
15 Església de Betlem
16 Fundació Antoni Tàpies
17 Fundació Joan Miró
18 La Pedrera
19 La Rambla
20 MACBA
21 Moco Museum
22 Mosaïc de Miró
23 Museu Picasso
24 Palau de la Generalitat
25 Palau de la Música Catalana
26 Palau Güell
27 Parc de la Ciutadella
28 Plaça de Sant Felip Neri
29 Platja de la Mar Bella
30 Platja de la Nova Icària
31 Platja de la Nova Mar Bella
32 Platja del Bogatell
33 Rambla del Poblenou

34 Recinte Modernista de Sant Pau
35 Temple d'August
36 Torre Glòries

🔴 ACTIVITIES

37 Runner Bean Tours

⚫ SLEEPING

38 Casa Bonay
39 Casa Mathilda
40 Generator Barcelona
41 Hotel Brummell
42 Hotel Neri

🟢 EATING

43 Bar Calders
44 Bar del Pla
45 Bar Mono
46 Bar Pimentel
47 Besta
48 Bodega la Peninsular
49 Buriti
50 Can Fisher
51 Cañete
52 Disfrutar
53 Fismuler
54 Funky Bakers Eatery
55 Gresca
56 Jai-Ca
57 La Cova Fumada
58 La Pubilla
59 Little Fern Café
60 Mont Bar
61 Xiringuito Escribà

🟢 DRINKING & NIGHTLIFE

62 Candy Darling
63 Carita Bonita
64 El Xampanyet
65 La Chapelle
66 La Vermuteria del Tano
67 La Violeta
68 Paradiso
69 Punto BCN
70 Sky Bar
71 Three Marks

🔴 SHOPPING

72 Mercat de la Concepció
73 Mercat de la Llibertat
74 Mercat de Sant Antoni
75 Mercat de Santa Caterina

continued from p555

stops everyone in their tracks. Despite the crowds, this is an unmissable, UNESCO-listed Barcelona highlight. The main construction is due to be completed in 2026. After taking over from original architect Francisco de Paula del Villar y Lozano in 1883, Gaudí (who is buried in the neo-Gothic **crypt**) spent 43 years of his life on the basilica. Above the main building there will eventually be 18 **towers**, some of them already open to visitors. The spectacularly sculpted **Façana del Naixement** (Nativity Facade) is the oldest of the basilica's three monumental facades; the 2018-completed **Façana de la Passió** (Passion Facade), depicting Christ's last days and death, is largely the recent work of the late sculptor Josep Maria Subirachs. Within, extraordinary leaning pillars evoke a natural forest.

On Passeig de Gràcia, the elegant boulevard that bisects L'Eixample, **Casa Batlló** *(casabatllo.es; adult/child €29/free)* is one of Barcelona's most beautiful and curious buildings. Created between 1904 and 1906, this is Gaudí at his fantastical best, from the playful facade with its bulging bone-like balconies and purple-blue *trencadís* tilework to the groundbreaking experiments in light and architectural form. The showstopper is the endlessly mesmerising rooftop.

Neighbouring Casa Milà is better known as **La Pedrera** *(lapedrera.com; adult/child €29/free)*, or the Quarry, because of its wave-like grey-stone facade. In the top tier of Gaudí's achievements, this madcap masterpiece with 33 balconies was built between 1905 and 1910 as a combined apartment and office block.

At UNESCO-listed **Park Güell** *(parkguell.barcelona; adult/child €18/13.50)*, just north of Gràcia, Gaudí turned his imagination to landscape gardening, creating an ingenious interplay between architecture and the natural world. Visiting the park's trail-laced northern part *(zona forestal)* is free. Best views? From 182m-high **Turó de les Tres Creus**, in the southwest corner.

For all Gaudí sights, book tickets ahead and arrive early or just before closing to beat the crowds. Guided tours are highly recommended.

Glowing Spires & Ancient Squares

Taste Ciutat Vella's long past

Sitting on the foundations of Roman Barcino, the Barri Gòtic is the oldest part of Barcelona and still the hub for festivities

EATING AROUND EL POBLENOU: OUR PICKS

Can Fisher: On Bogatell, reliably good seafood and a chic decor make this a good pick for a paella. *12.30-11pm Mon-Fri, from 10am Sat & Sun* €€

Little Fern Café: Expect a line on weekend mornings at this cafe beloved for its fresh aesthetic, granola bowls and avocado toasts. *9am-4pm* €

Xiringuito Escribà: An open-plan beach bar for digging into a classic, seafood or surf-and-turf paella or *fideuà* (paella-like fish and seafood noodle dish). *noon-10.30pm* €€€

Buriti: Get your morning energy jolt at this Brazilian restaurant with a healthy menu that delights both vegans and meat-eaters. *hours vary* €

Park Güell

BARCELONA'S MARKETS

In the 19th century, many *mercats* (markets) were redesigned by local architects. Today, stalls mingle with bars.

Mercat de la Boqueria: Famous, historic, busy, known for tapas bars such as El Quim.

Mercat de la Llibertat: Modernista hub of Gràcia life covered in 1893. Great tapas at Hermòs Bar de Peix.

Mercat de Santa Caterina: Designed by boundary-pushing architects Enric Miralles and Benedetta Tagliabue. Don't miss Bar Joan.

Mercat de Sant Antoni: Restored 1882 Modernista marvel anchoring Sant Antoni. Home to legendary Bar Pinotxo.

Mercat de la Concepció: Created in 1888 by Antoni Rovira i Trias. Popular for 24-hour flower shop Flores Navarro.

such as **Festes de la Mercè** in September. Extending northeast from the Barri Gòtic, La Ribera grew from the 10th century and became Barcelona's medieval commercial epicentre. Just east, palm-dotted **Parc de la Ciutadella** is central Barcelona's beloved green haven, created for the 1888 Universal Exposition on the site of the much-hated, long-demolished Ciutadella fortress (which had been built after the War of the Spanish Succession).

With its elaborate spires and neo-Gothic facade, the **Catedral de Barcelona** (*catedralbcn.org; adult/child €16/8*) rises in the heart of the Barri Gòtic, preserving a sacred crypt and a cloister that echoes with the honking of 13 white geese. Much of the building dates from the 13th and 14th centuries. Just across Via Laietana, La Ribera's harmonious **Basílica de Santa Maria del Mar** (*santamariadelmarbarcelona.org; adult/child from €5/free*) is Barcelona's most magnificent Catalan Gothic church, built between 1329 and 1382. Climb to the rooftop of either temple for exquisite views.

 EATING & DRINKING IN CIUTAT VELLA & SANT ANTONI: OUR PICKS

El Xampanyet: A legend of Barcelona's *cava* (sparkling wine) scene; arrive early for delicious tapas (tangy anchovies, gooey tortilla). *hours vary*	**Bar Mono:** Polished gastropub with all the classic tapas to check off your list, plus a good vegetarian menu. *11am-midnight Mon-Fri, to 1am Sat & Sun* €€	**Bar del Pla:** El Born favourite specialising in natural wines and creative tapas such as wasabi mushrooms. *noon-11pm* €€	**Bar Pimentel:** Understated tapas bar for *cava*, vermouth and wine; bites include tortilla and squid with lime mayo. *1-11pm Sun-Thu, to 11.30pm Fri & Sat* €€
Fismuler: El Bulli–trained chefs lead this innovative favourite where market menus change daily and wines are glorious. *hours vary* €€€	**Paradiso:** Named the globe's greatest bar in 2022 by The World's 50 Best Bars; try the mezcal-fuelled Cloud. *5pm-3am*	**Cañete:** Upmarket stylish bar for tapas and sharing plates like spicy octopus, oxtail stew and plump anchovies. *1pm-midnight Mon-Sat* €€	**Bar Calders:** Lively Sant Antoni bar for wines and vermouth paired with modern tapas from wraps and hummus to nachos. *hours vary* €

BEST GUIDED TOURS

Spanish Civil War Tours by Nick Lloyd: Historian-led tour of 1930s Barcelona, giving context to a complicated history. *(thespanishcivilwar. com)*

Barcelona Architecture Walks: Led by practising architects and architecture professors, including a Gaudí stroll. *(barcelona rchitecturewalks.com)*

Devour: Excellent food-focused tours supporting small businesses and local producers. *(devourtours.com)*

Runner Bean: Free daily tours led by knowledgeable guides. Bookings required; tips expected. *(runnerbean tours.com)*

Hidden City Tours: Social enterprise that trains guides who have been homeless; routes show a different side to modern-day Barcelona. *(hiddencity tours.com)*

Platja de la Barceloneta

The **Plaça de Sant Jaume** is home to the **Palau de la Generalitat** and the **Ajuntament** (City Hall). Remnants of Roman Barcino can still be seen at the **Temple d'August** *(free),* near pretty **Plaça de Sant Felip Neri**.

Strolling La Rambla
Barcelona's most famous boulevard

Ancient **La Rambla** connects Plaça de Catalunya to the waterfront, flanked by the Barri Gòtic and El Raval. Once the site of a stream outside the city walls, today it's undoubtedly busy and touristed, but look closely and you'll find centuries of Barcelona history. With five sections, you'll hear it referred to as Las Ramblas (Les Rambles in Catalan). Highlights include the **Església de Betlem**, a church built in the late 17th and 18th centuries; the colourful **Mosaic de Miró**; and the famed **Mercat de la Boqueria** (p559). Visit early and keep an eye on belongings.

 EATING & DRINKING IN L'EIXAMPLE & GRÀCIA: OUR PICKS

Gresca: At Gresca's open-plan kitchen, chef Rafa Peña reinvents seasonal produce alongside natural wines. *hours vary* €€

Besta: Exquisite menus blend Catalan and Galician flavours, mostly with a seafood focus (vegetarian options on request). *hours vary* €€

Disfrutar: Boundary-pushing, three-Michelin-star venue led by chefs Mateu Casañas, Oriol Castro and Eduard Xatruch. *12.45-2pm & 7.45-9pm Mon-Fri* €€€

Mont Bar: Bistro-style Michelin-starred restaurant with superb wines and next-level cooking using seasonal, organic produce. *1-2pm & 7-10pm Tue-Sat* €€€

Funky Bakers Eatery: Stylish cafe-deli for Barcelona-roasted coffee, delicious babkas, creative brunches and seasonal dishes. *hours vary* €€

Three Marks: Best coffee in town? Head to this speciality roastery in the Fort Pienc area and sit on the terrace. *8am-4pm Mon-Fri, 9.30am-5pm Sat & Sun*

La Pubilla: Alexis Peñalver's Gràcia kitchen has Catalan-style breakfasts and market-fresh menus. *9am-noon, 1-3.30pm & 8pm-midnight Tue-Sat* €€

La Vermuteria del Tano: Long-running favourite with decorative barrels, Perucchi vermouth and traditional conserves. *9am-9pm Tue- Fri, noon-4pm Sat & Sun*

For a more local-life experience, head to **Rambla del Poblenou** or L'Eixample's **Rambla de Catalunya**.

World of Picasso
Delve into the artist's early years

Five medieval palace-mansions on La Ribera's Carrer de Montcada create a striking setting for the **Museu Picasso** *(museupicassobcn.cat; adult/child €14/free)*. But what makes this landmark gallery truly impressive is its showcase of Málaga-born Pablo Picasso's formative years. The first two rooms display early oil paintings and sketches, including the famous *Portrait of Aunt Pepa,* done in 1896 in Málaga when Picasso was just 15. Room 3 houses one of the museum's star pieces, the enormous *Science and Charity,* from 1987. Subsequent rooms showcase the famous Blue Period (including *Woman with a Bonnet* from 1901, in room 8). In rooms 12 to 14, Picasso's 1957 series of renditions of Velázquez' 1656 masterpiece *Las meninas* dazzles among arches.

Fans of contemporary art will also enjoy the next-door **Moco Museum** *(mocomuseum.com; adult/child €17/14)*, L'Eixample's **Fundació Antoni Tàpies** *(museutapies.org; adult/child €12/free)* and El Raval's groundbreaking **MACBA** *(macba.cat; adult/child €11/free)*. The great-value **Articket Barcelona** *(articketbcn.org; €38)* covers six major galleries. Most museums close Monday.

Waterfront Fun
From beaches to cutting-edge architecture

Barcelona's waterfront stretches from the Port Vell marina near Montjuïc to the concrete sprawl of Parc del Fòrum. **Barceloneta** is a grid-like former fisherfolk's neighbourhood engineered in the 18th century, and is renowned for its tapas bars, like **Jai-Ca** *(barjaica.com),* **La Cova Fumada**, **La Violeta** and **Bodega La Peninsular**.

To the northeast, the sprawling **El Poblenou** is a former industrial area that has become one of the city's most fashionable hubs, home to the sky-high **Torre Glòries** *(miradortorreglories.com; adult/child €18/free)*. The best way to enjoy this area is by joining the runners, walkers, cyclists, paddleboarders, rollerbladers and beach-goers. The Poblenou-area beaches of **Nova Icària**, **Bogatell**, **Mar Bella** and **Nova Mar Bella** have a more relaxed feel than busy, central **Platja de la Barceloneta**.

Go Dancing in the Gaixample
Heart of Barcelona's LGBTIQ+ scene

Over in Esquerra de L'Eixample, the grid between Aragó, Gran Via, Balmes and Comte Urgell streets is popularly known as the 'Gaixample'. With its many bars, clubs, restaurants, bookshops and rainbow flags, this is the epicentre of Barcelona's LGBTIQ+ scene. Popular nightspots include **Punto BCN** for drinks and drag shows, and relaxed **La Chapelle**.

VERMOUTH HOUR

First brought to Spain from Italy in the mid-19th century, vermouth has experienced a dazzling revival in Barcelona over the last decade. Based on red or white wine, the drink is infused with botanicals and fortified with brandy. The best places serve it over ice with an olive and a thin slice of orange. It's ideally enjoyed with friends around midday, especially on weekends – *l'hora del vermut.* Vermouth is always accompanied by light snacks, such as salty crisps or a few tapas (anchovies, croquettes, *patates braves*). To *fer el vermut* (do a vermouth), choose from a wealth of *vermuterias* (vermouth bars), though most Barcelona bars now serve it. The Gràcia and Sant Antoni districts are particularly known for their vermouth-hour scenes.

FESTES DE LA MERCÈ

Held around 24 September, the **Festes de la Mercè** is Barcelona's greatest annual celebration. Honouring one of the city's two patron saints, festivities involve four days of concerts, dancing and street theatre. Much of the fun centres on the Barri Gòtic, particularly the **Basílica de la Mercè** *(basilicadelamerce. com),* Plaça de Sant Jaume, Via Laietana, La Rambla and the cathedral. But La Mercè is celebrated all over town. In La Ribera, the **Born Centre de Cultura i Memòria** *(barcelona. cat)* hosts displays and parades of fantastical Catalan creatures, while **Parc de la Ciutadella** (p559) has food markets and live music. Cultural highlights include *castells* (human towers), *gegants* (papier-mâché giants), *sardana* (folk dance) and *correfoc* (fire-running).

Museu Nacional d'Art de Catalunya

Weekends-only **Carita Bonita** is a hub for Barcelona's lesbian community. **Candy Darling** has drag shows and a cultural focus, while rooftop cocktails await at Axel Hotel's **Sky Bar** *(axelhotels.com).* In late June or early July, Barcelona hosts its packed two-week **Pride** *(pridebarcelona.org)* festival, with a Pride march on the Saturday.

Museums on the Mountain

Explore Montjuïc's terrific galleries

Rising up behind Poble Sec, pine-covered Montjuïc (173m) hosts some of Barcelona's finest museums, pretty gardens and an ancient hilltop **castle**. The spectacular neobaroque Palau Nacional, housing the **Museu Nacional d'Art de Catalunya** *(museunacional.cat; adult/child €12/free),* was built for the 1929 World Exhibition. Its vast collection of mostly Catalan art spans the early Middle Ages to the early 20th century. The high point is the extraordinary Romanesque frescoes, including the 12th-century *Christ in Majesty* (Sala 7) and *Virgin Mary and Christ Child* (Sala 9), both rescued from churches in northern Catalonia.

The nearby, light-flooded **Fundació Joan Miró** *(fmirobcn. org; adult/child €15/free)* is home to the world's greatest collection of artworks by the Catalan surrealist Joan Miró, and was designed by Miró's friend, the Catalan architect Josep Lluís Sert. Standouts include the huge 1979 tapestry of the *Fundació* and *Man and Woman in Front of a Pile of Excrement* (1935).

Beyond Barcelona

Parque Nacional de Ordesa y Monte Perdido
Toulouse
Parc Nacional d'Aigüestortes i Estany de Sant Maurici
Jaca
Tudela
Huesca
La Seu d'Urgell
Cadaqués
Zaragoza
Figueres
Lleida
Montserrat
Girona
Vic
Alcañiz
Tarragona
Barcelona
Amposta
Sitges
Vinarós

Uncover Catalonia's shimmering shores, dive into ancient cities or escape into some of the country's loveliest mountain terrain.

Barcelona's urban sprawl gives way to Catalonia's beloved coastlines. Just beyond Barcelona, Sitges has long been one of Spain's liveliest LGBTIQ+ friendly destinations, with beaches, parties and festivals year-round. On the central Costa Daurada, Tarragona was the first city to be settled by the Romans on the Iberian Peninsula. Northeast from Barcelona, the Costa Brava is one of the most dazzling parts of Spain's long shoreline, with culture-rich Girona awaiting just inland. If you only visit one place on the Costa Brava, Cadaqués – former home of Salvador Dalí – is the quintessential whitewashed village. Heading west into Aragón, the regional capital Zaragoza combines entrancing monuments with a great tapas scene. North of it all, the majestic Spanish Pyrenees straddle Catalonia, Aragón, Navarra and the Basque Country.

Places

Montserrat p563

Sitges p564

Tarragona p564

Cadaqués & the Costa Brava p566

Zaragoza p566

The Spanish Pyrenees p567

Montserrat
TIME FROM BARCELONA: 1½HR

Monastic mountain majesty

Attracting millions of visitors every year, Montserrat is Catalonia's most emblematic mountain. It's home to a historic mountain-side monastery and an ethereal natural landscape where curvaceous rock columns transform into sharp needle-like peaks at a distance, inspiring the Catalan name that translates as 'serrated mountain'.

Founded in 1025, the Benedictine **Monestir de Montserrat** (*montserratvisita.com; adult/child €20/10*) has been drawing pilgrims for centuries to see the icon of **La Moreneta** (the 'Little Brown One' or 'Black Virgin'), a wooden figure of the Virgin Mary prominently displayed at the centre of the

---

GETTING AROUND

Sitges has excellent *rodalies* (commuter train) connections to Barcelona (*rodalies.gencat. cat*). Tarragona and Zaragoza are linked to Barcelona and beyond by **Renfe** (*renfe.com*) trains. For the Costa Brava and the Pyrenees, it pays to have your own wheels, or use local buses (some routes only operate seasonally).

Some places restrict private-vehicle access during high season. For Montserrat, take the **FGC** (*fgc.cat*) R5 train from central Barcelona, then change to the Aeri cable car (*aeridemontserrat.com*) or Cremallera rack railway (*cremallerademontserrat.cat*).

THE CATALAN LANGUAGE

Prepare to be viciously side-eyed if you get caught calling Catalan a dialect of Spanish. Although it is a Romance language similar to both Spanish and French – you'll find that some words, such as *hola* and *merci* respectively, are identical – Catalan is distinct and spoken by over four million native speakers. Catalan is not only spoken in Catalonia, but also in parts of Valencia, the Balearic Islands, and even as far away as the Italian city of Alghero in Sardinia, which was colonised by the Catalans in the Middle Ages. Although most people in Catalonia are likely to speak Spanish as well, trying out a Catalan phrase here and there is usually appreciated.

altar. Despite the large tourist complex with shops, restaurants and museums, this is still a working monastery. With careful timing, you might catch a performance by the Escolania de Montserrat, one of the oldest boys' choirs in Europe.

Beyond the monastery complex, Montserrat is a natural park with many inspiring walking trails, including summitting the mountain (1236m) on the 10.3km **Sant Jeroni Loop**.

Sitges

TIME FROM BARCELONA: **35MIN**

A festive beach town

A popular day-trip escape from Barcelona, lively Sitges has a crop of beautiful beaches and a glitzy nightlife scene. Listen to the bells of the **Església de Sant Bartomeu i Santa Tecla** ring out as you lounge on the main strip of sandy beaches, or explore a little further up the coast to clothing-optional **Platja dels Balmins**.

Historically LGBTIQ+ friendly, Sitges traces its clubbing scene back to the 1980s. Catch the two largest celebrations of colour and love during Carnival in late February/early March or June's Pride parade.

Sitges also has a delightful, buzzy historic centre. Learn about one of the leading artists of Modernisme, Santiago Rusiñol, at the **Museu del Cau Ferrat** and the ornate **Palau de Maricel** *(museusdesitges.cat; adult/child €12/free);* they are closed on Mondays.

Tarragona

TIME FROM BARCELONA: **1–2HR**

Roman relics

Formerly known as Tárraco, Tarragona spent hundreds of years as the region's Roman capital. Today, well-preserved remnants of the ancient city are found throughout the old town of this vibrant, modern hub. A joint ticket *(tarragona. cat; adult/child €15/free)* offers access to all the major sites, which individually cost €5. Enter the history museum at **Torre de les Monges** and soon you'll be peering out over the **Circ Romà**, a partial preservation of a much larger chariot course. The museum continues underground, finishing at the **Torre del Pretori**, where you can climb to the top for a spectacular view of the sea-facing **Amfiteatre de Tarragona**, built in the 2nd century for up to 15,000 spectators.

Romans aside, the **Catedral de Tarragona** *(catedraldetar ragona.com; adult/child €12/8.50)* is one of the largest in Catalonia and features a blend of Gothic and Romanesque styles.

EATING IN GIRONA: OUR PICKS

Rocambolesc: Ice-cream shop with special flavours and fun popsicles; from the family of El Celler de Can Roca. *10.30am-11pm Sun-Thu, to midnight Fri & Sat* €

L'Argadà: Catalan steakhouse, where seasonal *calçots* (spring onions) are served in a traditional roof tile. *1.30-3.30pm & 8-10.30pm Mon-Sat, 1.30-3.30pm Sun* €€

Café Le Bistrot: Tables romantically arranged on the steps of Sant Domènec; book ahead. *1-4pm & 7.30pm-midnight Mon-Sat, 1-4pm Sun* €€

El Celler de Can Roca: World-famous and recognised for dramatic plating and gourmet cooking techniques. *12.30-9.30pm Wed-Sat, from 7.30pm Tue* €€€

GIRONA ARCHAEOLOGICAL WALK

Despite the contemporary city that surrounds it, Girona's old quarter maintains its medieval charm.

START	END	LENGTH
Museu d'Historia dels Jueus	Café Le Bistrot	2km; one hour

Just north of the Pont de Sant Agustí, you'll find the ❶ **Museu d'Historia dels Jueus**, located in a 13th-century Jewish home. Turn right on Carrer Sant Llorenç and walk up to a medieval fountain, ❷ **Font dels Lledoners**. Turn left through the plaza towards the steps of the Gothic-baroque ❸ **Catedral de Girona**, home to the *Tapestry of Creation* from the 11th or 12th century.

Trot down for a better look and go through the gate towards the ❹ **Basílica de Sant Feliu**. Take a right to pass the 12th-century ❺ **Banys Àrabs**. At the end of this road, find the ❻ **Plaça dels Jurats** and ❼ **Monestir de Sant Pere de Galligants**, which houses lovely cloisters and the archaeology museum. Climbing up the Passeig de la Reina Joana, follow the archaeological path to reach the ❽ **Jardins dels Alemanys** and access the ❾ **Muralles de Girona** for the walk along the walls, passing the towers of Gironella and Sant Domènec.

Descend the walls at Torre del General Peralta Bastion and continue until you pass the ❿ **Convent de Sant Domènec de Girona**. A huge convent founded in 1253, it now belongs to the university. Turn left on the Pujada de Sant Domènec and walk towards the picturesque stairs, where you might snag a table at ⓫ **Café Le Bistrot** (p564).

The **Museu d'Història de Girona**, housed within an 18th-century cloister, provides context about Girona through the ages.

0 — 200 m
0 — 0.1 miles
N

Plaça de Sant Pere

C del Bellaire

C de Santa Llúcia

Plaça de Sant Feliu

Pujda del Rei Martí

Ptge de la Reina Joana

Riu Galligants

Plaça de la Catedral

C dels Calderers

C de la Força

C de Rocaberti

C de les Ballesteríes

Riu Onyar

C de Belmirall

C d'Alemanys

Plaça de Sant Domènec

START

Plaça de l'Independència

Pont de Sant Agustí

C de Carreras Peralta

Pujada de Sant Domènec

Plaça de Josep Ferrater i Mora

⓫

END

C de Ciutadans

Next to the cathedral, the **Museu d'Art de Girona** has a sprawling collection, from religious Romanesque artworks to Modernisme.

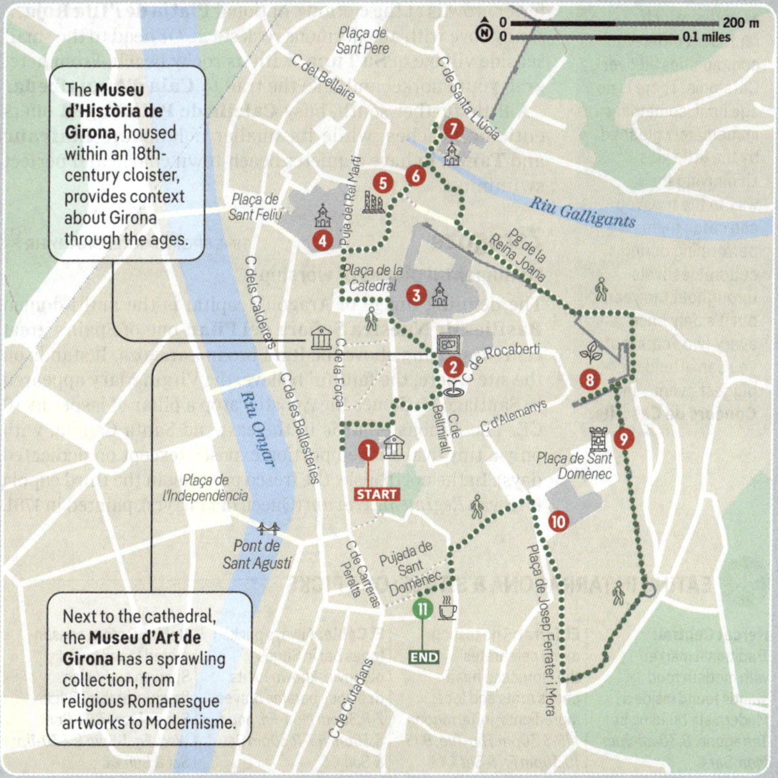

This uniquely Catalan tradition is a sight you won't soon forget. With its origins in an 18th-century Valencian folk dance, *castells* are all about creating the highest tower possible, often reaching heights of up to 15m. Just like the strong base of human power that holds the tower in place, the spirit of building human towers is all about community and groups of *castellers*, known as *colles*, which represent different communities all over Catalonia. There is no age limit, something immediately gleaned by the little kids shimmying their way to the top. You can catch them performing during cultural festivals throughout the year, but it's only once every two years that you can attend the biggest event – the **Concurs de Castells**.

Cadaqués & the Costa Brava
TIME FROM BARCELONA (CADAQUÉS): 2¼HR

Winds of Cap de Creus

Just north of Cadaqués, the **Parc Natural de Cap de Creus** (*parcsnaturals.gencat.cat*) is defined by its dry and weather-worn rocky landscape, filled with jagged and uncanny shapes that inspired the controversial surrealist artist Salvador Dalí throughout his life. Today it's a protected park with many marked walking paths, including an 8km route that you can follow from Cadaqués to the 19th-century lighthouse – **Far Cap de Creus** – at Spain's most eastern point. Venture to swimming spots **Cala Culip** and **Cala Jugadora**. During certain times of year, park roads close to vehicles, and a SARFA bus service (*moventis.es*) is offered from Cadaqués and the Corral d'en Morell car park.

Beach-hopping around Begur

Another of the Costa Brava's loveliest pockets is the cliff-edged shoreline around the charming town of **Begur**, 60km south of Cadaqués. The ruins of the 16th-century **Castell de Begur** provide one of the most majestic views of the Costa Brava; on clear days you can even see the Pyrenees. **Platja de Sa Riera** has plenty of sand to go around, but there are fewer crowds at the clothing-optional **Platja de l'Illa Roja**, a sandy cove with an enormous rock stack. Or head to the small seaside village of **Sa Tuna**, with its rocky beach. From here, grab your snorkel and take the trail to **Cala d'Aiguafreda**.

A little further south, busy **Calella de Palafrugell** offers enticing beaches, while its smaller neighbours **Llafranc** and **Tamariu** have a quieter beach-town charm and perfect swimming.

Zaragoza
TIME FROM BARCELONA: 1½HR

Monumental places of worship

The defining image of Aragón's capital is the multi-domed **Basílica de Nuestra Señora del Pilar**, one of Spain's great churches, rising above the Río Ebro in Zaragoza. It stands on the site where, the faithful believe, the Virgin Mary appeared to Santiago (St James the Apostle) atop a pillar of jasper in 40 CE. The famous pillar is in the east-end Santa Capilla, with only a tiny oval-shaped portion exposed (except on dedicated days). In the north aisle, the fresco painting in the third cupola is Goya's *Regina Martyrum* (Queen of Martyrs), painted in 1781.

EATING IN TARRAGONA & SITGES: OUR PICKS

Mercat Central: Traditional market with modern food stands found inside a Modernista building in Tarragona. *8.30am-9pm Mon-Sat €*

El Terrat: The tasting menu celebrates the Moroccan head chef's roots and local ingredients; in Tarragona. *1.15-3.30pm Thu-Tue, 8.15-10.30pm Fri & Sat €€€*

El Cable: Always packed tapas bar in Sitges' old town, known for its delicious *patates braves*. *7-11.30pm Mon-Fri, noon-3.30pm & 7-11.30pm Sat & Sun €€*

NeM: Creative, season-rooted tapas blend Spanish and Asian flavours at this stylish Sitges fave. *7.30-11pm Wed-Fri, 1-5pm & 7.30-11pm Sat & Sun €€*

La Seo, Zaragoza

THE COSTA BRAVA & DALÍ

Teatre-Museu Dalí: Topped by larger-than-life eggs, Dalí's theatre-museum opened in 1974 and is a centrepiece of the artist's hometown, Figueres.

Casa Museu Dalí: Just outside Cadaqués, the artist's labyrinthine house in Portlligat is unlike any historic home you've seen before, including his former workshop.

Cap de Creus: Dalí's painting *The Great Masturbator* mimics the shape of one of the cape's strangest rocks, located in Cala Culleró.

Castell Gala Dalí: Dalí's wife Gala is buried at the 14th-century castle he gifted to her, located between Girona and Palafrugell.

Expo Dalí: Small gallery in Cadaqués that showcases the artist's original prints.

Goya's earlier *Adoración del Nombre del Dios* adorns the ceiling of the choir at the church's far east end. Goya's work can also be seen at the **Museo Goya** *(museogoya.fundacionibercaja. es)* and the **Museo de Zaragoza** *(turismodearagon.com),* both slated to reopen in 2026 following renovations.

Though overshadowed in scale by the basilica, Zaragoza's **La Seo** cathedral is arguably a finer work of Christian architecture. Built between the 12th and 17th centuries, it stands on the site of Islamic Zaragoza's main mosque. A joint ticket covers both churches *(catedraldezaragoza.es; adut/child €10/free).*

High point of Islamic architecture

The dour castle-like exterior gives no hint of the ornate decorative joys within the **Aljafería** *(turismodearagon.com; adult/child €7/free).* Built as a fortified palace for Zaragoza's Islamic rulers in the 11th century, it passed into Christian hands in 1118, and in the 1490s the Reyes Católicos (Catholic Monarchs), Fernando and Isabel, tacked on their own palace. Wandering through its exquisitely sculpted courtyards and delicate interwoven archways, you can get a sense of the pomp and majesty of both the Islamic court and its Christian successors.

The Spanish Pyrenees TIME FROM BARCELONA: 3–4HR 🚗

Mountain hikes and other adventures

Some of Spain's most dramatic mountain country awaits in the Pyrenees, which spill over into France north of Zaragoza

 EATING IN CADAQUÉS & BEGUR: OUR PICKS

Compartir: Try the multicourse tasting menu from El Bulli alums for Catalan flavours made to share in Cadaqués. *1-3pm & 8-10pm Tue-Sat* €€€

Havana: Begur's Cuban connection results in authentic Caribbean flavours. *1-3.30pm & 7-10.30pm Thu-Mon, 7-10.30pm Wed* €€

Es Baluard: A family-run Cadaqués restaurant by the sea for traditional Catalan feasts and paella. *1-3.30pm & 8-10pm Wed-Sun, 1-3.30pm Mon* €€€

Lua: This cosy spot in Cadaqués serves Mediterranean and Asian fusion food like curry-covered pork meatballs. *1-3.30pm & 8-10.30pm* €€

PYRENEES PRACTICALITIES

The best walking season in Spain's Pyrenees is from about May to October. Warmest weather is generally from mid-June to early September; mountain streams and waterfalls are spectacular in spring; and October brings wonderful autumn colours. Book accommodation well ahead for July and August (the busiest season), and at any time of year if you're keen to stay in the *refugis* (mountain huts). Both national parks have wheelchair-accessible trails. Visit the park's visitor centres and information points for tips on hiking routes, weather conditions and seasonal transport. Stone villages dotted around the national park's fringes provide charming bases, including Torla, Broto, Aínsa and Bielsa for Monte Perdido and Espot, Taüll and Boí for Aigüestortes.

ILLIA SHVEDOV/SHUTTERSTOCK

Parc Nacional d'Aigüestortes i Estany de Sant Maurici

and Barcelona. Every corner of these undeveloped mountains is breathtaking in its majesty and inspiring in its beauty. Two pristine national parks provide the scenic high, with innumerable great walking trails and other adventure-activity opportunities.

In the north of Aragón, the 156-sq-km **Parque Nacional de Ordesa y Monte Perdido** *(miteco.gob.es)* encompasses limestone peaks, plunging canyons, thick forests, meadow pastures, rivers, waterfalls and turquoise mountain lakes. The park's **Valle de Ordesa** is one of the most spectacular canyons in Europe, with multiple walking routes including a classic 9km trail (one way).

Over in Catalonia's north, the 405-sq-km **Parc Nacional d'Aigüestortes i Estany de Sant Maurici** *(parcsnaturals. gencat.cat)* is rife with well-marked trails, welcoming *refugis* (huts) and impressive scenery at every turn. With over 200 lakes, overlooked by 3000m-high mountain peaks, the beauty of this glacier-carved realm feels downright cinematic. A standout hike (15.5km) is crossing the park in one day from Espot to Boí, connecting the Estany Llong and Estany d'Amitges routes through the **Portarró d'Espot** (2423m) pass. This area and its surrounds are also home to some of Spain's most popular ski slopes.

 EATING IN ZARAGOZA: OUR PICKS

La Clandestina: Stylish bistro known for its brunch (with *cava*), tasty vegetarian creations and great cheesecake. *hours vary* €€

Restaurante Palomeque: Rich, original Spanish dishes in a cosy dining room or streetside. *11am–midnight Mon-Fri, noon–6pm Sat* €€€

Bodegas Almau: All manner of tapas (anchovies a speciality), and hundreds of wine bottles at a 150-year-old bar. *11am–4pm & 7pm–midnight* €

Taberna Doña Casta: Join the crowds for tasty croquettes and *huevos rotos* (fried eggs with potatoes). *7pm–1am Tue, noon–4.30pm & 7pm–1am Wed-Sun* €

Northern Spain

DRAMATIC SCENERY | CULTURE-PACKED CITIES | GASTRONOMY

Often lyrically talked about as 'Green Spain', the northern stretch of the country feels a world away, with its rugged cliffs, verdant countryside, stone-built villages and wild surf beaches fronting the Bay of Biscay or the wide-open Atlantic. Each region has its own distinctive identity and, in most cases, language, and the culture-rich main cities are as enthralling as the quiet hills.

In the Basque Country, cows and sheep graze in valleys between lofty mountains, rocky coves are battered by furious Atlantic swells, while the cities buzz with art, gastronomy and nightlife. Many Basque people see their identity as strongly tied to the region they call Euskadi (País Vasco in Spanish), which officially includes the provinces of Vizcaya (and its capital Bilbao), Gipuzkoa (and its capital Donostia-San Sebastián) and Álava (and its capital Vitoria-Gasteiz). However, many Basques consider Euskal Herria ('the land of Basque speakers') to more broadly include Navarra and three provinces in southern France.

To the west, the autonomous region of Cantabria and the Principality of Asturias stretch just a little over 300km along the Bay of Biscay, yet encompass a dramatically beautiful world of Atlantic-whipped shores giving way to the snowcapped, adventure-laced Picos de Europa mountains. Galicia, Spain's northwest

☑ TOP TIP

Across the region, many shops (and some tourism activities) close for lunch during the 'siesta hours' (between about 2.30pm and 5pm). For budget-conscious dining, take advantage of *menús del día* (rarely served in evenings). Summer can be busy along Spain's northern coast; beaches are less packed in spring and autumn.

 GETTING AROUND

The north is well connected by air. Major towns have good bus and train connections; the narrow-gauge Renfe Cercanías Ancho Métrico *(renfe.com)* rattles across the north. For more remote destinations, hire a car or plan ahead to align with limited public transport services.

Many travellers explore this region on foot, taking advantage of local trails including the Camino del Norte variant of the Camino de Santiago. The main cities have enjoyably walkable old towns.

NORTHERN SPAIN

Atlantic
Ocean

Bay of
Biscay

Bordeaux

Arcachon

Santander

FRANCE

Viveiro
Ferrol
A Coruña
Ribadeo
Avilés
Gijón
Santillana
del Mar
Donostia-
San Sebastián
Fisterra
Vilalba
Luarca
Llanes
Laredo
Bayonne
Santiago de
Compostela
Lugo
Oviedo
Torre-
cerrado
Bilbao
Irún
Biarritz
Cabo
Fisterra
Noia
Peña
Ubiña
Picos de
Europa
Durango
Ribeira
Lalín
Ponferrada
León
Reinosa
Vitoria-
Gasteiz
Pamplona
Pontevedra
Ourense
Astorga
Aguilar de
Campóo
Miranda
de Ebro
Logroño
Vigo
Verín
Benavente
Palencia
Burgos
Calahorra
Viana do
Castelo
Braga
Chaves
Bragança
Zamora
Valladolid
Soria
Tudela
Porto
Vila Real
Tordesillas
Aranda de
Duero
Zaragoza

PORTUGAL

Salamanca

Río Miño
Río Duero
Río Ebro

0   100 km
0   50 miles

corner, combines the pilgrim magnet of Santiago de Compostela with a dramatic, wave-battered coastline.

Bilbao

Once defined by its steelworks and shipbuilding industries, Bilbao has seen a remarkable journey of regeneration since the 1990s. The staggering architecture, venerable dining scene, fascinating museums and endlessly creative cultural arena make Bilbao the most exciting urban centre in the Basque Country.

Arty Bilbao

The gleaming, titanium-clad **Museo Guggenheim Bilbao** (*guggenheim-bilbao.eus; adult/child €18/free*), on the banks of the Ría del Nervión, is the city's most striking building. Filled with pieces by some of the world's best contemporary artists, this extraordinary Frank Gehry–designed landmark is reason alone to visit Bilbao. Start your visit in the central atrium, a light-filled space in which the interior architecture can be admired. From here, three floors of galleries emerge, linked by staircases, catwalks and lifts. Check ahead for what's currently on show and any thrilling temporary exhibitions.

EATING IN BILBAO: OUR PICKS

La Viña del Ensanche: Mouthwatering morsels include ham, seared mackerel and crispy asparagus tempura. *10am-10.30pm Tue-Fri, from 1pm Sat* €

El Globo: Outstanding *pintxos* (labelled in English) that showcase the great bounty of the Basque countryside. *hours vary* €

Gure Toki: Many consider this Bilbao's best *pintxos*. Try mini pastry parcels filled with stir-fried veg and prawns. *10am-11pm Thu-Tue* €

Mina Restaurante: Serious creativity is on the tasting menu at this riverside restaurant, which some critics call Bilbao's best. *2-3pm & 9-10pm Wed-Sun* €€€

Exterior works to seek out include Louise Bourgeois' spider-like *Maman* and Anish Kapoor's *Tall Tree & the Eye,* both by the river; and Jeff Koons' *Puppy,* a 12m-tall Highland terrier made up of thousands of flowers.

But Bilbao's art scene extends beyond the Guggenheim. Don't miss the **Museo de Bellas Artes** *(bilbaomuseoa.eus; free),* which houses works by Murillo, El Greco and Goya. For a glimpse into the city's contemporary art scene, pop into riverside gallery **Uribitarte40** *(bilbaoarte.eus),* avant-garde Basque-focused **Sala Rekalde** *(salarekalde.bizkaia.net)* and **Azkuna Zentroa** (the Alhóndiga), a former wine-storage warehouse turned cultural centre *(azkunazentroa.eus).*

Donostia-San Sebastián

Officially named in both Basque (Donostia) and Spanish (San Sebastián), Donostia-San Sebastián is a city that celebrates the art of eating. Just as good as the food is San Sebastián's glamorous beachside setting. Little wonder, then, that over-tourism is a growing concern for locals. In 2023, mayor Eneko Goia announced a ban on the construction of new hotels to combat high visitor numbers.

Beach life

The crescent-shaped **Playa de la Concha** (and its westerly extension **Playa de Ondarreta**) is largely sheltered from Atlantic swells. Swim out to floating diving platforms or join in a volleyball match on the sand. At the eastern end of the beach, there are accessible hot showers, changing rooms and lockers and an accessible ramp down to the sand. From June to September, a free assisted bathing service is available.

Opposite Playa de la Concha is **Isla de Santa Clara**. In summer, **Motoras de la Isla** *(motorasdelaisla.com; €5)* runs boat trips to the island from the fishing port. You can also paddle to Santa Clara by SUP or kayak; rent them at **Club Deportivo Fortuna** *(cdfortunake.com; from €13 per hr).*

Fronting the Gros district, **Playa de la Zurriola** is the city's other beachy jewel, known for its surf waves (often beginner-friendly) and buzzing local scene. Don't miss **Mundaka**,

PAMPLONA

The Navarran capital of Pamplona (Iruña in Basque) combines a rich history and well-preserved old town with a youthful vibe and buzzing bar scene. It's easy to get a sense of Pamplona's past by wandering the cobbled streets, following the path of pilgrims walking the Camino de Santiago. At **Cafe Iruña**, you might expect former Ernest Hemingway to swing through the doors at any moment. But far from being caught up in the events of bygone years, Pamplona is a city that feels alive. Its most famous festivity is the raucous bull-running festival of **San Fermín**; it's important to note that the running of the bulls itself can be bloody and animal rights activists condemn its cruelty. There is a growing anti-bullfighting movement in many parts of Spain.

 EATING IN DONOSTIA-SAN SEBASTIÁN: PINTXOS & MICHELIN STARS

Bar Borda Berri: Perennially popular, old-school *pintxo* bar that lives up to the hype. *12.30-3.30pm Wed-Sat & 7.30-10.30pm Tue-Fri* €	**Paco Bueno:** This no-frills bar is the place to go for piping-hot battered prawns; order them at the counter. *11am-3pm* €	**La Viña:** Try the famous baked cheesecake, prepared daily and left to stand on shelves by the bar. *10.30am-4pm & 7-11pm Tue-Sun* €	**Ganbara:** This *pintxo* bar is highly regarded for its delectable plates and snacks; good wine list, too. *12.30-3.30pm & 7-11pm Tue-Sat* €
Txepetxa: Anchovies with various accompaniments are the house speciality at this traditional local bar. *noon-3pm & 7-11pm Tue-Sat* €	**Arzak:** Chefs draw on thousands of ingredients to create new dishes in 'the lab' at one of the world's best restaurants. *1.15-3.15pm & 8.45-10.30pm Tue-Sat* €€€	**Akelaŕe:** Three-Michelin-starred restaurant serving Basque nouvelle cuisine; located in the suburb of Igueldo. *1-2.30pm & 8.30-9.30pm Tue-Sat* €€€	**Martín Berasategui:** Chef Martín Berasategui takes a scientific approach at this triple-starred temple to food. *1-2.15pm Wed-Sun, 8.30-9.30pm Thu-Sat* €€€

100km west en route to Bilbao and a big name in the surf world due to its famous left-hand barrel; rent gear or book a lesson with **Mundaka Surf Shop** (*mundakasurfshop.com; rental from €10*).

Santillana del Mar

Just inland from the Bay of Biscay on Cantabria's western coast, Santillana del Mar is one of Spain's loveliest towns. Even high-season crowds seem to do little to diminish the charm of its cobbled lanes and plazas or its palaces and mansions built with wealth from South America.

Stepping into the past

Spain's most important prehistoric site, just outside Santillana del Mar, was discovered by an amateur archaeologist and his eight-year-old daughter in 1879. Magnificent **Altamira** (*cultura.gob.es; adult/child €3/free; closed Mon*) stands as a testament to the fact that humankind (extremely artistic humans at that) have called this area home for at least 35,500 years. The wonderfully executed animals (mostly created around 18,500 years ago) continue to thrill modern viewers with their artistic beauty as they gallop – sometimes larger than life-size – across the walls. Bison are curved cleverly across the rippled ceiling of the cave so that their muscles and contours are often revealed almost in three dimensions. It's unfortunate (if understandable) that the originals are under protection – viewed only occasionally by experts – but the incredibly realistic and interactive museum mock-up of the cave complex offers an unexpectedly fascinating experience.

Picos de Europa

Compact but dramatically varied, the 674-sq-km **Parque Nacional Picos de Europa** (*parquenacionalpicoseuropa.es*) is one of the favourite haunts for Spanish mountain enthusiasts. The park's three 2000m limestone massifs straddle the provinces of Cantabria, Asturias and Castilla y León. The pretty hill town of **Potes**, in the Cantabrian foothills of the Picos, and **Cangas de Onís** on the Asturian side make ideal bases.

Hiking the Picos

There are over 40 well-marked hiking routes across the Picos suited to all levels of energy, fitness and enthusiasm. Be prepared for squalls and carry waterproofs, warm gear, sunblock and a hat. Busy even on a winter's weekend, the **Ruta del Cares** is so popular it's often referred to as 'Spain's favourite hike'. Rich in flora and fauna and with fine mountain views, the 11km (one-way) route between **Poncebos** in Asturias and **Caín** in Castilla y León is an adventure, threading along ledges, passing through tunnels and crossing bridges in a gorge high above the Río Cares. The track is generally hiked from north to south.

The 753m-long **Teleférico de Fuente Dé** (*telefericodefuentede.com; adult/child from €13/6*) has been carrying visitors from **Fuente Dé** village (near Potes) to the top of the Picos

Altamira museum, Santillana del Mar

for more than 50 years. Weather permitting, you can hike down from an altitude of 1853m. The ride up to the cafe on the summit takes just four minutes but you should allow three to four hours for the 15km hike back down the slopes. If you opt to avoid the full walk back down, there are several (flatter) routes crisscrossing the higher peaks.

Santiago de Compostela

The destination of half a million people who follow the Camino de Santiago pilgrim trails every year, Santiago de Compostela is one of Spain's most beautiful cities and arguably the one where the aura of past centuries lives on strongest. It is also a thriving modern regional capital, with one of Spain's top universities.

Marvel at Santiago's cathedral

Entering magnificent **Praza do Obradoiro** for the first time, you'll stop dead in your tracks, just as many thousands of pilgrims do every year, eyes magnetised by the soaring Churrigueresque facade of the **Catedral de Santiago de Compostela** *(catedraldesantiago.es),* believed to house the tomb of Santiago (St James) the Apostle. Today's cathedral is one of Europe's architectural and historical highlights, and features a mix of an original Romanesque structure, constructed between 1075 and 1211, and later Gothic and baroque flourishes.

Inside, the **Altar Mayor** (High Altar) is a fantastically elaborate Churrigueresque confection with a statue of Santiago at its centre. The ambulatory (walkway) round behind the Altar Mayor passes the inside of the **Puerta Santa** (Holy Door), which opens only in holy years, and brings you round to a flight of steps descending to a view of the large 19th-century silver casket that contains, we're assured, Santiago's remains. Re-emerging, you can climb stairs up behind the Santiago statue, embrace him and make a wish.

JAMES JACKMAN/LONELY PLANET

CANTABRIA & ASTURIAS BEACHES

Playa de Somo: Across the bay from Cantabria's capital Santander, one of Spain's best surfing beaches has beginner-friendly waves in summer.

Playa de Torimbia: Near lively Llanes, Asturias' most famous *playa nudista* is a perfect arc of white sand bracketed by craggy headlands.

Playa del Silencio: Best for scenery (rather than swimming), this wild Asturian cove with jutting rock islets sits just west of pretty Cudillero.

Ribadesella: This easygoing Asturian fishing-and-beach town has a beautiful golden strand fronting the Río Sella estuary.

Playa de Langre: Sometimes described as Cantabria's most beautiful beach, this sandy cove and its smaller sister rest beneath spectacular cliffs.

TOLOBALAGUER.COM/SHUTTERSTOCK

Pórtico de la Gloria, Catedral de Santiago de Compostela (p573)

CATHEDRAL TIPS

At 7am, the Santiago cathedral is practically empty, even in peak summer months.

Entry to the Pórtico de la Gloria, Cubiertas (roof) and Museo Catedral is by ticket. Advance bookings, at least two weeks ahead for July and August, are essential for the first two.

Guided night tours (sometimes in English) are a treat. You'll enjoy stunning views from the Tribune, an upper-level balcony. Tickets *(€25)* go on sale 15 days ahead.

The popular **rooftop tour** *(adult/child €15/12)* provides a close-up look at the towers and their decorative adornments, plus tremendous city views. Be ready to climb over 150 steps.

The permanent collection of the **Museo Catedral** *(adult/child €7/free)* contains a sizeable section of Maestro Mateo's original carved-stone choir.

The cathedral's artistic high point, at the west end of the nave, the **Pórtico de la Gloria** features 200 Romanesque sculptures by Maestro Mateo, who was given charge of the cathedral-building programme in the late 12th century.

Prazas, museums and markets

At the northern end of Praza do Obradoiro, the **Hostal dos Reis Católicos** *(paradores.es)* was built in the 16th century as a pilgrim hostel by order of the Reyes Católicos. Today it's a *parador* (luxurious state-owned hotel), open for self-guided tours.

Opposite the cathedral, the elegant 18th-century **Pazo de Raxoi** is now Santiago's city hall. Head a few steps north to **Praza das Praterías** (Silversmiths' Square), centred on the 1825 **Fuente de los Caballos** and the excellent **Museo das Peregrinacións** *(museoperegrinacions.xunta.gal; free)*, which is closed on Mondays.

A bustling hub of Santiago life, the **Mercado de Abastos** *(closed Sun)* comprises 300-odd stalls piled high with fresh produce from Galicia's farms and coasts. Popular bars and restaurants line the street outside; inside, **Nave 5 Abastos** (Aisle 5) is set with long tables where you can sit down for well-priced meals cooked up in adjacent stalls.

EATING IN SANTIAGO DE COMPOSTELA: OUR PICKS

O Gato Negro: Old-school tavern (since 1922) with market-fresh seafood, empanadas and more. Be ready to eat standing. *12.30-3pm & 7.30-11pm Tue-Sat* €€

Café-Jardin Costa Vella: The garden cafe is a delightful breakfast spot. Also does light local-produce tapas, cakes and wines. *8am-12.30pm & 4.30-10.30pm* €

A Moa: Great mix of Galician and worldly fare in street-level wine bar, stone-walled restaurant and verdant garden. *1.30-3.45pm & 9-11pm Tue-Sat, 1.30-3.45pm Sun* €€

Abastos 2.0: Seafood dishes at marketside outdoor tables; daily-changing €50 *menú* at the indoor 'Barra' (reservations required). *noon-3.30pm & 8-11pm Mon-Sat* €€€

Cabo Fisterra & Around

Once believed by Europeans to be the western limit of the world, hilly, heather-clad Cabo Fisterra (Cape Finisterre) extends into the Atlantic 3km south of the fishing port Fisterra on Galicia's dramatic Costa da Morte. The cape is the final destination for particularly enthusiastic Camino de Santiago pilgrims who push on an extra 89km from Santiago de Compostela – and for those who walk the Camiño dos Faros along the Costa da Morte.

End-of-the-world lighthouse

Despite the crowds, **Cabo Fisterra** remains a wonderfully panoramic and atmospheric spot, topped by a squat 19th-century lighthouse, the **Faro de Fisterra**. Some who reach it on foot follow a tradition of burning worn-out old boots and socks on the rocks just below the lighthouse. The easiest and quickest way to walk from Fisterra to Cabo Fisterra is simply to head 3km along the AC445 road to the lighthouse, with the panoramas expanding as you go. Other, even more scenic paths lead here too, including over the top of **Monte do Facho** (242m), the promontory's highest point.

Walking the Camiño dos Faros

You can definitely enjoy the Costa da Morte pottering around by car, bicycle or motorbike, but you'll get the most intimate connection with its diverse scenes and moods by exploring on foot. A superb, often challenging, long-distance path, the **Camiño dos Faros** (*Lighthouse Way; caminodosfaros.com*) traces the whole coastline from Malpica de Bergantiños to Cabo Fisterra. Its eight stages are marked only in the Malpica-to-Fisterra direction (with small green arrows and paint blobs). Arguably most spectacular are Stage 7 (Muxía to Praia de Nemiña, 25km) and Stage 8 (Praia de Nemiña to Cabo Fisterra, 27km). Some people walk the whole trail in one trip; others do day walks. Expect sun, wind and rain: beware of fog rolling rapidly in, and avoid precipitous cliffs on gusty days.

NORTHERN WINES

Best known among characterful Galician wines are the fruity *albariño* whites from the Rías Baixas DO. Many good reds come from the native *mencía* grape, and in recent years winemakers have revived Galician grapes including *godello* (whites), *brancellao* and *merenzao* (reds). Produced using Hondarrabi Zuri grapes, Basque *txakoli* is a fresh, crisp, dry and slightly sparkling white wine that goes well with seafood or *pintxos* on sunny days. Wine aficionados the world over know the wines of La Rioja, where vines have been cultivated since Roman times. Cantabria, Asturias and the Basque Country are famous for their ciders, poured from up high for maximum fizz. Wineries across the north are open for tours and tastings; it's best to book. The *vendimia* (grape harvest) starts in August.

 EATING ON THE COSTA DA MORTE: OUR PICKS

O Pirata, Fisterra: The freshest of fish and seafood, traditionally prepared, at good prices and overlooking the harbour. *noon-5pm Tue-Sun* €

Etel & Pan, Fisterra Friendly cafe doing excellent burgers, *bocadillos* and salads, with plentiful vegetarian options. *noon-3.30pm & 7-10.30pm Fri-Tue* €

Casa Fontequeiroso, Nemiña Superb dinners based around traditional Galician recipes at a small rural hotel (p596). Non-guests should call first. *7-9pm* €€

Lonxa d'Alvaro, Muxía Fish *a la brasa* (char-grilled), seafood-stuffed *filloas* (crêpes) and lobster rice are the stars here. *hours vary* €€€

Valencia & Around

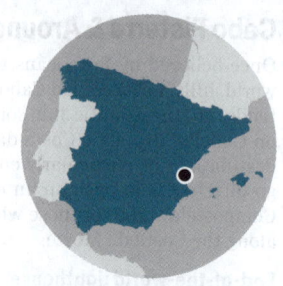

OTHERWORLDLY ARCHITECTURE | ELEGANT MARKETS | UPBEAT BEACHES

GETTING AROUND

Most of Valencia's sights are within easy reach of the main plaza and others are a short cycle or tram ride away. Taxis are affordable, costing around €10 from the centre to the beach. Bikes (around €15 per day) are a lovely way to explore the city. **Valenbisi** *(valenbisi. es)* is the city's bike scheme; a weekly ticket costs €13. While many parts of the surrounding Valencia region (including La Albufera) are easy to explore with public transport, hiring a car is useful.

☑ **TOP TIP**

Want to pack in a lot of sights? The **Valencia Tourist Card** *(€17/24/30 per 24/48/72 hr)* offers unlimited travel, discounts and a glass of wine at El Corte Inglés. Buy it from tourist information offices or access *visitvalencia.com* for 10% off.

With fun beaches, culture-packed cities and a fierce culinary heritage, Spain's east coast has an extraordinary feel-good factor. In recent years, the Valencia region has embraced urban regeneration, forward-thinking events and gorgeous green spaces (often guided by sustainability), attracting a new wave of visitors.

Over 2000 years of history have carved Valencia's warren-like old-town, from the Romans who founded it to the 20th-century architects who flexed their creativity. Ancient ruins have been painstakingly preserved, but the city isn't stuck in the past. Russafa is the creatives' *barrio,* with cool cafes, hidden galleries and brilliant restaurants; the seaside has a fresh feel with lively *chiringuitos* (snack bars). Further south, rewilding projects revive the dunes and ecosystems of La Albufera. Throw in a 9km-long park with bike routes, wildflowers and lemon trees, and it's clear Valencia is snapping at the heels of its Catalan neighbour. Among the city's many festivities, few rival the famous Las Fallas, held amid thundering pyrotechnics each March.

Taste Local Delicacies

Valencia's splendid Central Market

A feast of Valencia-grown produce awaits within the **Mercat Central** *(mercadocentralvalencia.es; closed on Sun),* a Valencian Art Nouveau–style market in the centre of Ciutat Vella. Inside, domed glass ceilings preside over pyramids of olives, fish and veg straight from the fields. A great way to get a taste for its buzzing, still-local atmosphere is by sipping a refreshing *horchata* (typical Valencian sugary cold drink made from tiger nuts) at the bar at **La Huertana**. Don't forget the *fartón,* an iced bun for dunking. **Les Tomates de Javier** sells the best Valencian tomatoes, **Retrogusto** *(retrogustocoffeemates.com)* brews cracking coffee, and **Solaz** sells cheesecake made by the

VALENCIA

★ HIGHLIGHTS
1 Catedral de Valencia
2 Ciutat de les Arts i les Ciències
3 Jardín del Túria
4 Mercado Central

● SIGHTS
5 CaixaForum
6 Museu de les Ciències
7 Palau de les Arts

● ACTIVITIES
8 Ana Illueca
9 Escuela Fictile
10 Valencia Bikes

● SLEEPING
11 Casa Clarita
12 YOURS

● EATING
13 2 Estaciones
14 Amor Amargo

15 Central Bar
16 Forastera Restaurant
17 La Cantina de Ruzafa
see 4 La Huertana
18 La Samorra
19 Maipi
20 Ostras Pedrín

● DRINKING & NIGHTLIFE
see 4 Retrogusto

● ENTERTAINMENT
21 Hemisfèric

● SHOPPING
22 Cuit
23 Konlakalma
see 4 Les Tomates de Javier
24 Plou Estudi
see 4 Solaz

VALENCIA POTTERY STUDIOS

Valencia has an ancient ceramics heritage, and modern artisans are throwing bold new shapes.

Cuit: Make your own mug in this chic Russafa studio to pick up the next month, or buy one readymade. *(cuit.es)*

Ana Illueca: The un-trendy area near Cabanyal is the unlikely home of this whip-smart pottery studio. *(anaillueca. com)*

Plou Estudi: Geometric shapes with pops of blue and yellow line shelves in this studio and shop.

Escuela Fictile: Japanese pottery has a huge influence on Macarena's pieces, found in her peaceful workshop.

Konlakalma: Katrin makes asymmetric vases and fluid sculptures using coil and slab building techniques. *(konlakalma.com)*

ROB TILLEY/GETTY IMAGES

Ciutat de les Arts i les Ciències

team of Ricard Camarena, owner of the two-Michelin-starred Ricard Camarena restaurant.

Find the Holy Grail

Spot a relic from 100 BCE

An impossible task? Not according to the **Catedral de Valencia** (*catedraldevalencia.es; adult/child €10/6*). Inside Valencia's Gothic cathedral is an agate goblet dating from 100 BCE. Dazzling gold handles and a base embellished with pearls, rubies and emeralds were added in the medieval era. But at just 17cm tall it's easy to miss: head towards the hushed 14th-century **Capilla del Santo Cáliz**. Constructed between the 13th and 15th centuries, the cathedral features splendid star vaulting and Renaissance-style frescoes above the main altar. A stomp up 207 spiral steps to the **bell tower** (*adult/ child €3/free*) is thrilling.

A Wondrous Complex

Dive into Santiago Calatrava's masterpiece

Establishing Valencia as a beacon of contemporary architecture, the astonishing **Ciutat de les Arts i les Ciències** (*cac.es*) is mostly the work of Valencian architect Santiago Calatrava.

 EATING IN RUSSAFA: OUR PICKS

Maipi: Old-school *taberna* serving whatever's fresh from the market, like sweet prawns or artichokes with *jamón*. *1.30-4pm & 8.30-11pm Mon-Fri* €

La Cantina de Ruzafa: Wholesome canteen famous for its stewed bull sandwich topped with fried eggs. *9.30am-5pm Mon-Thu, from 9am Fri* €

Amor Amargo: Cosy Art Nouveau interiors with ambitious cooking – the nine-hour ribs are heavenly. *noon-12.30am Tue-Sun, from 7pm Mon* €€

2 Estaciones: Meticulous food with seasonality at its core. The weekday *menú express* is fantastic value. *1.30-3.30pm & 8.30-10.30pm Wed-Sat* €€€

The architecture is a marvel in itself; a walk through the complex that occupies a vast swathe of the old Túria riverbed won't cost you a penny.

Calatrava balanced mighty, organic architecture by using ceramic mosaic tiles called *trencadís*. They're perhaps most striking on **Palau de les Arts**, an ultramodern performing-arts complex with four auditoriums. Tours run several times daily *(adult/child €18/14)*. To the south, the unblinking eye of the **Hemisfèric** houses an IMAX cinema with a 900-sq-metre screen. Across an expanse of water, **Museu de les Ciències** *(adult/child €9.40/7.20)* stretches out like a giant whale skeleton, housing an interactive science museum. Next up, resembling a huge purple mussel, the **CaixaForum** stages interesting exhibitions on diverse themes.

Bike to the Beach

Explore Valencia's loveliest gardens

Valencia's best park is found in an old riverbed that was diverted due to flooding. Snaking through the city for over 9km, **Jardín del Túria** is a delight to explore by bike. Inaugurated in 1986, today the riverbed is a haven of baobab and palm trees frequented by chattering parakeets and songbirds. On a leisurely route of around 12km (one way), it's possible to cycle all the way to pretty **Playa de la Patacona**, with its seafront restaurants and *chiringuitos*. Pick up wheels at **Valencia Bikes** *(valenciabikes.com; €15 per day)*, close to the Túria metro.

Boating & Bird-Spotting

Cruise La Albufera's waters

Just 15km south of Valencia proper, glorious La Albufera is the birthplace of paella, with much of the area protected by the peaceful **Parque Natural de la Albufera**. People have fished the freshwater lake here since prehistoric times, and the rice paddies have been around since at least the 15th century. This rice is used in the best paellas – try one at **Bon Aire** *(restaurantebonaire.com)* in **El Palmar**. A handful of boat trips join the local fisherfolk who use flat-bottomed boats and nets to harvest fish and eels from the shallow waters. Jaime, a La Albufera local, offers insightful trips with **Paseos en Barca El Pero** *(paseosenbarcaelpero.es; from €70)*. Sunsets are spectacular: book Jaime's sunset cruise or head to **Mirador El Pujol**.

SWIMMING SPOTS BEYOND VALENCIA

Around Xàbia: Cala del Portixol is famed as the most beautiful on the coastline. Cala Blanca and Cala de Dins are fairy-tale coves, accessible only by foot.

Dénia: Dénia's coastline has lots of little surprises. Swim in shimmering waters outside Cova Tallada, an artificial cave best accessed by kayak.

Fuente de los Baños: In the mountains around Montanejos, these emerald pools fed by hot springs are a dreamy wild-swimming spot.

Altea: Hilltop, whitewashed Altea, set between two protected natural parks, has lofty viewpoints, pebble beaches and turquoise waters.

La Devesa: Part of La Albufera's natural regeneration, La Devesa is accessed only by foot along a path bordered by rosemary and pines.

 EATING IN CIUTAT VELLA: OUR PICKS

Ostras Pedrín: Join a cool crowd out to get tipsy on *cava* and feast on a sea of oysters. *11am-midnight Mon-Sat, to 4pm Sun* €

La Samorra: Traditional tapas in a tiled *taberna*. Don't miss the *figatells* (meatballs). *7.30pm-midnight Wed-Sat, 12.30-5pm Thu-Sat, noon-5pm Sun* €€

Central Bar: Informal tapas bar among the fruit stalls of Mercat Central, with unbeatable cheesecake. *9am-3pm Mon-Thu, to 3.30pm Fri & Sat* €€

Forastera Restaurant: Dreamy dinner-date spot with a market-fresh tasting menu and wines from small artisanal producers. *hours vary Thu-Mon* €€€

Balearic Islands

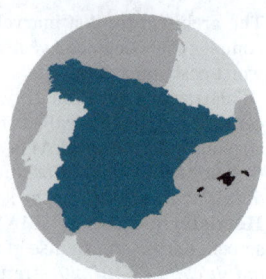

DREAM BEACHES | SOARING MOUNTAINS | CHARMING VILLAGES

 TOP TIP

In recent years, Mallorca and the other Balearics have suffered from growing overtourism concerns. Sidestep the summer crowds by visiting in shoulder season or winter. For Easter and summer, book well in advance. The opening hours provided here are for summer. Beyond Palma de Mallorca, many venues reduce hours or close in the off-season.

Etymologists may wrangle over the origins of their name, but there's no disputing the seductive magic of the Balearic Islands, clustered in the western Mediterranean off the east coast of Spain. Each of the four principal islands has its unique cultural identity, with a dialect related to Catalan, and own vibe.

Mallorca lives up to the social-media-worthy images of sun-warmed ochre buildings, scarlet bougainvillea in soulful hill towns and long beaches with aquamarine seas, but is also deeply enhanced by a contemporary outlook and rich culture. For Miró, it was the pure light. For hikers and cyclists, it's the Serra de Tramuntana's limestone spires. Foodies will love the markets and, of course, the chefs – inspired as much by their Mallorcan forebears as by contemporary Mediterranean cuisine. Meanwhile, beyond the built-up resorts, coves and white-sand bays rim the shoreline.

Menorca, the quieter pair to Mallorca, remains largely undeveloped, with brilliant, pristine beaches, megalithic ruins, two fascinating main towns (eastern Anglo-Spanish Maó and western mazelike Ciutadella) and dry stone walls crossing pastures. Ibiza's party-hard spirit draws crowds in summer, who relax on its beaches and hidden coves, and fill its somnolent, sunbaked white villages. Ibiza's part-

GETTING AROUND

Mallorca, Ibiza and Menorca have airports. Ferries (see *ferryhopper.com*) connect Alcúdia (Mallorca) with Ciutadella (Menorca) and Palma (Mallorca) with Ibiza Town; they also run to/from mainland destinations including Barcelona, Dénia and Valencia. Smaller ferries run between Ibiza and Formentera (30 minutes).

Car hire spikes seasonally so book well ahead, or use reliable local buses. Mallorca's **Ferrocarril de Sóller** (*trendesoller.com*) vintage train is a highlight. Well-marked cycling and walking paths crisscross the islands.

BALEARIC ISLANDS

ner (together, they are called the Pityuses or Pine Islands) Formentera, is pure bliss, with astonishing beaches and protected reserves.

Mallorca

History and art in the Mallorcan capital

Palma de Mallorca (universally shortened to Palma) is a stunner. Rising in sand-coloured stone from the broad still waters of the Badia de Palma, the city has been home to Christian Reconquistadors, Moors, Romans and, way back, the Talayotic people. All Palma visits begin best at the magnificent, waterfront **Catedral de Mallorca** *(catedraldemallorca.org; adult/child €10/free),* called 'La Seu'. Although the foundations went up in the 12th century on the site of the central mosque, most of the structure is predominantly Gothic. Continue your history lesson with the **Palau de l'Almudaina** *(patrimon ionacional.es; adult/child €7/4),* an Islamic fort converted into a royal residence in the 13th century, and the Moorish **Banys Àrabs** *(€3.50).*

Built with flair and innovation into the shell of the Renaissance-era seaward fortifications on the southwest side of Palma's old town, contemporary art gallery **Es Baluard** *(esbaluard.org; adult/child €6/free; closed Mon)* is one of the finest on the islands. Art lovers will want to make the pilgrimage to the wonderful hilltop compound and still-standing studios of Catalan artist Joan Miró, the **Fundació Pilar I Joan Miró** *(miromal lorca.com; adult/child €10/free; closed Mon).*

Off-the-beaten-track strands and coves

Mallorca's beaches are legendary. In the northeast, a 10km drive from castle-topped **Artà** through the mountainous

MALLORCA'S VILLAGES

Pollença: Attractive old quarter, historic religious sites, good food and easy beach or mountain access.

Artà & Capdepera: Each has superb medieval architecture overlooked by a walled, hilltop fortress.

Deià: Famous honey-coloured home to artists, writers (visit Casa Robert Graves) and musicians.

Biniaraix & Fornalutx: Walk from Sóller to these stone mountain villages blooming in subtropical flowers.

Banyalbufar: Moorish terraces with vineyards step to the sea.

Caimari & Campanet: Eat like royalty in foothill gateways to the Serra de Tramuntana.

HIKING THE SERRA DE TRAMUNTANA

Hikers come from far and wide for Mallorca's mix of soaring mountain peaks and cove-cracked coastline. You can hike year-round, though the best months are March to May and late September to October. Hiking UNESCO Reserve **Serra de Tramuntana** often involves some aspect of **Ruta de Pedra en Sec** (Dry Stone Route; GR221) – a 140km, 10-day hike between Sant Elm and Pollença. Well-marked and with accommodation at the end of each stage, this is a superb way to experience Mallorca far from the tourist crowds. A couple of favourite portions include the moderate Deià to Sóller hike (10km; four hours) and the famous **Camí de s'Arxiduc** (Path of the Archduke), a 13km circular route from Valldemossa.

woodland of Parc Natural de la Península de Llevant will bring you to wide, sandy **Cala Torta** (sometimes you have to walk down). Small, sheltered bays, **Cala Mitjana** and **Cala Estreta** (the latter is stone) are accessible down a rough track in the mountains. You can walk to them all from **Cala Mesquida** (about an hour to Estreta). Walk further north for **Cala Matzoc**. Often empty, this sandy beach is a timeless vision of Mediterranean coastline.

In the southeast, most beaches are fjord-like indents with sheets of white sand lapped by soft minty-blue waters. Just north of busy **Cales de Mallorca**, a walking trail leads several kilometres through woodland to a series of four pristine coves: **Cala Bota**, **Cala Virgili**, **Cala Pilota**, and just north, the best of the lot: **Cala Magraner**.

On the west coast, a Mallorcan highlight is to walk from a mountain village to its coastal *cala* (cove). Hardly a secret, but divine all the same, is the steep 2.5km (one-way) walk from Deià to **Cala Deià**, with famous restaurant **Ca's Patró March**.

Popular southern beaches include **Platja des Trenc**, **Cala Pi**, **Caló des Moro** and **Cala Mondragó**, but explore further and the aqua waters unfurl. **Platja d'Almunia** and **Platja de Ses Roquetes** are connected by a hiking trail. At **Cala Llombards**, a beach-hut bar, palm-leaf-shaded loungers and a ladder into the sea constitute the extent of human intervention.

Menorca

Menorca's dreamy beaches

Menorca's paper-white sands and jewel-blue waters are some of the Med's best, and authorities have taken measures to preserve their natural beauty. You'll usually need your own wheels to reach them (arrive early!), and then you often park and walk the final 1km to 3km. The loveliest beaches are strung along the south coast. Menorca's less-developed north coast is rugged and rocky, perforated with small, scenic coves.

Along with teeny **Cala Macarelleta**, the pair of exquisite horseshoe bays, **Cala Macarella** and **Cala Turqueta**, 13.5km southwest of Ciutadella, get very busy in summer for their bleach-blonde sands, unbelievably turquoise waters and cliffs cloaked in pines and holm oaks. It's a lovely 2km clifftop walk between the two via **Cala des Talaier** (accessible only on foot). Twin white-sand beaches of Banyuls and Bellavista make up **Platges de Son Saura**, 12km southeast of Ciutadella.

You'll be rewarded for the effort it takes to reach some of the island's quietest and most beautiful beaches, halfway along

EATING & DRINKING IN PALMA DE MALLORCA: OUR PICKS

El Perrito: Santa Catalina quarter's brunch mainstay: bagels, homemade cakes, fresh juices and hearty specials. *8am-4pm Mon-Sat, to 3.30pm Sun* €

La Rosa Vermuteria: Start your evening with a *vermut* (vermouth) and local-inspired tapas at this stylish spot. *noon-midnight* €€

El Camino: Stylish tapas bar: coffered ceilings, mosaic tiles and marble bar for watching your tasty bites prepared. *1-3.45pm & 6-10.45pm Tue-Sat* €€

DINS Santi Taura: Traditional Mallorcan cooking with a twist in this adults-only Michelin-star restaurant. *hours vary Tue-Sat* €€€

Cala Macarelleta, Menorca

HIKING MENORCA

Mystery-shrouded **Camí de Cavalls** (Path of Horses) loops 186km around the entire length of Menorca's coast. Connecting watchtowers, cannons and fortresses, it's believed to have been built in the 13th or 14th century to enable horseback patrols along the coastline and protect the island from sea invasions.

After years spent buried under scrub, the trail has been cleared and turned into a public footpath (GR223). It takes between seven and 10 days to hike, or you can do one of the 20 stages (5km to 14km each; outfitters can drop you off). Accommodation isn't always available at the end of each stage, meaning careful preplanning is required (see *camidecavalls.com*).

the southern coast. From **Sant Tomàs**, take the footpath west via **Platja Binigaus** to sublime **Cala Escorxada**, which has luminous waters, white sands and zero development. Continue west and you'll reach tiny **Cala Fustam**, which is a favourite of naturists. **Cala Mitjana** is most easily reached (1.5km) from **Cala Galdana** resort.

Ibiza & Formentera

Walking World-Heritage Dalt Vila

The heart and soul of the island, **Ibiza Town** (Eivissa) is a vivacious and elegant capital with a UNESCO World Heritage–listed fortified old quarter called **Dalt Vila** *(ibiza.travel)* set against a spectacular natural harbour. Its seven colossal, floodlit 16th-century bastions are visible from across southern Ibiza. Dalt Vila is tranquil and atmospheric, with many of its cobbled lanes accessible only on foot.

Enter via the **Portal de Ses Taules** gateway, just in from **Passeig Marítim** and behind neoclassical market **Mercat Vell**. All lanes lead steeply to **Castell d'Eivissa**, a walled district of historical buildings constructed over a 1000-year period, and **Catedral de Santa Maria de les Neus** on the summit. Sunset is gorgeous. Don't miss the wonderful **Museu d'Art**

EATING IN CIUTADELLA & MAÓ: OUR PICKS

Mercat de Peix: Tapas and *pintxos* bars fill this 1920s fish market, next to Maó's town market in the church cloisters. *11am-11pm Mon-Sat* €

Arjau Mao: Traditional Menorcan dishes and paella centring seafood and lobster, served portside. *1-3.30pm Thu-Mon* €€€

Pinzell: Contemporary remake of Mediterranean classics in Ciutadella. The squid stuffed with walnuts is exquisite. *1-3.30pm & 8-11.30pm Wed-Mon* €€

Pez Limón: Bold and unexpected culinary creations are the hallmark of this cosy Ciutadella tapas bar. *8-10.30pm Mon-Fri, 1-3pm & 8-10.30pm Sat* €€

IBIZA'S TOP CLUBS

Amnesia, Sant Rafel: Ibiza's most influential club, where DJ Alfredo pioneered Balearic Beat. *(amnesia.es)*

Hï Ibiza, Platja d'en Bossa: In 2022 and 2023, *DJ Magazine's* 'world's best club' with marquee DJ residencies. *(hiibiza. com)*

Pacha, Ibiza Town: Ibiza's original mega-club: multilevel dance floor, Funky Room for soul and disco. *(pacha.com)*

Ushuaïa, Platja d'en Bossa: Glitzy pool parties at Ibiza's hottest daytime club. *(theushuaiaexperien ce.com)*

DC 10, near the airport: Underground vibe and music-savvy crowd. *(dc10ibiza. com)*

Carrer de la Verge, Ibiza Town: Ibiza's main LGBTIQ+ village, with around 20 bars and clubs.

[UNVRS], Sant Rafel: World's largest club (formerly Privilege), regularly hosting thousands of clubbers. *(unvrs.com)*

Trucador Peninsula, Formentera

TOLOBALAGUER.COM/SHUTTERSTOCK

Contemporani d'Eivissa *(eivissa.es/mace; free),* housed in an 18th-century armoury.

Formentera's brilliant beaches

With sugar-white sands and perfectly clear turquoise water, the astonishing beauty of Formentera's pencil-slim **Trucador Peninsula** rivals that of the world's most glorious beaches. Walk or cycle along glittering **Ses Salines** (saltpans) to reach dirt tracks winding through steep sand dunes and emerge on the west side of this narrow sliver at dreamy **Platja Il-letes**. On the peninsula's east coast (just a few steps away) is equally gorgeous **Platja Llevant**. The beaches get packed, but they're still an essential Formentera experience. The Trucador Peninsula is part of the **Parc Natural de Ses Salines** *(car/ motorcycle €6/4).* Bring water, food and supplies.

The island's entire southern arc is necklaced with sandy alabaster bays lapped by aqua-tinted waters, known collectively as **Platja de Migjorn**. The best bits are at the southeastern end, around **Platja es Arenals**.

 EATING & DRINKING IN IBIZA TOWN: OUR PICKS

Can Costa: Reasonably priced grilled meats and paella make this a popular go-to in the Old Port. *1-3.30pm & 8-11pm Mon-Fri* €

La Barra de la Bientirada Ibiza: Hearty Spanish-fusion dishes in central Ibiza Town. Save room for killer cheesecake. *noon-midnight* €€

Bar Es Cafetí: Bar with eclectic decor in Dalt Vila, perfect for a pit stop with cocktails and finger foods. *10am-6pm Mon-Fri, noon-6pm Sat, to 4pm Sun*

Petit Vermut Eivissa: Cheerful vermouth, *apéro* and cocktails with tapas in a casual corner spot in the Old Port area. *4.30pm-late*

Seville

HERITAGE SITES | ARCHITECTURE | DINING

The Andalucian capital and jewel in the southern region's cultural crown, Seville is a luminous, romantic city. Its unique blend of artistic influences (Moorish, Jewish, Christian and Romani) infuses every detail from its magnificent Mudéjar architecture to the sultry notes of the flamenco guitar. This is a city built to explore on foot: a pleasant mesh of narrow cobbled streets and jaunty plazas, invigorated by the debonair nightlife that spills from tapas bars and bodegas.

Once-mighty civilisations, including the Romans, the Moors and the Reyes Católicos of the Spanish empire have left indelible marks on Seville, layered across the urban space. Countless generations of homebred *sevillanos* have treated Seville with reverence. As a result, the city's well-heeled past endures into the present, through impeccably preserved churches, aristocratic palaces, picturesque streets scented with orange blossom, and UNESCO-listed landmarks such as the imposing Gothic cathedral. Seville's fiestas are legendary, from the energetic Feria de Abril to more sombre Semana Santa.

☑ **TOP TIP**

Book tickets for the cathedral or the Real Alcázar as early as possible, but avoid visiting them on the same day (there's too much to take in). Admission is at a set time and can sell out days in advance. The cathedral is often closed for religious events and holidays.

A Royal Spectacle

Palaces, courtyards and gardens of the Real Alcázar

Since the 10th century, Moorish rulers and Spanish monarchs presided over their kingdoms from the exquisitely decorated

 GETTING AROUND

Much of Seville is best explored on foot, with sights clustered close together. For more spread-out attractions, rent bicycles from docking stations (Sevici app) or **Surf the City** *(surfthecity.es)*, along with electric scooters.

An electric tram line connects the San Sebastián bus station to the central Plaza Nueva. The main Plaza de Armas bus station serves major destinations across Andalucía. High-speed trains run from Sevilla Santa Justa. Buses link Sevilla Santa Justa train station to central Seville.

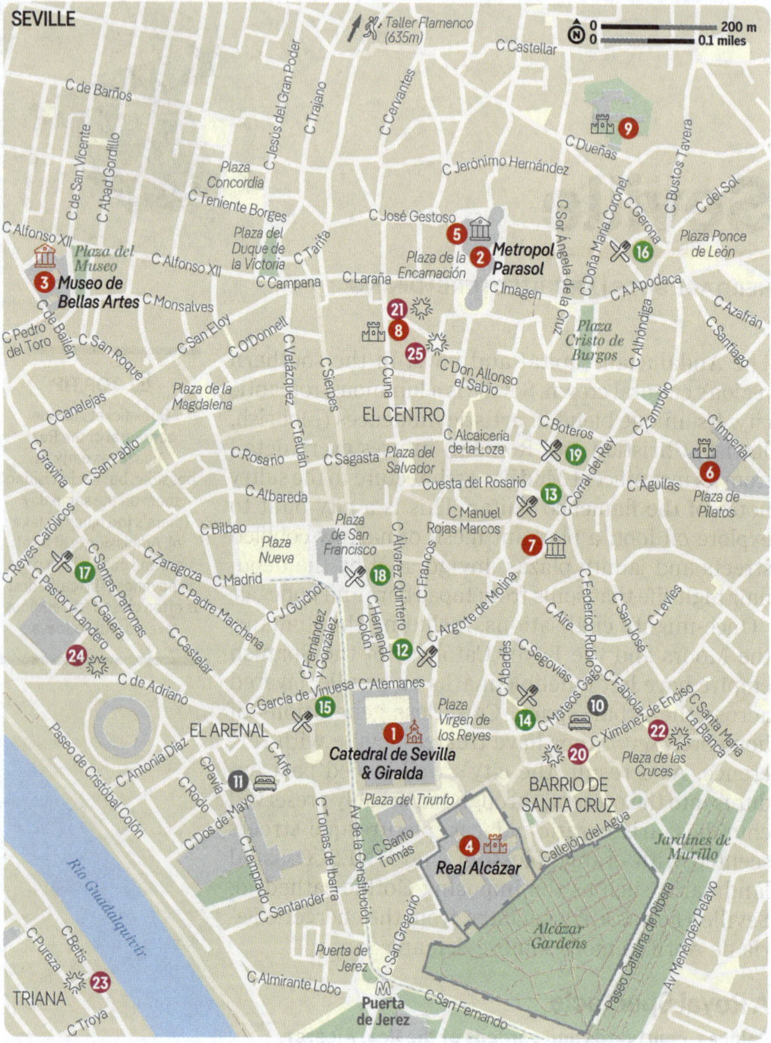

SEVILLE

Taller Flamenco
(635m)

C Castellar

0 ———— 200 m
N 0.1 miles

C de Barños

C de San Vicente
C Abad Gordillo
C Alfonso XII
C Teniente Borges
C Alfonso XII
C Monsalves
C Pedro del Toro
C de Bailén
C San Roque
C San Eloy
C O'Donnell
C Velázquez
C Canalejas
C Gravina
C San Pablo

Plaza Concordia
C Jesús del Gran Poder
C Trajano
C Cervantes
C Jerónimo Hernández
C Dueñas **9**

Plaza del Duque de la Victoria
C Tarifa
C Campana
C Laraña
C José Gestoso
5 **2**
Plaza de la Encarnación
Metropol Parasol
C Imagen
C Sor Ángela de la Cruz
C Doña María Coronel
C Gerona
C Bustos Tavera
C del Sol
Plaza Ponce de León
16
C A Apodaca
C Azafrán
C Santiago

3 **Museo de Bellas Artes**
Plaza del Museo

Plaza de la Magdalena
C Sierpes
C Rioja
C Sagasta
C Tetuán
C Cuna
21
8
25
C Don Alfonso el Sabio
Plaza Cristo de Burgos
C Alhóndiga
C Zamudio

EL CENTRO

C Alcaicería de la Loza
C Boteros
19
C Águilas
6
Plaza de Pilatos

C Canalejas
C Rosario
C Albareda
Plaza del Salvador
Cuesta del Rosario
C Corral del Rey
C Imperial

C Bilbao
Plaza de San Francisco
C Manuel Rojas Marcos
13
7

C Reyes Católicos
17
C Santas Patronas
C Zaragoza
C Madrid
C J Guichot
Plaza Nueva
C Álvarez Quintero
C Francos
18
C Argote de Molina
C Federico Rubio
C Aire
C San José
C Levíes

C Pastor y Landero
C Galera
C Padre Marchena
C Castelar
C Fernández y González
12
C Hernando Colón
C Abades
C Segovias
14
10
C Fabiola
C Ximénez de Enciso
22
C Santa María la Blanca

24
C de Adriano
C García de Vinuesa
C Atemanes
Plaza Virgen de los Reyes
C Mateos Gago
Plaza de las Cruces

EL ARENAL
C Antonia Díaz
C Arfe
C Rodo
C Dos de Mayo
15

Catedral de Sevilla & Giralda
Plaza del Triunfo
20

BARRIO DE SANTA CRUZ

Río Guadalquivir
Paseo de Cristóbal Colón
11
C Almirante Lobo
C Santo Tomas
Av de la Constitución
C Tomás de Ibarra
4 **Real Alcázar**
Callejón del Agua
Jardines de Murillo

TRIANA
C Pureza
C Betis
23
C Troya
Puerta de Jerez
C San Gregorio
C San Fernando
Alcázar Gardens
Paseo Catalina de Ribera
Av Menéndez Pelayo
Puerta de Jerez

Real Alcázar *(alcazarsevilla.org; adult/child €15.50/free)*, tearing down, augmenting and rebuilding sections of the labyrinthine complex.

The finest building overlooking the Patio de la Montería (Hunting Party's Courtyard) is the **Palacio de Don Pedro**. Built for King Pedro I (1350–69) with the help of Moorish Granada's finest artisans, it has an exquisite Mudéjar-style interior. Highlights include the golden-tiled dome ceiling of the Cuarto del Príncipe (Prince's Suite), and the spectacular Salón de Embajadores (Hall of the Ambassadors), originally Pedro I's throne room.

At the heart of this palace is the sublime central courtyard, the **Patio de las Doncellas** (Maidens' Courtyard). The sunken garden at its core, framed by carved arches, plasterwork and tiling, was uncovered by archaeologists in 2004. The Palacio Gótico (Gothic Palace), much remodelled for Carlos I in the 16th century, is now known as the **Salones de Carlos V**. The **Jardines de los Reales Alcázares** (Royal Alcazar Gardens) offer shaded paths between mazes of myrtle, fish-filled ponds and lofty palm trees.

Seville's Monumental Gothic Treasure

Tour the cathedral

When Castilian king Fernando III captured Seville from the Almohad dynasty in 1248, he ordered that the 12th-century great mosque be converted into a church. Flying buttresses, gargoyles and lavish ornamentation decorate the exterior of the world's largest Gothic building, Seville's **cathedral** *(cated raldesevilla.es; adult/child €13/free)*, officially known as the Catedral de Santa María de la Sede.

The visitor entrance is through the horseshoe arched doorway, **Puerta del Lagarto**. On your left, a gentle ramp swirls up through the **Giralda**, a former minaret repurposed as the cathedral's bell tower, with expansive views over Seville. The often-closed **Capilla Real** contains royal tombs, including the remains of Fernando III in a silver urn. Enter the series of rooms to your left to admire major art treasures, including

SEMANA SANTA IN SEVILLE

Seville puts on one of Spain's most elaborate manifestations of Christian Holy Week. From Palm Sunday to Easter Sunday, hooded *nazarenos* (penitents) carry huge *pasos* (floats holding revered statues, such as La Macarena) through the streets in ghostly solemnity. Parades lead from their home churches to the cathedral, often in the early evening. The *nazarenos* are members of the city's 50 *hermandades* or *cofradías* (religious brotherhoods, some of which include women), dressed in white robes with pointed conical hoods. The highlight of Semana Santa is La Madrugá in the early hours of Good Friday, when several of the city's most venerated statues make their appearances.

 EATING IN SEVILLE: OUR PICKS

Casa Morales: Family-run tapas bar notable for its sherry, *albóndigas* (meatballs) and croquettes. *noon-4pm & 8pm-midnight Mon-Sat, noon-4pm Sun* €€	**Bodega Santa Cruz:** The slow-cooked *montadito de pringá* (tender meats and sausage served on crusty bread) is a highlight. *8am-midnight* €	**Antigua Taberna de Las Escobas:** Seville's oldest tavern, around since 1386. Luminaries from Cervantes to Lord Byron have dined here. *noon-11pm* €€	**La Brunilda:** Enter through blue doors to a modern interior with inventive tapas, including an excellent mushroom risotto. *1.30-4.30pm & 8.30-11.30pm* €€€
Mamarracha: Trendy tapas place, with eclectic fare like *alcachofa a la brasa* (grilled artichokes). *1-5pm & 8pm-midnight Mon-Thu, 1pm-12.30am Fri-Sun* €€€	**Bar Alfalfa:** Snug bar with tasty tapas, including *salmorejo* (cold, tomato-based soup), overlooked by hundreds of dusty bottles. *9am-midnight* €€	**El Rinconcillo:** Purveyors of libations and tapas since 1670. Tabs are chalked onto the wood in front of you at the end. *1-5.30pm & 8pm-midnight Wed-Mon* €€€	**PETRA:** Inventive takes on popular tapas (meat, vegetarian and vegan). The gourmet experience isn't priced as such. *12.30-11.30pm Mon-Sat* €€

BEST PLACES TO EXPERIENCE FLAMENCO

La Casa del Flamenco: Three styles of flamenco, woven together by a virtuoso guitar performance.

Pura Esencia: The spiritual home of Seville's Roma flamenco practitioners.

Tablao Flamenco Andalusí: Passionate dancing backed by wistful vocals, guitar and *cajón* (percussion instrument).

Casa de la Memoria: The most intimate of shows, if you can bag a stage-side seat. In Lebrija palace's former stables.

Teatro Flamenco Sevilla: Larger shows bringing more performers onto the stage.

Casa de la Guitarra: Shows balance singing, guitar and dance, surrounded by antique flamenco guitars.

Museo del Baile Flamenco: Intriguing gallery that morphs into a performance venue at night.

Taller Flamenco: Fantastic classes, from dance and technique to *palmas* (clapping).

a Goya in the Sacristía de los Cálices, a Zurbarán in the Sacristía Mayor, and Murillo's shining *La inmaculada* in the Sala Capitular.

Hugging the exterior wall, the four figures carrying an ornately carved catafalque mark the **Tomb of Columbus**. It contains the famed voyager's remains, something which DNA testing in 2006 upheld as fact.

The Palaces of Barrio de Santa Cruz
Sumptuous mansions in the former Jewish quarter

The **Palacio de la Condesa de Lebrija** *(palaciodelebrija. com; adult/child €14/6)* condenses each of Seville's golden ages beneath one roof. Built in the Mudéjar-Renaissance style, its central courtyards are flanked by intricate plasterwork arches, *azulejos* and wide stairways. Head northeast to the bougainvillea-covered 15th-century **Palacio de las Dueñas** *(lasduenas.es; adult/child €14/10)*, residence of the late Duchess of Alba. It was also the birthplace of poet Antonio Machado. Further south lies the **Casa de Pilatos** *(fundacionmedinaceli. org; adult/child €12/free)*, with an exquisite *artesonado* (ceiling of interlaced beams).

From Ancient to Modern at Las Setas
Admire Museo Antiquarium and Metropol Parasol

Some of the best views of the cathedral come from atop one of Seville's more modern constructs. Officially called the **Metropol Parasol** *(setasdesevilla.com; adult/child €16/free)*, Las Setas (giant wooden mushrooms) straddle the broad Plaza de la Encarnación. Equally fascinating is the **Antiquarium** *(sevilla.org; adult/child €2/free; closed Mon)* beneath Las Setas: the ruins of Colonia Julia Romula Hispalis, the Roman iteration of Seville, date to around 40 CE.

Treasures of the Museo de Bellas Artes
Artistic masterpieces in a convent

The delightful mannerist palace housing Seville's **Museo de Bellas Artes** *(museosdeandalucia.es; EU/non-EU citizen free/€1.50)* exhibits 15th- to 20th-century artworks, but it's the Golden Age masterpieces that make this one of Spain's top art museums. Sala V contains the most impressive paintings, including Murillo's *Inmaculada concepción*. Highlights elsewhere include Zurbarán's *Cristo crucificado* (Sala VI and another in Sala X), El Greco's portrait of his son (Sala II), Velázquez' *Cabeza de apóstol* (Sala IV) and Goya's *Don José Duaso* (Sala XI).

Beyond Seville

Zafra
Huelva · **Seville** · Córdoba · Linares
Écija · Jaén
Parque Nacional · Lucena · Granada
de Doñana
Cádiz · Jerez de la · **Málaga** · Motril
Frontera
Costa de · Marbella · Adra
la Luz · Gibraltar (UK)
Tarifa
Tangier

Architectural wonders in some of Spain's oldest cities, evocative hill villages, glorious protected parks and a breathtaking coastline await around Andalucía.

With its wild Atlantic coastline and beloved Mediterranean shores, Andalucía evokes many of Spain's greatest calling cards. Much of this sunny, soulful region has passed through Phoenician, Greek, Carthaginian, Roman and Visigothic hands. It also tells the subsequent Al-Andalus story of the melding of three cultures – Moorish, Christian and Jewish – traceable in the ancient neighbourhoods of Córdoba, Granada, Cádiz and even Málaga, as well as the regional capital Seville. The buzzy coast and culture-packed cities give way to a mountainous interior filled with olive groves and pine forests, while sprawling nature reserves dot the countryside. Wander enchanting *pueblos blancos* (white towns) in the evening golden light, or glimpse Granada's Alhambra outlined against the snow-tipped Sierra Nevada, and you'll witness time standing still.

Parque Nacional de Doñana

TIME FROM SEVILLE (EL ROCÍO): 1HR

Lynx-spotting and exceptional birdwatching

The World Heritage–listed **Parque Nacional de Doñana** (*mite co.gob.es*), spread around the Río Guadalquivir delta, forms one of Europe's most extensive wetland areas, which is a haven for around 10,000 flamingos and over 500,000 other wintering birds. At this 601-sq-km park southeast of Huelva, together with the bordering Parque Natural de Doñana (which is under less strict protection), endangered creatures such as the Iberian lynx and Spanish imperial eagle have bounced back from the brink under close conservation. Visits to the national park are via accredited agency only, usually by 4WD; Seville-based **Doñana Wings** (*donanawings.com*) and **Naturanda** (*naturanda. com*) are recommended, as are local operators **Doñana Nature** (*donana-nature.com*), **Discovering Doñana** (*discovering donana.com*) and **Doñana Reservas** (*donanareservas.com*). If you're lucky, you have a good chance of spotting a lynx and her cubs in the mid-to late-summer months.

The main national park hub is the evocative Huelva province village of **El Rocío**, also known as the destination for Spain's greatest pilgrimage, the **Romería del Rocío** in May/

Places

GETTING AROUND

Córdoba, Málaga, Cádiz and Granada have efficient rail links *(renfe.com)*, including with Seville. The best way to enjoy them is on foot; apart from Granada (which has some hilly neighbourhoods), they're largely flat, compact cities. Málaga and Cádiz are ideal for cycling, too, with plenty of bike-hire options. Further afield, it's best to hire a car. Buses reach most destinations, with companies such as **Alsa** *(alsa.es)*, but services are limited and often reduced on weekends.

June. It's also possible to access Doñana from Sanlúcar de Barrameda in neighbouring Cádiz province.

Córdoba

TIME FROM SEVILLE: **50MIN**

A wonder of Islamic architecture

Jewel of the Moorish Caliphate when it was the Grand Mosque of Córdoba, and later one of Spain's great cathedrals, the **Mezquita** *(mezquita-catedraldecordoba.es; adult/child €13/ free)* is one of the world's most magnificent buildings. Free to access, the **Patio de los Naranjos** is the courtyard entrance to the Mezquita filled with palms, orange trees and ornate fountains, and overlooked by the 54m-high **Torre Campanario** (Bell Tower), which requires a separate ticket. Inside the Mezquita, a forest of arches stacks into the distance. It would have been a truly vast mosque upon its final enlargement in 994. The arches, resting on 856 columns (there were originally 1293), are striped strawberries-and-cream, mimicking the date palms of northern Africa.

At the southern wall is the building's pinnacle of Islamic-era decoration, the *maksura* (royal prayer enclosure). The geometric decoration of the arches and skylit domes are at their most lavish here. On the back wall is the *mihrab,* the decorative prayer niche facing Mecca, added along with the *maksura* during the extensions ordered by Al-Hakim II in the 960s. The gold mosaic cubes around its portal were created by a master sculptor from Byzantium. The construction of the current **Capilla Mayor** (main altar) and *coro* (choir) in the heart of the Mezquita began during the reign of Carlos I (1516–56) and was completed in 1766, with plateresque, Gothic, baroque and Renaissance motifs all at play.

Córdoba's other historical treasures include atmospheric **La Judería** (the Jewish quarter), the 14th-century **Alcázar de los Reyes Cristianos** *(cultura.cordoba.es; adult/child €7/free; closed Mon)* palace-fortress and the UNESCO-listed ruins of **Medina Azahara** *(museosdeandalucia.es; EU/non-EU citizen free/€1.50),* the palace-city just outside town built in the 10th century on the orders of Abd ar-Rahman III.

Cádiz

TIME FROM SEVILLE: **1¾HR**

Exploring Cádiz' buzzing *barrios*

Founded as Gadir by the Phoenicians in 1100 BCE, sultry Cádiz is Europe's oldest continuously inhabited settlement.

BLOOMING WONDERS

Among Córdoba's loveliest features are its famous flower-filled patios. In summer, Córdoba becomes a furnace, hence the millennia-old Roman and Moorish tradition of building houses with inner courtyards to facilitate airflow. Some courtyards are open to the public year-round, including the grand **Palacio de Viana** *(palaciodeviana.com);* others only during the **Fiesta de los Patios de Córdoba** (the first two weeks in May). Participating courtyard owners welcome visitors into their inner sanctums, where you can admire hanging plant pots, creeper-clad walls, fountains, quirky patio furnishings and exuberant flower arrangements. A great place to get started is the San Basilio (aka Alcázar Viejo) neighbourhood to the north and west of the Alcázar.

Runs great cooking classes and food tours too.

🍴 EATING & DRINKING IN CÓRDOBA: OUR PICKS

Nuur: Paco Morales gives centuries-old recipes such as pistachio soup the modern treatment; two Michelin stars. *1.30-6pm & 8.30-11.30pm Thu-Sat* **€€€**

Casa Pepe de la Judería: Around since 1920, Pepe's serves classic tapas such as *berenjenas con miel* (aubergines in honey). *1-4pm & 8pm-midnight* **€€**

Garum 2.1: Award-winning spot for imaginative takes on Cordoban dishes, like *salmorejo* with jelly sherry cubes. *1-4pm & 8pm-midnight Mon, Tue & Thu-Sat* **€€**

Jugo Vinos Vivos: Facing a tiny square and fountain, Jugo is all about live wines, sourced directly from small Andalucian producers. *hours vary*

RONDA & WHITE VILLAGES OF CÁDIZ

Andalucía's white villages and olive-tree-covered countryside are just as magical as the famed cities, especially around Ronda and Sierra de Grazalema.

START	END	LENGTH
Ronda	Arcos de la Frontera	140km; 1–2 days

Built astride a huge gash in the mountains carved out by the Río Guadalevín, **①** **Ronda** is a large *pueblo blanco* with a dramatic history. Soak it all up from the grand 1793 Puente Nuevo. Drive 20km north to **②** **Setenil de las Bodegas**, where buildings (homes, restaurants) are curled into cave-like streets beneath the ledges of the Río Trejo.

Zip 35km west, crossing from Málaga province into Cádiz province, to reach **③** **Zahara de la Sierra**. This fortified hill village of red-tiled white houses clusters beneath a ruined 12th-century Moorish castle, all overlooking a turquoise reservoir. From here, the sinuous CA9104 climbs high to the Puerto de las Palomas pass (1357m) before swooping down to **④** **Grazalema**, a

beautiful wool-producing village with sloping cobbled streets and delightful rural hotels for overnight stops.

Heading 20km southwest, travel along the A374 through cheese-making Villaluenga del Rosario (the province's loftiest village) to **⑤** **Benaocaz**, a former Moorish settlement and the jumping-off point for hiking the 3.3km Calzada Romana (an old Roman road to Ubrique). By car, it's just 7km downhill along corkscrew turns to leather-manufacturing **⑥** **Ubrique**, backed by the knife-edge Cruz de Tajo. A 40km spin northwest drops you in **⑦** **Arcos de la Frontera**, a cragtop beauty of a *pueblo blanco* whose origins predate the Romans.

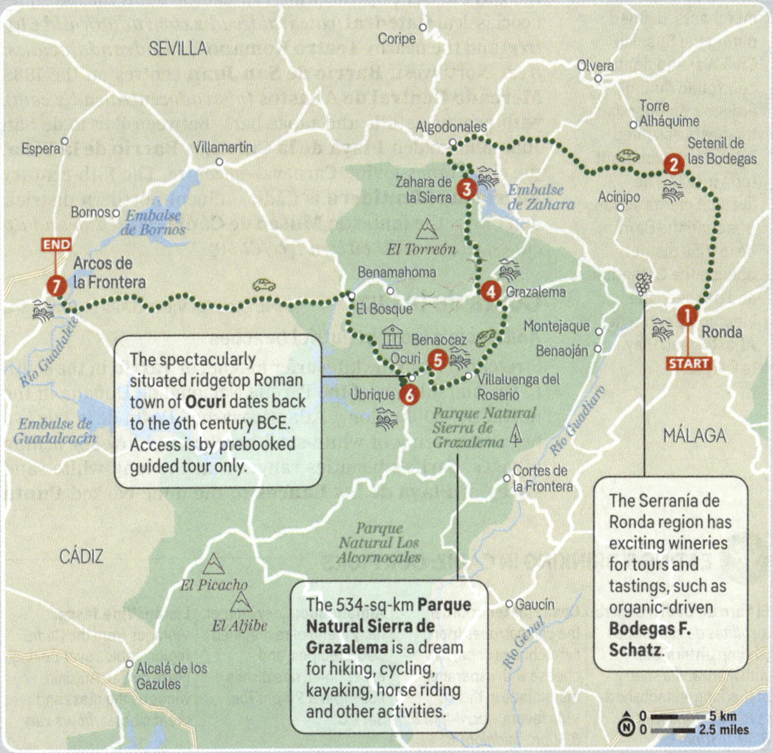

The spectacularly situated ridgetop Roman town of **Ocuri** dates back to the 6th century BCE. Access is by prebooked guided tour only.

The Serranía de Ronda region has exciting wineries for tours and tastings, such as organic-driven **Bodegas F. Schatz**.

The 534-sq-km **Parque Natural Sierra de Grazalema** is a dream for hiking, cycling, kayaking, horse riding and other activities.

SEVILLA
Coripe
Olvera
Torre Alháquime
Espera
Villamartín
Algodonales
Setenil de las Bodegas
Bornoso
Embalse de Bornos
Zahara de la Sierra
Embalse de Zahara
Acinipo
END ⑦ Arcos de la Frontera
El Torreón
Benamahoma
Grazalema
① Ronda **START**
El Bosque
Benaocaz
Montejaque
Benaoján
Ocuri
⑥ Ubrique ⑤
Villaluenga del Rosario
Parque Natural Sierra de Grazalema
MÁLAGA
Río Guadalete
Embalse de Guadalcacín
Cortes de la Frontera
Río Guadiaro
CÁDIZ
Parque Natural Los Alcornocales
El Picacho
El Aljibe
Gaucín
Río Genal
Alcalá de los Gazules

0 — 5 km
0 — 2.5 miles

CARNAVAL

If you're in Cádiz before Easter (in February or March, depending on the Easter dates), you'll be joining the *gaditanos* for Carnaval – Spain's biggest, liveliest, 10-day singing, dancing and drinking street party, complete with float parades, street food, fireworks and over 300 *murgas* (bands). Carnaval dates back to the 15th century, when costumed revelry was brought by homesick Genoese merchants. Banned during the Spanish Civil War and tightly controlled during Franco's dictatorship, the fiesta assumed its present exuberant form in 1977. The liveliest *murga* action is around the Barrio de la Viña district, outside the Cathedral, and between the Mercado Central de Abastos and Playa de la Caleta.

TRABANTOS/SHUTTERSTOCK

Generalife, Granada

The best way to dig into this appealing port city is by wandering its distinctive *barrios*. The **Barrio de Santa María** is the old Roma quarter, home to flamenco-world icon **La Perla** *(perladecadiz.com);* check for shows. Oldest of all is the **Barrio del Pópulo**, which spreads around the baroque-neoclassical **Catedral** *(catedraldecadiz.com; adult/child €10/ free)* and the nearby **Teatro Romano** *(juntadeandalucia.es; free).* Northwest, **Barrio de San Juan** centres on the 1838 **Mercado Central de Abastos** *(mercadocentralcadiz.com),* with produce stalls and tapas bars. Between Barrio de San Juan and golden **Playa de la Caleta** is **Barrio de la Viña**, the city's tapas-loving Carnaval epicentre. The 18th-century **Barrio del Mentidero** is Cádiz' affluent northern district; don't miss the fantastic **Museo de Cádiz** *(museosdeandalucia.es; EU/non-EU citizen free/€1.50).*

Costa de la Luz

TIME FROM SEVILLE (TARIFA): **2¼HR** 🚗

Andalucía's most beautiful beaches

Stretching from the kitesurfer magnet of **Tarifa** in the south to the marshlands of the Parque Nacional de Doñana in the north, the 200km-long, Atlantic-washed Costa de la Luz is a beguiling string of white-sand beaches and low-key fishing villages. Tarifa's beauties range from the long white-sand sweep of **Playa de los Lances** to the dune-backed **Punta**

 EATING & DRINKING IN CÁDIZ: OUR PICKS

El Faro de Cádiz: Superb *tortillitas de camarones* (shrimp fritters) pair with *manzanilla* sherry at this long-established favourite. *1-4.30pm & 8.30-11.30pm* €€

Casa Manteca: Order the *chicharrones* (pork scratchings) or *payoyo* cheese with asparagus marmalade in this La Viña tavern. *noon-4pm & 8.30pm-midnight* €

Almanaque: Cosy interior, daily menu of reimagined Cádiz recipes, and exceptional rice dishes. *1.30-4pm & 9-11pm Tue-Sat* €€

Listán Wine Tasca: Vintages from the Cádiz region, tables overlooking Plaza de San Antonio, wines by the glass and great nibbles. *hours vary*

Paloma and spectacular **Playa de Bolonia** with its 30m-high dune. North from Bolonia are the laid-back beach towns of **Zahara de los Atunes** and **Los Caños de Meca**, with long white-sand strands dotted with *chiringuitos* and surf schools. **El Palmar** has some of Andalucía's best surf waves and its own beach-bar scene, a quick hop away from **Vejer de la Frontera**, one of Andalucía's most exquisite *pueblos blancos*. Just north, seafront **Conil de la Frontera** is renowned for its many beaches, from the family-friendly strand of **Playa La Fontanilla** to the seven sheltered, nudist-friendly coves of **Calas de Poniente**. Pick your strand, bring a beach umbrella and join the fun.

Granada & Around

TIME FROM SEVILLE: 2½HR 🚗 + 🚆

The magical Alhambra

One of the most architecturally perfect buildings in existence, the Moorish palace-fortress of **Alhambra** *(alhambra-patronato.es)* sits high above Granada; its name derives from the Arabic *al-qala'a al-hamra* (the Red Castle). The 9th-century Alhambra was transformed during the 13th and 14th centuries by Granada's Nasrid rulers into the magnificent royal residence you see today.

Its walls carved with elegant Arabic inscriptions, the remarkable **Palacios Nazaríes** complex was originally divided into three parts: the Mexuar, Serallo and Harem. At the heart of the Serallo, where sultans conducted negotiations with Christian emissaries, is the **Patio de los Arrayanes**, named after the myrtle hedges around its rectangular pool and surrounded by marble-columned arcades. To the north, the Sala de la Barca, with a copy of its original cedar ceiling, leads into the **Salón de los Embajadores** – the largest, most striking chamber, with a domed marquetry ceiling symbolising the seven heavens of Islam. Continue to the **Patio de los Leones**, centred on an 11th-century fountain channelling water through the mouths of 12 marble lions.

The **Generalife**, the Nasrid rulers' summer estate, takes its name from the Arabic *jinan al-'arif*, meaning 'the overseer's gardens'. The Patio de la Acequia features immaculately tended gardens, while the Escalera del Agua is a marvel, with water channels running down stone balustrades.

Albayzín: Granada's UNESCO-listed old quarter

The cobbled alleyways, whitewashed mansions and scenic plazas of the UNESCO-listed Albayzín, Granada's old Moorish

ALHAMBRA TIPS

General tickets *(€22)* cover all areas; Gardens, Generalife and Alcazaba tickets *(€12)* exclude Palacios Nazaríes.

Access to Palacios Nazaríes is limited to 300 visitors every half-hour; book time-slot tickets as far in advance as possible.

Alhambra by night is a special experience: book Night Visit Palacios Nazaríes *(€12.70)* year-round or Night Visit Gardens & Generalife *(€8.50)* in April, May, September, October and November.

Bring ID that matches the name on your ticket – authorities are cracking down on scalpers buying up day tickets and reselling them to ticketless visitors by the gate.

🍴 EATING IN TARIFA & VEJER DE LA FRONTERA: OUR PICKS

El Jardín del Califa: Romantic Vejer spot with a creative Moroccan–Middle Eastern menu and Cádiz province vintages. Book ahead! *1-4pm & 7.30-11pm* €€

El Francés: At the standing-room-only bar or terrace tables in Tarifa, munch on classics with a twist. Also runs Silos 19. *12.30pm-midnight Fri-Tue* €€

El Lola: Stylish flamenco-themed tapas bar in old-town Tarifa, with dishes including seasonal *almadraba* tuna. *1-4.30pm & 7pm-midnight* €€

La Judería: Tucked away in a Vejer alleyway, this spot dazzles with its stellar rice dishes and goat's-cheese cheesecake with honey. *hours vary* €€

CABO DE GATA

Beach lovers dazzled by the Costa de la Luz are equally likely to fall for magical Cabo de Gata. At the opposite end of Andalucía (around two hours' drive from Granada), this wild stretch of the Almería coast is protected as the spectacular 340-sq-km **Parque Natural de Cabo de Gata-Níjar,** featuring some of Spain's most pristine, least crowded white-sand beaches, excellent scuba diving and other water sports, and a dramatic Mediterranean coastline ripe for exploration on foot or by bike. Between small, laid-back villages – like Rodalquilar, Las Negras, Pozo del Fraile and San José – trails weave across a desert-like volcanic landscape, taking in remote lighthouses, wind-battered capes and hidden-away coves that require a little more effort to reach.

quarter, occupy a hill facing the Alhambra. Allow a full day to explore, before dropping back down to the **Catedral de Granada** *(catedraldegranada.com; adult/child €7/free),* housing the tombs of the Reyes Católicos.

Off Carrera del Darro, the Albayzín's **Baños Árabes El Bañuelo** *(alhambra-patronato.es; €8.50)* is a well-preserved 11th-century Moorish public bath complex. Nearby, occupying the 16th-century Casa de Castril, the **Museo Arqueológico** *(museosdeandalucia.es; EU/non-EU citizen free/€1.50)* houses regional artefacts, from Palaeolithic to late Moorish times. Dominating the Plaza del Salvador near the top of the Albayzín, the 16th-century **Colegiata del Salvador** church was built atop a former mosque. A short wander southwest brings you to the **Mirador San Nicolás**, the famous viewpoint for sunset shots of the Alhambra silhouetted against the Sierra Nevada.

Hike into the Sierra Nevada

The 862-sq-km **Parque Nacional Sierra Nevada** *(miteco. gob.es)* – Spain's largest national park – is home to 2100 of Spain's 7000 plant species, as well as Andalucía's largest ibex population (around 15,000). It's also where you'll find **Mulhacén** (3479m), the highest point in mainland Spain. Ample day hikes (many doable from Granada) and multiday trails beckon walkers and mountaineers. The lower southern reaches – **Las Alpujarras** – and their dramatic valleys, dotted with age-old *pueblos blancos,* lend themselves beautifully to road-tripping and walking. The best months for hiking are April to mid-June and mid-September to early November for Las Alpujarras, while summer is good for the high Sierra Nevada. Along with summiting Mulhacén, highlights include walks around the three villages in the Barranco del Poqueira – Pampaneira, Bubión and Capileira – and lofty, *jamón*-making Trevélez. **Nevadensis** *(nevadensis.com)* can organise guided hikes.

Málaga

TIME FROM SEVILLE: 2¼ 🚗 + 🚆

City of artists

Begin your exploration of Málaga's artistic side at the **Museo Picasso Málaga** *(museopicassomalaga.org; adult/child €13/ free),* a must-visit in the city of the artist's birth. Among 200-plus works, highlights include a painting of Picasso's sister Lola, done when he was only 13, *Portrait of Paulo with White Hat* and *Olga Khokhlova with Mantilla.* The nearby **Museo**

 EATING & DRINKING IN GRANADA: OUR PICKS

Damasqueros: The tasting menu may feature aubergines with sardines and miso or veal sweetbreads. *1-3.30pm & 8.30-10.30pm Mon-Sat, 1-3.30pm Sun* €€€

Casa de Vinos La Brujidera: Wood-panelled bar with a superb wine cellar; most wines are available by the glass. *hours vary*

Taberna La Tana: Realejo favourite, serving over 500 Spanish wines alongside platters of cold cuts and other bites. *12.30-4pm & 8.30pm-midnight*

Bar Provincias: Old-school spot (around since 1945) perfect for people-watching as you munch on fried fish and seafood bites. *1-11.30pm*

ADIANY MONTELO/SHUTTERSTOCK

Parque Nacional Sierra Nevada

Casa Natal de Picasso (*museocasanatalpicasso.malaga.eu; adult/child €3/free*) is located in the house where the artist was born.

Continue on to the **Museo Carmen Thyssen** (*carmenthyssenmalaga.org; adult/child €12/free*), housed in an elegant 16th-century palace in the heart of the city's former Moorish quarter. A short walk away lies the **Museo de Málaga** (*museosdeandalucia.es; EU/non-EU citizen free/€1.50*), in the Palacio de la Aduana, which combines the former Museo Bellas Artes and the Museo Arqueológico.

As you pass through the neighbourhood of **Soho**, look for murals by the likes of Dean Stockton (D*Face), Shepard Fairey (OBEY) and ROA. Many museums close Monday.

MÁLAGA'S MULTICULTURAL HISTORY

Teatro Romano: Roman theatre built during the reign of Augustus in the 1st century CE and working up until the 3rd century.

Alcazaba: A winding pathway takes you through Arabic-style arched doorways, peaceful gardens and geometric-tiled courtyards at the city's 11th-century Moorish palatial fortress.

Castillo de Gibralfaro: Another vestige of Málaga's Moorish past, rising high above the city – you can hike up in 30 minutes.

Catedral de la Encarnación de Málaga: The colossal cathedral stands right in the centre of the city. Construction began in the 16th century on the site of a former mosque.

EATING & DRINKING IN MÁLAGA: OUR PICKS

Bodegas El Pimpi: In front of the Alcazaba, this fun bar has leafy courtyards, wine cellars and cosy rooms. The 'tunnel' is best for tapas. *noon-2am* €€

La Tranca: Elbow your way into this old-fashioned bar with vermouth and classic Andalucian tapas like tortilla and olives. *noon-1am* €

La Cosmo: Sleek modern dining by chef Dani Carnero. Try duck breast with barbecue sauce. *1.30-3.30pm & 8-11.30pm Mon-Sat* €€

Antigua Casa de Guardia: Old-school wine bar where muscatel and Pedro Ximénez are served straight from the barrel. *hours vary*

Places We Love to Stay

€ Budget €€ Midrange €€€ Top End

Madrid
MAP p542

Hostal La Zona € This stylish *hostal* has clean, bright rooms and breakfast is until noon.

Only YOU Atocha €€ Not only stylish but also sustainable, eschewing single-use plastics and offering electric-car charging.

Hotel Alicia €€ One of the landmark properties of the designer Room Mate chain, overlooking Plaza de Santa Ana.

Posada del Dragón €€ Remodelled La Latina inn with modern interiors retaining its traditional *corrala* courtyard.

Pestaña Plaza Mayor €€€ This sought-after address has been renovated with exposed brick, velvet walls and rooftop pool.

Toledo, Cáceres & Salamanca

Áurea Toledo €€ Five-star hotel spread across four historic courtyard houses with artefacts.

Hospes Palacio de San Esteban €€ In a 16th-century former Salamanca convent, with garden and pool.

Parador de Cáceres €€€ This old-town conglomeration of 14th-century Gothic palaces has stylish rooms.

Barcelona
MAP p556

Generator Barcelona € The switched-on Generator chain runs this large, social Gràcia hostel.

Hotel Brummell €€ In Poble Sec, this 20-room boutique hotel has an urban garden with a pool.

Casa Mathilda €€ Beautiful 1920s Eixample Dreta building converted into a 14-room boutique hideaway.

Casa Bonay €€€ A creatively restored 1896 Eixample building houses one of Barcelona's best boutique-design hotels.

Hotel Neri €€€ Two historic palaces merged to become this impeccable 22-room Relais & Chateaux property.

Costa Brava, Tarragona & Zaragoza

Tramuntana Hotel €€ Adults-only 11-room boutique hotel tucked away in old-town Cadaqués.

H10 Imperial Tarraco €€ Incredible views and a rooftop pool for recharging in Tarragona.

Hotel Sauce €€ Welcoming, family-run hotel in Zaragoza with fresh, cheerful rooms.

Bilbao & San Sebastián

Pensión Aida €€ Guests are made to feel welcome at this pensión with bright rooms.

Miró Hotel €€€ Opposite the Guggenheim, this contemporary design hotel charms art lovers.

Picos de Europa & Galicia

Hotel Costa Vella €€ Tranquil rooms, super-helpful staff and a lovely garden cafe overlooking Santiago.

Casa Fontequeiroso €€ Welcoming small hotel in deep Costa da Morte countryside, with superb home-cooked meals.

Valencia
MAP p577

Casa Clarita €€ Joyful interiors with colourful, chic murals by local artist Jaime Hayon.

YOURS €€€ Minimal design hotel scented with hand-poured candles. Plunge pool is heaven in summer.

Balearic Islands

Can Fuster, Sant Joan de Labritja €€€ Restored, eight-room, 150-year-old Ibizan farmhouse with pool.

Hotel Basilica, Palma de Mallorca €€€ Tear yourself away from your understated room for the rooftop pool with cathedral views.

Hotel Nou Sant Antoni, Ciutadella €€€ Spectacular Menorca boutique hotel in the heart of the old town.

Seville & Costa de la Luz
MAP p586

La Banda € Perennial Seville favourite for its stunning rooftop terrace, sociable ethos and evening events.

La Casa del Califa €€ North Africa–inspired rooms and fab restaurant in a 16th-century building in Vejer de la Frontera.

Casa del Poeta €€€ Deep in Seville's Barrio de Santa Cruz, stay at this restored 17th-century mansion.

Córdoba, Granada & Málaga

Patio del Posadero €€ Traditional Córdoba-Moorish touches and boutique design in a 15th-century property.

Hotel Casa 1800 Granada €€ Old-world coffered ceilings, contemporary rooms and beautiful courtyard within a 16th-century Granada building.

Hotel Boutique Teatro Romano €€ Light, contemporary rooms with views of Málaga's Roman theatre and Alcazaba.

Practicalities

HEATWAVES & WILDFIRES

In recent years, Spain has been experiencing increasingly intense heatwaves. Devastating wildfires and serious droughts often accompany them. If you're caught up in any of these, follow guidance from local authorities. Common restrictions during droughts might include beach showers and public fountains being switched off and bans on refilling swimming pools.

DANIEL FERRER PAEZ/SHUTTERSTOCK

SMOKING

Smoking is banned in enclosed public spaces, near hospitals and on over 660 beaches. Legislation to ban smoking on bar/restaurant terraces was in the works at the time of writing. Cannabis has been decriminalised for personal use, in small quantities.

LGBTIQ+ TRAVELLERS

In 2024, Spain ranked joint first place on the Spartacus Gay Travel Index of LGBTIQ+ friendly countries. It was the fourth country in the world to legalise same-sex marriage (in 2005), along with same-sex adoption. The 2023 Ley Trans brought groundbreaking legislation around rights for trans people. Spain's LGBTIQ+ hubs are Madrid, Barcelona, Sitges and Gran Canaria, though you'll find lively scenes countrywide.

TIPPING ETIQUETTE

Though tipping isn't obligatory, it's definitely appreciated. In restaurants, 5% to 10% (more common) is appropriate; for bars/cafes, people sometimes leave loose change. If paying by card, ask to add the tip to the bill total.

OPENING HOURS

Opening times vary seasonally and are typically more reduced in winter and/or peak summer months.
Banks 8.30am–2pm Monday to Friday
Cafes 7am–late
Bars Varies; often 6pm–late
Restaurants 1pm–4pm and 8.30pm–11pm or midnight
Shops 10am–2pm and 5pm–8pm Monday to Saturday

TOURISM TAX & PRIVATE RENTALS

Spain has experienced a surge in private short-term tourist rentals (especially apartments) in recent years, which many people link to growing overtourism issues. If booking one, check it's legally licensed. Some destinations also apply a tourism tax, usually added to accommodation bills.

PUBLIC HOLIDAYS

National holidays:
New Year's Day 1 January
Good Friday March/ April
Labour Day 1 May
Feast of the Assumption 15 August
Fiesta Nacional de España 12 October
All Saints' Day 1 November

Constitution Day 6 December
Christmas 25 December
Other common holidays:
Three Kings' Day 6 January
Maundy Thursday March/ April
Corpus Christi June
Feast of the Immaculate Conception 8 December

597

Language

English is quite widely spoken, especially in larger cities and popular tourist areas, but less so in rural villages and among older Spaniards. Spanish (Castilian) is the national language; Catalan, Galician and Basque are co-official regional languages. Learning a few words of the local language goes a long way.

Basics

Hello. Hola. *o·la*
Goodbye. Adiós. *Adiós*
Yes. Sí. *see*
No. No. *no*
Please. Por favor. *por fa·vor*
Thank you (very much). (Muchas) Gracias. *(moo·chos) gra·thyas*
Excuse me. Perdón. *per·don*
Sorry. Lo siento. *lo syen·to*
What's your name? ¿Cómo se llama usted? *ko·mo se lya·ma oo·ste*
My name is … Me llamo … *me lya·mo …*
Do you speak English? ¿Habla inglés? *a·bla een·gles*
I don't understand. No entiendo. *no en·tyen·do*

Signs

Abierto Open
Cerrado Closed
Entrada Entrance
Hombres Men
Mujeres Women
Prohibido Prohibited
Salida Exit
Servicios/Aseos Toilets

Time

What time is it? ¿Qué hora es? *ke o·ra es*

It's (10) o'clock. Son (las diez). *son (las dyeth)*
It's half past (one). Es (la una) y media. *es (la oo·na) ee me·dya*
yesterday ayer *a·yer*
today hoy *oy*
tomorrow mañana *ma·nya·na*

Emergencies

Help! ¡Socorro! *so·ko·ro*
Go away! ¡Vete! *ve·te*
Call the police! ¡Llame a la policía! *lya·me a la po·lee·thee·a*
Call a doctor! ¡Llame a un médico! *lya·me a oon me·dee·ko*

Menu Decoder

Menú del día Set lunch menu
Menú degustación Tasting menu
Tapas Small, savoury dishes
Pintxos Basque-style tapas, usually on bread
Ración or media ración Full-plate or half-plate portion of tapas
Marisco Seafood
Carne de cerdo Pork
Carne de vaca Beef
Pollo Chicken
Vegetariano Vegetarian
Vegano Vegan
Sin gluten Gluten-free

NUMBERS	
1	uno
2	dos
3	tres
4	cuatro
5	cinco
6	seis
7	siete
8	ocho
9	nueve
10	diez
20	veinte
50	cincuenta
100	cien

AVE train

Arriving & Getting Around

Spain's public transport is among Europe's best, with a fast and super-modern train system, an extensive domestic air network, a well-maintained road network, and buses that connect villages in the country's most remote corners.

Major Points of Entry
Most international travellers arrive into Madrid or Barcelona, though Málaga, Valencia, Mallorca, Ibiza, Alicante and the Canaries also have busy airports, particularly for hops within Europe. Transport to/ from airports is usually efficient.

Train
Renfe (renfe.com) is the national train system that runs most services in Spain, including the high-speed AVE trains. Private operators such as **Iryo** (iryo.eu) and **Ouigo** (ouigo. com) offer alternatives, often at lower prices. Most cities have local trains called *cercanías* (*rodalies* in Catalonia).

Bus
Most buses are geared towards local residents, which means weekend services are generally more limited. Tickets can often be booked online in advance, though for more remote routes you may need to pay in cash.

Car & Taxi
To rent a car in Spain, you must have a licence, be aged 21 or over and, in most cases, have a credit card (few places accept debit cards). Rates and availability vary enormously by season – book as far ahead as possible. Taxis are readily available in the big cities and main tourist destinations. Note that Uber doesn't operate in some places, though rideshare company **Cabify** (cabify.com) often fills the gap.

MONEY
Currency: Euro (€)

CARD & DIGITAL PAYMENT
All major credit and debit cards are widely accepted (including contactless payments and Apple/ Google Pay), though some places don't take Amex. There's sometimes a minimum spend and splitting bills isn't always an option. You may still occasionally need cash for small shops, flea markets, buses and tipping.

HOW TO SAVE A FEW EUROS
Many destinations offer tourist passes covering major sights at a discount, available at tourist offices, online or at the sights. Museums often have dedicated free-access days. Most sights offer discounted tickets for students, children and people over 65. Accommodation-wise, cut costs by skipping peak season (July/August and Easter) and weekends. Take advantage of lunchtime restaurant deals.

For places to stay in Switzerland, see p621

SAIKO3P/SHUTTERSTOCK

Above: Matterhorn (p615) and Zermatt (p614); Right: Eiger Express (p616), Wetterhorn and Grindelwald

Curated by
Nicola Williams

Switzerland

ALPINE TRADITION, OUTDOOR ACTION AND URBAN FUN

The Swiss don't do half measures: chocolate-box villages of film-set ilk, once-in-a-lifetime rail journeys, untamed nature off the charts...

No other place inspires exploration quite like Switzerland, a small country in western Europe that gave the world melt-in-the-mouth chocolate, cyberspace and an overdose of godlike landscapes. Where else can you follow flower trails around glittering lakes, cross glacial ice roped to a guide and corkscrew up vertiginous alpine passes like James Bond – all in one weekend?

How incredible and intoxicating it all is. But this is Sonderfall Schweiz ('special-case Switzerland'), a privileged neutral country, proudly idiosyncratic, insular and unique. Its four official languages alone speak volumes. French is spoken in Suisse Romande in the west, in Geneva and all around its lake, and in most of the split-personality canton of Valais. Moving east, Germanic

AARONCHENPS2/SHUTTERSTOCK

Switzerland baffles with Swiss-German in avant-garde Swiss capital Bern; in the flush of art-rich cities north; and across the Swiss Alps, from extreme-sports hub Interlaken in the Bernese Oberland to the glitterati-infused ski slopes of ritzy St Moritz in Graubünden. It is here, shouldering up to Austria and Italy in the country's southeast, that you might get to hear Romansh – Switzerland's fourth national language few have ever heard of (or heard). This is where the mountains get really wild – if you want to tiptoe off-grid, the protected Swiss National Park is the sweet spot. Then there is Ticino, a charismatic pocket of Italian-speaking exuberance and dolce vita in the hot south.

Sheer variety alone has you spellbound in Switzerland.

THE MAIN AREAS

GENEVA
Lakeside living and belle époque romance.
p604

NORTHERN SWITZERLAND
World-class art in culture-rich cities.
p609

THE SWISS ALPS
Bucket-list vistas and outdoor adventure.
p613

TICINO
The country's 'dolce' Italianate soul.
p618

Find Your Way

Switzerland's ravishing landscapes inspire immediate action – grab boots, leap on board, toot bike bell and let spirits rip. However you choose to get around, the going is typically smooth and the scenery is XXL magnificent.

Geneva, p604

Meet French-speaking Switzerland. 'Big bang' secrets, beachside DJs and chocolate-box old towns: Lake Geneva's eponymous town and its belle époque shores delight and surprise.

The Swiss Alps, p613

Soul-soaring mountain peaks, glacier, lakes and gorges stitch together this extraordinary swathe of the country, where the bulk of the action kicks off outside. Summer- or winter-sports fiends, this is your 'hood.

Northern Switzerland, p609

Feel the edgy urban pulse of the country's Germanic roots in a flush of northern cities, from one of Europe's least-known capitals to wealthy, hard-working and increasingly hip Zürich.

TRAIN, BUS, BOAT & CABLE CAR

Swiss trains, buses and paddle steamers on lakes all run like clockwork and connect seamlessly with mountain railways and cable cars. Transport is pricey – consider carefully the numerous discount-giving travel cards and tickets that are available.

CAR & MOTORCYCLE

A car is not essential, but can be useful for unearthing the country's nooks, crannies and most rural folds. Navigating steep relentless switchbacks is part of the joy of a summer road trip across high mountain passes in the Alps; check if open on *alpen-paesse.ch*.

Ticino, p618

Switzerland meets Italy: feast on pizza, gelato and a rich dose of dolce vita (the 'sweet life') in this Italian-speaking Swiss land of lakes, palm trees and more hours of sunshine than anywhere else in the country.

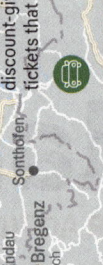

Jet d'Eau (p604) and Lake Geneva, Geneva

Plan Your Time

Despite the gravity-defying geographical terrain at times, Switzerland distances are manageable, variety is within easy reach and pretty much everything runs with clockwork precision and efficiency.

A Quick Taster

● Spend a day in Francophone **Geneva** (p604), enjoying old-town flanerie and a lake swim. Venture east along Lake Geneva by rail or paddle steamer, stopping in art-rich **Lausanne** (p607) or music-mad **Montreux** (p607). Cross the famous *Röstigraben* (Switzerland's linguistic, cultural divide) to capital city **Bern** (609). End on the Swiss-Italian Riviera (p620).

A Week in the Mountains

● Use metropolis **Zürich** (p611) as a stepping stone to **Grindelwald** (p616) for alpine scenery on skis or afoot, and take a ride of a lifetime up **Jungfraujoch** (p616). Consider a pit stop in **Lucerne** (p616), epitome of graceful lake living. Zip to **St Moritz** (p617) for more alpine action, then loop east into Italian Switzerland in medieval **Bellinzona** (p618).

SEASONAL HIGHLIGHTS

SPRING
Warm days: cafe terraces unfurl, flowers bloom along lake promenades, lake cruises spring into action.

SUMMER
Ski lifts open for hikers and mountain bikers, and high mountain passes are snow-free. Time to swim in lakes.

AUTUMN
Toast September's grape harvest at wine festivals. Ticino goes chestnut crazy. Mountain resorts hibernate in October.

WINTER
Carve through powder and scoff cheese fondue in an alpine resort. Ski season is mid-December to early April.

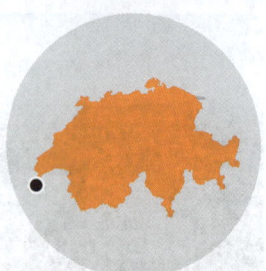

Geneva

CULTURE AND CHOCOLATE | OLD-TOWN FLANERIE | URBAN BEACHES

GETTING AROUND

Geneva is walkable, but **TPG** *(tpg.ch)* buses, trams and shuttle boats save tired legs; buy tickets *(three-stop single/hr/day Chf2/3/10)* at stops or on the TPG+ app.

Hotel guests receive a free **Geneva Transport Card**, covering unlimited public transport – also included in the **Geneva City Pass** *(geneve. com; Chf30/40/50 for 24/48/72hr)*. Rent a bike via the **Donkey Republic** *(donkey. bike)* app.

☑️ **TOP TIP**

To meet *chocolatiers* and taste their creations, buy a **Choco Pass** *(adult/ child Chf30/6)* at Geneva **tourist office** *(geneva.ch)* inside the train station or online; Chf1 goes towards Switzerland's climate protection/sustainable tourism. The 24-hour pass covers nine chocolate shops, Monday to Saturday.

French-speaking Geneva (Genève) is a rare breed. Glinting in the sun with the wealth of luxury jewellers, chocolate shops and investment banks, its flawless, glossy veneer can feel impenetrable. But meander away from the manicured lakeshore – into less touristy neighbourhoods like grungier Pâquis, village-like Carouge or along the postindustrial Rhône – and a rougher-cut diamond emerges, quietly humming with attitude.

A place of international diplomacy ever since persecuted Protestants from France sought refuge here during the Reformation in the 16th century, Geneva is home to 200-odd international and nongovernmental organisations, including the UN, World Health Organization and International Committee of the Red Cross. Getting a soaking on the pier beneath its emblematic Jet d'Eau pencil fountain, a 1951 rendition of the plume of water that shot into the sky for 15 minutes each Sunday to release pressure at the city's water station, is a rite of passage.

Feel Geneva's Antique Heartbeat

Explore the old town

Head to Gothic **Cathédrale St-Pierre** *(concerts-cathedrale. ch; towers adult/child Chf10/5)* and spiral up its towers to enjoy lake and old-town views. Next door at the **Musée International de la Réforme** *(musee-reforme.ch; adult/child Chf13/6),* closed Monday, learn how Geneva became a safe haven for Protestant refugees persecuted for their faith during the 16th-century Reformation. Uphill on **Grand-Rue**, philosopher Jean-Jacques Rousseau (1712–78) was born at the **Maison de Rousseau et de la Literature** *(m-r-l.ch/; adult/child Chf7/5).* End on **Place du Bourg-de-Four**, Roman forum, medieval-fair host and modern-day cafe-terrace hub.

GENEVA

Old Town

200 m
0.1 miles

Lake Geneva

Jet d'Eau

0   1 km
0   0.5 miles

⭐ **HIGHLIGHTS**
1 Jet d'Eau

🔴 **SIGHTS**
2 Cathédrale St-Pierre
3 Conservatoire et Jardin Botaniques
4 Grand-Rue
5 Horloge Fleurie

6 Maison de Rousseau et de la Literature
7 Musée International de la Réforme
8 Parc de la Perle du Lac
9 Place du Bourg-de-Four
10 Plage des Eaux-Vives
11 Quai du Mont Blanc

🔴 **ACTIVITIES**
12 Baby Plage
13 Bains des Pâquis
14 Bains du Jet d'Eau
15 Genève Plage
16 Quai de Cologny

⚫ **SLEEPING**
17 Hôtel Bel'Esperance

🟢 **EATING**
18 Bistrot des Halles
19 Buvette des Bains
20 Chez Ma Cousine
21 El Catrín

🔵 **INFORMATION**
22 Tourist Office

Venerate Mont Blanc

A waterfront walk along Quai du Mont Blanc

Satellites ensure Geneva's **Horloge Fleurie** (Flower Clock) next to **Pont du Mont Blanc** keeps perfect time, with the world's longest second hand (2.5m) and 6500 flowers. Across the bridge, views of Mont Blanc (4805m) encrust **Quai du Mont Blanc**. Promenade along the lakeshore to **Parc de la Perle du Lac**, where outdoor films are screened in summer *(cinetransat.ch; free)*. North again, the **Conservatoire et Jardin Botaniques** *(cjbg.ch; free)* showcases 11,000 species from around the world.

BEST LAKESIDE SWIM SPOTS

Genève Plage: May to September, this 1930s swimming-pool complex buzzes. *(geneve-plage.ch; adult/child Chf7/3.50)*

Bains des Pâquis: Vintage lake-water pool with retro vibe; sunrise concerts and full-moon swims in summer, saunas and lake dips in winter. *(aubp.ch; adult/child Chf2/1; extras Chf15–22)*

Bains du Jet d'Eau: Two small sleek pools in front of the Jet d'Eau, with lifeguards and snack bar. *(adult/child Chf2/1; Tue-Sun Jul-mid-Sep)*

Plage des Eaux-Vives: Human-made shingle beach with coffee trucks, showers, accessible ramps and family-friendly **Baby Plage** *(plagepublique deseauxvives.ge.ch; free).*

Quai de Cologny: Lounge on a ring-shaped wooden platform, suspended above the water.

DEYAN BARIC/ALAMY

CERN

Science Fest

Unravel the universe at CERN

Fathoming out particles that make up matter is what physicists at the European Organization for Nuclear Research or **CERN** do. This is where British scientist Tim Berners Lee invented the World Wide Web in 1989. **Science Gateway** *(visit.cern; free with online advance reservation)* shines light on CERN's incredulous work with science shows, films and exhibitions. Take tram 18 from Gare de Cornavin.

 EATING IN GENEVA: GOOD-VALUE DINING

Buvette des Bains: Grab breakfast, salads, oysters and a superlative cheese fondue at Bains des Pâquis' trendy, no-frills buvette (snack bar). *7am-10.30pm* €

Chez Ma Cousine: Generous portions of chicken, potatoes and salad at the old town's much-loved rotisserie. *11am-11.30pm Mon-Sat, to 10.30pm Sun* €

Bistrot des Halles: Join locals at the zinc bar for *côte de boeuf* (steak), calf kidneys and other bistro classics in the covered market. *7.30-7pm Mon-Fri, 6am-4pm Sat* €€

El Catrín: Authentic tacos and party vibe at this fun-loving Mexican hangout near the station. *6-11.30pm Wed, noon-2pm & 6-11.30pm Thu-Sun* €€

Beyond Geneva

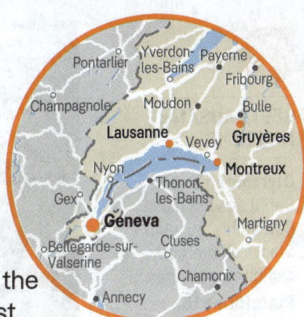

Gem villages, vineyards and castles bead the mythical northern shore of Europe's largest alpine lake.

Heading out of urban Geneva, join dots along the lakeshore between medieval villages, bijou pleasure ports and grassy 'beaches' cradling pebbly shores and summer bars. Rivalling Geneva in the dining and nightlife stakes is Lausanne (Switzerland's fourth-largest city), with an Olympian pedigree and vistas that pack a punch. A city of steps, its *escaliers* (staircases) link the hilltop old town and EPFL campus (Europe's version of Boston's MIT, where bold young scientists are engineering future brilliance) with belle époque beauty by the water. Continuing east, Lavaux vineyards so steep they are UNESCO-listed waltz along the shore to jazzy Montreux and the lake's emblematic château. Bicycle, e-bike or train, sailboat, vintage steamer or stand-up paddle: pick your means and level up with the local outdoor-action set.

Lausanne

TIME FROM GENEVA: **45MIN**

Meet the watch at the cathedral

Atop Lausanne's steeply pitched, medieval Old Town, **Cathédrale de Notre Dame** (*cathedrale-lausanne.ch; belfry adult/child €5/2*) might lack the lightness of French Gothic buildings, but its 'backstage' encounters thrill. Visit after dark when you can accompany the *guet* (nightwatch) – floppy black hat, candlelit lantern – on his nightly climb up 153 steps to his lookout and spartan bunk room atop the 79m-tall **Tour du Beffroi** (Belfry Tower). In keeping with a medieval tradition dating to 1405, the nightwatchman (or, since 2021, a female *guette*) calls out the hours into the night from 10pm to 2am.

Aim for a full moon or a night around midsummer when starlit views of the city laid out at your feet glow gold. To join *le guet/guette* at 10pm, you must call their 'office' (+41 21 312 74 91) to reserve for the following day.

Montreux

TIME FROM GENEVA: **65MIN**

Follow a trail of flowers to Château de Chillon

Art, music and natural beauty collide in Montreux, 30km southeast of Lausanne. The elegant lakeside town has been a magnet for artists and celebrities since the 19th century. Pink Floyd, David Bowie, Elton John and Ella Fitzgerald have all played at

Places

Lausanne p607
Montreux p607
Gruyères p608

GETTING AROUND

Regular SBB trains trundle along the lake from Geneva and Lausanne to Montreux and beyond. CGN steamers from Lausanne (1¾ hours) and Montreux (15 minutes) dock right in front of Château de Chillon.

Use Lausanne's metro, buses and trolleybuses to tackle city hills. Hotel guests get a free **Lausanne Transport Card** covering transport; otherwise buy tickets on the TL app *(t-l.ch)*. Cut sightseeing costs with a **Lausanne City Pass** *(1/2/3 days Chf30/40/50)*, also covering transport.

BEST LAUSANNE MUSEUMS

Olympic Museum:
Sprint against Usain Bolt at this museum. Stacks of interactive exhibits for all ages.

Plateforme 10:
Modern art in a trio of museums in an architecturally striking complex by Lausanne train station.

Collection de l'Art Brut: The world's original collection of Art Brut – subversive, 'raw art' by artists with no formal training – inside an 18th-century château.

Fondation de l'Hermitage:
A 19th-century mansion with art exhibitions, gardens and a family-friendly cafe-bistro.

Palais de Rumine:
Archaeology, geology and money museums inside the palace (1891–1906) where the treaty finalising the break-up of the Ottoman Empire after WWI was signed.

MARISA ESTIVILL/SHUTTERSTOCK

Château de Gruyères, Gruyères

Montreux's world-famous music festival, an annual fixture since 1967. Poking around the recording studio where rock band Queen recorded several albums at **Queen: The Studio Experience** *(mercuryphoenixtrust.org/studioexperience; free)* is a tearjerker.

Soak up summer splendour along the **Chemin Fleuri**. The Flower Path unfurls along the waterfront for 2.5km to Switzerland's best-preserved medieval fortress **Château de Chillon** *(chillon.ch; adult/child Chf15/7)*. Spellbinding floral displays are positively tropical, and views of alpine mountain peaks across the water in France are Disney movie stuff. In odd years during summer's **Biennale Montreux** *(biennale.ch; Aug–Nov)*, sculptures by Swiss sculptors dot the lake path.

Gruyères

TIME FROM GENEVA: **90MIN**

On the trail of cheesemakers

A classic day trip for Genevans, this tiny chocolate-box village seduces with cobbled streets, flower-strewn wooden houses and 13th-century **Château de Gruyères** *(chateau-gruyeres.ch; adult/child Chf13/5)*. Come summer weekends, you might catch alpenhorn players in the streets. But cheese is the cherry on the cake – AOP Gruyère, to be precise. Get up close to the production process at two very different dairies: industrial **La Maison du Gruyère** *(lamaisondugruyere.ch, adult/family Chf8/12)* next to Gruyères train station, and 17th-century rustic wooden chalet **Fromagerie d'Alpage de Moléson** *(moleson.ch; adult/child Chf5/3)*, 5km south, where cheesemaker François still heats the milk each morning in a cauldron over a wood fire and presses curds by hand into the moulds. Book at both to bag a spot.

 EATING & DRINKING IN LAUSANNE: OUR PICKS

Jetée de la Compagnie: Yoga, DJ sets, sunrise concerts at a 'beach' bar in an industrial container with tables by the water. *10am-midnight, from 9am Sun*

Great Escape: Grungy club-like interior and tree-shaded terrace above Place de Riponne. *10am-1am Mon-Thu, to 2am Fri, 11am-2am Sat, noon-1am Sun*

Le Barbare: Lausanne's best hot chocolate, plus superlative coffee, lunch and brunch year-round. *9am-midnight Tue & Wed, to 1am Thu-Sat, 10am-6pm Sun* €€

Café de l'Evêché: Dip into a traditional cheese fondue, laced with beer, in this old-school cafe by the cathedral. *7am-midnight Mon-Fri, from 11.30am Sat & Sun* €€

Northern Switzerland

ART AND ARCHITECTURE | CITIES | URBAN SWIMMING

Cradled by different beauty from the archetypal soaring mountains and alpine valleys, the Swiss Plateau in the north is Swisser than Swiss. Glacial meltwaters from the Bernese Alps trickle into the Aare River, a perfect ribbon of turquoise that wraps itself around Bern, the laid-back city few realise is Switzerland's capital. The holey cheese that couldn't be more Swiss if it tried hails from the surrounding Emmental countryside, as beautiful as Bern's cobbled picture-book Altstadt is enchanting.

Further north, velvety fields and rolling hills frame urban Basel. Nowhere is Switzerland's Franco-Germanic roots quite so apparent as in this multicultural powerhouse of a city, where Switzerland meets France and Germany at the heart of the Rhine confluence.

The metropolis vibes max out in Zürich, the country's hardworking financial centre which, being Swiss, softens the urban blow with a dreamy lake location and oversized nature right on its doorstep: the Rheinfall waterfall, mirrorlike Lake Constance, those whopping Swiss Alps on the horizon...

Bern

Bern will sweep you off your feet with its riverside location, World Heritage–listed **Altstadt** (Old Town), phenomenal art and views of snow-frosted Alps on the horizon. Catch bears,

---

☑ TOP TIP

August is the month for Zürich's **Street Parade** (*streetparade.com/en*), a techno celebration that has firmly become one of Europe's largest and wildest street parties. Join 800,000 revellers dancing to live music and DJ sets at one of eight stages and 29 'love mobiles'.

GETTING AROUND

Efficient SBB trains link all the main towns and cities; a car is only needed if you want to meander completely off the urban beaten track. Bern, Basel and Zürich are all a delight to explore on foot; buses, trams and local trains cover longer distances (download

public-transport apps at *bernmobil.ch, bvb.ch* and *svv.ch* respectively). Free or inexpensive bicycle-rental schemes make cycling fun – all three cities are part of the **PubliBike** (*publibike.ch*) bike-sharing scheme.

HOW SWISS CHEESE GETS ITS HOLES

Named for its birthplace in the Emme River valley, 15 minutes by train from Bern, Switzerland's Emmentaler cheese has a proud history dating back to the Middle Ages. Copycat cheesemakers around the world have appropriated the Emmental name, but only authentic Emmentaler Switzerland AOC conforms to the original production technique, using raw milk from grass-fed cows, cellar-ripened in giant wheels for at least 120 days.

Emmentaler's famous holes, known as 'eyes', result from the release of carbon-dioxide bubbles by bacteria during the ageing process. The larger the holes, the longer the cheese has matured, and the more pronounced its flavour.

a golden cockerel, jester and god of time Chronos twirling four minutes before the hour on Bern's historical **Zytglogge** clock tower.

Soak up Swiss art in technicolour

Take in Switzerland's answer to the Guggenheim. Rising like three rippling waves above farmland just outside town, Renzo Piano's striking **Zentrum Paul Klee** *(zpk.org; adult/child Chf20/7)* is a tribute to the visionary Swiss-German artist, born near Bern in 1879. Rotating exhibitions draw on a 4000-strong collection of Klee's colour-charged, music-inspired works, showcasing his prodigious career, from expressionism to Cubism and surrealism. Bus 12 runs from Bahnhof to the museum.

Swim down the Aare

Drifting past the historic landmarks of the Altstadt or dipping with locals during their lunch break in the city's shockingly cold turquoise water is a rite of passage. Providing you're an experienced swimmer, try the classic route: hike 2km upstream from **Marzili Pools** to **Camping Eichholz**, then drift back with the current to Marzili's brilliant (and free) lido to swim laps, sunbathe, play volleyball or grab an ice cream. The views of the domed **Bundeshaus** and the **Münster**'s medieval spire are spot on.

Basel

Basel draws culture fiends from far and wide with its exciting art museums, nightlife and cute Altstadt (Old Town) anchored by its colourful **Rathaus** and 13th-century Münster. One-third of its urban population being non-Swiss today assures a continuing international flavour.

Meet art masters at Basel's 'big three'

Basel's cultural scene is its biggest drawcard, with the **Kunstmuseum Basel** *(kunstmuseumbasel.ch; adult/child Chf30/12)* showcasing a world-class collection spread across three buildings in the heart of the city. Switzerland's largest collection of public art spans masters from the 15th century to present day.

Attack contemporary art next at the wacky **Museum Jean Tinguely** *(tinguely.ch; adult/child Chf18/free),* designed by Ticino architect Mario Botta. Arrive by ferry from the **Münster** (cathedral) or cross Mittlere Brücke (Middle Bridge) and walk east. The museum is above a pebble beach, pleasant for swimming or floating downstream with a *Wickelfisch* (sold at the tourist office) back to Mittlere Brücke.

EATING & DRINKING IN BERN: OUR PICKS

Altes Tramdepot: Cavernous tram hall pairing schnitzel and *Bauernrösti* (fried potatoes topped with an egg) with microbrews. *11am-12.30am* €€

Kornhauskeller: Dine beneath vaulted frescoed arches at this cellar restaurant championing Mediterranean cuisine. *11.30am-11.30pm Mon-Sat, to 10pm Sun* €€

On Tap: Atmospheric vaulted cellar with 12 craft beers on tap and more by the bottle. Pair with antipasti. *4-11.30pm Mon-Wed, to 12.30am Thu-Sat*

Abflugbar: Slick, stylish, speakeasy-style cellar bar with knockout cocktails. Try the basil smash. *7.30pm-12.30am Wed-Sun*

Rathaus, Basel

Final calling card is **Fondation Beyeler** *(fondationbeyel er.ch; adult/under 25 Chf25/free)*, in a light-filled, open-plan building by Italian architect Renzo Piano. Exhibitions rotate 19th- and 20th-century works and ethnographic art from Africa, Alaska and Oceania.

Zürich

MAP p610

With a gorgeous location at the meeting of the Limmat River and Zürichsee, Zürich is hip and culturally ambitious, too. Pair old-world lanes in the cathedral-pinned Old Town with postindustrial edge in the artsy Züri-West 'hood. May to mid-September, swim at a lake- or riverside *badi* (lido) and enjoy a lake cruise.

Gen up on Swiss history

Celebrate national history and culture at the **Landesmuseum Zürich** *(landesmuseum.ch; adult/child Chf10/free)*. Elaborately carved and painted sleds, traditional costumes, reconstructed historical rooms and more are beautifully presented at the main branch of the Swiss National Museum. Find exhibits on archaeology, and Zürich's history and national identity. The gift shop has one of the city's best choice of souvenirs.

 EATING & DRINKING IN ZÜRICH: OUR PICKS

MAP p610

Haus Hiltl: A buffet of meatless delights or dine formally upstairs at the world's oldest vegetarian restaurant (1898). *7am-10pm Mon-Fri, 8am-11pm Sat, 10am-10pm Sun* €

Old Inn: Homemade pastrami and other delicacies in antique-style gastropub in art nouveau building. *11.30am-2pm Mon-Fri, 6pm-midnight Tue-Sat* €€

Frau Gerolds Garten: A focal point of the city's alfresco summer drinking scene, in Züri-West. This is one of Europe's best grownup playgrounds. *hours vary*

Clouds: Survey the city from the heady heights of this sophisticated bar on the 35th floor of the Prime Tower. *5pm-midnight Wed & Thu, to 1am Fri & Sat, noon-8pm Sun*

BEST ZÜRICH CHOCOLATE SHOPPING

Lindt Home of Chocolate: Buy Lindt at factory prices at this educational experience with showpiece 9m chocolate fountain.

Café Sprüngli: Try pralines, Luxemburgerli macarons and Grand Cru Absolu, a chocolate made only with cocoa beans and cocoa pulp, at this historic cafe from 1836.

Max Chocolatier: Stylishly packaged bars, truffles and pralines, made with 100% natural ingredients.

Berg und Tal: Artisan grocery stocking several brands of locally produced bean-to-bar chocolate, including Taucherli and Garçoa.

La Flor: Specialising in single-origin bars made from sustainably grown cacao sourced directly from farmers.

HIGHLIGHTS
1 Kunsthaus - Moser Building

SIGHTS
2 Landesmuseum Zürich

EATING
3 Café Sprüngli
4 Haus Hiltl
5 Old Inn
6 Restaurant Markthalle

DRINKING & NIGHTLIFE
7 Clouds

8 Frau Gerolds Garten

SHOPPING
9 Berg & Tal
10 Freitag
11 Im Viadukt
12 La Flor
13 Max Chocolatier

Admire great art at the Kunsthaus

Explore Switzerland's largest art collection at the superlative **Kunsthaus** (*kunsthaus.ch; adult/child Chf24/free*) museum, where thought-provoking exhibits span two main buildings, linked by an underground tunnel with an Ólafur Elíasson sculptural artwork on its ceiling. Seek out its unparalleled collection of the works by titans of the Swiss art world, including Augusto and Alberto Giacometti and Ferdinand Hodler.

Feel the pulse of Züri-West

Züri-West's **Im Viadukt** (*im-viadukt.ch*) is a trendy shopping and dining complex beneath old stone railway bridges. Stroll the viaduct's three blocks between Limmatstrasse and Geroldstrasse to see what catches your eye. Grab breakfast or dinner at **Restaurant Markthalle** (*restaurant-markthalle.ch*). Inside a stack of shipping containers, **Freitag** (*freitag.ch*) sells colourful wallets and bags of all shapes and sizes made from recycled truck tarps.

The Swiss Alps

You have every right to feel petite in the Swiss Alps. Stretching from the canton of Valais above the Rhône Valley in the west to Graubünden in the east, they cut, slice and dice more than half of Switzerland into an astonishing outdoor playground of cloud-shredding snowy peaks, thunderous gorges, ice-blue glaciers and lakes – all ripe for summer hiking and winter skiing.

Switzerland's invisible *Röstigraben* (linguistic and cultural border) kicks in just beyond the French-speaking town of Verbier, where starlets sip cocktails and farmers craft AOP Raclette cheese. Arriving in Zermatt, tongues wag in Swiss-German as everyone stares, transfixed, at the famous Matterhorn. Moving north, the Bernese Oberland – shaped by a godlike hand – is another diva forcing visitors to constantly peer up in wonder. Whether flirting with mountaineering on a *via ferrata*, scaling new heights atop Jungfraujoch or thrilling out on Interlaken whitewater, be prepared to experience nature in overdrive.

Verbier

Ritzy Verbier is the diamond of the Valaisian Alps: small and expensive, it draws accomplished winter skiers and summertime mountain bikers. This French-speaking 'place to be' is an easy train from Geneva and its international airport to Verbier's valley station **Le Châble**, from where cable cars glide to the top.

Fly high on a Mont Fort sunrise

Watching the sun rise over pink peaks at dawn from **Mont Fort** (3330m) is a goosebump moment. If a 4.25am cable-car departure and Chf89 price tag (covering breakfast and all-day cable-car travel) is too extreme, ride a later bubble up to **Les Ruinettes** (2191m) and beyond to Mont Fort *(Chf22 with a free summertime VIP Pass, incl in hotel accommodation Jun-Oct)* from the **Médran cable-car station** on Verbier's main street. Harness the daredevil in you for the descent:

GETTING AROUND

There are excellent SBB train services from the rest of Switzerland to mountain resorts such as car-free Zermatt and Interlaken; funiculars often cover the final leg up to resorts. Cable cars typically close for servicing in late April and late October.

If you are driving in winter, carry snow chains or use winter tyres. In early and late summer, check if mountain passes are open (signs at the bottom of access roads usually say so).

☑ **TOP TIP**

Remember the *Glacier Express* and other panoramic lines are mountain trains: last-minute cancellations due to blocked lines by snow or rockfall happen (your reserved journey still takes place, but on regular lines).

at 100km/h on the 1.4km-long **Mont 4 Zipline** *(adult/child over 8 Chf45/20)*. The bird's-eye view over the Tortin Glacier is of once-in-a-lifetime experience.

Mountain-bike in an alpine playground

Ski-celeb Verbier morphs into bike central in summer. Whether you're tearing down the mountainside as a family on chunky *trottinettes* (hairnet and helmet included in fat-tyre scooter rental; from eight years) from the top of the Savoleyres or Les Ruinettes cable cars, or tackling technical jumps with expert mountain bikers in a dedicated bike park, there is something to suit most abilities. June to mid-October, mountain bikers can transport wheels on the Médran cable car and La Chaux Express chairlift from Les Ruinettes to access 19km of down-hill descents in **Verbier Bike Park** *(verbierbikepark.ch; day pass adult/child Chf55/28, with VIP Pass Chf28/14)*.

Zermatt

Nothing prepares you for that first intoxicating glimpse of car-free Zermatt's peak rising majestically above the town and ski slopes. Step off the train and a puff cloud invariably

---

 DRINKING IN VERBIER: BEST APRÈS-SKI

| **Ice Cube:** Summer or winter, watch paragliders paint rainbows in the sky from this slope-side 'cube' at Les Ruinettes. *9am-4.15pm Jun-Sep & Dec-Apr* | **Le Rouge:** Swoosh off the blue Le Rouge piste and into The Red for drinks, 'funky fondue' soirées and resident DJs spinning dance tunes. *noon-midnight* | **Pub Mont Fort:** Downtown's après-ski heavyweight: live music, DJ sets, terrace and pub grub (apricot chicken wings, fries in melted cheese). *3pm-2am* | **Farinet:** Less intimidating than other bars, the downtown lounge bar with sun terrace hosts a happy hour and live bands nightly in season. *3pm-2am* |

clings to the 4478m hooked summit, making the sudden pop-up brilliance of a cloudless Matterhorn all the more wondrous.

Summit 3883m and glide into Italy

Admire ice sculptures in a palace 15m deep in a glacier, whoosh down ice slides and snow-tube atop **Klein Matterhorn** (3883m), accessed from Zermatt town by three cable cars culminating with the **Matterhorn Glacier Paradise** (*matterhornparadise.ch; adult/child return Chf125/62.50*), the world's highest-altitude 3S cable car. The view of 14 glaciers and 35 other peaks over 4000m at the top is beyond breathtaking.

Assuming it's a bluebird day, hop aboard the 1.6km-long **Matterhorn Alpine Crossing** (*matterhornalpinecrossing. com; adult single/return from Zermatt Chf156/240*) for a spellbinding cable-car journey over a spectacular glacial world of ice – and across the world's highest alpine border crossing – to Testa Grigia (3458m) in Cervinia, Italy.

Ride Europe's highest cogwheel railway

The Matterhorn dominates the scenic ride aboard the **Gornergratbahn** (*gornergrat.ch; adult/child return summer Chf132/66, winter Chf96/48*) – an 1898 vintage – from Zermatt to **Gornergrat** (3089m). Larch forests and the Vispa River melt into snowfields as the train staggers up gradients of up to 20% for 9.4km. Alight at the top to a hypnotic panorama of the Gornergrat glacier, Monte Rosa massif and Switzerland's highest peak, Dufourspitze (Dufour Peak; 4634m). Toast your good fortune on the sun-blazed terrace of **Kulmhotel Gornergrat** (*gornergrat-kulm.ch*).

Interlaken

Victorian-era glamour meets big mountains in Interlaken, which thrills with just about every heart-pumping alpine sport. Squished between the glacier-fed lakes of Thun and Brienz, this is the springboard to the Alps' fabled Jungfrau Region.

Hook up with a guide

Capped by the pearly white peaks of Eiger, Mönch and Jungfrau, this petite alpine town is second only to Queenstown, New Zealand, when it comes to extreme sports. **Outdoor Interlaken** (*outdoor.ch*) is a one-stop adventure shop for pretty much every buzz-inducing activity imaginable: tandem paragliding or skydiving, bungee jumping from a mountain gondola above a dazzling alpine lake, whitewater rafting and canyon swinging between gorge walls at speeds of 120km/h.

THE GLACIER EXPRESS

Gorging on cinematic shots of peaks, lakes, racing whitewater and other natural landscapes is what a day aboard the bucket-list **Glacier Express** (*glacierexpress.ch; single 1st/2nd class Chf159/272, plus reservation fee Chf49*) is about. Pulled by steam engine when it first puffed out of Zermatt in 1930, the iconic red train traverses 91 tunnels and 291 bridges on its slow journey to St Moritz (p617). Creeping along at 10km/h at times, the average speed on its 290km-long journey is just 42km/h. On the final leg between Chur and St Moritz, the six-arch, 65m-high Landwasser Viaduct on the UNESCO World Heritage–listed Albula railway line razzle-dazzles.

EATING IN ZERMATT: OUR PICKS

Stefanie's Crêperie: Perfect crepes with sweet or savoury (cheese fondue with cherry brandy!) toppings. *1-7pm Mon & Tue, 11.30am-9.30pm Wed-Sun* €

Blatten: Follow a knowing crowd to this small family-run chalet cafe and prized lunch address, in Zermatt's peaceful Blatten hamlet since 1850. *10am-6pm* €

Zum See: Tuck into a cracking rösti and other top-drawer grassroots dishes at this centuries-old chalet in the Zum See hamlet. *8.30am-5pm* €€

Potato: With produce sourced within 99km and ceiling lamps crafted from wooden veg crates, you don't get more local – or brilliantly creative. *6-11pm Mon-Sat* €€€

MORE MYTHICAL TRAIN RIDES

Bernina Express: Plunge through 55 tunnels and across 196 bridges on this 156km journey through the Engadine, from Chur to Tirano (four hours) aboard panoramic coaches (*tickets.rhb.ch*).

Golden Pass Express: Variable-gauge bogies mean the journey between Interlaken and Montreux on Lake Geneva can be done in a single 3½-hour trip (*gpx.swiss*).

Centovalli Railway: Narrow-gauge line linking Locarno with Domodossola (Italy) in 1¾ hours (*vigezzina centovalli.com*).

Gotthard Panorama Express: Five-hour journey mixes a cruise across Lake Lucerne with a train through ravines and past mighty St Gotthard mountain range to Bellinzona and Lugano (*gotthard-panorama-express.ch*).

Grindelwald

Skiers and hikers cottoned onto the charms of this mountain resort in the late 19th century. The geranium-studded chalets, verdant pastures and Oscar-worthy backdrop (the Eiger's north face, glinting tongues of Oberer, crown-like peak of Wetterhorn) are as tantalising as ever.

Eternal ice at Europe's highest train station

Brave the crowds on the once-in-a-lifetime trip to Jungfraujoch, Europe's highest train station, at 3454m. From Grindelwald, the **Eiger Express** (*jungfrau.ch; round trip adult/child Chf97.80/20*) wings you up to Eigergletscher station, where you switch to the Jungfrau Railway up to UNESCO World Heritage–listed **Jungfraujoch** (*jungfrau.ch; round trip from Grindelwald adult/child Chf201/20*). The summit is always snow white. From the Sphinx observation deck, spot the **Aletsch Glacier**. Grindelwald's **Outdoor Mountaineering School** (*outdoor.ch; 2-day hike Chf395*) organises summer roped hikes on the 23km-long sea of ice with a guide.

Pick up speed at First

Rising above Grindelwald, the 2184m summit of First gets hearts thumping with up-close views of Eiger's ferocious north face and the 4078m fang of Schreckhorn from **First Cliff Walk by Tissot** (*jungfrau.ch; free*), a gravity-defying lookout platform jutting 45m into the void.

Less than an hour's walk from the First cable-car top station unveils the the calm sapphire waters of **Bachalpsee**. In winter, there's great powder for snowboarding and free-skiing. From **Faulhorn** (2681m), sledge 15km down to Grindelwald on the world's longest sledge run.

Lucerne

Lounging lakeside on the Swiss Alps' northernmost fringe, Lucerne (Luzern in German) has been on the map since the 13th century when merchants crossing the **St Gotthard Pass** traded their wares here. Mountains of myth ring its cobalt lake; Goethe, Queen Victoria, Wagner and more all waxed lyrical about the medieval Old Town.

Devour frescoes, fountains and medieval towers

Using the 14th-century covered wooden footbridge **Kapellbrücke**, cross the Reuss River into Lucerne's perfectly preserved **Altstadt**. Minutes from the train station, this warren

EATING IN GRINDELWALD: OUR PICKS

Cafe 3692: Grindelwald ingredients in tasty specials at this quirky, woodsy hut. Or try alpine teas with pastries. *9am-11pm Fri & Sat, to 6pm Sun €*

Stallbeizli-Heuboden: Fondue heaven at this mountain hut in a converted barn with summer terrace. *noon-10pm Tue-Sat, to 8pm Sun €€*

Glacier Fine Dining: Feast on foraged flowers, herbs and berries. Or Graubünden salmon marinated in gin made from Eiger glacier water. *6-11pm Thu-Mon €€€*

Airtime: In nearby Lauterbrunnen, chill over breakfast, gourmet sandwiches, coffee with cake and Staubbach beer. *9am-5pm Fri-Mon €*

Reuss River and Kapellbrücke, Lucerne

of cobbled streets hides ornate fountains and frescoes illustrating city history and culture. Fill your water bottle at the colourful **Fritschibrunnen** on Kapellplatz, admire painted facades on **Hirschenplatz**, and nod to the stone fountain on historic market square **Weinmarkt**. End by the river to confront roof panels depicting the Dance of Death on 15th-century covered timber bridge **Spreuerbrücke** (1408).

St Moritz

Switzerland's cradle of alpine tourism, St Moritz has been luring royals, celebrities and moneyed wannabes since 1864. With its aquamarine lake, emerald forests and aloof mountains, the town looks a million dollars. Beyond the glamour, vast swathes of the surrounding Graubünden region are remote and ripe for exploring.

Dare to try extreme bobsledding and tobogganing

For buzz, try careering headfirst down glass-smooth ice at 135km/h on St Moritz's **Olympic Bob Run** *(olympia-bobrun.ch; bobsleigh guest ride Chf269)*. Handcrafted from natural ice in Celerina near St Moritz, this 1722m-long ice channel is the world's oldest bobsleigh run, dating from 1904. Or torpedo headfirst down the **Cresta Run** *(cresta-run.com; 1st 5 rides Chf700)*, a tobogganing course created by British visitors in 1885. In a lying down position, you use a rake on special boots to brake and steer at speeds of up to 140km/h.

BEST LUCERNE MUSEUMS

Verkehrshaus: Switzerland's most visited museum, the interactive Swiss Museum of Transport is a family-must. *(verkehrshaus.ch)*

Sammlung Rosengart: View works by Paul Klee, Monet, Cézanne, Matisse and more in this world-class modern-art collection. *(rosengart.ch)*

Kunstmuseum Luzern: A hot spot for Swiss and international art. *(kunstmuseum luzern.ch)*

Zivilschutzanlage Sonnenberg: Tour a 1976 underground bunker large enough to accommodate 2000 people during the Cold War. *(unterir disch-ueberleben.ch)*

Bourbaki Panorama: Admire a huge circular painting by 19th-century Swiss artist Edouard Castres. *(bourbaki panorama.ch)*

DRINKING AROUND LAKE LUCERNE: IDYLLIC SPOTS

Rigi Kulm Hotel: Modern incarnation of Switzerland's oldest mountain hotel has superlative views from Rigi's peak. *9am-4.30pm Mon-Fri, 8.30am-5pm Sat & Sun*

Restaurant Seerose: The shady lakeside terrace makes this a tempting spot for a post-hike spritz or beer in Weggis. *noon-10pm*

Bürgenstock Resort: If you're feeling flush, take the boat and funicular up to this luxury resort for a cocktail in its Lakeview Bar. *10am-midnight Sun-Thu, to 1am Fri & Sat*

Seehotel Waldstätterhof: The lakeside terrace of this Brunnen hotel is ideal for an aperitif or dinner as the sun sets. *11.30am-2pm & 6.30-10pm*

Ticino

ITALIAN DOLCE VITA | LAKES | HISTORY

GETTING AROUND

Geography dictates how you can explore this southern tip of Switzerland. A car allows you to go deep into its least-ventured folds – the steep switchbacks won't be to the taste of uncertain drivers. SBB trains connect towns with the rest of Switzerland and nearby Milan in Italy. Boats join the dots year-round between towns and villages on Lago Maggiore *(navigazionelaghi.it)* and Lago di Lugano *(lagolugano.ch)*.

☑ **TOP TIP**

Locarno is the eastern terminus of the historic **Centovalli Railway** *(vigezzinacentovalli.com)*, which trundles in slow motion through burrows via 34 tunnels and across 83 bridges to Domodossola in Italy. Dramatic alpine vistas are nonstop and mesmerising.

The Swiss Alps make their final descent into Italy's sunny plains in Ticino, Switzerland's only entirely Italian-speaking canton where glaciers meet palm trees and Swiss efficiency fuses with Italian flair. Here, on the country's southern tip, olive trees and palms ring alpine lakes. Narrow, twisting valleys sport stone-built villages little changed in two centuries. Gone are the fondue and rösti – think pasta, risotto and polenta instead. Mediterranean winter means sunny days and snow-free lakeshores. In August's sizzling heat, dine in a grotto – a traditional rural dining venue, in a cool shady spot. Earthy autumn ushers in September's grape harvest and Castagnata in October when local chestnuts are picked and celebrated in every guise.

At the heart of the canton rises Bellinzona, Ticino's head-turning capital and a UNESCO World Heritage site, with its fortified ramparts and medieval magic. Venturing south, the tranquil lake waters of Lugano and Locarno on the shared-with-Italy shores of Lago Maggiore quietly seduce.

Ticino's Medieval Capital

Fortress-hop in Bellinzona

Begin at Bellinzona's mighty **Castelgrande** *(fortezzabellinzona.ch; adult/concession Chf28/18)*, with towers and ramparts free to scramble round. The defensive walls that barrel out for 450m to the west afford top-drawer panoramas of the town and mountains beyond. Continue up the other side of the valley to **Castello di Montebello**, with drawbridges, towers and archaeological exhibits. End with the long climb up switchbacks to **Castello di Sasso Corbaro**, perched high on a wooded hillside and exuding an austere beauty.

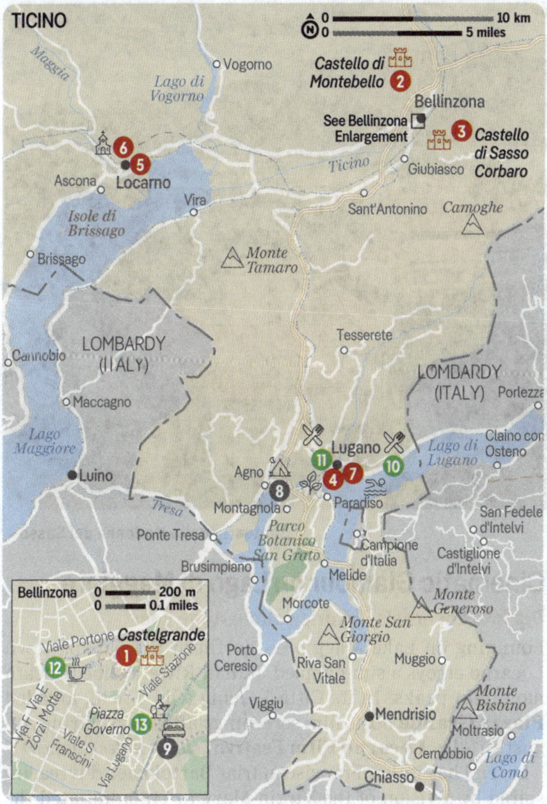

PALMS, PARROTS & ICY PEAKS

Welcome to the 'Sunshine Capital of Switzerland'! With around 2300 hours of sunshine per year, Locarno is hands-down Switzerland's sunniest town. Thanks to its protected location on the northern rim of Lago Maggiore, ringed by mountains that block cold winds while retaining warmth, sunny days combine with a microclimate to create an almost Mediterranean environment. Palm trees, banana plants, olive trees and tropical flowers thrive in the mild climate here, as does the odd escaped pet parakeet that you occasionally see squawking in trees in city parks. Winter temperatures rarely drop below freezing here, in sharp contrast to Ticino's ice-bound valleys just a short drive away.

Map labels:

TICINO

N
0 — 10 km
0 — 5 miles

Maggia
Lago di Vogorno
Vogorno
Castello di Montebello 2
Bellinzona
See Bellinzona Enlargement
6 5
Ascona Locarno
Vira
3 Castello di Sasso Corbaro
Giubiasco
Ticino
Sant'Antonino
Camoghe
Isole di Brissago
Brissago
Monte Tamaro
LOMBARDY (ITALY)
Cannobio
Maccagno
Tesserete
LOMBARDY (ITALY)
Porlezza
Lago Maggiore
Luino
Agno
11 Lugano
Lago di Lugano
Claino con Osteno
8
Montagnola
4 7
Paradiso
10
San Fedele d'Intelvi
Tresa
Ponte Tresa
Parco Botanico San Grato
Campione d'Italia
Castiglione d'Intelvi
Brusimpiano
Melide
Morcote
Monte Generoso

Bellinzona
0 — 200 m
0 — 0.1 miles
Viale Portone Castelgrande
1
12
Via F. Via E. Zorzi Motta
Piazza Governo
13
Viale S. Franscini
Via Lugano
9
Viale Stazione

Porto Ceresio
Riva San Vitale
Monte San Giorgio
Muggio
Viggiu
Mendrisio
Monte Bisbino
Moltrasio
Cernobbio
Lago di Como
Chiasso

⭐ HIGHLIGHTS
1 Castelgrande
2 Castello di Montebello
3 Castello di Sasso Corbaro

🔴 SIGHTS
4 Parco Ciani

5 Piazza Grande
6 Santuario della Madonna del Sasso

🔴 ACTIVITIES
7 Lido di Lugano

⚫ SLEEPING
8 Camping Lugano Lake

9 Ostello Montebello

🟢 EATING
10 Le Bucce di Gandria
11 Staglio

🟢 DRINKING & NIGHTLIFE
12 L'Arte del Caffè
13 Paprika Lounge Bar

Savour the Difference on a Passeggiata

Chill out in Lugano

One of the joys of staying in Lugano is an evening stroll along the promenade, with palm trees and flowerbeds lacing the sparkling waters of Lago di Lugano. Inland, sculpture-dotted **Parco Ciani** is a gorgeous place for a gelato or picnic on a red bench. On hot days, swim in pools or from the sandy beach at **Lido di Lugano** *(lugano.ch; adult/child Chf11/7)*. Meandering east, Piazza Manzoni anchors the old-world lanes and boutiques of the atmospheric **Old Town**.

TRABANTOS/SHUTTERSTOCK

Santuario della Madonna del Sasso

Cinematic Glamour on Lago di Maggiore

Dip into Locarno's historic cobblestone heart

Lounging on Lake Maggiore's northern tip, old spa town Locarno enjoys a sun-dappled 'Italian Riviera' vibe beneath mountain peaks. In its Città Vecchia (Old Town), arcaded **Piazza Grande** hosts film screenings after dark during August's 11-day **Locarno Film Festival** *(locarnofestival.ch)*.

Legend has it that Franciscan friar Bartolomeo d'Ivrea, inspired by a vision of the Virgin Mary in 1480, initiated the construction of **Santuario della Madonna del Sasso**, clinging to an outcrop in Locarno's Orselina suburb. To make the pilgrimage here, ride the Cardada **funicular** *(cardada.ch)* from just south of Locarno train station. Walk back down into town along the chapel-lined **Via Crucis** (Way of the Cross).

 EATING & DRINKING IN TICINO: OUR PICKS

Staglio: The best pizza slices in Lugano town that won't break the bank. Central location just back from the lakefront. *11am-9pm Mon-Thu, from noon Fri-Sun €*

Le Bucce di Gandria: In Gandria village above Lugano, feast on seasonal local flavours and sensational lake views. *7-10pm Thu-Sun, noon-2pm Sat & Sun €€*

Paprika Lounge Bar: Dive into inventive drinks and bites at this trendy spot in Bellinzona, perfect for a quick drink or lunch. *7am-10pm Mon-Fri, 8am-2pm Sat*

L'Arte del Caffè: This elegant cafe en route to Castelgrande is a great place for an Italian caffeine shot before the uphill castle hike. *8am-5.30pm Mon-Sat*

Places We Love to Stay

€ Budget €€ Midrange €€€ Top end

Geneva
MAP p605

TCS Camping Genève-Vésenaz € Campsite with cabins, tent pitches and van park overlooking a grassy beach on Pointe à la Bise, 7km north from downtown Geneva.

Hôtel Bel'Esperance €€ Single to family rooms sleeping four add extra appeal to this reliable midrange hotel. The icing on the cake: a rooftop terrace for lake-drooling.

Lausanne

Lausanne Jeunotel € Smart hostel a stone's throw from the lake, a Roman archaeological dig and the International Olympic Committee's shiny HQ. Dorms sleep two to six.

Mad House € The 'it' address in lively Flon (actually part of Accor's Ibis Styles brand), with rooftop bar, street-art deco and cool rooms from the team behind MAD club.

Montreux

Auberge de Jeunesse Montreux € Roll out of your bunk and into the lake at this modern hostel, midway between Montreux and Château de Chillon.

Hôtel La Rouvenaz €€ This boutique hotel–restaurant across from Montreux lakefront, with a down-to-earth contemporary ambience, is startling good value.

Gruyères

Fleur de Lys € Modern comfort with antique touches in a 17th-century building, plus a decent restaurant with a hidden terrace out the back.

Hotel de Gruyères €€ Cosy, traditional lodgings near the village entrance and car parks, with views of the surrounding mountains.

Bern

Am Pavillon € A pleasingly converted late-19th-century townhouse near the Hauptbahnhof, with bags of art-nouveau charm.

Hotel Marthahaus €€ In a leafy neighbourhood, this sweet and simple guesthouse is crisply designed, quiet and sprinkled with modern art.

Verbier

Map Hostel € Go vintage in the old vicarage, down the hill in Vieux Verbier. Bunk rooms sleep two to six.

Ride Inn €€ 'Chalet-style' B&B with shared bathrooms and summer garden. The bike-mad hosts are a mine of local information.

Zermatt

Jaëgerhof Hotel € Consistently reliable, this functional but attractive hotel sports three-star singles, doubles, twins and family rooms. Copious breakfast buffet.

Hotel Plateau Rose € Another brilliant deal, up a small hill by the Matterhorn Glacier Paradise cable car. Matterhorn views from its back garden are the finest in town.

Interlaken

Backpacker's Villa Sonnenhof € This slick, ecofriendly chalet and art-nouveau villa has immaculate dorms, a relaxed lounge and a well-equipped kitchen.

Salzano Hotel & Spa €€ This intimate chalet hotel on Interlaken's fringes has a quiet spa, big mountain views and outstanding Italian cooking.

Grindelwald

Gletschergarten €€ Brimming with pine, warmth and family heirlooms, this sweet family-run chalet has gorgeous mountain views.

Valley Hostel €€ A great activity base, this chilled hostel in Lauterbrunnen has pine-panelled dorms and a garden with compelling waterfall views.

Lucerne

Capsule Hotel € One-person enclosed sleeping booths, or 'capsules', in multi-capsule rooms, with shared bathrooms. Clean, comfortable alternative to dorm beds.

Hotel Continental Park €€ By pretty Vögeligärtli park in the new town, with stylish rooms and a Ticino-inspired restaurant. Bike hire available.

Mürren & Jungfrau

Mönchsjochhütte € Share the dinner table and dorm with rock climbers at Switzerland's highest serviced hut. Sensational sunrise.

Ticino
MAP p619

Ostello Montebello € Bellinzona's youth hostel occupies an enviable location between Castelgrande and Montebello. It has basic dorms and a large common room.

Camping Lugano Lake € One of four campsites clustered by Lake Lugano at the end of the runway of Lugano's small airport. High-standard facilities.

621

Practicalities

SAFE TRAVEL
Switzerland is very safe. Streets are well lit, and street crime and petty theft are uncommon. Check for ticks after a hike. As weather becomes increasingly fickle and extreme, a warming climate poses the greatest threat. Tap water is safe to drink; fill your bottle for free at fountains.

INSURANCE
If you're skiing, snowboarding or hiking, ensure your policy covers helicopter rescue and emergency repatriation.

Alternatively, summer or winter, when buying your lift pass online or in situ, most resorts offer optional insurance (usually Chf3 per day) covering emergency rescue off the mountain and medical care.

LGBTIQ+ TRAVELLERS
Switzerland is a tolerant country and reasonably progressive on LGBTIQ+ rights.

Zürich, Geneva, Lausanne, Bern and Lucerne have the liveliest LGBTIQ+ scenes. Pride kicks off on the snow in Verbier in April.

NATURAL DISASTERS
Download the Alert Swiss app or consult its website (alert. swiss) to receive national alerts, notifications, extreme weather warnings and information about a variety of hazards. The national service also issues relevant safety instructions.

LANGUAGES
German (p315), French (p245), Italian (p467) and Romansh are spoken in Switzerland.

AARONCHENPS2/SHUTTERSTOCK

ALPINE HAZARDS
Mountain risks include snowstorms, avalanches, landslides, flooding and thunderstorms. Keep up-to-date with *natural-hazards.ch*.

Summer or winter, alpine weather is notoriously fickle. Even in August it can feel like four seasons in a day, with sun, fog, storms and snow. Before heading into the mountains, check weather forecasts on *meteoswiss.admin.ch*. Subscribe to alerts for your specific location.

OPENING HOURS
Museums 10am–6pm; many close Monday or Tuesday and some stay open late Thursday
Restaurants noon–2.30pm and 6pm–9.30pm (7.30pm–10.30pm in French-speaking Switzerland and Ticino); closed one or two days per week.
Shops 10am–6pm Monday to Friday, to 4pm Saturday (6pm or later in French-speaking Switzerland).

PUBLIC HOLIDAYS
Some cantons observe other holidays and religious days, eg 2 January, Labour Day (1 May), Assumption (15 August) and All Saints' Day (1 November).
New Year's Day 1 January
Good Friday March/April
Easter Sunday and Monday March/April
Ascension 40th day after Easter
Whit Sunday and Monday Seventh week after Easter
Swiss National Day 1 August
Christmas Day 25 December
Boxing Day 26 December

ANTON GVOZDIKOV/SHUTTERSTOCK

Swiss International Air Lines

Arriving & Getting Around

Zürich Airport, 9km north of the city centre, and Geneva Airport, 4km northwest of the town centre, both have a mainline train station, with speedy trains into town plus regular public transport.

Arriving by Road
Bordering France, Germany, Austria, Liechtenstein and Italy, Switzerland is easily accessible by road. High alpine passes are snow-blocked and closed in winter (October to May/June). Roads signs for motorways are green.

Cycling & E-Biking
Well-signposted, scenic cycling routes spaghetti across the country; find cycling and mountain-biking pages on *schweizmobil.ch*. With SBB Rent-a-Bike *(rentabike.ch),* collect at one train station and return to another.

Driving Essentials
Drive on the right. Headlights must be turned on day and night. November to March, winter tyres are essential. Blood alcohol limit is 0.05%. To use motorways, pay an annual toll *(Chf40)* online at *vignette-schweiz.com.*

Trains, Buses & Cable Cars
Interconnected trains, boats, yellow PostBuses and cable cars have most of the country within easy, car-free reach. Consult routes and buy tickets on *swissrailways.com* and *travelswitzerland.com.* Download the SBB app *(sbb.ch)* for train timetables and tickets.

MONEY
Currency: Swiss franc (CHF or Chf)

CONTACTLESS PAYMENT
Almost every hotel, shop, restaurant, cafe, bar and business supports contactless payments and Apple Pay – there is no minimum payment amount.

CARDS & ATMS
Credit cards are widely accepted; EuroCard/MasterCard and Visa are the most popular. ATMs are widespread and accessible 24 hours.

CASH
Swiss francs are divided into 100 centimes (*Rappen* in German-speaking Switzerland). Many shops and small businesses don't accept large-denomination notes – 100, 200 and 1000 franc notes. Businesses throughout Switzerland accept cash payments in euros. Change will be given in Swiss francs at the rate of exchange calculated on the day.

MACIEJ SCHULZ/SHUTTERSTOCK

623

TOOLKIT

The chapters in this section cover the most important topics you'll need to know about in Western Europe. They're full of nuts-and-bolts information and valuable insights to help you understand and navigate Western Europe and get the most out of your trip.

Getting Around the Region
p626

Accommodation
p628

Family Travel
p630

Health & Safe Travel
p632

Women Travellers
p634

Food, Drink & Nightlife
p636

Responsible Travel
p638

LGBTIQ+ Travellers
p640

Accessible Travel
p641

Nuts & Bolts
p642

Sóller tram, Mallorca (p581), Spain
BORIS STROUJKO/SHUTTERSTOCK

Getting Around the Region

Western Europe has outstanding road, rail and plane connections. Ferries and flights connect the mainland to islands, and public transport is generally excellent, especially in cities and towns, becoming sparser in rural regions.

TRAVEL COSTS

Car rental
from €30 per day

Petrol
approx €1.60 per litre

Train
Milan–Rome from €65; London–Paris from £35

Metro ticket
from €1.50 in Madrid to €4.10 in Munich

Car

Driving yourself around in a rental car or your own vehicle gives you maximum flexibility, and it's almost always the best way to reach remote places. If, however, your visit involves major cities, you'll find a car can be complicated, even impractical due to traffic jams, parking issues and the ever-present danger of getting lost; head for your hotel, dump your bags and park your car for the duration of your stay. Some cities, such as London, Milan and Stockholm, have congestion charges.

Train

Western Europe's rail network is arguably the best and most extensive on earth. There's everything from luxury to local services and you can plan your entire trip around travelling by rail, safe in the knowledge that services will be quick, reliable and supremely comfortable. Many state railways have interactive websites publishing their timetables and fares. If you'll be taking the train on numerous legs of your journey, consider a rail pass.

Air

Travelling by air means you'll have more time in each destination, and it's a great way to see lots of far-flung places in a relatively short time period. You may even find that air travel can be comparable in cost to road or rail travel, especially if you travel off-season (eg avoiding mid-June to early September, Easter, Christmas and school holidays) and use low-cost airlines.

DRIVING ESSENTIALS

Drive on the right everywhere except Britain and Ireland.

Speed limit is typically 50km/h in cities and 120km/h on motorways.

Seatbelts are compulsory for all vehicle occupants.

BICYCLE HIRE

Much of Western Europe is ideally suited to cycling and bike hire is prevalent. Many Western European train stations have bike-rental counters, and major cities (including London, Paris, Berlin and Amsterdam) have bike- and e-bike-sharing schemes. Hostels are also good places to find cheap bike hire.

Tip

Going by train? **Man in Seat 61** (*seat61.com*) is comprehensive, while **DB Bahn** (*bahn.de*) provides excellent schedule and fare information in English for trains across Europe.

RAIL PASSES

Interrail *(interrail.eu)* offers a 'Global Pass' to European residents for unlimited rail travel through 33 European countries. Passes are valid for four, five or seven days in a month, or 10 or 15 days in two months. Interrail also offers One Country passes valid in the country of your choice for up to one month. The equivalent for residents of non-European countries are **Eurail** *(eurail.com)* passes. Prices and benefits are the same.

National rail operators might also offer their own passes, or at least a discount card, with substantial reductions on tickets purchased (eg the BahnCard in Germany or the Half-Fare Card in Switzerland).

With all passes, compare point-to-point charges and rail passes beforehand to make sure you'll break even.

Car Rental

It's usually cheaper to prebook a car online than hire one on arrival; at busy times, there may be no vehicles available if you leave it late. You'll generally find major car-hire companies at airports. The minimum age for hiring cars ranges from 18 to 25 years. A valid licence issued at least one year prior is necessary; carry an International Driving Permit (issued by your home automobile association) in case it's asked for. You should also purchase additional collision damage waiver (CDW) insurance.

Border Crossings

Border formalities have been relaxed in most of the EU, but still exist in all their original bureaucratic glory in the more far-flung parts of Eastern Europe, some of which border Western Europe.

In line with the Schengen Agreement, there are officially no passport controls at the borders between 29 European states, namely: Austria, Belgium, Bulgaria, Croatia, Czechia, Denmark, Estonia, Finland, France, Germany, Greece, Hungary, Iceland, Italy, Latvia, Liechtenstein, Lithuania, Luxembourg, Malta, the Netherlands, Norway, Poland, Portugal, Romania, Slovakia, Slovenia, Spain, Sweden and Switzerland.

Sometimes, however, there are spot-checks on trains crossing borders, so always have your passport. The UK was a nonsignatory to Schengen and thus maintains border controls over traffic from other EU countries (except Ireland, with which it shares an open border), although there is no customs control. The same applies to Ireland.

TAKING CARS ACROSS BORDERS

Be aware that some car-rental companies won't allow their vehicles to be taken across some borders; some major car companies will, for example, allow you to take a car from Germany into Slovenia, but not Croatia or Serbia.

In some countries, motorists must buy a motorway tax sticker (vignette in German and French; *contrassegno* in Italian) to display on the windscreen. Buy vignettes at petrol stations near the borders before crossing into the country.

Accommodation

From bare-bones hostels to boutique spa hotels in the Alps, from luxury villas by the Med and grand castle sleeps to family-run B&Bs and sky-high mountain huts, Western Europe has it all. Make where you stay an integral part of your experience.

Hotels

From sweet-and-simple family places to ultra-luxe spa hotels with dazzling sea views, hotels in Europe vary wildly in style and price, but there really is something for every budget. Cheap digs around bus and train stations can be convenient for late-night or early-morning arrivals and departures, but check the room beforehand. Top-end boutique and design hotels continue to punch high. Look out for creative options set in old castles, monasteries, palaces or even former prisons.

B&Bs

Guesthouses (*pension, Gasthaus, chambre d'hôte* etc) and B&Bs offer greater comfort than hostels for a marginally higher price. Most are simple affairs, normally with shared bathrooms. B&Bs in the UK and Ireland often aren't really budget accommodation and there's a new generation of boutique B&Bs, which are pretty flash.

Camping

Camping is popular in Europe, but given space constraints it's rarely a wilderness experience. Most camping grounds are some distance from city centres. Tourist offices provide lists of camping grounds and camping organisations. See **Hipcamp** *(hipcamp.com)* for details on prime campsites across Europe. There will usually be a charge per tent or site, per person and per vehicle. It's often necessary to book in advance.

Glamping

Glamping has soared in popularity across Europe and is a terrific (if pricier) way to slip back to nature without sacrificing creature comforts (we're talking proper beds, private toilets, even hot tubs...). And they're often green in every sense of the word.

Advance Reservations

During peak holiday periods, particularly Easter, summer and Christmas – and year-round in popular cities like London, Paris and Rome – it's wise to book ahead. Most places can be reserved online and can be cheaper through the hotel's own website.

Saving Money

Long-stay discounts are usually possible and hotel owners in southern Europe might even be open to a little haggling. It's common for business hotels to slash their rates on Friday and Saturday nights.

Farmstays

Fresh eggs from the hens for breakfast, animals to pet, walking trails on the doorstep, meals brimming with homegrown produce – farmstays are a terrific (and often inexpensive) way to get a true flavour of the land. Italy has a rich network of *agriturismi,* which are state-regulated. See *agriturismo.it* for more details. Elsewhere, visit *farmstayplanet.com.*

Hostels

If you're on a budget, Europe's hostels are ideal. Those affiliated to **Hostelling International** *(HI; hihostels.com)* usually offer the cheapest secure roof over your head. You need to be a YHA or HI member to use them, but non-members can stay by paying a few extra euros. There are also tonnes of private hostels and backpacker digs. These have fewer rules, more self-catering kitchens and fewer large, noisy school groups. If you aren't happy to share mixed dorms, ask when you book. **Europe's Famous Hostels** *(famoushostels. com)* has a selection of top independent backpacker hostels.

Wild Camping

If you prefer to head off on your lonesome into the wilds and camp where your fancy, be aware of the rules. In some countries, such as Austria, France and Germany, wild (aka free) camping is illegal on all but private land; in others, such as Greece, it's illegal altogether. Free camping is tolerated at some remote locations in Ireland and permissible in most places in Scotland, though not in England or Wales. Camping on private land is usually illegal without the permission of the landowner. If you are wild camping, be discreet, stay just one or two nights, decamp during the day and don't light a fire or leave rubbish.

Hay Hotels

Fancy hitting the hay? In Switzerland, Austria and Germany, you can properly get back to nature by swapping a bed for a barn or a *Heuhotel* (hay hotel). Farmers provide cotton undersheets (to avoid straw pricks) and woolly blankets for extra warmth, but you'll need your own sleeping bag and torch. For further details, visit **Schlafen im Stroh** *(myfarm.ch).*

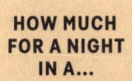

HOW MUCH FOR A NIGHT IN A...

hostel dorm bed
€15–40

farmstay
€100–120

campsite including tent
€15–30

boutique hotel
from €100

Memorable Luxe Stays

All over Europe you can stay in some incredible places if budget isn't an issue, with luxury hotels lodged in everything from castles to lavishly converted abbeys, vineyards and seafront fortresses. These vary from country to country, but include **Romantik Hotels** *(romantikhotels.com)* in Austria, Switzerland, Germany and Italy, **château** *(bienvenueauchateau. com)* stays in France, and Portugal's network of dreamy **pousadas** *(pousadas.pt).*

SUSTAINABLE CHOICES

Green sleeps are on the up in Europe. To tread lightly when travelling, look for the **EU Ecolabel** *(europa.eu)* and **Green Key** *(greenkey.global)* labels, which means the accommodation meets specific sustainable criteria, from renewable energy to waste management, water saving and recycling measures. Some will offer an incentive or discount if you arrive by public transport.

As a rule of thumb, camping and glamping sites, farmstays (including *agriturismi*) and mountain huts (of which the Alps has a vast network) tend to score highly when it comes to sustainability. An increasing number of hotels and B&Bs are also upping their green credentials. Check before booking.

Family Travel

Europe is a great place to travel with kids. Successful travel with young children requires some careful planning and effort. Don't try to overdo things; even for adults, packing too much sightseeing into your schedule can be counterproductive.

Pre-Trip Planning

Plan ahead and select a few big-ticket items aimed specifically at kids before you leave, such as Disneyland Paris. Don't write off the less obvious sights or smaller attractions. Many of Europe's art galleries and iconic monuments give out kids' activity books that lay out special interactive itineraries for children. Hit a festival. Many European festivals have a strong family bias and have been entertaining children for centuries, from Seville's Feria de Abril to France's Bastille Day.

Practicalities

Most car-hire firms in Western Europe have children's safety seats for hire at a nominal cost, but it's essential that you book in advance.

Highchairs and cots (cribs) are available in many restaurants and hotels but numbers are often limited.

Disposable nappies (diapers) are widely available, as is formula.

Babysitters are best sourced through your hotel.

Attitudes to breastfeeding in public vary; ask locally for advice.

Where to Stay

When planning your accommodation, consider whether your chosen place to stay is close to public transport, has lifts (elevators), green space and/or playgrounds nearby where kids can run free.

BEST ATTRACTIONS FOR FAMILIES

Eisriesenwelt (p61) Enjoy glittering chambers and frozen sculptures in the world's largest ice caves in Austria.

Cité de l'Espace (p239) Become a budding astronaut at Toulouse's space-fantastic museum.

Jacobite Steam Train (p164; pictured left) Cross the viaduct en route to Hogwarts as in the *Harry Potter* films.

Schloss Neuschwanstein (p288) Germany's fairy-tale fortress was the prototype for Disney's *Sleeping Beauty* castle.

Zoo Berlin (p262) One of the best zoos in Western Europe, with many species and fine conservation programs.

FAMILY TRAVEL ON A BUDGET

Saving money starts with picking the right accommodation. Cots are usually free of charge for babies and tots in hotels on request (book early). For cheap rooms, many hostels have at least one family room.

Lunch specials and fixed-price menus in restaurants tend to be inexpensive. Alternatively, street food in cities (from pizza to souvlaki) and picnics (raid local markets and supermarkets) can be great ways to economise.

Look out for free local guest cards, many of which reap excellent savings on activities. Kids under 12 (sometimes 18) often get free or reduced entry to sights and attractions.

FROM LEFT: NATALIA DERIABINA/SHUTTERSTOCK, RICHARD P LONG/SHUTTERSTOCK

MOVING AROUND

Rental-car companies can arrange child and booster seats, which, in some countries, are obligatory for children aged 12 and under (measuring between 135cm and 150cm). Newer public transport is often accessible for buggies and prams. In many countries in Western Europe, children under six travel free on public transport, or half-price until 15 years (proof of age may be required). To save, also keep an eye out for money-saving family passes.

Outdoor Fun

Winging you from seaside cove to cow-bobbled pasture, fast-flowing river to mountaintop, Western Europe is brilliant for families wanting to embrace the great outdoors. Many destinations offer gentle, well-marked family-friendly hiking and cycling trails, some of which are accessible to buggies (strollers) and prams. Most tourist offices can point out family-friendly hikes, from nature rambles to wildlife-spotting trails and coastal paths leading to hidden beaches. They can also advise about age-appropriate activities for adventurous kids, from surfing lessons to *vie ferrate* (mountain trails with permanent cables and ladders) and whitewater rafting (note that some activities have an age minimum). In winter, the Alps and Scandinavia are full-on winter wonderland stuff, with resorts offering ski lessons for children (generally aged four up), plus slope-side fun from snowshoeing to tobogganing, dogsledding and reindeer encounters.

> ### Tip
>
> Bring a light pram that easily folds, with thicker wheels to deal with cobblestones and public transport, and pack a baby carrier.

Outdoor Spaces

Many cities and towns across Western Europe feature parks with duck ponds and kids' play areas where the little ones can let off steam between sightseeing. Many lakes have supervised beaches, with kids' splash areas, slides and games. Even cities have lidos with activities from table tennis to volleyball and slides.

Child-Friendly Attractions

All over Europe, big-hitter museums and galleries have dedicated exhibitions, workshops, tours and activities for kids; some tourist offices have brochures and/or web pages devoted to such places. Museums can be fun as well as educational, such as London's hands-on Science Museum or Vienna's music-minded Haus Musik.

ADMISSION

Children aged between five and 18 get heavily discounted (usually half-price) entry on sights, attractions and tours. Kids four and under go free.

EATING OUT

Children are generally welcome in all but the most formal of restaurants in Europe, but check ahead.

Some restaurants have kids' menus, which are usually deep-fried, child-pleasing favourites. Others will make a half (small) portion of adult meals. From *frites* (fries) and crêpes in France to pizza and gelato in Italy and fish and chips in the UK, Europe has plenty of staples that appeal to little appetites.

Many family-friendly restaurants can provide highchairs or booster seats, but it's always worth checking when booking. You might want to bring along bibs, wipes, cutlery, books and toys.

Some countries make a particular fuss of little ones. Mediterranean countries, in particular, tend to make a real fuss of young children, from hair ruffling to extra sweets.

Attitudes relax the further south you go. In countries like Spain, Italy and Greece, expect to see local kids staying up late(ish) and eating at the same time as their parents. You're likely to see them playing in squares while parents are nearby having a drink.

Health & Safe Travel

Travelling in Western Europe is usually very safe. With comprehensive health care, political stability and generally low crime rates, you'd be unlucky to encounter any serious problems. The usual common-sense rules of having the right insurance and stashing away valuables apply.

VACCINATIONS & INFECTIOUS DISEASES

No jabs are necessary to visit Western Europe. However, the World Health Organization (WHO) recommends that all travellers be covered for diphtheria, tetanus, measles, mumps, rubella and polio, regardless of their destination. Since most vaccines don't produce immunity until at least two weeks after they're given, visit a physician at least six weeks before departure. There may be specific advice in relation to some areas; consult your doctor.

Health Insurance

It's unwise to travel anywhere in Western Europe without adequate travel insurance. A good policy should include comprehensive health insurance that covers medical care and emergency evacuation. If you are engaging in risky sports (whitewater rafting, paragliding, rock climbing, surfing, off-piste skiing and the like), you may need to pay for extra cover. Check the small print.

If you're an EU citizen or a citizen of Iceland, Liechtenstein, Norway or Switzerland, the free EHIC (European Health Insurance Card) covers you for most medical care in 32 European countries, including maternity care and care for chronic illnesses such as diabetes (though not for emergency repatriation). Offering the same benefits, the UK equivalent is the GHIC (Global Health Insurance Card). However, you will normally have to pay for medicine bought from pharmacies, even if prescribed, and perhaps for some tests and procedures. The EHIC and GHIC don't cover private medical consultations and treatment out of your home country; this includes nearly all dentists, and some of the better clinics and surgeries. In the UK, you can apply for an EHIC online, by telephone or by filling out a form available at post offices.

Non-EU citizens should find out if there's a reciprocal arrangement for free medical care between their country and the EU country they are visiting. Even if there is, don't skimp on health insurance.

Tap Water

Tap water is generally safe to drink in Western Europe. While bottled water is widely available, there's no need to buy it for health reasons; bring your own reusable water bottle and fill it straight from the tap. Do not drink water from rivers or lakes as it may contain bacteria or viruses. In Greece, the water is often safe to drink but doesn't taste pleasant. An increasing number of countries provide free water fountains at train stations, airports and dotted around major cities.

STINGING INSECTS

Wasps can be pesky in midsummer but are only dangerous for those with an allergy. Mosquitoes can be a nuisance around rivers and lakes. Bring repellent.

Health Care in Western Europe

Good health care is readily available in Western Europe, and pharmacists can give valuable advice for minor illnesses and sell over-the-counter medication. They can also advise if you need specialised help and point you in the right direction. The standard of dental care is usually good. If you use regular prescription medicine, bring enough for the duration of your trip, and carry with you the paper prescription, just in case.

Even if you're covered by reciprocal arrangements from your home country, travel insurance is a must.

Condoms are widely available in Western Europe; however, emergency contraception may not be, so take the necessary precautions.

Hiking Safety

Every year people die from landslides and avalanches in the Alps. Always check weather conditions before heading out; consider hiring a guide when skiing off-piste. Before going on challenging hikes, ensure you have the proper equipment and fitness. Inform someone at your accommodation where you're going and when you intend to return.

Online Resources

The **WHO** (who.int) publishes the free online book *International Travel and Health,* which is revised annually. **MD Travel Health** (mdtravelhealth.com) provides up-to-date travel-health recommendations for every country.

It's usually a good idea to consult your government's website before departure, if one is available:
Australia (smartraveller.gov.au)
Canada (phac-aspc.gc.ca)
UK (gov.uk/foreign-travel-advice)
USA (cdc.gov/travel)

HOT SUMMERS, COLD WINTERS

Summers in the south can be extremely hot, with temperatures soaring above 40°C in Spain, Italy and Greece. Be sure to seek shade from the midday sun, drink plenty of water to stay hydrated, wear sunblock and avoid overly exerting activities.

At the other extreme, winters can be cold in the Alps, so master the art of layering. On cold days, start with thermals or a warm underlayer, followed by wool or a warm fleece to keep the warmth in and a wind- and waterproof outer layer.

PICKPOCKETS & THIEVES

Theft is definitely a problem in parts of Europe. The key is to be sensible with your possessions. Pickpockets are most active in dense crowds, especially in busy train stations, around major tourist sites, and on public transport during peak hours. Most scams involve distracting you – either by kids running up to you, someone asking for directions or spilling something on you – while another person steals your wallet.

Don't store valuables in train-station lockers or luggage-storage counters. Don't leave valuables in your car, on train seats or in your room.

Never flaunt cameras, laptops or other expensive electronic goods. Consider using small zipper locks on your packs.

Spread valuables, cash and cards around your body or in different bags. A money belt with your essentials (passport, cash, credit cards, airline tickets) is usually a good idea.

Keep separate a photo of your passport's data pages. If you lose your passport, notify the police immediately to get a statement and contact your nearest consulate.

⚠ BEWARE ⚠
PICKPOCKET

633

Women Travellers

Travelling in Western Europe as a solo female traveller is a joy. Many cities and towns are small, walkable and safe. Countries topping gender-equality rankings include the Netherlands, Spain, Germany and Belgium, but with mindfulness, diligence and planning you shouldn't encounter problems elsewhere either. By Kerry Walker

Where to Stay

Where you stay matters. Book somewhere central and try to arrive during the daytime so you can easily get your bearings. For peace of mind, look out for hotels with 24-hour receptions (you might want to ask for an upper-floor room), hostels with women-only dorms and secure private rentals. Female-run and women-only hotels are also on the rise, so do your research.

What to Wear

Women might attract unwanted attention in rural Spain and Greece, and in southern Italy, especially Sicily, where many men view whistling and catcalling as flattery. Intense staring is common. Modest dress can help deter this. When entering Orthodox churches, women need to cover their hair, so having a scarf is useful.

Unwanted Attention

If ignoring unwanted male attention doesn't work, tell your interlocutor that you're waiting for your husband or boyfriend. If necessary, walk away. If you feel yourself being groped on a crowded bus or metro, be loud to draw attention to the incident. You can report incidents to the police, who are required to press charges.

Common Sense

In Western Europe, you should take all the usual precautions you would in any other part of the world. Walking alone at night is usually safe in well-lit, busy central areas. Avoid deserted streets and keep belongings close. Be aware of your surroundings and trust your gut – if it doesn't feel right, it probably isn't. Make a note of the local emergency number and keep your phone well charged.

Getting Around

Public transport is overall safe, but take greater care travelling in remote, quiet or poorly lit areas at night. Make sure taxis are registered or use a licensed rideshare app offering a women-only service such as Bolt and Uber. Hitchhiking alone is not recommended anywhere.

Tell a Friend

Stay connected. Let friends or family know where you are going and when you'll be back. One of the easiest ways to do this is with the **Find My Friends** (find-myfriends.com) app, which allows them to track your location in real time.

GROUP TOURS

Part of the fun of solo female travel is getting to socialise with like-minded people. **Solo Female Travelers Club** (solofemaletravelers.club), **Intrepid Travel** (intrepidtravel.com), **Insight Vacations** (insightvacations.com) and **Travel Queen** (travel-queen.co.uk) offer carefully tailored women-only group tours and expeditions that provide an easy road in. Food tours, city walking tours, cookery classes and guided activities can also be great ways to connect. **GetYourGuide** (getyourguide.com) is a good starting point.

Catedral de Santiago de Compostela (p573), Santiago de Compostela, Spain

Food, Drink & Nightlife

When to Eat

Lunch usually happens (and restaurants usually open) between noon and 2.30pm, with dinner between 6pm and 10pm.

In Spain, lunch can begin at 1pm (often 2pm or 2.30pm) and run until 4pm; dinner usually runs from around 9pm until 11pm or later, especially on weekends. Italy, Portugal and Greece are not quite as late but can be close, especially in summer.

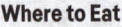

Where to Eat

Restaurants
Typically where you'll eat your evening meal, from cheap-and-cheerful to Michelin-starred restaurants.

Cafes
French cafes serve something more substantial, Austrian *Kaffeehäuser* are grandiose coffee houses, and Dutch *bruin cafés* ('brown cafes', ie pubs) often serve food.

Local variations
Each country has its own variation on the theme of restaurants: Spain's tapas bars, Greek tavernas, Italian *trattorie* and French bistros also offer lunch and dinner. Check individual destination coverage for more specific information.

MENU DECODER

FRANCE
Carte Menu

Menu Two- or three-course meal at a fixed price

Formule Cheaper lunchtime main course plus starter or dessert

Plat du jour Dish of the day

Entrée Starter/appetiser

Plat Main course

Dessert Just that, served after *fromage* (cheese)

ITALY
Piatto del giorno Dish of the day

Antipasto Hot or cold appetiser; for a tasting plate of different appetisers, request an *antipasto misto*

Primo First course

Secondo Second course

Contorno Side dish

Dolce Dessert

SPAIN
Menú del día Set lunch menu

Pintxos Basque-style tapas, usually on bread

Ración or **media ración** Full-plate or half-plate portion of tapas

Plato del día Dish of the day

Plato combinado Main-and-three-veg dish

Entrante Starter

Plato principal Main

Postre Dessert

HOW TO...

Order in France

Bread If a basket of complimentary bread is not automatically brought to the table after ordering, ask for some. Butter is a standard accompaniment with oysters and seafood (*demi-sel* or salted), and in top-end gastronomic restaurants (*doux* or unsalted). Except in top-end places, don't expect a side plate – simply put the bread on the table. And yes, mopping up sauce on your plate with a bread chunk is acceptable.

Coffee Order *un café* (espresso). Never end a meal with a cappuccino, *café au lait* (long milky coffee) or cup of tea, which, incidentally, never comes with milk in France. *Une tisane* (a herbal infusion) like mint or verbena is also acceptable.

The bill *L'addition* is only brought to the table when you ask for it. By law, the bill includes a 15% service charge; assuming you're happy with the service, tipping 5% to 10% of the bill is not expected but is much appreciated.

HOW MUCH FOR A...

Kaffee und Kuchen
(Austria, Germany)
€8–12

croissant
around €2

glass of wine
€4–12

bistro/*trattoria*/
taverna lunch
(France/Italy/
Greece)
€15–30

takeaway fish and
chips (UK/Ireland)
£12

three-course *menú
del día* (Spain)
€12–16

Michelin-starred
dinner
€50–250

pint of beer (UK)
£5

HOW TO... ### Order Tapas in Spain

Tapas are as much a way of life as they are Spain's most accessible culinary superstars. These bite-sized snacks are the accompaniment to countless Spanish nights of revelry and come in seemingly endless variations. Meanwhile, *pintxos* are piles of flavour often mounted on a slice of baguette with a toothpick, sometimes called 'high cuisine in miniature'. Unless you speak Spanish, ordering tapas and *pintxos* can seem like one of the dark arts of Spanish etiquette. Fear not – it's not as difficult as it first appears.

In the Basque Country, Zaragoza and many bars in Madrid, Barcelona and elsewhere, it couldn't be easier. With tapas and *pintxos* lined up along the bar, you either take a small plate and help yourself or point to the morsel you want. If you do this, it's customary to keep track of what you eat (by holding on to the toothpicks, for example) and then tell the bar staff how many you've had when it's time to pay. Otherwise, many places have a list of tapas on a menu or posted up behind the bar. Many places are known for a particular dish; ask for *la especialidad de la casa* (the house speciality).

Another way of eating tapas is to order *raciones* or *medias raciones,* usually to share. In some bars, mostly in Andalucía, you might get a small (free) tapa when you buy a drink.

The Origin of Tapas

A popular story says that a king was served a glass of wine in Cádiz with a slice of cheese or ham over the top as a *tapadera* (cover). The *tapa* (meaning 'lid') was born.

APERITIVO IN ITALY

Aperitivi are often described as 'before-meal drink and light snacks'. Don't be fooled. Italian happy hour can easily turn into a budget-friendly dinner disguised as a casual drink (otherwise known as *apericena*). This is particularly true of *aperitivi* accompanied by a buffet of antipasti, pasta salads, cold cuts and some hot dishes. As a result, *aperitivo* bars are popular places for first dates and singles looking to meet new people. You can methodically pillage buffets in cities – including Milan, Turin, Rome, Naples and Palermo – from about 5pm or 6pm to 8pm or 9pm for the price of a single drink, which crafty diners nurse for the duration. In Venice, locals enjoy *ombre* (half-glasses of wine) and bargain seafood *cicchetti* (Venetian tapas).

Despite its national popularity, Italy's *aperitivo* roots lie in Turin. It was in Piedmont's capital that, in 1786, Antonio Benedetto Carpano infused Moscato white wine with herbs and spices to create vermouth. The drink quickly gained a reputation for piquing the appetite, turning the bar in which Carpano worked into Turin's pre-dinner hotspot. These days, favourite *aperitivo* libations include the spritz – a mix of prosecco, soda water and either Aperol, Campari or the more herbacious Cynar. Not surprisingly, *aperitivi* are wildly popular among the many young Italians who can't afford to eat dinner out, but still want a place to enjoy food while schmoozing with friends – leave it to Italy to find a way to put the glam into budget.

Responsible Travel

Climate Change & Travel

It's impossible to ignore the impact we have when travelling; Lonely Planet urges all travellers to engage with their travel carbon footprint, which will mainly come from air travel. While there often isn't an alternative, travellers can look to minimise the number of flights they take, opt for newer aircrafts and use cleaner ground transport, such as trains. One proposed solution – purchasing carbon offsets – unfortunately does not cancel out the impact of individual flights. While most destinations will depend on air travel for the foreseeable future, for now, pursuing ground-based travel where possible is the best course of action.

The **UN Carbon Offset Calculator** shows how flying impacts a household's emissions.

The **ICAO's carbon emissions calculator** allows visitors to analyse the CO_2 generated by point-to-point journeys.

Germany's Emissions Sticker

To decrease air pollution caused by fine particles, most German cities now have low-emissions environmental zones that only cars displaying an *Umweltplakette* (emissions sticker, sometimes *Feinstaubplakette*) may enter – even foreign ones.

Green in Rotterdam

Rotterdam is the Dutch powerhouse of innovative, ecofriendly urban design. One of the highlights is Hofbogenpark, the Netherlands' longest, narrowest rooftop park, packed with boutiques, restaurants and cafes between greenery.

The **Refill** *(refill. org.uk)* app shows the nearest places to refill water bottles, get coffee in a reusable cup, bring a lunchbox for takeaway, as well as shops offering plastic-free refills.

Switzerland has some of the best air quality in Europe. Manure management and efficient livestock production have helped cut methane emissions, while particulate filter regulations for diesel engines have slashed black-carbon emissions.

SLOW FOOD IN ITALY

The **Slow Food** *(slowfood.it)* organisation promotes projects that protect culinary traditions and local ecosystems. Seek out restaurants recognised by Slow Food's guide *Osterie d'Italia* to support the organisation's ideals.

Over the past decade, the Greek island of Tilos has established itself as the Med's first green island, moving exclusively to renewal energy, promoting electrified transport and abolishing landfills. The island has a notable nature reserve.

Dine on Local French Ingredients

Choose restaurants that use local seasonal products; several in Paris get fruit and veg from rooftop farm **Nature Urbaine** *(nu-paris. com)*. Look for eateries with a *menu du marché* (market-sourced menu) or their own kitchen garden.

Ecofriendly Sleeps in France

Verfiy eco-credentials of hotels, campsites and B&Bs. France's **Clé Verte** *(Green Key; laclefverte.org),* the EU Ecolabel and Green Globe are common green labels. Search by 'gîte panda' to find green self-catering accommodation on *gites-de-france.com*.

Sustainable German Suburb

Visit Vauban in Freiburg, the world's first plus-energy, carbon-neutral sustainable residential community. Here, buildings like Green City Hotel generate and sell renewable energy; bike lanes and public transport make climate-friendly transit easy.

Tap water is safe to drink in most of Western Europe; bring a refillable water bottle to reduce plastic waste.

Pick up litter in Ireland with other volunteers on a community beach cleanup organised by **Clean Coasts** *(cleancoasts. org)*.

Sustainable Countries

According to the UN's *Sustainable Development Report 2025*, Germany (4th), France (5th) and Austria (6th) all came within the world's top 10 out of 193 UN member states.

Careful Where You Picnic

Don't picnic on or at historic steps, fountains, ruins or monuments, as the constant wear and spilled food causes damage. Also, make sure you dispose of rubbish in a bin.

Save Water

Water is a precious resource in much of southern Europe, especially in regions vulnerable to drought. Opt for shorter showers, reuse your towels and stick to the beach instead of hitting the big water parks.

RESOURCES

naturevolunteers. uk
Volunteering on a range of conservation projects

legambiente turismo.it
Italy's most important environmental association

fashionforgood. com
Dutch nonprofit inspiring sustainable fashion

germany.travel/ en/feel-good/ sustainability
Official resource for low-carbon German travel

LGBTIQ+ Travellers

In cosmopolitan centres in Western Europe you'll find very liberal attitudes towards homosexuality. Twelve of the 13 Western European countries have legalised same-sex marriages, and they all allow civil partnerships that grant all or most of the rights of marriage.

Gay Paris

Gay Paris lives up to its name. It's so open that there's less of a defined 'scene' here than in other French cities where it's more underground. Le Marais is the nightlife hub, but you'll find LGBTIQ+ venues attracting a mixed crowd city-wide.

Paris was the first European capital to vote in an openly gay mayor (Bertrand Delanoë, in office 2001–14). Same-sex couples commonly display affection in public and checking into a hotel room together is unlikely to raise eyebrows.

GAY ITALY

In Rome, the Colosseum end of Via di San Giovanni is a gay-friendly haunt, while in Milan, Via Lecco, Via Tadino and NoLo are popular LGBTIQ+ areas. Turin, Bologna, Genoa, Florence and Puglia all have thriving LGBTIQ+ nightlife scenes. Puglia's former president, Nichi Vendola, was one of Italy's first openly gay politicians. Attitudes tend to be more conservative in the country's south.

City vs Country

While LGBTIQ+ travellers enjoy full legal protections against discrimination, and liberal attitudes dominate throughout Western Europe, rural areas of Italy, Greece, Spain, Portugal and even Germany, France and Austria remain socially conservative where, outside larger cities, discretion is still wise.

BRITISH PRIDE

Between June and September, English cities and towns celebrate Pride with parades, concerts and parties. The biggest events are in London and Brighton, with huge parades and performances from big-name acts, but there are Pride events across the country on different weekends.

Legendary Gay Bar

Amsterdam's **Café 't Mandje** (*cafetmandje.amsterdam*) prides itself on allegedly being the world's oldest gay bar. Founded in 1927 by lesbian Bet van Beeren, it's provided a safe, judgment-free space for LGBTIQ+ folks and sex workers for decades.

SPAIN & LGBTIQ+ TRAVELLERS

Madrid hosts the largest Pride festival in Europe, drawing around two million people annually. There are important Pride celebrations in Barcelona, Sitges, Seville, Palma, Badajoz and Ibiza. In Madrid, it's all about the lively Chueca district; in Barcelona, it's 'Gaixample' in L'Eixample. Elsewhere, the beach resorts of Sitges (Catalonia), Torremolinos (Andalucía), Maspalomas (Gran Canaria) and Ibiza are also key to the LGBTIQ+ scene.

Accessible Travel

Western Europe's historic buildings and streetscapes can pose problems for travellers with disabilities or limited mobility, due to steep hills, cobblestones, stairs and lack of lifts in many older buildings (it's worth asking if a freight lift is available). Bathrooms and hotels in restaurants may not be accessible for wheelchairs; check when making reservations.

Passenger Assist

Railway networks in most countries offer mobility assistance if you need help navigating a station or boarding a train. You'll usually need to call or book through an app at least 24 hours ahead.

Airport

Major airports have staff who can assist passengers with reduced mobility. Services range from barrier-free shopping to parking and transfers. Notify your airline for assistance at least 48 hours before departure, and head to the Special Assistance desk in Arrivals.

Accommodation

Small guesthouses and B&Bs (especially those in historic buildings) are often unable to provide services for guests with reduced mobility. Larger, more expensive hotels (four-star or above, usually) have a small number of rooms set up for travellers with disabilities.

ACCESSIBLE MUSEUMS

Accessibility is on the rise at many galleries and museums in Western European cities, with ramps, lifts and well-spaced exhibitions. Some (like London's Science Museum) even have quiet times, ear defenders, sensory maps, Braille signs and audio description.

MUSEUM DISCOUNTS

If you have an obvious disability and/or appropriate ID, some sights offer free or discounted admission. It's worth contacting them in advance of your visit to smooth your way through the entry process.

Cobblestone Streets

Western Europe's historic city centres are often paved with uneven cobblestones and lanes that can be narrow and difficult to navigate for wheelchair users or the vision-impaired, particularly when crowded in the summer season.

Public Transport

Congested inner cities and old underground subway systems with few elevators can make Europe a tricky destination for people with mobility issues. However, newer trains tend to be good and buses often have low floors, ramps and lifts.

RESOURCES

AccessAble (accessable.co.uk) Detailed access information for thousands of venues across the UK and Ireland.

AccessiblEurope (accessibleurope.com) Specialist European tours with van transport.

Society for Accessible Tourism & Hospitality (SATH; sath.org) Reams of information for travellers with disabilities.

Sage Traveling (sagetraveling.com) Great resource for finding accessible hotels in cities all over Europe.

Limitless Travel (limitlesstravel.org) Accessible holidays in Europe, from cruises to coach tours.

Madrid's **Museo Tiflológico** (museo.once.es) has touchable exhibits such as paintings, sculptures and tapestries, as well as more than 40 scale models of world monuments, including Madrid's Palacio Real and Cibeles fountain, Granada's Alhambra and Segovia's aqueduct.

Nuts & Bolts

COUNTRY CODE

Austria +43
Belgium +32
Britain +44
France +33
Germany +49
Greece +30
Ireland +353
Italy +39
Luxembourg +352
Netherlands +31
Portugal +351
Spain +34
Switzerland +41

EMERGENCY NUMBER

112

POPULATION

Austria 9 million
Belgium 12 million
Britain 69 million
France 68 million
Germany 83 million
Greece 10 million
Ireland 5 million
Italy 59 million
Luxembourg 677,000
Netherlands 18 million
Portugal 10 million
Spain 49 million
Switzerland 9 million

Time

Western Europe is divided into three time zones. From west to east:
Greenwich Mean Time/UTC UK, Ireland, Portugal, Canary Islands (Spain)
Central European Time/CET (GMT/UTC + 1) Austria, Belgium, France, Germany, Italy, Luxembourg, the Netherlands, Spain (except Canary Islands), Switzerland
Eastern European Time/EET (GMT/UTC + 2) Greece

All of Western Europe observes daylight saving time on synchronised dates in late March (clocks go forward an hour) and late October (clocks go back an hour).

Internet Access

Internet access varies enormously across Europe. In most places you'll be able to find wi-fi (also called WLAN in some countries). It's usually free, but don't be surprised if you find the occasional hold-out. Internet cafes are increasingly rare but not impossible to find.

OPENING HOURS

These vary from country to country, and can differ between cities and villages, but generally:

Banks 9.30am to 3pm or 5pm Monday to Friday

Cafes 8am to 11pm

Pubs/bars Noon to midnight; to 1am Friday and Saturday

Restaurants Lunch noon to 2.30pm, dinner 6pm to 10pm (later in cities); in Spain, lunch/dinner can start as late as 2.30pm/9pm

Shops 9am to 5.30pm (6pm in cities) Monday to Saturday, 10am to 5pm Sunday; big-city convenience stores open 24/7

Electricity

Europe generally runs on 220V, 50Hz AC, but the UK runs on 230/240V, 50Hz AC. If your home country has a vastly different voltage, you'll need a transformer.

The UK and Ireland use three-pin square plugs. Most of Europe uses the 'europlug' with two round pins. Greece, Italy and Switzerland use a third round pin in a way that the two-pin plug usually – but not always in Italy and Switzerland – fits. Buy an adapter before leaving home or at the airport.

Type C
220V/50Hz

Type G
230V/50Hz

SIM Cards

Even if you're not staying in Europe long, it's more cost-effective for travellers visiting from outside Europe to purchase a prepaid local SIM (eSIM cards are increasingly popular). That's because call and data costs can be prohibitive unless you're using an EU phone and network (residents of Western European countries don't pay extra for data if travelling in another EU country). In several countries you need your passport to buy a SIM card.

Toilets

Many public toilets require a small fee, either deposited in a box or given to the attendant. Availability of toilets varies. If you can't find one, simply drop into a hotel or restaurant and ask to use theirs, or make a nominal purchase at a cafe.

Visas

Citizens of the US, Canada, Australia, New Zealand and the UK currently need only a valid passport to enter all countries in Western Europe, but check requirements before travelling. Citizens of these same countries don't need visas for stays of up to 90 days out of every six-month period.

In late 2026, the EU is introducing a new visa-waiver scheme called ETIAS (European Travel Information and Authorisation System). Citizens of visa-exempt countries will subsequently have to fill in an online application and pay €20 (free for those under 18 or over 70). The authorisation will be valid for three years.

ETIQUETTE

Politeness goes a long way. The same applies to greetings in the local language. Master enough of the local language to be able to say the basics, such as 'hello', 'please', 'thank you' and 'goodbye' in shops, cafes and restaurants.

Take your cue from locals in terms of dress. Beachwear is usually not acceptable at restaurants and in cities.

Dress modestly at religious sites. Bring a shawl or wrap to cover shoulders in churches. In mosques and Orthodox churches, women should also cover their hair.

Avoid visiting religious sites at key times (such as services) if you're sightseeing only.

Raise a toast by saying 'cheers' in the local language, clinking glasses and making eye contact.

In Italy, eat spaghetti with a fork, not a spoon, and never order coffee with your lunch or dinner.

PUBLIC HOLIDAYS

Each country in Western Europe observes its own public holidays and national days, but widely celebrated ones include the following. In Greece, many religious holidays follow the Orthodox calendar (usually two weeks later than elsewhere).

New Year's Day 1 January

Epiphany 6 January

Easter Monday March/April

Labour Day 1 May

Whit Monday 6th Monday after Easter

Ascension Day 6th Thursday after Easter

Corpus Christi 2nd Thursday after Whitsunday

Assumption 15 August

All Saints' Day 1 November

Immaculate Conception 8 December

Christmas Day 25 December

Boxing Day 26 December

THE WESTERN EUROPE
STORYBOOK

Our writers delve deep into different aspects of Western European life

A History of Western Europe in 15 places

Western Europe is an epic story. It begins in dark caves with simple paintings on walls.

Anthony Ham

p646

Wild Nature in Western Europe

Western Europe has an abundance of wild corners and expanses.

Anthony Ham

p650

Western Europe's Swimmable Urban Centres

More and more citizens are demanding access to their natural waters.

Vesna Maric

p652

Catedral de Santiago de Compostela (p573), Santiago de Compostela, Spain
FOTOGRO/SHUTTERSTOCK

A HISTORY OF WESTERN EUROPE IN
15 PLACES

Western Europe is an epic story. It begins in dark caves with simple paintings on walls, rises to great heights of civilisation, endures the tumult of revolutions and catastrophic wars, only for the continent to emerge more unified than ever. Read on to anchor your history lessons in some of Western Europe's most storied attractions. By Anthony Ham

TENS OF THOUSANDS of years ago, the human story was one in which nature held sway and humankind huddled in caves, painting the story of their world on rock walls by the flicker of firelight. And yet, the descendants of these cave dwellers would forge a very different story of sophistication in the empires of Rome and Ancient Greece. Others would join the story, bringing Islam and the latest scientific and artistic traditions to Iberia and changing the continent forever. These grand tales echo down through the centuries – in architecture, in cultural and culinary traditions, and in systems of government.

More recent stories struggle between revolutionary upheavals, astonishing scientific advancement and conflict on an unprecedented scale, culminating in a century in which world wars ravaged the continent. With such destruction on a previously unimaginable scale, the continent seemed broken beyond repair. And yet, Western Europe's capacity (some would say, special penchant) for enlightened reinvention has seen its people and leaders forge a new path of unity. No matter how much it frays around the edges, that unity offers great hope that Western Europe's near future could be somewhat less destructive than its past.

1. Altamira
PREHISTORIC CAVE ART

In 1879, when historian and scientist Marcelino Sanz de Sautuola and his eight-year-old daughter María uncovered intricate coloured-in paintings of bison, horses, deer and other beasts in a cave in the Cantabrian countryside, they instantly knew it was something special. The Cueva de Altamira, near Santillana del Mar, conceals Spain's finest prehistoric art, etched between 13,000 and 35,000 years ago using the natural rock relief. Though the original cave is closed to visitors for conservation purposes, the wonderful replica cave is a marvel of contemporary creativity in its own right.

For more on Altamira, see p572.

2. Stonehenge
BRITAIN'S FAVOURITE STONE CIRCLE

England's most famous ancient monument has dominated Salisbury Plain for some 5000 years, but its story is still shrouded in mystery. The henge likely started life as a burial site for Neolithic peoples, but the mighty standing stones were stacked up in phases, with evidence suggesting some were hauled from as far away as northeast Scotland. The stone circle was constructed to align with sunrise on the summer solstice and used for pagan ceremonies throughout the Bronze Age and into the Iron Age – the involvement of druids and the wizard Merlin, however, is purely latter-day conjecture.

For more on Stonehenge, see p136.

3. Ancient Delphi
SPIRITUAL CENTREPIECE FOR ANCIENT GREECE

Ancient Delphi has an incredibly potent spirit. Centred on the hillside Temple of Apollo, home to the ancient world's most renowned oracle (also known as the Pythia), this sacred spot was never a city. To this day, the haunting ruins on the slopes of Mt Parnassus look out over an unbroken expanse of olive trees, sloping down to the Gulf of Corinth. Rich and powerful petitioners flocked to Delphi from the 8th century BCE onwards, erecting opulent monuments. The priestess would make often-cryptic pronouncements, which were then interpreted by a priest into verse.

For more on Delphi, see p330.

4. Roman Forum
CAESAR'S RISE AND FALL

Rome was said to have been founded by Romulus in 753 BCE, but it would come into its own centuries later. By the time Julius Caesar was born in 100 BCE, Rome controlled all of present-day Italy and large chunks of the Mediterranean coast. Caesar would greatly extend Rome's borders, invading modern-day France and Britain.

Stonehenge (p136), Britain

But in 49 BCE he defied the Senate, sparked a civil war and assumed dictatorial powers after returning to Rome victorious. As the centre of Roman life, the Forum was the site of many historic events including, in 44 BCE, Ceasar's cremation.

For more on the Roman Forum, see p404.

5. Mezquita de Córdoba
THE GOLDEN AGE OF ISLAMIC SPAIN

The armies of Islam crossed into Spain from North Africa in 711, and they remained for more than seven centuries. On the banks of the Río Guadalquivir, at the heart of ancient Córdoba, lies one of the world's great Islamic buildings – a relic of a time when Córdoba ranked among Europe's most cultured cities. The caliphate was established in 929 by Abd ar-Rahman III, who added the minaret to the astonishing horseshoe-arched mosque; other highlights include the citrus-scented Patio de los Naranjos and a shimmering *mihrab* (prayer niche) adorned with gold mosaics.

For more on the Mezquita, see p590.

6. Palazzo Ducale, Venice
THE RISE OF CITY STATES

Venice's glittering ducal palace is a testimony to the wealth and power of Italy's northern city states that arose following the fall of Rome and decline of Byzantine power. Venice broke free of Byzantine rule in the 8th century and became a seafaring republic that spread along the Adriatic through Dalmatia to Greece and as far as Cyprus. Its greatest maritime rival was Genoa, but other powerful city states included Milan, Florence and Pisa. The Venetians gained a reputation as wily operators, striking deals that facilitated trade with such competing powers as the Byzantine, Ottoman and Holy Roman Empires.

For more on the Palazzo Ducale, see p429.

7. Tower of London
JEWEL IN BRITAIN'S CROWN

When William the Conqueror had the White Tower built as the centrepiece of his London fortress during the 1066 Norman Conquest, it was the ultimate muscle-flexing symbol of pomp and power. With its riot of towers and battlements overlooking the Thames, the iconic tower gallivants through 1000 years of history. It has been a fortress, a royal residence, a treasury, a mint, an arsenal and a prison. The Crown Jewels (protected by the red-coated Yeomen Warders, or Beefeaters, and a flock of fabled ravens) dazzle with the world's biggest diamonds. And its walls whisper of murdered princes and beheaded queens.

For more on the Tower of London, see p123.

8. Hofburg, Vienna
HOME OF THE HABSBURGS
Imagine what you could do with unlimited riches and Austria's top architects at hand for 640 years, and you'll have the Vienna of the Habsburgs. The tour de force is the Hofburg, HQ of the imperial family from 1273 to 1918, with a flabbergasting stash of cultural and art treasures. The oldest section is the 13th-century Schweizerhof (Swiss Courtyard), named after the Swiss guards who protected its precincts. Feel the weight of the Austro-Hungarian Empire while marvelling at the treasury's imperial crowns and precious religious relics, the equine ballet of snow-white Lipizzaner stallions at the Spanische Hofreitschule and the chandelier-lit apartments.

For more on the Hofburg, see p52.

9. Granada & the Alhambra
ANDALUCÍA CHANGES HANDS
Above all others, the Alhambra is Spain's great Moorish relic, a fantastical palace-fortress laced with fragrant gardens, interlocking patios and rushing water features, perfected under the Islamic Nasrid emirs, particularly Mohammed V. The celebrated Palacios Nazaríes (a high point in Islamic architecture) and elegant Generalife were created in the 14th century. Famously, it was the fall of Nasrid Granada on 2 January 1492 that marked the end of the Reconquista, the battle by Spain's Reyes Católicos (Catholic Monarchs) to liberate the peninsula from Muslim rulers.

For more on Granada and the Alhambra, see p593.

10. Château de Versailles
SYMBOL OF FRENCH EXCESS
Louis XIV (r 1643–1715), better known as Le Roi Soleil (the Sun King), ascended the

throne aged five. Bolstered by claims of divine right, he involved the kingdom of France in a series of costly wars with Holland, Austria and England. Louis XIV built the most extravagant palace on French soil at Versailles in 1663. The king forced his 6000 courtiers to compete with each other for royal favour, thus quashing the feuding aristocracy and creating the first centralised French state. The French Revolution would follow little more than a century later.

For more on Versailles, see p192.

11. Salzburg
MOZART'S BAROQUE HOMETOWN
Set against the backdrop of the Alps, Salzburg has long been a city of grand designs. But it was Wolf Dietrich von Raitenau, prince-archbishop of Salzburg from 1587 to 1612, that gave the Altstadt (old town) its magic baroque touch. The UNESCO World Heritage–listed historic centre dazzles with brilliance: from the copper-domed, twin-spired Dom, a masterpiece of baroque art, to the Residenz, a stately baroque palace, and the resplendent, fountain-adorned Residenzplatz. Appropriately, this beacon of sophistication was the birthplace of Wolfgang Amadeus Mozart in 1756, and echoes of Salzburg's favourite son are everywhere.

For more on Salzburg, see p57.

Alhambra (p593), Spain

FROM LEFT: FOTO PARA TI/SHUTTERSTOCK, HAVANA1234/GETTY IMAGES

Woods Cemetery, Flanders Fields, Ypres (p99)

12. Wittenberg

BIRTHPLACE OF THE REFORMATION

Wittenberg is Germany's spiritual lodestar. The jury's out on whether former Augustinian monk Martin Luther actually nailed his incendiary *Ninety-Five Theses* to Wittenberg's Schlosskirche (All Saints' Church) on 31 October 1517. What's not in dispute is the fact that Luther's points, challenging articles of faith that underpinned the Catholic Church's authority, kick-started the Protestant Reformation. The original doors were destroyed by fire in the 18th century, but their vast, 19th-century bronze replacements, inscribed with Luther's theses in Latin, remain a focal point for pilgrims to Wittenberg, sometimes known as 'the Rome of the Protestants'.

For more on Wittenberg, see p304.

13. Ypres & Flanders Fields

WWI KILLING FIELDS

One of the most glorious medieval buildings in Belgium is the huge, fanciful cloth hall in Ypres (Ieper) – although, what you see was totally rebuilt after WWI when it had been left as rubble after endless bombardment. Whole villages in these parts disappeared into the mud where for several years soldiers rotted in sodden trenches in Flanders fields. The course of WWI could have been very different if plucky Liège had not previously delayed German advances by 12 valuable days. It's a soulful place haunted by more than 150,000 ghosts.

For more about Ypres and Flanders Fields, see p99.

14. Buchenwald

STORIES OF WWII HORROR

Buchenwald, one of the first, largest and most notorious of all Nazi concentration camps, occupies the blackest possible niche of German history. It was established in 1937 and was among the longest-running of the camps, operating under the Nazis until its liberation by US forces on 11 April 1945; earlier the same day, Buchenwald's prisoners had seized control of the camp. Initially, it housed political enemies of the Nazis, making room in time for Jews, Roma and prisoners of war. Tens of thousands of people died there. Today, the camp is preserved largely as it was at the moment of liberation.

For more on Buchenwald, see p304.

15. Berlin Wall

THE 20TH CENTURY CHANGES COURSE

For 28 years, from 1961 to 1989, the Berlin Wall was the paramount symbol of the Cold War. A complete circuit, some 155km in circumference, it was built around West Berlin by the German Democratic Republic (GDR) to close off the route via which more than 3.5 million of its citizens had defected to the West. The 'Fall of the Wall', officially dated to 9 November 1989, was the culmination of a wave of events, including the waning of Soviet power in the Eastern Bloc countries, which led to the collapse of Eastern European communism and the reunification of Germany on 3 October 1990.

For more on the Berlin Wall, see p261.

WILD NATURE
IN WESTERN EUROPE

Western Europe may be better known for its human history, culture and architecture, but this beautiful region has an abundance of wild corners and expanses. National parks offer brilliant opportunities to explore on foot and provide refuge for a surprising variety of wildlife. By Anthony Ham

National Parks

At last count, the 13 countries of Western Europe had 140 national parks. By sheer numbers, Italy (25 national parks), the Netherlands (21), Germany (16), Spain (16), Britain (15) and Greece (15) had the most parks.

But of greater importance is the percentage of each country's territory that is locked away and protected. By this latter standard, France was the clear winner with 11 national parks covering 9.5% of mainland France, followed by Britain (8.2%) and Italy (5%).

The poorest performers when it came to setting aside national parks were Switzerland (one park covering just 0.4% of the country), Portugal (one park, 0.8%), Spain (16 parks, but also just 0.8% of national territory) and Ireland (six parks protecting just 0.9%).

Many Western European national parks provide important protection for wildlife, including flora; Spain's Parc Nacional d'Aigüestortes i Estany de Sant Maurici, for example, is home to 600-year-old pine trees that predate Christopher Columbus' voyages to the Americas. But the parks' priorities extend beyond conservation to making some of the continent's most beautiful corners accessible for recreational tourism.

Wildlife

France leads the way when it comes to wildlife diversity – it has more mammal species (135) than any other Western European country. When it comes to birds, Britain leads the way with 562 different species, followed by Spain (550) and France (522).

The most celebrated mammals in Western Europe tend to be the most charismatic – the Eurasian wolf, the brown bear, and the Eurasian and Iberian lynxes. Otherwise, there are lots of ibexes (a wild goat), chamois (a small antelope), red foxes, squirrels marmots and all manner of smaller species.

Mountain regions protect the continent's many birds of prey, which include golden eagles, falcons and vultures (both bearded and griffin). Western Europe also has hundreds of Ramsar-certified wetlands – Britain alone has 176 – which provide ideal habitat for waterbirds.

Eurasian Wolf

The grey or Eurasian wolf is present throughout Western Europe, with the largest populations thought to be in Italy (3300), Spain (2300), Germany (1600) and Greece (1000).

Thanks to historically strict EU laws prohibiting the hunting and killing of wolves, wolf numbers have been increasing across Western Europe. While it's good for the species – between 12,000 and 20,000 wolves roam Europe – there's a growing backlash against wolves whenever they prey on pets and valuable domestic livestock.

In 2024, the German government, under pressure from farmers and the powerful hunting lobby, voted in favour of an EU law to downgrade the protection of wolves, making it easier for governments to permit the shooting of wolves to protect livestock. Surprisingly, the move was approved by then Environment Minister Steffi Lemke, a member of the Green Party.

Brown Bear

The Eurasian brown bear is Western Europe's largest mammal by a long shot – a male in prime condition can weigh 480kg and stand 2.5m tall. One of the most common of all bear species (although sightings are rare), it ranges from Scandinavia and Russia down through the heart of Western Europe to Spain's Pyrenees and into Eastern Europe. The Eurasian brown bear is easily recognisable, with its fur colour ranging from a yellowish-brown to near-black. Brown bears are omnivorous, and meat accounts for no more than 15% of their diet.

An estimated 15,000 inhabit the continent in fragmented populations. In Western Europe, they're found in Spain (in both the Pyrenees and the Picos de Europa), Italy and Greece.

There's no resident brown bear population in Germany, although individuals occasionally turn up. In 2006, a bear nicknamed Bruno crossed the border from Austria into Germany and was believed to be the first brown bear to set foot on German soil in 170 years. After much media coverage, Bruno was shot in southern Bavaria after he began feeding on domestic pets and livestock.

Iberian & Eurasian Lynx

Two of the four species of lynx (a genus of medium-sized cats with spotted coats and affecting pixie-like ear tufts) live in Western Europe. The most widespread is the Eurasian lynx, whose range extends from Western Europe across Russia to East Asia. After being hunted to local extinction, Eurasian lynxes have been reintroduced into Germany, Austria, Switzerland, Italy and France, and small populations persist in each country, as well as in the Netherlands and Belgium.

Smaller than the Eurasian lynx and a different species, the Iberian lynx (*lince ibérico* in Spanish) is an astonishing conservation success story. A century ago, there were perhaps 100,000 Iberian lynxes in the wild in Iberia. So plentiful was the lynx that the Spanish government classed it as vermin, encouraging hunters to kill the animals. By 1960 only 500 remained. Over the decades that followed, there were fears that the Iberian lynx would become the first cat species to fall extinct since the sabre-toothed tiger, 10,000 years ago. By the early 21st century, numbers were down to just 94, in Andalucía, in the Parque Nacional de Doñana and in the Sierra Morena.

A captive breeding program began, with young captive-born lynx being released into the wild. By 2015, numbers had risen to about 400 and the Iberian lynx was taken off the International Union for Conservation of Nature's 'critically endangered' list. As of 2025, the Iberian lynx has been downgraded to 'vulnerable' with more than 2000 wild lynxes across large areas of Spain and parts of Portugal.

WESTERN EUROPE'S SWIMMABLE URBAN CENTRES

Things are looking up for Western Europe's urban swimmers, as more and more citizens are demanding access to their natural waters. By Vesna Maric

WESTERN EUROPE'S TEMPERATURES are soaring every summer and, with global temperatures on the rise, are likely to get hotter each year. It's a rare urban centre in the region that doesn't turn into a hot cauldron from July to September, and cleaning up the rivers for urban swimming has become a legitimate, welcome and somewhat urgent concern. And while many cities face stubborn barriers to becoming swimmable – such as historical legal frameworks prohibiting swimming in urban rivers by default, or insurance concerns and fear of litigation keeping the authorities from opening access to their waters – the perfect example of how things are changing from the ground up is the **Swimmable Cities Alliance** (*swimmablecities.org*), a citizen-powered organisation that has been doing some worthy lobbying to clean up the many river waters across Europe and beyond. Launched just before the start of the 2024 Paris Olympics, Swimmable Cities has grown into a global platform with 2025 seeing signatory organisations from more than 80 cities and towns, and 30 countries around the world.

Swimming in Paris

One of the highest-profile such cases is the River Seine. While nude swimming in the Seine was common practice in the 17th century, the last hundred years had seen a ban on bathing in the river because of high levels of contamination by human waste. The city authorities spent nearly €1.4 billion to build giant stormwater basins for wastewater management, treatment plants and filtering stations to lower the river's bacterial contamination from faecal waste. The project to clean up this murky river was one of the major parts of the 2024 Paris Olympics preparations – and as of July 2025, 1000 swimmers a day are allowed access to three bathing sites on the banks of the Seine for free. The city is explicit that bathers can't just jump into the Seine at random spots outside the designated zones, due to safety issues. The spots where swimming is allowed are found near the finance ministry at Bercy, in the east of the city, Grenelle in the west of the city (with a view of the Eiffel Tower!), and near Pont de Sully, looking on to the Île St-Louis. The Seine swimming season is open from early July to the end of August.

Bathing in Berlin

Similarly to the Seine, swimming in Berlin's Spree River was common a century ago, giving us an indication of the level

of toxicity that industrial development has imposed onto Western Europe's natural world since that time. The ban on swimming in the Spree was introduced in 1925, when a combination of the city's industrial boom and huge population increase turned the river water into a human health hazard. Since 2012, Berlin's citizens have been campaigning for the Spree to become swimmable again. The **Flussbad Berlin** (*flussbad-berlin.de*) project was launched in order to turn a section of the river, the Spree Canal, into a filtered, free public swimming pool with integrated wetland zones to clean the water naturally, making the river a natural resource in the heart of the city. According to activists, the river water is swimmable most days of the year, except during and after heavy rainfall when the river turns toxic with overflowing human waste from the sewage system and oil and tyre rubber being washed from streets into the Spree. City officials have also cited the potential hazard of wartime munitions lodged in the riverbed, although activists reject this as a real danger since, allegedly, wartime munitions may be lodged in lakes too. It remains to be seen how fast and how far the Flussbad Berlin project will go.

Splashing in Rotterdam & Amsterdam

Rotterdam's Rijnhaven port is a success story. The city was the host of the 2025 Swimmable Cities Summit, where 150 participants from four continents gathered to garner, according to the organisers, 'bold action in climate adaptation, community wellbeing and urban waterfront regeneration'. Once an industrial port on the south bank of the Nieuwe Maas river, Rijnhaven is now a designated swimming area, with an accompanying floating park and lots of enthusiastic locals. At the time of writing, it was the only legal place to swim in Rotterdam's city centre, but who's to say the citizens won't organise for more.

Amsterdam hasn't had to go through any major battles to organise its waterways for the locals and the many tourists the city sees every year. There are several city beaches, and six million visitors a year swim, sail or row in the lakes of the planted forest, Amsterdamse Bos, where water quality is measured for bacteria and algae. A website (*zwemwater.nl*) gives indicators of the city's – and country's – water cleanliness, temperature, and the location of facilities such as bike parking and public toilets. If you're thinking of swimming in Amsterdam's canals, the idea is best left alone due to pollution, except for the annual **Amsterdam City Swim** (*amsterdamcityswim.nl*), held in September, when thousands swim from the Keizersgracht to the Marineterrein harbourside.

Dipping in Barcelona, London & Zürich

Finally, several of Western Europe's major cities have always had their swimming opportunities at hand. The most obvious and popular urban destination in the region for a dip is, of course, Barcelona. There are several good beaches, Platja de la Barceloneta being the most famous one, the most central and practically always packed. Platja del Bogatell, Platja de Sant Sebastià and Platja de la Nova Mar Bella are slightly more free of crowds. If you get on one of the regional trains, you can access emptier sandy beaches only minutes away from the centre.

Away from the Mediterranean, London has excellent swimming opportunities – believe it or not (it's not what most visitors expect). Lovers of natural waters can choose between swimming at the Hampstead Heath bathing ponds, where there are a women's pond, men's pond and a mixed pond, and Hyde Park's Serpentine Lido – all of these are in the middle of incredibly beautiful London parks. There are various spots where swimmers can bathe in the Thames, but this is generally outside the city centre. Switzerland's Zürich and Geneva have swimming opportunities galore, in both their urban rivers and lakes, which are heavenly on hot midsummer days.

INDEX

Map Pages **000**

INDEX

F-I

> "The perfect market keepsake in Gouda (p484) was snapping a photo of my one-year-old sitting on stacked round cheese blocks."
>
> **BARBARA WOOLSEY**

> "Watching flower-garlanded cows descend from their summer pastures (p72) in Tyrol's Zillertal in the golden light of a late-September day was a beautiful glimpse of Alpine before tourism got a grip."
>
> **KERRY WALKER**

Mapping data sources:
© Lonely Planet
© OpenStreetMap http://openstreetmap.org/copyright

THIS BOOK

This guidebook was produced by the following:

Destination Editor
Shauna Daly

Production Editor
Kathryn Rowan

Image Editor
Dermot Hegarty

Cartographer
Anthony Phelan

Coordinating Editor
Brana Vladisavljevic

Assisting Editors
Imogen Bannister, Nigel Chin, Melanie Dankel, Helen Koehne, Anne Mulvaney, Karyn Noble

Assisting Cartographers
Dorothy Davidson, Mark Griffiths, Chris Lee Ack, Daniela Machová

Contributing Writers
Rudolf Abraham, Isabel Albiston, Alexis Averbuck, Kat Barber, Oliver Berry, Joe Bindloss, Caroline Bishop, Abigail Blasi, Federica Bocco, Jean-Bernard Carillet, Daniel James Clarke, Fionn Davenport, Marc Di Duca, Natalia Diaz, Virginia DiGaetano, Jamie Ditaranto, Kathy Donaghy, Peter Dragicevich, Keith Drew, Mark Elliott, Becki Enright, Mark Eveleigh, Daniel Fahey, Fabienne Fong Yan, Esme Fox, Michael Frankel, Duncan Garwood, Benedetta Geddo, Kay Gillespie, Laurie Goodlad, Anthony Haywood, Sandra Henriques, Rooksana Hossenally, Felicity Hughes, Sarah Irving, Anna Kaminski, Lauren Keith, Cyrena Lee, Daphné Leprince-Ringuet, Lucy Lovell, Emily Luxton, Mike MacEacheran, Vesna Maric, Marlene Marques, Chrissie McClatchie, Hugh McNaughtan, Mélissa Monaco, Mary Winston Nicklin, John Noble, Nanjala Nyabola, Stephanie Ong, Lorna Parkes, Ashley Parsons, Marisa Megan Paska, Samantha Priestley, Leonid Ragozin, Kevin Raub, Joseph Reaney, Simon Richmond, Daniel Robinson, Madeleine Rothery, Eva Sandoval, Andrea Schulte-Peevers, Sarah Souli, Regis St Louis, Paul Stafford, Nicola Leigh Stewart, Rowan Twine, Sara van Geloven, Ryan Ver Berkmoes, Tasmin Waby, Neil Wilson, Peter Yeung, Angelo Zinna

Cover Researcher
Stefanie Delgado

Thanks
Jeremy Toynbee

FROM LEFT: SURIADY WIJTAN/SHUTTERSTOCK, POSITIVETRAVELART/SHUTTERSTOCK

MIX
Paper | Supporting responsible forestry
FSC™ C021741

Paper in this book is certified against the Forest Stewardship Council™ standards. FSC™ promotes environmentally responsible, socially beneficial and economically viable management of the world's forests.

Published by Lonely Planet Global Limited
CRN 554153
16th edition – Jun 2026
ISBN 978 1 83869 389 3
© Lonely Planet 2026 Photographs © as indicated 2026
10 9 8 7 6 5 4 3 2 1
Printed in Malaysia